AF541048

Jammu and Kashmir

Past Tense, Present Imperfect and Future Indefinite

जम्मू कश्मीर की दलदल पूर्ण समस्या का साकार रूप

भूत व्यग्र, वर्तमान विकृत एवं भविष्य संदिग्ध तथा अनिश्चित्

Jammu and Kashmir

Past Tense, Present Imperfect and Future Indefinite

जम्मू कश्मीर की दलदल पूर्ण समस्या का साकार रूप

भूत व्यग्र, वर्तमान विकृत एवं भविष्य संदिग्ध तथा अनिश्चित्

Professor Dr. K.L. Bhatia
B.A. (Hons.); LL.M., Ph.D. (Pune)
DAAD and Max Planck Fellow and Alumni
Emeritus Professor of Law,
College of Legal Studies
University of Petroleum and Energy Studies
V&PO Bidholi, via Premnagar, Dehradun. Uttrakhand
[Former Head & Dean, Faculty of Law, and Director
The Law School, University of Jammu and Director, Amity Law School]

DEEP & DEEP PUBLICATIONS PVT. LTD.
F-159, Rajouri Garden, New Delhi - 110027

JAMMU AND KASHMIR
Past Tense, Present Imperfect and Future Indefinite

ISBN 978-81-8450-387-6

Typeset by THE LASER PRINTERS
8/15, 3rd Floor, Subhash Nagar, New Delhi-110027

Printed in India at MAYUR ENTERPRISES, WZ Plot No. 3, Gujjar Market, Tihar Village, New Delhi - 110 018

Published by DEEP & DEEP PUBLICATIONS PVT. LTD.
F-159, Rajouri Garden, New Delhi-110027.
Phones: 25435369, 25440916
Sales Showroom: 2/13, Ansari Road, Daryaganj, New Delhi-110002
Phone/Fax: 23245122

Contents

Preface

Being a conscientious citizen of India, I have tried, with diffidence, modesty and humility, to analyze the open or veiled game plans that not only throw a new light on certain aspects of the Jammu-Kashmir issue, but also unfold the contrived plans of those who have made a 'no-problem Jammu-Kashmir' a 'problem Jammu-Kashmir'. It has become a new challenge in the context of an internal as well as external security problem. The subject-matter of Jammu-Kashmir has been close to my heart. After an in depth study of different game plans being projected at different levels the world over, I thought it as my duty to make a critique analysis of the issues with the sole objective in mind let "We the People of India" know the reality of veiled and contrived fictions. In this tiny bilingual write up I have made a modest analysis of such contrived fictions with the sole object as to how to come out of this cobweb. Jammu-Kashmir is an integral and irrevocable part of Indian "Sovereign, Socialist, Secular, Democratic, Republic". My sole modest endeavor has been to present that the State of Jammu-Kashmir ought not to have been a contending issue because she has immutably and imperishably been a part of Indian Nation historically, morally, ethically, legally, socially, constitutionally and internationally. However, it has been confounded and complicated by those actors whose contrived plots that are full of tragedies, have been striving hard to reverse this historical truth and trying to make us believe globally the truth of their lies. Such actors' open or veiled efforts have speciously succeeded to make the "no-dispute" a "dispute", and making honest nationalists the victims of situational crisis. This monograph shows the games of such planners replacing "simple Kashmir" into "Kashmir imbroglio". It also narrates the saga of events, which have not only embittered

Indo-Pakistan relations, but also converted "communal harmony" into "communal disharmony". My only object through this succinct write up has been "save Jammu-Kashmir" from the hands of those actors whose only approach has been to disintegrate Jammu-Kashmir from Union of India that is *Bharat*.

I express my sincere tributes to all my warm and dear friends who have sharpened my analysis-visions with their wise suggestions.

PROFESSOR DR. K.L BHATIA
Professor Emeritus

प्रस्तावना

जम्मू–कश्मीर का विषम विषय मेरा मार्मिक हार्दिक विषय है। भारत का एक जागरुक नागरिक होने के नाते विषय का सही दिशा में विश्लेषण करना मैं अपना कर्तव्य समझता हूं। जम्मू–कश्मीर समस्या ना होकर भी एक जटिल समस्या है। यह जटिल समस्या कई विकृत प्रवृत्तियों का परिणाम है। अतैव आन्तरिक और बाह्य सुरक्षा का अहम विषय है।

जम्मू–कश्मीर विकृत प्रवृत्तियों के हाथों अनेकानेक प्रकार के प्रयोगों के अध्यन का विषय बन गया है एवं अंततोगत्वा यह अनेकानेक खिलाड़ियों के हाथों कठपुतली है। मैने इन सबका भारतीयता एवं भारतीय दृष्टि के माध्यम से विश्लेषण करने का विनम्र प्रयास किया है। यह विनम्र प्रयास विकृत प्रवृत्तियों की विचारधाराओं को चेतना हेतु है कि जम्मू–कश्मीर भारत गणराज्य का अभिन्न एवं अटूट अंग है।

मैं उन सर्व बन्धुओं एवं मित्रगण का आभार प्रकट करता हूं जिन्होंने मेरे इस विनम्र प्रयास में सहयोग दिया है।

प्रो० डॉ० के०एल० भाटिया

Introduction

The internal as well as external political complications and complexities that have beset Jammu and Kashmir are matters of common knowledge the world over. I do not cherish any intention to covering them. However, the modest approach in this write up is purely as well as exclusively that of a student of law.

Is Jammu and Kashmir a problem? If there is problem, it is a problem of unrealistic contrived contrivances of contrived plots that are full of tragedies. Jammu and Kashmir State is a problem of contrived history of modern era. The conviviality begins with the accession of Jammu and Kashmir with the Union of India as her integral part on 26th and 27th October 1947, and since then the State has been a contentious issue internally as well as externally. It, thus, is conceived of social, economic, political, national and international dimensions. Besides, it seems that Jammu and Kashmir problem is the consequence of obstinate approach by some people at different times. It has been confounded and complicated unconscientiously by those who have had varying and inconsistent behaviour pattern. In this quicksand is it easy to find out a solution satisfying the audacity of all? Besides the political gimmicks, it has been off the line notoriety in the hands of those who have aspired and loved to remain out of the main streamline of the Nation. It has been a bone of contention between the integrationists and disintegrationists. Fairly speaking, the State of Jammu and Kashmir ought not to have been a contending issue because she has immutably been a part of Indian Nation historically, religiously, morally, ethically, legally, constitutionally, and internationally [The State of J&K along with other States of India has had *de jure* recognition by international community on the declaration of India's independence and State's accession]. The disintegrationists have been striving hard to reverse this historical truth, and trying to make us all believe globally the truth of their million dollars lies. It has been an abode of *Devatas, Saints, Sages, Seers, Faqirs, and Peers* and that precisely seems to be the reason that is heaven on the earth. It is a place of *Shrines* of all faiths and beliefs symbolizing the communal harmony of the region. It is also a place of *Shiva Shrines* located in the serene and picturesque cascading environ that unequivocally indicates the emergence, growth and existence of a widespread cult of *Shiva*. Be that as it may, the malign charter starts with the launch of mischievous movements with multi-dimensional consequences. The State of Jammu and Kashmir has been presented only with one gloss of school of thought and that school of thought was so much of one sided that it adopted those soft strategies to resolve the unknotted J&K problem that virtually made J&K knotty. In the backdrop of this, it may be no exageration to submit that J&K is a riddle wrapped in mystery inside an enigma. How to come out of this riddle there has to be a roadmap with new strategies, advanced visions, and farsighted perceptions. In the making of a roadmap, it may be appropriate to have a deep peep into the conduct of those who have been responsible to quagmire a quark.

Backgrounder

The quagmire started with the launch of movements against the ruler of the State [Maharaja Hari Singh] by those who had dreamt to be in the shoes of the ruler by overthrowing him out of power. The Maharaja had maintained opposition to such conscriptions, because the opponents were behaving against the ruler, as he seemed to be a foreigner ruler on the Indian soil. And, the attempts to equate such movements with the Indian freedom movement seem to be unnatural, specious, fictitious, factious and anti-national. Besides, varying and inconsistent statements of stands of 1931, 1942, 1947, 1949, 1950, 1953 by those who aspired to be loyal with Pakistan treating the Valley of Kashmir as their *affaire de Coeur*.

The voluminous literature on Kashmir shows sordid intrigue and treachery that has battered relations between India and Pakistan on the one hand, and India and Kashmiri psyche on the other hand. It also unfolds the endeavours, open or veiled, by Super Powers to make the no-dispute a dispute to serve the ends of the power block. It also makes the revelations of the haplessness and helplessness of Sardar Patel, Gopalaswami Ayyanger, Hari Singh, M.C. Mahajan, and host of others who were victims of situational crisis. It shows the replacement of "simple Kashmir" into "Kashmir Imbroglio". It narrates the saga of events that "a vehement exponent of accession to India seems to have been converted to 'independent Kashmir'." It also reflects the impetus on certain aspects of the Kashmir issue, which have not only embittered perpetually India-Pakistan relations, but also converted "communal harmony" into "communal disharmony". In the backdrop of it, it shall be appropriate to mention about the sequence of events that throw a new light on certain aspects of the Kashmir issue.

The State of J&K, covering an area of 86,024 square miles (222,236 square km), has a strategic importance as its territory [the Valley of Kashmir, Jammu, Ladakh, Balitstan, Gilgit, Hunza and Nagar] shares borders with Pakistan in the west, Afghanistan in the north, China in the north and east. Besides, it is close to the Soviet border in the North-West, and is the old trade route to Central Asia.

The modern history is testimony to the fact that a new era in the history of the State of J&K had begun with the enthronement of Maharajah Hari Singh in September 1925 who succeeded the royal power and sovereignty status as a linear descendent of the Dogra Maharajah Gulab Singh who created the State of Jammu and Kashmir under the treaty of Amritsar in March 1846 by paying rupees 75 lakhs as war indemnity to the British colonial government after the demise of Maharajah Ranjit Singh in 1839. [C. Joseph Chacko: India's Contribution to the Field of International Law Concepts, 1958]. The movement known as "Kashmir for Kashmiris" launched under the leadership of Shankarlal Koul could be conceded a black lung chapter in the history of J&K as it induced Hari Singh to enact the "State Subject Law, 1927" imposing restrictions on the entry of non-Kashmiris in Government jobs and on the sale of immovable property to them. [Premnath Bazaz: Kashmir in Crucible]. Reading Room Party organization founded in 1930 in Srinagar by a few Muslim graduates of which Sheikh Mohammed Abdullah was also a member seems to be the foundation stone of the feeling of alienation mainly not only from the government of Hari Singh, but also the rest of the non-Muslim population. This gave birth to isolation and escapism. This was furthered by the foundation of the Muslim Conference under the chairmanship of Sheikh Abdullah who began the fight for democratic rights for Muslims alone. It led to tension between Hindus and Muslims and to communal riots in Srinagar in June 1931. Hindus suffered heavily. Why Sheikh Abdullah did not raise his voice and concern for non-Muslims who, too, were the significant components of the population? Communal disturbances sowed the seeds of communal disharmony. In August 1945, Sheikh Abdullah, as Chairman of National Conference, spelt out his program for building a new Kashmir. Why did he not spell out his module for the entire State? Another phase of opposition to the Hari Singh

Government was the launch of "Quit Kashmir" agitation speciously equating it with the "Quit India" movement. The Indian Independence Act, 1947 provided for transfer of power to two newly created Dominions from one Indian Continent, viz., India and Pakistan. Vide that law; a plan/roadmap for Indian Princely States was defined by which the Princely States were to accede to either Dominion by 15th August 1947. Paramountcy lapsed on 15th August 1947. All but three Princely States had acceded to either India or Pakistan. Incidents of belated accession of Princely States of Hyderabad and Junagad are meaningfully well placed in history, and, perhaps, that indecisiveness had been the root cause of unpleasantness. Be that as it may, *Afridis*/ tribesmen, soldiers in plain clothes, and desperadoes with modern weapons, from North-West-Frontier Province of West Pakistan, with the connivance and active support of Pakistan's Government invaded Kashmir on 22nd October 1947 as a consequence to coerce Hari Singh to accede to Pakistan. This crisis made Hari Singh to listen to the advice of several Indian leaders of different shades and ideology to accede to India and seek Indian Government's help to uproot the invaders/aggressors from Kashmir. Under these special circumstances, the sovereign Hari Singh like other sovereigns of about 560 Indian Princely States acceded to India by signing the unconditional Instrument of Accession on 26th October 1947 and accepted by the Governor-General Mountbatten on 27th October 1947. In the backdrop of this, a reference to sections of Maharajah Hari Singh's letter as the independent sovereign ruler of his State to Lord Mountbatten is significant: "My dear Lord Mountbatten, I have to inform Your Excellency that a grave emergency has arisen in my State and request immediate assistance of your Government. . . . Your Government was aware that the State of Jammu and Kashmir has not acceded to either the Dominion of India or to Pakistan. I wanted to take time to decide to which Dominion I should accede, whether it is not in the best interest of both the dominions and my State to stand independent, of course with friendly and cordial relations with both. Though my State had a 'Standstill Agreement' with the Pakistan Government, that Government permitted steady and increasing strangulation of supplies like food, salt and petrol to my State. . . . Afridis, soldiers in plain clothes, and desperadoes with modern weapons had been allowed to infiltrate into my

State. These enemies . . . were engaged in the wanton destruction of life and property and were marching on with the aim of capturing Srinagar, the summer capital of my Government, as a first step to over-running the whole State. . . . The mass infiltration of tribesmen . . . in motor trucks . . . and fully armed with up-to-date weapons cannot possibly be done without the knowledge of the Provincial Government of the Northwest Frontier Province and the Government of Pakistan. . . . [With such conditions prevailing in my State], I have no option but to ask for help from the Indian Dominion. Naturally they [the Indian Dominion] cannot send the help asked for by me without my State acceding to the Dominion of India. I have accordingly decided to do so and I attach the Instrument of Accession for acceptance by your Government". [C. Joseph Chacko, *Ibid.*].

Lord Mountbatten, the last British Governor-General and the first Governor-General of free Independent India, promptly accepted the Instrument of Accession and replied vide his letter dated 27th October 1947: "In the special circumstances mentioned by Your Highness, my Government have decided to accept the accession of Kashmir State to the Dominion of India. . . . It is my Government's wish that, as soon as law and order have been restored in Kashmir and her soil cleared of the invaders, the question of the State's accession should be settled by a reference to the people". [C. Joseph Chacko, *Ibid.*].

The Maharajah Hari Singh of Jammu and Kashmir State acceded to India on 26th October 1947; the accession was accepted by the Government of India on 27th October 1947; and, on 28th October 1947 the Prime Minister of India Pandit Jawaharlal Nehru wired to the Prime Minister of Pakistan informing him that "action Government of India has taken has been forced upon them by circumstances and imminent and grave danger to Srinagar. . . . In regard to accession also it has been made clear that this is subject to reference to people of State and their decision. Government of India has no desire to impose any decision and will abide by people's wishes. But these cannot be ascertained till peace and law and order prevail . . ." [C. Joseph Chacko, *Ibid.*].

Jammu and Kashmir's accession to India is final and irrevocable and in conformity with International Law. The Maharajah of the State of Jammu and Kashmir was an independent sovereign as per Indian Independence Act, 1947.

Oppenheim, an international jurist, appears to submit the tests: "In every monarchy the monarch appears as the representative of the sovereignty of the State, and thereby becomes a sovereign himself; and this fact is recognized in international law . . . International law recognizes all monarchs as equally sovereign . . ." [Oppenheim, *International Law*, Vol. I, p. 758]. Hence, all such sovereigns represent their States and they are International Persons or subjects of International Law.

Professor Philip C. Jessup, an outstanding jurist of International Law of Columbia University, has recognized the marks of statehood: (a) a permanent population; (b) a defined territory; (c) a government; and (d) capacity to enter into relations with other States. [U.N. Security Council Records, 383rd meeting, December 2, 1948, p. 9.].

In the backdrop of these tests, it may be conclusively submitted that the Maharajah of Jammu and Kashmir representing his State had all the requisite attributes of an International Person/ Subject in International Law on and after August 15, 1947.

In this context, a reference to the decision of J&K High Court rendered by Justice Shamiri in *Magher Singh* v. *Principal Secretary, Jammu and Kashmir* [A.I.R. 1953, J&K 25] may be made that unequivocally neatly discusses the status of Maharajah of Jammu and Kashmir prior and subsequent to the Indian Independence Act, 1947:

> "Previous to the partition of British India into two Dominions of Pakistan and India there was no doubt that the Ruler of Jammu and Kashmir was under the suzerainty of the British Crown inasmuch as foreign relations were under the exclusive control of the Crown Representative. But insofar as the internal sovereignty of the ruler was concerned it was absolutely unlimited and there were no fetters on it. In this connection it would be relevant to reproduce sections 4 and 5 of the Jammu and Kashmir Constitution Act . . . as they stood amended in November, 1951.
>
> 'Section 4: The territories for the time being vested in H.H. are governed by and in the name of H.H. and all rights, authorities and jurisdiction which appertain or are incidental to the government of such territories are exercisable by H.H.'

'Section 5: Notwithstanding anything contained in this or any other Act all powers, legislative, executive and judicial in relation to the State and its government are hereby declared to be and to have always been inherent in and possessed and retained by His Highness and nothing contained in this or any other Act shall affect or be deemed to have affected the right, or prerogative of His Highness to make laws, and issue proclamations, orders and ordinances by virtue of his inherent authority'."

The High Court, thus, decreed that (1) so far as the internal sovereignty of the State was concerned, the powers of the ruler were similar to those of the British Parliament; (2) with the passage of section 7 of the Indian Independence Act of 1947 the State of Jammu and Kashmir "became an independent and sovereign State in the full sense of international law"; (3) consequently, "His Highness became an uncontrolled and absolute sovereign"; (4) the signature and submission of the Instrument of Accession to the Government of India was "subject always to the terms thereof", and for no other purpose, and that therefore; (5) the proclamation of His Highness transferring and entrusting his powers to "Shree Yuvraj [Yuvaraj Karan Singh] was perfectly valid and constitutional".

In the backdrop of the above, it unequivocally seems that the action of Maharajah Hari Singh as an independent and absolute Monarch of an independent State of Jammu and Kashmir is beyond any doubt thoroughly, legally, politically, socially, ethically, and morally compatible with all points of international law, and is not open to challenge from the standpoint of the international law governing sovereign entities at any international forum. In my humble opinion the accession of Jammu and Kashmir, therefore, to the Indian Union in terms of Instrument of Accession was an act of legal plenitude. If this act of accession is questioned on the grounds of its possible illegality, unconstitutionality, then all accessions whether to India or Pakistan would be open to similar objections that may consequently lead to disintegration inviting a Pandora box of intrigues as well as incongruities. It may also be pertinent to deal with the oft-hackneyed offer of plebiscite which India is alleged to have made with a view of finding a solution to a dispute between India and Pakistan with reference to Kashmir. The acceding Monarch Maharajah Hari Singh had never used the term plebiscite or any other condition in his Instrument of Accession to the Government of India.

However, the contentious point that needs in depth probing seems to be pondered, viz., but for unilateral cease-fire, the Indian soldiers of Indian defense forces when were in winning position could have uprooted the tribesmen from the Indian soil of Kashmir, and, further, could not have been the soaring cause for the creation of POK. Nehru-Mountbatten duo personal promises to finalize the accession through the will of the people, that is, plebiscite, [Durga Das: Sardar Patel's Correspondence: 1971: pp. 73, 81, 257, 341] was incompatible legally, constitutionally, politically, ethically, socially, and morally, and as such self-created difficulties by unnecessarily volunteering for "in accordance with the wishes of the people" or "question of accession should be settled by a reference to the people", mischievously and speciously construed as plebiscite, has been responsible for muddling and making Kashmir a highly intricate problem as well as playing for high stakes. Under Mountbatten's encouragement Jawaharlal Nehru taking the Kashmir case to UNO further made a local/ National issue an International one and opened a floodgate for the intervention of UK, USA, Russia, China, Muslim countries, Militants as well as terrorist groups, Terrorist Training Centers in POK, and Pakistan, Jamat-e-Islami, a Hard Core Pro-Pak group, Hurriyyat, a conglomeration of some Militant groups, to wean India and seems to be inclined to bleed India to the last drop; UN Resolutions, Tashkent Agreement, Simla Agreement, Lahore Declaration, Islamabad Declaration have yielded no results except the prize we are fighting for is the Valley of Kashmir. The cumulative impetus is fraught with both danger and disaster, and there has been a debit balance throughout so far as achievements are concerned with *coup de grace* results.

Propositions: Internal and External

What type of an action is needed to finally end that has been getting worse, a number of methods have been presented locally, nationally, and internationally to jettison the conditions so that the coming events may not further weaken the situation.

LOCAL GAME PLAN

The most regrettable happening of the past presented by Sheikh Abdullah and his National Conference has been the New Kashmir Module whereby Jammu Region could have three districts of Jammu, Udhampur and Kathua and leaving the rest of the territory of J&K to a Muslim republic like Pakistan. [Durga Das: *Id.* at p. 128]. This module presents the mindset of those people who have had narrower vision to resolve the Kashmir issue. Neo New Kashmir modules have been in the framework of Pre-1953, autonomy—greater autonomy and regional autonomy. Pre-1953 and autonomy are the two sides of the same coin. They are like mistress at their home without any checks and balances. In the autonomy reports it has *a multo fortiori* been recommended to have Pre-1953 position, viz., what was the political, legal and constitutional status of J&K before the detention of Sheikh Abdullah that should be restored. The provisions of the Indian Constitution were extended to the State of J&K vide Constitutional (Application to the State of J&K) Order 1954 that superseded the Constitutional (Application to the State of J&K) Order 1950. By 1950 Constitutional Order the provisions of Articles 1 and 370 of the Constitution of India were extended to the State of J&K with the adoption and enforcement of the Constitution of India. Subsequently, the Constituent Assembly of

J&K in 1956 in *proprio vigore* ratified the accession of J&K with the Union of India as one of her integral federal unit and also adopted as well as enforced Constitution of J&K. [C. Joseph Chacko, *Ibid*]. Besides, over 370 Central Laws have been extended to the State of J&K so that the people of J&K, too, have the equal fruits of those laws by that the citizens of India have the profits. Pre-1953 proposition is fraught with dangerous consequences. First, it shall be step forward to the rescinding of the provisions of the Constitution of India as well as the Constitution of J&K that shall leap backward to the Constitutional status of 1933. Once this happens it shall automatically mean J&K ceasing to be an integral part of India as per Article 1 and Schedules I and IV of the Constitution of India, and Section 3 of the Constitution of J&K. Second, the permanent residents of J&K shall cease to be the citizens of India thus depriving them the benefits of the rights, the Basic rights, and the Fundamental rights of the citizenry. Third, it shall amount to an invitation for resettlement of those who left the country voluntarily to settle in other sovereign State by giving up Indian citizenship and permanent residence of J&K for their loyalty to Pakistan. Such people have fought 1947, 1965, 1971 wars against India and fighting proxy war against India as Militants, terrorists, secessionists, wagers of war, infiltrators, incinerators inciting, instigating and coercing the people of the State of J&K to join hands with them for the perpetuation of their unholy acts of omissions and commission with pernicious effects. This proposition is incompatible with all social, political, legal, constitutional, and international norms, namely, what is not constitutionally permissible to do directly that is not permitted to do indirectly. Fourth, it shall deprive the people of J&K the national integration profits enjoined under the Constitution of India such as Supreme Court jurisdiction (original, appellate, and PIL), over 370 Central Laws, Comptroller and Auditor General, Election Commission, and a host of others. Fifth, it shall lead to the superimposition of another fiefdom and serfdom.

The propagators of 'self-rule' seem to be ignorant about the in depth meaning of the phrase they have coined as a solution to the naughty knotty J&K problem. Self-rule was a movement launched by *Swarajists* (freedom fighters) against the British rulers in India for the restoration of self-rule by democratic means by the Indians, for the Indians, and of the Indians. In J&K, her people have been exercising their enfranchisements since 1957 by democratic means for the self-rule by them, for them and of them. What more does self-rule mean? It is nothing but a mischievious propagation to misguide the people. Similarly, healing touch proposition has yielded negative results as it encouraged militants/terrorists and secessionists to squeeze maximum benefits from government chest at the cost of nationalists. The State Governments have failed to provide meaningful healing touch to the West Pak refugees and internally displaced persons who have been living as strangers in their own home. Article 370 is adopted version of the draft Article 306-A. It was adopted by the Constituent Assembly unanimously and without a single dissentient voice and without a speech from anybody raising any note of criticism including the four representatives from J&K in the Constituent Assembly, viz., Sheikh Mohammed Abdullah, Mirza Afzal Beig, Moulana Masoodi, and M.R. Baigra who were signatories (24th January 1950) to the adopted text of the Constitution of India on 26th November 1949. [CAD, Vols. X-XII, 1989 Ed., pp. 421-29]. Article 370 was enjoined in the Constitution of India as a temporary measure to eventually meet the special situations created by special unforeseen circumstances with the sole objective that it should rescind with the ceasing of the special hostile situations and never making it as an entrenched one. But working with the provisions of Article 370, it seems, has generated the feeling of alienation. Its language ought to have been similar to the language of Article 371, viz., as a special measure for the development of non-developed/under developed spatial areas of the Indian territory so that such areas, too, get an equal opportunity to come up in the streamline of the Indian Nation with the feeling of equalization. Alienation has permeated an attitude of secessionism, separatism, militancy and terrorism. This also is responsible for an idea of an independent Kashmir mooted by those who have perhaps proved to be one of the greatest betrayals in history of modern India. [Durga Das, *op. cit.* at pp. 266-68]. Their hurting and injurious language is "Accession to either side cannot bring peace. We want to live in friendship with both Dominions. Perhaps a middle path between them, with economic co-operation with each, will be the only way of doing it. But Britain, the United States and other members of the United Nations must guarantee not only by India and Pakistan but an independent Kashmir also. . . ." [Vide Sheikh Abdullah in an interview with Michael Davidson, quoted in Durga Das, *Ibid.*] Besides, it is difficult to define what ordinary Kashmiris want/aspire/desire. Many express that they want/aspire to be masters of their own will or destiny without any checks and balances. Many express the view that they only want to be left alone but do not define what would that entail. Be that as it may, no one should be misled by this hotch potch. This seems to be the real mindset of all those who are perpetuating the suspected plan in the garb of hard-core and soft-core conglomerates. And, Article 370 is responsible for the permeation of this type of behaviour pattern. Erasing of it has become non-practical because it has been allowed to oscillate between political will and legal viability. To me, it seems that the retention of Article 370 and alienation perpetuity has been due to those who may have desired to evaporate it but could not do so because when the flesh is weak, the spirit however willing cannot execute.

What has been the impetus of all the above-mentioned movements/proposals/propositions? What results have they yielded so far? The experiments have yielded no meaningful results for the only reason that the propositions have been presented insincerely, unconscientiously, and superciliously.

PAKISTAN GAME PLAN

Pakistan has only one game plan to have Kashmir within her fold by any foul play that is visible in the incidents of aggression caused by Pakistan in 1947, 1965, 1971, Kargil invasion 1999, and Proxy war occasioned by the ticklish tactics of militancy, terrorism, terrorists training camps on her soil, Jihad, and her militants' or terrorists' attack in Mumbai on 26.11.2008. Pakistan aspires to destabilize India with her supercilious approach and as such has dishonoured all peace rapprochements of UN Resolutions, Tashkent Agreement, Simla Agreement, Lahore Declaration, etc. However, it has come to be sensitive to Confidence Building Measures after Islamabad Declaration that is the reiteration of Lahore Declaration. Besides, political pronouncements "putting the Kashmir problem in hibernation for the generation next", and "conflict management and simultaneous creation of trading bloc in South Asia as part of efforts to settle outstanding issues with

India like the Kashmir problem" are inasmuch as unclear as that of deficiency of sound mind.

INTERNATIONAL GAME PLAN

International Game Plan emanates from the thesis of Postcolonial perceptions having base on the carving out of artificial boundaries through European conquests and settlements establishing the destabilizing legacy in the Third World whereby the boundaries of the State and those of the ethnic nation did not coincide. Kashmir problem, perhaps, may have to be perceived as an example of such British legacy worked out by Mountbatten by encouraging Jawaharlal Nehru to declare unilateral ceasefire that culminated into the artificial creation of POK. This unequivocally seems to have opened floodgate of international interventionists in Kashmir affairs like a harlot, the Kashmir problem is at the disposal of everyone. International modules, thus, are based on "Strategic Interdependence" perceptions. "Strategic Interdependence" relates to international security issues that primarily involve the defense capabilities and deterrence postures adopted by States against threats from each other under conditions of strategic interdependence. "Strategic Interdependence" denotes the relative power distributions among States, although the constitution and measurement of power remain subject to debate. [Raju, G.C. Thomas, "What is Third World Security?" *Annual Review of Political Science*, 6(1) 2003, 205-32]. Measurement of power refers to existing military capabilities and mobilization potential based on a State's economic and technological capacities and capabilities. Be that as it may, military capability and potential as a measurement of power was complicated by the "advent of nuclear weapons" that made "traditional" "measurement of power" of "absolute capabilities" as irrelevancy and the psychology and motivation to deter an attack became the more important factor in the calculus of power. [*Ibid*.]. This new model has permeated "Strategic Interdependence", which has come up as India started perceiving some utility in acquiring or preserving a nuclear deterrent capability in case of interventionists intervention in Kashmir affairs that affect India's internal, external or regional security interests. [*Ibid*.].

In the backdrop of this, it is imperative to have perceptions of international modules directed to resolve Kashmir issue as "Back Channel Diplomacy" or "Quiet Diplomacy". The authors of "Kashmir: The Road to Peace" argue that the "modules can be useful to all those who want to replace violençe with diplomacy and bring peace to the people of Kashmir". [Public International Law Policy Group]. The module is debatable from Indian perspective because that raises many debatable issues. However, the proposed module presents "model language" of the "proposed agreements" between *Kashmir* v. *India* v. *Pakistan* to be incorporated in a "Constitutional Framework" as follows:

Abbreviation	*Official Name of Agreement*
1. Burundi Agreement	Arusha Peace and Reconciliation Agreement for Burundi, August 20, 2000.
2. Dayton Accords	The General Framework Agreement for Peace in Bosnia and Herzegovina (initiated in Dayton on 21 November 1995 and signed in Paris on 14 December 1995.
3. East Timor Agreement	Agreement between the Republic of Indonesia and the Portuguese Republic on the Question of East Timor, 5 May 1999.
4. El Salvador Agreement	El Salvador Peace Agreement 16 January 1992.
5. Guatemala Agreement	Guatemala Agreement on Identity and Rights of Indigenous Peoples, March 31, 1995.
6. KFOR Agreement	Military Technical Agreement between the International Security Force (KFOR) and the Governments of Federal Republic of Yugoslavia and the Republic of Serbia, June 9, 1999.
7. Kosovo Interim Agreement	The Interim Agreement for Peace and Self-Government in Kosovo, February 23, 1999.
8. Lahore Declaration	Lahore Declaration by the Prime Ministers of the Republic of India and the Islamic Republic of Pakistan, February 21, 1999.
9. Northern Ireland Agreement	The Northern Ireland Peace Agreement: The Agreement Reached in the multi-party Negotiations, October 4, 1998.

10. Papua New Guinea Agreement	Bougainvillea Peace Agreement, August 30, 2001.
11. Sierra Leone Agreement	Peace Agreement between the Government of Sierra Leone and the Revolutionary United Front of Sierra Leone, Lome', Togo, May 25 to July 7, 1999.
12. Simla Agreement	Simla Agreement on Bilateral Relations between India and Pakistan signed by Prime Minister of India Mrs. Indira Gandhi and President of Pakistan Z.A. Bhutto, July 3, 1972.
13. South African Constitution	Constitution of the Republic of South Africa, May 8, 1996.
14. Sudan Protocol	Sudan's Machakos Protocol, July 20, 2002.
15. Tashkent Declaration	Tashkent Declaration, January 10, 1996.
16. Angola Ceasefire	Angola-Unita Ceasefire Agreement, April 2002.
17. Lusaka Protocol	Angola-Lusaka Protocol, Lusaka, Zambia, November 15, 1994.
18. Somalia Ceasefire	Somalia Agreement on Implementing the ceasefire and on modalities of disarmament (Supplement to the General Agreement signed in Addis Ababa, on January 8, 1993.

THE GIST OF THE ABOVE MODULE

A. Constitutional Status of Article 370

1. Article 370 of the Constitution of India shall be made permanent. Deleting the term "temporary" from the Article as well as references to Article 370 and replacing it with the word "special" shall accomplish this.
2. All Presidential Orders restricting the scope of Article 370 shall be rescinded. There shall be no further acts by the Indian Government to create ambiguity as to the Status of Kashmir.
3. The rights created herein for the self-governance of the semi-autonomous region of Kashmir are non-derogable.

B. Governance Retained by India

All powers not delegated to India by this Agreement are reserved to Kashmir, respectively, or to its people.

(a) Defense

1. The Indian Government will continue to exercise competence over the external defense of Kashmir. The State of Kashmir continues to be a part of India and as such India still maintains control over its defense. Indian military presence in Kashmir. shall be reactionary only.
2. Kashmir shall closely supervise any Indian defense force in Kashmir to prevent abuses by the Indian force. If such abuses, as those prescribed in this Agreement's section on human rights, do take place, the Kashmir legislature shall have the authority to submit the issue to the Human Rights Committee for adjudication.

(b) Foreign Affairs

1. The Indian Government will continue to exercise control over the foreign affairs of the region.
2. The Indian Government shall consult with the Kashmir legislature regarding any foreign affairs decisions affecting the region. The Kashmir legislature shall approve any decisions of India that relate specifically and singularly to the foreign affairs of Kashmir but to no other region.

(c) Fiscal Policy

1. Kashmir will still require continued support from the Central Government and as such the Indian Government should continue to exercise control over monetary policy of the region.
2. India shall also retain control over national taxation. The government of Kashmir shall control regional taxation for Kashmir.
3. The Indian Government shall ensure the full economic development of Kashmir. This shall entail increased investment in the region and the strengthening of economic growth programs through education and

monetary support. India shall also continue to govern Kashmiri participation in the Indian common market, with the objective to continue active participation.

C. Status of Kashmir Borders

(a) The border of Kashmir shall not change as a result of this agreement. The Line of Control (LOC) will be the official border, as defined by the 1972 Simla Agreement that separates Azad Kashmir from Kashmir. The northern, southern, and eastern borders shall not vary from what they are at the time of the signature of the agreement.

(b) Azad Kashmir shall not be considered a part of the new special autonomous region. If the populous of Azad Kashmir expresses an interest in joining the special autonomous region of Kashmir, Kashmir shall support a referendum and give credence to its outcome.

D. Kashmiri Participation in Central Government

(a) Kashmir shall continue to participate in the structure of the Indian Government so far as those structures affect Kashmir. This determination shall be based on those powers retained by the Indian Government as detailed in this Agreement.

(b) Selection of Kashmiri representatives shall not change from the existing methods.

(c) The government of Kashmir shall be consulted by the Government of India for the purpose of taking Kashmiri views into account on issues within the Indian Government of particular relevance to the Kashmir.

E. Determination of Kashmiri Citizenship and Symbols of Identity

1. All the people living in Kashmir for a minimum of 7 years at the time of signing of the Agreement shall be considered citizens of Kashmir.
2. All people living in Kashmir for less than 7 years at the time of the signing of the Agreement shall be granted Kashmiri citizenship after fulfilling 7 year residency requirement.

3. There shall be no denial of citizenship based on the race, religion or sex of an individual. The Kashmiri legislature shall ensure the grant of citizenship to all those requesting it.
4. Accusations of discrimination for citizenship shall be adjudicated as a type of discrimination before the International Criminal Court.
5. The Constitutional Congress or new Kashmiri government will set the regulations for issuance of identity documents such as passport.
6. There shall be no denial of identity documents based on race, religion or sex.
7. The Constitutional Congress, or new Kashmiri government, shall determine the symbols of national identity such as flag and coat of arms. The Indian flag shall continue to fly at national ceremonies and other legally required events.

F. Mechanism for Enforcement of Special Autonomy Status

Upon an allegation by either Kashmir or Pakistan that the principles for heightened autonomy provided for in this section are being abused, a committee appointed by the United Nations Secretary General, comprised of internationals, will investigate the allegation. If the appoint committee determines that there is a violation, the Human Rights Committee of Kashmir will attempt to resolve the situation. If the Committee determines that it is beyond its capabilities to remedy the situation, the United Nations High Commissioner for Human Rights will bring the issue to the United Nations Security Council for immediate resolution.

G. Constitutional Status of Kashmir

The Kashmir government shall be granted full competence over all matters not controlled by the Central Government as specified above. This will mean full, meaningful and exclusive control over all matters concerning the establishment of all legal, political, social, cultural and educational policies in Kashmir.

H. Legislation

The Kashmir government shall be granted complete competence over the enactment, repeal and reform of laws in the region in conformity with its Constitution. This power shall not be fettered in any way by the Indian Government except in its spheres of influence as specified above. Any legislation passed must, however, not be contrary to the spirit of the Indian Constitution.

I. Financial Matters

The Kashmir government shall be granted control over local taxation and shall be responsible for the manner in which State funds are allocated. The exercise of this power must be done in an equitable manner and with no prejudice to members of minority groups.

J. Policy-making

The government of Kashmir shall be accorded authority for formulating and implementing measures concerning all aspects of the region's social, cultural, educational and scientific policy.

K. Corruption

The government of Kashmir is called upon to address the problem of corruption through the enforcement of anti-corruption measures, including prompt and impartial investigation and prosecution of offenders.

L. Elections

(a) Both parties shall ensure that the conditions exist for the conduct of free and fair elections in the region. This will include ensuring an open and free political environment for all citizens, a safe and secure environment that ensures freedom of assembly, association and expression, the access to all available resources to all candidates without prejudice. Both parties must also ensure free exercise of media for campaigning candidates.

(b) The Indian Government shall accept the presence of an

international election observer body to monitor the conduct of the elections and to certify that the elections have been free and fair.

(c) This international body must be accorded full access to all aspects of the electoral process including voter registration, access to polling centers and dissemination of ballots following the election.

(d) The body shall work in conjunction with Electoral Commission of India to ensure that secure and transparent voting procedures are followed.

(e) Any allegations of violation of procedures must be investigated and any parties found to be guilty shall have penalties imposed on them including removing the candidate from the party list.

M. Candidates

A person's past political associations or activities shall not be a bar to holding office. All candidates must, however, renounce all use of violence.

N. Human Rights

1. Kashmir agrees to promote and protect human rights in the region. To this end, it will give full force and effect to the international human rights treaties to which it is bound through the ratification of the treaties by the Government of India, namely, Universal Declaration of Human Rights; International Covenants on Civil and Political Rights, and Economic, Social and Cultural Rights; Convention on the Elimination of All Forms of Discrimination against Women; Convention on the Rights of the Child.
2. In addition to the international treaties listed above, other Conventions that India has not acceded to will be adopted by the Kashmiri government, namely, Convention against torture and other Cruel, Inhuman or Degrading Treatment or Punishment; declaration on the Elimination of all Forms of Intolerance and of Discrimination Based on Religion or Belief.
3. Fundamental Rights of All Kashmiri People:

(i) The rights and duties proclaimed and guaranteed inter alia by the Universal Declaration of Human Rights, the International Covenants on Human Rights, the Convention on the Elimination of All Forms of Discrimination against Women and the Convention on the Rights of the Child shall form an integral part of the Constitution of Kashmir as a Bill of Rights that receives the same pre-eminence in judicial matters as the Constitution itself. These fundamental rights, both in the treaties named above and the provisions specifically enumerated below, shall not be limited or derogated from, except in justifiable circumstances acceptable in international law and set forth in the Constitution.

(ii) All citizens shall have rights and obligations.

(iii) Human dignity shall be respected and protected.

(iv) All women and men shall be equal. No one may be discriminated against, *inter alia*, on grounds of origin, race, ethnicity, gender, color, language, social situation, or religious, philosophical or political convictions, or by reason of a physical or mental handicap. All citizens shall enjoy equal protection of the law, as well as equal treatment under the law.

(v) The State or its organs shall arbitrarily deal with no person.

(vi) All women and men shall have the right to life.

(vii) All women and men shall have the right to personal freedom, including to physical and mental integrity, and to freedom of movement. Torture and any other kind of cruel, inhuman, degrading treatment or punishment shall be prohibited. Everyone shall have the right to be free from violence from either public or private sources.

(viii) The State shall to the extent possible ensure that all citizens have the means to lead an existence consistent with human dignity.

(ix) All women and men shall have the right to respect for their private and family life, residence and personal communications.

(x) Freedom of expression and of the media shall be

guaranteed. The State shall respect freedom of religion, belief, conscience and opinion.

(xi) No one shall be arbitrarily deprived of her/his nationality or denied the right to change it.

(xii) No one may be denied access to basic education. The State shall organize public education, and shall develop and promote access to secondary and post-secondary education.

(xiii) All citizens shall have the right to move and settle freely anywhere in the regional territory, as well as to leave it and return to it.

(xiv) Everyone shall have the right, in judicial or administrative proceedings, for her/his case to be dealt with equitably and decided within a reasonable time limit. Everyone shall have the right to due process and fair trial.

(xv) No one may be deprived of her/his liberty other than in conformity with the law.

(xvi) Each individual shall have the duty to respect and show consideration for her/his fellow citizens without any discrimination.

(xvii) Any restriction of a fundamental right must have a legal basis; it must be justified by the public interest or by the protection of another person's fundamental right; it must be proportional to the objective pursued.

(xviii) Fundamental rights must be respected throughout the legal, administrative and institutional order. The Constitution shall be the supreme law and must be upheld by the Legislature, the Executive and the Judiciary. Any law that is not in conformity with the Constitution shall be invalid.

O. Religious Minority: Freedom of Religion

1. Every person shall have the right to freedom of conscience, religion, thought, belief, and opinion.
2. No one shall be subject to coercion, which would impair his or her freedom to have a religion or belief of his choice.
3. Freedom to manifest one's religion or belief may be

subject only to such limitations as are prescribed by law and are necessary to protect public safety, order, health or morals or the fundamental rights and freedoms of others.

4. Without derogating from the generality of sub-section (1), religious observances may be conducted at State or State-aided institutions under rules established by an appropriate authority for that purpose, provided that such religious observances are conducted on an equitable basis and attendance at them is free and voluntary.
5. Nothing in this Article shall preclude legislation recognizing:
   - a system of personal and family law adhered to by persons professing a particular religion; and
   - the validity of marriages concluded under a system of religious law subject to specified procedures.
6. The right to freedom of thought, conscience, religion or belief shall include, *inter alia*, the following freedoms:
   - To worship or assemble in connection with a religion or belief, and to establish and maintain places for these purposes;
   - To establish and maintain appropriate charitable or humanitarian institutions;
   - To make, acquire and use to an adequate extent the necessary articles and materials related to the rites or customs of a religion or belief;
   - To write, issue and disseminate relevant publications in these areas;
   - To teach a religion or belief in places suitable for these purposes;
   - To solicit and receive voluntary financial and other contributions from individuals and institutions;
   - To train, appoint, elect or designate by succession appropriate leaders called for by the requirements and standards of any religion or belief;
   - To observe days or rest and to celebrate holidays and ceremonies in accordance with the precepts of one's religion or belief; and
   - To establish and maintain communications with

individuals and communities in matters of religion and belief at the national and international levels.

7. Religion may be considered in hiring practices to the extent that under-represented groups are promoted to achieve proper representation within the economic community.
8. Any written or verbal incitement, through media or otherwise, of ethnic or religious hostility or hatred shall be prohibited and, if communicated, promptly suppressed with perpetrators subjected to prison term that shall be incorporated into the criminal laws of Kashmir.

P. Women's Rights

It is recognized that women are practically vulnerable, being confronted with discrimination as women, and also having to deal with a social situation characterized by intense poverty, exploitation, and violence. The government undertakes to take the following measures to ensure the protection of women's human rights.

(a) Governmental

(i) Establish a Division of Women's Rights within the Department of Human Rights, with the participation of such women, including legal advice services and social services, to ensure the right of women to full and equal participation in political, civil, economic, social, and cultural life.

(ii) Ensure that the Division of Women's Rights is afforded the opportunity to integrate gender concerns into all levels of the government bureaucracy.

(iii) Promote the dissemination and faithful implementation of the Convention on the Elimination of All Forms of Discrimination against Women.

(b) Legal

(i) Review and update the penalties imposed by current legislation for sexual crimes, harassment against women, and intra-family violence, and prosecute these crimes.

(ii) The equal status of the human rights of men and women shall be guaranteed.

(iii) Enable women to participate freely and willingly in any gender empowering legal measures directly affecting their society and rights as human beings under the Geneva Conv:ntions.

(iv) As the health and safety of women and children are fundamental in the sustainability of the Kashmiri people, the rights of women should be honored and respected in Kashmiri society. As such, any treaty concerning the general rights of the Kashmiri people shall be included and represented in any future decision about the legal statutes of Kashmir.

(c) Political

(i) Ensure that social and political organizations adopt specific policies to enhance and promote the role of women in the process of strengthening civilian power.

(ii) Ensure that at all times in the exercise of power, women, whether organized or not, are provided with and guaranteed opportunities to participate.

(iii) Women shall enjoy representation in any governmental body that rules Kashmir through the visible and elected representation of female leaders.

(iv) Women shall be given significant representation in both governmental and civil bodies.

(v) The role of women in civil society and community life shall not be undermined or silences.

(vi) Women shall equally participate in democratic institutions.

(d) Civil

(i) Women not participating in combat shall be respected as civilians. As such, they are outside of the conflict and shall not be engaged by combatants. Women and children shall not be utilized as shields in war.

(ii) Guarantee women and girls participation at all levels of public life by ensuring their fundamental rights to education, work, health care, political participation, freedom of movement, and equitable treatment under the law.

(iii) Education for women is of paramount importance to the future generations of Kashmiris. Women and girls shall not be denied access to education based on gender.

Q. Chlidren's Rights

(i) Every child has an inherent right to life, and to the fundamental freedoms enumerated above, to the extent practicable in accordance with the age and maturity of the child.

(ii) Every child shall have his or her rights upheld, without discrimination of any kind, as set forth in the UN Convention on the Rights of the Child.

(iii) Every child shall have the right to special measures to protect or promote her/his care, welfare, health and physical security, and to be protected from maltreatment, abuse or exploitation.

(iv) Young people should be employed in public service projects as well as income-generating projects that provide social assistance to youth in certain difficult circumstances such as orphans, street children, and abandoned.

(v) A child shall not be separated from his or her parents against their will, except when competent authorities subject to judicial review determine, in accordance with applicable law and procedures, that such separation is necessary for the best interests of the child. Such determination may be necessary in a particular case such as one involving abuse or neglect of the child by parents, or one where the parents are living separately and a decision must be made as to the child's place of residence.

(vi) Measures shall be taken to combat the illicit transfer and non-return of children abroad.

R. Education

(i) Illiteracy shall be eradicated among youth through compulsory education for the first nine years of schooling (Basic Education) and the government shall endeavor to provide free schooling for a further three years.

(ii) Peace shall be taught as a facet of other disciplines throughout elementary school, and taught as a separate subject in the secondary school level, with a mandatory minimum one-class requirement for graduation.

(iii) The government shall offer vocational and technical training to those youth over 9 that do not attend school that will allow them carry out projects that will contribute to their personal development and to the economic and social development of Kashmir.

(iv) A region-wise campaign will be conducted via the Education Division to help the various groups in the population live together again in peace. The campaign shall endeavor to raise awareness of the issues involved with peaceful co-existence and the capability, through various forms of non-violent action, to fulfil that promise.

(v) Political and administrative leaders and economic agents shall receive additional training in the peaceful settlement of disputes.

S. Refugees

(i) All Kashmiri refugees and displaced persons, located outside Kashmir, shall have the right to return and live in safety, and dignity, free from intimidation or coercion of any kind.

(ii) Individuals who left Kashmir prior to 1990 shall receive financial compensation for the loss of their property and are welcome to resettle within Kashmir.

(iii) Individuals who left Kashmir after 1990 may also receive financial compensation for the lost property, but may file claims to receive the property itself if they choose.

(iv) The claims of refugees shall be investigated and confirmed through the Refugee Division. Any financial compensation that will be granted shall be processed via the Refugee Division.

(v) The Refugee Division shall help returnees recover their

property and bank accounts whose existence has been duly proven that were left in Kashmir before their exile.

T. Department of Human Rights

The government of Kashmir shall add a new Department of Human Rights to the existing government structure. In furtherance of the goal of an effective and functioning human rights body, technical and material assistance may be sought from the United Nations Special Commission on Human Rights, the United Nations Center for Human Rights, and other relevant international organizations.

1. Powers and Responsibilities of the Department: The Department of Human Rights shall:

   (i) receive, consider and follow-up with complaints regarding possible human rights violations;
   (ii) carry out the necessary investigations autonomously, effectively and in accordance with the political constitution of the Jammu and Kashmir State and international norms regarding human rights;
   (iii) determine whether or not a violation of human rights has occurred on the basis of all the information it is able to obtain in the exercise of the powers referred to herein, taking into consideration any investigations that the competent constitutional institutions may carry out; and
   (iv) the Department shall be empowered to establish itself and move freely throughout Kashmir; interview any person or group of persons freely and privately for the proper performance of its functions; collect whatever information may be relevant for the implementation of its mandate; disseminate information relating to its functions and activities to the Kashmiri public through the mass media.

2. In the performance of its functions the Department shall take into account the situation of the most vulnerable groups of society and to the population directly affected

by the armed confrontation (including displaced persona, refugees and returnees).

3. In verifying the observance of human rights, the Department shall pay particular attention to rights to life, integrity and security of person, liberty, due process, freedom of expression, freedom of movement, freedom of association, and political rights.
4. The Department shall conduct its activities on a permanent and ongoing basis. With the exception of the activities of the Indian soldiers and police force during the years prior to the signing of the Agreement, which will be investigated by the Division of Religious Minorities, all human rights violations occurring prior to the signature are investigated through the Reconciliation Divisions and not through the permanent or other *ad-hoc* Divisions of the Department.
5. A Kashmiri native agreed upon by both the Kashmir Legislative Council and Kashmir Legislative Assembly shall head the Department. The individual should be selected based on the strength of his or her reputation for fairness, integrity, quality of work, and knowledge/ background in the human rights field. The individual shall be an eminent person of high moral standing who possesses a demonstrated commitment to human rights and the rights of members of regional communities. His or her term shall last for six years, with the possibility of one re-appointment.
6. The Department shall have its own offices, adequate communication facilities and secretarial support staff. The Department shall be housed in the summertime in Srinagar, and during wintertime reside in Jammu. Support staff for the Department can be hired through the regular civil servant hiring process, while ensuring that the staff comprises a representative selection of the population including women, members of both religious majorities and any minority groups in the region.
7. The Department will include Divisions responsible for Fundamental Human Rights, Religious Minority, Women, Children, Refugees, Education, and Reconciliation.

8. A consortium of local human rights and civil society groups in Kashmir shall be encouraged to help monitor human rights observance. This group will have the authority to investigate claims and allegations regarding the performance of the Department, and verify that the hiring goals are met.

A succinct glance at the abovementioned proposed module shows that it has hidden agenda that encourages secessionism. And, for that reason alone, the proposed module can't be conceded as peace module but encouraging secessionism/ seceding module, interventionist module interfering with the sovereignty of the country, an interventionist foreign Constituent Assembly dictating changes in the Indian Constitutional Framework that itself is against the Basic Structure of the Constitution of India, and it should not be encouraged for several reasons. First, the proposed solution-module encourages heightened autonomy, which has since been rejected by the Parliament of India as the State of J&K enjoys maximum autonomy enjoined under Article 370, with the possibility of independence in the near future. Second, it shall open the re-examination and re-determination of accession. The authors of the proposed module should remember that the Instrument of Accession were matter of past history, and past history is a dead history, and any endeavors to revive it should be fraught with dangerous consequences by giving fuel to the fire. This shall lead to the revival of all the documents of accession did the successors of about 560 Indian Princely States so desire. God forbids that this does not happen because that may lead to bloodbath. Third, Kashmir and Kashmiris are unable to defend itself from nationalists and integrationists interested in the unity and integrity of India, its territory, and its people. Fourth, the proposed module is Kashmir as well as Kashmiri centric. It nowhere represents the concern of Ladakh and Ladakhiat, and Jammu and Jammuiat. It shall only escalate alienation amidst three regions—*Kashmir Valley* v. *Jammu* v. *Ladakh like Kashmir* v. *India* v. *Pakistan*. Fifth, seceding is incompatible with constitutional permissibility, because the integration is so well neatly woven in the language of Article 1 of the Constitution of India "India that is Bharat shall be the Union of States" that makes seceding and secession impossible, non-workable and impractical. (C.A.D., Vol. VII, p. 43; *In re Berubari*, A.I.R. 1960 S.C. 845; *Maganbhai* v. *Union of India*, A.I.R. 1969 S.C. 783; *Union of India* v. *Sukumar Sen Gupta*, A.I.R. 1990 S.C. 1692). Sixth, secession is rarely recognized in the international community under the aegis of International Law. Secession will *a fortiori* cause a grant secessionist movement in India that would escalate militancy, terrorism, and violence in the country.

NATIONAL GAME PLAN

India faces challenges to her integrity, sovereignty, security both internal and external, and defense from the propagators/ perpetrators/authors of the abovementioned Local, Pakistan, and International Game Plans. Besides, India has successfully been combating as well as quelling the ticklish game plans thrust by militant/terrorist groups like Jammu & Kashmir Liberation Front (JKLF 1977), All Parties Hurriyyat Conference: 1993: a coalition and conglomeration of 26 guerilla and political groups (some claim that it is actually a creation of the United States Institution of Peace—a Washington-based think tank), Muttahida Jihad Council, Hizb-ul-Mujahidin, Jaish-e-Mohammed, Lashkkar-e-Tayyiba, through Armed Forces, Politically, Diplomatically, and strategically by caring the respect for the observance of human rights to human dignity of those who are not the propagators or perpetrators or vouchers of secessionism, separatism, terrorism, and militancy. Another challenge that India faces is Pakistan's contempt for Accords/Agreements be that UN Resolutions of 1948, 1949, Tashkent Declaration 1966, Simla Agreement 1972, Lahore Declaration 1999. These Accords were meant to ease the tension between India and Pakistan over Kashmir. These Accords were to be a milestone in the development of synergic relationship. Had those Accords been honored there ought to have, it is assumed, developed a model SAARC like model European Union and EURO.

It may be argued that Pakistan signed the Accords/ Agreements with the least intention to adhere to them. [Brahama Chellaney, Why The Agreements Failed, *The Hindustan Times*, Sep. 8, 1999]. The contemptuous behavior of Pakistan was visible of planning the Kargil invasion while it signed the Lahore

Declaration (*Ibid.*). It has unequivocally *a multo fortiori* been opined that Pakistan has been the ultimate hypocrite by continuing to swear by the 1948 and 1949 UN Resolutions while at the same time violating them by refusing to withdraw from J&K (*Ibid.*). It may, however, be expressed that the only Accords/Agreements Pakistan have enforced that placed the onus of compliance on India for reasons not far to seek.

Encountered by these challenges, Islamabad Declaration reiterating Lahore Declaration, India and Pakistan initiated Confidence Building Measures to restore peace and normalcy in the region by initiating several measures in this perspective such as people to people contact through Muzfarabad Kaman Amman Setu route, Wagha route, Khokhara route, road and railway routes, exchange of journalists, cultural troops, etc. through the aegis of Social Sciences Study Center and other agencies.

Besides, India initiated internal CBM by holding First Jammu and Kashmir Round Table Conference in Delhi in February 2006, and Second Jammu and Kashmir Round Table Conference in Srinagar on 24th and 25th May 2006. The Prime Minister of India, Dr. Manmohan Singh, declared the strategic policy plan by identifying five issues for an in-depth examination by five Committees, namely,

Group I: Confidence Building Measures Across Segments of Society in the State: Headed by Mr. Mohd. Ansari

The Group will evolve:

- Measures to improve the condition of people affected by militancy.
- Schemes to rehabilitate all orphans and widows affected by militancy.
- Issues relating to the relaxation of conditions for persons who have foresworn militancy.
- An effective rehabilitation policy, including employment, for Kashmiri Pandit migrants.
- An approach considering issues relating to return of Kashmiri youth from areas controlled by Pakistan.
- Measures to protect and preserve the unique cultural and religious heritage of the State.

Group II: Strengthening Relations Across the Line of Control: Headed by Mr. M.K. Rasgotra

To recommend measures to:

- Simplify procedures to facilitate travel across the Line of Control.
- Increase goods traffic.
- Expand people-to-people contact.
- Open up new routes such as Kargil, Skardu, etc.

Group III: Economic Development: Headed by Dr. C. Rangarajan

To evolve strategy that ensures:

- Balanced economic development and employment generation.
- Balanced regional and sub-regional development within the State.

Group IV: Ensuring Good Governance: Headed by Mr. N.C. Saxena

To consider effective measures to:

- Increase responsiveness, accountability and transparency of the administration.
- Strengthen local self-government.
- Effectively monitor development programs.
- Institute zero tolerance for human rights violations.
- Strengthen the Right to Information.
- Provide adequate security to all segments of society, particularly the minority communities.

Group V: Strengthening Relations between the State and the Centre: Headed by Justice Sageer Ahmad

To deliberate on:

- Matters relating to the special status of Jammu and Kashmir within the Indian Union.
- Methods of strengthening democracy, secularism and the rule of law in the State.
- Deliberate on effective devolution of powers among

different regions to meet regional, sub-regional and ethnic aspirations.

Representation of almost all political parties has been taken care of, but the Report (Annexures 1-5) ignores the consensus of views of all the representatives. It is a "Quiet Diplomacy" to "quietus of genesis of Centre-State issues." It was consisted of 21 member. The Group had only met for the first and the last time on 2-3 September, 2007 with a consensus opinion to meet again to deliberate upon the issues. Suddenly and surprisingly, Justice Sageer Ahmad submitted the "Summary of Recommendations" without the signatures of the Chairman of the Group Justice Sageer Ahmad as well as 21 members. This is disrespect to the members. A Justice has done injustice to the issues. The recommendations show a "de-strengthening approach" in place of "strengthening Relations between the State and the Centre." With all diffidence, modesty and humility, it is submitted that the report is 'judicially mockery, political gimmicks and socio-ethic joke'. It is devoid of all cannons of socio-judicious ethics. Justice Sageer Ahmad's report sounds bad because it proposes bad reforms and, therefore, not beautiful. Its recommendations are bad for the country and worse for the State. The reasons are not far to seek. The working of Centre-State relations does not depend on the independence approach, but on the "functional reciprocal dependence" approach that shall culminate into the success of strengthening of Centre-State relations within Constitutional scheme, Constitutional values, Constitutional culture, and Constitutional morality.

Critical Observations and Concluding Summations

Indian Game Plan seems to be of new strategy to come out of the cobweb of Local, Pakistan and International Game Plans, which are Kashmir Valley centric with least concern for the nationalist feelings of Jammu and Ladakh populace. The above tripartite approach is coupled with blow hot and blow cold behavior pattern. Be that as it may, the most important issue is that the Indian Game Plan ought not to fall prey of the abovementioned tripartite Game plans. India has to be tactics in her synergic strategy planning lest it becomes the victim in the trapping of tripartite deceptive Game Plans. India's Game Plan ought to be modeled in safeguarding her boundaries, sovereignty, integrity, internal and external security, and defense. She has to evolve new strategies to combat the challenges that are threats to her internal as well as external security. The security threats are multifaceted nature that spring from the problems of Postcolonial world, namely, interethnic, racial, quasi-racial, ideological, strategic, economic, social, and neo-political alignments. These Groups, four out of five, seem to have addressed themselves certain penetrating questions to plug loopholes in the system and suggested remedial measures in improving the system. This appears may not have been an easy task. It seems a Herculean task, because in the restoration of the confidence of all, including the politicians, have to be conscientious, sincere and above politicking in their behavior pattern. Whether their recommendations are another docket for the cupboards as well as the spiders to weave enchanting deceptive fabric, the time would only speak. However, in my opinion, these Groups have not addressed minutely the basic question why, how and under what circumstances did confidence loose? Who is in the garb of whom? In the answer of these million dollar questions alone lay the perpetual confidence building strategy. Militancy, terrorism and proxy war thrust on India from across the borders are responsible to give rise to matters of internal as well as external contentions and are responsible obstacles in confidence building measures. Successive State governments have not been considering State of J&K as one composite unit, but in three different units, and as such a contributory factor in simmering the confidence. Lack of good governance, accountability, and transparency are equally responsible for the loss of confidence of the populace in the functioning of the system, and, hence, obstacles in sustainable governance. The regressive corruption is on the ascendancy and progressive corruption on the decay, and 'care me not' responsive as well as responsible attitudes having been developing resentment, dissatisfaction and belying faith. Emergence, perpetuation, and continuation of fundamentalism are another factor for simmering the confidence. Exodus of Hindus in majority from the Valley has not only changed the demography but also has been responsible for the loss of confidence and faith of the said populace, designated as internally displaced persons, in the governments and their style of functioning. Exodus of Hindus, due to the impetus of terrorism, from other parts of the State and her apathy/impassiveness for such internally displaced persons seems another cause of loss of confidence. Maligning the security forces in the pretext of human rights as well as International Humanitarian Laws violations sloganeering gives boost to the militants, terrorists, propagators of proxy war to escalate in their nefarious activities, and demoralization of security forces as well as nationalists. This aspect as required to be addressed has not gained that sort of intensity as was expected, and as such leaves a wide void to be filled in when seems to be a futuristic strategy. There is no uniform rehabilitation or resettlement policy for internally displaced persons, displaced persons and refugees from West Pakistan of 1947, and, naturally, lack of confidence as well as faith. The Working Group on

Confidence Building Measures in its Report of January 2007 has, *inter alia*, recommended that "the rehabilitation problems of refugees of 1947 who came over from adjoining areas of Pakistan across International border need to be examined and settled once for all. These persons are not eligible for being permanent residents of the State". The status of such refugee-persons has been addressed with deceptive as well as contemptuous *lingua fauna*. The status of such refugee-persons continues to be that of homeless persons; non-domicile persons, and speaks volumes about their fate. The Working Group on the Confidence Building Measures has evaporated the soup and sauce of the confidence of such refugee-persona. We aspire for External Confidence Building Measures, but give least to the Internal Confidence Building Measures, seem to be a big paradox. We appear to have missed the opportunity once again by loosing the confidence of such persona who have confidence in us in the long cherished hope that they would cease to be homeless as well as non-domiciliary. The Vth Working Group on Centre-State Relations on the subject matter has failed to address the problem in the right perspectives; rather its language seems to be of artificiality and contrived paradigms because of its minimal insights into the mutual coordination of Law and Morality. The Working Group appears to have made this law and morality knot a riddle wrapped in mystery inside an enigma. Its recommendation seems to be lost of farsightedness, because it permeates the Othello's Sword to hang on the heads of such refugee-persona. Its maximalists' perception appears to leave the problem unresolved in the hands of those who failed to resolve it. This seems, in my opinion, the matter in the hands of those who though may have the desire to contribute but could not do so because when the flesh is weak, the spirit however willing cannot execute. Self-rule and autonomy are political ideologies of two different political parties, which do not carry majority support from all the regions of the State. Self-rule and autonomy stand rejected by Parliament of India, and as such cannot be conceded as viable solutions to the confidence building. Jammu and Ladakh regions represent nationalist and integrationist behavior pattern to remain in coordination as well as cooperation with the Union of India, whereas Valley presents otherwise. What a paradox in confidence building measures! Coordination between delimitation and communalization has belied confidence-building hopes of straightening demographic imbalances. Inclusion of Article 370 in the text of the Constitution of India has never been the aspiration of "We the people of J&K and India", and as such its continuation belies hopes of confidence building. Working with the Constitution and democracy have been examined as well as re-examined with reiterations by Sarkaria Commission and Venkatachallia Commission that any interference with the working of the Constitution and democracy will offend the Basic Structure of the Constitutional culture. The endeavors of the Working Group have to be to strengthen coordinative as well as cooperative federal culture and that alone will bring strength in the Unity and Integrity of the Indian Nation. And, the only efforts that are required in this direction are to not to belittle the present working of Center-State relations' confidence. Equitable Developments and financial allocations on the basis of equalization in the three regions of the State shall develop faith and confidence in the whole populace of the State. Eco-tourism (economic and ecological) shall be the focus for the whole State. Promotion of pilgrimages like Shardapeeth will yield confidence. Confidence building on *ad hoc* basis amidst one section of the populace shall be at the cost of entire populace that shall not yield meaningful results. Groups like Hurriyyat, JKLF, etc. that do not represent the voice of the entire population of the State must not be encouraged, otherwise that shall cost heavily in confidence building measures. Any political mileage if given to any political party shall be disastrous; the only mileage that has to be worked out will be for the Unity and Integrity of the Indian Nation, and nothing less, nothing more. To enhance confidence, there have to be no compromise—internally and externally. The "Havana Joint Mechanism to Terrorism Statement" of September 2006 both by Prime Minister of India Dr. Manmohan Singh and President of Pakistan General Pervez Musharraff seems to be susceptible and has many hidden compromises, and as such has to be perceived as well as pursued with utmost caution. It is quintessential to submit that proposed local, Pakistan and international modules are not short of quagmire because those modules encourage self-determination, self-rule, autonomy, independence, secessionism, ceding on the basis of 'Back Channel Diplomacy' conceived in four comprehensive formulae, namely, Northern Ireland, Kosovo, East Timor, American Think Tank. It may be niche to submit that India has to some time pursue hard-state policies as well as strategies in place of soft-state policies through dialogue in order to resolve inconclusive dispute with synergic strategies lest it becomes indefinite. Synergic strategy and comity in the South Asia region [SAARC] to developing trade, commerce, culture relationship, academia exchange, may yield positive results, this synergic comity shall only strengthen South Asia region and may be an envious harbinger for the others to emulate. This needs courageous strategies to work out perpetual peace solutions for the good of human beings, for the happiness of human beings, for the prosperous development of human beings. This is the only synergic strategy to keep the history in the past and march progressively like pilgrimage progress for everlasting peace and prosperity. This is the only human right module that may have to be worked out with synergic strategy. We must keep before our eyes the wise saying. "Eternal vigilance is the price of liberty". We must behave in such a manner that it might not ever be said in repentance of us that:

> *"Khola Kafas To Taqate Parwaz Hi Nahin*
> *Bulbul Tere Nasib Ko Sayyad Kya Kare".*

REFERENCES

1. Durga Das, Sardar Patel's Correspondence New Light on Kashmir, 1945-1950, Vol. I, 1971.
2. Collier's Encyclopedia: http://www.mtholyoke.edu/acad/interl/colkash.htm
3. K.L. Bhatia, Jammu and Kashmir Article 370 of the Constitution of India, 1997.
4. htt://www.criisweb.org/showreport.cfm?reportid; Somini Sen Gupta, The India-Pakistan Tension: The Background; Struggle for Kashmir is Fueled by Clashing, *New York Times*, January 13, 2002.
5. U.N. Documents on the Kashmir Issue can be procured at the UN Website www.un.org

6. C. Joseph Chacko, India's Contribution to International Law, Kashmir and International Law, Rescueil Des Cours, 1958.
7. South Asia Terrorism Portal Statement: htt://www.satp.org/satporgtp/countries/India/states/jandk/terrorist outfits/Hurriyat.htm
8. John Gershman, Crisis Watch Profile: Kashmir at http://www.selfdetermine.org/conflicts/kashmir/html
9. Howard B. Schaffer, Reconsidering the US Role, *The Washington Quarterly*, Spring (2001).
10. International Crisis Group, Kashmir: Confrontation and Miscalculation, Asia Report No: 35 (2002).
11. Somini Sengupta, The India-Pakistan Tension, *op. cit.*
12. Brahma Chellenay, Pakistan's Contempt for Accords, *The Hindustan Times*, September 8, 1999, www.jammu-kashmir.com/archives/archives1999/99september08.html
13. Ajay Singh and Anthony Davis, *Asia Week*, Unaligned Line of Control: Why India and Pakistan Differ over the Border, www.asiaweek.com/news/990709/nat3.html
14. Kuldip Nayar, Pak May Challenge Siachen Control, www.rediff.com/news/1999/jul/16nayar.htm
15. John Gerhman, Overview of Self-Determination Issues, Self-Determination on Forcus, http://www.selfdetermine.org/conflicts/Kashmir body.html
16. Strobe Talbot, Talbot on Self-Determination in an Interdependent World, Foreign Policy, Spring 2000, http://www.usembassy.
17. EU Report on Kashmir backs India's Stand, 2007.
18. Jammu and Kashmir: Self-Determination. Demands for a Plebiscite and Secession: Examining the Contradictions, http://www.members.tripod.com
19. Eric Kolodner, The Future of the Right to Self-Determination, 10 *Conn. J. Int'l. L.*, 153 (1994).
20. Yves Beigbeder, International Monitoring of Plebiscite, Referenda and National Elections: Self-Determination and Transition to Democracy, 1994.
21. Irrma Foley, Karen Heymann, Susan Kagondu, Catherine Kihara and Lynne Madnick, Kashmir: The Road to Peace, Public International Law and Policy Group, www.publicinternationallaw.org
22. Jammu and Kashmir Government and Administration, http://www.jammukashmir.nic.in/govt/welcome.html
23. Article 370: Law and Politics, *Frontline*, Volume 17, September 2000, http://www.flonnet.com
24. Arvind Lavakare, The Indeterminate Life of Article 370, II, June 2002.
25. J&K Autonomy Committee Report, Vols. I and II, 2000, http://www.indiainfo.com/news/2000/06/20/constitution.html

26. Election Commission of India: Background Information on Jammu and Kashmir, http://www.eci.gov.in
27. Raju G.C. Thomas, What is Third World Security?, Department of Political Science, Marquette University, Milwaukee, Wisconsin, *Annual Review of Political Science*, Vol. 6: 205-32, 2003, http://www.arjournals.annualreviews.org
28. Prem Nath Bazaz, Kashmir in Crucible.
29. C.A.D., Vol. VII, p. 43.
30. C.A.D., Vols. X-XII, 1989 Ed., Reprint, pp. 421-29.
31. *Magher Singh* v. *Principal Secretary, Jammu and Kashmir*, A.I.R. 1953, J&K 25.
32. *In re Berubari*, A.I.R. 1960 S.C. 845.
33. *Maganbhai* v. *Union of India*, A.I.R. 1969, S.C. 783.
34. *Union of India* v. *Sukumar Sen Gupta*, A.I.R. 1990, S.C. 1629.

The Constitution of Jammu & Kashmir : The Genesis of Crisis— Past Tense, Present Imperfect and Future Indefinite

I feel honoured to be fortunate enough to present the views in the august gathering in the presence of respected Lt. Gen. (Rtd.) Shri S.K. Sinha, the former Governor of J&K State, and Shri Arun Jaitely, the Honourable Member of Parliament and the Leader of Opposition in the Rajya Sabha, on the most unfortunate topic of the day, which is of contrived nature.

THE DISTURBING QUESTIONS

- Why a special Constitutional treatment to only one Federal Unit of the Indian Federation that is Union of States?
- Why a separate Constitution of J&K within the federal structure of the Constitution of India when all the States of Union of India work within the Constitutional scheme of India?

THE GENESIS OF THE CONSTITUTION OF J&K

The Genesis of the Constitution of J&K is Article 370 of the Constitution of India moved by Shri Gopalaswamy Ayyanger as Article 306-A in the Constituent Assembly of India on Monday, 17 October, 1949.

Article 306-A was not originally a part of the "Draft Constitution" prepared by the Drafting Committee headed by

Dr. B.R. Ambedkar and presented in the Constituent Assembly of India under the Chairmanship of Dr. Rajendra Prasad.

At the outset; it may be submitted that the four representatives of J&K in the Constituent Assembly, namely, Mr. Sheikh Mohd. Abdullaha, Mr. Afzal Beg, Mr. Maulana Masoodi, and Mr. M.R. Baigra, did not overtly and covertly utter a single word on the extent and language of Article 306-A irrespective of the fact that they were present physically in the Constituent Assembly on the day of its presentation in the Constituent Assembly. [They were the signatories to the final adopted Constitution of India]

It is also a matter of historical fact that there was no word from Dr. B.R. Ambedkar, because he was not in favour of a separate and special constitutional status to J&K. He reportedly happened to convey: "You want India to defend Kashmir, give Kashmiris equal rights all over India, but you want to deny India and Indians all rights in Kashmir. I am Law Minister of India. I can't be a party to such a betrayal of National interest".

It is also a matter of history that except Mr. Gopalaswamy Ayyanger and Mr. Maulana Hasrat Mohani, no other Member of the Constituent assembly did participate in the debate on the extent and content of Article 306-A.

A SEPARATE CONSTITUTION OF J&K A BY PRODUCT OF ARTICLE 370!

- It is a known fact that the separate Constitution of J&K is the by product of Article 370.
- It creates a sovereignty within a sovereign [Indian] permeating the feelings of a separate country as well as separatism.
- It is against the basic structure of the Constitution of India and, hence, legally and constitutionally incompatible, and not permissible.

WHAT DOES ARTICLE 370 ENJOIN?

The language of Article 370 (original 306-A) is inasmuch as deceitful as the beautiful language of Constitution of J&K is deceitful and the root cause of separatism.

1. Article 238 shall not apply in relation to the State of J&K. [Paradox: Article 238 originally related to Part B States in the original constitutional language, which was repealed from the Constitution of India by Seventh Amendment Act, 1956 as a consequence of States Reorganization Act, 1956 doing away with Part A,B,C states. Unfortunately, this Article continues to occupy a place in the language of Article 370)!
2. The power of Parliament to make laws for the State of J&K shall be limited to
   (i) those matters in the Union List and Concurrent List which, in consultation with the Government of the State, are declared by the President to correspond to matters specified in the Instrument of Accession governing the accession of the State to India, i.e., Defence, Foreign Affairs, and Communication.
   (ii) such other matters in the said List as, with the concurrence of the Government of the State, the President may by order specify, i.e., Central Laws in terms of matters enumerated in the Union List and Concurrent List shall not extend to the State of J&K without the concurrence of the State Government.
3. The provisions of Article 1 of Constitution of India shall apply in relation to the State of J&K. [Article 1 states India that is BHARAT shall be the Union of States — Schedule I and Schedule IV. Article 1 became operative on the date of the adoption of the Constitution of India, i.e., 26 November, 1949; Accession on 26/27 October, 1947, J&K like other Native/Princely States part of Indian Federal Democratic Republic on the date of adoption of the Constitution of India, i.e., 26 November, 1949].
4. Such of the other provisions of the Indian Constitution and subject to such exceptions and modifications shall apply in relation to the State of J&K as the President may by Order specify. (Constitutional Application Order, 1950: Articles 1 and 5-11, i.e., Citizenship of India — All permanent residents of J&K became citizens of India

under it; Constitution Application Orders 1954,1962, 1966 and 1985—extended provisions of the Indian Constitution from time to time with certain modifications; Article 35-A added as fundamental right for J&K giving special privileges to the permanent residents of J&K].

Pre-1953 or Pre-1947 or autonomy or Azadi demands amount to the cessation of Article 1 (J&K no more federal unit of Indian federation) and withdrawal of Citizenship right to the people of J&K.

5. The President may, by public notification, declare that this Article shall cease to be operative or shall be operative only with such exceptions and modifications and from such date as he may specify: *Provided that the recommendations of the Constituent Assembly of the State shall be necessary before the President issues such notification.*
   - This is the root for the establishment of the Constituent Assembly for the making of J&K Constitution.
   - This Article can be abrogated by the State Assembly as it enjoys constituent making power by amending J&K Constitution. (Section 147 of J&K Constitution). The Governor of the State during first six months' governor's rule under J&K Constitution can recommend for its deletion [as legislative and executive powers are vested in the Governor]. The Governor during the operation of President's rule under Article 356 of the Constitution of India can recommend for its deletion or abrogation and the Parliament of India can play such role.
   - It facilitates the growth of secessionism, terrorism, militancy, subversion and demand for independence *Azadi*, self rule, pre-1953, pre-1947, autonomy and internal autonomy.
   - It also facilitates the growth and continuation of corrupt oligarchies, and personal aberrations.
   - It puts false and fictitious notions and hopes in the minds of the youth.

- It gives rise to regional tensions and conflicts [three regions of the State: Jammu, Kashmir and Ladakh].
- It makes the nationalists and integrationists of Jammu and Ladakh regions people to suffer.
- It makes an inroad for autonomy assumed to be available just on the stroke of pen pushing, which is otherwise incompatible and not attainable in practice under the constitutional provisions, constitutional practices and conventions.

WHAT DOES AUTONOMY OR PRE-1953 OR PRE-1947 OR SELF RULE POSITION IMPLY?

- It amounts to deprivation of right of Indian citizenship to the permanent residents of J&K, thus depriving them the fruits of fundamental rights.
- It shall amount to the deprivation of the status of J&K State within the framework of the Constitution of India, which declares India that is Bharat shall be the Union of State.
- It shall amount to the propagators of Azadi or autonomy or pre-1953 or pre-1947 to say: "You will send and I will spend without accountability; you will have no say even if I build a corrupt and callous oligarchy and cause a situation in which Damocles sword of secession, subversion, militancy, terrorism, self rule, loyalties across the border, pre-1953, pre-1947 could be kept hanging permanently on your head".

HOW FAR J&K CONSTITUTION THE ROOT CAUSE FOR SUBVERSIVE, SECESSIONIST, TERRORIST, MILITANCY ACTIVITIES

See the Preamble language of the Indian Constitution and J&K Constitution:

- Indian Constitution: "We the People of India ..."
- J&K Constitution: "We the People of J&K..."
- How people of J&K are different from the people of India? This language gives the impression as people of J&K are different from the people of India. This seems to be the root cause of subversion, secessionism,

separatism, terrorism, militancy, pre-1953 or pre-1947 or self rule or autonomy.

- Sections 6-9 of he J&K Constitution are also the root cause of secessionism, subversion, etc. The language of these sections could have been summed up in one Section, viz., the permanent residents of J&K shall be the permanent citizens of India. This could have facilitated all citizens of India to integrate culminating into the complete integration of J&K to India, and there ought not have been the direct consequences of subversion, secessionism, separatism, militancy, terrorism, and across border loyalties.
- In the backdrop of this, the Instrument of Accession became a thing of the past, and a dead past could not have been the bone of contention every now and then. Hence, it can't be reopened.
- Besides, a specious or fictitious impression has been created that all princely States except the State of J&K agreed to integrate themselves to India by accepting the Constitution of India that would come. I quote Hari Singh's announcement of 15 July, 194 as mentioned in Durga Dass, Sardar Patel's Correspondence, Vol. I, pp. 66-68 and 13-15:
- "... Naturally we are interested in the progress of India as a whole. *My views on the subject are well known and on more than one occasion I have Riven expression to them. They are briefly that we look forward to taking our due place in the new constitutional structure of India*, whereby we hope that India will be able to take its proper place as a great nation, one of the brotherhood of nations, and to wield great influence in the affairs of the world, thus adding to human civilization those aspects of our great culture which will help to solve the problems of mankind".
- *Had this announcement of Hari Singh taken conscientiously and seriously, there ought not have born Article 370 and a separate Constitution of J&K breeding secessionism, subversion, pre-1953, pre-1947, autonomy, terrorism, self rule, militancy, and across border loyalties.*

ARTICLE 370 AND J&K CONSTITUTION *MOGNA CORTO OF DISCRIMINATION*

Mr. Maulana Hasrat Mohani asked in the Constituent Assembly—Why this discrimination? To which Mr. Gopalaswamy Ayyengar replied—may be speciously relevant then but not now—that Kashmir's conditions were special and required special treatment. Special conditions were:

1. War was going on within the limits of J&K.
2. There was cease fire agreed; but the conditions in the State were unusual. Normalcy was to be restored.
3. Part of the State was in the hands of rebels and enemies [(POK): Azadi, self rule, autonomy could have been liberation of POK and its complete integration to India in terms of Instrument of Accession since POK happened to be the integral geographical and territorial part of J&K sending unequivocal signals to the rulers across the border].
4. We were engaged with U.N. in regard to J&K. Freedom from entanglement was possible when the Kashmir problem was satisfactorily settled [J&K disputant reference to U.N. now is redundant].
5. Government of India had committed themselves to the people of Kashmir to ascertain whether they will remain with the Republic of India or wish to go out of it. Government of India committed to the will of the people by means of plebiscite provided that peaceful and normal conditions were restored and the impartiality of the plebiscite could be guaranteed [This is the price We the People of India are paying].
6. Praja Sabha was dead.
7. We had also agreed that the will of the people, through the instrument of a Constituent Assembly, will determine the Constitution of the state as well as the sphere of Union jurisdiction over the State [This speaks bankruptcy of farsightedness by conceiving a separate Constitution for the State with the disastrous consequences like Azadi or self rule or autonomy or pre-

1953 or pre-1947 or subversive activities or secessionism or militancy or terrorism or loyalties across the border, and the price We the People of India are paying the Valley of Kashmir].

8. It was inevitable to establish an interim system and Article 306-A (370) was an attempt to establish interim system. It could have come to an end as soon as normalcy was restored, peace was established, and Constituent Assembly accepted the Instrument of Accession. [This had already happened. The Constituent Assembly of J&K had already accepted in unequivocal language the Instrument of Accession, and the Constitution of J&K by its Preamble language: " We the people of J&K having solemnly resolved, in pursuance of accession of this State to India which took place on 26th day of October, 1947, to further define the existing relationship of the State with the Union of India as an integral part thereof, ... and assuring the Unity of the Nation". Hereafter, it ought to have mentioned, by a reference to the contents of the letter of Maharaja Hari Singh as mentioned above, to further define the existing relationship of the State of J&K with the Union of India as its integral federal Unit within the framework of the Constitution of India that shall apply and extend to the State of J&K as it applies and extends to other UNION OF STATES of India that is BHARAT. Here, we lost the golden opportunity and thus paying the price of our past follies the Valley of Kashmir at the sufferance of the citizens of Jammu and Ladakh who have no links with secessionism or separatism or azadi or autonomy or pre-1953 or pre-1947 or self rule or militancy or terrorism or loyalties across the border taking instructions from them for subversive activities or notorious proxy war activities].

SUBMISSIONS

1. Political will lacked farsightedness and committed a mistake by moving and adopting Article 306-A (370).

2. It was unwise to recommend and propose a separate Constituent Assembly for J&K, which gave a separate Constitution of J&K, thus, sowing the seeds for generating separate feelings of secessionism or subversion or pre-1953 or pre-1947 or azadi or autonomy or self-rule.

3. How there could be two sovereign bodies (Constituent Assemblies—one for India and another for J&K) within one federal democratic republic India that is BHARAT. Hence, against the basic structure of the Constitutional spirit.

4. It disturbs to assure the Unity and Integrity of One Nation in the maintenance of uniformity.

5. Remodel the language of Article 370 by replacing its language empowering the Governor of the State to take steps to develop those areas of the State which have thus far been neglected to bringing them in the mainstream as provided in the constitutional language of Articles 371 and 371A-371I [temporary and special provisions for the States of Maharashtra and Gujarat, Nagaland, Assam, Manipur, Andhra Pradesh, Sikkim, Mizoram, Arunachal Pradesh, Goa].

6. To bring full moon integration, to recommend to scrap a separate Constitution of J&K to do away with the psyches of separatism or secessionism or subversion or pre-1953 or pre-1947 or autonomy or azadi or self rule or across border loyalties.

7. To achieve, let us solemnly resolve to generate public opinion in the country lest:

"Khola Kafas To Taqote Porwoz Hi Nahin
Bulbul Tere Nasib Ko Sayyad Kya Kare"

प्रस्तावना

जम्मू और कश्मीर को घेरने वाली आंतरिक और बाह्य राजनीतिक उलझनों और जटिलताओं से विश्व परिचित है। मेरा अभिप्रायः इन्हें ढकने का नहीं है। यह आलेख विशुद्ध रूप से और मात्र रूप से एक विधि विद्यार्थी ज्ञाता के नाते एक विनम्र प्रयास है ताकि पाठक इससे परिचित हो सकें।

क्या जम्मू कश्मीर एक समस्या है? यदि यह समस्या है तो यह समस्या कृत्रिम विकारयुक्त काल्पनिक नीतियों का सामूहिक परिणाम है। वास्तव में जम्मू कश्मीर समस्या आधुनिक इतिहास के विकृत तथ्यों का स्वरूप प्रस्तुत करता है। 26–27 अक्तूबर 1947 को इस विकृति का प्रारंभ जम्मू कश्मीर का भारत गणराज्य के साथ विलय होने पर आरंभ हुआ जब यह राज्य भारत का अटूट अंग बना। तबसे लेकर यह विषय आंतरिक और बाह्य दृष्टि के अनेकानेक उलझनों का शिकार होता गया। इसके अतिरिक्त यह लगता है कि अलग–अलग समय पर कुछ लोगों की हठधर्मी के कारण जम्मू कश्मीर की यह समस्या विकट से विकटतम् होती गई। यह परिस्थिति उन सत्ता आसीन लोगों के कारण बन गई जिनका व्यवहार हमेशा अस्थिर एवं काल्पनिक बना रहा। ऐसे लोग जो भारत की मुख्य धारा से बाहर रहना चाहते थे, उन लोगों के षड्यंत्रों का शिकार बन गया। कश्मीर समस्या विलयवादी और अलगाववादी शक्तियों के बीच के संघर्ष का परिणाम है। जम्मू कश्मीर का विलय विवाद का विषय नहीं बनना चाहिए था क्योंकि यह ऐतिहासिक, धार्मिक, नैतिक, संवैधानिक और कानूनी दृष्टि से भारत का अभिन्न अंग बन चुका था। अलगाववादी भरसक प्रयास कर रहे थे कि इस ऐतिहासिक सत्य के अपने झूठे प्रचार से विश्व को भ्रम में डाल सकें। इसमें कोई संदेह नहीं कि कश्मीर समस्या का आधार झूठ, निरंतर झूठ और कोरे झूठ से उत्पन्न हुआ है। ग्रेटर कश्मीर, नया कश्मीर, जनमत संग्रह, स्वशासन, स्वाययत्ता और पुनर्वास की घोषणाओं ने इसको और उलझा कर रख दिया है। कश्मीर देवी–देवताओं, संतों, ऋषियों, फकीरों और पीरों की पूज्य स्थली रही है और इसलिए इसको

धरती पर स्वर्ग कहा जाता है। जहां पर भिन्न मतों और आस्था रखने वालों के अपने–अपने श्रद्धा स्थल रहे हैं। जिसके कारण यहां सदैव धार्मिक सद्भावना बनी रही है। यह क्षेत्र भगवान शिव के पवित्र स्थानों से भरा है, इसलिए इस धरती पर 'शैवमत' का प्रादुर्भाव हुआ और यह मत फल फूलकर भारत के एक महान दर्शन के रूप में प्रस्थापित हुआ है। जम्मू कश्मीर की तथाकथित समस्या एक पक्षीय विचार से उपजी और इसके समाधान के लिए ऐसी नरम नीतियां अपनाई गईं जिसके कारण यह समस्या सुलझने की बजाए और अधिक उलझ गई। यह कहना गलत न होगा कि हमारे नीति निर्धारकों ने स्वयं ही इस सीधे सादे प्रश्न को एक ऐसी पहेली बना दिया कि जिससे बाहर निकल पाना आसान नहीं रहा। इस वक्त यह उपयुक्त होगा कि जिन लोगों ने इस साधारण समस्या को उलझा दिया है उनके विचार और व्यवहार का विश्लेषण किया जाए। 1931, 1942, 1947, 1949, 1950, 1953 में जिन सांप्रदायिक और अलगाववादी मुस्लिम कश्मीरी नेताओं और उनके समर्थकों ने इस राज्य को पाकिस्तान में मिलाने, जनमत संग्रह करवाने तथा जम्मू कश्मीर पर भारत की प्रभुसत्ता को कम करने के लिए षड्यंत्र रचे, उनके प्रति हमारी नीतियां कभी भी सुदृढ़ एवं निर्णायक नहीं रही। कश्मीर के अंदर ऐसा विषैला साहित्य छपता और बहता रहा जिसके कारण कई भारत विरोधी षड्यंत्र बनते रहे और परिणाम स्वरूप भारत और पाकिस्तान की दूरियां बढ़ती रहीं। दूसरी ओर, कश्मीर की मानसिकता विकृत होती रही। महा शक्तियों की प्रत्यक्ष और गुप्त नीतियां भी इस परिस्थिति को अधिक भयावह बनाने के लिए अपना योगदान देती रहीं। इन घटनाओं से कुछेक ऐसे तथ्यों का भी उद्घाटन होता है जिसके कारण सरदार पटेल, गोपालास्वामी अईअंगर, महाराजा हरीसिंह, मेहरचंद महाजन और इन सरीखों अनेकानेक दूसरे महत्वपूर्ण लोग भी परिस्थितियों का शिकार बनते रहे हैं। एक साधारण कश्मीर विषय को उलझा हुआ जटिल कश्मीर विषय बना दिया। यह चीज भी सामने आ जाती है कि इन परिस्थितियों के कारण जम्मू कश्मीर के भारत के साथ विलय के कट्टर समर्थक भी एक स्वतंत्र कश्मीर की बात सोचने लग पड़े। एक सीधा एवं सरल कश्मीर ऐसा विकृत हुआ जिसने भारत और पाकिस्तान के संबंधों को सदा के लिए कड़वाहट से भर दिया और दूसरी ओर परस्पर धार्मिक सद्भावना के स्थान पर धार्मिक संघर्ष का वातावरण बना दिया। इन तथ्यों की पृष्ठभूमि में यह युक्तियुक्त होगा कि उन घटनाओं की श्रृंखला का उल्लेख किया जाए जो कश्मीर समस्या के कई पक्षों पर प्रकाश डालने वाले हैं।

घटनाओं की पृष्ठभूमि

जम्मू कश्मीर राज्य का क्षेत्रफल 86024 वर्ग मील है (2,22,236 स्क. कि. मी.)। यह राज्य कश्मीर घाटी, जम्मू, लद्दाख, बालितस्तान, गिलगित, हूजां और नगर क्षेत्रों को मिलाकर बना है। इस क्षेत्र का सामरिक महत्व है। इसकी सीमाएं पश्चिम में पाकिस्तान और उत्तर में अफगानिस्तान, उत्तर–पूर्व में चीन के साथ मिलती हैं। इसके अतिरिक्त यह रूस के बहुत निकट पड़ता है। मध्य एशिया को जाने वाला मार्ग इसी क्षेत्र से गुजरता है। आधुनिक इतिहास इस बात का साक्षी है कि सितंबर 1925 में महाराजा हरीसिंह के सत्तारूढ़ होने पर जम्मू कश्मीर राज्य में एक नए युग का प्रारंभ हुआ। 'कश्मीर कश्मीरियों के लिए' का आंदोलन जो शंकरलाल कौल की अध्यक्षता में आरंभ किया गया वह जम्मू कश्मीर के इतिहास के ऊपर एक काला धब्बा है। महाराजा हरीसिंह ने 1927 में स्टेट सब्जेक्ट कानून लागू करके कश्मीर से बाहर लोगों के लिए सरकारी नौकरियों और अचल संपत्ति खरीदने पर पाबंदी लगा दी थी। (प्रेमनाथ बजाज : कश्मीर इन करूसीबल)

1930 में श्रीनगर के कुछ मुस्लिम स्नातकों ने जिसमें शेख मुहम्मद अब्दुल्ला भी शामिल थे, एक रीडिंग रूम नाम की पार्टी का गठन किया। रीडिंग रूम पार्टी का गठन ही कश्मीर के मुसलमानों को महाराजा हरीसिंह के राज्य से दूर करने और मुस्लिम जनसंख्या से दूर रखने का कारण बन गया। इस घटना ने कश्मीरी मुसलमानों को सबसे अलग–थलग रहने का भाव पैदा कर दिया। शेख मुहम्मद अब्दुल्ला द्वारा 'मुस्लिम कान्फ्रेंस के गठन के कारण यह अलगाववाद की धारणा और सुदृढ़ हुई और शेख अब्दुल्ला ने महाराजा हरीसिंह के विरुद्ध मुसलमानों के प्रजातांत्रिक अधिकारों का संघर्ष शुरु कर दिया। इसके कारण हिंदू और मुसलमानों में मनमुटाव शुरु हो गया। जून 1931 में कश्मीर के अंदर सांप्रदायिक दंगे प्रारंभ हो गए। इन सांप्रदायिक दंगों में हिंदूओं

की बड़ी हानि हुई। तब हिंदू जनसंख्या के हित हेतु शेख मुहम्मद अब्दुल्ला ने कोई आवाज़ क्यों नहीं उठाई ? वह केवल मुस्लिम जनसंख्या के हित हेतु ही अपनी आवाज़ पुरज़ोर उठाते रहे। क्यों ? क्या इससे उनकी मानसिकता स्पष्ट नहीं होती है। इन दंगों ने राज्य में सांप्रदायिक संघर्ष का बीज बो दिया। अगस्त 1945 में जब शेख अब्दुल्ला नेशनल कान्फ्रेंस के अध्यक्ष थे, ने 'नया कश्मीर' की रूपरेखा बनाना आरंभ कर दिया। उसने समस्त जम्मू कश्मीर राज्य के लिए कोई रूपरेखा क्यों तैयार नहीं की ? शेख मुहम्मद अब्दुल्ला ने महाराजा हरीसिंह का विरोध करने के लिए ''भारत छोड़ो'' की तर्ज़ पर ''कश्मीर छोड़ो'' आंदोलन शुरू कर दिया। इंडियन इन्डिपेंडेंट एक्ट 1947 के माध्यम से ब्रिटिश पारलियामेंट ने हिंदूस्तान और पाकिस्तान को सत्ता हस्तांतरण का कानून बनाया। उसमें राजाओं द्वारा शासित राज्यों के लिए यह प्रावधान रखा गया कि वह भारत अन्यथा पाकिस्तान में से किसी के साथ अपने राज्य का विलय कर सकते हैं। 15 अगस्त 1947 को अंग्रेज़ों की प्रभुसत्ता समाप्त हो गई। तीन रियासतों को छोड़कर बाकी सब रियासतों का विलय हिंदूस्तान या पाकिस्तान के साथ हो गया। हैदराबाद और जूनागढ़ की रियासतों का विलय अनेक कारणों से विलंब से हुआ। परंतु आज तक इस बारे में कोई झगड़ा अथवा प्रश्नचिह्न नहीं हुआ है। जम्मू कश्मीर के महाराजा हरीसिंह भी समय पर निर्णय नहीं कर पा रहे थे। संभवता यही विलंब निर्णय बाद के संघर्ष का कारण बना। 22 अक्तूबर 1947 को उत्तर पश्चिम सीमा प्रान्त के कबालियों ने पाकिस्तान की सक्रिय सहायता और सांठ–गांठ से कश्मीर घाटी पर आक्रमण किया ताकि महाराजा हरीसिंह को पाकिस्तान के साथ अपने राज्य का विलय करने के लिए मजबूर कर दिया जाए। इस विकट परिस्थिति ने महाराजा हरीसिंह को मजबूर कर दिया कि वह भारत के अनेक नेताओं की बात माने और कश्मीर के आक्रमणकारियों को उखाड़ फेंकने के लिए भारत सरकार की सहायता ले। इन विशेष परिस्थितियों में महाराजा हरीसिंह ने अन्य लगभग 560 स्वतंत्र राज्यों की तरह बिना शर्त विलय पत्र पर हस्ताक्षर करके 26 अक्तूबर 1947 को भारत के साथ विलय किया जिसको 27 अक्तूबर 1947 को गवर्नर जनरल माउंटबेटन ने स्वीकार कर लिया। (सी० जोसेफ चेको, भारत का अन्तर्राष्ट्रीय विधि विचार–विनिमय में योगदान, 1958)

28 अक्तूबर 1947 को भारत के प्रधानमंत्री पंडित जवाहरलाल नेहरु ने पाकिस्तान के प्रधानमंत्री को तार करके सूचना दी कि, ''भारतीय सरकार ने

जो कार्यवाही की है, वह श्रीनगर पर आने वाले संकट की परिस्थितियों को देखते हुए उन पर थोपा गया है। राज्यारोहण के संदर्भ में यह भी स्पष्ट कर दिया गया है कि यह सब राज्य के लोगों के निर्णय और उनके संदर्भ के अधीन है। भारतीय सरकार उन पर अपना निर्णय थोपने की कोई इच्छा नहीं रखती और लोगों की इच्छाओं को स्वीकार करेगी। पर यह सब तब तक संभव नहीं है जब तक शांति और कानून की व्यवस्था लागू न हो जाए।'' (सी० जोसेफ चेको, भारत का अन्तर्राष्ट्रीय विधि विचार–विनिमय में योगदान, 1958)

जम्मू और कश्मीर का राज्यारोहण भारत में अंतिम और अटल है। अन्य कोई विकल्प नहीं है; यह अन्तर्राष्ट्रीय विधि को दृढ़ करता है। भारतीय स्वाधीनता अधिनियम, 1947 के अनुसार जम्मू और कश्मीर राज्य के महाराजा एक स्वतंत्र राजा हैं। अन्तर्राष्ट्रीय विधिशास्त्री ओप्पेंहेइम ने कहा, हर राज्य का राजा अपने राज्य के अधिपति के रूप में होता है और स्वयं प्रशासक बन जाता है। (ओप्पेंहेइम, अन्तर्राष्ट्रीय विधि, खंड एक, पृ० 758) यह तथ्य अतर्राष्ट्रीय विधि में अभिज्ञात हैं कि सभी शासक एक समान हैं और प्रभुसत्ता के प्रतिनिधि के रूप में प्रतीत होते हैं। वे अन्तर्राष्ट्रीय व्यक्ति हैं और अन्तर्राष्ट्रीय विधि का विषय हैं। कोलम्बिया विश्वविद्यालय के अन्तर्राष्ट्रीय विधि के उत्कृष्ट विधिशास्त्री आचार्य फिलप सी. जेस्सुप ने राज्य के अधिराजे को कुछ चिह्न देकर प्रमाणित किया है :

1. स्थायी जनसंख्या।
2. परिभाषित राज्यक्षेत्र।
3. सरकार ; और
4. अन्य राज्यों के साथ रिश्ता बनाने की क्षमता।

(यू.एन. सुरक्षा परिषद्, काउंसिल रिकार्ड्स्, 383 बैठक, दिसंबर 2, 1948, पृ० 9)

इन सबकी पृष्ठभूमि में यह निश्चय के साथ कहा जा सकता है कि जम्मू और कश्मीर के महाराजा अपने राज्य का नेतृत्व करते थे, 15 अगस्त 1947 से पहले भी तथा बाद में भी उनके पास अन्तर्राष्ट्रीय विधि का अन्तर्राष्ट्रीय विषय–चिह्न बनने के सारे गुण थे। इस विषय में जम्मू और कश्मीर उच्च न्यायालय के न्यायधीश शामीरी द्वारा दिए निर्णय ''मघेर सिंह बनाम प्रिंसिपल सेक्रेटरी जम्मू–कश्मीर'' (ए०आई०आर० 1953, जम्मू–कश्मीर 25) का संदर्भ दिया जा सकता है : ''निस्संदेह जम्मू–कश्मीर के महाराजा की स्थिति भारतीय

स्वाधीनता अधिनियम से पूर्व और बाद में स्वच्छता की परिचर्चा करती है। ब्रिटिश भारत के दो राज्यों भारत–पाकिस्तान के विभाजन से पहले कोई शक नहीं था कि जम्मू–कश्मीर का शासक ब्रिटिश राज की सूजरेनिटी के उतना ही अंदर था, जितना कि उसके अंदर विदेशी रिश्ते थे। लेकिन अब तक आंतरिक राजा का राज्य बिल्कुल सीमाहीन था। उस पर कोई बंधन नहीं था। इस संदर्भ में सैक्शन 4 और सैक्शन 5 जम्मू–कश्मीर संविधान अधिनियम को बनाना सही था जो नवंबर 1951 में संशोधित हुआ।''

''सैक्शन 4 : इस समय जो राज्य एच०एच० में हैं, वो उनके द्वारा और उन्हीं के नाम पर नियंत्रित हैं। सारे आकस्मिक अधिकार कुछ ऐसे राज्यों की तरफ हैं, जिन पर एच०एच० काम कर सकता है।''

''सैक्शन 5 : सैक्शन 5 या किसी अन्य अधिनियम का साथ यदि हम न दे तो राज्य और उसकी सरकार से संदर्भित सारे अधिकार जो व्यवस्थापक, निर्वाहक और न्यायिक हैं, स्वाभाविक होने के कारण हमेशा से महामहिम के द्वारा अपनाए गए हैं और रखे गए हैं। इस सैक्शन या किसी भी अन्य अधिनियम ने महामहिम के परम अधिकार को विधि बनाने के लिए, घोषणा करने और आज्ञा देने के लिए तथा नियुक्ति करने और उनके स्वाभाविक प्राधिकार की हैसियत से प्रभावित नहीं किया है और न ही करेंगे।''

इसलिए उच्च न्यायालय ने यह आदेश दिया कि :

''1. जहां तक आंतरिक राज्य के प्रभुत्व की बात है, शासक के अधिकार ब्रिटिश संसद के समान थे।''

''2. भारतीय स्वाधीनता अधिनियम 1947 के सैक्शन 7 के अंश के साथ जम्मू और कश्मीर राज्य अन्तर्राष्ट्रीय विधि की संपूर्णता में एक स्वतंत्र और प्रधान राज्य बन गया।''

''3. इस संपूर्णता में महत्वपूर्ण बन गए लोग अनियंत्रित हो गए।''

''4. हस्ताक्षर और राज्यारोहण की आज्ञा भारतीय सरकार की स्थिति पर आधारित थी और किसी और लक्ष्य के लिए थी।''

''5. महत्वपूर्ण बन गए लोग ने विश्वास के साथ स्थानांतरण की घोषणा की। उनके द्वारा अपना अधिकार युवराज कर्णसिंह को देना संवैधानिक दृष्टि से बिल्कुल सही था।''

यदि एकतरफा युद्धबंदी का फैसला न लिया होता तो भारत की सुरक्षा सेनाएं जो कश्मीर की धरती से कबालियों को उखाड़ कर बाहर फेंकने में

सक्षम थीं, सफल होतीं और बाद में विवादास्पद पाक अधिकृत क्षेत्र (पी०ओ०के०) न बन पाता। पंडित जवाहरलाल नेहरु और माउंटबेटन दोनों के ''लोगों की इच्छा जानकर'' विलय को अंतिम रूप देने के वायदे ''जनमतसंग्रह'' की मांग के रूप में सामने आए (दुर्गादास, सरदार पटेल का पत्रकला : 1971, पृ० 73, 81, 257, 341)। ''जनमत संग्रह'' की बात कानूनी एवं संवैधानिक रूप से राज्य के और भारत के संविधान के साथ मेल नहीं खाती। इस तरह हमने स्वयंमेव जनमत संग्रह की बात करके एक मुफ्त का सिरदर्द अपने लिए पैदा कर लिया जिसके कारण यह समस्या उलझनों से भर गई और अनेक बड़े खतरे पैदा हो गए। माउंटबेटन के उकसाने पर पंडित जवाहरलाल नेहरु कश्मीर का मामला यू०एन०ओ० में ले गए और हमने एक राष्ट्रीय विवाद को अन्ततोगत्वा एक अन्तर्राष्ट्रीय विषय बना दिया और इंग्लैंड, अमेरीका, रूस, चीन और मुस्लिम देशों द्वारा हस्तक्षेप के दरवाज़े खोल दिए। विवादास्पद पाक अधिकृत क्षेत्र में आतंकवादियों के प्रशिक्षण शिविर और पाकिस्तान जमाते इस्लामी के कट्टरवाद पाक समर्थक गुट और अनेक अलगाववादी संगठनों का झुंड जिसे हुर्रियत के नाम से जाना जाता है, कश्मीर को भारत से अलग करने और भारत के खून का आखिरी कतरा तक निकालने के लिए संघर्षरत हैं। यू०एन०ओ० का प्रस्ताव, ताशकंद समझौता, शिमला समझौता, लाहौर और इस्लामाबाद की घोषणाएं सब निश्फल साबित हुए और इनका कोई परिणाम नहीं निकला। इसका एक मुख्य कारण पाकिस्तान की हठधर्मी और 'मैं न मानूं' विकृत। परिणामस्वरूप हम आज भी कश्मीर घाटी के लिए लड़ रहे हैं। इन सब बातों का सामूहिक परिणाम हमारे लिए घाटा ही घाटा है। इनके अतिरिक्त अन्य अनेकानेक भयानक तथा भयावह परिस्थितियां पैदा हो चुकी हैं।

आंतरिक और बाह्य समस्याएं

अंततोगत्वा विचार करने की बात यह है कि जो परिस्थितियां बिगड़ चुकी हैं, उनका हल क्या निकाला जाए। स्थानीय, राष्ट्रीय और अन्तर्राष्ट्रीय स्तर पर ऐसे हल प्रस्तुत किए जा रहे हैं जिससे बिगड़ती हुई परिस्थिति को और अधिक न बिगड़ने दिया जाए। उपर्युक्त तीन पक्षीय हलों का आलोचनात्मक विश्लेषण इस प्रकार है।

इसका आकलन करना अनिवार्य है ताकि भारत की संप्रभुता एवं अखंडता बनी रहे। इन खेलों/योजनाओं की भीतरी सच्चाईयों का सही अवलोकन अनिवार्य है।

स्थानीय प्रतिरूपक

भूतकाल में शेख मुहम्मद अब्दुल्ला और उनकी नेशनल कान्फ्रेंस ने प्रतिरूपक प्रस्तुत किया था जिसके अन्तर्गत जम्मू क्षेत्र के पास जम्मू, उधमपुर, कठुआ के तीन जिले रहे और बाकी राज्य का समस्त क्षेत्र पाकिस्तान की तरह मुस्लिम गणराज्य के लिए छोड़ दिया जाए (दुर्गादास, पृ० 128)। यह प्रतिरूपक उन लोगों की तंग मानसिकता को प्रस्तुत करता है जो कश्मीर समस्या को एक प्रकार से हल करना चाहते हैं। नयी कश्मीर प्रतिरूपक, 1953 के पूर्व की स्थिति अटानमी अथवा स्वाययत्ता की कल्पना है – बृहत्त स्वाययत्ता और क्षेत्रीय स्वाययत्ता।1953 के पूर्व की स्थिति अथवा स्वाययत्ता दोनों ही स्थिति के दो पहलू हैं। यह कल्पना अपने घर में पूरा ऐसा मालिक बनकर बैठने की है जिसमें कोई जबावदेही, पूछताछ, पारदर्शिता और संतुलन न हो। दूसरे शब्दों में 1953 से पूर्व की मांग राज्य में राजनैतिक, कानूनी और संवैधानिक उस स्थिति को बहाल करने की इंगित है जो शेख मुहममद अब्दुल्ला की नज़रबंदी से पहले की स्थिति थी। भारत के संविधान के कुछ अंश जम्मू कश्मीर

पर लागू किए गए थे (1954 का संविधान आर्डर जिसके अन्तर्गत संविधान घोषणा 1950 की संवैधानिक व्यवस्था को निरस्त कर दिया था)। 1950 के संवैधानिक आर्डर के द्वारा भारतीय संविधान की धारा एक और धारा 370 को जम्मू कश्मीर में लागू कर दिया था जिस समय भारत के संविधान को संपूर्ण देश में लागू किया गया था। तदुपरांत जम्मू कश्मीर की संविधान सभा ने जम्मू कश्मीर के भारत गणराज्य संघ के साथ स्थाई विलय पर अपनी मोहर लगाई थी और जम्मू कश्मीर भारतीय संघ की एक स्थाई इकाई बन गई। जम्मू कश्मीर का संविधान भी धारा 3 के अन्तर्गत इसकी पुष्टि करता है। भारतीय संविधान की धारा 370 की व्यवस्था अनुसार केंद्र के लगभग 370 के अधिक कानून जम्मू कश्मीर में भी लागू हुए ताकि जम्मू कश्मीर के लोग भी भारत गणराज्य संघ की मुख्य धारा में प्रवाहित होकर वह सारे लाभ उठा सकें जो समस्त भारत के नागरिक लाभ उठा रहे हैं। 1953 के पूर्व की स्थिति मांग को लागू करने पर कई अनेकानेक भयंकर परिणाम हो सकते हैं जिनकी कल्पना मात्र से ही सिहरन होती है। यह एक ऐसा कदम होगा जो भारत के संविधान के लागू अंशों को राज्य से हटाने की बात होगी और अन्ततोगत्वा उसे 1933 के संविधान की स्थिति में लाने की बात होगी। अगर यह एक बार कर दिया गया, जम्मू कश्मीर धीरे–धीरे भारत का एक अभिन्न अटूट अंग बनने की बजाए इससे अलग होने की स्थिति में आ जाएगा जिसका उल्लेख भारतीय संविधान की धारा 1 और शड्यूल 1 और 4 में दिया गया है। इसी तरह से जम्मू कश्मीर संविधान की धारा 3 भी प्रभावित होगी। दूसरी बात यह है कि जम्मू कश्मीर के स्थाई नागरिक भारत के नागरिक होना बंद हो जाएंगे। तीसरी बात यह है कि यह कदम उन लोगों को दुबारा आकर बसने का निमंत्रण हो जाएगा जिन्होंने अपनी इच्छा से यह देश छोड़ दिया था और दूसरे देश जाकर आबाद हो गए थे क्योंकि वह पाकिस्तान के वफादार थे। इन्हीं लोगों ने 1947, 1965, 1971 में भारत के खिलाफ युद्ध लड़े थे और आज भी छद्म युद्ध कर रहे हैं। इन लोगों के लिए आतंकवादी, उग्रवादी, अलगाववादी और युद्ध पिपासे घुसपैठिए शब्द–संज्ञा इस्तेमाल किए गए हैं। यह तत्व जम्मू कश्मीर के लोगों को अपनी गतिविधियों से मज़बूर कर दें कि वह पाकिस्तान के साथ हाथ मिलाएं और देशद्रोह की गतिविधियों में संलग्न होएं। अन्तर्राष्ट्रीय कानून और संविधान से खिलवाड़ करके अलगाववादी और पाकिस्तान के द्वारा आतंकवाद, आतंकवादी एवं घुसपैठियों को निरंतर प्रोत्साहित करने के हथकंडे अपनाए जा रहे हैं।

चौथी बात यह है कि यदि इन व्यवस्थाओं को मान लिया जाए तो जम्मू कश्मीर भारत के संविधान के सब लाभों से वंचित हो जाएगा जिसको बाकी देश के लोग उठा रहे हैं जैसे भारत का उच्चतम न्यायालय और उसकी मौलिक एपीलेट और पी०आई०एल० ऑथोरिटी और ऐसे 370 के लगभग केंद्रीय कानून, नियंत्रक ऑडिटर, जनरल, चुनाव आयोग और भारतीय संविधान की अनेक धाराएं। यह तत्व जम्मू कश्मीर के लोगों को अपनी गतिविधियों से मज़बूर कर दे कि वह पाकिस्तान के साथ हाथ मिलाए और देशद्रोह की गतिविधियों में संलग्न होए। अन्तर्राष्ट्रीय कानून और संविधान की धज्जियां उड़ा करके अलगाववादी और पाकिस्तान के द्वारा यह हथकंडे हथियाए जा रहे हैं। पांचवी बात यह है कि जम्मू कश्मीर के ऊपर एक ओर नबावशाही या सुलतानशाही लाद दी जाएगी। स्वशासन के ढिंढोलची इस बात से पूर्णतया अनभिज्ञ हैं कि स्वशासन का अर्थ क्या है और स्वशासन ही जम्मू कश्मीर की समस्या का हल कैसे ? स्वराज्य का आंदोलन स्वराज्यवादियों ने ब्रिटिश हुकुमरानों के विरुद्ध शुरु किया था और मांग की थी कि भारत के ऊपर भारतीयों का राज्य भारतीयों के द्वारा भारतीयों के वास्ते ही हो। परंतु जम्मू कश्मीर के अंदर लोग पहले से ही अपने मतों का उपयोग करके अपनी चुनी हुई सरकारें बना रहे हैं। 1957 से वह अपने मतों का इस्तेमाल करके अपने लिए अपनी सरकार चुन रहे हैं। इससे अधिक स्वशासन और क्या हो सकता है ! यह लोगों को भ्रम में डालने के लिए एक शरारतपूर्ण प्रचार है। दूसरी तरफ हीलिंग टच के नारे ने भी लोगों को भ्रमित किया है। राज्य सरकार पश्चिमी पंजाब के शरणार्थियों और राज्य के अंदर के ही बेघर हुए लोगों को हीलिंग टच देने में असफल हुई है और वह लोग आज भी अपने घरों में बेगानों की तरह रह रहे हैं। धारा 370 ड्राफ्ट धारा 306 ए का अंतिम रूप है जिसको संविधान सभा ने बिना किसी आपत्ति के मत से पारित किया। किसी ने भी इसकी आलोचना नहीं की और न ही कोई अन्य आपत्ति उठाई। भारत की संविधान सभा ने शेख मुहम्मद अब्दुल्ला, मिर्जा अफज़ल बेग, मौलाना मासूदी और मोती राम बैगरा चार सदस्य बैठे हुए थे। इन्होंने 26 नवंबर 1949 को संविधान को अपनाया तथा अन्य समस्त सदस्यों के साथ संविधान की मूल प्रति पर 24.01.1950 अपने हस्ताक्षर किए। धारा 370 को भारत के संविधान में एक अस्थाई प्रावधान के रूप में रखा गया ताकि समय–समय पर उत्पन्न होने वाली विशेष परिस्थितियों में उसका उपयोग किया जा सके और इस बात का आश्वासन दिया गया कि विशेष विकट

परिस्थितियां समाप्त होने पर इसे समाप्त कर दिया जाएगा। परंतु दुर्भाग्य से धारा 370 के कारण देश से अलग होने की भावना ही प्रबल हुई। धारा 370 की भाषा वास्तव धारा 371 की तरह होनी चाहिए थी। इसको इस रूप में प्रस्तुत किया जाना चाहिए था कि यह विशेष कदम अविकसित तथा अर्धविकसित क्षेत्रों के पूर्ण विकास हेतु उठा सके ताकि उन क्षेत्रों के निवासी भी जीवन में अपना विकास करने के लिए समान अवसर प्राप्त कर सकें और बाकी समाज के साथ बराबरी की सतह पर आ सकें। परंतु दुःख का विषय है कि इस धारा 370 के कारण देश से अलग होने आतंकवाद और अलगाववाद का भाव ही पनपा है। स्वतंत्र कश्मीर की मांग भी इसी के कारण बड़ी है। यह भारत के आधुनिक इतिहास का सबसे बड़ा विश्वासघात है। उनकी भाषा बड़ी घातक और दुःख पहुंचाने वाली है। "दोनों में से किसी देश के साथ विलय शांति नहीं ला सकता। हम दोनों कंधों के साथ दोस्त बनकर रहना चाहते हैं। शायद उनके दिमाग में यह एक बीच का रास्ता है जिसके अन्तर्गत परस्पर आर्थिक सहयोग ही एक रास्ता होगा ऐसी व्यवस्था बनाने का। स्वतंत्र कश्मीर की गारंटी केवल भारत और पाकिस्तान ही नहीं, अपितु अमेरीका, ब्रिटेन और संयुक्त राष्ट्र संघ के अन्य सदस्य भी दें।" (द्वारा शेख अब्दुल्ला : दुर्गादास में प्रस्तुत)। इसके अतिरिक्त यह कहना कठिन है कि सर्वसाधारण कश्मीरी की क्या इच्छा है और वह क्या चाहता है। एक विचार तो यह है कि कश्मीरी स्वयं ही अपने भाग्य का विधाता बनना चाहता है और उसके ऊपर कोई भी नियंत्रण उसे संतुलित रखने के लिए न हो। कुछ लोगों का मत है कि कश्मीरी बिल्कुल अलग रहना चाहता है यह जाने बगैर कि यह स्थिति उसे कहां पहुंचाएगी। परंतु यह अनेक उलझन भरे सुझाव गलत रास्ते पर डालने वाले हैं। ऐसा प्रतीत होता है कि कुछ लोग इस विषय में नर्मदल के हैं और कुछ गर्मदल के हैं। इन सब परिस्थितियों के लिए धारा 370 जिम्मेदार है। इस धारा को भारत के संविधान से पूर्णतया निरस्त करना ही देश और राज्य के हित में है और जम्मू कश्मीर की समस्या के समाधान में लाभकारी है। परंतु इसका निरस्तीकरण राजनैतिक इच्छा और कानूनी व्यवस्था के बीच त्रिशंकु की तरह लटक रहा है।

उपरोक्त सब सुझावों का क्या परिणाम हुआ है, यह देखने की और चिंतन की बात है। अभी तक जितने प्रयोग हुए हैं, उनका कोई परिणाम नहीं निकला है। इसका कारण यह है कि इन सभी सुझावों के पीछे कोई प्रामाणिकता नहीं है।

पाकिस्तान रणनीति (गेम प्लान)

पाकिस्तान तो चाहता है कि कश्मीर किसी तरह भी उसके अधिकार क्षेत्र में आ जाए। पाकिस्तान की यह इच्छा 1947, 1965, 1971 और 1999 के कारगिल पर किए गए आक्रमण से सिद्ध होती है। पाकिस्तान ने कश्मीर पर अधिकार प्राप्त करने के लिए आतंकवाद और जेहाद का रास्ता चुना है जिसके द्वारा वह अपनी भूमि पर आतंकवादियों के प्रशिक्षण शिविर चलाकर कश्मीर में बल्कि देश भर में राजनैतिक अस्थिरता पैदा करने में लगा हुआ है। पाकिस्तान ने आज तक हिन्दूस्तान के साथ किसी भी समझौते की कदर नहीं की वह चाहे यू०एन० का प्रस्ताव (संयुक्त राष्ट्र संकल्प) हो, ताशकंद या शिमला समझौता हो अथवा लाहौर की घोषणा। आज तक हिंदूस्तान और पाकिस्तान के बीच विश्वास का सेतु निर्माण करने के लिए पाकिस्तान ने बड़ी बेशर्मी से उनको तोड़ा।

अन्तर्राष्ट्रीय रणनीति (गेम प्लान)

द्वितीय महायुद्ध के बाद अनेक यूरोपीय देशों को जो विदित क्षेत्र मजबूरन छोड़ने पड़े, वहां उन्होंने स्वतंत्र होने वाले अनेक देशों की सीमा निर्धारण करने का काम अपने ढंग से शुरु किया। कश्मीर की समस्या ब्रिटिश सरकार की इस नीति का ही परिणाम है जिसका नक्शा लार्ड माउंटबेटन ने नेहरु को प्रोत्साहन देकर तैयार किया। इसी कारण एक तरफा युद्ध विराम की घोषणा हुई और एक बनावटी पी०ओ०के० की स्थापना हुई। इसी नीति के कारण कश्मीर में अन्तर्राष्ट्रीय शक्तियों द्वारा दखल देने के कारण दरवाजे खुल गए और उन्होंने कश्मीर समस्या के हल के लिए कई विदेशी मॉड्यूल प्रस्तुत करने प्रारंभ कर दिए। सबसे पहले इस समस्या के समाधान के लिए स्ट्रेटेजिक इंडीपेंडेंस मॉड्यूल का सुझाव प्रस्तुत किया। इस सुरक्षा का संबंध अन्तर्राष्ट्रीय सुरक्षा के साथ है। बुनियादी तौर पर एक राज्य की अपनी सुरक्षा और दूसरे राज्य के द्वारा आक्रमण की स्थिति में उनको निरस्त करने की क्षमता का प्रावधान है जिसे स्ट्रेटेजिक इंडीपेंडेंस का नाम दिया गया है। स्ट्रेटेजिक इंडीपेंडेंस स्टेट्स राज्यों के बीच (मध्य) शक्तियों के विभाजन की व्यवस्था करता है जबकि इसका संविधान और परस्पर शक्तियों का विभाजन एक विवाद का विषय है (राजू जी०सी० थामस : व्हॉट इज थर्ड वर्ल्ड सिक्योरिटी)।

तीसरी विश्व सुरक्षा

शक्तियों का माप सैनिक क्षमताओं से संबंधित है और उसका आधार राज्य की आर्थिक और तकनीकी क्षमताओं पर निर्भर करता है। चाहे वह सैनिक क्षमता हो या अन्य प्रकार की क्षमता हो, परंतु आणविक हत्यारों के सामने आ जाने के बाद सैनिक शक्ति को परंपरागत ढंग से मापने का सारा सिलसिला ही बदल गया है। सैन्य शक्ति को मापने का पुराना तरीका बिल्कुल बेकार हो गया है और अब इसी आणविक आक्रमण को रोकने की मानसिकता निर्माण करना ज़्यादा आवश्यक हो गया है। अब स्ट्रेटेजिक इंडीपेंडेंस इस नए मॉड्यूल की कल्पना से भारत की सैन्य शक्ति न्यूकलियर क्षमता प्राप्त करने के बाद बदल गई है और इसके बीच में दखल देने वाली शक्तियों को भारत के आंतरिक, बाह्य और क्षेत्रीय सुरक्षात्मक समस्याओं का भी विचार करना है। इन नई परिस्थितियों में कभी कश्मीर समस्या के समाधान के लिए ''बैक चैनल डिप्लोमेसी'' का भी प्रारंभ हुआ है। 'कश्मीर रोड टू पीस' के लेखक–निर्माता तर्क देते हैं कि ''बैक चैनल डिप्लोमेसी'' उन सब के लिए लाभदायक हो सकती है जो शक्ति प्रयोग के स्थान पर कूटनीति को कश्मीर के शान्ति स्थापन करने के लिए प्रयोग में लाना चाहते हैं। भारत की दृष्टि से एक मॉड्यूल के ऊपर बहस हो सकती है क्योंकि इससे अनेक विवाद योग्य विषय निकल सकते हैं। इस तरह से जो मॉड्यूल प्रस्तुत किया गया है और जिस तरह के कश्मीर भारत पाकिस्तान के बीच में समझौते हुए हैं, उनको एक संवैधानिक ढांचे में इस प्रकार से रखा जा सकता है।

ढांचे का स्वरूप	**समझौते का आधिकारिक नाम**
1. बुरुंडी एग्रीमेंट	अरुषा पीस एंड रीकॉनसाईलेशन एग्रीमेंट फॉर बुरुंडी, अगस्त 20, 2000.
2. डेटोन एकोर्ड्स	द जनरल फ्रेमवर्क एग्रीमेंट फॉर पीस इन बोसनिया एंड हरज़ीगोविना (इनीशिएटिड इन डेटोन ऑन 21 नवंबर 1995 एंड साइंड इन पैरिस ऑन 14 दिसंबर 1995।)
3. ईस्ट टाईमोर एग्रीमेंट	एग्रीमेंट बिटविन द रिपब्लिक ऑफ इनडोनेशिया एंड द पोरच्यूग्यूईस रिपब्लिक ऑन द क्यूशचन ऑफ ईस्ट टाईमोर, 5 मई 1999.
4. इल सल्वेडोर एग्रीमेंट	इल सल्वेडोर पीस एग्रीमेंट, 16 जनवरी 1992.

5. ग्यूएटमाला एग्रीमेंट	ग्यूएटमाला एग्रीमेंट ऑन आइडेंटिटी एंड राईट्स ऑफ इनडीजीनियस पिपील्स मार्च 31, 1995.
6. केफौर एग्रीमेंट	मीलिटरी टेक्नीकल एग्रीमेंट बिटविन द इंटरनेशनल सिक्योरिटी फोर्स (केफौर) एंड द गवर्नमेंट्स ऑफ फीडरल रिपब्लिक ऑफ यूगोस्लाविया एंड द रिपब्लिक ऑफ सरबिया, जून 9, 1999.
7. कोसोवो इनटीरिम एग्रीमेंट	द इनटीरिम एग्रीमेंट फॉर पीस एंड सैल्फ गवर्नमेंट इन कोसोवो, फरवरी 23, 1999.
8. लाहौर डेकलेरेशन	लाहौर डेकलेरेशन बाय द प्राइमीनिस्टर्स ऑफ द रिपब्लिक ऑफ इंडिया एंड द इस्लामिक रिपब्लिक ऑफ पाकिस्तान, फरवरी 21, 1999.
9. नॉरदन आईरलैंड एग्रीमेंट	द नॉरदन आईरलैंड पीस एग्रीमेंट : द एग्रीमेंट रीचड् इन द मल्टी–पार्टी नीगोशिएशन्स, अक्तूबर 4, 1998.
10. पपूआ न्यू गूईनिया एग्रीमेंट	बोउगेनविलिया पीस एग्रीमेंट अगस्त 30, 2001.
11. साईर्रा लीओनी एग्रीमेंट	पीस एग्रीमेंट बिटवीन द गवर्नमेंट ऑफ साईर्रा लीओनी एंड द रीवोल्यूशनरी यूनाईटेड फ्रंट ऑफ साईर्रा लीओनी, लोम, टोगो, मई 25 टू जुलाई 7, 1999.
12. शिमला एग्रीमेंट	शिमला एग्रीमेंट ऑन बीलेटरल रीलेशन्स बिटवीन इंडिया एंड पाकिस्तान साइंड बाई प्राईमीनिस्टर ऑफ इंडिया मिसेस इंदिरा गांधी एंड प्रेसीडेंट ऑफ पाकिस्तान जेड०ए० भुट्टो, जुलाई 3, 1972.
13. साउथ अफ्रीकन कॉन्सटीट्यूशन	कॉन्सटीट्यूशन ऑफ द रिपब्लिक ऑफ साउथ अफ्रीका, मई 8, 1996.
14. सूडन प्रोटोकोल	सूडन्स मेकहेकोस प्रोटोकोल, जुलाई 20, 2002.
15. तशकेंट डेकलेरेशन	तशकेंट डेकलेरेशन, जनवरी 10, 1996.
16. एंगोला, सीज़फायर	एंगोला–उनीता सीज़फायर एग्रीमेंट, अप्रैल 2002.
17. लूसाका प्रोटोकोल	एंगोला–लूसाका प्रोटोकोल, लूसाका, जंबिया, नवंबर 15, 1994.

18. सोमालिया सीज़फायर — सोमालिया एग्रीमेंट ऑन इंप्लीमेंटिंग द सीज़फायर एंड ऑन मोडेलिटीस ऑफ डीसारमेमेंट (सप्लीमेंट टू द जनरल एग्रीमेंट साइंड इन एडिस एबाबा, ऑन जनवरी 8, 1993)

उपरोक्त मॉड्यूल का सार

(क) धारा 370 का संवैधानिक स्वरूप

भारत के संविधान की धारा 370 को स्थाई प्रावधान बनाया जाए और इस धारा से अस्थाई शब्द को निकाल दिया जाए। और इसमें एक शब्द ''विशेष'' या स्पेशल जोड़ दिया जाए। धारा 370 की क्षमताओं को कम करने वाले सारे प्रेसीडेंशियल नार्म्स को निरस्त किया जाए। आगे भारत सरकार की ओर से कश्मीर के संवैधानिक स्टेटस को साथ छेड़–छाड़ करके किसी प्रकार की एमबीगूयिटी न पैदा की जाए। इस तरह से जो कश्मीर को स्वाययत्ता के अधिकार मिले, उनके बीच में कभी भी कोई दखलअंदाजी न की जाए।

(ख) भारत द्वारा कायम किया गया शासन

इस समझौते के अन्तर्गत जो अधिकार भारत को न मिले हों, वह कश्मीर और यहां के लोगों के लिए सुरक्षित रखे जाएं।

(1) सुरक्षा

कश्मीर की बाह्य सुरक्षा के लिए सब शक्तियां पहले की तरह भारत सरकार के हाथ में रही। जम्मू कश्मीर राज्य भारत का अंग है इसलिए कश्मीर की सुरक्षा के ऊपर भारत का ही आधिपत्य रहे। कश्मीर में भारतीय सेना की उपस्थिति केवल आवश्यकता तक ही सीमित रहे। कश्मीर बड़े ध्यान से भारत की सुरक्षा सेना के ऊपर नज़र रखे ताकि सेना शक्ति का दुरुपयोग न कर पाए। अगर इस तरह का दुरुपयोग होता है तो समझौते के अन्तर्गत का नवाधिकार रक्षा के प्रावधान के अन्तर्गत कश्मीर विधानसभा को अधिकार हो कि वह यह मामला फैसला करने के लिए मानवाधिकार (ह्यूमन राइट्स) कमेटी के सामने रख सके।

(2) विदेशी मामलात

भारत सरकार इस क्षेत्र के विदेशी मामलात पर अपना नियंत्रण जारी रखेगी।

भारत सरकार किसी भी विदेशी मामले के साथ विषय पर जिसका असर इस क्षेत्र को प्रभावित करता है, कश्मीर विधानसभा के साथ परामर्श करेगी। कश्मीर की विधानसभा भारत के किसी फैसले को स्वीकार करेगी जिसका संबंध केवल विशेष रूप से एकमेव कश्मीर के विदेशी मामले के साथ होगा और भारत की ओर किसी परदेश के साथ नहीं होगा।

(3) आर्थिक नीति

1. कश्मीर को अभी भी केन्द्रीय सरकार के समर्थन की जरूरत पड़ेगी और ऐसे ही भारतीय सरकार को भी राज्य की आर्थिक नीति पर नियंत्रण रखना जारी रखना चाहिए।
2. भारत को राष्ट्रीय कर निर्धारण पर भी नियंत्रण रखना चाहिए। कश्मीर सरकार को कश्मीर के लिए राज्य कर निर्धारण पर संयम रखना चाहिए।
3. भारतीय सरकार को कश्मीर के पूरे आर्थिक विकास को आश्वस्त करना चाहिए। यह राज्य के बढ़ते हुए निवेश को स्थिर करेगा और ज्ञान तथा आर्थिक सहारे से आर्थिक विकास कार्यक्रम को प्रबल करेगा। कश्मीर का भारत के सामान्य बाज़ार में भाग लेने पर भारत इस उद्देश्य के साथ शासन करना जारी रखेगा कि कश्मीर का सक्रिय सहयोग मिलता रहे।

(ग) कश्मीर बार्डर की वस्तुस्थिति

1. इस करार की वजह से कश्मीर की सीमा बदलनी नहीं चाहिए। लाइन ऑफ कन्ट्रोल (LOC) इसकी व्यावहारिक सीमा होगी। जिस तरह 1972 शिमला करार में कहा गया है, जो आज़ाद कश्मीर को कश्मीर से अलग करता है। उत्तर, पूर्व और दक्षिणी सीमाएं तबसे हैं, जबसे इस करार पर हस्ताक्षर हुए हैं ; उन्हें बदलना नहीं चाहिए।
2. आजाद कश्मीर को नए विशेष स्वतंत्र राज्य का भाग नहीं मानना चाहिए। अगर स्वतंत्र कश्मीर की आबादी कश्मीर के विशेष स्वतंत्र राज्य से जुड़ने की अपनी रुचि दिखाती है, तो कश्मीर की जनता की सम्मति लेनी चाहिए (refrendum) और उसके परिणाम पर विश्वास रखना चाहिए।

(घ) केन्द्रीय सरकार द्वारा कश्मीर विभाजन

1. कश्मीर को भारतीय सरकार द्वारा बनाए ढांचे में भाग लेना चाहिए जब तक कि वह कश्मीर को प्रभावित करे। इस करार के अनुसार, यह दृढ़ता भारतीय सरकार द्वारा कायम शक्तियों पर आधारित होनी चाहिए।
2. कश्मीरी प्रतिनिधि का चुनाव अब भी तकनीकों से बदलना नहीं चाहिए।
3. भारतीय सरकार को कश्मीरी दृष्टिकोण के संदर्भ में कश्मीर सरकार की सम्मति लेनी चाहिए।

(ड.) कश्मीरी नागरिकता की पहचान और पहचान चिह्न

1. सभी लोग जो कश्मीर में करार के हस्ताक्षर के समय कम से कम 7 वर्षों से रह रहे हैं, उन्हें कश्मीर का नागरिक मानना चाहिए।
2. सभी लोग जो कश्मीर में करार के हस्ताक्षर के समय 7 वर्षों से कम रहे हैं, उन्हें 7 साल में नागरिक जरूरतों के बाद कश्मीरी नागरिकता मिलनी चाहिए।
3. कौम, धर्म और लिंग के आधार पर किसी भी तरह की नागरिकता की मनाही नहीं होनी चाहिए। कश्मीरी विधानसभा को उन सभी को आश्वस्त करना चाहिए जो नागरिकता की मांग कर रहे हैं।
4. नागरिकता के लिए भेदभाव के आरोप पर अन्तर्राष्ट्रीय अपराधी न्यायालय के सामने निर्णयादेश देना चाहिए।
5. संवैधानिक कांग्रेस या नयी कश्मीरी सरकार ही पहचान–पत्र कायदे बनाएगी जैसे पासपोर्ट के प्रकाशन पर !
6. किसी तरह की मनाही पहचान–पत्र के लिए कौम, धर्म या लिंग के आधार पर नहीं होनी चाहिए।
7. संवैधानिक कांग्रेस या नयी कश्मीरी सरकार को राष्ट्रीय पहचान के चिह्न बनाने चाहिए जैसे ध्वज और हाथों की परत। भारतीय ध्वज को राष्ट्रीय तथा दूसरे विधिक समारोह पर फहराते रहना चाहिए।

(च) स्वायतता अन्यथा स्वतंत्रता की विशिष्ट वस्तुस्थिति लागू होने की प्रक्रिया

कश्मीर या पाकिस्तान द्वारा बढ़ते हुए स्वयंसिद्धांतों अथवा स्वायतता अन्यथा स्वतंत्रता का आरोप, जो इस भाग में दिए गए हैं, को आरोपित अपशब्द

कहे गए हैं, यूनाइटेड नेशन सेक्रेटरी जनरल द्वारा बनाई गई अन्तर्राष्ट्रीय समिति ऐसे आरोप की जांच करेगी। अगर बनाई गई समिति खंडन को दृढ़ करती है, तो मानव अधिकार समिति इस स्थिति को हल करने की कोशिश करेगी। अगर समिति की सामर्थ्य इस स्थिति को हल करने की क्षमताओं से परे है, तो यूनाइटेड नेशन हाई कमीशन मानव अधिकार हेतु इस विषय को जल्दी से जल्दी हल करने के लिए यूनाइटेड नेशन सिक्योरिटी काउंसिल के सामने लाएगी।

(छ) कश्मीर की संवैधानिक वस्तुस्थिति

कश्मीर सरकार को उन विषयों के लिए पूरे अधिकार मिलने चाहिए जो केन्द्रीय सरकार के नियंत्रण में नहीं हैं। मतलब, कश्मीर स्थापना को लेकर सभी विषयों पर पूरा, अर्थपूर्ण और स्वतंत्र नियंत्रण जो विधि, राजनीतिक, सामाजिक, सांस्कृतिक और शैक्षिक राजनीति से संबद्ध होंगे।

(ज) व्यवस्थापना

कश्मीर सरकार को राज्य में संविधान की सहमति के साथ विधिक अधिनियम, खंडन और उन्नति की ओर उन्मुख करने का पूरा अधिकार मिलना चाहिए। भारतीय सरकार द्वारा उसके प्रभावित होने वाले क्षेत्र के अतिरिक्त इस शक्ति पर किसी प्रकार का बंधन नहीं होना चाहिए। वस्तुतः कोई भी विधान सभा कोई भी विधि–विधान विधान द्वारा पारित भारतीय संविधान की मुख्य धारा के विपरीत नहीं होना चाहिए।

(झ) आर्थिक विषय

कश्मीर सरकार को स्थानीय कर निर्धारण का नियंत्रण मिलना चाहिए और उसे राज्य की निधि का बंटवारा होने के लिए जिम्मेदार होना चाहिए। इस शक्ति का अभ्यास अल्पसंख्यक लोगों के साथ निष्पक्ष रूप से होना चाहिए।

(ञ) नीति निर्माण

कश्मीर सरकार को उन मापदंडों तथा रणनीति को बनाने और अमल में लाने के लिए अधिकार मिलना चाहिए जो राज्य की सामाजिक, शैक्षिक, सांस्कृतिक और वैज्ञानिक नीतियों से संबंध रखता है।

(ट) भ्रष्टाचार

कशमीर सरकार भ्रष्टाचार विरुद्ध मापदंडों को अपनाए और अपराधियों का तत्पर और निष्पक्ष अनुसरण करे एवं उसे भ्रष्टाचार की समस्या को उपयुक्त दिशा निर्धारित करने हेतु सम्बोधित करने का प्रयास करना चाहिए।

(ठ) चुनाव

1. दोनों दलों को यह आश्वस्त करना चाहिए कि राज्य में मुक्त और स्वच्छ चुनाव की स्थिति कायम रहे। इसमें खुला और मुक्त राजनीतिक वातावरण बनाना नागरिकों के लिए आश्वासन होगा। एक सुरक्षित वातावरण जिसमें सभी उम्मीदवारों को बिना किसी हस्तक्षेप के मौजूद साधनों के आंतरिक सम्मेलन, सभा और उक्ति की आजादी होगी। दोनों दलों को मीडिया का अभ्यास कराना आंदोलनकारी उम्मीदवार के लिए निश्चित करना चाहिए।
2. भारतीय सरकार को अन्तर्राष्ट्रीय चुनावी प्रेक्षक समिति की उपस्थिति को स्वीकार करना चाहिए जो चुनाव के संचालन पर निगरानी रखेगी और यह प्रमाणित करेगी कि चुनाव मुक्त और स्वच्छ धरातल पर हो।
3. चयन केंद्र में प्रवेश और मतदान का प्रसार चुनाव होने के बाद हो। इस अन्तर्राष्ट्रीय समिति को चुनावी प्रक्रिया के सभी विभागों में वोटर के पंजीकरण को मिलाकर पूरा स्वागत मिलना चाहिए।
4. इस समिति को यह आश्वस्त करने के लिए इलेक्शन कमीशन ऑफ इंडिया के साथ_संयोजित होकर काम करना चाहिए कि चुनावी प्रक्रिया सुरक्षित और पारदर्शी है।

(ड) उम्मीदवार

किसी व्यक्ति का पुराना राजनीतिक संबंध या गतिविधियां अधिकारित कार्यालय में बाधा नहीं होनी चाहिए। हलांकि सभी उम्मीदवारों को हिंसा को अस्वीकार एवं तज्य/त्याग करना चाहिए।

(ण) मानवाधिकार

1. कश्मीर मानव अधिकारों को प्रोत्साहित और सुरक्षा करने के लिए सहमत है। अंततः यह भारत सरकार द्वारा संधि की संपुष्टि से अन्तर्राष्ट्रीय मानव

संधि को बल और परिणाम प्रदान करेगा तथा मानवीय अधिकारों की सार्वभौमिक घोषणा, मानवीय अधिकारों पर अन्तर्राष्ट्रीय प्रसंविदाएं, महिलाओं पर से सभी प्रकार के भेद–भाव को हटाने का प्रयास तथा बच्चों के अधिकार आदि विषयों पर अधिकार और दायित्व की घोषणा करेगा।

2. कश्मीर सरकार द्वारा अन्तर्राष्ट्रीय मानवाधिकार उन सभी संधि के साथ ही दूसरी प्रथाएं प्रताड़ना, क्रूरता, अमानवीय या क्षति करने वाला व्यवहार, सभी प्रकार की सजा या धर्म और विश्वास के आधार पर भेदभाव आदि भी अपनाई जाएंगी जिसे भारत ने अभी तक नहीं अपनाया है।

सभी कश्मीरी लोगों के मूलभूत अधिकार

1. मानवीय अधिकारों की सार्वभौमिक घोषणा, मानवीय अधिकारों पर अन्तर्राष्ट्रीय प्रसंविदाएं, महिलाओं पर से सभी प्रकार के भेद–भाव को हटाने का प्रयास तथा बच्चों के अधिकार आदि विषयों पर अधिकार और दायित्व की घोषणा तथा गारंटी कश्मीर के संविधान का एक संपूर्ण पात्र है। जिसे अधिकारों के अनुरूप उसी प्रकार की श्रेष्ठता मिली है जिस तरह संविधान को मिली है। अन्तर्राष्ट्रीय विधि के तहत अपनाई गई क्षमा करने योग्य घटनाएं जिन्हें संविधान में आगे रखा गया है, के अतिरिक्त ऊपर दिए गए संधि–पत्र का मूलभूत व्यवहार और नीचे दी गई व्यवस्था सीमित या अप्रतिष्ठित नहीं होनी चाहिए।
2. सभी नागरिकों के अधिकार और दायित्व होने चाहिए।
3. मानवीय गौरव की गरिमा का मान और सुरक्षा होनी चाहिए।
4. सभी महिलाएं और पुरुष एक समान होने चाहिए। जन्म, परंपरा, जाति, लिंग, रंग, भाषा, सामाजिक स्थिति, दर्शन, धार्मिक या राजनैतिक धारणा अथवा शारीरिक या मानसिक असहायता की वजह से किसी के विरुद्ध भी भेदभाव नहीं होना चाहिए। कानून के अनुसार, सभी नागरिकों को समान सुरक्षा और समान व्यवहार का लाभ उठाना चाहिए।
5. राज्य या उसके अंग को मनमाने ढंग से किसी से बात नहीं करना चाहिए।
6. सभी महिलाओं और पुरुषों को जीवन जीने का अधिकार होना चाहिए।
7. सभी महिलाओं और पुरुषों को व्यक्तिगत आजादी का व्यवहार होना चाहिए। जिसमें शारीरिक और मानसिक अखंडता और कुछ करने का

अधिकार भी सम्मिलित है। किसी भी प्रकार की क्रूर, अमानवीय, अपमानजनक व्यवहार, सज़ा और यातना वर्णित होनी चाहिए। हर किसी के पास यह अधिकार होना चाहिए कि वह सामाजिक या व्यक्तिगत हिंसा से मुक्त हो।

8. राज्य को एक सीमा तक यह आश्वासन होना चाहिए कि सभी नागरिकों के पास साधन हों जिससे वे मानवीय गौरव के अनुकूल रह सकें।
9. सभी महिलाओं और पुरुषों को अपने निजी और पारिवारिक जीवन, निवास और व्यक्तिगत वार्तालाप का आदर करने का अधिकार है।
10. अभिव्यक्ति और संचार की स्वतंत्रता का आश्वासन दिया जाना चाहिए। राज्य को धर्म, विश्वास, विवेक और विचारों का सम्मान करना चाहिए।
11. किसी को भी मनमाने ढंग से उसकी राष्ट्रीयता से वंचित करने या उसे बदलने के अधिकार से मनाही नहीं होनी चाहिए।
12. किसी को भी मूल शिक्षा प्राप्त करने की मनाही नहीं होनी चाहिए। राज्य को आम जनता की शिक्षा का प्रबंध करना चाहिए तथा माध्यमिक और उत्तर माध्यमिक शिक्षा का विकास और प्रोत्साहन होना चाहिए।
13. सभी नागरिकों को यह अधिकार होना चाहिए कि वे राज्य के क्षेत्र में मुक्त होकर कहीं भी घूम सकें, उसे छोड़ सकें या वापस आ सकें।
14. न्यायसंबंधी प्रशासनिक प्रक्रिया में सभी को यह अधिकार है कि उनका केस निष्पक्ष और निर्धारित समय सीमा में हो।
15. नियमों के समर्थन के अतिरिक्त कोई भी अपनी आजादी से वंचित नहीं रहना चाहिए।
16. सभी लोगों का यह कर्तव्य है कि वे अपने सहनागरिकों का आदर करें और बिना किसी भेदभाव के अपने सहनागरिकों पर ध्यान दें।
17. मूलभूत अधिकारों के लिए किसी भी प्रकार की पाबंदी पर एक न्यायिक धरातल होना चाहिए। यह जनता के हित के लिए या दूसरे व्यक्ति के मूलभूत अधिकारों की रक्षा के लिए होना चाहिए। लक्ष्य का अनुसरण इसके अनुरूप होना चाहिए।
18. न्यायिक, प्रशासनिक और संस्थानिक आदेश के तहत मूलभूत अधिकारों का सम्मान होना चाहिए। संविधान ही परम कानून होना चाहिए तथा विधानसभा, प्रबंधकर्ता और न्याय के धरातल पर इसकी पुष्टि होनी चाहिए।

(त) धार्मिक अल्पसंख्यक : स्वतंत्रता और धर्म

1. हर व्यक्ति को अपने विवेक, धर्म, सोच, विश्वास और विचार की स्वतंत्रता का अधिकार होना चाहिए।
2. किसी पर भी बलप्रयोग नहीं होना चाहिए कि धर्म या विश्वास का पालन की उसकी स्वतंत्रता को नष्ट कर दे।
3. अपने धर्म या विश्वास को व्यक्त करने की स्वतंत्रता कानून के बताए अनुसार सीमित रहनी चाहिए जो जनता की सुरक्षा, आदेश, स्वास्थ्य, सिद्धांतों, मूलभूत अधिकार और दूसरों की स्वतंत्रता के लिए आवश्यक है।
4. राज्य या राज्य के संस्थानों में उन नियमों के अनुसार सबसैक्शन (1) की जैनरेलिटी को अप्रतिष्ठित किए बिना धार्मिक अनुसरण किए जा सकते हैं जो इसी के लिए उचित समिति द्वारा बनाए गए हैं। पर इन धार्मिक अनुसरण को एक समान धरातल पर किया जाना चाहिए और उसमें भाग लेने के लिए मुक्त और स्वतंत्रता होनी चाहिए।
5. इस धारा में कुछ भी विधानसभा को वंचित न करें, जो कि सामने लाती हैं :–
   (अ) व्यक्तिगत और पारिवारिक न्याय जिससे एक विशिष्ट धर्म का अनुसरण करने वाले लोग जुड़े हुए हैं।
   (ब) विवाह की मान्यता को बताए गए व्यवहार (प्रोसीड्यूर) की तरह ही काम करना चाहिए। इसका निष्कर्ष धार्मिक कानून के सिस्टम के अन्तर्गत निकाला गया है।
6. चिंतन, धर्म और विश्वास की स्वतंत्रता के अधिकार को सम्मिलित करना चाहिए जिसे अनेक विषयों की स्वतंत्रता है : –
   (क) धर्म या विश्वास के संदर्भ में संगठित होना तथा इन चीजों के लिए जगह बनाना और उसे संभाले रखना।
   (ख) आवश्यक धमार्थ और मानवीय संस्थानों को बनाना और देखभाल करना।
   (ग) आवश्यक चीजों और बातों को बनाना, अपनाना और उपयोग करना जो किसी धर्म या विश्वास के सिद्धांतों से संबंध रखते हैं।
   (घ) इन क्षेत्रों में आवश्यक पत्र लिखना, विवाद करना, और विस्तार करना।

(ड) उपयुक्त स्थानों पर धर्म या विश्वास के बारे में सिखाना।

(च) याचना करना और अपनी इच्छा से व्यक्ति और संस्थानों से आर्थिक या किसी और प्रकार की सहायता लेना।

(छ) धर्म और विश्वास की जरूरत के लिए बुलाए गए नेता को सिखाना, चुनना और पदनामित करना।

(ज) प्रत्येक धर्म और विश्वास के अनुसार आराम करना, छुट्यिों, समारोह को मनाना।

(झ) धर्म और विश्वास के संदर्भ में राष्ट्रीय और अन्तर्राष्ट्रीय स्तरों पर व्यक्ति और समाज से वार्तालाप करना और उसे संभाले रखना।

7. किराए पर दिए जाने के अभ्यास में धर्म अर्थात पंथ को उस हद तक सहमत करना जब तक कि अप्रस्तुत ग्रुप को प्रोत्साहन मिले ताकि वह आर्थिक समूह में अच्छी प्रस्तुति पा सके।
8. परंपरावादी, धार्मिक विरोध या नफरत को संचार या किसी भी अन्य माध्यम द्वारा लिखित या मौलिक रूप से उकसाना प्रतिबन्धित होना चाहिए। कश्मीर के आपराधिक नियमों में ऐसे अपराधों के लिए जेल अथवा सज़ा का प्रावधान अनिवार्य हो।

(त) स्त्रियों के अधिकार

यह प्रमाणित है कि महिलाएं व्यवहार में अतिसंवेदनशील होती हैं और महिला होने के कारण भेदभाव का सामना करना तथा गरीबी, शोषण, हिंसा आदि सामाजिक स्थिति का सामना भी वे करती हैं। सरकार निम्न बातों का संकल्प ले जिससे महिलाओं के मानवीय अधिकारों की सुरक्षा निश्चित हो जाएः

(अ) सरकारी

1. मानवीय अधिकार विभाग के तहत कानूनी सलाह, सेवा और समाज सेवा में रत महिलाओं के सहयोग से महिलाओं के अधिकारों को निश्चित करना जिससे उन्हें समान सहयोग मिले तथा राजनैतिक, असैनिक, आर्थिक, सामाजिक और सांस्कृतिक जीवन का अंग बनें।
2. यह निश्चित हो कि महिलाओं के अधिकारों को यह अवसर मिले कि वह सरकारी तंत्र की सभी सीमाओं तक लिंग संबंधी बातों का अनुकलन करें।

3. महिलाओं के विरुद्ध होने वाले भेदभाव को हटाने के समझौते को विश्वसनीय माना जाए तथा उसके विस्तार को प्रोत्साहित किया जाए।

(आ) न्यायिक

1. सेक्सुअल अपराध, महिलाओं के विरुद्ध छेड़छाड़, पारिवारिक हिंसा आदि अपराधों पर विधानसभा द्वारा लगाए गए दंड को दुबारा देखना और अपडेट करना चाहिए।
2. महिलाओं और पुरुषों के मानवीय अधिकारों को समान ओहदा मिलना चाहिए।
3. महिलाओं को काबिल बनाना जिससे वह किसी भी लिंग शक्ति निधि माप में मुक्त होकर अपनी इच्छा से सहयोग दे। जनेवा समझोते के अन्तर्गत जो समाज और अधिकारों को प्रभावित कर रहा हो।
4. महिलाओं और बच्चों का स्वास्थ्य और सुरक्षा कश्मीरी लोगों के चिरस्थाई होने के लिए मूलभूत है। कश्मीरी समाज में महिलाओं के अधिकारों को प्रतिष्ठा और सम्मान मिलना चाहिए। भविष्य के किसी भी निर्णय में कश्मीर की विधिक अवस्था को देखते हुए कश्मीरी लोगों के आम अधिकारों से संबंध रखने वाला कोई भी संधि–पत्र सम्मिलित और प्रस्तुत होना चाहिए।

(इ) राजनैतिक

1. प्रशासनिक शक्ति को मज़बूत करने की प्रक्रिया में महिलाओं की भूमिका को बढ़ावा देने हेतु यह निश्चित हो कि सामाजिक और राजनीतिक संस्थाएं विशेष नीतियां अपनाएं।
2. यह निश्चित हो कि शक्ति के अभ्यास में महिलाएं व्यवस्थित हों या न हो, उन्हें भाग लेने का अवसर और अधिकार मिलने चाहिए।
3. कश्मीर पर शासन कर रहे किसी भी सरकारी तंत्र में स्वयं को प्रस्तुत करने का लाभ महिलाओं को उठाना चाहिए।
4. सरकारी और प्रशासनिक तंत्र में भी महिलाओं को प्रस्तुति का अधिकार मिलना चाहिए।
5. सभ्य समाज और वर्ग में महिलाओं की भूमिका को दबाना और शांत नहीं करना चाहिए।
6. लोकतांत्रिक संस्थाओं में महिलाओं को समान सहयोग देना चाहिए।

(ई) सभ्यता

1. युद्ध में भाग न लेने वाली महिलाओं का प्रशासनिक तौर पर सामाजिक सम्मान होना चाहिए। वैसे ही वह लड़ाई से बांहर है। विरोध करने वालों द्वारा वह बांधी नहीं जानी चाहिए। महिलाओं और बच्चों को युद्ध में ढाल की तरह प्रयोग नहीं करना चाहिए।
2. कानून के अन्तर्गत महिलाओं और लड़कियों को शिक्षा, नौकरी, मूलभूत अधिकार, स्वास्थ्य रक्षा, राजनीतिक सहयोग, काम करने की स्वतंत्रता आदि सामाजिक जीवन के हर धरातल पर सहयोग देना चाहिए।
3. कश्मीरीयों की भावी पीढ़ी के लिए महिला शिक्षा का महत्व प्रधानतम है। लिंग भेद के आधार पर महिलाओं और लड़कियों को शिक्षा से वंचित नहीं करना चाहिए।

(थ) बच्चों के अधिकार

1. बच्चे की अवस्था और परिपक्वता के हिसाब से हर बच्चे को जीने का और मूलभूत स्वतंत्रता प्राप्त करने का स्वाभाविक अधिकार है।
2. बिना किसी प्रकार के भेद–भाव के हर बच्चे के अधिकार की पुष्टि होनी चाहिए। जैसे यू०एन०ओ० समझौता बच्चे के अधिकारों के लिए दिया गया है।
3. सभी बच्चों को विशेष प्रबंधों को प्राप्त करने का अधिकार होना चाहिए जो दुर्व्यवहार, अपमान और शोषण से मुक्त कर उनकी देखभाल, स्वास्थ्य रक्षा और शारीरिक सुरक्षा को बढ़ावा दे।
4. अनाथ, सड़क पर छोड़े हुए बच्चों आदि मुश्किल परिस्थितियां झेल रहे युवाओं को सामाजिक सहयोग देने के लिए जनता सेवा योजना तथा जनसंख्या की आय से संबंधित योजना में नौकरी देनी चाहिए।
5. किसी बच्चे को उसकी इच्छा के विरुद्ध उसके मां–बाप से अलग नहीं करना चाहिए। इसके अतिरिक्त योग्य अधिकारी न्यायिक तौर पर देखकर उपर्युक्त नियम व कानून के अनुसार यह दृढ़ करें कि बच्चे के हित के लिए अलगाव जरूरी है या नहीं। मां–बाप द्वारा अपमान या अनदेखा करने जैसी विशिष्ट परिस्थिति में या मां–बाप के अलग होने पर बच्चे के रहने की जगह का निर्णय लेना हो, तब ऐसी दृढ़ता जरूरी है।

(द) शिक्षा

1. अनिवार्य शिक्षा के द्वारा युवाओं के बीच अशिक्षा को समाप्त कर देना चाहिए। प्राथमिक शिक्षा के पहले नौ सालों के दौरान् सरकार की कोशिश होनी चाहिए कि आगे के तीन सालों के लिए मुफ्त शिक्षा दे।
2. प्राथमिक शिक्षा के दौरान् दूसरे अनुशासन का पहलू शांति हो। स्नातक के लिए एक क्लास जरूरत के लिए माध्यमिक शिक्षा को एक अलग विषय की तरह पढ़ाना चाहिए।
3. नौ वर्ष से ज्यादा अवस्था के बच्चों को जो स्कूल नहीं जाते, सरकार को व्यावसायिक और तकनीति शिक्षा देनी चाहिए। यह उन्हें अपना व्यक्तिगत विकास करने के लिए उस तरह के प्रोजेक्ट को करने के प्रति प्रेरित करेगा जो कश्मीर के आर्थिक और सामाजिक विकास में मदद करेगा।
4. शिक्षा विभाग द्वारा एक क्षेत्रीय आंदोलन किया जाएगा जो आबादी के अलग–अलग समूहों को एक साथ रहने में मदद करेगा। इस तरह का आंदोलन अलग–अलग प्रकार की अहिंसक गतिविधियों द्वारा शांतिपूर्वक रहने के साथ–साथ क्षमताओं के बारे में जागरूकता पैदा करने की कोशिश करेगा।
5. युद्ध को शांतिपूर्वक स्थिरता में बदलने के लिए राजनैतिक और प्रशासनिक नेताओं और आर्थिकतावादियों को अतिरिक्त शिक्षा देनी चाहिए।

(ध) शरणार्थी

1. कश्मीर से बाहर स्थित सभी कश्मीरी शरणार्थियों और स्थानांतरित लोगों को लौटने का सभी धमकियों और जबरदस्ती से मुक्त होकर तथा सुरक्षा और गौरव के साथ जीने का अधिकार होना चाहिए।
2. 1990 से पहले कश्मीर छोड़ने वाले सभी उनकी खोई हुई संपत्ति के लिए तथा कश्मीर में फिर से स्थापित होने के लिए आर्थिक सहारा मिलना चाहिए तथा उनका स्वागत होना चाहिए।
3. 1990 के बाद कश्मीर छोड़ने वाले सभी लोगों को अपनी खोई हुई संपत्ति के लिए तथा उस संपत्ति को वापस पाने के लिए आर्थिक प्रतिफल मिलना चाहिए।
4. शरणार्थी विभाग द्वारा शरणार्थियों के दावों की तहकीकात होना निश्चित

होना चाहिए। किसी भी प्रकार के आर्थिक प्रतिफल पर शरणार्थी विभाग द्वारा काम किया जाना चाहिए।

5. जिन शरणार्थियों की संपत्ति को मान्यता प्रमाणित की गई है वह कश्मीर में रह गई है, शरणार्थी विभाग को वापस आने वालों की संपत्ति और बैंक खाते वसूलने में उनकी मदद करनी चाहिए।

(न) मानवाधिकार विभाग

उपयोगी और कार्यशील मानवीय अधिकार विभाग के लक्ष्य को बढ़ाते हुए कश्मीर सरकार को सरकारी ढांचे में मानवीय अधिकारों के लिए एक नया विभाग जोड़ना चाहिए। इसके लिए मानव अधिकार पर संयुक्त राष्ट्र का विशेष अधिकार तथा मानव अधिकार का संयुक्त राष्ट्र केंद्र आदि अन्तर्राष्ट्रीय संस्थानों से तकनीकी और भौतिक सहयोग लिया जा सकता है।

(क) मानव अधिकार विभाग की शक्तियां और दायित्व

1. मानवीय अधिकारों के उल्लंघन से संबंधित शिकायतों पर ध्यान देना चाहिए और काम करना चाहिए।
2. मानवाधिकारों के बारे में अन्तर्राष्ट्रीय मापांक के राजनैतिक संविधान के अनुसार प्रभाव और स्वतंत्रता के साथ जरूरी तहकीकात करना चाहिए।
3. शक्ति के अभ्यास के दौरान् उचित संवैधानिक संस्थाओं द्वारा जानकारी के आधार पर इस तहकीकात को ध्यान में रखना चाहिए कि निर्दिष्ट मानवाधिकारों का उल्लंघन हुआ है कि नही।
4. कश्मीरी जनता के बीच संचार द्वारा किसी भी व्यक्ति और समूह का उन्मुक्त और व्यावहारिक साक्षात्कार करना, अपने कार्यों की अच्छी प्रस्तुति और आदेश के अमल के लिए उचित जानकारी इकट्ठी करना, अपने कार्यों और गतिविधियों से संबंधित जानकारी फैलाना आदि को ध्यान में रख विभाग को खुद को स्थापित करने और कश्मीर में मुक्त होकर घूमने का अधिकार होना चाहिए।
5. अपने कार्यों की प्रस्तुति में विभाग को सबसे संवेदनशील समूह की स्थिति का तथा सेना से प्रभावित हो रही आबादी (स्थानांतरित, शरणार्थी और वापस लौटने वाले) का ध्यान रखना चाहिए।
6. मानवीय अधिकारों के अनुसरण को स्थापित करने में विभाग को व्यक्ति

के जीवन, अखंडता, सुरक्षा, स्वतंत्रता, अभिव्यक्ति, घूमने और संगठित होने की स्वतंत्रता और राजनैतिक अधिकारों पर विशिष्ट ध्यान देना चाहिए।

7. भारतीय सैनिक और सुरक्षा बल की गतिविधियां जो करार पर हस्ताक्षर करने के पूर्व हुई, वे धार्मिक अल्पसंख्यक विभाग द्वारा जांची जाएंगी। सभी मानवीय अधिकारों का उल्लंघन जो हस्ताक्षर से पहले हुआ, उसे मैत्री विभाग द्वारा पुनः जांचा जाएगा। विभाग को अपनी गतिविधियां स्थाई आधार पर तीव्र गति से करना चाहिए।
8. कश्मीर विधान परिषद् और कश्मीर विधानसभा संगठन द्वारा सहमति दिए गए कश्मीर मूल निवासी को ही विभाग का नेतृत्व करना चाहिए। उसकी प्रतिष्ठा की ताकत, निष्पक्षता, अखंडता, काम की विशिष्टता, ज्ञान की पृष्ठभूमि आदि मानवाधिकारों के आधार पर होना चाहिए। उस व्यक्ति को श्रेष्ठ होना चाहिए जिसके सिद्धांत ऊचे हों, जिसकी प्रतिबद्धता क्षेत्रीय समाज के सदस्यों तथा मानवाधिकारों की तरफ हो। उसकी अवधि दुबारा नियुक्ति के आश्वासन के साथ 6 साल की हो।
9. विभाग के पास अपने कार्यालय, संचार–साधन और लिपीकीय सहायक अधिकारी होने चाहिए। विभाग का स्थायित्व ग्रीष्म ऋतु में श्रीनगर में और शरद ऋतु में जम्मू में होना चाहिए। सिविलियन सेवक को किराए पर लेने की प्रक्रिया से सहायक अधिकारी को विभाग के लिए लिया जा सकता है इस निश्चितता के साथ कि आबादी (जिसमें महिलाएं, धार्मिक बहुमत के सदस्य आर किसी भी क्षेत्र का अल्पसंख्यक समूह) सहायक अधिकारी की प्रस्तुति के चुनाव में सम्मिलित है।
10. विभाग उन परिमाणों का ध्यान रखेगा जो मूलभूत मानवाधिकारों, धार्मिक अल्पसंख्यक, महिलाओं, बच्चों, शरणार्थी, शिक्षा और पुनः मैत्री आदि के लिए जिम्मेदार होगा।
11. स्थानीय मानवाधिकारों के संघ और असैनिक समाज समूह को कश्मीर में बढ़ावा मिलना चाहिए जो मानवाधिकारों के अनुसरण पर दृष्टि रखें। इस समूह का अधिकार विभाग की प्रस्तुति के संदर्भ में दावों और आरोपों की जांच करना और यह पुष्ट करना होगा कि सभी लक्ष्य पूरे हों।

ऊपर दिए गए मापांक पर एक संक्षिप्त एवं विहंगम दृष्टि डालें तो इसमें निहित कार्यक्रम सिर्फ इस कारण से फूट की भावना को बढ़ावा देगा। और

इस वजह से दिए गए मापदंड को शांति मापदंड नहीं माना जा सकता बल्कि इसे हस्तक्षेप मापदंड माना जा सकता है जो देश की सत्ता में दखल दे रहा है। हस्तक्षेप करने वाला विदेशी संवैधानिक संगठन जो भारतीय संवैधानिक ढांचे को बदलने की कोशिश कर रहा है और भारतीय संविधान के प्राथमिक ढांचे के खिलाफ है, उसे अनेक कारणों से बढ़ावा नहीं मिलना चाहिए। पहला, मापदंड का प्रस्तुत किया गया समाधान बढ़ती स्वायतता एवं स्वतंत्रता को बढ़ावा देता है जो भारत के संसद द्वारा त्याग दिया गया है। धारा 370 के निर्देशानुसार, जम्मू–कश्मीर का राज्य भविष्य में विशेष तौर पर अधिकतम स्वायतता के आसार के साथ अधिकतम स्वतंत्रता का आनंद लेता है। दूसरा, इसे (instrument of accession) स्वीकृति के निरीक्षण और पुनः निरीक्षण को दुबारा नहीं खोलना चाहिए। प्रस्तुत किए गए मापांक में लेखक उन सभी नकारात्मक खिलाड़ियों को यह याद दिलाना चाहता है कि स्वीकृति का यंत्र ऐतिहासिक अतीत का विषय है। ऐतिहासिक अतीत एक निर्जीव इतिहास है और कोई भी कोशिश उसे आग में घी डालने के समान खतरनाक परिणामों से पुनर्जीवित करने के लिए पर्याप्त होगी। स्वीकृति के सभी दास्तावेजों को पुनर्जीवित करने का भयावह दुष्परिणाम लगभग 560 भारतीय राजसी राज्यों के उत्तराधिकारियों को सुप्त शेर को जगाने के समान है। भगवान की कृपा से यह नहीं हुआ क्योंकि ऐसी दुर्घटना खून की होली एवं खून की नदी बहाव को जन्म देता। तीसरा, कश्मीर और कश्मीरी खुद को राष्ट्रीय तौर पर जोड़ने वाले लोगों, जो भारत और भारतीयों की एकता और अखंडता में रुचि रखते हैं, से खुद को बचाने में असहाय हैं। चौथा, प्रस्तुत मापदंड कश्मीर और कश्मीरियों पर आधारित है। यह कहीं भी लद्दाख और लद्दाखियों तथा जम्मू और जम्मूवासियों के विषय को नहीं दिखाता। यह सिर्फ तीन क्षेत्रों के बीच विराग को बढ़ावा देता है – कश्मीर घाटी बनाम जम्मू बनाम लद्दाख जैसे कि कश्मीर बनाम भारत बनाम पाकिस्तान। पांचवा, संवैधानिक अनुमति के अनुसार अलग होना अयोग्यता है क्योंकि जोड़ने की प्रक्रिया को इतने अच्छे से बुना गया है। भारतीय संविधान के धारा 1 की भाषा में, "भारत के राज्यों का संगठन होना चाहिए," जो अलग होने को नामुमकिन, अक्रियान्वन और अव्यावहारिक है। (सी०ए०डी० वोल्यूम, VII, p. 43 ; इन री बैरूबरी, ए०आई०आर० 1960, एस०सी० 845 ; मगनभाई, ए०आई०आर० 1990, एस०सी० 1692)

छठा, अन्तर्राष्ट्रीय कानून के संरक्षण के अन्तर्गत अलग होना अन्तर्राष्ट्रीय समाज में मुश्किल से माना जाता है। अलग होना पूरे भारत में अलगाववाद की भावना पैदा करेगा जो देश में उग्रवाद, आतंकवाद और हिंसा को बढ़ावा देगा।

राष्ट्रीय रणनीति

भारत अपनी अखंडता, स्वतंत्रता, प्रभुसत्ता, आंतरिक और बाहरी सुरक्षा, स्थानीय, पाकिस्तान, अन्तर्राष्ट्रीय लेखकीय सुरक्षा और रणनीति के अपराधकर्ताओं को सह रहा है और इन सबसे जूझ रहा है। इसके अलावा भारत कामयाबी से विरोध कर रहा है और अस्थिर रणनीतियों का मुकाबला कर रहा है और आतंकवाद तथा उग्रवाद को समाप्त करने का भरसक प्रयास कर रहा है जो कि आतंकवादी समूहों जैसे जम्मू और कश्मीर मुक्ति फ्रंट है (जे०के०एल०एफ० 1977)। हुर्रियत सम्मेलन 1993 अनेक समूहों का गठजोड़ जिसमें अनेक संगठनीकरण 26 गोरिल्ला और राजनीतिक समूहों का गढ़ है {कुछ लोग दावा करते हैं कि यह वास्तव में यूनाइटेड स्टेट्स के शांति संस्थान (वांशिंगटन में स्थापित शांति संस्था) का आविष्कार है।}, मुत्ताहिदा जिहाद सभा, हिज्ब–उल–मुजाहिदिन, जैशै–ए–मुहम्मद, लश्कर–ए–तोईबा आदि का अस्तित्व, सशक्त सेनाओं द्वारा राजनैतिक व्यवहार कुशलता और कूटनीति द्वारा मानवीय अधिकारों के अनुसरण के विरुद्ध एवं विरोध में है। पाकिस्तान के अवमानना समझौते की चुनौती को भी भारत सह रहा है। भारत और पाकिस्तान के बीच के तनाव को शांत करने के लिए कश्मीर को लेकर यू०एन० रीजोल्यूशन 1948–49, ताशकेंट डकलेरेशन, शिमला एग्रीमेंट 1972, लेहोर डेक्लेरेशन 1999 बना था। समन्वित रिश्तेदारी के विकास में यह समझौते एक मील के पत्थर साबित होने थे। अगर यह समझौते मान्य होते तो यूरोपियन संगठन मॉडल और यूरो की तरह सर्च मॉडल बनता। यह तर्क किया जा सकता है कि पाकिस्तान ने करार पर हस्ताक्षर किए यह सोचकर कि वह उनके साथ कदापि नहीं रहेगा (ब्रहामा चीलैनी, द हिंदुसतान टाईम्स, सितंबर 8. 1999)। पाकिस्तान ने जब लाहौर घोषणा पर हस्ताक्षर किए तो उसका घृणायुक्त व्यवहार कारगिल आक्रमण की योजना को दिखाता था। निसंदेह यह कहा जा सकता है कि 1948 और 1949 रीजोल्यूशन की शपथ को लेते समय पाकिस्तान आखिर तक पाखंड को अपनाए रहा ; जम्मू–कश्मीर को न छोड़कर उस समय वह उसका उल्लंघन भी कर रहा था। हलांकि यह जताया जा

सकता है कि वह करार जिन्हें पाकिस्तान ने लागू किया है जिनको प्रमाणित करने का भार भारत पर ही रहा है। उन वजहों को ढूंढने में अधिक मुश्किल भी नहीं है।

इन चुनौतियों से जूझने के बाद, इस्लामाबाद घोषणा लाहौर घोषणा को दोहराती है। भारत–पाकिस्तान ने राज्य में शांति और सामान्य स्थिति वापस लाने के लिए व्यक्ति से व्यक्ति का संपर्क, मुजफराबाद कमान आमान सेतु मार्ग, वागहा मार्ग, खोखारा मार्ग, सड़क और रेलवे मार्ग, पत्रकारों का आदान–प्रदान, सांस्कृतिक दल, सामाजिक विज्ञान, शिक्षा केंन्द्र, दूसरे कार्यालयों के संरक्षण इत्यादि द्वारा आत्मविश्वास बनाए रखने वाले बहुत से उपाय अपनाने आरंभ किए। इसके अलावा भारत ने आंतरिक सी०बी०एम, पहली जम्मू–कश्मीर राउंड टेबल सम्मेलन, दिल्ली में फरवरी 2006 और श्रीनगर में 24 व 25 मई 2006 जम्मू–कश्मीर राउंड टेबल सम्मेलन आरंभ किया। भारत के प्रधानमंत्री डॉ० मनमोहन सिंह ने पंच कमेटी द्वारा उन्हें अंदरूनी जांच के लिए भेजा और कूटनीति योजना की घोषणा की।

समूह 1

राज्य में, समाज के अलग–अलग भागों में आत्मविश्वास बढ़ाने वाले उपायः श्री मोहम्मद अंसारी के नेतृत्व मेंः–

1. सेना द्वारा प्रभावित लोगों की स्थिति सुधारने के उपाय।
2. सेना द्वारा प्रभावित विधवाओं और अनाथों को पूर्व अवस्था में लाने की योजनाएं।
3. उन लोगों की स्थिति में शिथिलता जिन्होंने सैनिक बनने की सौगन्ध ली है।
4. पूर्व अवस्था में एक असरदार प्रभाव लाने की नीति जिसमें स्थानांतरित कश्मीरी पंडित के लिए रोजगारी सम्मिलित हो।
5. एक सिफारिश उन कश्मीरी युवाओं के लिए जो पाकिस्तान के अधीन क्षेत्रों से संबंध रखते हैं।
6. राज्य की अद्भुत सांस्कृतिक और धार्मिक परंपरा को सुरक्षित रखने के उपाय।

समूह 2

एल०ओ०सी० के आर–पार के रिश्तों को मज़बूत करना : श्री एम०के० रस्गोत्रा के नेतृत्व में उपायों का सुझाव देना :

1. उस प्रक्रिया को सरल करना जो एल०ओ०सी० के आर–पार यात्रा करने को सहज बनाएं।
2. समानों के व्यापार को बढ़ाना।
3. व्यक्ति से व्यक्ति का संपर्क बढ़ाना।
4. नए रास्तों को खोलना जैसे कि कारगिल, शकरदू आदि।

समूह 3

डॉ० सी० रंगराजन के नेतृत्व में आर्थिक विकास :

1. उन नीतियों को उभारना जो संतुलित आर्थिक प्रादुर्भाव और रोजगार को आश्वस्त करें।
2. नियंत्रित आर्थिक विकास और रोजगार पैदा करना।
3. राज्य में नियंत्रित क्षेत्रीय और उप–क्षेत्रीय विकास।

समूह 4

श्री एन०सी० सक्सेना के नेतृत्व में अच्छे अधिकारों को आश्वासन देना : प्रभावशाली उपायों को ध्यान में रखना जिससे :–

1. प्रशासन की जवाबदारी, उत्तरदायित्व और पारदर्शिता बढ़े।
2. स्थानीय स्व–सरकार को मज़बूत करना।
3. विकासशील कार्यक्रमों को प्रभावशाली ढंग से देखना।
4. मानवाधिकारों का उल्लंघन करने वालों के लिए सहनशक्ति को शून्य मनस्कता का बनाना।
5. जानकारी के आधार को मज़बूत करना।
6. समाज के सभी वर्गों, विशेष रूप से अल्पसंख्यक को उपयुक्त सुरक्षा प्रदान करना।

समूह 5

केंद्र और राज्य के रिश्तों को मज़बूत करना :

सावधानी रखना :

1. जो विषय जम्मू–कश्मीर के विशिष्ट पद से भारतीय संघ के अन्तर्गत संबंध रखते हैं।
2. विधियां, जो लोकतंत्र, सांप्रदायिकता और कानून के क्षेत्र को मज़बूत करती हैं।
3. विभिन्न राज्यों के मध्य, क्षेत्रीय, उपक्षेत्रीय और पौराणिक इच्छाओं इच्छाओं को पाने के लिए शक्ति के प्रभावशाली आक्रमण के प्रति सावधान होना। सभी राजनैतिक दलों के प्रस्तुतिकरण पर ध्यान रखा गया है।

आलोचनात्मक विश्लेषण और निष्कर्ष का सार

स्थानीय, पाकिस्तान और अन्तर्राष्ट्रीय रणनीति के जाल से बाहर आने के लिए भारतीय रणनीति एक नई कूटनीति अपना रहा है जो कश्मीर घाटी के आस–पास सीमित है और जम्मू और लद्दाख के जनसाधारण से बहुत कम ताल्लुक रखते हैं। यह त्रिभागी पहुंच बहुत गरम और बहुंत ठंडे व्यवहार प्रतिरूप के साथ आती है। सबसे महत्वपूर्ण बात यह है कि भारतीय रणनीति कहीं इस त्रिभागी रणनीति का शिकार न हो जाए। भारत को अपनी समन्वित व्यूह रचना की योजना में चालाक होना पड़ेगा वरना शायद वह त्रिभागीय कपटी राजनीति के जाल का शिकार बन जाएगा। भारतीय रणनीति का ऐसा प्रतिरूप होना चाहिए जो उसकी सीमाओं, प्रभुत्व, अखंडता, अंदर और बाहर की सुरक्षा और रक्षा की सुरक्षा करे। उसको उन चुनौतियों से जूझने के लिए नई योजनाएं बनानी पड़ेंगी जो उसकी अंदर और बाहर की सुरक्षा के लिए खतरा है। यह सुरक्षा का खतरा बहुआयामी व्यवहार है जो पोस्ट–संघजीवी दुनिया की परेशानियों से पैदा होता है। जैसे – पारंपरिक जाति संबंधी, प्रायः जाति–संबंधी, विचार पद्धति, कूटनीति, आर्थिक, सामाजिक और नव–राजनैतिक पंक्तियां। इस समूह में पांच में से चार ने अपने–आप को पहचान दी है, कुछ प्रश्नों को समझाया है और सिस्टम को सुधारने के सुखदायक उपाय दिए जिससे वह सिस्टम के छिद्रों को बंद कर सके। यह एक आसान कार्य नहीं रहा होगा। यह एक अतिकठिन काम लगता है क्योंकि नेताओं सहित सभी के आत्मविश्वास को वापस लाने के लिए अपने निष्कपट व्यवहार और सद्विवेक से राजनीति से ऊपर उठना होगा। उनके सुझाव दूसरे अफसरों की अलमारी के लिए चिट्ठी है। यह मकड़ी के मनोहर धोखा देने वाले वस्त्रों की तरह होंगे या नहीं, यह समय ही बताएगा। इन समूहों ने बारीकी से यह मूल प्रश्न नहीं उठाया कि कैसे, क्यों और किन स्थितियों में आत्मविश्वास खत्म हुआ ! कौन किसके वश

में है ! अगर निरंतर आत्मविश्वास पैदा करें तो इन बहुमूल्य प्रश्नों के जबाव अकेले ही दिए जा सकते हैं। उग्रवाद, आतंकवाद और छद्मयुद्ध लड़ाई सीमापार से भारत पर प्रहार कर रही है। यह अंदर और बाहर के विवाद के विषयों को पैदा करने के लिए जिम्मेदार है और आत्मविश्वास पैदा करने के उपायों में विघ्न डालने के लिए जिम्मेदार हैं। अलग–अलग राज्य सरकारें जम्मू और कश्मीर को पृथक विभागों से निर्मित एक भाग नहीं मान रहीं बल्कि तीन भागों में मान रही हैं और यह आत्मविश्वास को कम करने में सहायक है। अच्छा शासन, उत्तरदायित्व और पारदर्शिता की कमी भी जनसामान्य के आत्मविश्वास के खोने में समान रूप से जिम्मेदार है। और इसीलिए जीवन धारण करने योग्य अधिकार में बाधा है। जो हमें पीछे ले जाए, वो भ्रष्टाचार बढ़ रहा है और आगे बढ़ाने वाला रुख कम हो रहा है। क्रोध, असंतोष में लिपटा हुआ सच 'मेरी चिंता छोड़ो' जैसा जबाव और जिम्मेदारी भरा भाव पैदा कर रहे हैं। जल्दी, स्थिरता और प्रधानता को आगे बढ़ाना आत्मविश्वास को घटाने के दूसरे फैक्टर हैं। घाटी से हिंदू जनसंख्या की विदाई ने न सिर्फ सामाजिक स्थिति बदल दी है बल्कि लोगों के आत्मविश्वास और विश्वास के खोने के लिए भी जिम्मेदार है। सरकार और उसके काम करने की शैली में अंदर से हटाए लोगों का ब्यौरा दिया गया है। बढ़ते आतंकवाद को देखते हुए राज्यों के भागों से हिंदुओं का विदा होना, सरकार की अचेतना और उदासीनता आदि स्थितियां उनका आत्मविश्वास घटने का एक कारण है। मानवीय अधिकारों के बहाने अर्न्तराष्ट्रीय मानवीय कानून का उल्लंघन हुआ है और इससे सुरक्षा दलों की बदनामी हुई है। इसने आतंकवाद और प्रतिनिधि युद्ध को बढ़ावा दिया है जिससे वह अपनी उच्छृंखल गतिविधियों, सुरक्षा बलों और राष्ट्रवादियों के उत्साह भंग में आगे बढ़ सके। यह पक्ष जिस तरह से रखा जाना चाहिए था, उतनी तीव्रता से रखा नहीं गया। इससे यह एक ऐसा बड़ा सा रिक्त स्थान छोड़ गया जिसे भरना भविष्य संबंधी नीति है। कश्मीर घाटी तथा प्रदेश के अन्य भागों से घर से बेघर (शरणार्थियों) और 1947 के पश्चिमी पाकिस्तान के शरणार्थियों के आत्मविश्वास की कमी कों दूर करने के लिए कोई भी पुनः सुधार या पुनरुद्धार नीति नहीं है। आत्मविश्वास बढ़ाने के उपायों पर कार्यरत समूह ने जनवरी 2007 की अपनी रिपोर्ट में यह सुझाव दिया कि, ''पाकिस्तान का जो निकटरस्थ क्षेत्र है, उसके पार की अर्न्तराष्ट्रीय सीमा से आए शरणार्थियों की पुनरुद्धार समस्या का निरीक्षण होना चाहिए तथा उसका निर्णय हो जाना

चाहिए। ये लोग राज्य के स्थायी नागरिक बनने के योग्य नहीं हैं। ऐसे शरणार्थियों की वस्तुस्थिति को कपट तथा अपमानजनक ढंग से प्रस्तुत किया गया है। इनकी स्थिति जो अब भी बेघर और अस्थानीय लोगों की है, उनके भविष्य के बारे में बताती है। आत्मविश्वास बढ़ाने के उपायों पर कार्यरत समूहों ने ऐसे शरणार्थियों के आत्मविश्वास को समाप्त कर दिया है। हम बाह्य आत्मविश्वास बढ़ाने का उपाय चाहते हैं और आंतरिक आत्मविश्वास को बढ़ाने पर कम ध्यान देते हैं। उनके मन में संजोई आशा थी और हम पर विश्वास था कि अब वे बेघर और अस्थानीय नहीं रहेंगे। उनके आत्मविश्वास को खोकर हमने एक बार फिर उनके विश्वास को प्राप्त करने का मौका खो दिया है। इस विषय को सही दृष्टि से सामने रखने में कार्यरत समूह असफल हो गया। उनकी भाषा बनावटी लगती है क्योंकि वह कानून और सद्भावना के आपसी संगठन का न्यूनतम निरीक्षण कर पाया। कार्यरत समूह ने कानून और पुण्यशीलता के इस संबंध को एक ऐसी पहेली बना दिया जो रहस्मयी तरीके से प्रहेलिका में लिपटी है। उसके सुझाव दूरदर्शिता को ध्यान में रखकर नहीं दिए गए क्योंकि यह ओथेलो की तलवार की तरह शणार्थियों के सिर पर लटकने के लिए सहमति दे रही है। उसके विप्लववादी ज्ञान ने समस्या को सुलझाए बिना ही उन लोगों के हाथ में छोड़ दिया जो इसे सुलझा नहीं सके। मेरे विचार से यह विषय उन लोगों के हाथ में है जो योगदान देना चाहते थे पर नहीं दे पाए क्योंकि जब शरीर कमज़ोर होता है तो आत्मा चाह कर भी काम नहीं कर सकती। स्वराज्य और स्वतंत्रता दो अलग–अलग राजनैतिक दलों के राजनैतिक आदर्श हैं जिन्हें राज्य के किसी भी क्षेत्र से लोगों का सहयोग नहीं मिला। स्व–राज्य और स्वतंत्रता अन्यथा स्वायतता भारत के संसद द्वारा नकार एवं ठुकरा दिए गए हैं। जम्मू और लद्दाख क्षेत्र खुद को राष्ट्रवादी, अखंडता और एकता से पूर्ण दिखाते हैं जो भारत के संगठन के साथ संबंध और सहयोग बनाए हुए हैं। कश्मीर घाटी इसको अलग ढंग से प्रस्तुत करती है कि आत्मविश्वास पैदा करने वाले उपायों से असत्याभास झलकता है।

सीमांकन और सामुदायिकता के बीच का संबंध परस्पर जुड़ा हुआ है। इसने आत्मविश्वास बनाए रखने की आशा को अनियंत्रित, कठोर सामाजिक स्थिति से जोड़ दिया है। धारा 370 को सम्मिलित करना भारतीय संविधान के लेख में कभी भी 'भारत और जम्मू कश्मीर के नागरिकों की इच्छा' नहीं रही। आत्मविश्वास बढ़ाने के लिए आगे बढ़ने की उनकी इच्छा उन्हें अपने साथ

जोड़ लेती है। सरकारिया कमीशन ने, वेंकटाचेलिया कमीशन ने संविधान और लोकतंत्र के साथ काम करने का निरीक्षण और पुनःनिरीक्षण किया है। और माना है कि संविधान और लोकतंत्र के काम में दखल देना संवैधानिक संस्कृति के मूल ढांचे का उल्लंघन करेगा। कार्यरत समूह को उद्यमी होना चाहिए जिससे समकक्ष और सहायक संघीय संस्कृति मज़बूत हो। यह अकेले ही भारतीय राष्ट्र की एकता और अखंडता में मज़बूती लाएगी। इस दिशा में सिर्फ इतना प्रयास करना है कि केन्द्रीय राज्य संबंधी आत्मविश्वास को बनाए रखने के लिए किए जा रहे वर्तमान कार्यों का अनादर न हो। एक समान विकास और आर्थिक बंटवारे को, जो राज्य के तीनों क्षेत्रों में निष्पक्षता के आधार पर हुआ है, राज्य के सामान्यजन में विश्वास और आत्मविश्वास पैदा करना चाहिए। पूरे राज्य का ध्यान पर्यावरण–पर्यटन (आर्थिक और अर्थशास्त्री) पर होना चाहिए। शारदापीठ जैसी तीर्थयात्रा को बढ़ावा देना आत्मविश्वास से भरेगा। किंतु इसका परिणाम स्वार्थ से भरा नहीं होना चाहिए। हुर्रियत और जे०के०एल०एफ० जैसे समूह को बढ़ावा नहीं मिलना चाहिए जो राज्य की पूरी जनसंख्या की आवाज़ को संबोधित नहीं करते हैं। इस बात को बढ़ावा मिला तो यह आत्मविश्वास बढ़ाने के उपायों को प्रभावित करेगा। किसी भी राजनैतिक दल को राजनैतिक भत्ते का मिलना हानिकारक होगा। सिर्फ ऐसे भत्ते पर काम होना चाहिए जो भारतीय राष्ट्र की एकता और अखंडता के लिए हो। इसमें आंतरिक और बाह्य स्तर पर कोई समझौता नहीं होना चाहिए। सितंबर 2006 का 'हवाना ज्वाइंट मैकेनिज़्म टू टूरिस्ट स्टेटमेंट' भारत के प्रधानमंत्री डॉ० मनमोहन सिंह तथा पाकिस्तान के राष्ट्रपति जनरल मुशर्रफ द्वारा ग्रहणीय है और बहुत से छुपे हुए समझौतों से युक्त है। अधिकाधिक सावधानी के साथ इसे ऐसे ही देखा जाना चाहिए और अनुसरण किया जाना चाहिए जैसे Quiet Diplomacy को। यह बताना सर्वोत्कृष्ट है कि प्रस्तुत स्थानीय, पाकिस्तान और अन्तर्राष्ट्रीय मापदंड दलदल से कम नहीं है क्योंकि यह सुदृढ़ता, स्वराज्य, स्वतंत्रता, स्वायतता, आज़ादी और उग्रवाद एवं अलगाववाद को बढ़ावा देता है। यह बैक चैनल डिप्लोमेसी के रूप में ग्रहण किया गया है जो चार विस्तृत फार्मूलों – 'नॉरदन आईरलैंड, कोसोवो, ईस्ट टाइमोर, अमेरिकन थिंक टैंक' में है। यह बताना ताक पर रखने के समान होगा कि भारत को कभी–कभी सरल राजनीतियों की जगह कठिन राजनैतिक

और कूटनीतिक पद्धतियां अपनानी चाहिए जिससे समन्वित नीतियों के साथ बिना किसी परिणाम के विवाद सुलझ सके। अन्यथा यह अनियमित हो जाएगा। साउथ एशिया में समन्वित नीति और शिष्टाचार, व्यापार, क्रय–विक्रय, सांस्कृतिक रिश्ता और शैक्षिक आदान–प्रदान का बढ़ना अच्छे परिणाम देगा। यह समन्वित शिष्टाचार सिर्फ साउथ एशिया क्षेत्र को मज़बूत करेगा। दूसरों की बराबरी करेगा इसलिए कि एवं सद्भावना द्वेष फैलाने वाला अग्रदूत होगा। मानव की खुशी, उसकी सफलता और विकास के लिए, शांति परिणामों पर निरंतर काम करने के लिए इसे साहसी नीतियां चाहिए। इतिहास को भूतकाल में रखने के लिए और तीर्थयात्री की तरह आगे बढ़ने के लिए, हमेशा की शांति और समृद्धि के लिए सिर्फ यही एक समन्वित नीति, एक मानव अधिकार मापदंड है। हमें अपने सामने यह उक्ति रखनी चाहिए कि, ''अनंत सावधानी स्वतंत्रता का मोल होता है।'' हमें इस तरह व्यवहार करना चाहिए कि हमारे लिए यह कभी दुबारा न कहा जाए कि ––

''खोला कफ़स तो ताकते परवाज़ ही नहीं,
बुलबुल तेरे नसीब को सैयाद क्या करे !!''

APPENDICES

APPENDIX I

Summary of Reports of Five Working Groups on Jammu and Kashmir

SUMMARY OF REPORT OF WORKING GROUP-I ON CONFIDENCE BUILDING MEASURES ACROSS SEGMENTS OF SOCIETY IN THE STATE

The Working group on confidence building measures across segments of society in the State was chaired by Shri Mohammad Hamid Ansari and comprised of 17 other members (list attached) drawn from across the political spectrum and other spheres of life. The Working Group held three meetings on 27.07.2006, 15.09.2006 and 24.11.2006.

2. The Group had the following agenda:

- Measures to improve the condition of people affected by militancy.
- Schemes to rehabilitate all orphans and widows affected by militancy.
- Issues relating to the relaxation of conditions for persons who have forsworn militancy.
- An effective rehabilitation policy, including employment, for Kashmiri Pandit migrants.
- An approach considering issues relating to return of Kashmiri youth from areas controlled by Pakistan.

3. After consolidating all the view points and identifying the items of convergence the recommendations were finalized after thorough discussions.

4. The Group expressed serious concern over the incidents of human rights violations in Jammu and Kashmir. The necessity of curbing human rights violations are considered to be one of the most important measures to be taken so that the innocent persons do not become victims of counter-insurgency measures. It was also felt that this would also help to enhance India's International image. The Group therefore recommended strengthening of the State Human Rights Commission along the lines of the NHRC, revitalization of its functioning and setting up of an Empowered Committee for monitoring the Action Taken Report on its recommendations.

5. The Working Group recommended administering the relief to the victims of militancy prescribing an order of priority for the victims to receive relief assistance. Considering the limitation on the numbers of Government jobs available it is necessary to prioritize normative conditions in the provision for jobs to victims' families. The Working Group was of the view that wherever it is not possible to provide Government jobs, a one-time compensation of Rs. 5.00 lacs be given. A rehabilitation package for the injured victims and relief/compensation for victims of the Kargil War was also suggested.

6. The Group recommended review and revocation of laws that impinge on fundamental rights of common citizen, such as Armed Forces Special Powers Act. Law and order was to be maintained through normal laws to the maximum extent.

7. The Group deliberated on the conditions of widows and orphans of those killed in militancy-related violence. It was considered necessary to set-up a special cell to get complete data including wives and children of persons missing or presumed dead for making effective rehabilitation schemes. They should complete the work within 3 months. The widow relief of Rs. 500 at present should be revised and orphans provided scholarships to cover cost of education and their livelihood concern by a suitable scheme. Orphans of killed militants with no other source of income should be included as a goodwill gesture. Relief measures should be monitored regularly and malpractices curbed effectively.

8. The Group felt that there is a need to create conditions for persons who have forsworn the path of militancy to avoid reversion back to militancy and to provide them a definite policy/

package for their rehabilitation. They should be treated in a dignified manner. The Group has recommended that the security forces should be instructed to keep a check on fake encounters and fake recovery of arms. Cases of all persons in jails should be reviewed and those who are under trial for minor offences should be given general amnesty.

9. The Group also recommended devising an effective rehabilitation policy including employment for Kashmiri Pandit migrants. Further, it has been recommended that the rights of Kashmiri Pandit migrants to return to the places of their original residence should be recognized and a comprehensive package devised in consultation with their representatives. This should be based on comprehensive collection of database. It should include other militancy affected migrants of Jammu region. Jobs for Kashmiri Pandits should be identified in Police and other Civil Service vacancies besides Government of India offices located in J&K. Relief to NoKs who could not be provided jobs as prescribed under SRO-43 should be increased from Rs. 1 lakh to Rs. 5 lakhs. An inventory of their properties should be prepared to examine illegal occupation. Adequate compensation/rent should be provided to the properties of migrants occupied by SFs. All camp migrants should be provided living conditions and accommodation. Kashmiri Pandits living in the Valley should also be provided opportunities of education and employment. It is also necessary to start a dialogue with the representatives of Kashmiri Pandit migrants with a view to design a package for their return and rehabilitation within next three years. The Working Group also recommended setting up of a Minority Commission for J&K.

10. The Working Group recommended to categorize youth into those who joined militancy for misguided ideological reasons, monetary considerations and forced circumstances. It suggested consideration of a policy within a framework of CBM enunciated in the RTC and after verifying the identity of persons returning from the other side within a time frame to be decided. Such persons should be given a rehabilitation package and treated with dignity to join the mainstream similar to para 8 above.

11. The recommendations of the Group included preparation of a comprehensive policy to preserve monuments, sites, building structures, objects and landscapes that are significant in indigenous history, architecture, archaeology, engineering and

traditional art forms by a body of experts through an autonomous institution.

12. The Group recommended that problems being faced by the refugees who came from West Pakistan in 1947 such as State Subject Status should be settled once for all. The Working Group expressed concern and need for further relief and rehabilitation of refugees of 1965 and 1971 wars who have not been fully rehabilitated living mostly in Jammu Division.

13. The Working Group touched upon balanced regional development, economic development of certain communities and the need for more power projects.

14. The Group also suggested the following steps to stop migration:

(i) Centre and State Government to consider application of internationally accepted policy in consultation with experts.

(ii) To start unconditional dialogue process with militant groups for finding sustainable solutions to the problems of militancy.

(iii) To examine the role of media in generating an image of the people of the State so as to lessen the indignity and suspicion that the people face outside the State.

Composition of Working Group-I

1.	Shri Mohammad Hamid Ansari, Chairperson, National Commission of Minorities	Chairman
2.	Shri Ali Mohammad Sagar, MLA (Ex-Minister J&K) National Conference	Member
3.	Shri Molvi Iftikhar Ansari, Ex-Minister, J&K People's Democratic Party	Member
4.	Peerzada Mohammad Sayeed, Minister for School Education, IT, Science & Technology, Haj & Auqaf President, J&K PCC	Member
5.	Prof. Chaman Lal Gupta, Ex-MoS, Govt. of India, BJP	Member
6.	Shri Omkar Nath Trisal, Advocate, CPI (M)	Member
7.	Shri Hakeem Mohd. Yaseen, Minister of Transport, J&K, PDF	Member

8.	Shri Yashpal Kundal, MLA, Panthers Party	Member
9.	Shri Tsering Dorjee, Chairman, LAHDC, Leh	Member
10.	Shri Asgar Hussain Karbalai, Chairman, LAHDC, Kargil	Member
11.	Dr. Agni Shekhar, Panun Kashmir Movement	Member
12.	Shri Taj Mohi-ud-Din, Minister for Consumer Affairs, J&K	Member
13.	Shri Shabir Khan, Vice Chairman, State Pahari Board	Member
14.	Sardar T.S. Wazir, President, Shiromani Gurudwara Prabandhak Committee, Jammu	Member
15.	Shri R.S. Chib, Ex-Minister, J&K	Member
16.	Shri Gh. Nabi Khayal, Journalist	Member
17.	Master Tassaduq Hussain, Ex-MLC	Member
18.	Sheikh Abdul Rehman, Ex-MP & Ex-MLA	Member

SUMMARY OF RECOMMENDATIONS OF WORKING GROUP-II ON STRENGTHENING RELATIONS ACROSS THE LINE OF CONTROL (LOC): JAMMU AND KASHMIR

The Working Group submitted the report in January 2007 on the following agenda taken up for deliberation:

1. 'Measures to simplify procedures to facilitate travel across the Line of Control'.
2. 'Measures to increase goods traffic'.
3. 'Measures to expand people-to-people contacts, including promotion of pilgrimage and group tourism'.
4. 'Measures to open up new routes such as Kargil-Skardu'.

Methodology and Guiding Principles Adopted by the Group

The Group recognized and was motivated in their efforts on the importance of people-to-people contacts and free travel facilities for the purpose of persons residing on two sides of the LoC thereby resulting in promotion of friendly and beneficial cooperation and the strengthening of peace in the region. The Working Group was guided by the belief that the opening of routes for trade and commerce would help in not only improving the economic conditions on both sides but also it would be an important step towards normalization of the situation.

The Working Group has made the following important recommendations on the issues concerned in pursuance to agenda:

1 (a) Expand Eligibility for Travel and Visit Across LoC

The Working Group recommended that the category of persons eligible to travel across the LoC from among divided families be not restricted to relations only, but to expand and cover persons who want to visit places of religious interest, tourism, and those requiring medical aid. However, tourism was to be allowed in groups only.

1 (b) Simplify and Speed up Procedure for Travel Across the LoC

All residents of Jammu and Kashmir may be required to obtain Permanent Resident Certificate (PRC). The PRC should be taken as the basic document on the strength of which travel permit is issued and Security clearance completed within a maximum period of two months. Traders should be issued multiple entry/exit permit valid for a minimum period of one year. Priority for clearance should be given for Emergency cases like serious illness, death or marriage in the family. Applications for travel permit should be accepted and disposed of in more number of places beginning Anantnag, Baramullah, Poonch and Rajouri besides Jammu and Srinagar and relations permitted to go upto the border.

2. Measures to Increase Trade and Commerce between Two Sides

The Working Group recommended the Provision of a Joint Consultative Machinery of officials and representative of trade and commerce from both sides to resolve difficulties. The eligible list of items for export should include handicrafts, fruits and other items manufactured by SSIs in J&K, and similar list finalized for imports from the other side. The hazardous goods should be allowed to be transported in a special vehicle and authorized to travel across LoC direct to the destination or earmarked transport depots at the LoC. Provision should be made for effective and quick mechanism for unloading, checking, etc. Concerted efforts may be taken to improve infrastructure support for goods and passengers traffic. The Working Group also suggested reciprocal waiver of customs duties for 3 years, promotion of trade fairs, Common Free Trade Area and reasonable levy of state Tax on goods traded.

3. Measures to expand people-to-people contact, including promotion of pilgrimage and group tourism

The Working Group recommendations suggested Exchange visits between students and faculty members of the Universities on two sides of the LoC; Organized visit of school students; Short-term courses in certain specific subjects; Consideration for the grant of admission to PoK students in J&K Universities; Exchange visits of groups of journalists, academicians, lawyers, etc. Cultural trips in the fields of music, dance, etc. After due consideration of security aspects the landline and mobile communication should also be permitted.

4. Measures to Open up New Routes Across the LoC

The Working Group recommended opening up of additional routes viz., Kargil-Skardu; Jammu-Sialkote; Turtuk-Khapulu, Chhamb-Jorian to Mirpur; Gurez-Astroor-Gilgit; Titwal-Chilhan; Jhangar (Nowshera)-Mirpur and Kotli. Additional contact points need to be established and in the Ladakh region Hundurman and any suitable point in Turtuk-Khapulu route was suggested. The Initiative to open new routes, should be taken unilaterally, integrated check post set-up to facilitate trade. Persons holding passport and visas should be allowed to travel on Jammu- Sialkote route for which appropriate mechanism are to be created.

5. Additional Recommendations on other Issues

The Working Group recommended constitution of a Joint Consultative Group of 10 numbers of the legislatures on both sides and to exchange views periodically on social, economic, cultural and trade-related matters of mutual interest. The Working Group recommended consultation, as necessary, for the provision of disaster and relief measures, exchange visits of groups of professionals for horticulture, tourism promotion etc., programme for the removal of land mines for better utilization of agricultural and grazing lands, consideration for opening of Leh-Xinjiang route across LOC with China and Leh to be promoted as an alternative for the Kailash-Mansarovar yatra.

The Working Group also noted that it understands and appreciates that in implementing its recommendations the Central and the State Governments will have to take into account the prevailing security situation.

Composition of Working Group-II

1.	Shri M. Rasgotra	Chairman
2.	Choudhary Mian Aitaf, MLA (Ex. Minister), National Conference	Member
3.	Shri Tariq Hamid Qara, Minister for Finance, J&K, People's Democratic Party	Member
4.	Shri Abdul Gani Vakil, MLC, Senior Vice-President, J&K PCC Congress	Member
5.	Shri Ashok Khajuria, State President, Bhartiya Janta Party, J&K	Member
6.	Shri Ghulam Nabi Malik, CPI(M)	Member
7.	Prof. Bhim Singh, MLC, President, Panthers Party	Member
8.	Shri Haji Nissar Ali, Minister for Social Welfare, J&K	Member
9.	Prof Ashok Aima	Member
10.	Qazi Mehboob Illahi	Member
11.	Shri Mohd. Yousuf Bhat, CPI	Member

SUMMARY OF REPORT OF WORKING GROUP-III ON ECONOMIC DEVELOPMENT OF JAMMU & KASHMIR

The Working Group on Economic Development was chaired by Dr. C. Rangrajan and comprised of 11 other Members drawn from across the political spectrum. The composition of the Working Group is given in the annexure. The Working Group held three meetings and identified sectors which will have the maximum impact on growth and employment generation. The specific focus is on inclusive growth and balanced economic development of three regions. The Working Group was of the view that the development challenges of J&K can be identified by the following six objectives:

(i) Reconstruction and maintenance of existing physical assets.
(ii) Investment in physical infrastructure particularly power and roads.
(iii) Investment in social infrastructure.
(iv) Creating a conducive climate for private investment.
(v) Balanced regional development.
(vi) Comprehensive fiscal adjustment.

2. The Working Group accordingly, came up with a number of recommendations for achievement of the above mentioned objectives. To achieve the first objective of Reconstruction and maintenance of existing physical assets, the working group has felt that what needs to be done is to have three sub-plans within the state plan. The first sub-plan will focus on completing ongoing projects, the second sub-plan to bring all existing assets to working order, and the third sub-plan focused on capacity creation in the infrastructure sector.

3. To achieve the second objective of investment in physical infrastructure particularly power and roads, the working group has made recommendations relating to augmenting capacity and efficient management of power sector, improvement in road connectivity including rural roads to facilitate movement of goods to major markets. The recommendations relate to solving the power shortage problem in the short-term (transfer of Dulhasti HEP) and in the long-term (transfer of Bursar HEP), strengthening of infrastructure and power sector reforms. In power sector, the working group has recommended transfer of 390 MW Dulhasti HEP to State Government (financial implication Rs. 4933 crore) and transfer of 1020 MW Bursar Project for execution by the State Government instead of NHPC. The group has also made recommendations relating to enhancement of states share of free power in Central Projects, simplification of procedures for various clearances, acquiring stake in thermal projects and exploiting Geo-Thermal and Micro-Hydel Projects to reduce dependency on Hydel Power. The group has also made recommendations relating

to power sector reforms such as functioning of State Electricity Regulatory Commission reducing transmission and distribution losses and rationalization of tariff, establishing distribution regions/circles, improving Accelerated Power Development and Reform Programme fund utilization.

4. The group made the following recommendations regarding development of Communications, Rural Roads and Telecom. The recommendations include according high priority to four-laning and repairing National Highways, early completion of the railway project on extending the railhead from Udhampur to Katra and from there to Kashmir Valley early, improving rural connectivity and redress the imbalance in rural road density across districts, revising unit cost norms of road construction per km length, specifically taking into account the hilly terrain of J&K, including the cost of land acquisition as a part of the project in the road construction schemes of the Government of India, land acquisition law to be modified such that the owners get a fair value for their land, implementing reduction in stamp duty to encourage sellers and buyers to indicate the correct value of transactions, revising the subsidy policy of Government of India for rural telephony, reducing entry tax on telecom equipment and sorting out inter-connection impasse by Department of Telecommunication.

5. To achieve the third objective of investment in social infrastructure, the working group made the following recommendations relating to Health, Employment and Education. The recommendations pertaining to health are implementation of the National Rural Health Mission without further delay by completing all preparatory work, setting up Mobile Diagnostic and Primary Clinics at the block level, setting up advanced mobile units with emergency care facilities for dealing with injuries from IED blasts, grenade explosions and other such militancy-related emergencies, creating a telemedicine network, designing and implementing an appropriate health insurance scheme for BPL families.

6. The recommendations relating to Employment and Education are upgrading existing vocational and technical training institutions and making them fully functional by providing them with building, equipment and trained faculty, expeditiously establishing 13 new ITIs, creating an incentive structure for encouraging the private sector to open IT training institutes in the

state, delivering the adult literacy programme through "literacy volunteers" drawn from the ranks of the educated unemployed in the state and appointing agricultural graduates in all the 2700 Panchayats in the state for agricultural extension effort.

7. To achieve the fourth objective of creating conducive climate for private investment, the working group made recommendations relating to industrial development and commerce. The recommendations include creation of Special Investment Zone with world class infrastructure, captive power generation and distribution, high quality services and utilities, dedicated infrastructure facilities, fast track and single window clearances, and liberalized labour laws, leveraging the special concession package announced by the Centre to attract investments to the state, Special package for revival of sick industrial units both in the public sector and the private sector, constructing and air cargo complex and a container depot (which could possibly be located in Jammu), revitalizing handicraft sector through targeted investment and skill upgradation of artisans, exploring the potential for trade across the border and scope for co-operation on subjects of common interest, upgradation and rehabilitation of industrial estates and creation of an Asset Reconstruction Company. The financial implication of the major proposals amount to Rs. 475 crore.

8. To achieve the fifth objective of balanced regional development of three regions of the State, the Working Group felt that the three regions of the state have different comparative advantages and the development strategies for each region has to be consistent with these the advantages. The Group recommended that resources should be deployed in such a way that no region feels aggrieved or left behind. The recommendations include adopting the participative and inclusive process inherent in the State Finance Commission to give fillip to balanced regional development, making District Development Boards more inclusive by including elected representatives and prominent person from among the backward communities, carrying out functions like minor roads, lanes, drainage, local level water supply schemes, primary education, rural health through the local bodies, involving public representatives in the process of allocations from the State Plan, examining establishment of a separate Directorate for Gujjars and Bakkerwals.

9. To achieve the sixth objective of comprehensive fiscal adjustment, the Working Group has recommended re-structuring public finances of the state to generate resources for development by pruning the unproductive expenditure, and redesigning the flow of central assistance to finance development expenditure rather than filling non-plan revenue gap.

10. The Working Group also made recommendations relating to development of other sectors of economy. The recommendations relating to Tourism are preparation of tourism vision document and a master plan based on sustainable tourism, exploiting state's rich cultural heritage and developing modern allurements like shopping, food courts, multiplexes, music festivals and sports events. The recommendations relating to Agriculture, Irrigation and Forest are diversifying production and adopting market-oriented products, encouraging new avenues like floriculture, aromatic and medicinal plant cultivation, completing on going irrigation projects, tapping the main rivers per minor irrigation projects, reforestation of degraded forests and using fallow land for fast growing trees. The Group also made recommendations relating to Horticulture such as market development schemes for fruit and fruit processing, better sorting, grading, packaging, and cold chain storage facilities to improve price realization.

11. Apart from the above, The Working Group also made recommendations on the other issues such as restoring properties occupied by the Army and Central paramilitary forces to owners or paying compensation, giving attention to internal roads in areas of tourist importance like Patnitop, Katra, Sonmarg, Yusmarg, etc. and expediting the work on Mughal Road, development of lakes and ponds for fisheries development by Panchayats, exploring an alternate route through Ladakh for the Kailash-Mansarovar pilgrimage, giving a special package for better drinking water facilities in *Kandi* areas, exploring possibility of relocation of business activities in Srinagar to other places in view of the congestion, conducting survey of mineral resources and relaxing eligibility norms for police and para military forces for aspirants from the state.

12. Finally, the Working Group recommended setting of a small monitoring authority for implementation of these recommendations. The financial implication of the major

recommendations of the Working Group amount to Rs. 7947 crore.

Composition of Working Group-III

1. **Dr. C. Rangarajan, Chairman, Prime Minister's Economic Advisory Council** — **Chairman**
2. Shri Omar Abdullah, M.P., President, National Conference — Member
3. Shri Muzaffar Hussain Baig, MLA, Ex. Deputy Chief Minister, Peoples Democratic Party (PDP) — Member
4. Shri Gulchain Singh Charak, MLC, Minister for Public Works Deptt., J&K Congress (INC) (Representing Dogra Sadar Sabha) — Member
5. Shri Nirmal Singh, Ex. State President BJP, J&K — Member
6. Shri Shyam Prasad Kesar, Member, State Committee CPI (M) — Member
7. Shri Ghulam Mohd. Sheikh, CPI — Member
8. Shri Balwant Singh Mankotia, MLA, Panthers Party — Member
9. Shri Nawang Rigzin Jora, Minister for Power, Representing Ladakh — Member
10. Thakur Puran Singh, MLA, Ex MoS(J), Representing Paharis — Member
11. Shri Nizam-ud-din Khatana, Representing Gujjars & Bakkerwals — Member
12. Shri Mohd. Sharief Niaz, Ex. Minister — Member

SUMMARY OF RECOMMENDATIONS OF WORKING GROUP-IV ON ENSURING GOOD GOVERNANCE IN J&K

The Working Group on ensuring good governance submitted the report in March 2007.

The Working Group held its meetings on 8.8.2006, 20.11.2006 and 10.02.2007 at Srinagar, Jammu.

(1) The Working Group recommended the appointment of the Chief Information Commissioner of the State, the

Appellate Authorities and the Departmental Information Officers for effective implementation of the Right to Information Act.

(2) The Working Group recommended the introduction of e-governance in the State for the purposes of computerization of the functioning of government departments and public services such as Land records; Sub-Registrars Offices; Treasury operations; Electoral rolls; issue of Certificates, etc. The capacity of Information Technology department must be built to serve such purpose. The Working Group laid stress on introducing Information Kiosks at key service delivery institutions and to introduce Single Window Payment system for utilities like water, electricity, telephone, etc. Websites and on-line redressal methods should be incorporated in all government departments.

(3) The Working Group recommended Review of laws and Simplification of rules and procedures in departments which have a large public interface, e.g. Land Acquisition Act, land use changes, etc. Levy of fees should be more for commercial and industrial use in land use; digitized photographs of buyers and sellers be made compulsory; making Stakeholder benefits a reality in project rehabilitation are among the other suggestions of the Working Group. The Working Group suggested measures to promote entrepreneurship; formatting and standardization of forms and certificates; adoption of Single File system to bring about transparency in Government.

(4) The Working Group recommended independent Committees to assess performance of Police, Municipalities and Revenue departments once in 3 years.

(5) The Working Group recommended a 3 year tenure for officials, bringing down the weightage to interview in recruitments of teachers, review of qualifications in tune with higher specialization, fixing of responsibility and accountability, merit based promotions, etc. The Working Group recommended dual signing of Government orders to eliminate fake orders.

(6) The Working Group prescribed formulation of Citizens Charter and their review of implementation besides a system of public hearings at the District and State levels for increasing government visibility and people participation.

(7) The Working Group also recommended self-assessment of department by presenting a Report card by the Ministers and performance review of outcomes and expenditure, public perception surveys, institutional strengthening, public-private partnership, social audit and fiscal reform, etc. The budget cycle should be 2 years and a roll over facility followed for the unspent balances at the end of 1 year.

(8) The Working Group recommended implementation of Panchayati Raj Act in letter and spirit giving them appropriate devolution as per advice of State Finance Commission. J&K Government should examine extending of the 73rd Amendment. Capacity building of functionaries, mobilization of community leadership as partners and effective transfer of funds and functions are among the important suggestions in this regard.

(9) Programme implementation should be made more transparent by the use of Information Technology, e.g. tendering process could be made on-line. For proper monitoring the Working Group suggested elimination of overlapping jurisdictions, measurement of outcomes, and timely receipt of funds by the departments, etc.

(10) The Working Group considered measures to institute Zero-tolerance of Human Rights violations. For this purpose the Working Group recommended strengthening of the State Human Rights Commission (SHRC) for speedy redressal of complaints. There should also be comprehensive training for law enforcement Agencies on the subject. Political and civil society members should be part of a High Powered Committee to enforce Human rights, ensure accountability and implementation of laws. The State Government should act on all the

recommendations of SHRC and there should be a speaking order for non-acceptance on any account.

(11) The Working Group recommended that there should be sensitization of the RTI Act, biannual review of the application filed to bring about transparency in Government.

(12) The Working Group recommended Security Forces to adopt a Citizen Friendly approach; Safeguarding the life and property of innocents; Offering Special protection to minority residential areas; Activating local bodies to have a system of community watch on elements who pose a threat and isolating them besides setting up of a Minority Commission to look into their problems.

(13) A High Level State Committee reporting to the Highest authority should oversee the implementation of the recommendations was suggested by the Working Group and also the setting up of an Special Purpose Vehicle for their delivery.

Composition of Working Group-IV

1.	**Shri N.C. Saxena**	**Chairman**
2.	Shri Ajay Sadhotra, MLA, (Ex-Minister, J&K), National Conference	Member
3.	Sardar Rangil Singh, Ex-Minister, J&K People's Democratic Party	Member
4.	Pandit Mangat Ram Sharma, Minister for Health & Labour, J&K Congress (INC)	Member
5.	Prof. Hari Om, State Vice-President, BJP, J&K	Member
6.	Shri Abdul Gani Hafiz, State Committee, CPI(M)	Member
7.	Prof. K.S. Jamwal, Panthers Party	Member
8.	Shri P. Namgyal, MLC (Ex-Minister, GoI)	Member
9.	Shri Amar Nath, Kashmiri Pandit Samiti, Vaishnavi	Member
10.	Mohd. Shafi Pandit, Chairman, State Public Service Commission	Member
11.	Shri Nizam-ud-Din, MLC, J&K	Member
12.	Shri Bashir Ahmad Dar, Ex-Secretary, Board of School Education	Member

JAMMU AND KASHMIR
CONFIDENCE BUILDING MEASURES ACROSS SEGMENTS OF SOCIETY IN THE STATE
Report of the Working Group
January 2007

CONTENTS

THE WORKING GROUP

1. Shri Mohammad Hamid Ansari	Chairperson, National Commission for Minorities.	Chairman
2. Shri Ali Mohammad Sagar	ML A, (Ex-Minister, J&K) National Conference	Member
3. Shri Molvi Iftikhar Ansari	Ex-Minister, J&K People's Democratic Party	Member
4. Peerzada Mohammad Sayeed	Minister for School Education, IT, Science & Technology, Haj & Auqaf President, J&K PCC	Member
5. Prof. Chaman Lal Gupta	Ex-MoS, Govt. of India, BJP	Member
6. Shri Omkar Nath Trisal	Advocate, CPI(M)	Member
7. Shri Hakeem Mohammad Yaseen	Minister for Transport J&K, PDF	Member
8. Shri Yashpal Kundal	MLA, Panthers Party	Member
9. Shri Tsering, Dorjee	Chairman, Ladakh Autonomous Hill Development Council, Leh	Member
10. Shri Asgar Hussain Karbalai	Chairman, Ladakh Autonomous Hill Development Council, Kargil	Member
11. Dr. Agni Shekhar	Panun Kashmir Movement	Member

12.	Shri Taj Mohi-ud-Din	Minister for Consumer Affairs, J&K	Member
13.	Shri Shabir Khan	Vice-Chairman, State Pahari Board	Member
14.	Sardar T.S. Wazir	President, Shiromani Gurudwara Prabandhak Committee, Jammu	Member
15.	Shri R.S. Chib	Ex-Minister, J&K	Member
16.	Shri Gh. Nabi Khayal	Journalist	Member
17.	Master Tassaduq Hussain	Ex-MLC	Member
18.	Sheikh Abdul Rehman	Ex-MP & Ex-MLA	Member

The Working Group was constituted after an announcement was made by Dr. Manmohan Singh, the Hon'ble Prime Minister of India in the Round Table Conference held at Srinagar on 24th and 25th May, 2006.

The Group had the following Agenda before it:

1. Measures to improve the condition of people affected by militancy.
2. Schemes to rehabilitate all orphans and widows affected by militancy.
3. Issues relating to the relaxation of conditions for persons who have foresworn militancy.
4. An effective rehabilitation policy, including employment, for Kashmiri Pandit migrants.
5. An approach considering issues relating to return of Kashmiri youth from areas controlled by Pakistan.
6. Measures to protect and preserve the unique cultural and religious heritage of the State.

Methodology Adopted by the Group

The Working Group in the 1st meeting decided that there will be a consensus approach to the issues placed before the Group and that the Group members should try to find a solution in public interest and above party considerations. Accordingly, the remarks and comments from each member were obtained on different issues. Thereafter, the suggestions made by the members were classified with reference to the agenda items and placed before the Group for further considerations.

The Chairman had extensive discussions with senior representatives of National and State political parties as also journalists and other opinion makers. After consolidating all view points and identifying the items of convergence, a set of draft recommendations were prepared and placed before the Working Group for consideration and final approval. The recommendations were finalized after thorough discussions and are now presented in the form of this report.

The Chairman also made field visits to migrant camps to examine the situation on ground for an appropriate consideration and appreciation of the Working Group in its deliberations.

Some other issues were raised by the members which are not strictly within the purview of the Working Group but recommendations about them have also been made. It was decided that some of the issues would be referred to other Working Groups for detailed examination and their recommendations.

Meetings

The Working Group held three meetings on the dates and places mentioned against each:

I. 27.07.2006 Srinagar. Sher-i-Kashmir International Convention Complex
II. 15. 09.2006 Jammu. Govt. Guest House, Canal Road.
III. 24.11.2006 Jammu. Govt. Guest House, Canal Road.

Background of the Issues

Issue No. 1—Measures to improve the conditions of people affected by militancy

The State has been facing the problem of militancy from 1989 onwards which has continued to date. During this period a large number of militants crafted over from across the border who included foreign Nationals mainly from Pakistan and Afghanistan, youth who have gone from the State and received extensive training in the use of arms and ammunition across the line of control and certain other persons who provided local assistance to the militants. The militants and their acts caused extensive damage to the infrastructure in the State and damaged a large number of public and private buildings, Government schools and colleges, hospitals, bridges, besides causing damage to a large number of religious and historically important monuments.

A large number of persons belonging to all communities were killed by being deliberately targeted or in cross fire and the situation lead to the migration of more than 90% of Kashmiri Pandits from Kashmir valley as also some Kashmiri Muslims and Sikhs.

Logically the entire population of Jammu and Kashmir can be termed to have been affected by militancy in one way or the other, but *for the purpose of this issue the Working Group has considered only those who have been directly affected*. The Working Group concerns itself only with the rehabilitation and improvement of conditions of the militancy victims and did not go deeper into the causes or the genesis of the militancy in the State.

Issue No. 2—Schemes to rehabilitate all orphans and widows affected by militancy

As a direct result of militancy a large number of persons were killed due to various reasons based on community and political affiliations and also such persons termed as being Government informers or mixed up with security force. Another important category is that of the security persons both from within the State and outside who fell victim in directly fighting the militants or sometimes being targeted specifically. This has resulted into a number of widows and orphans requiring rehabilitation measures in the State. The number of such persons is, however, not exactly available and the Working Group has recommended that full information should be collected.

Issue No. 3—Issues relating to relaxation of conditions for persons who have forsworn militancy

During the years of militancy a large number of persons are reported to have come across the line of control who were of Nationalities other than Indian. But a large number of local youth also got involved in militancy by getting training across the border or remaining within the State. As a result of peace process some of them have now forsworn militancy and surrendered before the political leaders or the security forces. The Working Group has examined their special problems of rehabilitation, and their joining the mainstream.

Issue No. 4—An effective rehabilitation policy, including employment for Kashmiri Pandit migrants.

With the start of militancy in 1989 there was a large scale migration of Kashmiri Pandits from Kashmir valley. This process had started towards the end of 1989 and continued for the next one and half years in full force. Thereafter, the migration continued but the number was not as large as initially. It is estimated that a total number of more than three lakh persons migrated, who now are mainly based in Jammu, Kathua and Udhampur districts in Jammu division and New Delhi outside the State. Some of the families migrated to other places also but their number is comparatively not very large.

While migrating, the Kashmiri Pandits carried their belongings wherewithal and also some moveable assets. The houses and buildings remained unattended, which were locked at the lime of migration.

After 1995-96 a trend started when the property in Kashmir valley was disposed off initially, which can be termed as a distress sale, but in later years a fair price was obtained. As the transactions took place individually, figures in detail are not available, but most of the transactions are legally valid.

The migrants started getting relief, which included cash, and free rations for which different types of scales were sanctioned from time to time. At present the migrants who are living in camps in Jammu are getting the cash assistance and other facilities as follows:

Cash Relief	Rs. 750 per head (Maximum ceiling Rs. 3000 per family)
Ration	9 Kg rice per person per month
	2 Kg Atta per person per month
	1 Kg sugar per ration ticket/card

The total number of families registered as migrants by the office of the Relief Commissioner, Jammu amounts to 34,131 that include 5,889 living in camps in Jammu and 28,242 as non-camp migrants. Of these 30,206 families are Hindus, 2,170 are Muslims, 1,749 are Sikhs and 06 families are registered as others.

Whereas it cannot be denied that Kashmiri Pandits have a right to go back to their places but rehabilitation, avenues of employment and other facilities are required which have been examined by the Working Group.

It is estimated that the total population of Kashmiri Pandits in the Valley before migration was about 3.50 lakh. While the majority migrated, about 18,000 persons still remained as in 1997.

Issue No. 5—An approach considering issues relating to return of Kashmiri Youth from areas controlled by Pakistan

It has been expressed in a number of quarters that Kashmiri youth who went across the line of control for getting training and creating acts of militancy came back during the last many years, but a number of them are still remaining in areas under the control of Pakistan. Some visitors who went across have reported that many of the youth who were earlier disillusioned are now keen to return back to their native places and lead a normal life. Although this issue has international dimensions, the Working Group has examined whether a peaceful return and rehabilitation would be feasible.

The number of such persons is not known but their existence is substantiated by various reports.

Issue No. 6—Measures to protect and preserve the unique cultural and religious heritage of the State

Jammu and Kashmir presents the unique picture of a land where unity transcends the innumerable varieties and diversities of race, religions, language: and culture.

The grand past of the state is exemplified by the presence of several temples, shrines. Gompas of Ladakh, the Buddhist Viharas, for example, the remains of prehistoric settlements in Burzahom in Kashmir: the architectural ruins of Avantipura temples on the right bank of the Jhelum; the ruins of Martand temple, dedicated to the sun-god, situated four miles from Anantnag; and the temple ruins of Pandrethan, Paraspur and that of Pari Mahal. The Makdum Shah Shrine, the Chrar-I-Sharief Shrine and the Shah Hamdan mosque are one of the richest illustrations of the all-pervasive religious and architectural sense in the State. Besides, the spread of Budhism in the North-Western part of the subcontinent in evident from the 3rd great Buddhist council that was held in Kashmir during the time of King Kanishka.

Kashmir hits inherited a rich cultural and literary legacy, with one of its greatest pieces as *Raj Tarangini* or 'the River of Kings' by Kalhana and *Tarikh-Wagai-Kashmiri by* Mulla Ahmad Kashmiri. The Kashmiris speak 13 different languages and dialects, the chief amongst these being Dogri, Kashmiri. Pahari, Ladakhi and Dardi.

The rich music tradition of Kashmir includes classical and folk music, as well as the vocal and instrumental. Kashmiri classical music is usually called *'Soofiana Kalam'*, meaning 'mystical poetry', the wording being usually in Persian. The Ladakhis are mainly Buddhists; their monastries play an important part in their cultural and artistic activities. Then there is Pahari music of the plains. There are unique folk-dances of Kud, Bhaderwah, etc. *'Chakri'* a kind of folk-music and folk-dance combined together is the most popular and most widely played-music of the people of Kashmir.

Besides, the exquisite workmanship of the Kashimiri shawl and the elegant and graceful miniature art in the form of Basohli paintings representing the Pahari School of paintings render even more colour and richness to the culture and art of the State.

The State boasts of elaborate wood-carving in walnut, the art of Paper-machic, the silver-ware, the Kashmiri carpets and rugs; the silk and silk embroidery, that are world famous.

Needless to say, the great forest wealth, abundance of limestone and presence of gold and precious stones in the State simply add to its invaluable possessions.

With such a rich cultural and religious heritage, there is all the more necessity for its preservation as one of the best illustrations of composite culture in the world.

Recommendations of the Working Group

Issue No. 1. "Measures to improve the conditions of people affected by militancy"

The necessity of curbing human rights violations was stressed by most members of the Working Group. Emphasis was placed on Prime Minister's assurance of 'zero tolerance' for human rights violations, as on India's international commitments and international image. It was considered imperative to develop a mechanism in which responsibility for specific human rights violations can be fixed and derelict officials identified and proceeded against.

In this context, the need for strengthening the Human Rights Commission of J&K, and revitalizing it's functioning, was repeatedly stressed.

Recommendation No. 1.1

Human rights awareness should be inculcated in all civil and military government functionaries, and in the public. The State Human Rights Commission should be strengthened, along the lines of the NHRC, to enable it to ensure that innocent persons do not become victims of counter-insurgency measures. The following specific measures be taken:

(a) Investigative machinery, independent of the regular police, be provided to the Commission.
(b) Implementation of the recommendations of the Commission be made obligatory. In case a recommendation cannot be accepted, a Speaking Order should indicate reasons thereof.
(c) An Empowered Committee be appointed to report regularly on the action taken by the Government on the recommendations of the Commission.

Recommendation No. 1.2

While all victims of militancy stand in need of relief and assistance, the actual administration of relief/provision of jobs may be undertaken in the following order:

(a) Next of kin of persons—political workers/personalities, Government functionaries, police and para-military personnel—who were specifically targeted by the militants.
(b) Next of kin of those who were not involved in militancy and who lost their lives due to being caught in crossfire in counter-insurgency operation.
(c) Innocent persons who suffered injury due to acts of militancy.
(d) Persons rendered invalid due to mine blasts.

(e) Persons having suffered loss of livelihood due to agricultural land being taken over by the security forces/army, or in border fencing and laying of land mines.

(f) Criteria for the above-mentioned categories are prescribed in SRO-43. However, limitations on the number of available government jobs necessitate prescribing of priorities. The following norms should be considered for this purpose:
   - For families having no source of income, the beneficiary should be a direct dependent and an immediate family member of the deceased;
   - The beneficiary should be totally unemployed, Self-employed persons should not be considered eligible for this purpose;
   - In those cases, where employment cannot be provided as per the above criteria, a one time compensation of Rs. 5 lakhs be given and the case closed; and
   - Government may provide for 30% reservation for SRO-43 cases for vacancies in Class IV, Junior Assistant or equivalent. Wherever a technical qualification is necessary, the beneficiary should possess it.

(g) Persons injured due to militant action should be provided full rehabilitation package for treatment. They should also be assisted in rehabilitating the business/economic activity they were engaged in prior to getting injured.

(h) Relief/compensation as per established, precedents, mid-procedures, should be extended to victims of the Kargil War, including persons rendered invalid due to cross-firing and mine blast; and those who suffered loss of crops due to army taking over agricultural land or border fencing and land mines.

Recommendation No. 1.3

Certain laws made operational during the period of militancy (e.g. Armed Forces Special Powers Act, Disturbed Areas Act) impinge on fundamental rights of citizens and adversely affect the public. They should be reviewed and revoked. Law and order matters should be dealt with, to the maximum extent possible, through normal laws.

Issue No. 2—"Schemes to rehabilitate all orphans and widows affected by militancy"

Recommendation No. 2.1

Complete data of widows and orphans; affected by militancy, should be collected for making effective schemes for their rehabilitation. The data should also include wives and children of persons missing or presumed dead. Setting up of a special cell for their identification and rehabilitation should be considered. This cell will complete the collection of this data within a period of three months.

Recommendation No. 2.2

(i) The widows and orphans who are covered under the provisions of SRO-43 should be provided relief as in the case of victims of militancy under issue No. 1.

(ii) Relief to certain widows, which presently amounts to only Rs. 500 is inadequate and should be raised to a realistic level.

(iii) A suitable scheme of providing scholarship to orphans who are of school going age may be prepared. The scholarship should cover to the cost of education as also the financial requirements of the orphan.

(iv) The State Government, as a matter of policy, may consider extending the scheme of scholarship mentioned above to orphans of killed militants whose family has no other source of income. This would only be a good will gesture.

Recommendation No. 2.3

Administrative delays/malpractices in reaching relief to the concerned should be curbed. All Additional Deputy Commissioners or any other officer designated at the district level be empowered to ensure that relief measures are monitored regularly. Any person entitled to relief should be able to approach this officer.

Issue No. 3.—"Issues relating to relaxation of conditions for persons who have forsworn militancy"

Recommendation No. 3.1

The following may be considered by the State Government:

(i) A definite policy/package for rehabilitation is required so as to discourage any reverting back to militancy.

(ii) Persons who have forsworn militancy and wish to join the mainstream should be treated with dignity and a conscious effort made to prevent undignified treatment being accorded to them.

(iii) Security Forces should be instructed to keep a check on fake encounters and fake recovery of arms.

(iv) Cases of all persons in jail should be reviewed, and general amnesty given to those under-trial for minor offences or who are innocent.

Issue No. 4.—An effective rehabilitation policy, including employment for Kashmiri Pandit migrants"

Recommendation No. 4.1

(i) The rights of Kashmiri Pandit migrants to return to the places of their original residence should be recognized without any ambiguity and made a part of the State policy.

(ii) A comprehensive package should be prepared for rehabilitation of migrants in consultation with their representatives. Apart from Kashmiri migrants, militancy-affected migrants within Jammu region, namely in Rajouri, Poonch and Doda also need to be rehabilitated. However, collection of complete data on these migrants is a pre-requisite for devising of any rehabilitation package.

Recommendation No. 4.2

The following specific notions may be considered:

(A) Job Opportunities

(i) Jobs to the Kashmiri Pandit migrants may be provided against retirement vacancies for which certain organizations can be earmarked including Police, and offices of HODs and Civil Secretariat which have in built security arrangements.

(ii) The job opportunities in the State being limited, the GoI may, in their offices located in J&K, accommodate SRO-43 candidates of the State belonging to Kashmiri Pandits.

(iii) Relief in SRO-43 cases should be increased from Rs. 1 lakh to Rs. 5 lakh as one-time compensation so as to enable the jobless migrants to engage in self-employment. [As also recommended at No. 1.2 (f)].

(B) Migrants' Properties

(a) An inventory of properties, including orchards of migrants, should be generated and examined for illegal occupation, if any, and full compensation of the properties be given once regaining of ownership is ruled out and the property is appropriately valued for.

(b) The property of migrants in Kashmir valley, which is presently under the occupation of security forces, should make the owners eligible to receive adequate rent or compensation for the use of such properties including lands and buildings.

(C) Other Matters

(a) All Camp migrants should be provided living conditions and accommodation in accordance with the package already approved by the Hon'ble Prime Minister. A number of residential buildings on that account are being constructed at Jammu. The same pattern should be followed for all camp migrants.

(b) While the State Government may take all the measures as recommended for rehabilitation and improving living conditions of migrants it must not ignore the fact that a small number continue to live in Kashmir Valley and did not leave their places of residence. It would be necessary to ensure that they may continue to live in peace and have ample opportunities of employment and education. Special problems faced by them regarding safeguard of their property or other assets should be looked into.

(c) Setting up of Minorities Commission for Jammu & Kashmir should be considered.

Recommendation No. 4.3

The following may be considered for arriving at a long/ medium-term policy:

(i) A dialogue should be started with the representatives of Kashmiri Pandit migrants for a detailed scheme regarding the future of rehabilitation aid and assistance to camp migrants and those who are receiving cash/ kind relief/grants.

(ii) A dialogue should also be started with representatives of migrant community for designing a package for return and rehabilitation of migrants including identification of such categories who will return in the next three years.

Issue No. 5.—An approach considering issues relating to return of Kashmiri youth from areas controlled by Pakistan"

The youth who have gone into militancy have to be considered under the following categories:

(a) Youth who joined militancy for misguided ideological reasons;

(b) Youth who have gone for monetary considerations; and

(c) Youth who have been forced into militancy.

A careful assessment of their number is necessary in the first instance for taking a view on a long-term basis.

Recommendation No. 5.1

A policy on this question be made keeping in view the following:

(a) It be within the framework of the Confidence-Building Measures enunciated by Hon'ble Prime Minister in the Round Table Conference.
(b) An effective method be adopted for proper verification of the identity of the persons who returns from the other side.
(c) Once a person is allowed to return, he should be extended the benefit of recommendation 3.1(i) and 3.1 (ii) above.
(d) The offer to permit return should within a time frame to be determined politically to maximize its impact.

Issue No. 6.—"Measures to Protect and preserve the unique cultural and religious heritage of the State"

Recommendation No. 6.1

(a) Cultural and religious heritage include monuments, sites, building structures, objects and landscapes that are significant in indigenous history, architecture, archeology, engineering and culture. Historically, architecturally, and culturally, they make a major contribution to the society and should, therefore, be preserved.
(b) A comprehensive policy on preservation of cultural and religious heritage of the State is required and the work of preservation should be assigned to some autonomous institution
(c) Steps should be taken to preserve and continue traditional art forms like sufiana music, miniature paintings, folk dances, etc. A comprehensive plan should be got prepared by a body of expects in the field which could include those who have served with the Academy

of Art and Culture and persons who have sufficient local knowledge in this behalf.

Other Issues

The main issues on the agenda of the Working Group have been covered broadly as above. Certain other issues were also raised by members which the Working Group regards as worth considering at the level of the Government of India and the State Government. These issues and the recommendation of the Working Group are as below:

Issue No. 7.—The rehabilitation problems of refugees of 1947 who came over from adjoining areas of Pakistan across International border need to be examined and settled once for all. These persons are not eligible for being permanent residents of the state.

Issue No. 8.—There are certain refugees who have not been provided full rehabilitation after the wars with Pakistan in 1965 and 1971. They are mostly concentrated in the Jammu division and their status as also requirements of further relief or rehabilitation should be addressed to.

Issue No. 9.—For balanced development and redress of the feeling that there is discrimination against certain region or sub-regions within the State, it was suggested that the systems of Regional or Sub-regional Councils be examined. Since this issue also falls in the purview of Working Group No. III on "Economic Development", the same has been posed to that Working Group with the suggestion that this Working Group considers that the settlement of this issue is of prime importance.

Issue No. 10.—Another important item of the requirement of accelerated economic development of certain communities which have been deprived for a long time like Gujjars, Bakkerwals and the Pahari-speaking people. This issue has also been referred to the Working Group No. III on "Economic Development".

Issue No. 11.—An important issue related to all sections of the society is availability of power, which is very vital for industrial development as also for a decent living in all households. All possibilities for setting up of new power projects within the framework of Indus Water Treaty should be considered.

Issue No. 12.—The State has been facing problems relating to migration in which the Working Group has proposed case specific recommendations of immediate nature. In addition, it may be necessary to examine in detail the reasons and the problems related to migration and steps that any recurrence should not take place.

The following may therefore be considered:

(a) It has to be recognized that the problem of militancy and alienation of some sections of the society has to be tackled in a very broad framework in this behalf. Central and State Governments may consider application of internationally accepted policies; in consultation with experts.

(b) An unconditional dialogue process should be started with militant groups for finding a sustainable solution to the problem of militancy in the State.

(c) The probable role of media should be examined in generating an image of the people of the State so as to lessen the indignity and suspicion that the people, especially youth face outside the State.

Acknowledgements

The Chairman was assisted in convening the Working Group meetings, recording the proceedings, making all other arrangements for Group's work including the preparation of the records of various meetings and Group's final report by a team of officers headed by Shri Ajit Kumar, IAS, Financial Commissioner (Coordination) and including officers and staff of the office of the Resident Commissioner, New Delhi, Commissioner/Secy. General Administration Department and the Hospitality and Protocol Department of the State Govt.

(MOHAMMAD HAMID ANSARI)

New Delhi
Dated January 10, 2007

ECONOMIC DEVELOPMENT OF JAMMU AND KASHMIR

Report of Working Group No. III

March 2007

Working Group No. III on "Economic Development" of Jammu and Kashmir

1.	Dr. C. Rangarajan, Chairman, Prime Minister's Economic Advisory Council	Chairman
2.	Shri Omar Abdullah, MP President National Conference	Member
3.	Shri Muzaffar Hussain Baig, MLA Ex. Deputy Chief Minister People's Democratic Party (PDP)	Member
4.	Shri Gulchain Singh Charak, MLC Minister for Public Works Dept., J&K Congress (INC) (Representing Dogra Sadar Sabha)	Member
5.	Shri Nirrnal Singh Ex. State President BJP, J&K, BJP	Member
6.	Shri Shyam Prasad Kesar Member State Committee CPI(M)	Member
7.	Shri Ghulam Mohd. Sheikh, CPI	Member
8.	Shri Balwant Singh Mankotia, MLA, Panthers Party	Member
9.	Shri Nawang Rigzin Jora, Minister for Power Representing Ladakh	Member
10.	Thakur Puran Singh, MLA, Ex MoS, Representing Paharis	Member
11.	Shri Nizam-ud-din Khatana Representing Gujjars & Bakkerwals	Member
12.	Shri Mohd. Sharief Niaz, Ex. Minister	Member

The Working Group was constituted following an announcement made by the Prime Minister in the Round Table

Conference at Srinagar on 24th and 28th May, 2006. The Working Group held three meetings in all between Aug. 2006 to Feb. 2007 (Schedule of meetings at Appendix 3). It also held consultations with the Chief Minister of J&K at Srinagar on Aug. 29, 2006. The Working Group wishes to thank the (officers of Government of Jammu and Kashmir for their advice and the officers of Economic Advisory Council to PM for assistance throughout this task.

CONTENTS

INTRODUCTION AND OVERVIEW

Approach of the Working Group

1.1 The State Plan provides the platform for Jammu and Kashmir (J&K) to pursue its development. Besides, there is the large initiative through the Prime Minister's Reconstruction Plan, with an outlay of Rs. 24000 crores, aimed at three basic thrust areas: (i) expanding economic infrastructure; (ii) expanding the provision of basic services; and (iii) employment and income generation.

1.2 In another important initiative, the Prime Minister had constituted a Task Force under the chairmanship of Dr. C. Rangarajan on the 'Development of Jammu and Kashmir'. The Task Force, whose report was submitted to the Prime Minister in December 2006, made comprehensive recommendations on growth generating initiatives for the state focusing on important sectors like power, rural roads, telecom, tourism, horticulture and food processing, health as also some quick yielding projects. The Working Group has studied the report of the Task Force and supports the recommendations made therein.

1.3 Rapid and sustained economic development of J&K is the common agenda of both the Working Group and the Task Force; hence some overlap in recommendations is inevitable, and perhaps also desirable. However, the mandate of the Working Group extends beyond that of the Task Force especially with respect to the thrust on balanced regional and sub-regional development and employment generation. Accordingly, the Working Group has identified sectors which will have the maximum impact on growth and employment generation in Jammu and Kashmir. The specific focus of the recommendations is on inclusive growth and on balanced economic development.

Development Challenge

1.4 Long-term development of Jammu and Kashmir (J&K) is a formidable challenge in many ways. The state has to reconstruct an economy ravaged by two decades of militancy and terrorism and at the same time deliver quickly on growth and poverty reduction which, in the ultimate analysis, is the most sustainable solution to restoring peace and order. J&K has some unique economic disadvantages arising out of remoteness and poor connectivity, hilly and often inhospitable terrain, vulnerability to natural disasters, a weak resource base, poor infrastructure, sparse population density, shallow markets and most importantly a law and order situation threatened by militancy. Taken together, all these factors have resulted in a classic "backwardness trap" of low economic activity, low employment and low-income generation.

1.5 The economic disadvantage indicated above has substantial implications for the size and nature of the development problem and for the approach to be adopted. First, the internal market is too small to take advantage of scale economies in production. The alternative of scaling up production to viable levels by exporting to markets outside the state is infeasible because of poor connectivity. Second, unit costs of service delivery are high because of high costs of inputs as also low population densities. Third, the private sector, which should be the engine of growth, has not taken off in part because of low supply and demand linkages and in part because of inhibition of the private sector on account of security concerns. Consequently, the burden of generating economic activity has had to be borne almost exclusively by the public sector. Fourth, the virtual absence of the private sector has meant a low tax base. Fifth, the beneficial impact of public expenditure has been lost to some extent. Such benefits have tended to spill over beyond the state as much of the contractors' payments are transferred and purchases are made beyond the state—a phenomenon referred to as the 'missing multiplier'. Finally, excessive and prolonged dependence on central assistance has led to a complacent attitude towards resource generation, fiscal responsibility and accountability for results.

1.6 The above analysis suggests that the approach to long-term development of J&K should focus on generating economic activity within the state and on mainstreaming the state into the national and the global economy. The most efficient way of doing this is to focus on sectors and projects that yield quick results while at the same time laying the foundation for long-term growth. The immediate priority in this regard is repair and reconstruction of assets damaged by militancy and terrorism. Next, long-term development requires investment in physical and social infrastructure. This does not mean only creation of new assets but it also means operation and maintenance (O&M) of existing assets. Experience shows that O&M of existing assets yields a much higher return for every rupee spent than creation of new assets. In practical terms this means repair and maintenance of existing roads, irrigation and drinking water works as well as staffing and equipping schools and health centers.

1.7 Inclusive growth means ensuring that the benefits of growth translate into poverty reduction. In other words, growth should be such that the poor contribute to growth and the poor benefit from growth. This requires better education and health. The Government has a critical responsibility in improving the reach and quality of education and health. Investment in social infrastructure therefore assumes significance in this context.

1.8 Low level of employment opportunities is a dominant and vocal concern in J&K. This results in the common argument that there should be a frontal thrust on explicit employment generation programmes. Experience of the last 50 years has however shown that the most effective way of generating sustainable employment is through accelerating growth; special employment programmes through incentives and subsidies have been both costly and ineffective. While heightened economic activity creates the demand for jobs, state intervention will be required to improve the employability of the job-seekers so as to match the emerging demand with appropriate supply.

1.9 Like most large states, J&K too faces the problem of regional imbalances which are not only inimical to growth but also engender political tensions. Balanced regional development of the three regions of the state—Jammu, Kashmir and Ladakh should also receive priority attention.

Agenda—Six Objectives

1.10 Accordingly, the development challenges of J&K can be defined by six objectives:

(i) Reconstruction and maintenance of existing physical assets

1.11 There is an urgent need to change the methodology of the plan. Currently there is too much focus on creation of new assets at the expense of maintaining existing assets although the latter yield better value for money. In the case of J&K what needs to be done is to have three sub-plans within the state plan. The first sub-plan will focus on completing ongoing projects. Like in every state the tendency in J&K too has been to shut new projects every year without completing the ongoing ones. The result has been a large work programme, thin spreading of available resources and consequent inefficiencies in public resource allocation. The problem has been compounded in J&K because of the law and order situation over the last several years. Efficiency demands that the ongoing works have the first charge on available resources. The Working Group has been informed that the Government is already working on this sub-plan. The second is a "comprehensive maintenance" sub-plan to bring all capital assets to working order. The third is a "new capital sub-plan" focused on capacity creation in the infrastructure sector.

(ii) Investment in physical infrastructure—power and roads

1.12 Power is by far the most crucial infrastructure sector for J&K. Almost every other development initiative of the Government is linked in some way to improving the power situation in the state. In fact, if expenditure on power purchase and receipts are netted out of the revenue account of the Government, the state will not only balance the revenue account but also will in fact generate a surplus for capital spending. The key priorities in the power sector are augmenting capacity and more efficient management of the sector.

1.13 Improvement in road connectivity is another infrastructure priority. The road density in the state is among the lowest in the country and what roads exist are in poor shape. Improving and expanding the highway corridors is important. Equally important is connecting the villages and towns to the main corridors through an internal road network so as to facilitate movement of goods from the farms and firms to the major markets and also to redress the imbalances in road density across the state.

1.14 In terms of expenditure allocations, it is best for the state to use the funds under centrally sponsored schemes, in particular Bharat Nirman, to create the road infrastructure. Both the PM's Reconstruction Programme and the ADB assistance have components for roads. The state plan should therefore, focus on filling gaps in areas outside of these programmes, particularly to balance the road density across the state.

(iii) Investment in social infrastructure

1.15 Investment in education and health is a priority across the country, but it has greater urgency in a state like J&K where the delivery systems have atrophied on account of the law and order problems. Education and health are not only important for human resource development but also for restoring the faith of the people in the institutions of governance.

(iv) Conducive climate for private investment

1.16 No matter how successful the fiscal adjustment, public resources will be limited. The Government should use its scarce resources in areas where it alone can operate such as in providing public goods and merit goods and leave the rest of economic space to the private sector. For the private sector to respond to this initiative by stepping up investment, the state needs to create a policy and physical environment conducive to private sector development. This will be the route to sustainable development of the state.

1.17 Even as the India growth story is the global toast, much of the positive benefits of this are bypassing J&K. The most important reason is the negative investor perception about the security situation in the state. Second, competition, among the states for attracting both domestic and foreign investment is very fierce and J&K is handicapped in joining this competition because of its poor infrastructure situation and remoteness from markets. The third reason is the land ownership issue which prohibits non-Kashmiris from owning property in the state.

1.18 J&K is trying to overcome many of these problems. The perception on the security situation can only improve over time as positive information percolates. What J&K needs are a couple of demonstrable successes. For this purpose, the state needs to attract some large and medium industrial houses to invest in the state. Second, some of the geographical handicaps of J&K are sought to be neutralized by the tax incentive package announced by the Center. However, J&K has not benefited as much from this package as have some other states, which too have a similar package such as Himachal Pradesh and Uttaranchal. Here again, improving perceptions will help. Third, the state government has relaxed some of the regulations relating to land lease like extending the lease period to 90 years. It will help if the government launches a vigorous promotion drive to disseminate information and correct the misperceptions. Finally, the state government should review all economic legislation on the statute book and weed out all legislation that is no longer relevant.

(v) Balanced regional development

1.19 Balanced regional development is important for every state but particularly so for J&K. It is far easier to restore law and order and give a sense of security when every region feels 'included' in the process of growth. The three regions of the state —Jammu, Kashmir Valley and Ladakh—have different comparative advantages and the development strategy for each region has to be consistent with these differences. Importantly, resources should also be deployed in such a way that no region feels aggrieved or left behind.

(vi) Comprehensive fiscal adjustment

1.20 The nature and size of the development problem cast a significant fiscal burden on the state. Fiscal adjustment in the state has to proceed at two levels. The first is to restructure public finances to generate resources for development. This requires generating own revenues, pruning unproductive expenditure and redirecting expenditures to productive uses. While investments in new physical and social infrastructure is necessary, it is equally important to spend on maintaining existing assets as that will provide good value for money.

1.21 The second level of adjustment is to redesign the flow of central assistance. Although; J&K has been receiving a fair measure of central assistance, much of it has gone to fill the non-plan revenue gap of the state rather than finance development expenditure. This is not advisable. The state government should have the undivided responsibility of managing its non-plan gap. Central assistance should be devoted entirely to development where the end use can be monitored and where the outcomes can be more concretely defined.

POWER SECTOR

Current Scenario

2.1 The rich water resources of Jammu and Kashmir offer immense potential for commercial hydropower generation of as much as 14,000 MW. Only 10% of this has been exploited so far.

2.2 The power sector of the state is characterized by huge revenue losses, vast supply-demand gaps, weak infrastructure and very high T & D losses. The T&D losses are in the range of 68% among the highest in the country. As of March 2006, the state faced peak deficit of 418 MW (26%) and energy deficit of 352 MU (35%) in power supply.

2.3 J&K has 14 hydroelectric projects with a total capacity of 1474 MW (304 in the state sector and 1101 MW in the central sector). Two hydroelectric projects, namely, Dulhasti (390 MW) and Baglihar (450 MW), are under construction. 7 more Hydroelectric Projects with an installed capacity of 2839 MW have been handed over to NHPC for implementation.

Initiatives

2.4 The recommendation of the Task Force on the transfer of Dulhasti HE project, presently in the central sector, to J&K is a welcome step. While this will provide some comfort on the generation side, there will still be pressing need to augment capacity further. To meet this need, it will be imperative to take up new power projects under the Prime Minister's 50,000 MW hydro initiative. The projects that can be taken up immediately are the following:

(i)	Sawalkote	600 MW
(ii)	Kiru	430 MW
(iii)	Kawar	320 MW
(iv)	Ralte	560 MW
(v)	Shamnot	370 MW

2.5 The pre-feasibility reports for these projects are available and follow-up action for implementation of these projects needs to be initiated urgently. These would be in addition to the seven projects with NHPC, out of which one of the projects, i.e. Bursar

Storage Scheme (1020 MW) (under the PMs Reconstruction Plan) has been recommended by the Task Force for transfer to J&K for execution in the state sector. The Working Group supports this recommendation, as it will mean that the full benefit of the allocation under the Prime Minister's Reconstruction Plan will accrue to the state as opposed to just 12% share in the power, that would be the case if the project is implemented in the central sector. Transfer of Dulhasti and Bursar will neutralize to some extent the disadvantages the state faces in developing its hydro potential. Nonetheless, there is a strong case for additional support. One option is to slightly enhance J&K's share in central hydro projects based on the state's rivers beyond the current norm of 12%.

2.6 The long delays in execution of power projects are a major concern. NHPC and the state power sector must expeditiously complete these projects and an immediate step would be simplification of procedures for various clearances like forest, pollution control, etc.

Thermal, Geothermal and Micro Hydel Projects

2.7 J&K is currently excessively dependent on hydropower. Correcting this imbalance is important for managing the demand-supply imbalances. It will therefore be advisable for J&K to acquire a stake in a few thermal projects including IPPs outside the state. This will ensure supply of thermal power on a long-term and assured basis. To go forward with this proposal, the state can seek the help of a power trading company.

2.8 Studies show that J&K has potential geothermal energy contained in its underground reservoirs of steam/water and hot dry rocks. Its uses include power generation, direct use of heat for space heating, agriculture, aquaculture, industrial processes, balneology, tourism, etc. Geothermal energy is particularly useful in hilly and remote areas in J&K where cost of conventional energy is high. In the state, geothermal resources have been identified in Puga-Chhumathang in Ladakh. Commercial potential for a 50 MW geothermal plant was identified but the project is yet to take off. Implementation of this pilot project can provide a platform for mainstreaming geothermal source of energy during the 11th Plan period.

2.9 J&K should exploit its significant micro, mini and small hydel potential for local supply which will reduce the dependence on grid supply. These decentralized plants will be more economical in remote hilly areas.

Reforms

2.10 Augmenting power generation capacity is necessary but not sufficient. There cannot be sustainable results unless efforts to increase generation capacity are accompanied by reforms in transmission and distribution. The State Electricity Regulatory Commission needs to be made fully functional. There is a need to establish a Transmission Utility for reduction of T&D losses and efficient management of power supply. A long-term plan will be necessary which would include establishment of distribution regions/circles and energy audit.

2.11 Under the Accelerated Power Development and Reform Programme (APDRP), the state has an allocation of Rs. 1100 crores. The schemes sanctioned should be implemented quickly and progress monitored on a regular basis.

2.12 The state should ensure rationalization of tariff, time bound loss reduction and close monitoring for stoppage of power misutilization and theft.

2.13 Besides high T&D losses, the gap in revenue recovered affects the overall finances of the state. Moreover, the new generation projects will entail additional debt servicing obligations. These obligations cannot be met unless the financial position of the power sector is strengthened. This requires fiduciary controls by way of fully accounting for all the power that is generated, diligently billing and collecting the dues.

COMMUNICATION, RURAL ROADS AND TELECOM

Context

3.1 The problem of connectivity in Jammu and Kashmir operates at two levels: the problem of road connectivity to J&K—the state is connected to the rest of the country through just one highway; and the problem of road connectivity within J&K—there is a huge disparity in the road density across districts in the state especially the rural roads sector.

3.2 To address the first problem, a high priority has to be accorded to four laning the National Highway, which extends from Jalandhar to Jammu and further to Srinagar. High priority must also be accorded to undertaking repairs on the highway especially at Panthal arid Ramban where frequent landslides lead to closure of the highway for extended periods. The feasibility of constructing by-passes for these stretches can be examined. The National Highway is already a part of the North-South corridor and work on four-laning this needs to be accelerated. The other thrust area would be the early completion of the railway project of extending the railhead from Udhampur to Katra and from thereon to the Kashmir Valley for which the schedule is already laid down.

3.3 Regarding the second problem of road connectivity within J&K, the Working Group is of the view that rural roads should be the focus area for the state and all efforts must be made to leverage the funds available under the Bharat Nirman scheme of the centre. Some equalization of road density will come about through the Rural Road Connectivity Scheme of Bharat Nirman which aims at connecting every habitation with a population of 1000 in the plains and population of 500 in the hilly areas. There is need to revise these norms downwards for J&K keeping in view its terrain and the highly scattered population.

Rural Roads

3.4 At 13% the road density (road length per 100 sq kms) in J&K is amongst the lowest in the country. Moreover, there are huge inter-district variations in road density ranging from a high of 81.8% in Budgam to a low of 5% in Doda. Bringing places like Rajouri and Doda to state level average let alone the national-level average requires great effort and sizeable investment. Using the ballpark norm that it takes Rs. 2.43 crore per unit "index of road", the investment needed to equalize the road density across the state will be of the order of Rs. 1750 crores.

3.5 While estimating the requirement for investment, it is essential that the norms for unit cost of road for km length, as estimated for the rest of the country, be revised specifically taking into account the hilly terrain of J&K. Suitable modifications may also need to be made for difficult terrain within the state.

3.6 A major constraint in implementing road projects is land acquisition. Due to the hilly terrain, the land acquisition requirement is comparatively higher. Since land holdings are small and the rural populace is heavily dependent on subsistence farming, there is great resistance to parting with the land for road construction. The problem is further exacerbated by theiow price at which the land is acquired by the state authorities who fix the price based on the sale deeds in the area. There is a tendency to understate the value of the land to avoid the heavy stamp duty.

3.7 Owing to these constraints, and inadequate budgets, the state government is unable to make land available on time for central projects and the road construction programme suffers. A two-pronged strategy is required to resolve the problem. Firstly, the Government of India road construction schemes must include the cost of land acquisition as a part of the project. Secondly, the land acquisition law must be modified such that the owners get a fair value for their land. An important parameter in fixing the fair price would be the fact that whenever an area is opened up for road construction, the cost of adjoining lands increases manifold but the person who sacrifices the land for road construction seldom benefits from this beneficiation. Thus 'fair value' must be based on the prospective (post-project) value of land rather than past sale transactions. The recent decision of the state government to reduce stamp duty from 20% to 10% in rural areas and 14% to 7% in urban areas is a welcome step. This will encourage land transactions to disclose the correct transaction value on the sale deeds and hence aid the determination of a 'fair value'. However, the implementation of this reduction has been hampered by the non-completion of 'zoning' which must be expedited.

Telecom

3.8 Development of the telecom infrastructure holds out considerable promise for the development of J&K not only because of the economic benefits it will bring but also because it will deepen J&K's integration with the rest of the country thereby strengthening social and emotional ties.

3.9 With mobile services launched only in August 2003, J&K has been a late entrant into the telecom sector. Even so the state has caught up with the rest of the country—the teledensity of J&K as of June 2006 at 11.0 was only marginally short of the national average of 13.7. Disaggregated figures however show that telecom penetration has been uneven across the urban and rural segments with the latter performing substantially below the national average. Growth in Internet connections and quality of connectivity is poor. Similarly, Broadband services, a crucial infrastructure for a knowledge economy and for IT enabled services have been recently launched only in two major cities, i.e. Jammu and Srinagar. As against a total of 1.32 million connections in the country (March 2006), only 4612 connections are working in the state. There is need to actively promote Broadband since this has the potential to trigger the IT-BPO sector which is employment intensive.

3.10 The main constraint to telecom growth in J&K emanates from the supply side, namely high rollout costs, lack of adequate connectivity between the operators, security concerns, high entry cost burden and bureaucratic delays. To overcome these, first the subsidy policy of GoI for rural telephony must be revised for J&K in view of the difficult terrain and the security situation. Second, the high entry tax on telecom equipment should be reduced to incentivize investments in the state. Third, the state government must streamline the issue of clearances (like forest, municipal and local bodies) to minimize the transaction costs for the service providers. Finally, the Department of Telecom must sort out the issue of interconnect between operators to improve the quality of service and drive down costs.

TOURISM

Issues and Status

4.1 J&K was a mainstream tourist destination long before tourism in the modern form emerged as a growth industry. The state's scenic beauty, its temples and shrines and its rugged terrain offered broad-based attraction for tourists across the entire spectrum, and tourism had for long remained the backbone of J&K economy. This healthy growth got derailed in the wake of the insurgency of the 1990s. Over the last two years, tourism has begun to recover, but it is still a far way-off from becoming the preeminent engine of growth that it once was. This is an opportune time for J&K to aggressively reposition itself as a tourist destination riding on the back of the economic buoyancy around the world and at home in India. The state needs to market itself in three distinct niches—leisure tourism in the valley, religious tourism in Jammu and adventure tourism in Ladakh.

4.2 The Valley attracted 7 lakh tourists in 1988/89, averaging a growth rate of 10+%. This healthy progress was jolted by the insurgency in the 90s and tourism went on a decline. There were early signs of recovery in 2003 when tourist arrivals touched 1.9 lakhs. The recovery accelerated in the following two years with tourist arrivals of 3.8 lakhs in 2004 and 6.1 lakhs in 2005: Sporadic incidents of violence through 2006 have dampened the growth in 2006 with arrivals of 3.8 lakhs up to August 2006. Security is after all a pre-requisite for tourism to flourish.

4.3 If there were no insurgency, tourism would have maintained its growth track and it is estimated that annual tourist arrivals today would have been in the range of 15-18 lakhs. Tourism's share of the state's GSDP, which was 10% in 1988/89; would have gone up to 5%-20% if not higher.

4.4 As per available figures available, in the Valley there are 18,000 beds in hotels and houseboats but most of them require upgrading and proper maintenance. The valley needs another 6,000 beds by 2010 and 3,000 more thereafter up to 2015.

4.5 The present accommodation in Jammu and Katra is 15,000 beds, but the bulk of them are below required standard and inadequate to meet the need. In the next 10 years, 10,000 additional beds will be needed.

4.6 In Ladakh, 5,400 beds are available which are inadequate and there is an urgent requirement of 2,000 beds.

Creating Infrastructure

4.7 For upgradation of infrastructure including hotel rooms, the state has to find resources under the State Plan and also help the industry in getting appropriate loans from the banking sector. To accelerate renovations and new constructions of houseboats, hotels, and shikaras, a sum of Rs. 30 crore may be allocated for immediate disbursement as soft loans with an appropriate monitoring mechanism.

4.8 Even with finance in place, development of permanent infrastructure will take time. Development of paying guest accommodation should be explored as an interim measure. Across the world and now also in India, paying guest accommodation for domestic and international tourists at important tourist centers is helping to supplement the existing accommodation. The concept offers visiting tourists an opportunity to stay with a local family, experience the local way of life and to discover local culture and cuisine. A three-stage approach would be required to exploit this opportunity in the state. First, eligibility norms for categorizing an existing facility as 'paying guest' accommodation must be evolved. Though there are some norms established by the tourism ministry, these may need to be customized for J&K. Second, the process of registration of paying guest accommodation must commence. Third, soft loans must be extended to the house owners to enable them to refurbish the facilities as per the norms. This initiative will, apart from providing affordable accommodation, also involve the local people and generate employment opportunities.

Initiatives

4.9 To achieve the tourism targets, the state needs (a) Vision Document; and (b) a Master Plan based on research by a reputed organization. Support can be obtained from international agencies. This would be very necessary in view of environmental considerations.

4.10 Tourism is also related to better road connectivity which has to be addressed on a priority basis.

4.11 The facilities and check points at airports, railway stations and bus stands need to be tourist-friendly.

4.12 Effort will need to be made to attract entrepreneurs from the rest of the country with incentives like single window clearance and easy availability of land for projects in and around Srinagar and other places of tourist interest. Wherever possible, land should be made available on long-term lease. Should that not be possible, government should join as partner in the venture with land as its equity contribution while the private partner brings in the investment and management expertise.

4.13 The State needs to spend more on tourism promotion

and develop facilities for golf, convention centers and heli-skiing to attract tourists in high-income brackets.

4.14 Although J&K's natural beauty and religious shrines are large tourist draws, they need to be supplemented by facilities also for entertainment and recreation. It will be necessary to create facilities like shopping complexes, food courts, and multiplex music festivals and sports events. The issue of heritage tourism needs to be examined in a larger context especially in the Ladakh area which could prove attractive for tourists from South East Asia.

4.15 Many beautiful spots in the state with tourism potential are outside the tourist circuit because of lack of connectivity and infrastructure. It will be necessary to identify such places located in all three regions of the state—Jammu, Kashmir and Ladakh—and connect them with good roads and build hotels and lodges to attract tourists.

AGRICULTURE, IRRIGATION AND FOREST

Context

5.1 Agriculture, engaging 65% of the population, is an important contributor to the state economy. However, heavy dependence on cereals, small peasant holdings and subsistence farming have all created a sub-optimal cycle of low productivity and low investment, which is reflected by the low contribution of this sector (27%) to the GSDP.

5.2 The productivity of most crops is below the national average, and the state has a deficit in food crops, oilseeds and vegetables. Over 80% of the net sown area is under food crops and only 42% of the area is under irrigation.

Improving Productivity

5.3 The state has three main agro-climatic zones and various micro agro-climatic zones. There is an immediate need to evolve sub-regional strategies for investment and growth. Diversification of production and adoption of market-oriented products are natural corollaries of the sub-regional strategy.

5.4 In addition, improving availability of inputs like seeds, fertilizer, pesticides and most importantly micro-credit are other important initiatives which are important for raising agricultural production.

5.5 Another important strategy would be to actively encourage new avenues like floriculture, aromatic and medicinal plant cultivation, especially those with low volume and high values as these have the potential to enhance economic activity and increase incomes. Horticulture is particularly suitable for hilly areas which are anyway unsuitable for traditional agriculture.

Irrigation

5.6 Intensive agriculture will depend on availability of assured irrigation, which is a precondition for improvements in agricultural production and productivity. With less than half the cultivable area under irrigation, there is need to complete the ongoing irrigation projects expeditiously. The state should explore the options for claiming the full share of water from Thein Dam in the Ravi Canal Project.

5.7 Despite the restrictive nature of the Indus Water Treaty, it is possible to exploit tributaries of main rivers to increase the area under irrigation. The main rivers like Ujh, Tawi, Ante (Rajouri), Basantar and streams in Doda district can be tapped for local minor irrigation projects. This will enable herbal farming in the Shivalik region. Another initiative in the region of Shiwalik Hill (Udhampur and Kathua) would be to explore rainwater harvesting in tanks and ponds for both irrigation as also domestic use.

Animal Husbandry and Pasture Development

5.8 A large number of people in the state, especially Gujjars and Bakkerwals are dependent on cattle rearing and sheep breeding. However, the productivity in the sector is low and the state still depends on imports for animal products. Despite a high ratio of 900 animals per 1000 persons, only 4% of the gross cropped area is under fodder cultivation. Pasture development, especially in the hilly areas, and cultivation of high yield grasses are two immediate initiatives that would boost growth in the sector.

5.9 A significant concern of the pastoralists who depend on rearing of livestock, is the need for protection mechanism against loss of animals due to death. Currently, there is a Livestock Insurance Scheme under the 10th FYP which is being implemented on a pilot basis; in Jammu and Pulwama.[1] Under the scheme, Government gives a 50% subsidy on the insurance premium for crossbred and high yielding cattle and buffaloes. The scheme will be extended to the whole country and more species of livestock in the 11th FYP, depending on its performance during the pilot period (2005-06 and 2006-07). The state must urgency expedite the implementation of the Scheme and set-up district committees to review and suggest appropriate modifications to enable the scheme to be implemented in the whole state.

5.10 Since the closure of Himalayan Wool Combers, there are no facilities for processing of wool in the state. The producers are unable to get a fair price, hence an important initiative would be to encourage investments in production and local value addition by way of primary processing of wool especially for the high value 'pashmina'.

Forests and Environment

5.11 Forests are a lifeline of the state be it for tourism, hydropower generation or for refurbishing the ground water table. In addition, they contribute to creating a dust-free Switzerland-like climate in the state beyond Patnitop, which may be conducive for setting up 'footloose industries' like electronics which are employment intensive.

5.12 Up to the 1980s, the forests were a revenue-generating sector. This position changed subsequently due to heavy felling of trees, degradation of the forests and encroachment into forest area. Returns became non-commensurate with investment. To reverse the situation and to meet the demand for timber and minor forest produce like 'kattha' and charcoal, reforestation of the degraded forests, strengthening the forest demarcation division and using fallow land for fast growing trees are three important strategies. The last strategy was implemented in the form of the 'social forestry' project. Under this plan scheme a number of plantations and village wood lots were raised by using fast growing species having timber value. The project was successful

1. The scheme is being implemented on a pilot basis in 100 selected districts all over the country.

in the initial implementation and did succeed in greening fallow land. However, the panchayats and the local communities were unable to maintain the plantations once the project was handed over. The project has a lot of potential and can be revived on a pilot basis in some identified areas. However, community training and handholding for some period after completion of the project may yield better results.

HORTICULTURE

Issues and Status

6.1 Horticulture and food processing have tremendous potential of being growth engines. An estimated 25 lakh persons are connected directly or indirectly with the horticulture sector. Fruit production expanded from 0.93 million tons in 1999/2000 to 1.4 million tons by 2005/06. Productivity, however, remains low compared to international levels: for apples, the main horticulture commodity, productivity has been hovering at 10 tons/hectare compared to 26 tons in USA, Australia and New Zealand. The sector as a whole is locked in a sub-optimal cycle of low productivity and low investment.

6.2 The problems that horticulture sector faces are locational disadvantage, the poor condition of National Highway, the presence of many layers of intermediation in the distribution and virtual absence of post-harvest infrastructure.

Initiatives

6.3 About 30% of apple production in the state is low-grade fruit, which requires processing rather than direct sale. The capacity for the food processing has therefore to increase from the present 65,000 tons to 3 lakh tons in a short time. An immediate initiative would be a market development scheme for processing horticulture produce, which should cover apple pulp, jams, jellies, squashes, juices, etc. This should ideally be done in public-private partnership or through joint ventures with grower's participation.

6.4 Certain minor fruit products can be encouraged in wasteland areas, which are not otherwise suitable for high value fruit crops, commonly known as Kandi area in the Jammu Division.

6.5 For better pricing of fruit, it is necessary to have better sorting, grading and packaging, which automatically increases price advantage. Besides a plan for establishment of cold chain storage has to be quickly formulated and implemented.

6.6 It is necessary to train farmers to increase capacity in high value products like aromatic and medicinal plants, organic vegetables and better quality fruit, in addition to traditional horticultural produce.

INDUSTRIAL DEVELOPMENT AND COMMERCE

Special Industrial Zone

7.1 Creating employment opportunities is one of the biggest challenges for J&K. Although agriculture will need focus, bulk of the employment generation for the educated youth will have to emanate from the industrial sector.

7.2 What J&K needs is a big banner initiative—one that will raise the profile of the state among potential investors. The best option in this regard is an SEZ. However, the viability of an SEZ is doubtful given the state's land locked geography, infrastructure deficit and distance from the ports. Instead what J&K should attempt is a Special Industrial Zone (SIZ). The SIZ will mimic all the physical attributes and governance structures of SEZs but not necessarily their fiscal and statutory dimensions. Like SEZs, the SIZ top will be a large area with world class infrastructure, captive power generation and distribution, high quality services and utilities, dedicated infrastructure facilities, fast track and single window clearances, and to the extent possible liberalized labour laws, Units in an SIZ however will have neither tax concessions nor export obligations. They will be free to sell in the country or export. The main effort should be to provide a hassle free environment where entrepreneurs are free of all the disadvantages that cripple their productivity and efficiency and are enabled to compete at the global level from a level playing field.

7.3 The most compelling argument for an SIZ is that it is by far the most efficient way for J&K to spend its limited resources to attract investment. Ideally, the Government should improve infrastructure across board but given its fiscal pressures, that is hardly possible. On the other hand, spreading the available resources too thin is sub-optimal. What will be optimal will be for the Government to concentrate its resources in one focal area.

7.4 The SIZ is a model that other states too can adopt. But it is particularly appropriate! for J&K as the SIZ will make it possible to ring fence the zone in a physical sense to protect against security threats. The Working Group recommends Rs. 200 crore outlay by the Centre for this.

Special Concession Package

7.5 In order to encourage investment, in 2002 the Centre announced a special concession package for industries set-up in J&K. However, the impact of the package as measured by fresh investment has been limited as compared to a similar incentive package for investment in the neighbouring state of Uttaranchal. In a welcome measure, the 2007-08 budget extended the income tax and central excise exemptions for investments in J&K up to 2012. What this means is that there will be a window of time between 2010 and 2012 when central excise exemption would be available exclusively in J&K (not in the other two states).

7.6 The other concessions available for investments in J&K are the 3% interest subsidy on working capital, insurance cover on capital investment and the income tax exemptions of 100% for 10 years.[2] The state government must launch a vigorous promotion drive to disseminate information about the concession package, specially emphasizing the additional benefits. The other complementary measures that the state must initiate are review of the existing land policy, offering matching concessions for priority sectors by way of reduction in state taxes and development of industrial estates by leveraging the funds under the PM's Reconstruction Plan. Another priority would be review and reform in the procedure for various clearances which go a long way in reducing the transaction costs for the investors. Most importantly the state must actively woo large industrial houses, as even a couple of successes will have a large demonstration effect.

2. The income tax exemption for Himachal and Uttaranchal was 100% for the first five years and thereafter 30% for companies and 25% for other than companies for the next five years

Other Initiatives

7.7 J&K also needs a special package for revival of sick industrial units both in the public sector (e.g. ITI and HMT) and the private sector.

7.8 Inadequate access is a major constraint to industrial growth. J&K immediately needs an air cargo complex and a container depot which could possibly be located in Jammu.

7.9 Non-availability of credit is a major bottleneck for local entrepreneurs. The public sector banks and the J&K Bank Ltd. should be encouraged to take a lead in this regard.

Revitalizing Handicrafts

7.10 J&K, once famous for its handicrafts, has lost its niche in this segment owing to neglect and lack of an organized effort to keep up with the changing market dynamics. Revival of the handicrafts through an artisan development programme is potentially an important avenue for improving the livelihood of a sizable segment of the rural population. This requires interventions across the entire chain—skill upgradation, organization of production, finance and marketing.

7.11 The Confederation of Indian Industry (CII) had recently undertaken a project by forming Kiran, a self-help group with 45 women in the 18-25 age group. The project was supported through a tripartite agreement between CII, Dastkar and Sadbhavana Trust. An internal assessment by CII found that the project had lost its momentum in the second year itself primarily due to two factors—design and marketing. Other constraints identified were inadequate government initiatives, lack of facilities for skill upgradation (which affected both quality and consistency) and limited number of NGOs which could assist in capacity building and commercial development.

7.12 The CII experience suggests that the two key challenges to be addressed for moving forward are: (i) reestablishing the niche for J&K handicrafts in both domestic and external Markets; and (ii) improving the skill endowment. This calls for a two-stage approach.

7.13 The first stage effort which can yield quick wins is to find markets for what is already being produced. The focus is on market development by working with the Directorate of

Handicrafts; Export Promotion Council (the key player in the Moradabad brassware success story) and adequately stocking and refurbishing the J&K State emporia across the country.

7.14 The second stage approach with a medium-term focus will be to identify consumer demand in domestic and external markets so as to reorient supply to match this demand. This would ideally start with a market survey followed by creating an enabling infrastructure in the state to have international buying houses to visit the production facilities in the state. The key priorities from the supply side will be capacity building aimed at improving the skill endowment, raising productivity, and enhancing quality followed by finance and marketing support. This is an initiative ideally done in a PPP mode. The state government should identify a high profile corporate house which will invest in the soft and hard infrastructure with an eye on long-term sustainable profits.

Trade Across the Border

7.15 The peace initiative between Pakistan and India and the opening of bus routes across the LOC are welcome developments. If trading is permitted across the border, it will open up immense opportunities not only with PoK but also with Pakistan and other Central Asian countries. There is great potential for trade in handicrafts, horticulture products, shawls, garments, carpets and dry fruits. The other potentially profitable items of trade are export of construction material and medicines. It would be useful to identify items that can be imported from PoK and also explore scope for co-operation on subjects of common interest like environment protection, water management, natural disaster management and forestry. To convert this opportunity, a major initiative on construction and refurbishing of border roads will have to be undertaken. Some potential candidate routes are Jammu-Suchetgarh-Sialkot, Kargil-Skardu, Nowshera-Mirpur and Tangdhar across the Neelam valley.

Small Scale Industry

7.16 Despite internal problems, the SSI sector of J&K has witnessed rapid growth. The total of around 73,000 SSI units in the state, out of which 67% are located in rural areas, provide employment to a lakh and half people. The small scale industries cover traditional areas like carpet weaving, handlooms, handicrafts as also new areas like food processing, bulk drugs, metallic and non-metallic products, etc.

7.17 The Units are not evenly distributed across the state. They are largely concentrated in Jammu, Srinagar and Kathua followed by Baramullah, Anantnag and Pulwama. With only a few units, Ladakh lags way behind in SSI development.

7.18 The operations of the small scale sector have however been hampered by a host of factors such as poor infrastructure like power, roads and transport, shortage of industrial sheds and plots, lack of adequate credit, non-availability of skilled manpower and the law and order situation. The state government has attempted to correct the situation by refurbishing infrastructure and setting up industrial estates, a 'growth centre', and an export promotion industrial park. In addition, the state government offers a host of incentives to the SSI sector like exemption of GST on purchase of raw material and sale of finished goods, price preference in government procurement and toll tax exemption.

7.19 Reviving the SSI sector has a high development payoff because of its employment intensity and export potential. While the above incentives by the state government help, they are by no means adequate to revive the SSI sector. They need to be supplemented by at least one major initiative by the Centre.

7.20 One possible initiative is to help revive the industrial estates in the state. Many of them need immediate comprehensive maintenance and upgradation by way of repair of roads, drainage systems, creation of landfils for disposal of hazardous waste, water and power supply. The existing Industrial Infrastructure Scheme (IIUS) of Government of India provides for upgradation and rehabilitation of industrial estates at a total cost of up to Rs. 50 crore per estate provided the concerned SSI units within the estate and the state government make matching contribution to the extent of 15% and 10% respectively. In other words, GoI will provide up to Rs. 37.50 crore per estate provided the state government and the estate together contribute Rs. 12.50 crore. Currently, J&K is unable to take advantage of the scheme as neither the state government nor the SSI units are in a position to mobilize their required contributions. The Working Group recommends that the Center waive the requirement of counterpart contribution and help revive the industrial estates. This can be tried on a pilot basis for six estates well distributed across the state. The additional contribution from GoI will be Rs. 75 crore at the rate of Rs. 12.50 crore per estate.

7.21 Industrial sickness is rampant, and as per a recent report, as many as 22,000 SSI units have closed down. This sickness, in turn, has corrupted the balance sheets of the financial institutions (FIs). Providing a way out for the FIs to clean up their balance sheets is therefore a necessary precondition for revival of sick units. Most of the FIs in J&K were working well till 1989. The J&K State Financial Corporation (JKSFC) which was the lead financial institution for term lending to industry was earning cash profits till 1989. However, the viability of JKSFC was severely dented by the militancy in the valley. A large number of small-scale units closed down and consequently defaulted on their loan repayments which in turn eroded the financial viability of JKSFC. Between 1990 and 1997, the non-performing asset (NPA) portfolio of JKSFC increased by a whopping 645%. The track record of SIDCO, the State Industrial Development Corporation was similar. Its NPA accounts rose from 8 in 1990 to 68 in 1997 with the infected assets accounting for Rs. 198 crores. The only financial institution operating at full capacity presently is the J&K Bank. With the collapse of the public sector FIs, most of the financing for trade and some minimal production activity is coming from the informal sector which is both limited and costly.

7.22 As recommended by the Task Force on Development of J&K, revival of the financial sector of the state calls for the setting up of an Asset Reconstruction Company. The ARC will take over the infected assets of the state level FIs. This will clean up the balance sheets of the FIs, restore their viability and make them eligible for drawing refinance from central institutions. It is proposed that the initial corpus of the ARC can be Rs. 300 crores with a contribution of Rs. 200 crores from the Center and a contribution of Rs. 100 crores from the FIs in J&K.

HEALTH

Issues and Status

8.1 Human capital, as characterized by good education and good health, is an important determinant of economic growth. In

J&K, health care delivery is important not only for human resource development but also for restoring the faith of the people in the institutions of governance.

8.2 As compared to the national average, the aggregate health indicators like birth rate, death rate, infant mortality rate and maternal health indicators present a satisfactory picture but practically on every parameter, J&K lags behind the best performing state in the country. The main reason for this is that the public health care delivery system of the state has atrophied over the years of militancy forcing people to buy health care from the private sector. There is an immediate need for revitalizing health delivery particularly targeted at poorer segments of the population who cannot afford private health care.

8.3 The health infrastructure in J&K at all levels (primary, secondary and tertiary) suffers from shortages that are both qualitative and quantitative in nature which is made worse by the acute manpower shortage of paramedics, doctors and specialists. The non-availability is more acute in rural areas.

On-going Initiatives

8.4 The on-going initiatives in the state include the Prime Minister's Reconstruction Plan which has schemes for setting up of Anganwadi centers, increased outlay under National Rural Health Mission, construction of Rural Health Centre buildings and two prestigious projects of upgrading the Jammu Medical College and Srinagar Medical College with allocations of Rs. 120 crore each.

Way Forward

8.5 The NRHM with its focus on quality health care and community-based approach needs to be implemented to ensure achievement of clearly defined and measurable targets. The Scheme should be monitored for completion in time.

8.6 It would be necessary to take up, as a short-term measure, setting up of mobile clinics, which should have Doctors and paramedics and other facilities like X-ray, ECG and Ultra Sound. These could have specific route and schedule that is pre-determined to ensure availability of services to uncovered population. It would be desirable to have one such unit for each block, i.e. 107 such units for the state as a whole. These units would not only improve access and coverage but also optimize utilization of healthcare services. At an estimated capital cost of Rs. 30 lakhs per unit, each consisting of one vehicle for the staff and one for the equipment, the total capital cost for 100 units will be Rs. 30 crore. The operating cost will be Rs. 23 lakhs per unit or a total of Rs. 23 crores for 100 units[3].

8.7 We recommend an allocation of Rs. 30 crore for this scheme to cover the capital cost phased over three years. The release should be linked to progress under NRHM as measured by predetermined and agreed criteria and should also be subject to the state government making the corresponding allocation in the budget for the recurring costs.

8.8 In addition to the above it is extremely important to set-up advanced mobile units with emergency care facilities for dealing with injuries from IED blasts, grenade explosions and other such militancy-related emergencies. These mobile units must be stationed at strategic locations and be capable of rushing to site of militant attack on an emergence drill protocol similar to that of fire tenders. These units will not only provide physical relief to the victims but also enable the State to score a psychological win over the militants.

8.9 Other important initiatives in improving healthcare would be encouraging PPP for setting up (secondary and tertiary healthcare facilities, establishing a telemedicine network and health insurance for covering medical expenses for BPL families.

EDUCATION AND EMPLOYMENT CONTEXT

9.1 Low level of employment opportunities is a dominant and vocal concern in J&K. The long years of militancy have eroded the industrial base completely. Most PSUs are closed down and private investment shied away due to the disturbed law and order conditions. In addition, there is no reliable data on employment which makes it difficult to design appropriate interventions.

9.2 The most effective way of generating sustainable employment is through accelerating economic growth, which has been the dominant concern of this Working Group. While heightened economic activity creates the demand for jobs, state intervention

3. Figures taken from the NRHM document.

will be required to improve the employability of the job-seekers so as to match the emerging demand with appropriate supply.

Training

9.3 To improve employability both in the public and private sectors, training and skill upgradation are essential. The existing institutions lack essential infrastructure including the most crucial one—qualified teachers. While it is important to build new institutes, it is equally important to upgrade the existing vocational and technical training institutions and make them fully functional by providing them with building, equipment and trained faculty. In this regard, the expeditious establishment of the 13 ITIs which have been in the pipeline forlong is important.

9.4 The BPO revolution in the country has leveraged the IT skills of young people. However, the youth of Jammu and Kashmir have been unable to share this uptrend due to lack of adequate IT training facilities in the state. This vital gap needs to be bridged at the earliest through active intervention by the state to make it attractive for institutes like NUT, WIPRO and others to open training centers in the state.

Adult Literacy Volunteers

9.5 Adult Literacy is an important instrument in economic development as also for curbing militancy. It not only improves the livelihood of the poor but also gives them a stake in societal progress. One way of delivering the programme is through literacy volunteers' drawn from the ranks of the educated unemployed in the state.

9.6 At the rate one for 30 adults, the requirement will be for 85000 literacy volunteers. At a consolidated stipend of Rs. 2000 per month, the total bill will be of the order of Rs. 17 crores per month or Rs. 200 crores per year. If necessary the programme could be started on a pilot basis in 2-3 districts and rolled out in phases after building in the lessons of experience.

9.7 The programme can be linked to skill upgradation in five sectors, which are employment intensive—tourism, horticulture/floriculture, handicrafts, food processing and environment. The programme structured this way will deliver several benefits. It will improve adult literacy, it will improve the income earning capacity of the poor, and it will mitigate the problem of educated unemployment.

9.8 The Employment of these literacy volunteers' will be limited to two years whereafter the programme will be gradually wound down. By then other employment avenues should open up to provide alternate avenues to the disbanded volunteers. This literacy volunteer programme will go a long way to meet the foremost concern of the state—that of providing employment avenues to the educated unemployed.

Agricultural Extension Workers

9.9 Agricultural extension effort in J&K has suffered over the last 20 years in part because of the pressures of militancy and in part for want of adequate staff. This is a vital gap that needs to be filled on a priority basis. One cost effective way of doing this is to appoint an agricultural graduate in each of the 2700 panchayats in the state. Their main responsibility will be to set-up an agri-clinic in the respective panchayat for disseminating improved agricultural technologies and practices. They would also be responsible for supplying seeds, fertilizers and pesticides. We recommend an allocation of Rs. 250 crores for this phased over three years.

REGIONAL DEVELOPMENT

Context

10.1 Like every other state in the country, J&K too suffers from regional imbalances. The root cause of such imbalances is the inequitable distribution of natural resources and economic opportunities, and they tend to get aggravated over time unless corrective action is taken to redress them. Regional imbalances are not unique to India; they exist in all large countries and have been the source of a lot of political strife and discontent. Redressing regional imbalances has all along been a central aim of our development effort, but the success has not been uniform nor the results always sustained. Demonstrable striving to redress regional imbalances is particularly important in a state like J&K not only for the economic benefits it offers but also for the positive externalities it will have by way of restoring law and order and inspiring the trust and confidence of people.

10.2 During its meetings, the Working Group noted that

there is a widespread feeling amongst the three regions—Kashmir, Jammu and Ladakh, that the fruits of economic development have not been shared equally. (This feeling is more pronounced in the case of the latter two). At the sub-regional level, there are numerous backward areas. Some of them which found mention during deliberations were Chenab valley, parts of Doda district, Rajouri, Poonch and certain areas of Udhampur and Kathua districts like Gulabgarh and Basholi in Jammu, districts of Kupwara, Tangdhar and Gurez in Kashmir and practically the whole of Ladakh.

10.3 For balanced regional development, it is important that the development initiatives identified in this report are implemented effectively and quickly. Beyond that it is also necessary to put in place institutional arrangements that give a sense of involvement and participation to the people in the development process.

Institutional Arrangements

10.4 An important initiative in establishing institutional arrangements is the passing of the J&K State Finance Commission Act which mandates and authorizes the Government to establish a State Finance Commission. The terms of reference of the proposed SFC are far more extensive than those of other state SFCs and give special emphasis to identifying backward districts and assessing the extent of backwardness and suggesting remedial measures. The analysis and recommendations of the SFC should provide a platform not only for financial devolution to the municipalities and panchayats but also for administrative and functional decentralization. The participatory and inclusive processes inherent therein will give a fillip to balanced regional development.

10.5 The District Development Boards (DDBs), functioning in the state since 1978, are an important arrangement and already have people's representatives taking stock of development requirements and the progress achieved by various programmes in the district. To make the DDBs more inclusive, it may be useful to include elected representatives from Panchayati Raj Institutions and local bodies in the DDB's. In areas where Panchayats are not functional, prominent persons from the local communities may be taken on board the DDB. In the case of backward communities like Gujjars, Bakkerwals and Gaddis, wherever their population is sizeable, prominent persons from their community must be inducted as members of the respective DDB.

10.6 To improve community participation in development, local bodies like Panchayats, City Corporations and Municipalities should be strengthened. A number of functions like minor roads, lanes, drainage, local level water supply schemes, primary education and rural health care should be carried out through the local bodies. These local bodies can also be centers of economic activity promotion.

10.7 Panchayati Raj institutions in J&K are being revived after two decades. Much of the institutional and physical infrastructure has crumbled or been destroyed. It is difficult to revive panchayats without providing some basic infrastructure and facilities. We recommend a grant of Rs. 100,000 for each panchayat to build basic facilities and provide some minimal administrative infrastructure. The total cost for the 2700 panchayats of the state will work out to Rs. 27 crores.

10.8 Presently, state plan allocations are divided into state and district components in the ratio of 60:40. There was a suggestion in the Working Group that districts should be provided larger funding and that this ratio should be revised to 50:50. The state plan provides for relatively large infrastructure projects whose benefits typically extend beyond the borders of a single district, oftentimes encompassing the entire state. A District Plan, on the other hand, provides for schemes with localized benefits. There is an obvious trade-off here. The state government may consider this suggestion of the Working Group along with all its implications.

Backward Communities

10.9 There was a unanimous view in the Working Group that the development process bypasses some communities and groups despite a lot of pronouncements and indeed good intentions for Improving their lot. They remain trapped in backwardness because of locational disadvantage, traditional occupation patterns or sheer lack of opportunities. Particularly mentioned in this regard were the Gujjars, Bakkerwals[4], Gaddis, Panaris and people

4. Chairman visited a colony of Doodhi Gujjars and noted their lack of access to basic amenities.

living in hilly areas and Kandi belts. There was a view that the mandate to improve the lot of these extremely backward groups gets diluted as it gets clubbed; with development of backward classes and tribes. A dominant suggestion was that there must be a separate Directorate for development of Gujjars and Bakkerwals with separate funding and that this Directorate must be housed in the Planning Department. The Government may examine this suggestion.

OTHER ISSUES AND RECOMMENDATIONS

11.1 The recommendations made in the previous sections address the core sectors that have a multiplier effect on the economy. In addition, the following stand alone recommendations made by members of the Working Group warrant urgent consideration—

(a) Army and paramilitary forces have reportedly occupied land, orchards, houses and other buildings like schools and public health facilities in militancy infested areas. This has deprived the owners of a source of income, and in some cases of a source of livelihood. It is important to restore the properties to the owners by providing alternate accommodation for the security forces. If that is not possible, at least payment of rent on a regular basis must be ensured.

(b) Internal roads in areas of tourist importance like Patni Top, Katra, Sonmarg, Yusmarg, etc. must be given attention. Needing high priority are the roads in the upper reaches, including the ones with the Border Roads Organization. The four laning of the national highway must be extended up to Baramullah. This will be important if the trade route from Baramullah-Uri-Muzzafarabad is opened.

(c) The 'Mughal Road', a proposed alternative to the national highway, which will go from Jammu to Rajouri, Poonch and to Kashmir Valley should be completed as quickly as possible.

(d) The state has a number of local lakes and ponds, which could be developed by Panchayats for Fisheries

Development. They would also add to better environment protection and ground water recharge.

(e) An alternate route for the Kailash Mansarovar Pilgrimage through Ladakh should be explored. Because of the large multiplier effect of tourism, this will give a fillip to economic development of Ladakh.

(f) There are about 70,000 families of 1947 refugees from west Pakistan who do not enjoy the status of permanent residents of the state. This issue needs resolution. It is understood that this is being examined by two other Working Groups.

(g) A special package for better drinking water facilities in Kandi areas should be prepared.

(h) Over the last several years, the cities of Srinagar and Jammu have become highly congested. A decongestion plan aimed at shifting businesses and offices that do not have public dealing on a regular basis must be designed and implemented.

(i) The state has a very large area under forests and cold desert in Ladakh. An extensive survey of mineral resources can be made for exploitation of the economic mineral belt.

(j) Many aspirants from the state are unable to join the police and paramilitary forces because they do not meet the eligibility criteria by way of education. However, giving access to local people in security enforcement can have a demonstrably benign effect on the security situation. The Center must examine a way of providing recruitment access to these people by relaxing the eligibility norms.

IMPLEMENTATION AND MONITORING

12.1 The Working Group urges the Government to set-up a Monitoring Committee to oversee the translation of its recommendations into concreter schemes, their approval with appropriate financing and the effective utilization of funds. The Monitoring Committee will report periodically to the Chief Minister.

APPENDIX I—1

Working Group Recommendations—Summary

1. Power Sector

- Transfer of 390 MW Dulhasti Hydel Power Project from NHPC to J&K (para 2.4)
- Projects to be undertaken on priority—Sawalkot (600 MW), Kiru (430 MW), Kawar (320 MW), Ralte (560 MW) and Shamnot (370 MW) (para 2.4)
- Transfer of 1020 MW Bursar Storage Scheme from NHPC to J&K for execution in the state sector (para 2.5)
- Slightly enhance J&K share of free power in central hydel projects (para 2.5)
- Simplification of procedures for various clearances, like forest and pollution control (para 2.6)
- Acquire stake in thermal projects and exploit geothermal potential in the state (para 2.7 and 2.8)
- Exploit micro, mini and small hydro potential (para 2.9)
- The States Electricity Regulatory Commission to be made fully functional (para 2.10)
- Establish a Transmission Utility for reduction of T&D losses and efficient management of power supply (para 2.10)
- Establish distribution regions/circles (para 2.10)
- Improve Accelerated Power Development and Reform Programme fund utilization (para 2.11)
- Rationalization of tariff, time bound loss reduction and close monitoring for stoppage of power misutilization and theft (para 2.12)

2. Communication, Rural Roads and Telecom

- High priority to be accorded to four laning and repairing the National Highway (para 3.2)
- Early completion of the railway project of extending the railhead from Udhampur to Katra and thereon to Kashmir Valley (para 3.2)
- Improve rural connectivity and redress the imbalance in rural road density across districts of the state (para 3.4)

- Norms for unit cost of road for km length, as estimated for the rest of the country, be revised and specifically take into account the hilly terrain of J&K (para 3.5)
- Government of India road construction schemes to include the cost of land acquisition as a part of the project (para 3.7)
- Land acquisition law to be modified such that the owners get a fair value for their land (para 3.7)
- Implement the reduction in stamp duty to encourage the sellers and buyers to indicate the correct transaction value (para 3.7)
- Revise subsidy policy of the Government of India for rural telephony (para 3.11)
- Reduce entry tax on telecom equipment (para 3.11)
- DoT to sort out the interconnection impasse (para 3.11)

3. Tourism Sector

- Renovations and new constructions of house boats, hotels, and shikaras (para 4.7)
- Develop 'paying guest' accommodation (para 4.8)
- Prepare a tourism vision document and a master plan based on sustainable tourism (para 4.9)
- Improve road connectivity (para 4.10)
- Tourist friendly facilities and check points at airports, railway stations and bus stands (para 4.11)
- Attract entrepreneurs with easy availability of land and single window clearance (para 4.12)
- Need to increase expenditure on promotions (para 4.13)
- Exploit state's rich cultural heritage and develop modern allurements like shopping, food courts, multiplexes, music festivals and sports events (para 4.14)
- Harness heritage tourism (para 4.14)

4. Agriculture, Irrigation and Forest

- Evolve sub-regional strategies for investment and growth (para 5.3)
- Diversify production and adopt market-oriented products (para 5.3)
- Improve availability of inputs like seeds, fertilizer, pesticides and micro-credit (para 5.4)

- Encourage new avenues like floriculture, aromatic and medicinal plant cultivation (para 5.5)
- Complete the ongoing irrigation projects expeditiously (para 5.6)
- Explore the options for claiming the full share of water from Thein Dam in the Ravi Canal Project (para 5.6)
- Tap the main rivers for minor irrigation projects (para 5.7)
- Pasture development, especially in the hilly areas and cultivation of high yield grasses (para 5.8)
- Expedite implementation of Livestock Insurance Scheme (para 5.9)
- Set-up a processing center for wool (para 5.10)
- Need for reforestation of the degraded forests and using fallow land for fast growing trees (para 5.12)

5. Horticulture

- Market development scheme for fruit and fruit processing (para 6.3)
- Encourage minor fruit products in wasteland areas (para 6.4)
- Better sorting and grading, packaging and cold chain storage facilities to improve price realization (para 6.5)
- Train farmers to increase capacity in high value products (para 6.6)

6. Industrial Development and Commerce

- Create a Special Investment Zone with world class infrastructure, captive power generation and distribution, high quality services and utilities, dedicated infrastructure facilities, fast track and single window clearances, and liberalized labour laws (para 7.2)
- Leverage the special concession package announced by the Centre, to attract investments within the state (para 7.6)
- Special package for revival of sick industrial units both in the public sector and the private sector (para 7.7)
- An air cargo complex and a container depot which could possibly be located in Jammu (para 7.8)
- Revitalize handicraft sector through targeted investment and skill upgradation of artisans (para 7.12)
- Explore the potential for trade across the border and scope for

co-operation on subjects of common interest (para 7.15)
- Upgradation and rehabilitation of industrial estates (para 7.20)
- Setting up an Asset Reconstruction Company (para 7.22)

7. Health Sector

- Get implementation of National Rural Health Mission started without further delay by completing all preparatory work (para 8.5)
- Set-up Mobile Diagnostic and Primary Clinics at block level (para 8.6)
- Set-up advanced mobile units with emergency care facilities for dealing with injuries from IED blasts, grenade explosions and other such militancy-related emergencies (para 8.8)
- Create a telemedicine network (para 8.9)
- Design and implement an appropriate health insurance scheme for BPL families (para 8.9)

8. Employment and Education

- Upgrade the existing vocational and technical training institutions and make them fully functional by providing them with building, equipment and trained faculty (para 9.3)
- Expeditious establishment of 13 ITI's (para 9.3)
- Create an incentive structure for encouraging private sector to open IT training institutes in the state (para 9.4)
- Deliver the adult literacy programme through 'literacy volunteers' drawn from the ranks of the educated unemployed in the state (para 9.5)
- Appoint agricultural graduates in the 2700 Panchayats in the state for agricultural extension effort (para 9.9)

9. Regional Development

- The participative and inclusive process inherent in the State Finance Commission to give fillip to balanced regional development (para 10.4)
- Male the District Development Boards more inclusive by including elected representatives and prominent people from backward communities (para 10.5)
- Functions like minor roads, lanes, drainage, local level water supply schemes, primary education, rural health care to be

carried out through the local bodies (para 10.6)
- Involve public representatives in the process of allocations under the state plan (para 10.8)
- Examine the establishment of a separate Directorate for Gujjars and Bakkerwals (para 10.9)

10. Other Issues and Recommendations (para 11.1)

- Properties occupied by army and paramilitary forces to be restored to owners or compensation paid
- Internal roads in areas of tourist importance like Patni Top, Katra, Sonmarg, Yusmarg, etc. be given attention and work on Mughal road be expedited
- Panchayats to develop local lakes and ponds, for Fisheries Development
- Explore an alternate route through Ladakh for the Kailash Mansarovar Pilgrimage
- Special package for better drinking water facilities in Kandi areas
- In view of the congestion in Srinagar and Jammu explore possibility of relocation of business activity at other places
- Survey of mineral resources to be undertaken
- Relax eligibility norms for police and paramilitary forces for aspirants from the state.

11. Implementation and Monitoring

- Set-up a small monitoring authority for implementation of these recommendations and translating the same into financial terms (para 12.1)

APPENDIX I—2

Financial Package Implicit in Working Group Recommendations

(Rupees crore)

1.	Transfer of Dulhasti Hydel Power Project (para 2.4)	4933 *
2.	Rural Roads Improvement (para 3.4)	1750
3.	Renovation and new construction of houseboats, hotels and shikara's (para 4.7)	30
4.	Market Development Scheme (Fruit and fruit processing) (para 6.3)	50
5.	Industrial Development	
	(i) Development of SIZ (para 7.4)	200
	(ii) Revival of Industrial Estates (para 7.20)	75
	(iii) Asset Reconstruction Company (para 7.22)	200
6.	Health	
	(i) Mobile Clinics (para 8.6)	30
	(ii) Telemedicine (para 8.9)	2
7.	Adult Literacy and creating Urban Employment (para 9.6) @ Rs. 200 p.a	400
8.	Agricultural extension workers (para 9.9)	250
9.	Strengthening of Panchayati Raj Institutions by making 2700 Panchayat offices functional (para 10.7)	27
	Total	7947

* The net present value (at 7% discount rate) of GoI's liability is Rs. 4933 crore and would involve a cash outflow of Rs. 984 crores in the first year tapering off to Rs. 321 crores in the 10th year).

APPENDIX I—3

Meetings of the Working Group

1st Meeting	Srinagar	29 August 2006
2nd Meeting	Jammu	1 December 2006
3rd Meeting	Jammu	23 February 2007

WORKING GROUP ON ENSURING GOOD GOVERNANCE IN JAMMU AND KASHMIR

Final Report
March 2007

REPORT OF THE WORKING GROUP ON GOOD GOVERNANCE

Table of Contents

List of Tables and Diagrams

List of Boxes

The Working Group

1. Shri N.C. Saxena	Chairman	
2. Shri Ajay Sadhotra	MLA, (Ex-Minister, J&K) National Conference	Member
3. Sardar Rangil Singh	Ex-Minister, J&K People's Democratic Party	Member
4. Pandit Mangat Ram Sharma	Minister for Health & Labour, J&K Congress (INC)	Member
5. Prof. Hari Om	State Vice-President, BJP, J&K	Member
6. Shri Abdul Gani Hafiz	Member, State Committee, CPI (M)	Member
7. Prof. K.S. Jamwal	Panthers Party	Member
8. Shri P. Namgyal	MLC, (Ex-Minister, GoI)	Member
9. Shri Amar Nath Vaishnavi	Kashmiri Pandit Samiti	Member
10. Mohd. Shafi Pandit	Chairman State Public Service Commission	Member
11. Shri Nizam-ud-Din	MLC, J&K	Member
12. Shri Bashir Ahmad Dar	Ex-Secretary, Board of School Education	Member

The Working Group was constituted in implementation of the decision concerning the establishment of five working groups announced by the Prime Minister of India at the Round Table Conference held at Srinagar on 24th and 25th May, 2006.

The Group had the following Agenda before it:

To consider effective measures to:

1. Increase responsiveness, accountability and transparency of the administration
2. Strengthen local self-government

3. Effectively monitor development programmes
4. Institute zero-tolerance for human rights violations
5. Strengthen the Right to Information
6. Provide adequate security to all segments of society, particularly the minority communities

Meetings

I	8. 8.2006	Srinagar	Sher-i-Kashmir International Convention Complex
II	20.11.2006	Jammu	State Guest House, Canal Road
III	10.02.2007	Jammu	State Guest House, Canal Road

Summary of the Recommendations

Issue No. 1—To consider effective measures to increase responsiveness, accountability and transparency of the administration

Recommendation No. 1

Appointment of **Chief Information Commissioner** of the State, the Appellate Authorities and the Departmental Information Officers for effective implementation of the Right to Information.

Encouraging people to make use of the Right to Information Act by creating awareness. For this purpose, an awareness campaign should be launched through print and electronic media for which budget provision should also be made.

Recommendation No. 2

Introduction of **e-governance** in the State may be attempted in the following areas:

(a) Building up the capacity of the Information Technology Department by instituting a Directorate and field organisations.
(b) Land records may be computerized and placed on a web site to enable landholders to got the information without the need to approach Government officials.
(c) Sub-Registrar's offices should be computerized and brought under the control of the Revenue Department

and merging it ultimately with the Tehsil office.

(d) Treasury operations should also be fully computerized.

(e) Computerization of service delivery procedures should be undertaken for issue of certificates. Electoral rolls in Urdu for all 87 Assembly constituencies have been computerized by the NIC, J&K. This data-base could be used for speedy disbursal of certificates.

(f) Setting up of Information Kiosks at key service delivery institution such as Revenue offices, Registration offices and Police Stations will facilitate giving basic information on procedures to be followed for availing services in the respective Departments.

(g) Mass training in the use of computers should be given to the Government functionaries who would actually be operating the system. Thereafter, they should not be frequently transferred.

(h) The Government may introduce IT enabled single window payment systems for utilities like water, electricity rents and telephones etc.

(i) The process of developing web sites for each of the Government departments should be speeded up and an on-line grievance redressal mechanism should be incorporated to make administration more visible.

(j) An attempt towards introducing e-governance in Police procedures for filing FIRs and for getting police verification done for passport, etc. can be considered to be made.

Recommendation No. 3

Simplification of Rules and Procedures

Review of laws should be attempted in Departments, which have a large public interface (such as revenue laws) so that procedures can be simplified. For example, the Land acquisition and some other laws could be simplified on the following lines:

(a) The present Land Acquisition Act is unfair to the people, as it does not give a fair value and hence creates resistance to the acquisition for public purposes among the owners. The following amendments to the J&K Land Acquisition Act need to be brought into force at the earliest:

I. Consent award could be the primary mode of settling the amount of compensation, which should not be less than the value calculated on the basis of the principle enunciated in the main text.

II. Whenever land acquired for a public purpose is transferred to an individual or a company for a consideration, 25 per cent of the difference between such consideration and the compensation will be given to the original land owners.

III. The rate of solatium should be increased from the present 15% of the market value to 30% as is prevalent in the rest of the country.

IV. A time limit of maximum of 18 months to be fixed for the completion of the acquisition proceedings from the date of notification of the Act under Section 4 of the Act. Presently there is no such time limit except 2 year's time limit from the date of publication of declaration under Section 6 of the Act.

V. Whenever the quantum of land being procured exceeds a certain limit/percentage of land of the owner/tiller then there should be adequate measures for proper rehabilitation of the persons affected by the project by way of employment, skill-upgradation, sharing stakes in the benefits of the project, e.g. the person whose land is being acquired for irrigation purposes should be provided an alternative piece of land in the command area of the irrigation project.

VI. Presently there is no fee charged by the Government for the conversion of agriculture land for non-agriculture purposes as is done in the rest of the country. Conversion of agriculture land puts premium on the society as the Government will be obliged to ensure food security despite reduction in the area under cultivation and thus cost will ultimately fall on the society through taxation. It is, therefore, desirable that reasonable amount of conversion fee should be levied for conversion of agriculture land to non-agriculture purposes. The levy should be more for the land put to commercial or industrial use.

VII. The Ministry of Rural Development, GoI is likely to come up with a revised draft of the Land Acquisition Act, as well as a Rehabilitation Policy. J&K government should study the draft and model its policy on the GOI pattern.

VIII. It should be compulsory to put digitized photographs of the buyers and the sellers on the Sale/ Purchase Deeds relating to immovable property. This practice is being followed now in Haryana and Delhi.

IX. Instead of acquiring land sometimes it may be more convenient, for both the farmers and government, to take land on a long-term lease by the government from the owners by paying two times the gross value of current annual production.

(b) A Committee should be set-up to identify specific laws and rules that hamper entrepreneurship. A systematic review needs to be undertaken for areas from where Government must withdraw, in a phased manner, its role and also define the Departments, which do not now serve any public purpose, which need to be wound up. A study in respect of Public Sector Undertakings would also be necessary.

(c) Formats for various certificates must be standardized and simplified. The already existing data for BPL census, electoral rolls may be used for computerization of the data.

(d) **Pe-regulation** has made almost no impact at the state level. The systems of buying and selling land, getting a ration card of security back, and Rent Control Acts, all need a thorough revision. One can set-up an industry worth billions of Rupees in India without any license today, but a farmer can neither set-up a brick kiln unit, nor a rice shelling plant, and not even cut a tree standing on his own private field without bribing several officials. It is a sad commentary on our laws that the informal sector, which provides maximum employment, is mostly declared as illegal and subject to the whims of law enforcing agencies. A Committee should be set-up to identify specific laws and rules, which hamper entrepreneurship.

(e) **File movement**—More emphasis need to be placed on a system like that of the 'Desk Officer' where the operating level concerned is responsible for the maintenance of record. This would lead to an increase in result-orientation, the possibility of flatter organisations and a reduction in dependence on lower levels. Up to Special Secretaries to the State Government, officers should be encouraged to keep the most important files in their personal cupboard, so as to expedite the process of decision-making, increase transparency, and reduce the chances of corruption by the lower functionaries. A single filing system should be followed in dealing with proposals from Head of the Department. This will also encourage transparency within government.

Recommendation No. 4

Departments such as the Police and Revenue, which have more public dealing, should be assessed in terms of their policies and performance once in three years by an independent Committee consisting of professionals, stakeholders in the relevant fields and prominent citizens.

Recommendation No. 5

(a) A new Transfer Policy should be formulated stressing that the officials are in place for at least three years and the Policy is adhered to strictly. The Transfer policy should have the following objectives:
- The need to curb the overall incidence of premature/untimely transfers.
- Eliminate transfer industry and transfers resulting from political interference.

- The policy should be seen as fair, objective, and leading to career development.
- The aptitude and experience of officers should be kept in view while giving a posting.
- Non-cadre persons should not be allowed to occupy cadre posts beyond a fixed time of six months or one year.

(b) In the recruitment by the Public Service Commission the amount of discretion can be brought down, for example, by reducing the weightage given to the interview for recruitment of teachers. The prescribed qualifications for various posts should be reviewed from time to time keeping with the rising trend of specialization and higher qualifications.

(c) (i) For the sake of fixing responsibility and accountability, it should be mentioned in each Government order the level at which the decision has been taken. The reason for disallowing a petition should be fully mentioned and the reasons for delay in disposal of the petitions should be fully explained. There may be a system of clear Job Descriptions in every department for every post to increase accountability levels.

(ii) To eliminate fake orders, every Government order must be signed by two officers of the Department.

(d) All promotions shall be merit based, seniority alone should not be the criteria. There should be an effective system of writing APRs (Confidential Reports), which should be regularly maintained and not written up only at the time of promotion.

Recommendation No. 6

(a) Every Department should prepare and publish a Citizens' Charter in a time-bound manner. Periodic review of the Departments adherence to the Citizens Charters may be undertaken by the GAD, but preferably through independent agencies. The guidelines for formulating Citizens Charters may be prepared by GAD and disseminated. An ideal charter should have the following components:

1. Clear responsibility—who will provide the service?
2. What does the citizen need to do—application, fee, information, etc.
3. What is the time frame in which the service shall be delivered.
4. What is the compensation for delay.
5. What is the redressal mechanism.

(b) A system of **public hearings** both at the district level as well as State level would be useful in strengthening accountability, increasing government visibility and ensuring people's participation.

(c) **Self-Assessment:** At the end of the Financial year, the concerned Ministers may present a complete Report Card or self-assessment giving various details, which could, *inter-alia,* include the performance of the Department including expenditure incurred, the outcomes obtained, details of performance; including underachievement, austerity measure or resource savings and the innovations introduced.

(d) **Surveys:** Government departments should also mount surveys of the perceptions and experiences of the ordinary people and civil society in sectors which have a public interface. These surveys will both measure public perception and experience of the integrity of staff interacting with the public and overall performance in the delivery of services.

(e) **Institutional strengthening:** As a part of the capacity building, periodic training programmes may be made mandatory for all Government officials on subjects such as service delivery improvement, leadership, change management and performance management. Before this, the basic infrastructure crucial to service delivery must be in place. Redeployment and right sizing of staff would assist in good governance.

(f) **People's participation:** The basic building block of good governance is the people's participation. The

Government could go in for using governance-reform tools like building public-private partnerships, social audit and citizens' score card. Government could identify and select a few dedicated NGOs based on pre-determined criteria to partner in strengthening public service delivery.

(g) **Performance Management:** Each Department, in consultation with various stakeholders, should set 3 to 5 outcomes that it would like to achieve in the next 2 to 3 years and work towards achieving those. In this process each Department should prepare a Status Paper of services it offers to citizens, plan for improving services and then set the outcomes to achieve.

(h) **Fiscal Management:** Fiscal reform is a critical component of good governance. The State of J&K has its specific problems of budget cycles and utilization of finances. There should be some mechanism to monitor whether the current year's expenditure is more or less over the past few years. The budget cycle is too short for full utilization of funds for capital works. Expenditure budget should be valid for two years, so that capital expenditure can be completed without surrender of funds. The practice of releasing large amounts of funds at the end of financial year, resulting in many irregularities in booking the expenditure, should be done away with. A "Roll-over" facility may be followed with the unspent of one year being carried over to the next without having to go through the elaborate annual plan and budgeting process, thereby preventing waste of time that is spent on replanning during the first few months of the following year.

Issue No. 2.—To consider effective measures to strengthen local self-government

Recommendation No. 7

The Panchayati Raj Act needs to be implemented in letter and spirit and for this purpose the Panchayats and the Block Panchayat Boards, etc. should be given appropriate devolution of the State revenue, as per the advice of the State Finance Commission. Some of the assets of the Government and local institutions like primary and middle schools, water supply schemes should also be transferred to the local Panchayats for management on sustainable basis.

The Godbole Committee Report had suggested that J&K should consider extending the provisions of the 73rd Amendment of the Indian Constitution, this should be examined. For reviving the institutions of local Self-Government, some of the suggestions could be as follows:

- A comprehensive capacity assessment exercise followed by a capacity building.
- Effective transfer of funds, functions and functionaries to the Panchayats would have to be taken up on priority.
- Activity Mapping exercise being followed in other States and rationalization of schemes to be implemented by PRIs.
- Capacity building of Panchayat members may also be undertaken simultaneously by organizing training courses.
- Mobilization of community to be partners in local governance has to be taken up through local leadership.

Issue No. 3.—To consider measures to effectively monitor development programmes.

Recommendation No. 8

The State and district administration should be streamlined by way of sincere attempts in clarifying roles and responsibilities, and eliminating overlapping jurisdictions to strengthen the capacity to clearly pinpoint responsibility. Efforts should be made to ensure linkages between activities undertaken and actually delivered to the common man. The outcome should be more regularly measured and their determinants analyzed. Initially, measurement of outcomes may just be for information, and the sake of openness. Over time, such measures could be used to hold districts and departments accountable for improvements.

Information should not only be collected and submitted but should also be used for taking corrective and remedial action.

As regards utilization of funds received from Government of India review should be made every month whether the entitled funds are being received in the State by the concerned Departments.

District level programme implementation could be made more transparent by the use of Information Technology. For instance, the tendering process for carrying out works and procurement could be made on line.

Issue No. 4.—To consider effective measures to institute zero-tolerance for human rights violations.

Recommendation No. 9

(a) The State Human Rights Commission requires to be strengthened as the body enforcing respect for human rights. The press and civil society organization can act as watchdogs and help ensure speedy redressal of complaints of human rights violations. Also comprehensive training must be imparted to the law enforcing agencies on what comprises human rights and its violations.

(b) There should be a high-powered Committee (including political representatives and civil society members) for enforcing human rights and emphasis on rule of law, accountability and proper implementation of laws.

(c) All recommendations should be acted upon by the State Government and in case any recommendation is not accepted, reasons for the same should be given through a speaking order.

Issue No. 5.—To consider effective measures to strengthen the Right to Information

Recommendation No. 10

With the introduction of the Right to Information Act, it is necessary that officers belonging to State Government and Local Self-Government Institutions (LSGIs) be suitably sensitized and trained in this respect.

Further dissemination of the contents of the Right to Information Act and biannual review or the applications filed under RTI and the status thereof should also find place in the efforts to improve transparency in administration.

This issue has also been examined and recommendation made at Issue No. 1: Recommendation No. 1.

Issue No. 6.—To consider effective measures to provide adequate security to all segments of society, particularly the minority communities.

Recommendation No. 11

(a) The security forces have to adopt a citizen-friendly approach and ensure that while militancy and law and order are adequately tackled, innocent persons should not be harmed and their life and property adequately protected.

(b) The areas having residence of minorities or others who have a threat should be identified and provided with special protection. Help of para military forces should also be taken in this regard and their units located in vulnerable areas.

(c) Local Panchayats and other bodies should be asked to have a system of community watch to ensure that elements who pose a threat are identified in advance and are unable to get any local support.

(d) Setting up of a Minorities Commission to regularly look into the problems of Minorities should be examined.

Implementation

The recommendations of the Working Group have been arrived at after careful thought to examine in depth the issues placed before it. For translating the recommendations in focused action it would be necessary to appoint a Committee (reporting directly to the highest authority in the State) to oversee the implementation of the recommendations. The strategy would include sequencing of reform, a definitive administrative set-up for implementation, getting the Departments on board for undertaking reform, comprehensive, mass training on good governance and the monitoring of the implementation processes itself. What would be required would be a Special Purpose Vehicle for delivery of reforms.

CHAPTER I

Introduction

The Working Group on Ensuring Good Governance is part of the five groups set-up as an outcome of the second Round Table Conference of the Prime Minister on Jammu and Kashmir (May 2006). The mandate of the Working Group is to consider effective measures to increase responsiveness, accountability and transparency of the administration, strengthen local self-government, monitor development programmes, strengthen the right to information, institute zero tolerance for human rights violations and provide adequate security to all segments of society.

Keeping in mind the mandate of the Group, the present report outlines a good governance agenda for J&K. The suggestions presented in this document are the outcome of a series of deliberations undertaken by the Group members on the status of governance and administrative systems in the State. The focus of reform and the end outcome, it was discussed, would be improved services to the citizens—this would be brought about by instituting measures to make administration more effective and empower citizens with information and knowledge.

Background

Reforms in governance of the State of J&K are coming at an opportune time. As it is, the state is in the best of times and worst of times. It is in the worst of times as in the last few years citizens have been complaining about the state of administration, there has been a sense of unease over the trend that public service provision has been taking, leading to a pessimistic view of the future. Citizen's apathy towards the government has grown, fuelled by the instability caused by the militancy situation. The government's position has been unenviable as it has battled with this instability and the citizens' perceptions of the absence of any "visible" improvement in government services. However, the brighter side belongs to the beginnings of recognition of the need for reform and some major steps undertaken towards revitalizing administration by the State government. If the latter trend is supported there is every reason to believe that the current pessimism will be short-lived and J&K will be well on its way into treating a model in governance-focused on citizen-centric administration.

A brief overview of the development indicators of the state are in order. Despite the fact that the proportion of people below the poverty line in J&K is least of all the states in India, the State has not done well in terms of many other socio-economic indicators. Nearly 80% of the population lives in rural areas and 70% is employed in the agricultural sector.[1] The industrial and infrastructural base of the state is also unsatisfactory with coverage of roads and railways being amongst the lowest in the country.

The comparative picture for J&K and India as a whole on some indicators is shown in the following tables:

TABLE 1

Literacy Rates—All India and J&K (1951-2001)

(per cent)

Sl. No.	*Year*	*All India*	*J&K*
1.	1951	16.67	—
2.	1961	24.02	11.03
3.	1971	29.45	—
4.	1981	36.03	32.68
5.	1991	52.21	—
6.	2001	65.38	54.46

In literacy, J&K ranks third from the bottom compared to other states and the only states with lower literacy rates are Bihar and Jharkhand.

In health, too, its achievements have been modest. Basic indicators such as birth and death rates show that much remains to be done to bring the state at par with higher ranking states in the country. The crude birth rate per 1000 was 13.27% during 1999-2000 and the crude death rate was 3.03% during the same period. The state-wise Infant Mortality Rate is shown below:

1. *Source:* Directorate of Economics and Statistic, Government of J&K.

Box 1: IMR in 2004

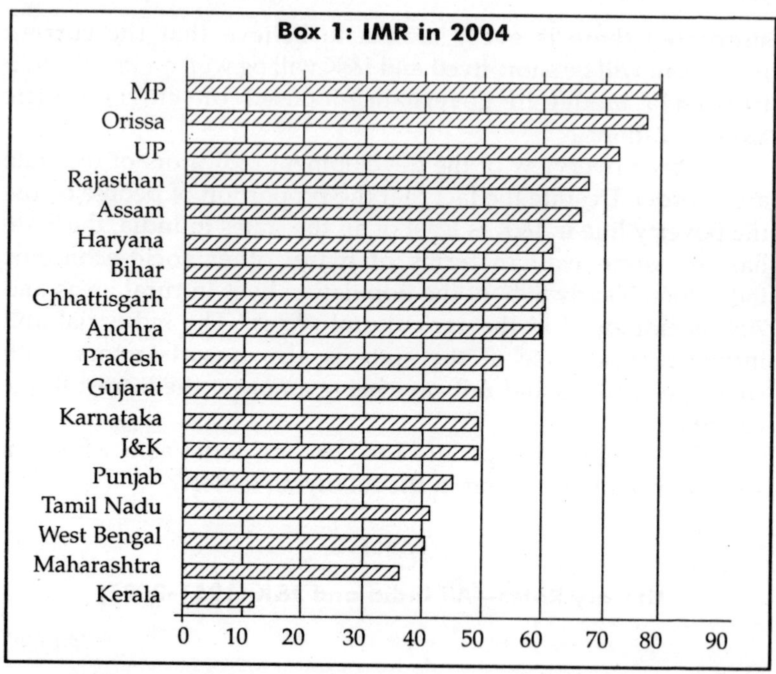

The change in percentage of malnourished children below three years between 1998 and 2006 is shown below, based on NFHS II and NFHS III findings (Box 2).

The Table 2 depicts, in brief, the comparative standing of J&K amongst the various states of India in terms of development indicators:

As shown in Table 2, although the overall achievement rating for J&K is 'B', the achievements in other indicators are inadequate, with social well-being ranking at 'E'. It can be seen that in almost every aspect of the human development indices J&K is nearer the bottom than the top in both the ranks and the ratings.

The inadequacy of social development is also evident from the trend in development spending. It is apparent that the expenditure on establishment, maintenance and services has been on the increase in the state, while less emphasis has been placed on investments and growth-oriented development expenditure. This trend is reflected in the Budget for 2005-06 as well where capital expenditure is placed at Rs. 3828 crores as against revenue

Box 2: Child Malnutrition in 1998 and 2006

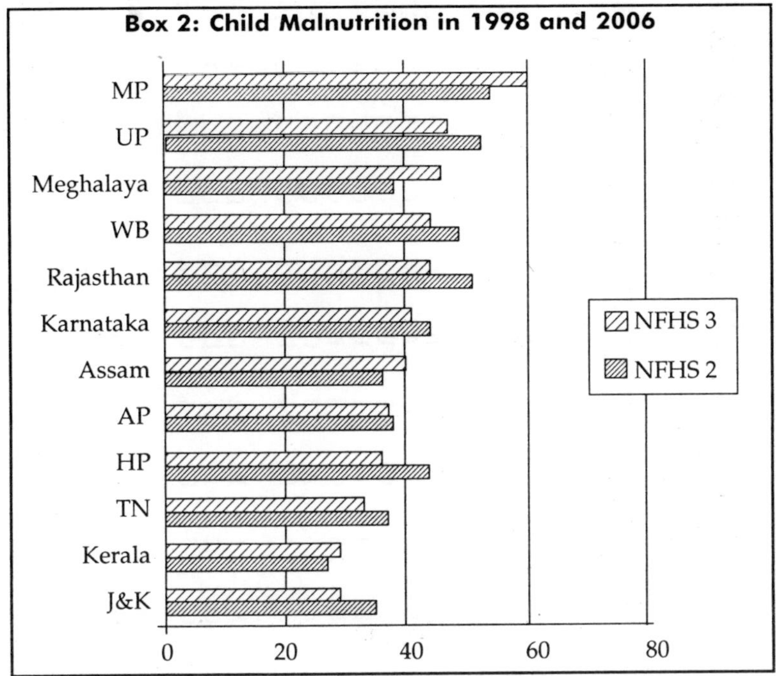

expenditure of Rs. 9117 crores.[2] Development spending clearly has taken a back seat. This fact, however, has not escaped the concern of the Government which has put in process initiatives to check mounting revenue expenditure (such as restructuring PSUs) and improve revenue receipts (such as promoting tourism).

The Process of Governance Reform

Reforms Already Initiated

There is a keen focus on governance reform already present in the state. Many initiatives to enhance efficiency of government procedures and development programmes have been put in place[3]. This is a heartening development and the initiatives are listed below:

1. Work Culture in government offices: a circular has been

2. Govt. of J&K, Budget at a Glance, 2005-06.
3. *Source:* General Administration Department, Government of J&K.

TABLE 2

Ranking and Rating for Major 20 States in India based on the Performance in some Development Indicators

States	*Infrastructure Reservation*										*High Value Agriculture*		*Personal Finance*				*General*	
1	*2*	*3*	*4*	*5*	*6*	*7*	*8*	*9*	*10*	*11*	*12*	*13*	*14*	*15*	*16*	*17*	*18*	*19*
Kerala	A	2.5	A	1.5	A	4	A	3.1	B	2.5	A	1.4	A	2.7	A	2.8	A	2.7
Himachal Pradesh	B	1.6	A	1.8	B	3	B	2.2	B	2.4	A	1.5	B	2.2	A	2.5	C	1.7
Punjab	A	2.5	C	0.7	B	2.4	D	0.2	B	2.3	C	0.2	A	2.9	A	2.3	A	2.7
Haryana	B	2	C	0.8	C	2.3	B	1.6	C	1.4	C	0.7	B	2.1	B	2.3	A	2.9
Jammu & Kashmir	C	1.5	B	1.2	E	2.2	C	1.3	C	1.4	A	1.5	B	2	C	1.9	B	2.3
Maharashtra	A	2.8	B	1	A	2	B	1.2	B	2.5	B	1	A	2.6	C	1.5	A	2.5
Uttarakhand	B	2	B	3	B	2.6	C	1.3	C	1.9	C	0.7	B	2.1	C	1.8	B	2.1
Karnataka	A	2.4	C	0.5	C	2.3	B	2	B	2.3	B	1.2	B	1.9	C	1.7	B	2.5
Gujarat	A	2.3	B	1.1	C	2.4	B	2.3	B	2.5	C	0.8	B	2.1	C	1.3	A	2.6
Tamil Nadu	A	2.6	A	1.4	B	2.4	B	2.5	B	2.6	A	1.3	C	1.8	C	1.8	A	2.7
Rajasthan	C	1.3	D	0.4	D	1.3	B	2.2	C	1.6	D	2.4	D	1.2	C	1.5	C	1.4
Andhra Pradesh	B	2.1	C	0.9	D	1.6	C	1.4	B	2.1	B	1.2	D	1.4	D	1.3	B	2.3
Uttar Pradesh	C	1	D	0.4	D	1.2	D	0.9	D	1.2	E	0.4	D	1.2	D	1.2	D	1
West Bengal	B	2	D	0.3	C	2.4	C	1.3	C	1.5	D	0.4	C	1.6	D	1.1	C	1.6
Madhya Pradesh	C	1.2	C	0.8	D	1.3	B	2.3	D	1.1	C	0.5	B	1.1	D	0.3	C	1.4
Jharkhand	D	0.6	C	0.4	E	0.3	D	0.9	D	1	C	0.8	D	1.3	D	0.5	D	0.7
Orissa	D	0.5	D	0.4	D	1.3	B	2.1	D	0.5	C	0.7	D	0.6	E	0.5	D	0.3
Chandigarh	C	1.1	C	0.3	D	2	B	2.2	D	1	C	0.7	D	0.8	E	0.4	C	1.1
Assam	C	1.1	C	0.5	D	1.2	D	0.4	D	0.5	C	0.6	D	1	E	0.3	C	1.3
Bihar	E	0	E	0	E	0	D	0.3	D	0.1	E	0.2	D	0.2	E	0	E	0

issued regarding punctuality in government offices, redressal of public grievances, checking of wasteful expenditure, checking corruption, monitoring of development works in quantifiable terms and against physical and financial targets, touring by officials in districts and outlying areas for inspection and redressal of problems.

2. The Right to Information Act has been passed and Accountability Commission set up.
3. Monitoring system for development schemes is being institutionalized by placing Additional District Development Commissioners in each district.
4. Internal vigilance has been strengthened by nomination of Departmental Vigilance Officers.
5. The process of introduction of computers in government offices has begun; efforts are on to computerize treasuries for better financial management.
6. Departments have been asked to notify Citizens Charters.
7. Chief Minister's Gold Medal is being awarded to officials with high integrity.
8. Declared policy of Zero Tolerance for Human Rights Violations

Ensuring Good Governance—Improving Public Services

It is recognized universally that good governance entails improving services by the government to the public through efficient administrative systems, timeliness, reducing corruption and effective implementation of development programmes. The role of the state in efficient provision of basic services is crucial, more so in a developing nation. The need for government's interest and involvement in the social development is captured by this quote from the *World Development Report—2004.*

"Services—A Public Responsibility

By financing, providing, or regulating the services that contribute to health and education outcomes, governments around the world demonstrate a responsibility for the health and education of their people. Why? First, these services are replete with market failures—with externalities, as when an infected child spreads the disease to playmates, or a farmer benefits from a neighbour's ability to read. So the private sector, left to its devices, will not achieve the level of health and education that society desires. Second, basic health and basic education are considered fundamental human rights. The Universal Declaration of Human Rights asserts an individual's right to "a standard of living adequate for the health and well-being of himself and of his family, inducing...medical care...[and a right to education that is] . . . free, at least in the elementary and fundamental stages." No matter how daunting the problems of delivery maybe. Therefore, the public sector cannot walk away from health and education. The challenge is to see how the government, in collaboration with the private sector, communities and outside partners, can meet this fundamental responsibility."

The Working Group on Good Governance has been instituted at an opportune time, when the process of governance reform is already in its incipient stage. The mandate of the Group clarifies the path that the reform process must naturally take and the themes of accountability, transparency, responsiveness in administration fit neatly into the vision of the State Government, while the focus on strengthening local self-government, strengthening the right to information and instituting zero tolerance for human rights violations underscore the citizen-centric approach to governance. What follows is a description of the proposals for good governance worked out by the Group. The ensuing chapters are organized around the following themes:

- Proposals for Good Governance in Jammu and Kashmir
- Implementation Arrangements.

CHAPTER 2
Proposals for Good Governance in Jammu & Kashmir

One of democracy's key roles is to deliver essential public services effectively. These services or public goods mostly relate to the rights of citizens viz. shelter, food, health and education and security. Translated into specific services these include housing and property rights, public distribution of essential food items, free and compulsory education upto secondary level, provision of basic health services including drinking water and sanitation facilities and maintenance of law and order.

These services are provided by various departments like Revenue, Registration, Education, Health, Rural development and police. As part of the reforms in governance many of these services are also supposed to be delivered under the aegis of rural and urban local governments. The local governments in India, generally, and in J&K specifically have not yet taken sufficient roots. While it is agreed generally that the transfer of the 3 Fs—funds, functions and functionaries are essential, there is neither complete agreement nor blueprints available for a quick and efficient transfer of the same.

Not only do public services need to be delivered efficiently in a democracy, they also have to be done so in a manner that is transparent and accountable to the citizens. The aspect of transparency has been strengthened by the legislation on Right to Information. Some features of this legislation are of immense value to civil society in monitoring not only the progress of various schemes and plans but also in understanding how decisions have been arrived at. The positive aspect of this for the government itself is that decision-makers will become more introspective when demand for information comes from below.

This introspection should ideally lead to a review of relevance of policies, procedures and practices arising in a particular context to a different one. While most of the procedures and practices are dictated by, for instance, a paper-based society; the current society itself lies in an era of sweeping technological changes that warrant reforms.

The mandate of the Group covers all these aspects of governance. Therefore, this chapter outlines a set of reforms covering the following areas:

(1) e-governance, simplification of rules and procedures (Mandate: responsiveness and efficiency in administration).
(2) Transparency and accountability in administration, Institutional strengthening, performance ; management (Mandate: accountability, transparency, responsiveness).

(3) Fiscal Management.
(4) Programme monitoring and implementation.
(5) Enforcing zero tolerance; for human rights violations and security to all sections of society.
(6) Strengthening local self-government.

The reforms being suggested by the Group are accompanied by examples of similar initiatives in other states."[4]

I. E-governance

Introduction of computers in various service delivery procedures and in functioning of government departments has been attempted successfully in many states (including Andhra Pradesh, Kerala, Karnataka, Uttar Pradesh and Madhya Pradesh). These initiatives have not only enhanced efficiency but reduced the direct contact of the public with the government machinery to the benefit of both. Some of the ways in which it may be applied to J&K follow.

Building up the capacity of the Information Technology Department.—At present the IT Department is functioning without a Directorate and field organizations. This lack of capacity has stalled the implementation of the few projects taken up by the Department for automation of administrative processes. Consequently, funds allocated under various schemes by the State Government and the GoI are going unspent. For instance, an amount of Rs. 5.92 crores under ACA in the outlay for 2005-06 was surrendered, as it could not be spent.

Computerization of land records.—Land records may be computerized and placed on a dedicated website so that they are available to the citizens at the click of a button, without approaching government officials. At present, the Survey Settlement operation is in progress in four tehsils of Kashmir. The data is stored in flash memory cards and brought to Srinagar for integration into special software. The process of computerization requires being undertaken on a wide scale and connectivity built up so that land records are accessible easily.

Computerization of Sub-Registrar's Office, and then bringing it

4. A set of best practices from across Indian states may be viewed in Annexure I.

under the control of the Revenue Department (sequencing is important here; one should not attempt changing the department unless all records have been computerized and placed on website), and merging it ultimately with the Tahsil Office. At present, the Registration Department is under the judicial wing, which creates anomalies in administration.

Computerization of service delivery procedures such as issue of certificates—Entry of father's name in the electoral roll and a copy of land records downloaded from the website should be sufficient proof of a person's native status, and he/she should be given a certificate accordingly without any further enquiry. Electoral Rolls in Urdu for all 87 Assembly constituencies have been computerized by the NIC J&K; this database could be used for speedy disbursal of certificates.

Setting up Information Kiosks at key service delivery institutions such as Revenue offices, Registration offices and Police Stations. This will facilitate giving basic information on procedures to be followed for availing services in the respective departments. Apart from reducing the workload on officials, this step would make information easily accessible to citizens. At present, Community Information Centres have been set-up at 60 Blocks in J&K (in Phase 1). The need is to focus on the specific service delivery points such as in the above-mentioned Departments so that common services are easily accessible to citizens.

Outsourcing some of the functions, such as data entry, to reduce burden on service delivery officials.

Mass training to government functionaries on the use of computers as in the states of Kerala, Tamil Nadu, Andhra Pradesh, Karnataka and Gujarat.

IT-enabled single window payment systems for utilities like water, electricity, telephones (on the lines of e-Seva in Andhra Pradesh and FRIENDS in Kerala).

Websites for each of the government departments with an online grievance redressal mechanism to make administration more visible and bring it closer to the citizens (This has been attempted under the Lokvani project in Sitapur District in Uttar Pradesh and Bangalore City Corporation). Another method of grievance-redressal could be the use of media for public interface (such as CM Online of Gujarat and Sutharyakerala of the Kerala government). At present the J&K government Departments are in the process of developing websites, this effort should be speeded up.

By introducing e-governance in Police procedures for filing FIRs, or for getting police verification done for passport, etc. may be simplified. For instance, if the list of those who have been convicted or prosecuted for serious offences is computerized it may be possible to do away with field verification of a person's reputation through constables for the purpose of issue of a passport, and verification formalities could be completed centrally on the basis of the computerized database. Similarly, it may be examined if FIRs could be accepted through fax, or through e-mail. The objective should be to reduce personal contact with the Police personnel to the extent possible. A system of on-line receipt of such applications could be introduced for which the petitioner needs to go only to a kiosk, and send his/her application by e-mail. Even copies of documents can be scanned and sent along with the application. The applicant should immediately within seconds get an acknowledgement with a particular number so that he could trace the movement of his application on the computer itself.

Treasury operations must also be computerized in order to save on time and reduce cumbersome procedures.

Box 3

Friends Project: Kerala

The FRIENDS project has been implemented by the Information Technology Department, Government of Kerala in collaboration with various departments like the Kerala State Electricity Board, Kerala Water Authority, BSNL, Revenue Department, Civil Supplies Department, Motor Vehicles Department, Universities and the Local Bodies of the State. It is a "Single Window Scheme" giving the citizens the option of paying for the common services rendered to them under a single roof. FRIENDS is a multiple agency bill collection system. The FRIENDS project envisages facilitating the collection of various payments pertaining to payees within specified area limits like corporation, municipality, etc. at a single centre.

FRIENDS is an example of improving access, timeliness, reduction in the channels of citizen-government interface—all through the effective use of Information Technology.

II. Simplification of Rules and Procedures

Rules and procedures governing various administrative procedures must be reviewed in order to increase timeliness in service delivery. Some of the suggestions in this regard are:

Review of laws in departments with public interface (such as Revenue Laws) so that procedures can be simplified. For instance, the problem in land acquisition for schemes such as Bharat Nirman is due to complicated rules. One solution could be that instead of acquiring land it may be taken on a long-term lease by the government from the owners by paying two times the gross value of current annual production. Other simplifications in the Land Acquisition Law could be as follows:

1. For determining the market value of land the Collector could take recourse to three different modes of assessment. Firstly, on the basis of existing sale deeds as has been done in most cases so far. Secondly, the Collector may take into account the scheduled rates for that category of land fixed under the Indian Stamps Act for registration of sale deeds. Thirdly, the Collector may calculate the gross annual production from each plot and fix the compensation as 20 times the gross value of annual production. The final market value for assessment will be the highest among the three amounts arrived at by these three methods.
2. Consent award could be the primary mode of settling the amount of compensation, which should not be less than the value calculated on the basis of the principle enunciated above.
3. Whenever land acquired for a public purpose is transferred to an individual or a company for a consideration, 25 per cent of the difference between such consideration and the compensation will be given to the original land owners.
4. The rate of solatium should be increased from the present 15% of the market value to 30% as is prevalent in the rest of the country.
5. A time limit of maximum of 18 months to be fixed for the completion of the acquisition proceedings from the

date of notification of the Act under Section 4 of the Act. Presently, there is no such time limit except 2 years' time limit from the date of publication of declaration under Section 6 of the Act.

6. Whenever the quantum of land being procured exceeds a certain limit/percentage of land of the owner/tiller then there should be adequate measures for proper rehabilitation of the persons affected by the project by way of employment, skill-upgradation, sharing stakes in the benefits of the project e.g. the person whose land is being acquired for irrigation purposes should be provided an alternative piece of land in the command area of the irrigation project.
7. Presently there is no fee charged by the Government for the conversion of agriculture land for non-agriculture purposes as is done in the rest of the country. Conversion of agriculture land puts premium on the society as the Government will be obliged to ensure food security despite reduction in the area under cultivation and thus cost will ultimately fall on the society through taxation. It is, therefore, desirable that reasonable amount of conversion fee should be levied for conversion of agriculture land to non-agriculture purposes. The levy should be more for the land put to commercial or industrial use.

The Ministry of Rural Development, GOI is likely to come up with a revised draft of the Land Acquisition Act, as well as a Rehabilitation Policy. J&K government should study the draft and model its policy on the GOI pattern.

De-regulation has made almost no impact at the state level. The systems of buying and selling land, getting a ration card or security back, and Rent Control Acts, all need a thorough revision. One can set-up an industry worth billions of Rupees in India without any license today, but a farmer can neither set-up a brick kiln unit, nor a rice shelling plant, and not even cut a tree standing on his own private field without bribing several officials. It is a sad commentary on our laws that the informal sector which provides maximum employment is mostly declared as illegal and subject to the whims of law enforcing agencies. A Committee should be set-up to identify specific laws and rules which hamper entrepreneurship. A systematic review needs to be undertaken to review the areas in which government must withdraw, albeit in a phased manner, and departments which need to be wound up should be defined.

Formats for various certificates must be standardized and simplified—Such certificates are needed for Ration Card, caste, backward area, income, etc. Computerizing the data for all families will sort out the problem once for all. The already existing data for BPL census may be used. Help of village panchayat and electoral rolls may also be taken in compiling the data.

File movement—More emphasis needs to be placed on a system like that of the 'Desk Officer' where the operating level concerned is responsible for the maintenance of record. This would lead to an increase in result-orientation, the possibility of flatter organisations and a reduction in dependence on lower levels. Up to Special Secretaries to the State Government, officers should be encouraged to keep the most important files in their personal cupboard, so as to expedite the process of decision-making, increase transparency, and reduce the chances of corruption by the lower functionaries. A single filing system should be followed in dealing with proposals from Head of the Department. This will also encourage transparency within government.

Orders under the Essential Commodities Act—There are a large number of licenses and permits to be obtained from the authorities under the EC Act. Apart from this a large number of registers are to be maintained and returns filed periodically. Inspections are carried out regularly to ensure adherences to the licenses obtained. These have increased bureaucratic rents and the operational costs of supply of essential commodities. The controls and restrictions, imposed by the State Government under the EC Act, are dis-incentives to production and distribution of essential commodities. A committee should be set-up to examine this so as to reduce corruption by curtailing the influence of various inspectors and their discretionary activities.

III. Transparency and Accountability in Administration

Corruption = Monopoly + Discretion – Transparency (in governance)

Accountability is essential for greater responsiveness to the needs of the public and thus to improve service quality—whether it is the individual civil servant who is directly accountable, or the department as a whole. Priorities for enhancing both internal and external civil service accountability should include: improved information systems and accountability for inputs; better audit; face-to-face meetings with consumers and user groups; publishing budget summaries in a form accessible to the public; a stronger performance evaluation system; scrutiny and active use of quarterly and annual reports; and selective use of contractual appointments.

Departmental Assessments—Departments such as the Police and Revenue, which have more dealings with the people, should be assessed once in three years by an Independent Committee, consisting of professionals such as journalists, retired judges or members of the armed forces, academicians, activists, NGOs, and even retired government servants. These should look at their policies and performance, and suggest constructive steps for their improvement. At present the systems of internal inspection are elaborate (although fallen into disuse) but often preclude the possibility of a 'fresh look' as they are totally governmental and rigid. The system should be made more; open so that the civil service can gain from the expertise of outsiders in the mode of donor agency evaluations of projects. The teams would undertake surveys of quality of service delivery in key areas; scrutinize policies, programs and delivery mechanisms. The civil servant's views on work constraints and reporting fraud and corruption should be elicited. The reviews conducted should also form the basis of time bound changes and improvements which should be monitored.

Review of Transfer Policy—There is immense pressure for transfers in most departments such as Education, Revenue and Health. The Transfer Policy must be reviewed so that officials are in place for at least three years and the Policy adhered to strictly. A system of Cadre Management Authorities as set-up by the Karnataka government and a blanket ban on general transfers is an example. A good transfer policy should have several objectives, such as:

- the need to curb the overall incidence of transfers,
- eliminate 'transfer industry' and politicized transfers,
- the policy should be seen as fair, objective, and leading to career development,
- the aptitude and experience of officers should be kept in view while giving a posting, and
- non-cadre persons should not be allowed to occupy cadre posts beyond a fixed time of six months or one year.

To begin with, GAD should calculate the average tenure of Principal Secretaries, Secretaries and Deputy Commissioners/ Superintendent of Police every quarter, and publicize this fact, so that political consensus is built up on the need for longer tenures.

There should be adequate publicity about who can transfer officials at various levels in government. This will ensure that government does not meddle with the transfers of low level officials. Powers of transfers of all Class II officers should be with the HOD, and not government.

Stability index should be calculated for important posts, such as Secretaries, Deputy Commissioners, and District Superintendent of Police. An average of at least two years for each group should be fixed, so that although government would be free to transfer an officer before two years without calling for explanation, the average must be maintained above two years.

At least for higher ranks of the civil services, e.g. Chief Secretary and DGP, postings may be made contractual for a fixed period of at least two years, and officers be monetarily compensated if removed before the period of the contract without their consent or explanation.

The recent Supreme Court order on Police Reforms should be strictly implemented in letter and in spirit.

At the same time it must be recognized that some posts would have more attraction for the employees than others. These may be due to better location where good schools or cheap government housing is available, more challenges, the pull of private practice for doctors, or simply more opportunities to make money. Except for the Indian Foreign Service no other service categorises posts according to its demand so as to ensure that everyone gets a fair chance to serve on both important and difficult (such as in remote and disturbed areas) assignments. Posts should be categorised in each department according to the nature of duties and geographical location into A, B and C posts, and the kind of mix that should dictate the average officer's span of career should be charted out. It should be possible to know through websites that total transparency is being observed and whether some 'well connected' officials have not been able to get 'plum' postings and avoid difficult areas. It is noteworthy that the region of Ladakh already has its transfer policy which had an incentive system for postings in difficult areas.

Box 4

Review of Transfer Policy in Karnataka

The critical problem of frequent transfers has plagued many state governments by hampering the efficiency and effectiveness of public services. The problem had reached gigantic proportions in Karnataka during 2000-01 and the Departments accounting for most transfers were crucial ones such as Police, PWD and frontline officials in departments such as Health and Education. After imposing a blanket ban on transfers in 2001-02, the government decided to create a committee system to address requests for transfers at all levels. The innovation in this scheme was that Cadre Management Authorities were created for A, B, C, and D category posts. The new transfer rules raised minimum tenures across groups and certain cadres were exempt from transfers altogether. These measures reduced political interference to a large extent by creating a system of rules and increasing transparency by creating a database to track transfers over time.

Recruitments: In recruitments by the Public Service Commission the amount of discretion can be brought down. For instance, as against the 20% marks set aside for the interview for recruitment of teachers, the weightage may be brought down to 10% first, and then ultimately to zero. Also the list of selected candidates along with the aggregate marks secured by them may be published twice—once before the interview and again after, so that transparency of the process is increased as also the satisfaction level of the applicants.

In order to tackle the large number of writs and cases filed with respect to government appointments, contractual employees may be hired with the specific purpose of following up and getting such cases disposed. Simultaneously, Service Rules may also be revised.

There should be a survey of all government servants, which should be computerized and put on a website. This will help in eliminating various people who are still drawing salaries from government, though their age is more than 60, or they were recruited as cooks or orderlies for officers who have retired. High wages with little accountability for actual service delivery has made public sector agencies and bodies an obvious target for patronage hiring, which results in massive over-staffing. It appears that Government is committed to public service providers, but not to public service provision.

At present a large number of *adhoc* appointments have been made in gross violation of Service Rules. Non-cadre people are occupying cadre posts. There are instances in J&K where Chief Engineers retire, but their substantive post is only as Assistant Engineer, because regular appointments are not made. Therefore, a department-wise drive should be organized to regularize appointments. This will also need simplification of PSC procedures. The state government will recruit a large number of teachers, AWWs, ANMs, and other medical staff in the coming years. Some states are able to complete recruitment with minimum complaints or litigation, because they follow a fair and transparent procedure. If appointment is for a particular post (and not to the cadre), postings to remote and difficult places does not pose a problem. To eliminate take orders, every Government order must be signed by two officers of the Department

Fixing responsibility and accountability: The control that the politicians exercise on the civil servants often amounts to backseat driving. In the present system it is difficult to fix responsibility for decisions, or for not taking decisions. The term public interest is most abused today, as it is used to cover hidden and malafide motives knowing fully well that the public is not in a position to challenge the bonafides of decision-makers. It is here that a fundamental change is required in the Rules of Business. It should be mentioned in each government order the level at which decision has been taken.

- The reasons for disallowing a petition should be fully mentioned, that is, it should be a speaking order, and the reasons for delay in disposal of petitions should be fully explained.

There may be a system of clear Job Descriptions in every department for every post. This would increase accountability levels.

There should be an effective system of writing APRs (Confidential Reports), which should be regularly maintained and not written up only at the time of promotion.

Reducing corruption: In particular, property and tax returns of all senior officers should be available for scrutiny by the public. These could be put on a 'home page' of the government on the Internet, so that anyone having access to Internet could access such information and get in touch with government if the stated facts are contrary to his knowledge.

Annual awards for whistle-blowers—Governments should in each department institute annual awards for recognition of the contribution made by such persons in exposing wrong-doings in the government.

Citizens Charter: Every Department should prepare and publish a Citizens' Charter in a time-bound manner. Periodic review of the Departments adherence to Citizens' Charters may be undertaken by GAD, preferably through independent agencies. The guidelines for formulating Citizens' Charters may be prepared by GAD and disseminated. An ideal charter should have the following components:

1. Clear responsibility—who will provide the service?
2. What does the citizen need to do—application, fee, information, etc.
3. What is the time frame in which the service shall be delivered.
4. What is the compensation for delay.
5. What is the redressal mechanism.

During introduction of citizens' charters, it should be noted that merely notifying citizen's charters should not be an end in itself. Each department should organise large-scale capacity building programmes to bring in attitudinal change in their employees. Officials should interface with public on at least one fixed day in addition to routine interaction, so that a system is devised for ensuring a speedy disposal of grievances at all levels of governance. At present, there is no institutionalized system in J&K for monitoring the progress on redressal of grievances (how many complaints received, how many disposed-off to the satisfaction of the complainant, how many pending, etc.), although J&K officers are very open to public and receive their applications without grudge.

Proactive publication and display of information by various Departments on services delivered and pending is a must, so as to reduce the number of applications for grievance redressal.

Face to face meetings of officials with citizens: A system of public hearings both at the District level as well as Departmental level would be useful in strengthening accountability, increasing government visibility and increasing peoples' participation. The experience of Nationalized Banks could be a pointer in this direction.

Report Cards: At the end of the Financial year, the concerned Ministers ought to present a complete Report Card or self-assessment giving various details, which could, *inter-alia,* include their performance including expenditure incurred, the outcomes obtained, details of performance, including under-achievement, austerity measure or resource savings, if any and innovations introduced. This should be telecast live on all TV channels and also have representative Sarpanches of Gram Panchayats, randomly selected to be present and give their assessment or appraisal.

Strengthening the Right to Information: With the introduction of the Right to Information Act, it is necessary that officers belonging to State Government and Local Self-Government Institutions (LSGIs) be suitably sensitized and trained in this respect. With a view to bringing in transparency and accountability, such capacity building programmes can be held by the Training Division or the GAD. Similarly, using e-Governance, most of the information pertaining to each office can be published on the web. This will make the process of responding to requests from citizens for information easier and faster. The aim of the Department should be to publish information that meets the three Rs: *reliable, relevant* and *regular.*

Appointment of Chief Information Commissioner of the State, the Appellate Authorities and the Departmental Information Officers for effective implementation of the Right to Information may also be done.

Also people should be encouraged to make use of the Right to Information Act by creating awareness. For this purpose, an awareness campaign should be launched through print and electronic media for which budget provision should also be made.

In the context of development works enforcing the rule that all muster rolls and bills are regularly read out and explained to the people in the village, and put on the web (at least in some places on a pilot basis) would provide the necessary (empowering) information to the public. To do this, no radical change in official rules is required. On the contrary, existing rules already provide for such sharing of vital relevant information with the public and village panchayats. However, such rules are mostly observed in the breach, because it suits the bureaucracy to conceal such information to enable its arbitrary and nepotistic exercise of power.

Further dissemination of the contents of the Right to Information Act and biannual review of the applications filed under RTI and the status thereof should also find place in the efforts to improve transparency in administration.

Surveys: Government departments should also mount surveys of the perceptions and experiences of the ordinary people and civil society in sectors that have a public interface. These surveys will both measure public perception and experience of the integrity of staff interacting with the public and overall performance in the delivery of services. Surveys should be carried out by an independent institute/survey body of recognized survey experience and integrity, and the results be published in a time bound manner. Implementation of the recommendations of these surveys should be ensured. Similarly, publication of reports of state-sponsored commissions and key policy papers should be compulsory. It is not enough that the J&K government departments and the state governments use professional and academic organisations to undertake impact studies from time to time. Their findings must be publicised and discussed with key stakeholders so that improvements in design and delivery can be effected at the earliest. Government should also put on its website findings of the impact studies, and distribute these in the workshops it organizes. Dissemination of results is critical for use. Results that are not widely disseminated, through mechanisms tailored to different groups in civil society, will not be used, and the resources that were spent in getting such results will be wasted.

Exit polls: There should be periodical exit polls of all government offices which have large interlace with public. Some of the questions could be: How long did it take to have a citizen's work attended to? Did he/she receive courteous and helpful treatment? Was he/she asked to pay any bribe? These would help in assessing satisfaction levels of citizens and would serve as important outcome indicators.

IV. Institutional Strengthening

To carry out reforms leading to good governance, it is essential that the required capacities in knowledge, skills and aptitude be developed amongst government functionaries through a well designed and sustained strengthening of institutions and individuals.

Capacity building: Periodic Training programmes may be made mandatory for all government officials on subjects such as design of programmes and monitoring, results-based management, service delivery improvement, leadership, change management and performance management. The capacity of State-based training institutions may be enhanced and Faculty may be called from other Institutions in the country to impart training.

Infrastructure: Many of the frontline service delivery Institutions lack adequate infrastructure for effective citizen-centric service delivery. Basic infrastructure, adequate space, provision of computers and other items crucial to service delivery must be in place even before an attempt is made to bring about attitudinal change in government functionaries for good governance.

Human Resources: There is a widespread belief that government institutions are overstaffed and downsizing is the order of the day. While in many instances government departments are overstaffed as Clerks, peons and drivers, at the same time service departments are woefully understaffed at the frontline level, for instance, as teachers, doctors and para-medical staff. A study of the frontline service delivery institutions is necessary in order to assess the situation at the ground level. Redeployment and 'rightsizing' would assist in good governance. J&K has a specific problem in this regard as employees are unwilling to serve in areas that are prone to militancy with the result that primary health centres, primary schools and other frontline service delivery institutions fall short of staff. For doctors, practice in rural areas as a first posting may be made mandatory with increased remuneration. In addition setting up of paid clinics in Government Hospitals with sharing of fees by doctors and hospitals may be considered as an option for ensuring attendance.

V. Peoples' Participation

Peoples' participation is the basic building block of good governance and is now widely recognized as a crucial ingredient in governance reform. Some of the ways of enhancing peoples' participation could be:

Building public-private partnerships: Government could identify and select a few dedicated NGOs based on pre-determined criteria to partner in strengthening public service delivery. These could be particularly useful in the social sector—for instance in motivating girl children to attend school, in disseminating information on health programmes and in IEC for sanitation programmes. The Education Department has already got the Hole in the Wall initiative of NIIT working in some schools. Other NGOs and private sector organizations could be identified with specific areas of work to augment the State's activities and programme implementation.

Social Audit: At the State level social audit of the Government could be conducted by accredited panels of eminent citizens of unimpeachable integrity and social commitment and be identified jointly by all political parties, ruling and opposition. They may be empowered to co-opt experts. The reports of the Audit should be made public.

Citizens' Scorecard: Monitoring of government provision of services may be undertaken in the form of a Citizens' Scorecard (as done in the case of Bangalore Municipal Corporation) and community scorecards. In Bangalore the satisfaction from public hospitals improved from 25 to 34 percent between 1994-99, but jumped to 78 per cent in 2003. This highlights the importance of regular information flows in ensuring standards of public service delivery. A similar initiative could be undertaken on a pilot basis for selected government institutions in J&K.

Box 5

Kudumbasree—An Example of Peoples' Participation

Kudumbasree is a poverty eradication project launched by the Government of Kerala with the active support of the Centre and NABARD with the aim of wiping out absolute poverty from the State within 10 years.

The project is implemented by the State Poverty Eradication Mission of the State government through local self-governing bodies. In this model, nine non-economic indicators are used to identify the beneficiary 'at risk' families -possession of a *kutcha* house, no access to safe drinking water and sanitation, presence of illiterate adults in the family with not more than one earning member, family barely getting two meals a day or less, presence of children below the age of five, presence of an alcoholic or drug addict member in the family and persons belonging to the Scheduled Caste or Scheduled Tribe. In 1994 the Community Based Nutrition Programme and Poverty Alleviation Project (CBNP & PAP) started functioning with UNICEF assistance and participation of the local community in the area of Malappuram, considered the most backward district of Kerala. Over 4000 neighbourhood self-help groups were formed under this project. These SHGs started mobilising savings and were linked to various commercial banks under the Linkage Banking Programme of NABARD. The implementation of various government-sponsored programmes for improving health and sanitation in Malappuram District was channelled through these SHGs. Besides empowering women through community organisation, Kudumbasree encourages and guides them in starting small livelihood earning enterprises. Products manufactured by such enterprises are sold through the rural marketing network.

The Kudumbasree network has expanded in Kerala and has been a model for community mobilization and self-help initiatives all over the State. It is also an example of active peoples' participation, women's empowerment and constructive linkages between the government and citizens.

VI. Performance Management

Each Department, in consultation with various stakeholders, should set 3 to 5 outcomes that it would like to achieve in the next 2 to 3 years and work towards achieving those. For instance, these could be reducing absenteeism of doctors and teachers in remote areas, completing all engineering works on which 50% work has already been done, increasing the utilization of budget for centrally sponsored schemes to 95% or more, measuring and improving the satisfaction level from public services (such as PDS, tahsils, etc.) to at least 50%. In this process each Department should prepare a Status Paper of services it offers to citizens (which should be freely available), plan for improving services and then set the outcomes to achieve.

Each Department may be given the option of volunteering for a "Charter Mark" Certification in achieving standards in service delivery. (This has been an initiative of the GoI in many States) Charter Mark is a quality standard which encourages and rewards improvements in public service with reference to the commitments and standards notified in the Citizens' Charter. Those agencies which are implementing their Charters exemplarily and are providing an excellent standard of service receive certification/recognition in the form of a 'Charter Mark' after an independent assessment. The Kerala government has over the last two years got a few of the Departments to work towards the Charter mark

The promotion system must reward performance and penalize (and correct) under-performance.

Each Department may also be encouraged to produce the best website in the State for which an award may be instituted by the Government.

VII. Fiscal Management

Fiscal reform is another critical component of good governance. This is especially important for J&K given its specific problems of budget cycles and utilization of finances.

There is no tradition in J&K of monitoring social sector expenditure, and find out whether the current year's expenditure is more or less (as % of total expenditure, or as % of NSDP) as compared to previous years. For instance, the Reserve Bank data given below shows that expenditure on Education and Health did not increase in J&K (this was also the pattern in most Indian states) over the past few years. However, during our interviews we got the impression that senior officers were not aware of such a trend.

Changes in Expenditure on Education and Health as % of Total Expenditure (J&K and all states)

Box 6

Year	Education		Health	
	J&K	*All States*	*J&K*	*All States*
2000-01	11.1	17.4	4.9	4.7
2001-02	11.6	16.1	5.5	4.4
2002-03	10.9	15	5.2	4.1
2003-04	8.9	12.6	4.4	3.6
2004-05	8.9	13.4	4.5	3.8

Budget: Release of budget is neither certain nor timely. The budget cycle is too short for full utilisation of funds for capital works. Expenditure budget should be valid for two years, so that capital expenditure can be completed without surrender of funds. Similarly for centrally sponsored schemes, approval of the state legislature should not be necessary for using central funds that are transferred to the state consolidated fund.

Funds allocated to the departments in the state budgets are not released during the year in an orderly manner and that far too many references have to be made to the Finance Department (FD) for prior approval for release of funds on ways and means considerations. The same is found to be true in respect of release of funds to District Boards Large funds are released at the end of the financial year resulting in many irregularities in booking the expenditure. Government of J&K should publicise for each department the percentage of funds spent each year in the last month, week, and last day of the year.

The delay in release of central funds to departments is because of fiscal stress and consequently funds being used for purposes other than intended, mainly to meet state's other exigencies. This is reflected by the fairly large backlog in audit certificates, to be submitted by the state for CSS. As J&K follows a cash basis of accounting, releases to implementing units are treated as expenditure and reported back to the GoI, which is not conducive to good management. This accounting policy has in-built incentive for the state to 'spend' the budget for fear of lapse of budgets, without sufficient focus on utilisation of the funds. This is evidenced by the large fund releases in the last quarter of the financial year. It also creates conditions for transfer of funds to lower level implementing units and often results in funds lying idle at various levels with little oversight. There is no pressure on the state to obtain expenditures reports, utilization certificates and audit assurance on the actual utilization of funds.

Roll-over Plans: Annual Plans, Budgets and Allocations have the disadvantage of the process starting all over again the following year with a few more months spent on re-planning. A "Roll-over" facility may be followed with the unspent budget of one year being carried over to the next without having to go through the elaborate annual plan and budgeting process. The GoI may be requested to try out a few pilot projects based on this concept. This concept is used very often in the corporate sector.

Transparency: Again, as in other administrative functions, transparency in financial management requires: (i) publication of program performance reports, and (ii) feedback mechanisms to elicit client feedback on the quality of services provided.

VIII. Programme Monitoring and Implementation

Officials at all levels spend a great deal of time in collecting and submitting information, but these are not used for taking corrective and remedial action or for analysis, but only for forwarding it to a higher level, or for answering Assembly Questions. Field staff reports only on activities, it is not involved in impact assessment, or in qualitative monitoring. The concept of stakeholder monitoring is unknown. No indicators exist for assessing public participation or their awareness.

Emphasis is laid only on the initial or current expenses. After five years, little is done or monitored. Secondly, when money has been allocated for a particular activity in a particular area, it is assumed that the work in question has been done, and that it was sufficient. This ignores the fact that either of the above assumptions could be wrong. The primary monitoring activities have to do with fiscal accountability. While it is necessary, it should not be allowed to overshadow the need for technical and resource monitoring and planning work accordingly. At present, there is great pressure on the field staff as a whole to account for funds utilized, but not in terms of longer-term results, because those are not monitored. Thus financial planning is divorced from physical planning.

In some cases academic institutions are asked to review the schemes. Their approach emphasizes rigour, but often its completion requires years and policy-makers lose their patience with their work. There are also reports by professional consulting organisations, especially on centrally sponsored schemes. However, the Departments look upon giving of funds to consulting organisations as a patronage activity. Little interest is taken in ensuring the quality of the report, or in following up on their recommendations.

Therefore, it is not enough that the government departments use professional and academic organisations to undertake impact studies from time to time. Their findings must be publicised and discussed with key stakeholders so that improvements in design and delivery can be effected at the earliest. Governments should also put on its website findings of the impact studies, and distribute these in the workshops it organizes. Dissemination of results is critical for use. Results that are not widely disseminated, through mechanisms tailored to different groups in civil society, will not be used, and the resources that were spent in getting such results will be wasted.

To sum up, weaknesses in public expenditure management —both budget programming and budget execution—have reduced the effectiveness of public spending. Expenditure programming has been approached as an accounting exercise, rather than as a tool for achieving policy objectives. The focus has been on inputs rather than outputs and outcomes, with departments asked to explain where they would spend money, but not held to account for delivery against performance indicators. On the other hand, the nature and extent of risk of fraud, waste and abuse of public funds is growing.

Streamlining State and District Administration: A recent report on decentralization in Karnataka reveals the astounding fact that there are over 400 'plan' schemes in each of the state's 27 districts, many of which constitute only small trickles of money but enough to justify the continuation of posts and salaries to administer such 'programs'. In total, there are about 658 budget heads in the average Karnataka district budget operated by the district authorities directly, and another 1,000 heads operated by the state government in the district.[5] The confusion in districts across much of India generated by the proliferation of schemes, budget heads, and related establishments costs is compounded by overlapping and poorly defined functions involving a plethora of line departments, elected councils, and planning authorities. There could be similarly a large number of schemes in J&K. Without a serious attempt at streamlining state and district administration, clarifying roles and responsibilities, and eliminating overlapping jurisdictions, confusion, and an accompanying loss of the capacity to clearly pinpoint responsibility, will become near permanent features of governance in India. Disentangling this maze, particularly developing clearer and shorter paths for the flow of funds as well as for taking decisions among center, state, and local government, is thus an important factor in enforcing accountability across the system.

Programme monitoring: Monitoring of programmes is critical to ensure proper fund utilization and measure outcomes. The recent J&K government initiative of introducing Additional District Development Commissioners in the Districts as independent programme monitoring agencies is a welcome move. Further efforts for ensuring linkages between activities undertaken and actually delivered would strengthen programme monitoring to a great extent.

Outcome Measurement: Apart from generating and disseminating information regarding services and their progress (as discussed in the section on Transparency above), providers and policy-makers should know (and be constantly learning) about what works,. This requires outcomes to be more regularly measured and their determinants analyzed. One critical role of the state government, when districts and departments have the primary responsibility for the delivery of publicly-funded services,

5. Government of Karnataka, Department of Rural Development and Panchayat Raj, Report of the Working Group on Decentralisation, (Bangalore: Department of Rural Development and Panchayat Raj, 2002), p. 101.

is to be an independent source for this measurement. Initially, measurement of outcomes may just be for information and the sake of openness. Over time, such measures could be used to hold districts and departments accountable for improvements—perhaps to the extent of conditioning fiscal transfers to District Boards based on progress. It is in the experimentation that such flexibility allows that solutions to the problem of implementation can be found. Lessons learned will help all districts and departments improve their performance.

Documentation and dissemination: Being able to document what actually happens is absolutely critical to an outcome orientation. Without good information on what has happened, a focus on results is impossible. And for good information, one requires monitoring or tracking of progress in accordance with objectives and indicators, along with evaluation that can look at broader considerations.

Capture district-wise data to fix accountability: Often data on performance reaches late, or is not available district-wise, with the result that accountability cannot be fixed. On the other hand, state governments do not discourage reporting of inflated figures from the districts, which again renders monitoring ineffective. For instance, the Rapid Household Survey, conducted in 1998-99 and repeated in 2002-03 indicates a fall in full immunisations across the country from 54.2 per cent in 1998-99 to 48.2 per cent in 2002-03, with rapid decline in the poorer states, as shown in Table 3. Similarly, delivery at public institutions has declined from 24% to 18.5%, and ANM making home visit within two weeks from 14.1 to 12.7% during the same period.

TABLE 3

Full Immunisation under Universal Immunisation Programme

(*per cent*)

	1998-99	*2002-03*
Uttar Pradesh	43.7	29.8
Andhra Pradesh	74.5	61.6
Assam	46.7	27.6
Haryana	66	57.9
Madhya Pradesh	48.4	34

(MTA X Plan)

Had this data been available timely and for each district, it would be easy to fix responsibility and help in outcome monitoring. On the other hand, as data is often not verified or collected through independent sources, no action is taken against officers indulgirig in bogus reporting. Similarly, district-wise data on IMR needs to be made available for every year in J&K.

According to an article in Indian Pediatrics (August 17, 2005), results of a survey in district Kargil showed that only 65% of infants received full primary immunization, with rural areas fairing worse (62%) than the urban areas (72%). Coverage rates were similar in boys and girls. Antigen-wise, the highest coverage (92.5%) was seen for BCG, and the poorest (65%) for measles vaccine. The attrition from the first to third dose of DPT and OPV (from 89% to 83%) was remarkable; drop-out rates from the 3rd priming dose (83%) to booster (31%) at 16-24 months were far steeper. Some 7.5% of the infants remained completely un-immunized, while 28.5% were only partially primed. However, since the results of such honest surveys are not known to district authorities, no action is taken to improve the situation.

Fund utilization: The Chief Secretary should review every month whether the entitled funds from GoI are being received in the state by the concerned departments. Information on SGRY for 2005-06 (Table 4) shows that as against an allocation of 26 crores, districts could receive only 15 crores, presumably because of delay in submission in UCs. The data for SGSY reveals a similar picture (Table 5). Similarly, gross underutilization has also been reported. For instance in SGSY, as against the total availability of funds to the tune of Rs. 72 crore during 2005-06, expenditure was only Rs. 36 crore. As for the Total Sanitation Campaign, as against the availability of Rs. 130 crores, expenditure was nil.[6] In fact J&K has the dubious distinction of recording poorest performance in construction of household toilets, as shown below:

Transparency in programme implementation: District-level programme implementation could be made more transparent by the use of Information Technology. For instance, the tendering process for carrying out works and procurement could be made online. Many States in India have experimented with this initiative. Punjab has for example implemented electronic

6. Rural Development Department, Government of J&K.

Box 7
% Achievement of Construction of IHHL

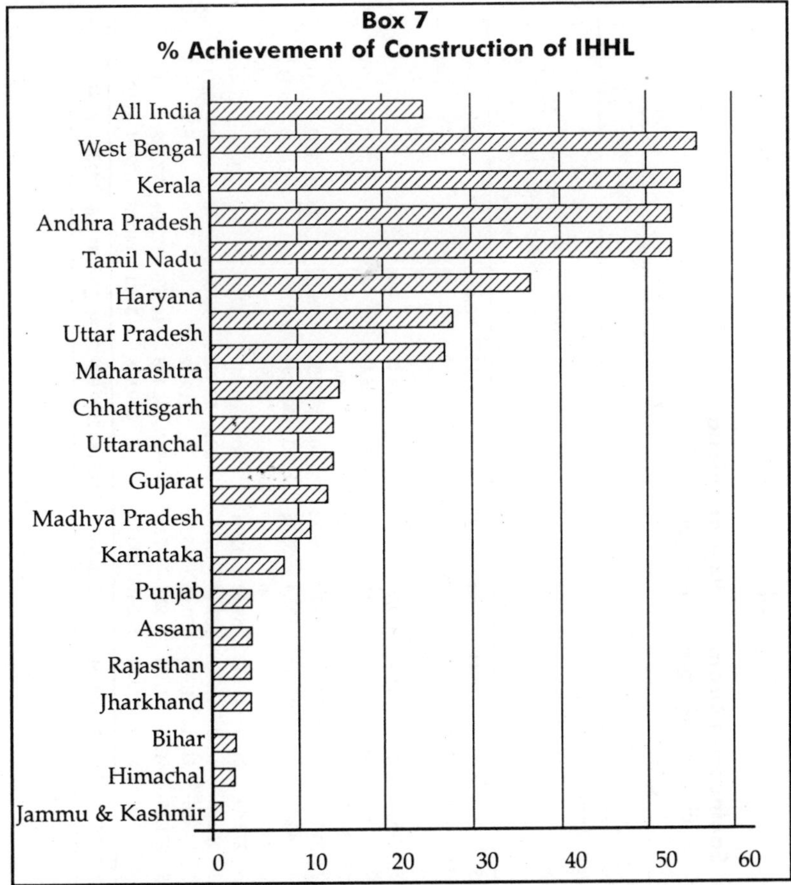

tendering or e-tendering, whereby traditional tendering processes are carried but using the internet. The scheme covers the full cycle of purchasing from indent to receipt of goods and connects buyers and suppliers through electronic exchange of information. Such processes would ensure greater transparency in administration and reduce the opportunities for siphoning funds by various actors in the process.

IX. Enforcing zero tolerance for human rights violations and security to all sections of society

Policy decision: A recent *India Today* Survey on the State of the

TABLE 4

Sampoorna Grameen Rozgar Yojana
Financial Progress, Year 2005-06

S. No.	District	Till Month	Opening Balance	Allocation			Central RIs	Releases			Misc. Receipt	Total Availability	Utilization				
				Centre	State	Total	Last Yr. red. this Year	Centre	State	Total			Gen. Works	SC/ST		Maintenance	Train
														Ind. Beneficiaries	Habi.		
1.	Anantnag	March	32.49	390.7	138.5	529.2	0	356.44	138.5	494.94	1.77	520.2	385.652	0	82.44	6.83	0
2.	Badgam	March	0	0	0	0	0	0	0	0	0	0	0	0	0	0	0
3.	Baramulla	March	0	0	0	0	0	0	0	0	0	0	0	0	0	0	0
4.	Doda	June	0	259.96	86.65	346.61	0	114.38	105.09	219.47	0	219.47	0	0	0	0	0
5.	Jammu	June	14.26	321	107	428	26.79	0	81.88	81.88	0.48	123.41	0	0	0	0	0
6.	Kargil	Nov.	74.26	163.74	100.7	338.7	0	163.74	100.7	264.44	0	338.7	119.76	0	0	0	0
7.	Kathua	Dec.	0.634	227.89	82.42	310.31	0	136.73	61.79	196.52	0	199.154	78.13	2.28	51.33	0	0
8.	Kupwara	March	44.901	219.63	123.4	343.03	0	131.78	123.4	255.18	1.213	301.294	260.883	0	0	11	0
9.	Leh	June	23.99	193.79	64.6	258.39	0	0	0	0	0	23.99	0	0	0	0	0
10.	Pulwama	Feb.	2.015	199.13	79.5	278.63	24.93	119.48	59.62	179.1	0	206.045	117.49	3.2	37.85	0	0
11.	Punch	Dec.	6.11	193.81	68.22	262.03	0	116.29	51.16	167.45	24.27	197.83	48.07	0	0	50.13	0
12.	Rajouri	June	0.17	263.1	87.7	350.8	32.94	115.76	70.15	185.91	0	219.02	0	0	0	0	0
13.	Srinagar	Mar.	3.322	168.93	62.5	231.43	61.58	110.4	62.5	172.9	4.386	242.188	144.576	12.104	72.888	0	0
14.	Udhampur	Nov.	3.658	0	0	0	0	133.54	102.41	235.95	0	239.608	34.21	14.113	27.51	1.934	0
	Total		205.81	2601.68	1001.19	3677.13	146.24	1498.54	957.2	2455.74	32.119	2839.909	1188.771	31.697	272.018	69.894	0

TABLE 5

Swarnajayanti Gram Swarozgar Yojana
Financial Progress, Year 2005-06

S. No.	District	Till Month	Opening Balance	Allocation			Releases		Misc. Receipts				Total funds Available	Utilization of Funds
				Centre	State	Total	Central (%)	State	Interest incurred	Return of subsidy	Others	Total		
1	2	3	4	5	6	7	8	9	10	11	12	13	14	15
1.	Anantnag	03	32.46	73.31	24.437	96.31	35.11 (47.89)	23	1.5	2.53	0	4.03	94.6	56.56
2.	Baramulla	03	40.82	77	25.667	121.85	56.9 (73.9)	0	0	0	0	0	97.72	75.57
3.	Badgam	03	32.65	48.41	16.137	69.26	26.34 (54.41)	20.85	0	0	0	0	79.84	50.58
4.	Doda	03	17.53	133.8	44.6	178.4	30.74 (22.97)	44.6	1.39	2.025	0	3.415	96.285	76.8
5.	Jammu	03	9.01	51.68	17.227	81.48	24.75 (47.89)	29.81	3.02	1.85	0	4.87	68.44	58.83
6.	Kargil	03	4.48	7.11	2.37	7.11	4.8 (67.51)	7	0.09	0.77	0	0.86	17.14	15.85

(Contd.)

TABLE 5 (*Contd.*)

1	2	3	4	5	6	7	8	9	10	11	12	13	14	15
7.	Kathua	03	3.38	28.44	9.48	43.19	13.62 (47.89)	14.75	1.27	0	0	1.27	33.02	32.56
8.	Kupwara	03	10	38.86	12.953	60.76	33.26 (85.59)	21.9	0.34	0	0	0.34	65.5	41.6
9.	Leh	03	1.89	6.34	2.113	6.34	8.22 (129.65)	2.74	0.02	1.71	0	1.73	14.58	14.16
10.	Punch	03	4.59	33.86	11.287	53.51	16.23 (47.93)	19.65	0.13	0.25	0	0.38	40.85	36.64
11.	Pulwama	03	5.59	30.41	10.137	46.26	30.41 (100)	15.85	0.21	0	0	0.21	52.06	36.03
12.	Rajouri	03	0.05	50.36	16.787	73.76	51.41 (102.08)	23.4	0.43	0.08	0	0.51	75.37	65.98
13.	Srinagar	03	5.72	22.89	7.63	34.44	10.96 (47.88)	8.66	0.45	1.81	0	2.26	27.6	27.43
14.	Udhampur	03	11.93	68.07	22.69	68.07	65.67 (96.47)	30	0.008	10.742	0	10.75	118.35	152.5
	Total		180.1	670.54	223.515	940.74	408.42 (60.91)	262.21	8.858	21.767	0	30.625	881.355	740.7

States[7] shows that among all the States, J&K has the largest police force relative to its population: 3,740 policemen per million people. In the same survey, J&K is ranked 17 out of 20 big Indian States. J&K has continuously been in the limelight for human rights violations by its security forces (including armed forces and police). Recently a Human Rights Watch Report alleged that the State's failure to end widespread human rights abuses by security forces and militants was responsible for fuelling the cycle of violence in the State. Clearly human rights violations have been a major issue of concern in the State and the declared (by the State government) policy of 'zero tolerance for human rights violations' comes at an appropriate time.

Capacity Building: The State Human Rights Commission requires strengthening as the body enforcing respect for human rights. That awareness about the Commission has grown is evident by the increase in the number of complaints it has received —from 395 in 2001 to 474 in 2002. However, it suffers from resource constraints and requires more teeth to carry out its tasks. Applications should be disposed in a time-bound manner. All recommendations should be acted upon by the State Government and in case any recommendation is not accepted, reasons for the same should be given through a speaking order. There should be a high-powered Committee (including political representatives and civil society members) for enforcing human rights and emphasis on rule of law, accountability and proper implementation of laws.

Awareness generation: The Press and civil society organizations can be brought into the picture for awareness generation activities and positive reporting on human rights issues. These agencies can act as watchdogs and help ensure speedy redressal of complaints of human rights violations. Also comprehensive training must be imparted to the law enforcing agencies on what comprises human rights and its violations.

X. Strengthening Local Self-Government

State Finance Commission: J&K has set-up a State Finance

7. *India Today*, Special Issue, 'State of the States', September 11, 2006.
8. Entitled 'Everyone Lives in Fear: Patterns of Impunity in Jammu and Kashmir'.

Commission and this is a move towards analyzing the problems in Panchayats and redressing them. The Godbole Committee Report had suggested that J&K should consider extending the provisions of the 73rd Amendment of the Indian Constitution to the State for reviving these institutions.

Status: The following tables show the status of Panchayati Raj in the State after the 2001 elections. (Table 6)

The Table 6 show that in Kashmir Division more than 50% of the seats for Panches are lying vacant. The panchayats in the States are not functioning as instruments of vigorous local self-government. This is evidenced by the following facts:

1. Halqa Panchayats have very limited powers of taxation. They also do not have the necessary apparatus for decentralized planning—neither functions nor functionaries.
2. Halqa Panchayats have limited activities under their jurisdiction. Many areas considered important to be governed at the local level, such as primary education, are in limited purview of the Hatqa Panchayats.
3. There is no independent Election Commission in the State.
4. Members of District Development Boards are not directly elected.
5. There are no Block Development Councils.

In this situation a reconsideration of the State PR Act is required. Some of the suggestions for strengthening local self-government could be:

(i) A comprehensive capacity assessment exercise followed by a capacity building one.
(ii) Effective transfer of funds, functions and functionaries to the Panchayats would have to be taken up on priority.
(iii) Activity Mapping exercise on the lines of that which is being carried out in other states and rationalization of schemes to be implemented by PRIs.
(iv) Training for capacity building of Panchayat members may also be undertaken simultaneously.

TABLE 6

Information Regarding Panchayat Election, J&K, 2001[9]

District	*No. of Blocks*	*No. of Panches*	*No. of Sarpanches elected*	*No. of Sarpanches vacancies*	*Total No. of Panches to be elected*	*No. of Panches elected*	*No. of vacancies of Panches*	*No. of Pyts. Notified by Govt.*	*No. of Pyts. yet to be notified*
A. Kashmir Division									
Kupwara	9	224	168	58	1471	915	556	95	129
Baramulla	14	276	162	114	2148	902	1246	93	178
Leh	6	68	68	—	448	448	—	67	1
Kargil	7	65	65	—	453	453	—	65	—
Budgam	8	199	61	138	1444	315	1129	25	174
Srinagar	4	93	67	2(3	666	247	419	21	72
Anantnag	10	309	251	58	2242	1191	1051	121	188
Pulwama	6	236	202	34	1586	684	902	26	210
Total	64	1470	1042	428	10458	5155	5303	518	952
B. Jammu Division									
Jammu	11	295	294	01	2448	2443	05	295	0
Kathua	08	183	182	01	1394	1391	03	182	1
Poonch	05	115	115	—	1028	1026	02	114	1
Udhampur	12	21	212	03	1840	1792	48	210	5
Doda	14	262	216	29	2004	1698	306	216	46
Rajouri	07	160	160	—	1376	1364	12	160	0
Total	57	12 30	1196	34	10090	9714	376	1177	53

Source: Reconstructed from the information received from Directorate of Rural Development, Srinagar/Jammu.

9. State Development Report, Planning Commission, GoI.

(v) Mobilization of community to be partners in local governance.

XI. Measures to Provide Adequate Security to all Segments of Society, Particularly the Minority Communities

(1) The security forces have to adopt a citizen-friendly approach and ensure that while militancy and law and order are adequately tackled, innocent persons should not be harmed and their life and property adequately protected.

(2) The areas having residence of minorities or others who have a threat should be identified and provided with special protection. Help of para military forces should also be taken in this regard and their units located in vulnerable areas.

(3) Local Panchayats and other bodies should be asked to have a system of community watch to ensure that elements who pose a threat are identified in advance and are unable to get any local support.

(4) Setting up of a Minorities Commission to regularly look into the problems of Minorities should be examined.

Conclusion

The above-mentioned proposals have been made keeping in mind the specific task given to the Working Group. In addition, the Group also observed that reform of legislature and judiciary is also important apart from that of administration. However, implementation is the key to success of good governance initiatives. Full implementation of these suggestions is what would make for good governance. Therefore; the Group felt that it is necessary that a set of guiding principles and steps to be followed for implementation are listed out separately. The next chapter sets out these guidelines and action steps for J&K state.

CHAPTER 3

Implementation of the Good Governance Initiatives

The initiatives suggested by the Working Group would require strategic changes at the line department level and at the level of the frontline service delivery institutions. It is imperative that staff actually get to know and practice good governance principles. The Government of J&K's good governance planning process should have as its basic premise and as a *sine qua non* that all efforts should be aimed at providing quality services to the citizens, especially the poor and the marginalized. The following may be viewed as the key ingredients for success of good governance initiatives:

- That all government departments and institutions have the capacity to carry out the implementation of the initiatives.
- That the concept of citizen-centric service delivery is firmly engrained as the basic premise on which institutions base their working.
- That standards are set for each department and institution so that improvement in service delivery becomes clearly measurable, and
- That good governance is sustained over time.

Strategy Outline

The initiatives suggested by the Working Group may be implemented in a structured manner. Not only is it essential that the sequencing of reform be undertaken, implementation may be undertaken in comprehensive manner to ensure service delivery improvement, administrative efficiency and sustainability of reform. The strategy would include a definitive administrative set-up for implementation, getting the Departments on board for undertaking reform, comprehensive, mass training on good governance and citizen-centric service delivery and the monitoring of the implementation processes itself (through external means and by the state government itself). What would be required would be a Special Purpose Vehicle for delivery of reforms, support systems for implementation and purposive training. At a later stage in the process, standards could be ensured through a baseline survey, a citizens' survey and a social audit. Monitoring and impact evaluation for the reforms may be in the form of a Social Audit, post-implementation as a longer term vision. All these steps would need to be preceded by policy change adopting good governance as the stated policy. Some of these arrangements and requirements are discussed in some detail below. Diagram 1 depicts the strategy for reform (please refer page 38)

A Special Purpose Vehicle for Good Governance Implementation

The Government of J&K may think of establishing a "Special Purpose Vehicle" (SPV) on good governance management on the lines of a 'Centre for Modernizing Government'. This could be an independent training-*cum*-implementation Centre or may be part of GAD. If independent, the SPV could have wider participation from the community on its governing structure and should have as its main goal enabling the government to ensure it delivers on the basic issues of governance and services. One wing of the Centre could be responsible for undertaking IT-related administrative reforms and implementing them and the other could be devoted to Training of officials for capacity building. A High level Committee chaired by the Chief Secretary should monitor the progress periodically. The Centre may be responsible for developing a Results-Based Management strategy for implementing the reforms suggested.

In addition, for the concept of good governance to be ingrained across board, the strategy could be to use extensive training in a "mass instruction" mode. The instruction material may include tailor-made mass-communication-based modules on good governance and service delivery management that could be beamed through television, sent as compact disks, could be transmitted as streaming videos through the Internet, delivered through personal contact sessions by paid and volunteer instructors to the government institutions. In addition, the Government of J&K would have to ensure one very important feature: that is, all instruction materials relate to the local conditions and features.

This SPV should also be able to conceptualize and carry forward the utilization of the mass instruction mentioned above by providing grassroots support in implementation of initiatives. It is evident from the case of other states, that the current thinking and capacity of State Institutes of Administration are not adequately geared to address these tasks. The need for a new approach may be stated here, and it may be suggested that this area could be one where a Public-Private Partnership could bear fruits.

Support Systems for Implementation

Software for tracking implementation: A part of the implementation arrangements may be the development of software for tracking progress of the initiatives. What is required, especially considering the need for sustainability is an IT tool that would not only show progress but also give analytical inputs to a decision-maker. What could be thought of as the implementation progresses is custom-made software going beyond standard ERP for business enterprises. It should have at least the following features: on-line data capture, 'user-friendly rules for decision-making, real-time data on infrastructure, human resource, finances, procedures and processes, analytical information—including easy features for aggregation and dis-aggregation on various parameters—that would aid managerial decision-making, a platform for sharing information across departments and institutions, quick-search facility, successful case studies, unique features that need to be factored in for exceptional cases, etc. The depth and breadth of data and information requirements would vary according to where in the hierarchy of government a user fits in, and hence; the design would have to be multi-layered.

Programme Support Executives: At the level of the department or the district, implementation could be undertaken by a separate cadre of people posted in each of the districts. This could be in the nature of Support Executives—a cadre of young trained and qualified men and women who have basic managerial skills and qualifications. This would serve the dual purpose of implementing the initiatives and providing employment to qualified youth in the state. The Support Executives may be hired by the SPV (suggested above) and could be stationed in the District headquarters or in the selected departments to carry out implementation and report progress to the implementing agency.

Reform Champions: No service can be reconstructed without the support of a champion who is usually an experienced manager. For champions to succeed, they usually need political support to insulate themselves from pressures to reverse changes that reduce rent-seeking opportunities for politicians, employees, and, in some cases, consumers as well. Strong support from the Chief Minister in the case of both Andhra Pradesh and Karnataka in the past has made it possible for IT initiatives to succeed without major employee resistance. It is also hard to imagine the innovations introduced to control transfers in Karnataka, especially mass transfers, without the support of the Chief Minister. In Maharashtra, the reform of the Stamps and Registration Department, which generates substantial annual revenues, was overseen by a dedicated manager who had the support of the Cabinet, which approved his restructuring package, including turning over core functions in the Department to the private sector. Managerial champions thus require well-honed political skills to convince politicians to take risks, while reform-minded politicians require good managers to implement their larger goals.

Annual Index of Good Governance: The concept of good governance needs to be translated into a quantifiable annual index, and measured for each district, on the basis of certain agreed indicators such as infant mortality rate, extent of immunisation, literacy rate for women, availability of safe drinking water supply, electrification of rural households, extent of power dues recovered, rural and urban unemployment, percentage of girls married below 18 years, percentage of villages not connected by all weather roads, number of class I government officials prosecuted and convicted for corruption, and so on. Some universally accepted criteria for good budgetary practices may also be included in the index. Once these figures are publicized, districts may get into a competitive mode towards improving their score. Financial transfers to the districts should be linked to such an index.

Political and Administrative Will: Needless to say that such comprehensive reforms need for their sustenance strong political and administrative will from the top. In its absence, reforms remain only on paper.

Sequencing of reform: Government of J&K should decide the sequencing of the suggestions given in this report. Not all reforms can be undertaken simultaneously. Government should take up those where the negative side-effects are minimal. These are like the low hanging fruits where benefits far outweigh the costs.

A good civil service is necessary but not sufficient for good governance; a bad civil service is sufficient but not necessary for bad governance. Hence the paramount necessity of improving the performance of the civil service, without which services will never reach the 'Aam Admi'.

DIAGRAM 1

Implementation Arrangements

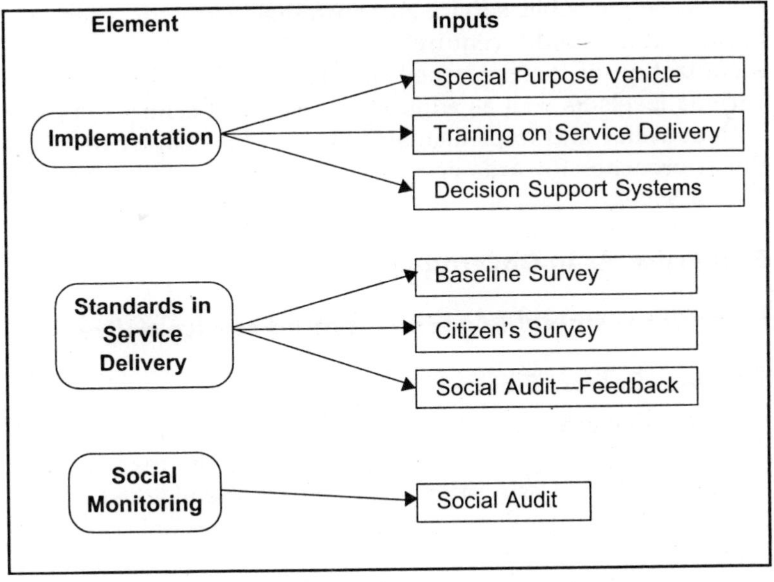

APPENDIX I—4

Best Practices in Governance Across Indian States

Introduction

Achieving good governance implies that the operational arms of the government or government institutions that directly interface with the citizens will plan and act in such a way as to achieve better public service and sustainable growth. These two broad aims would require interventions in the realm of organization of the concerned departments and institutions at various levels as well as adoption of a citizen-centric approach both at policy and implementation level. This chapter describes the approaches towards good governance adopted in various Indian States.

Best Practices in Governance

I. Kerala: sustainable people-centred service delivery

1. Service Delivery Project

The Government of Kerala identified service delivery improvement, particularly to the poor and the marginalized sections of society as a priority. In 2003-04 it embarked upon a major Service delivery improvement programme and within this context developed a now policy for service delivery that was capable of application to all public services provided by state and local self-governments. The Service Delivery Project (SDP) became one of the action-research fast track projects designed to test out the ground level realities in putting into action the superstructure of results-based management system through the Service Delivery Policy. The SDP seeks to create 2585 model institutions in 8 departments and 22 categories of Institutions. The key focus areas in SDP have been setting standards, implementation, relating resource allocation to services provided and social monitoring. The project involves the preparation of service delivery (improvement plans by frontline officials in the selected institutions, and implementation of those plans on a fast track basis through an intense process of identifying existing and new services through consultation, assessing requirements and budgeting for improvements - all at the frontline service delivery level. This has been the first effort of its kind in India for a State government to attempt sustainability of its public services on such a large scale through participatory planning. The process of mapping services across departments and planning for improvement on this large scale may be a model for other States to follow.

2. DC Suite

The District of Palakkad in Kerala became in 2002-03 the first IT enabled district headquarters in India. The district collectorate underwent total computerization, which was part of the Modernizing of Government Programme (MGP) of the Kerala Government. The objective of the exercise was to make the services of the collectorate more citizen-friendly. DC Suite is a web enabled centralized and integrated service delivery system consisting of a set of applications covering 21 functional areas of work in the Collectorate. These include an electronic file management system, revenue recovery management and public grievance monitoring system. It enables the public to retrieve information through multi-channel service delivery access points like touch screen kiosks, interactive voice response system, SMS, service counters, e-mail, internet kiosks. It has the scope of interconnectivity with other IT enabled development projects in the State, thus taking services to the grassroots level, improving access and promoting transparency in administrative systems.

3. Kudumbasree

Kudumbdsree is a poverty eradication project launched by the Government of Kerala with the active support of the Centre and NABARD with the aim of wiping out absolute poverty from the State within 10 years.

The project is implemented by the State Poverty Eradication Mission of the State government through local self-governing bodies. In this model, nine non-economic indicators are used to identify the beneficiary 'at risk' families—possession of a *kutcha* house, no access to safe drinking water and sanitation, presence of illiterate adults in the family with not more than one earning member, family barely getting two meals a day or less, presence of children below the age of five, presence of an alcoholic or drug addict member in the family and persons belonging to the Scheduled Caste or Scheduled Tribe. In 1994 the Community Based Nutrition Programme and Poverty Alleviation Project (CBNP & PAP) started functioning with UNICEF assistance and participation of the local community in the area of Malappuram, considered the most backward district of-Kerala. Over 4000 neighbourhood self-help groups were formed under this project. These SHGs started mobilising savings and were linked to various commercial banks under the Linkage Banking Programme of NABARD. The implementation of various government-sponsored programmes for improving health and sanitation in Malappuram District was channelled through these SHGs. Besides empowering women through community organisation, Kudumbasree encourages and guides them in starting small livelihood earning enterprises. Products manufactured by such enterprises are sold through the rural marketing network.

The Kudumbasree network has expanded in Kerala and has been a model for community mobilization and self-help initiatives all over the State. It is also an example of active peoples' participation, women's empowerment and constructive linkages between the government and citizens.

4. FRIENDS

The FRIENDS project has been implemented by the Information Technology Department, Government of Kerala in collaboration with various departments like the Kerala State Electricity Board, Kerala Water Authority, BSNL Revenue Department, Civil Supplies Department, Motor Vehicles Department, Universities and the Local Bodies of the State. It is a "Single Window Scheme" giving the citizens the option of paying for the common services rendered to them under a single roof. FRIENDS is a multiple agency bill collection system. The FRIENDS project envisages facilitating the collection of various payments pertaining to payees within specified area limits like corporation municipality etc. at a single centre.

FRIENDS is an example of improving access, timeliness, reduction in the channel of citizen-government interface—all through the effective use of Information Technology.

II. Experiences from Andhra Pradesh

I. The Indira Kranti Pratham Project

The extremely poor groups in Andhra Pradesh were organized under the Velugu scheme in 2000 (recently renamed Indira Kranti Pratham). It is another example of successfully organizing communities (especially women members) into self-help groups to enhance their resource management capacities. To date approximately 6 million rural poor women have been organized into self-help groups and village organizations at the village level, Mandal Samakhyas at the block level, and Zilla Samakhyas at the district level. According to a recent World Bank Report (2006) Velugu has significantly increased the access of self-help groups to commercial credit. Total annual credit to poor households and their groups has increased twelve-fold from Rs. 2.3 crore in 2000 to Rs. 27.6 crore in 2005. The total credit flow from commercial banks to these groups since 2000 has grown to Rs. 63.1 crore and is expected to reach 100 crore by the time the project closes. As in the case of Kudumbasree of Kerala, Velugu has been used extensively for the implementation of development projects at the district level.

2. e-Seva

e-Seva is an e-governance tool built on the public-private partnership model. It provides citizens with a transparent, efficient and effective administrative system and is a one-stop shop for a range of citizen-friendly services. The services include those of the State, Local, Central government and private business. Connection with all departments online enables transactions at an e-Seva centre to be simultaneously updated in the servers of participating departments

III. Maharashtra: Examples of Good Governance

1. SETHU

This project implemented in the Thane Collectorate has involved delegation of certificate issuing powers from the Collector to the Deputy Collector, SDM and Tahsildar for the entire district. This system has been a good example of simplification of government procedure in favour of the citizens availing the services. It has significantly reduced transaction time and made the procedure transparent since the initial processing of applications is done on a computer through a cooperative society. The citizen is able to correct mistakes in data entry on the spot and the decision on his/her application is made within 24 hours.

The SETHU project is an example of private-public partnership with the involvement of civil society actors in processing applications and in initial funding of the set-up. It is also yet another instance of IT leading to improvement in service delivery by cutting time and reducing the margin for errors.

2. Upgradation of Stamps and Registration Department

Modernization of sub-registries in the State has been brought about through extensive employee consultation. Subsequently, office maintenance was given out to private contractors for maintenance for five years. The element of discretion involved in the acceptance of applications by the sub-registrar has been done away with and documents are required to be automatically accepted and returned within a set standard time. The Ready Reckoner manual for determining property values has been computerized reducing the time taking in generating stamp values. This effort has made the standardization of service delivery possible across all sub-registries simultaneously. Facilities have been put in place for online interaction of the citizens with the department, thus taking services closer to the people.

IV. Reform in Karnataka

1. Rules for transfers of civil servants

The critical problem of frequent transfers has plagued many state governments by hampering the efficiency and effectiveness of public services. The problem had reached gigantic proportions in Karnataka during 2000-01 and the Departments accounting for most transfers were crucial ones such as Police, PWD and frontline officials in departments such as Health and Education. After imposing a blanket ban on transfers in 2001-02, the government decided to create a committee system to address requests for transfers at all levels. The innovation in this scheme was that Cadre Management Authorities were created for A, B, C, and D category posts. The new transfer rules raised minimum tenures across groups and certain cadres were exempt from transfers altogether. These measures reduced political interference to a large extent by creating a system of rules and increasing transparency by creating a database to track transfers over time.

2. The Learning Guarantee Programme

The Learning Guarantee Programme (LGP) is an example of public-private partnership in the education sector. An initiative of the Azim Premji Foundation from 2003-05, the aim of the project was to improve the quality of primary education by focusing on learning outcomes. The foundation worked with the State government in north-east Karnataka to support experimentation with innovative approaches on a large scale so that the lessons learnt could be successfully integrated into the large educational system. The difference in this programme was that it went beyond the issues of access to education to focus on pedagogical approaches and ultimately on the learning levels of cognitive and non-cognitive competencies. The focus was thus on the effectively assessing outcomes of learning in an area where high drop out rates and grade repetition rates had almost become a norm. The programme was also an innovation where it went beyond emphasizing inputs to analyzing outcomes.

The LGP used an incentive-based approach to optimize the ability of schools to achieve the objectives of universal enrolment, retention and enhanced learning levels. The success factors wore communicated from one school to all participating schools to motivate teachers, students and community members to strive for learning guarantee.

V. One Day Governance in Gujarat

The Gujarat government has initiated a number of e-governance schemes including e-grama and SWAGAT (State-wide attention of grievances by application of Technology) in recent times. One initiative that has won acclaim in the State has been the 'One Day Governance' scheme. The Scheme has entailed setting up of civic facilitation centres (Nagarik Seva Kendras) in Municipalities, Municipal Corporations, Taluka Offices and Collectorates. These centres are like the one-stop counters adopted by other states (like Maharashtra, Andhra Pradesh mentioned already). Wherein citizens can apply for various certificates like income, caste, domicile certificates, file affidavits, apply for Arms License Renewal, and many other documents and expect to get their documents within a few hours. This has resulted in cutting delays, reducing arbitrariness in service delivery and greater efficiency through the use of Information Technology.

VI. Tamil Nadu Good Governance

Public-private partnership in health care in Tamil Nadu

This good governance initiative in Tamil Nadu came about in 1997 by a realization by the government that resources were simply not enough for adequate upkeep and upgradation of health care institutions. The government therefore initiated a programme of industrial participation for maintenance of government health care facilities. Gaps in the public health system were identified and institutions requiring immediate attention identified. Industrialists were requested to volunteer to 'adopt' institutions and contribute to the infrastructure of that facility. The other models were of 'partial adoption', each differing from the other in terms of capital investment.

Apart from attracting investment in healthcare facilities, the programme resulted in facilitating local ownership and supervision and in developing important inter-sectoral linkages. It also created the much-needed asset base for medical facilities in the State.

VII. Examples from Madhya Pradesh

1. Gyandoot

Gyandoot is the Stockholm Challenge IT Award (2000) winning e-governance initiative of the Government of Madhya Pradesh. Initiated in the Dhar district—a tribal dominated district—the programme installed computer networks in the district connecting 31 village centres. The project provided online services including land revenue transactions, public grievance redressal, a matrimonial site, employment news and free e-mail facility on social issues. This helped improve interface between citizens and government and enabled knowledge access in a region populated by the marginalized tribal peoples.

2. Rogi Kalyan Samiti

The Rogi Kalyan Samiti project began in 1994 and involved management of public hospitals through community participation. Conceived as a response to local problems to improve the availability and quality of hospital infrastructure and services, a Samiti is set-up as a registered society but with active participation of the State government. It can use the premises and assets of the hospital it has been set-up for, raise additional resources and spend them in running the hospital and improving its services. Additional resources are usually raised through donations from the community and by levying user charges graded by peoples' ability to pay. The network of Rogi Kalyan Samiti has expanded significantly in Madhya Pradesh and has shown that even the poor are willing to pay user charges for better quality health care. It is also an example of community empowerment and participation in development. The project won the Global Development Network Award for the most innovative development project in 2001.

VIII. The Uttar Pradesh Example: Lokvani

Lokvani is an e-governance project one of the first of its kind in the State of Uttar Pradesh. The project, launched in Sitapur District of U.P. provides various e-governance services to the citizens. What is noteworthy in the project is that it provides an online grievance redressal mechanism in the form of online submission, monitoring and disposal of complaints. The system has been easy to access and operate a fact underscored by the popularity of the online public grievances redressal which received 11,000 complaints by March 2005 (it was launched in 2004). Lokvani also provides details of various government schemes, government prescribed forms, details of developmental work in the district, lists of old age pensioners, lists of scholarship beneficiaries, Funds allotted in various government schemes, allotment of foodgrains to kotedars, allotments of funds to gram panchayats, etc. The project has benefited citizens in a big way as it has enabled access to services at the Block, tehsil and town level, so citizens no longer have to travel all the way to the District office.

IX. Private Sector Initiatives to Improve Rural Livelihood[10]

1. ICICI banking services for the poor

To address the rural poor's unequal access to finance, ICICI Bank has led multiple initiatives to provide banking services at an affordable cost to the poor. ICICI has partnered with others to co-locate automatic teller machines with rural Internet kiosks and explore SmartCard technology to provide secure, low-cost transactions and loan management. More important, ICICI Bank has created a network of 8,000 self-help groups, covering about 160,000 women, to serve as the vehicle for creating successful, micro-financed businesses. In the process, ICICI Bank has given these women the means to transform their social and economic lives, their families, and their villages.

2. ITC e-Choupal

ITC e-Choupal illustrates how improvements in technology and communications infrastructure can be good for both equity and efficiency in product markets. ITC e-Choupal today reaches out to and empowers over 3.5 million farmers in 31,000 villages by enabling them to readily access crop-specific, customized, and comprehensive information in their local language. Vernacular websites provide real-time information to even the smallest marginal farmers on the prevailing Indian and international prices and price trends for their crop, expert knowledge on best farming practices, and micro-level weather forecast. This significantly improves the farmers' decision-making ability, thereby helping them better align their agricultural produce to market demand and ensure better quality, productivity, and price discovery. The ITC e-Choupal model has been specifically designed to tackle the challenges posed by the unique features of Indian agriculture, which is characterized by fragmented farms, weak infrastructure, information asymmetry, and numerous intermediaries. Over the next decade, the ITC e-Choupal network aims to cover more than 100,000 Indian villages, representing a sixth of rural India, and to create more than 10 million e-farmers.

[10] From the World Bank Development Policy Review, 2006.

ACKNOWLEDGEMENT

The Working Group on Good Governance was set-up by the Hon. Prime Minister as an outcome of the Second Round Table Conference on Jammu & Kashmir (J&K). The constitution of the Group and the terms of reference were detailed by the Hon. Chief Minister, Shri Ghulam Nabi Azad. The Group was charged with the mandate of considering effective measures to improve accountability, responsiveness and transparency in administration, enforce the Right to Information, improving monitoring and implementation of development programmes, strengthen local self-government and institute zero tolerance for human rights violations in the state.

Accordingly, the Group held a preliminary meeting in August 2006 at Srinagar to chalk out a plan of action and identify the important issues in governance of the state. Preliminary data collection including examples of good governance from other states was completed prior to consultations with the members of the Group. Subsequently, a series of meetings were held with senior officials of the Government of J&K to discuss the various policies, programmes and schemes of crucial sectors such as health, education, rural development, finance, etc. Based on these deliberations, a draft of the suggestions for good governance was prepared and presented at the second meeting of the Group in Jammu in November 2006. The present report is based on consensus that was developed during this meeting.

This report would not have been possible but for the keen interest shown by the Hon. Chief Minister Shri Ghulam Nabi Azad in the development of the state of Jammu & Kashmir. We are grateful to him for all the support and even more so for the wonderful hospitality we received in J&K.

Thanks are due to all the members of the Working Group on Good Governance who actively participated in the various meetings and also provided us their written comments and suggestions.

We were fortunate to have had senior officials from various departments sharing their analysis and insights about the outstanding issues in J&K with us. I am indebted to them for this. For reasons of space I am not individually naming them here.

A work of this nature required close coordination, which was ably provided by Shri Ajit Kumar, Financial Commissioner (Coordination), ably supported by Ms. Shally Ranjan, OSD. We are thankful to them for this as also for managing our logistics.

I am thankful to Ms. Tina Mathur, Consultant to the Group, for providing various intellectual inputs as also the initial drafts of the presentations and the report.

Above all, I would like to thank the people of J&K for the warmth that they showed us and I do hope that we have suggested measures for good governance in this report which will ultimately benefit them.

NARESH CHANDRA SAXENA
Chairman

APPENDIX I—5

Working Group V

SUMMARY OF RECOMMENDATIONS

1. Article 370 of the Constitution of India

It is for the people of the State of Jammu and Kashmir to decide how long to continue Article 370 in its present form and when to make it permanent of abrogate. The matter being 60 years old, should be settled once for all.

2. Demand of Autonomy by National Conference

The question of "Autonomy" and its demand can be examined in the light of the 'Kashmir Accord' or in some other manner or on the basis of some other formula as the present Prime Minister may deem fit and appropriate so as to restore the 'Autonomy[1] to the extent possible.

The question of appointment of the Governor and dismissal of the popular Government by the Governor may be considered and resolved.

3. Demand of Self Rule

Mr. M.H. Beg on behalf of PDP explained orally the concept of "Self Rule" but the 'Self Rule' as proposed by the PDP could not be considered in all its detail as the document containing the various aspects of the 'Self Rule' were not provided to the Working Group as promised by POP during the course of the proceedings.

Basically it appears to relate to 'Autonomy' in a wider context, which requires to be considered by the Central Government if and when approached with documents containing specific proposals of the "Self Rule". This document should be on record.

4. Term of Legislative Assembly of the State

Any change in the term of the Assembly will require political consensus among the various political parties in the State and it can be effected only through a Constitutional Amendment.

5. Representation/Reservation for Scheduled Tribe and Women in the Assembly

On this issue, the national pattern may be a good guide subject to political consensus.

6. Abolition of State Legislative Council

The present position may be maintained.

7. Increase in the number of Assembly seats and De-limitation Commission

Since the Constitutional provisions do not allow any change upto the year 2026, the present position may be maintained till then.

8. Strength of the Council of Ministers

Formation of the Ministry and strength of the Council of Ministers is the exclusive prerogative of the Chief Minister within the provisions of the Constitution.

9. Strengthening of the Democratic Process

Regular elections to democratic bodies including Panchayats and Municipalities etc. should be held.

10. Human Rights

The Human Right violations must not be tolerated and the State Government should take steps to strengthen institutions which are involved in safeguarding the human rights including the State Human Rights Commission.

Additional staff as recommended in the body of the report be sanctioned, which will work under the direct control of the Commission.

11. Right to Information Act and Accountability Commission

The positions vacant in the Accountability Commission may be filled up and the Commission should be made fully functional.

12. Armed Forces Special Powers Act

A group of Central Government and the State Government officers and peoples representatives may be constituted which will review the application of the Act to various parts of the State regularly to explore the possibility whether the Act can be withdrawn from any part of the State.

13. Issues relating to Kashmiri Migrants

The Central and State Governments must take all steps to implement the relief and rehabilitation packages sanctioned in this regard including the package announced by the present Prime Minister. The progress made should be regularly reviewed by a Group of Senior Officers from the Government of India and the State Government. Migrant employees should be encouraged to return to the Valley on guarantee of their children being admitted to educational/training institutions and they and their families be provided full security.

Large industrial units like ITI/HMT should be revived and migrants can also be housed in secure zones in these campuses, and also given employment.

Migrants within the Jammu Region may also be provided relief on the same pattern as the Kashmiri Migrants.

14. Issues relating to Refugees of 1947, 1965 and 1971 and other Migrants within Jammu Region

The recommendations of the Wadhwa Committee Report be implemented and an Empowered Group of Senior officers of Government of India/State Government be appointed to monitor the implementation of these recommendations and other measures as may be sanctioned by the State Government.

State Government may consider providing relief to the Refugees from West Pakistan as permissible under the Constitution. Otherwise an alternative package providing cash relief as one-time settlement be considered.

State Government may provide a limited number of seats to the children of the refugees from West Pakistan in technical institutions and the Government of India may provide employment to them in Central Government offices located in Jammu and Kashmir to the extent of 2%.

Other refugees and border migrants displaced as a result of conflict at international border/LOC be given suitable compensation and proper steps taken for their rehabilitation. Similarly those who were displaced in 1999 (after Kargil conflict) should be properly settled.

15. Under representation of Jammu in Legislative Assembly

Since there is Constitutional constraint to make any changes till the year 2026, as a new Delimitation Commission can be set up only thereafter, the present position may continue.

16. Discrimination against Jammu

The recommendations made by Gajendragadkar Commission and Sikri Commission may be kept in view while making out policies.

Planned Expenditure in the Jammu and Kashmir Regions and District sectors does not indicate any discrimination and this situation be maintained. (See detailed reasons)

The daily wage rate in all areas should be on the basis of 'Equal Pay for Equal Work' and there shall not be any discrimination.

State Government should take steps to ensure that viable projects under IRDF or any other scheme are prepared for consideration.

A Dogri Channel may be set up on the lines of Kashir Channel of the Doordarshan.

For improvement in technical education, the NIT at Srinagar and Government Engineering College at Jammu be upgraded to I IT level. Similarly the Central Government may also establish an MM in the State.

Steps be taken to promote IT Industry in both Jammu and Kashmir regions to open up the employment opportunities for technically qualified youth.

The Finance Commission recently set up by the State Government will be an appropriate forum to address any left out grievances of any regions of the State. The Scope of Work given to the Finance Commission needs to be effectively taken up for finding permanent solution.

Although the recommendations of The Gajendragadkar

Commission, The Sikri Commission and The Wazir Commission have largely been implemented, the State Government may examine if any further action is required so as to remove any apprehension about discrimination against any part of the state as brought out by some of the members.

The State Government may also look into the statement that the Civil Secretariate and H.O.D. offices have a proportionately high number of non-gazetted employees from The Kashmir Valley and if so this may be corrected through appropriate measure.

17. Union Territory Status for Ladakh

It is not recommended that the unity and integrity of the State of Jammu and Kashmir be compromised and the Union Territory Status for Ladakh is not recommended.

The functioning of Ladakh Autonomous Hill Development Council has been very successful and it may continue its commendable work.

Regarding higher cost of construction in Ladakh, the State Government/Finance Commission should make appropriate budget allocation for this region.

A separate university for Ladakh can be considered to be set up.

18. Position of Chief Minister, Dy. Chief Minister and Ministers from Ladakh

No specific recommendation is made except that the elected government should ensure that adequate representation is given to all regions of the State at appropriate levels, and may also consider the question of appointment of Dy. CM. either from Jammu/Kashmir or Ladakh depending on the region to which the Chief Minister belongs.

19. Representation in the Supreme Court

The High Court of Jammu and Kashmir has benches in both Jammu and Srinagar and are functional round the year, it will be appropriate and advisable in view of the Special Status of the State That Judges to the Supreme Court are elevated from both Jammu and Srinagar.

20. Regional Councils

The State may set up a State Planning and Development Board, which will be advisory in nature and could consider formulation of schemes for the state sector, assign priority to such schemes and also monitor their effective implementation. The Board will have MLAs, experts, representatives of backward regions as members.

21. Local Self-Governance

All Panchayati Raj institutions should be strengthened and the 73rd and 74th Amendments to the Constitution of India should be considered by the State for adaptation or making a similar provision in the State Constitution.

For backward areas, better infrastructure, road network and health and educational institutions should be provided. A special plan for backward areas within the overall State/District plans should be considered.

22. Reservation in services/promotions/professional institutions.

The Jammu and Kashmir State Backward Classes Commission will be the appropriate forum to deal with the issues of reservation for backward communities and backward areas.

The issue of providing reservation to the residents of areas adjoining international border at the same level as LOC may be considered by the State Government.

23. Other Issues

Certain other issues not within the terms of reference of the Working Group V, which were raised by various members, have been listed which may be considered for appropriate action.

This is only a summary of the recommendations made by the Working Group and for full appreciation of the recommendations and the background in which they have been made, the main report may be referred to.

APPENDIX II

Report of the State Autonomy Committee

Jammu, April 1999

CHAPTER I

Introduction

Centre-State relations have remained on centre stage of Indian political scenario for quite a length of time, before 1950 when the present Republican Constitution was adopted and enacted in its entirety on 26-01-1950 and even thereafter. Right from 1919, the future of India was seen as a Federal State. In fact Simon Commission put it on record unambiguously:

"Apart together from any question of an ultimate Federal Union between the Indian States and British India, there are, we think very strong reasons for the reconstruction of the Indian Constitution on a Federal basis. It is only in a Federal structure that sufficient elasticity can be obtained for the Union of elements of diverse internal conditions and the communities at very different stage of development and culture."

The developments till enactment of Government of India Act, 1935 ultimately led to constitutional framework for future federal polity of the country. The build up of this federal polity, of necessity, could not follow the pattern of formation of Federation of American States, Australia or Canada but, even so, the federal polity envisaged for India was to consist of Indian Provinces and Indian States, as units. The Joint Parliamentary Committee on Indian Reforms recorded as under:

"Federations have commonly resulted from an agreement between

independent or at least autonomous governments surrendering a definite part of their sovereignty to a new Central Organism . . . we are faced with the necessity of creating autonomous units and combining them into a Federation by one and the same Act."

The Federation was to consist of all British Provinces, till then centrally administered both in legislative as well as executive wings, and the Indian states which were to accede in respect of some subjects for legislative purposes to Federal/Union Legislature and to the extent of the surrender of those subjects to accept executive functioning of the Centre as well. States had the option to join or not to join the Federation. The Act of 1935 provided the instrumentality for exercise of this choice by providing for an Instrument of Accession.

The sequence of events after enforcement of 1935 Act in April 1937, elections in British provinces and formation of governments by Indian Parties, World War 1939-45. India's insistence on independence, equally shrill cries for partition of India, non-exercise of option by Indian States to join the Constituent Assembly, continued refusal of the Muslim League to sit in the Constituent Assembly, quick developments leading to departure of Lord Wavell and incoming of Lord the, preponing of the date of independence from 1948 to 1947 for the country, ultimate passage of the Indian Independence Act, 1947 on 4th July, 1947, declaring 15th August, 1947 as "appointed day" when Dominions of India and Pakistan were to be formed—all these developments took place at breathtaking pace. The Indian States had even so the option to join one or the other Dominion, India or Pakistan.

Indian States, with the lapse of paramountcy on the "appointed day", i.e. 15th August, 1947 as sovereign entities could go the way they chose to exercise the option. Their joining had to be voluntary and at the time of joining they were under no obligation to accept any future Constitution except by voluntary acceptance or supplementary agreement. They had the right to accept or not to accept provisions of the Constitution that either Dominion would adopt for itself.

Partition in 1947 did effect a slight change in the perception about future Constitution that would be adopted for the country. From truly federal polity, it took a turn towards making this federal polity such that Centre retains some extraordinary powers too. This seemingly was to ensure a strong Centre. It was regarded to be an "imperative necessity." In fact, even the Second Report of the Union Powers Committee placed on record the following:

> *"Now the partition is a settled fact. We are unanimously of the view that it would be injurious to the interests of the country to provide for a weak Central authority which would be uncapable of ensuring peace, in coordinating vital matters of common concern and of speaking effectively for the whole country in the international sphere."*

Earlier perception was creation, in a way, of the mandate of Cabinet Mission Plan which had discarded partition but partition having been announced the earlier perception was held to be non-binding. Indian Federation in the new context was to have a strong Centre, of course, retaining all the necessary features of a federal polity.

This primarily was the kind of difference in treatment which became inevitable in regard to Indian Provinces. Indian States who had to be part of either of the Dominions by their own choice were on a different footing. They constituted the real units choosing to be part of a federal system in that the unit, upon exercise of voluntary choice in favour of either of the two Dominions, would accept federal authority in some fields of governance.

How other Indian States exercised this choice, how they participated in Constitution framing and in what form did they adopt it, is not our concern today. This shall be referred to wherever necessary in the pages to follow. But it is relevant to mention here that whereas other Princely States signed the Instrument of Accession to India and subsequently the instruments of merger, the accession of J&K State was limited only to the areas of Defence, External Affairs and Communication.

Uniquely, Jammu and Kashmir State is the only one to have negotiated the terms of its membership of the Union. Right till the Delhi Agreement of 1952, it did not accept any provisions of the Constitution of India other than those agreed to in the Instrument of Accession and retained its autonomy.

Autonomy has remained, since the days of accession, the heart-beat of the people of the State. Today we find that the State has lost all resemblance to autonomy. Its erosion is the primary cause for Kashmir discontent. Keeping this in view, Shri Narasimha Rao, 'the then Prime Minister of India announced in 1995 that the Union Government would be prepared to consider autonomy "short of independence" for Jammu and Kashmir. Welcoming this on behalf of Jammu and Kashmir National Conference, Dr. Farooq Abdullah asked the Union Government to issue an order under Article 370 to restore the state's autonomy in terms of the Delhi Agreement of 1952. When this did not happen, the National Conference boycotted the Parliamentary poll in 1996.

Mr. Deve Gowda as Prime Minister, offered Jammu and Kashmir "maximum autonomy" which perusaded Dr. Farooq Abdullah and his party National Conference to participate in the Assembly elections. The Party fought these elections on autonomy plank and was returned with a thumping majority. Following the resumption of office as Chief Minister. Dr. Farooq Abdullah with the approval of his Cabinet promptly constituted a Committee to examine and recommend measures for the restoration of autonomy. This was exactly in accordance with the mandate given to him by the people of the State as also the assurances held out by the Union Government.

CHAPTER II

Constitution of State Autonomy Committee

The State Government set-up a Committee to examine the question of restoration of autonomy to the State of Jammu and Kashmir vide Government Order No. 1164-GAD of 1996 Dated 29-11-1996 with the following composition:

(1) Dr. Karan Singh	Chairman
(2) Sh. Mohi-ud-Din Shah	Member
(3) Sh. Abdul Ahad Vakil	-do-
(4) Sh. Abdul Rahim Rather	-do-
(5) Sh. Piyaray Lal Handoo	-do-
(6) Sh. Bodh Raj Bali	-do-
(7) Molvi Iftikhar Hussain Ansari	-do-
(8) Kushok Thiksay	-do-
(9) Shri Teja Singh	-do-

By a subsequent Government Order No. 263-GAD of 1997

dated 21-02-1997, it was ordered that Shri Teja Singh shall be Member/Convernor of the above committee. Dr. Karan Singh resigned as Chairman on July 31, 1997 and vide Government Order No. 1303-GAD of 1997 dated 19-08-1997, Shri Ghulam Mohi-ud-Din Shah, PWD Minister. J&K Government was appointed as Chairman w.e.f. the date Dr. Karan Singh resigned. By another Government Ordcr No. 1413 of 1997 dated 05-09-1997 Mirza Abdul Rashid, former Speaker of J&K Legislative Assembly was nominated as member of the Committee.

Terms of Reference

The terms of reference of the Committee are as follows:

- (i) To examine and recommend measures for the restoration of autonomy to the State of Jammu and Kashmir consistent with the Instrument of Accession, the Constitution Application Order, 1950 and the Delhi Agreement of 1952.
- (ii) To examine and recommend safeguards that be regarded necessary for incorporation in the Union/State Constitution to ensure that the Constitutional arrangement that is finally evolved in pursuance of the recommendations of this Committee is inviolable.
- (iii) To also examine and recommend measures to ensure a harmonious relationship for the future between the State and the Union.

Four features of these terms of reference deserve particularly to be noted. First, implicit in the exercise is acknowledgement of the fact that the State's autonomy, guaranteed by Article 370 of the Constitution of India, was eroded in breach of its provisions, of those of the Instrument of Accession to which Article 370 gave full recognition of the Constitution (Application to Jammu and Kashmir) Order, made under Article 370, by the President of India on January 26, 1950, extending to the State specified provisions of the Constitution of India which had come into force on the same day, and of the Delhi Agreement of July, 1952. It is this erosion which has necessitated "the restoration of autonomy" to the State. As we shall point out, till now 94 of the 97 entries in the Union

List have been applied to the State, 26 entries in the Concurrent List have also been applied, 6 more with modifications. Even in 1954 the Concurrent List did not apply at all. The process did not cease. It was accelerated. The Constitutional relationship that was thus established was contrary to and went far beyond the Delhi Agreement.

Secondly, if this exercise is to be worthwhile, it would be necessary to devise appropriate effective constitutional safeguards against any repetition of that unfortunate phase of erosion in future. Any Constitutional arrangement that is evolved to this end must have finality and be "inviolable".

Thirdly, the exercise has a definite limit and a clear objective. It seeks in effect the full enforcement of the historic Delhi Agreement concluded between the Prime Minister of India, Pt. Jawaharlal Nehru, and the Prime Minister (as he was then called) of the State, Sheikh Mohammed Abdullah, the two foremost architects of the State's accession to the Union of India. Implementing their mutual pledges in that Agreement is, at once, the bottom line and the high ideal we have placed before ourselves.

Lastly, but not least, it follows necessarily from the foregoing that efforts in these directions will "ensure a harmonious relationship for the future between the State and the Union", of which it is a member, by redressing the grievances of the past and the strains they so needlessly created in the relationship. It will strengthen, not weaken, the relationship. Far from being inconsistent with each other, the autonomy of the State will strengthen the ties that bind it to the Union and, with them, the unity of India.

Our nation is rich in its diversities and we are justly proud of it as we are of the bonds that weld us into one nation. The Constitution of India reflects both the unity and the diversities. Besides the fundamental rights which protect all citizens, there are fundamental rights for the protection specifically of the "language, script or culture" of any section of the citizens (Article 29) and of the right of minorities as such "based on religion or language" to establish or administer educational institutions of their choice (Article 30).

There is a whole part (XVI) containing provisions for reservation of seats for Scheduled Castes, Scheduled Tribes and

Anglo-Indians in the Lok Sabha and in public services as well as provisions for the protection of Scheduled Tribes.

Regional diversities are reflected in special provisions with respect to the States of Nagaland {Article 371-A), Sikkim (Article 371-F), Mizoram (Article 371-G) and Arunachal Pradesh (Article 371-H) which confer "special status" on these states. There are other "special provisions" with respect to some states concerning certain areas within those states, for example. Article 371 relating to the States of Maharashtra and Gujarat. In respect of Nagaland and Mizoram, Parliament is barred not only from altering religious or social practices but also "customary law and procedure", "administration of civil and criminal justice" according to such law and ownership and transfer of land.

The State of Jammu and Kashmir is, thus, not the only one to enjoy "a special status" under Article 370. In turn, the State is a mosaic of diversities in its regions, groups and communities. Protection of minorities and regional interests is a prime duty. Mindful of this fact, the Government of the State appointed, simultaneously with this Committee, a Committee on Regional Autonomy.

The Report we submit to the Government, is addressed to the people of the State and, also, to the country. We have been fully alive to the hopes and expectations aroused by our work as well as the misgivings expressed in some quarters. The State has passed through a grim ordeal in the last decade. To any who honestly felt alienated or frustrated, for whatever reason, our Report will provide assurance that the democratic framework does provide avenues of redress.

We have heard a large cross-section of people within and outside the State and received memoranda from many persons and also held discussions with leaders of political parties, eminent jurists, journalists and members of Parliament from Jammu and Kashmir in November 1997. Their names are listed in Appendix I and II respectively. To all of them we express our deep gratitude. We have consulted pertinent literature on the State's constitutional history since independence in order to understand why and how things went wrong after the initial years of promise. It is our firm belief that that happy phase can yet be recalled and repeated if the mistakes and misjudgments that led to its termination are corrected. Our faith in the future of the State as a willing, content and enthusiastic member of the Union of India remains undiminished. We are beset with problems, misunderstandings and obstacles. We shall overcome them. All must cooperate earnestly in that endeavour.

CHAPTER III

Pre-Independence Scenario

Situation as it obtained on 14th and 15th August, 1947 in the State of Jammu and Kashmir was that a movement had been launched by the premier political party (National Conference) in May, 1946 and the slogan of "Quit Kashmir" had been echoed all over India. This slogan asked for transfer of power from the Ruler to the people of Jammu and Kashmir. The movement claimed the right of the people to end discontent and dissatisfaction created by enforcement of the undemocratic J&K Constitution Act of 1939 promulgated by the Maharaja of Jammu and Kashmir on September 7, 1939. It had gone underground after the desperate Ruler chose to ruthlessly suppress it. As in the past, Jenab Sheikh Mohammad Abdullah and other leaders of this movement were imprisoned. On the dawn of independence Jenab Sheikh Sahib was lodged in the State Army Cantonment in Badami Bagh, Srinagar, serving the sentence imposed by trial judge for sedition, other leaders of the movement were either in exile or underground.

India became independent on August 15, 1947. Section 1 of the Indian Independence Act, 1947 said that as from that date, "two independent Dominions shall be set-up in India, to be known respectively as India and Pakistan". It proceeded to define their territories. But they were confined to the provinces under direct British rule. Section 7(1)(b) declared that the suzerainty of the British Crown over the Indian States lapsed and with it all the treaties and agreements between them and the Crown. Section 8(2) of the Act provided that until the Constituent Assemblies of both States framed their respective constitutions, each of them "shall be governed as nearly as may be in accordance with the Government of India Act. 1935". Section 9(1)(c) empowered the Governor-General to make changes in the Act in its application to the separate new States.

Accordingly, on August 14, 1947, the Governor General made

the India (Provisional Constitution) order adapting the Government of India Act, 1935 as the interim Constitution of India with the changes specified in the Act. Section 6 of the Act provided that "an Indian State shall be deemed to have acceded to the Dominion if the Governor General has signified his acceptance of an Instrument of Accession executed by the Ruler thereof. It proceeded to lay down the minimum essential contents of such an Instrument. Simply put three matters were to be specified in the Instrument of Accession in order to conform to Section 6. First, acceptance of the functions of the central authorities as laid down in the Act; namely, the Governor General, the Dominion Legislature, the Federal Court and any other Dominion authority established by or under the Act. Secondly, the Ruler had to undertake to give effect to the provisions of the Government of India Act, 1935 within his State "so far as they are applicable therein by virtue of the Instrument of Accession". Lastly, the Instrument had to "specify the matters" which the Ruler accepted as ones with respect to which the Dominion Legislature may make laws for the State and correspondingly, the executive authority of the Dominion in the State. In respect of all the three the Instrument could specify the limitations as well.

The Indian Independence Act of 1947 enacted by the British Parliament leading to formation of the Indian Dominion and the Dominion of Pakistan had of necessity to recognise that with the surrender of imperial power their paramountcy over Indian States would, in the process, also lapse and with that lapse Indian states' rulers could become sovereign unto themselves. India faced yet another difficult period of history. The sub-continent had as many as 554 states known as native Indian states and fear and apprehensions were lurking in all minds keen to have a united India as to how the native rulers would behave in the event of freedom. March to Independence saw such fears gradually removed. Quite in good time hundreds of these native states by covenants/agreements got merged with the Indian Union giving up their right to freedom or to separate constitutions. They agreed to what the constitution would give to them via the Constituent Assembly of the Union.

After the adoption of the programme of "New Kashmir" (Naya Kashmir) in September, 1944 and its presentation to the Ruler, yet another experiment was launched by him to ensure popular association with the administration. In pursuance of a notification issued on 2nd October, 1944 a nominee of the National Conference and another member of Praja Sabha were appointed as Ministers in the Cabinet but this experiment did not last long. The experiment failed when the National Conference nominee resigned. It sharpened the struggle for ultimate changes in Kashmir. By the time this farce of dyarchy ended with resignation of National Conference nominee from the Cabinet, the Cabinet Mission was stated to arrive in India to negotiate transfer of power and the future constitution for the country. The premier political party in the State, All J&K National Conference, recognised that paramountcy of the British would lapse and that time had come when on such lapse the peoples' right to exercise the sovereign right for governance must take precedence over everything else. The party demanded that the Treaty of Amritsar dated 16th March 1846 signed between Maharaja Gulab Singh and the then British Government in India which was in the nature of a sale deed and was thus an insult to the people of the State must go lock, stock and barrel. This became the theme. The "Quit Kashmir" movement was launched in early 1946 (April-May). A memorial was submitted to the Cabinet Mission claiming the right to have sovereignty restored to the people rather than the Ruler.

Chapter IV

Accession to India

The State of Jammu and Kashmir acceded to the Dominion of India on October 26, 1947 when its Ruler, Maharaja Hari Singh, signed an Instrument of Accession and the Governor General of India, Lord Mountbatten, accepted the Instrument. The texts of the letters exchanged between the Maharaja and Lord Mountbatten and the Instrument of Accession as well as the circumstances in which they were executed are set out in the Government of India's White Paper on Jammu and Kashmir (1948). The three documents, viz. the Maharaja's letter and the Governor General's reply accepting the Instrument of Accession and the Instrument of Accession are appended as Appendix III.

By the Instrument of Accession, the Maharaja of Jammu and Kashmir accepted three subjects as ones on which the Dominion Legislature "may make laws for the State". They were: Defence,

External Affairs and Communications. A schedule to the Instrument listed precisely 16 topics of legislation that fell under those three heads. There was another section (D) in the Schedule on matters "Ancillary". Four were listed—elections to the Dominion Legislature, offences against laws made under the above subjects, inquiries and statistics concerning them; and "jurisdiction and powers of all courts with respect to any of the aforesaid matters but except with the consent of the Ruler of the Acceding State, not so as to confer any jurisdiction or powers upon any courts other than courts ordinarily exercising jurisdiction in or in relation to that State."

By the Instrument, the Maharaja also accepted, as Section 6 of the Act required, the functions conferred on the Dominion authorities by the Act, namely, the Governor General, the Dominion Legislature and the Federal Court.

For the federal machinery to function properly any document of adherence executed, either before or after the establishment of the federation, must specify the subjects it yields to the federal union and the provisions of the Constitution which it accepts. The Government of India Act, 1935 provided the basics of a federation. It was readily available for adaptation by all concerned. The Constitution of India is a more elaborate document. Article 370 had perforce to empower the President of India to make orders separately in order to specify both the Union subjects and provisions concerning the federal structure. The State was careful to ensure right till the Delhi Agreement that it did not accept all the provisions and retained its own institutions and its autonomy. Significantly, Clause 5 of the Instrument provided against any variation of its terms without the Ruler's consent. Clause 7 read thus: "Nothing in this Instrument shall be deemed to commit me in any way to acceptance of any future Constitution of India or fetter my discretion to enter into arrangements with the Government of India under any such future Constitution". Clause 8 said: "Nothing in this Instrument affects the continuance of my Sovereignty in and over this State, or, save as provided by or under this Instrument, the exercise of any powers, authority and rights now enjoyed by me as Ruler of this State or the validity of any law at present in force in this State".

The State of Jammu and Kashmir was then governed by the Jammu and Kashmir Constitution Act, 1939. Justice Dr. A.S.

Anand, a distinguished Judge of the Supreme Court, now Chief Justice of India opined in his book. The Development of the Constitution of Jammu and Kashmir: "The Government of Jammu and Kashmir did not accept the Constitution of India as a Constitution for the State. Despite the accession, the State was still to be governed by the old Constitution Act, 1939. This was because the Government of India had given an undertaking that the people of Kashmir could frame their own Constitution. The Government of India could not force the State to accept the Constitution (of India), for that would violate the agreed terms of the association of Kashmir with India. The State had voluntarily surrendered three matters only and the Government of India could not enlarge the sphere of its jurisdiction at its own discretion."[1] (Universal Book Traders, Delhi, Third Edition, 1994, page 99)

The Maharaja made an order on October 30, 1947 appointing Sheikh Mohammed Abdullah as "the Head of the Administration with power to deal with the emergency'" and appointed a twenty-three member Emergency Council "pending the formation of the Interim Government". By a proclamation issued on March 5, 1948 the Maharaja decided "to replace the Emergency Administration by a popular Interim Government and to provide for its powers, duties and functions, pending the formation of a fully democratic Constitution".

Sheikh Mohammed Abdullah was appointed Prime Minister. The Council of Ministers was to function "on the principle of joint responsibility." It was enjoined to convene "a National Assembly based upon adult suffrage" to frame a Constitution. The Assembly was to submit the Constitution "through the Council of Ministers for my acceptance."

This was a reference to a Constitution for the State. Right from the beginning in 1948, there was no doubt in any quarter that, regardless of the arrangements in respect of other former Indian States, the State of Jammu and Kashmir would have its own Constitution as a member of the Indian Union. Uniquely, the State is the only one to have negotiated the terms of its membership of the Union. The negotiations were spread over five months.

Negotiations on the provisions in the proposed Constitution

1. Justice A.S. Anand, The Development of the Constitution of Jammu & Kashmir, 3rd Edition, 1994, p. 99

of India that would embody the terms of the State's membership of the Union began when a conference of the leaders of the National Conference and of the leaders at the Centre was held in Delhi on May 15 and 16, 1949. Pt. Jawahar Lal Nehru recorded the issues discussed in a letter to Sheikh Saheb on 18th May. The State was to have its own Constitution and *"it will be for the Constituent Assembly of the State, when convened, to determine in respect of what other subjects the state may accede."* On May 27, 1949, a member of its Drafting Committee, Sir N. Gopalaswamy Ayyangar moved an amendment to the Assembly's Rules empowering "the Ruler of Kashmir on the advice of his Prime Minister" to nominate the State's four representatives to the Constituent Assembly of India. The State's legislature, the Praja Sabha, had not met since April 1947 and was now "dead". The National Assembly of the State was yet to be elected. On June 16, 1949 Sheikh Mohammad Abdullah, Mirza Mohammed Afzal Beg, Maulana Mohammed Saeed Masoodi and Moti Ram Baigra took the pledge and signed the Register of Members of the Constituent Assembly of India.

It must be mentioned at the outset in all fairness that the texts of Sheikh Mohammed Abdullah's letters of October 12 and 15, 1949 are not available, whereas those of Mr. Ayyangar and Sardar Vallabhbhai Patel's letters to him and to each other. On October 12, Sheikh Saheb complained to Mr. Ayyangar, as he recalled in his letter of 17th October, that the draft Article 306-A (with modifications, the present Article 370) which he had given to Mr. M.A. Beg "failed to implement the pledges given to us" and was, therefore, unacceptable. Two meetings followed on October 15. After the first, Mr. Ayyangar wrote to Sardar Patel enclosing his draft of the Article. It did not provide a finality to further acquisition of power by the Centre by stipulating that the concurrence of the State Government to such acquisition shall be ratified by the Constituent Assembly.

Mr. Ayyangar presented another draft later on October 15, which drew a protest from Patel and rejection by Sheikh Saheb, both, on 16th October. Mr. Ayyangar prepared yet another draft in consultation with Kashmir's representatives. It was finalized on the afternoon of October 16, 1949. On the assurance that the agreed draft would be moved, Mr. Beg withdrew his own amendment. Sheikh Mohammad Abdullah recorded the agreement in another letter of 16th October and thanked Ayyangar for his pains.

On October 16, 1949 a "Final Draft" of Article 306-A was settled between Mr. N. Gopalaswamy Ayyangar, Mirza Mohammed Afzal Beg and Mr. M.A. Shahmiri. It read thus:

Final Draft of Article 306-A (Jammu & Kashmir) as Settled Between the Hon'ble Shri N. Gopalswamy Ayyangar on the one side and Messers Beg and Shahmiri on the other on October 16, 1949.

306-A (1) Notwithstanding anything contained in this Constitution,

(a) the provisions of Article 211-A of this Constitution shall not apply in relation to the State of Jammu and Kashmir;

(b) the power of Parliament to make laws for the State shall be limited to—

(i) those matters in the Union List and the Concurrent List which, in consultation with the Government of State, are declared by the President to correspond to matters specified in the Instrument of Accession governing the accession of the State to the Dominion of India as the matters with respect to which the Dominion Legislature may make laws for the State; and

(ii) such other matters in the said Lists as with the concurrence of the Government of the State, the President may by order specify;

Explanation:—For the purposes of this article, the Government of the State means the person for the time being recognized by the Union as the Maharaja of Jammu and Kashmir acting on the advice of the Council of Ministers appointed under the Maharaja's Proclamation dated the 5th March 1948.

(c) the provisions of Article 1 of this Constitution shall apply in relation to the State;

(d) such of the other provisions of this Constitution and subject to such exceptions and modifications shall apply in relation to the State as the President may by order specify:

Provided that no such order which relates to the matters

specified in the Instrument of Accession of the State aforesaid shall be issued except in consultation with the Government of State:

Provided further that no such order which relates to matters other than those referred to in the preceding proviso shall be issued except with the concurrence of that Government;

(2) If the concurrence of the Government of the State referred to in sub-clause (b)(ii) or in the second proviso of sub-clause (d) of clause (1) was given before the Constituent Assembly for the purpose of framing the Constitution of the State is convened, it shall be placed before such Assembly for such decision as it may take thereon;

(3) Notwithstanding anything in the preceding clauses of this article, the President may, by public notification, declare that this article shall cease to be operative or shall be operative only with such exceptions and modifications and from such date as he may specify:

Provided that the recommendation of the Constituent Assembly of the State shall be necessary before the President issues such a notification.

This draft was finally agreed on October 16, 1949. What happened next day, October 17, 1949 in the Constituent Assembly was recorded immediately thereafter that very day by Sheikh Saheb in a letter to Mr. Gopalaswamy Ayyangar.

"This morning when we expected the final draft, which had appeared in the List of Amendments circulated by the Secretary of the Constituent Assembly, to come up before the Assembly, you and Mualana (Azad) Sahib came to me and asked me if I could accept an important change in the Explanation to Sub-clause (b) of Clause (1) of the draft Article 306-A, as appearing in the List of Amendments. After careful consideration of the proposed amendment in the Explanation, my colleagues and I told you both in the lobby that it was not possible for us to accept this change in the final draft and you and Mauiana Sahib left us while we were still discussing the matter in the lobby amongst ourselves, the draft Article 306-A was moved by you in the Constituent Assembly, and, when part of your speech was over, we were told by someone that the draft Article had been taken up by the Assembly, and, therefore, we took our seats in the Assembly Hall. We could not conceive that any amendment in the final draft, as circulated in the List of Amendments, would be made by you without conveying your final decision in the matter to us, and so we took it for granted that the final draft Article 306-A was presented before the Assembly in the form in which it had our consent; and, therefore, when it was passed by the Assembly, we did not take part in the debate. While Maulana Sahib and you came to us to discuss the matter with us in the lobby. I clearly told you that in the event of any change in the finalized draft Article 306-A. We should be at liberty to move the amendment, of which notice had been given by Mr. Beg and his two other colleagues and which had been withdrawn on the express assurance given by you yesterday. In these circumstances, it was not possible for us to move any amendment and we did not get an occasion to express our views on the matter before the open House."

Sheikh Saheb threatened to resign from the Constituent Assembly. Mr. Ayyangar replied on October 18. He did not deny that the draft had been unilaterally changed. "It is true that after having unsuccessfully attempted, alongwith Maulana Azad, to persuade you to agree willingly to the substitution of the words 'for the time being in office' for the word 'appointed', I did move the article with that amendment after obtaining the permission of the President to do so. He argued that it was "a trivial change" in response to the desire expressed by a large number of the leading Members of the House. The Prime Minister Pt. Nehru was abroad then. Mr. Ayyangar himself recorded that "the words in the Explanation as agreed to between us are Council of Ministers appointed under the Maharaja's Proclamation dated March 5, 1948." The words appearing in the Article as passed yesterday are "the Council of Ministers for the time being in office under the Maharaja's Proclamation dated March 5, 1948." His plea that "the change of words does not constitute the slightest change in sense or substance" was wrong. Under the agreed Explanation. Sheikh Saheb's dismissal in 1953 would have been a Constitutional impossibility.

In his letter to the Prime Minister Pt. Jawaharlal Nehru on November 3, 1949 on his return from the United States of America. Sardar Patel also admitted that the draft "was modified to cover not merely the first Ministry so appointed but any subsequent Ministries which may be appointed under that proclamation."

The Constituent Assembly adopted the Constitution of India

on November 26, 1949. (C.A.D.: Vol. 12, p. 995). It repealed the Government of India Act, 1935. Article 394 provided that most of its provisions would come into force from January 26, 1950. On November 25, 1949 the Maharaja of Jammu and Kashmir made a proclamation declaring that "the Constitution of India shortly to be adopted by the Constituent Assembly of India shall in so far as it is applicable to the State of Jammu and Kashmir, govern the Constitutional relationship between this State and the contemplated Union of India. . ."[1] On January 26, 1950 the President of India made the first Constitution (Application to Jammu and Kashmir) Order, 1950[2] under Article 370 of the Constitution of India. It conformed strictly to the Instrument of Accession.

CHAPTER V

Article 370 of the Constitution of India

Article 370 of the Constitution reads thus:

370. Temporary Provisions with respect to the State of Jammu and Kashmir—(1) Notwithstanding anything in this Constitution—

(a) the provisions of Article 238 shall not apply in relation to the State of Jammu and Kashmir;

(b) the power of Parliament to make laws for the said State shall be limited to—

(i) those matters in the Union List and the Concurrent List which, in consultation with the Government of the State, are declared by the President to correspond to matters specified in the Instrument of Accession governing the accession of the State to the Dominion of India as the matters with respect to which the Dominion Legislature may make laws for that State;

(ii) Such other matters in the said Lists, as, with the concurrence of the Government of the State, the President may by order specify.

Explanation:—For the purposes of this article, the Government of the State means the person for the time being recognised by the

1. (White paper on Indian States; Government of India, Ministry of States, New Delhi, 1950, p. 371).
2. See Appendix IV.

President as the Maharaja of Jammu and Kashmir acting on the advice of the Council of Ministers for the time being in office under the Maharaja's Proclamation dated the fifth day of March, 1948;

(c) the provisions of Article 1 and of this article shall apply in relation to that State;

(d) Such of the other provisions of this Constitution shall apply in relation to that State subject to such exceptions and modifications as the President may by order specify:

Provided that no such order which relates to the matters specified in the Instrument of Accession of the State referred to in paragraph (i) of sub-clause (b) shall be issued except in consultation with the Government of the State:

Provided further that no such order which relates to matters other than those referred to in the last preceding proviso shall be issued except with the concurrence of that Government.

(2) If the concurrence of the Government of the State referred to in paragraph (ii) of sub-clause (b) of clause (1) or in the second proviso to sub-clause (d) of that clause be given before the Constituent Assembly for the purpose of framing the Constitution of the State is convened, it shall be placed before such Assembly for such decision as it may take thereon.

(3) Notwithstanding anything in the foregoing provisions of this article, the President may, by public notification, declare that this article shall cease to be operative or shall be operative only with such exceptions and modifications and from such date as he may specify:

Provided that the recommendation of the Constituent Assembly of the State referred to in clause (2) shall be necessary before the President issues such a notification.

A careful study of the text reveals six special provisions for Jammu and Kashmir. First, it exempted the State totally from the provisions of the Constitution of India providing for the governance of the states. It was allowed to have its own Constitution within the Indian Union.

Second, Parliament's legislative power over the State was restricted to three subjects—defence, external affairs and communications. The President could extend to it other provisions of the Constitution to provide a constitutional framework if they related to the matters specified in the Instrument of Accession. For all this, only "consultation" with the State Government was required since the State had already accepted them in 1947 by the Instrument of Accession.

Third, if other "constitutional" provisions and other Union powers are to be extended to the State of Jammu and Kashmir the prior "concurrence" of the State Government was required.

The fourth feature is that even that concurrence alone did not suffice. It had to be ratified by the State's Constituent Assembly. This is often overlooked. Article 370 (2) says clearly: "If the concurrence of the Government of the State ... be given before the Constituent Assembly for the purpose of framing the Constitution of the State is convened, it shall be placed before such Assembly for such decision as it may take thereon."

The fifth feature is that the State Government's authority to give the "concurrence" lasts only till the State's Constituent Assembly is "convened". It is an "interim" power. Once the Constituent Assembly met, the State Government cannot give its own "concurrence". Still less, after the Assembly met and dispersed. Moreover, the President cannot exercise his powers to extend the Indian Constitution to Jammu and Kashmir indefinitely. The power has to stop at the point the State's Constituent Assembly drafted the State's Constitution and decided finally what additional subjects to confer on the Union and what other provisions of the Constitution of India it should get extended to the State rather than having their counterparts embodied in the State Constitution itself. Once the State's Constituent Assembly has finalized the scheme and dispersed the President's extending powers ended completely.

The sixth special feature, the last step in the process, is that Article 370(3) empowers the President to make an order abrogating or amending it. But for this, also "the recommendation" of the State's Constituent Assembly "shall be necessary before the President issues such a notification".

Article 370 cannot be abrogated or amended by recourse to the amending provisions of the Constitution which apply to all the other states because Article 368 has a proviso which says that no constitutional amendment "shall have effect in relation to the State of Jammu and Kashmir" unless applied by order of the President under Article 370. That requires first the concurrence of the State government and subsequent ratification by its Constituent Assembly.

Article 1(1) of the Constitution of India says that India shall be a Union of States. Sub-clause (2) adds that the states shall be specified in the First Schedule, this schedule mentions the State of Jammu and Kashmir. But, it is extended to the State only through Article 370(1)(c) which says: "The provisions of Article 1 and of this Article shall apply in relation to that State." This is not without legal significance and consequence. Mr. G.L. Nanda was, therefore, right in pointing out, as Union Home Minister, on 4th December, 1964 in the Lok Sabha, that it would be "totally wrong to assume that with the repeal of the Article all Constitutional provisions would automatically apply to Kashmir". Mr. S.B. Chavan made similar comments on March 1, 1993.

Article 370 was authoritatively explained by its mover in the Constituent Assembly. Mr. N. Gopalaswamy Ayyangar, contemporaneously and in 1952 by the President of the Assembly who became the first President of India, Dr. Rajendra Prasad.

Mr. Ayyangar said in the Constituent Assembly on October 17, 1949, "We have also agreed that the will of the people through the instrument of the Constituent Assembly will determine the Constitution of the State as well as the sphere of Union jurisdiction over the State ... You will remember that several of these clauses provide for the concurrence of the Government of Jammu and Kashmir State. Now, these relate particularly to matters which are not mentioned in the Instrument of Accession, and it is one of our commitments to the people and Government of Kashmir *that no such additions should he made except with the consent of the Constituent Assembly which may he called in the State for the purpose of framing its Constitution. In other words, what we are committed to is that these additions are matters for the determination of the Constituent Assembly of the State."*

Mr. Ayyangar explained that, "the provision is made that when the Constituent Assembly of the State has met and taken its decision both on the Constitution for the State and on the range of federal jurisdiction over the State, the President may on the recommendation of that Constituent Assembly issue an order that this Article 306A shall either cease to be operative or shall be operative, only subject to such exceptions and modifications as may be specified by him. But before he issued any order of that kind the recommendation of the Constituent Assembly will be a condition precedent.

This unique process of Presidential orders altering Constitutional provisions by an executive order ends with the final decision of the State's Constituent Assembly. "When it has come to a decision on the different matters, it will make a recommendation to the President who will either abrogate Article 306A or direct that it shall apply with such modifications and exceptions as the Constituent Assembly may recommend." Mr. Ayyangar repeatedly said that the Government's concurrence alone will not do. "That concurrence should be placed before the Constituent Assembly when it meets and the Constituent Assembly may take whatever decisions it likes on those matters."[1]

The White paper on Indian States made an important exposition of the Constitutional changes in para 221 at page 113 in chapter XI entitled, "Indian States under the New Constitution". Referring to Article 370 it said, "Steps will be taken for the purpose of convenient a Constituent Assembly which will go into these matters in detail and when it comes to a decision on them, it will make a recommendation to the President who will either abrogate Article 370 or direct that it shall apply with such modifications and exceptions as he may specify." Thus, the State's Constituent Assembly's decision was to mark a finality to the exercise of the President's powers under Article 370.

On July 29, 1952 Sheikh Saheb wrote to Pt. Nehru to inform him that the Constituent Assembly proposed to elect the State's Head of the State on August 16, 1952 and he wished that the necessary Order under Article 370 should be issued by the President in time to make it possible. Pt. Nehru replied immediately that very day. His letter of July 29, 1952 is very instructive. It is reproduced below:

New Delhi
July 29, 1952

My dear Shaikh Saheb,

I have just received your letter of the 29th July about the Head of the State. I do not see how we can go through all the various processes about this matter before the 16th August. It is not a perfectly clear matter from the legal point of view how far the President can issue notifications under Article 370 several times. In any event, it would be desirable to include in one notification such present changes that we have decided

1. C.A.D., Vol. 8, pp. 424-427.

to make. To have repeated notifications following one another in fairly quick succession would be odd, apart from the possible difficulty about their legality. We are having this matter examined.

There is also the question of how the present Maharaja should be dealt with. The obviously easy and decorous course is for him to abdicate. I hope he will do so. If not, then it may become necessary for the President to take some steps. All this has to be thought out.

In this matter you will appreciate that we have to proceed with the concurrence of the President. The final decision, no doubt, is that of the Government. But we cannot hustle the President.

I am sending your letter to Dr. Katju and Gopalaswami Ayyangar.

Yours sincerely,
Jawaharlal Nehru

Evidently, the President, Dr. Rajendra Prasad, one of the leaders of the Patna Bar, had expressed his doubts about the legality of successive orders under Article 370. This impression, which Pt. Nehru's letter conveys, is fully borne out by Dr. Prasad's note to Pt. Nehru sent under a covering letter dated September 6, 1952. It was first published only in 1991.[1] In view of its high relevance we reproduce this authoritative document in full as Appendix VIII.

The President pointed out the uniqueness as well as the incongruity of amending a Constitution by mere executive order. *"Nowhere else, as far as I can see is there any provision authorizing the executive government to make amendments in the Constitution......"* The crucial issue was whether the President's power to make such orders under Article 370 "is exercisable from time to time or is exhausted by a single exercise thereof. *Judging by the language employed and by the very exceptional nature of the power conferred, I have little doubt myself that the intention is that the power is to be exercised only once, for then alone would it be possible to determine with precision which particular provisions should be excepted and which modified. The fact that the President is also required to specify the date from* which the notification is to take effect also lends to confirm this view."

1. Dr. Rajendra Prasad: Correspondence and Select Documents Edited by Valmiki Choudhary, Allied Publishers Ltd., New Delhi, Volume 15, pp. 104-08.

Precisely for this reason, the marginal note to Article 370 described its nature as "Temporary provisions with respect to the State of Jammu and Kashmir". They were temporary in point of time and not as a half way house to the State losing its special status, eventually. Elaborating on his reasoning the President concluded:

> "The correct view appears to be that recourse is to be had to this clause [(cl. 3) of Article 370] only when the Constituent Assembly of the State (sic. he meant clearly the Constitution) has been fully framed".

This interpretation accords with the terms of the provision, Article 370, with its author Mr. N. Gopalaswamy Ayyangar to exposition in the Constituent Assembly, with Prime Minister Jawaharlal Nehru's letter of July 29, 1952 and his other pronouncements, with Sheikh Mohammad Abdullah's understanding of Article 370, and, induced, with the entire process before and after the adoption of Article 370. On the other hand, not one contemporaneous document contradicts thus interpretation or supports the unconstitutional practice that later came into vogue. Pt. Nehru's letter to Sheikh Saheb on August 1, 1952 mentioned the aspect of propriety besides legality. "As I have written to you, there is doubt here as to whether we can issue a succession of President orders dealing with these questions piecemeal. Apart from the legality there is also the question of propriety"

Sheikh Saheb told the State's Constituent Assembly on August 11, 1952 that "the fact that Article 370 has been mentioned as temporary provision in the Constitution does not mean that it is capable of being abrogated, modified or replaced unilaterally. In actual fact, the temporary nature of this Article arises merely from the fact that *the power to finalise the Constitutional relationship between the State and the Union has been specifically rested in the Jammu and Kashmir Constituent Assembly.* This power ceases to be one of imparting finality if, even after the Assembly's dispersal, modifications to the Constitution and amassment of power by the Centre can take place with the concurrence of another executive body of the State Government. Later, orders under Article 370 were passed even with the concurrence of the Governor alone, who is removable from office by the Centre at any moment. He, thus, accorded "concurrence" to the centre at its bidding as, indeed, did some Chief Ministers of the State.

Sheikh Saheb continued: *"It follows that whatever modifications, amendments or exceptions that may become necessary either to Article 370, or any other Article in the Constitution of India in their application to the Jammu and Kashmir State, are subject to the decisions* of this sovereign body". Obviously, once this body disperses after completion of its task, no amendments to the Constitution of India could be made in their application to the State for the simple reason that the sovereign and appointed ratifying body no longer existed. Any other interpretation would reduce the terms of Article 370 to a naught and the entire exercise to a farce by making permanent what was meant to be a transitory arrangement till the Constituent Assembly of Jammu and Kashmir finalised (a) The State's Constitution, and (b) its corresponding recommendations to the President, as envisaged by Article 370.

Sheikh Saheb warned: "I would like to make it clear that any suggestions of altering arbitrarily this basis of our relationship with India would not only constitute breach of the spirit and letter of the Constitution, but it may invite serious consequences for a harmonious association of our State with India."

At its fourth session on August 20, 1952 the State's Constituent Assembly passed a detailed Resolution in implementation of its Resolution of June 10, 1952 on the Head of the State.

The President of India persisted with his objections till as late as November 7, 1952 insisting that the Constituent Assembly "should come to a decision on all matters relating to the State's Constitution...."[1] The Prime Minister of India was in bind. He had agreed with the President's views on the legality but termination of the royal dynasty was also part of the Delhi Agreement. He was under pressure from Sheikh Saheb and his colleagues. Pt. Nehru, therefore, wrote to the President on the same day, November 7, 1952: "I can only repeal what I have said above that we have considered every aspect of this question and come to certain conclusions which have to be given effect to now. We cannot reopen six month's discussions".

1. V. Choudhary; Vol. 20, p. 395, footnote 3.

Accordingly, on November 15, 1952 Constitution Order No. 44 was made by the President under Article 370: "In exercise of the powers conferred by this article the President, on the recommendation of the Constituent Assembly of the State of Jammu and Kashmir, declared that, as from the 17th day of November, 1952 the said Article 370 shall be operative with the modification that for the explanation in clause (I) thereof, the following explanation is substituted namely:

"*Explanation*—For the purposes of this article, the Government of the state means the person for the time being recognized by the President on the recommendation of the Legislative Assembly of the State as the Sadar-i-Riyasat of Jammu and Kashmir, acting on the advice of the council of Ministers of the state for the time being in office."[1]

CHAPTER VI

Convening of the J&K Constituent Assembly

After adoption of the Constitution of India and its application to the State of Jammu and Kashmir pursuant to proclamation dated 25th November, 1949 and enforcement of the Constitution on 26th of January, 1950 the constitutional relationship of the state with the Union of India was shaped by the Constitution (Application to Jammu and Kashmir) Order of 1950. This order specified matters corresponding to those in respect of which the State had acceded to the Indian Union according to the terms of the Instrument of Accession. These are given in the 1st Schedule to the aforesaid Order.

This Order further mentioned that in addition to the provisions of Article 1 and Article 370 of the Constitution the only other provisions of the Constitution shall apply in relation to the state of Jammu and Kashmir shall be those specified in the Second Schedule to this Order and shall so apply subject to the exceptions and modifications specified in the Second Schedule.

The jurisdiction of the Union Parliament to legislate with respect to our State was thus clearly defined consistently with the position that emerged as a result of having ceded the powers pursuant to Instrument of Accession. The rest of it was left for the

1. Ministry of Law Order No. C.O. 44, dated the 15th November, 1952.

State to take care of in its own Constitution.

While this was so, the need for a constitution for the State of Jammu and Kashmir was also very intensely fell not only for the reason of defining the state's legislative power but also for other reasons. Total uncertainty on the political horizon was eating into the vitals of the social fabric. The future of the ruling dynasty also required to be settled. Rightly had the Article 170 of Constitution of India consistent with the National Conference stand throughout in respect of the right of the Jammu and Kashmir State to frame its own constitution envisaged a Constituent Assembly. Kashmir has its own history of freedom movement and as we have seen above, "New Kashmir" programme had envisaged a National Assembly for the State of Jammu and Kashmir and attachment of the people with the perception was so well recognised that even in the declaration of 5th March 1948, the Maharaja of Jammu and Kashmir had proclaimed as under:

> "I have already appointed the popular leader of my people Sheikh Mohamad Abdullah as the Head of the Emergency Administration.
>
> It is now my desire to replace the emergency administration by a popular interim Government and to provide for its powers, duties and functions, pending the formation of a fully democratic constitution.
>
> My council of Ministers shall take appropriate steps, as soon as restoration of normal conditions has been completed, to convene a National Assembly based upon adult suffrage, having due regard to the principle that the number of representatives from each voting area should, as for as practicable, be proportionate to the population of the area.
>
> The constitution to be framed by the National Assembly shall provide adequate safeguards for the minorities and contain appropriate provisions guaranteeing freedom of conscience, freedom of speech and freedom of assembly".

Vuvraj Karan Singh functioning as Regent, therefore, issued a proclamation of 20th April, 1951 setting the ball rolling for the convening of the Constituent Assembly for the state of Jammu and Kashmir to decide the future Constitution of the State. The

Proclamation directed that the Constituent Assembly consisting of representatives of people elected on the basis of adult franchise shall be constituted for the purpose.

Elections were thus held in terms of the Proclamation, hopes rose high, Constituent Assembly met on 31st October, 1951.

In his inaugural speech in the State Constituent Assembly on 5th November, 1951 Jenab Sheikh Mohammad Abdullah, the then Prime Minister of Jammu and Kashmir State, echoing the aspirations of the people, made the following observations:

> "We must remember that our struggle for power has now reached its successful climax in the convening of this Constituent Assembly. It is for you to translate the vision of New Kashmir into reality and I would remind you of its opening words which will inspire our labours.
>
> 'We the people of Jammu, Kashmir, Ladakh and Frontier regions, including Poonch and Chenani illaqas commonly known as Jammu and Kashmir State in order to perfect our union in the fullest equality and self-determination, to raise ourselves and our children for ever from the abyss of oppression and poverty, degradation and suppression, from medieval darkness and ignorance into the sunlit valleys of plenty, ruled by freedom, science and honest toil, in worthy participation of the historic resurgence of the peoples of the East, and the working masses of the world, and in determination to make this our country a dazzling gem of the snowy bosom of Asia, do propose and propound the following Constitution of our State.'
>
> You are the sovereign authority in this State of Jammu and Kashmir; what you decide has the irrevocable force of law. The basic democratic principle of sovereignty of the nation, embodied ably in the American and French constitutions is once again given the shape in our midst. I shall quote the. famous words of Article 3 of the French Constitution of 1791.
>
> 'The source of all sovereignty resides fundamentally in the nation.... Sovereignty is one and indivisible, inalienable and imprescriptible. It belongs to the nation."
>
> We should be clear about the responsibilities that this power invests us with. In front of us lie decisions of the highest

national importance which we shall be called upon to take upon the correctness of our decisions depends not only the happiness of our land and people now, but the fate as well of generations to come."[1]

He set the following four tasks before the Constituent Assembly for deliberation:

(i) Devising Constitution for the future governance of the country which he called very difficult and a detailed one.

(ii) The future of the royal dynasty: The decision he said had to be taken with urgency and wisdom since on that decision depended the future form and the character of the State.

(iii) The third major issue which awaited deliberations of members of the Constituent Assembly arose out of the Land Reforms which the Government carried out with vigour and determination. A decision had also to be given by the members on the landowners' demand for compensation.

(iv) Fourth and what he called the final matter was to be reasoned conclusion of the Constituent Assembly regarding accession after full consideration of the three alternatives he would state later in the Assembly.

On each of these tasks he set the parameters in the inaugural speech itself.

He indicated that the future political set up had to be based on the highest principles of the democratic constitutions of the world and therefore the Assembly has to base its work on principles of equality, liberty, social justice, these being regarded as integral features of progressive constitutions. Rule of Law as in the rest of democratic would had to be the cornerstone of the political mechanism for governance of the State. Equality before law and independence of judiciary were vital to the whole fabric. Besides, freedom of the individual in the matter of speech, movement and association should be guaranteed. "Freedom of the press and opinion would also be features of our constitution", he

1. For full text of Sheikh Saheb's speech, see Appendix V.

said. Basis was provided in the outline embodied in "New Kashmir" programme. He described democracy as an "apparatus of social organisation wherein people govern through their own chosen representatives and are themselves guaranteed political and civil liberties".

In this regard we may place on record the following in relation to the then constitutional ties between the State and the Union of India:

> "The Constitution of India has provided for a federal union and in the distribution of sovereign powers has treated us differently from other constitutional units. With the exception of the items grouped under Defence, Foreign Affairs and Communications in the Instrument of Accession, we have complete freedom to frame our Constitution in the manner we like. In order to live and prosper as good partners in a common endeavour for the advancement of our peoples, I would advise that, while safeguarding our autonomy to the fullest extent so as to enable us to have the liberty to build our country according to the best traditions and genius of our people, we may also by suitable constitutional arrangements with the Union establish our right to seek and compel federal cooperation and assistance in this great task, as well as offer our fullest cooperation and assistance to the Union".

After describing the essential background that required to be taken into consideration in order to facilitate taking of final decision on the issues referred to above. Sheikh Saheb reminded the Hon'ble members of what he had said in the course of his trial for sedition at Badamibagh cantonment in the following words:

> 'The future constitutional set-up in the State of Jammu and Kashmir cannot derive authority from the old source of relationship, which was expiring and was bound to end soon. The set-up could only rest on the active will of the people of the state, conferring on the head of the State the title and authority drawn from the true and abiding source of sovereignty that is the people.'

From the above description of the task before the Constituent-

Assembly it is abundantly clear that Sheikh Saheb envisaged State Union relationship as "one of partners in common endeavour for the advancement of the people" and therefore, regarded "safeguarding of our autonomy to the fullest extent" and suitable "constitutional arrangement with the Union" as two cornerstones to ensure fullest cooperation and assistance between partners.

CHAPTER VII

Delhi Agreement of July, 1952

The Constituent Assembly, convened on 31st October, 1951, thus was not only to frame the Constitution for the State but was to give certain more important decisions regarding the future relationship of the State with the Union. It started its work in the right earnest and as days passed by, need for a decision on certain important matters relating to framing of the Constitution and any further application of the Union Constitution to the State was felt. Besides, questions arising out of the need to settle the future of the ruling dynasty and of arriving at a concrete solution about the fundamentals of the Constitution of the State as an integral part of India had also to be considered.

1952 proved a very important year in the State's constitutional evolution. It witnessed the conclusion of the historic Agreement between Pt. Jawahar Lal Nehru and Sheikh Saheb which was announced at a press conference in Delhi on July 24, 1952. It culminated in the President's second Order under Article 370 on November 15, 1952 but the first made on the recommendation of the Constituent Assembly of Jammu and Kashmir. Its constitutional significance emerges clearly if its background is borne in mind.

The National Conference led by Sheikh Saheb was pledged to radical programme covering a wide range of subjects such as land reforms. It included termination of hereditary rulership in the State. By 1952 it had ended in the other former princely States. Maharaja Hari Singh had virtually abdicated as ruler in favour of his son Yuvraj Karan Singh although the proclamation of June 9, 1949 merely said that since he was leaving the State for reasons of health his powers and functions shall he "exercisable" by the Yuvraj, thus making him Regent. Sheikh Saheb mentioned in his address to the Assembly that "another issue of vital import to the nation involves the future of the Royal Dynasty."

Events picked up speed in June. On June 10, 1952 the Basic Principles Committee submitted its Report to the State's Constituent Assembly. It provided *inter alia* that the "institution of hereditary Rulership shall be terminated" and that "the office of the Head of the State shall be elective." The Constituent Assembly accepted the Report on June 12, 1952.

It is against this background that the Delhi agreement was concluded after prolonged discussions; first, from June 14 to 20, 1952 and, next, from July 20 to 24, 1952.[1] Its terms were announced by Pt. Jawahar Lal Nehru in Lok Sabha on July 24, 1952[2] and in the Rajya Sabha on August 5, 1952.[3]

The terms of the agreement were explained to the Constituent Assembly of Jammu and Kashmir by the State's Prime Minister, Sheikh Mohammed Abdullah on August 11, 1952.[4]

Both leaders provided the background and highlighted the significance of the agreement. Pt. Nehru told the Lok Sabha:

> "The position since the Constitution was framed is thus contained in the Article 370 and in the President's Order following it. Article 370 was obviously of a transitional nature, and it allowed the President to make any additions to it, any variations to it, later on, the object being that if any change or addition was required, we need not have to go through the cumbrous process of amending our Constitution, but the President was given the authority to amend it in the sense of adding a subject, part of a subject, whatever, *it was to the other subjects, in regard to Kashmir. But in Article 370 the old principle was repeated and emphasized that all these changes or any change, required the approval of the Constituent Assembly of the Jammu and Kashmir State.*
>
> When this was put down in our Constitution, there was

1. S. Gopal (Editor), Selected works of Jawahar Lal Nehru, Vol. 19, p. 211.
2. Parliamentary Debates, Lok Sabha, Official Report Part II, Vol. III, No. 15, Cols. 4501-4521.
3. Rajya Sabha Debates, Vol. 1, Nos. 24-31 (July 28–August 5, 1952): Cols. 2970-2995.
4. For full text of Sheikh Saheb's speech see Appendix VI.

no Constituent Assembly of Jammu and Kashmir State, but we envisaged it. We had envisaged it for a long time. *And if the Constituent Assembly was not there, then it required the consent of the Jammu and Kashmir Government. So that was the position.*"[1]

The implication is plain. Additional subjects could be acquired by the Centre only with the approval of the State's Constituent Assembly.

Briefly the Delhi Agreement covered ten points. It was agreed that residuary powers would continue to vest in the State as provided in Article 370; within the ambit of Indian citizenship, the State legislature would have the power to regulate the rights and privileges of permanent residents or "State Subjects" as defined in a 1927 State Order, the Fundamental Rights chapter of the Indian Constitution be applied to the State with modifications and exceptions such as enabling transfer of land to the tiller without payment of compensation; the jurisdiction of the Supreme Court would extend to the State; the State flag would not be a rival to the national tricolour which would occupy a supremely distinctive place in the State, the power to grant reprieve and commute sentences would vest in the President of India; with the abolition of hereditary rulership, the Head of the State of Jammu and Kashmir shall be recognized by the President on the recommendations of the Legislative Assembly of the State; a financial arrangement between the State and the Union be evolved; with regard to emergency powers, Article 352 be modified to provide for its promulgation in case of external aggression but in case of internal disturbance only at the request of or with the concurrence of the State Government; and the Election Commission will conduct elections to Parliament and to the offices of President and Vice-President.

During the course of negotiations as had become necessary after the presentation of the interim report of the Basic Principles Committee in the circumstances referred to hereinbefore, certain agreements were arrived at, details of which were placed before the House by Jenab Sheikh Sahib on 11th of August, 1952. He said:

"The Government of India held the view that the fact that

1. For relevant extracts from Pt. Jawahar Lal Nehru's speech in the Lok Sabha on July 24, 1952 see Appendix VII.

J&K State was the Constituent Unit of the Union of India led inevitably to certain consequences in regard to certain matters, namely: (a) Residuary Powers, (b) Citizenship, (c) Fundamental Rights, (d) Supreme Court, (e) National Flag, (f) The President of India, (g) The Headship of the State, (h) Financial Integration, (i) Emergency Provisions, and (j) Conduct of Election to Houses of Parliament." Sheikh Saheb informed the House about its agreement arrived at in respect of each of them as follows:

Residuary Powers

It was agreed that while under the present Indian Constitution the Residuary Powers vested with the Centre in respect of all States other than Jammu and Kashmir, in the case of our State they vested in the State itself and should continue as such. In this regard, Sheikh Sahib observed as follows:

> "We have always held that the ultimate source of sovereignty resides in the people. *It is, therefore, from the people that all powers can flow. Under these circumstances, it is upto the people of Kashmir through this Assembly to transfer more powers for mutual advantage to the custody of the Union/Centre."*

Citizenship

In this connection, Sheikh Sahib informed the Assembly:

> "It was agreed that in accordance with Article 5 of the Indian Constitution persons who have their domicile in the Jammu and Kashmir State shall be the citizens of India. It was further agreed that the State Legislature shall have power to define and regulate the rights and privileges of the permanent residents of the State, more especially in regard to acquisition of immovable property, appointment to service and like matters. Till then the existing state law would apply."

> "It was also agreed that special provisions will be made in the laws governing citizenship to provide for the return of those permanent residents of J&K State who went to Pakistan in connection with the disturbances of 1947 or in fear of them as well as of those who have left for Pakistan earlier but could

not return. If they return, they should be entitled to the rights, privileges and obligations of citizenship".

Indicating the special reasons for the protection of State Subjects, he said as follows:

"Hon'ble Members are perhaps aware that in the late twenties people of J&K agitated for the protection of their bonafide rights against superior competing interests of the non-residents of the State. It was in response to this popular demand that the Government of the day promulgated a Notification in 1927 by which a strict definition of the term "State Subject" was provided. I am glad to say that Government of India appreciated the need for such a safeguard".

Fundamental Rights

In this regard, Sheikh Sahib observed as follows:

"It is obvious that while our Constitution is being framed the fundamental rights and duties of a citizen have necessarily got to be defined. It was agreed, however, that the Fundamental Rights, which are contained in the Constitution of India could not be conferred on the residents of J&K State in their entirety taking into account the economic, social and political character of our movement as enunciated in the New Kashmir Plan. The need for providing suitable modifications, amendments and exceptions as the case may be in the Fundamental Rights Chapter of the Indian Constitution in order to harmonize those provisions with the pattern of our principles was admitted".

The main point, Sheikh Sahib indicated, that remained to be determined was whether the Chapter of Fundamental Rights should form part of the Constitution of Jammu and Kashmir or that of the Union Constitution. On this aspect there was no agreement.

Supreme Court

It was agreed that Supreme Court should have original

jurisdiction in respect of disputes mentioned in Article 131 of the Constitution of India. It was further agreed that Supreme Court should have jurisdiction in regard to Fundamental Rights which are agreed to by the State. It was recommended on behalf of the Government of India that the Advisory Board in the State, designated as "His Highness's Board of Judicial Advisors" should be abolished and the jurisdiction exercised by it should be vested in the Supreme Court of India. The State Government felt that this would need a detailed examination and consequently it was agreed that it should have time to consider it further.

National Flag

For historical and other reasons connected with the freedom struggle in the State, the need for the continuance of the State flag was recognized. It was agreed that the Union Flag to which all owed allegiance as part of the Union will occupy supremely distinctive place in the State.

President of India

It was decided that powers to grant reprieve and commute death sentences, etc. should also belong to the President of the Union.

Headship of the State

The Government of India appreciated the principle proposed by the Basic Principles Committee as adopted by the Assembly in regard to the abolition of the hereditary rulership of the State. The following arrangement was mutually agreed upon in this regard:

(i) "The Head of the State shall be the person recognized by the President of the Union on the recommendation of the Legislature of the State.

(ii) He shall hold office during the pleasure of the President.

(iii) He may, by writing under his hand addressed to the President, resign his office.

(iv) Subject to the foregoing provisions the Head of the State shall hold office for a term of five years from the date he enters upon his office."

Financial Integration

It was recognized that while it would be necessary to evolve some sort of financial arrangement between the State and the Union, in view of the far-reaching consequences involved therein, it was agreed that a detailed examination of the subject would be necessary before doing that.

Emergency Powers

On behalf of the Government of India it was stated that Article 352 of the Constitution was necessary as it related to vital matters affecting the security of the State. The Government of India did run press for application of Article 356 or even Article 360. Item 1 in the Seventh Schedule relating to the defence of India applied and the Government of India would have full authority to take any steps in connection with defence, etc. The State representatives indicated that they were averse to internal disturbance being referred to in this connection as even petty internal disorder might be considered sufficient for application of Article 352. To meet the State's point of view it was therefore decided that Article 352 might be accepted with addition of the following words at the end of the first paragraph:

> "But in regard to internal disturbance at the request or with the concurrence of the Government of the State."

It was also agreed that the whole matter of application of Article 353, 354, 358 and 359 will be further examined.

Conduct of Elections to Houses of Parliament

Article 324 of the Indian Constitution was already applicable so far as it relates to elections to Parliament and in the offices of the President and the Vice-President of India.

This is how the leader of the Constituent Assembly Sheikh Mohammad Abdullah introduced the Delhi Agreement to the Assembly which was adopted unanimously on 19th August, 1952.

Consequent thereupon, the Drafting Committee of the State Constituent Assembly formed to work out and prepare proposals regarding termination of the hereditary rulership in the State presented its report.

Resolution for adoption by the House was introduced in the following words:

"Now, therefore, in pursuance of the resolution dated the 12th June, 1952, and having considered the report of the Drafting Committee the Assembly resolves:

1. (i) that the Head of the State shall be the person recognized by the President of the Union on the recommendations of the Legislative Assembly of the State;
   (ii) he shall hold office during the pleasure of the President;
   (iii) he may, by writing in his hand, addressed to the President, resign his office; and
   (iv) subject to the foregoing provisions, the Head of the State shall hold office for a term of five years from the date he enters upon his office:

   Provided that he shall, notwithstanding the expiration of his term, continue to hold the office until his successor enters upon his office;
2. that the recommendation of Legislative Assembly of the State in respect of the recognition of the Head of the State specified in sub-para (I) of paragraph 1, shall be made by election;
3. that the method of election to qualifications for and all other matters pertaining to the office of the Head of the State shall be prescribed, in the Constitution, and until these are so prescribed, shall be as set out in the rules contained in the schedule annexed to this resolution;
4. that the Head of the State shall be designated as the Sadar-i-Riyasat;
5. that the Sadar-i-Riyasat shall be entitled in such emoluments, allowances and privileges as may be prescribed in the Constitution and pending the framing of the Constitution, to such emoluments, allowances and privileges as may be decided by this Assembly by separate resolution;
6. that the Sadar-i-Riyasat shall exercise such powers and

perform such functions as may be prescribed in the Constitution to be framed by this Constituent Assembly, and until such Constitution is framed, he shall exercise such powers and perform such functions as have hitherto been exercised by His Highness under the Jammu and Kashmir Constitution Act, 1996, as amended by Act No. XVII of 2008;

7. That in the event of the occurrence of a casual vacancy in the office of the Sadar-i-Riyasat by reason of his death, resignation or otherwise, the powers and functions exercisable by the Sadar-i-Riyasat shall, until the assumption of office by the newly elected Sadar-i-Riyasat in accordance with the procedure laid down in this resolution, be exercised and performed by the person recommended by the State Government for recognition as officiating Sadar-i-Riyasat to the President of India; and
8. That this Assembly shall in due course provide a suitable remedy in respect of violation of the Constitution or gross misconduct by the person for the time being holding the office of the Sadar-i-Riyasal.

The Assembly further Resolves:

That the Prime Minister of Jammu and Kashmir State is authorized to communicate a copy of this resolution to "the Government of India for favour of appropriate action to enable its being given effect to."

This resolution was unanimously adopted after a formal amendment of changing the words, President of Union in sub-clause (1) of para 1 of the Resolution to President of India. Bill effecting the change based on this Resolution was introduced and passed on 10th November, 1952. This Act became Jammu and Kashmir Constitution Amendment Act of 2009.

CHAPTER VIII

Dismissal of Sheikh Mohammad Abdullah and its Aftermath

Then came the unfortunate and unconstitutional dismissal of Sheikh Mohammad Abdullah, the then duly elected Prime

Minister of the State on August 8, 1953 and his imprisonment simultaneously. This was without reference to the Legislature of the State that had exercised its right to elect its Sadar-i-Riyasal only a short time ago in pursuance of agreed proposition of Government of Jammu and Kashmir and Government of India. It is again grievously tragic in that the dismissal was not only of the Prime Minister without reference to the Legislature but also of the leader of the Constituent Assembly having sovereign task of framing the Constitution of the State as also of shaping the future relationship of Jammu and Kashmir State with the Indian Union. This happened at the hands of those in whom the people had reposed their trust and faith and while the Constitution-making process was still under way. This traumatic experience was the first major shock received by the people of the State after the new relationship. It justified the fears Sheikh Saheb had entertained on October 17, 1949 when an agreed draft was unilaterally altered by the leaders at the Centre. It also proved true, as later events showed, the warning he had delivered on August 11, 1952 against unilateral changes to Article 370. Sheikh Mohammad Abdullah was unconstitutionally dismissed from office as Prime Minister of the State of Jammu and Kashmir and put in prison along with his colleagues. A reign of terror was let loose. An era of corruption began. So did a phase of unconstitutionality.

The situation that followed this unfortunate event was neither in the national interest nor that of the State. During this period, besides what happened to the constitutional relationship between the Union and the State, India faced 1965 war followed by 1971 war and signed the Tashkent Agreement of 1966 and the Simla Agreement of 1972. Yet peace and development eluded it.

Highly controversial elections to the State legislative Assembly were held. Each election deepened the distress among the people and dislike for the managers of the election. Elections of 1957, the first held after the unfortunate incident of 1953, were internationally decried; 1962 elections were again on a similar pattern; rarely did these two so called general elections see anyone contesting or in any way being allowed to raise fundamental questions of why and how of developments of 1953. Elections of 1967 saw an additional change that had come about in Kashmir in that official National Conference had for the first time become a branch of the Indian National Congress in the State. In these elections, the people of the State lasted the first fruit and how bitter it was of the Congress entering into State politics as a substitute for the official National Conference. A dissident section of National Conference had by 1966 refused to continue to be part of the National Congress and constituted itself into Jammu and Kashmir National Conference over again. It sought to challenge the Indian National Congress in the battle for electoral confidence and having realized that the situation might become serious, a fraudulent drama of so-called scrutiny of papers was ensured on the table of the Returning Officer. Nomination papers of 22 contestants from as many Constituencies contesting against Indian National Congress candidates were rejected and Indian National Congress Candidates declared elected without having to ask for vote from these Constituencies. Curiously enough in Kashmir Valley in constituencies where contest was allowed. Congress cut a very sorry figure whether it was in the Parliamentary Constituency of Srinagar or Assembly Constituencies of Safakadal, Zadibal, Budgam, Banihal, Shopian and Tral. Of all the fifteen seats in Anantnag district only two seats were allowed to be contested not by National Conference but two young independent political activists and these were dismally lost by the Indian National Congress. This arbitrary and undemocratic manner of conduct of elections gravely shook the faith of the people.

The 1972 elections after Pakistan's debacle in Bangladesh had started assuming great importance because of widespread feeling that the erstwhile Jammu and Kashmir National Conference under the leadership of Jenab Sheikh Mohammad Abdullah was seriously considering that the public loss of faith in democratic process needs to be checked. But before this self-examination of various political options could be allowed to crystalize into a course of action decisively in favour of the people for regeneration of their faith, the Congress Government in the State inflicted a blow to this process of reappraisal by thoughtlessly enacting a law which banned participation in election by anyone who had at any time in the past been a member of a political party declined an unlawful association under the said law. In this way, they prevented the mass of the people from entering into the electoral process.

1972 election was over but it set in a realization that the

situation in Kashmir will not improve on any front whatsoever if Sheikh Saheb and all his loyal followers who spent most of the period from 1958 to 1975 in prisons did not become part of the national mainstream. Efforts to ensure this were set in motion. Negotiations continued for long. During the negotiations, an agonizing reappraisal of the sordid events of 1953 and onwards upto 1975—a long period of 22 years was undertaken. There were people who said the clock cannot be tuned back but there were also people who advocated that not only must the clock be turned back but it might be necessary to replace it if the purpose was to stem the rot that had set in after the arrest of Sheikh Saheb.

CHAPTER IX
Constitution (Application to Jammu & Kashmir) Order, 1954 and Beginning of Erosion of the State Autonomy

On February 11, 1954 Syed Mir Qasim presented to the Constituent Assembly the report of the Drafting Committee. The annexure to the Report indicated "in detail provisions of the Constitution of India which generally correspond to Defence, Foreign Affairs and Communications and such other matters as are considered essential concomitants of the fact of accession."

On February 15, 1954 the Constituent Assembly adopted the following resolution unanimously: Resolved that "(a) having adopted the report of the drafting committee this day, the 15th February, 1954, and (b) having thus given its concurrence to the application of the provisions for the Constitution of India in the manner indicated in the Annexure to the aforesaid report this Assembly authorize the Government of the State to forward a copy of the said Annexure to the Government of India for appropriate action".

This resolution was defective in form. It was not addressed to the President, as it should have been. But it was a substantial compliance with the requirement of a recommendation to him under Article 370. On May 14, 1954 the President made thereunder C.O. 48 the Constitution (Application to Jammu and Kashmir) Order, 1954. Its preamble says that it was made "with the concurrence of the Government of the State of Jammu and Kashmir". Once the Constituent Assembly was convened, the State government lost the power to accord any such concurrence.

However, the order may be said to be valid in so far as it conform to the Annexure to the report of the Constituent Assembly's Drafting Committee only, and, no further. The Order of 1954 does conform in the Annexure to the Report. This Order superseded the Order of 1950 and has been treated as the parent order to which subsequently amendments were made by Orders by the President under Article 370.

In view of its importance, the Order of May 14, 1954 is reproduced in full as Appendix VIII. The entries in the Union list I in the Seventh Schedule as applied to the State by this Order did not, unfortunately, conform strictly to the Instrument of Accession and the Delhi Agreement. However, the State List as well as the Concurrent List were entirely excluded. The State's right to all residuary subjects other than the ones in the Union List which were conferred on the Union was fully accepted. For the rest, certain provisions of the Constitution of India were applied in full; some with modifications, while the rest were omitted.

Before we proceed further and see how to evolve a consensus for action consistent with earnest desire to win back people solidly for participation in the national mainstream politics, it will be necessary to see how things had been allowed to go a drift after August 1953 till 1965 and after 1965 till 1975. It will be interesting to note that after inauguration of the Indian National Congress in the State when it substituted the National Conference and made it a branch of the National party with Sheikh Saheb and his colleagues still in jail and later facing alleged cases of conspiracy and treason, how maximum assault was launched upon Kashmir's special position, its autonomous character, its sovereign character and all this only to realise in 1975 that things had gone out of gear and people had lost whatever faith and confidence they had in the democratic relationship, issues deferred at the time of Delhi Agreement could not be negotiated any further till the Constituent Assembly itself was flawed by putting the real leadership of the people behind the bars arbitrarily and unconstitutionally. Even casual examination of the first Constitution (Application to Jammu and Kashmir) Order, 1954 that came into existence after these traumatic changes of 1953 will show that a path different from the one aspired to be chosen by the people of Kashmir State under the leadership of Sheikh Mohammad Abdullah was far different from the one envisaged by the Instrument of Accession and all that had gone with it. Jurisdiction of Union Parliament was extended from three subjects—Defense, External Affairs and Communications, to almost all the subjects—Defense, External Affairs and Communications, to almost all the subjects in the Union List. This constituted a first encroachment on the powers of legislation of the State by widening of those of the Union. We have seen the entries of the List 1 of Seventh Schedule which were made applicable by the Constitution Application Order of 1950 and also the entries which were not applicable to the State of Jammu and Kashmir. The Constitution Application Order of 1954 reversed the Order and made Union Parliament capable of legislating in respect of almost all the entries in the List, of course, with some exceptions and modifications. While the 1950 Order made some parts besides Articles 1 and 370 applicable—making exceptions and modifications also, 1954 Order made many more parts applicable with or without modifications. The important Article made thus applicable was Article 3 in which a proviso has been added for its modified application. The proviso required that "no bill for increasing or diminishing the area of Jammu and Kashmir or for altering the name of boundaries of the State shall be introduced in Parliament without the consent of the Legislature of the State." Part II of the Constitution of India now became applicable as a result of 1954 Order, with some modifications based upon letter and spirit of Delhi Agreement. Part III of the Constitution relating to Fundamental Rights was made applicable by 1954 Order. The question that remained to be determined was whether the chapter on Fundamental Rights of the Indian Constitution should form a part of the State Constitution or of the Constitution of India as applicable to the State. As it happened, a new Committee on Fundamental Rights was constituted after 9th August, 1953. The reconstituted committees both on Basic Principles as also on Citizenship and Fundamental Rights submitted their report to the Constituent Assembly on 3 February, 1954. The report of the Drafting Committee appointed by the Constituent Assembly in conformity with the recommendations of the two aforesaid committees was presented to the Assembly on 11th February, 1954. The annexure to that report indicated details of the provisions in the Constitution of India to be made applicable to the State. In accordance with the directions contained in the two reports, the sphere of Union jurisdiction was determined/refixed keeping intact all along the residuary powers of the State. It is this annexure to the report, which ultimately formed the Constitution (Application to J&K) Order of 1954 and made applicable parts of the Constitution of India to our State.

Part V dealing with Union had already been made applicable with some exceptions and modifications and additionally, Articles 54, 55, 73, 134, 139 and 150 were applied with modifications. Thereafter, from Part XI Article 246, 250, 251, 253, 254, 256, 261 were made applicable with modifications. Since this chapter deals with legislative powers of Parliament and residuary powers of legislation it may be worthwhile to notice changes brought about in the chapter in its application to the State of Jammu and Kashmir by 1954 Order.

Whereas under the 1960 Order, Parliament could make laws for the State in respect of only such matters in the Union list which correspond to the matters specified in the Instrument of Accession, by the 1954 Order, as a consequence of omission of the words "Subject to the provisions of paragraph 2", occurring in the 1950 Order, the Parliament could thereafter make laws in respect of all matters specified in the Union List. As if that was not enough, the Article was further modified in its application to the State vide C.O. No. 66 dated 28th September, 1963, enabling Parliament to make laws for the State in respect of matters in the Concurrent List also. Most important thing in the Seventh Schedule according to the Order of 1954 was continuance of what had been the feature of the earlier order of 1950 that the State List and the Concurrent List in their application to the State of Jammu and Kashmir were excluded. Regarding rest of the Articles from the important chapter dealing with legislative relations of the Union and the State it has been noted that the Articles 248 and 249 dealing with the residuary powers of the legislation and also power of Parliament to legislate in respect of matters in the State List in the national interest were not applicable to the State. Article 250 was also not applicable to the State under 1950 Order but was applied in a modified form by 1954 Order vesting the Parliament with the power to make laws for the State in respect of matters not enumerated in the Union List.

It may thus cover areas which are part of residuary powers of legislation or strictly powers of Legislature of the State. Article

251 in its application to Jammu and Kashmir State in view of non-application of Article 249 in the Order of 1954 had to remain confined to Article 250 alone in its application to the State. Vide Article 253 in its modified form it was made obligatory that after commencement of the Constitution (Application to J&K) Order of 1954 no decision affecting the disposition of the State of Jammu and Kashmir could be made by the Government of India without the consent of the Government of the State. Article 755 was omitted from application to Jammu and Kashmir State and Article 354 applied with modifications. The article as applicable to Jammu and Kashmir state at that time read as follows:

> "If any provision of law made by the Legislature of a State is repugnant to any provisions of law made by Parliament which Parliament is competent to enact, law made by Parliament whether passed before or after the law made by the Legislature of the State prevail and law made by the Legislature of the State shall to the extent of repugnancy be void."

Clause (2) of the Article as in the Union Constitution was omitted in relation to the J&K State.

From Chapter II of this Part dealing with Administrative Relations, while 1950 Order made Article 256 applicable to the State without any modifications or exceptions and applied Article 257 with the exceptions of clauses (3) and (4) thereof, Articles 260, 262 and 263 were excepted under the 1954 Order. Article 256 was renumbered as clause (1) of that Article and the following new clause (2) was added thereto, namely:

> "The State of Jammu and Kashmir shall so exercise its executive power as to facilitate the discharge by the Union of its duties and responsibilities under the Constitution in relation to that State; and in particular, the said State shall, if so required by the Union, acquire or requisition properly on behalf of and at the expense of the Union on such terms as may be agreed, or in default of agreement, as may be determined by an arbitrator appointed by the Chief Justice of India."

Article 259 in its application was omitted and Article 261 applied with minor modifications. In Clause (2) thereof the words 'made by Parliament' were ordered to be omitted. After this change, clause (2) of Article 261 in its application to J&K reads as under:

> "The manner in which and the conditions under which the acts, records and proceedings referred to in clause (1) shall be proved and the effect thereof determined shall be as provided by law.

The next chapter, namely Chapter XII deals with Finance, Property, Contracts and Suits. We have seen how Constitution Application Order of 1950 had dealt with this Chapter in its application to the State of Jammu and Kashmir. Exception was made in respect of Articles 264, 265, clause (2) of Articles 267, 268 and 281, clause (2) of Article 283, Articles 286 to 291, 293, 295, 296 and 297. Articles 266, 282, 284, 298, 299 and 300 were applied in modified form. 1954 Order did radically change the situation in so far as application of this chapter was concerned. This despite the fact that Delhi Agreement had not recorded any conclusions regarding financial relationship between the State and the Union and the matter had been deferred for final solution. The negotiations did not conclude at all between the real representatives of the State and the Government of India till introduction of the report of the Basic Principles Committee and Advisory Committee on Fundamental Rights in the Assembly in the manner described above. 1954 Order, however, affirmed omission of clause (2) of Article 267, clause (2) of Article 283 as in the 1950 Order and again repeated that Articles 266, 282, 284, 298, 299 and 300 would apply in identical terms as in 1950 Order. This would mean that reference in these Articles to State or States shall be construed as not including reference to the State of Jammu and Kashmir. In Article 277 and 295 commencement of Constitution was to be construed as commencement of Constitution (Application to J&K) Order of 1954.

The changes in Article 303, Part XIII deleted reference to any entry relating to trade and commerce in any list in Seventh Schedule as providing authority of restriction on legislative power of Union and of States in regard to trade and commerce and reference to Article 306 is not necessary since by now this provision stands deleted.

In Part XIV, provisions regarding All India Services (Art. 312) were not applicable to the State even under 1954 Order dated 14th May, 1954.

The next Part XV dealing with elections and Article 324 thereof was made applicable only in relation to elections to Parliament and to offices of President and Vice-President. Rest of the Articles 325, 326, 327, 328 and 329 were omitted from application to this State.

In Part XVI reference to Scheduled Tribes was omitted in relation to J&K. Articles 331, 332, 333, 336, 337, 339, 342 stood omitted and references to the State or States in Articles 334 and 335 were to be construed as not including references to the State of Jammu and Kashmir.

Part dealing with official languages, i.e. Part XVII in its application to State of Jammu and Kashmir had to remain related to:

(a) The official language of the Union;
(b) The official language for communication between one State and another, or between a State and the Union; and
(c) The Language of the proceedings in the Supreme Court.

That takes us to another important part namely Part XVIII relating to EMERGENCY PROVISIONS. Articles 352 to 360 are included in this Part.

This chapter was not mentioned in the Constitution (Application to J&K) Order of 1950. A new clause was added which became sub-clause (4) of Article 352 in the year 1954 as it then was. The sub-clause read as under:

> "No proclamation of emergency made on grounds only of internal disturbance or imminent danger thereof shall have effect in relation to the State of Jammu and Kashmir (except as respects Article 354) unless it is made at the request or with the concurrence of Government of that State."

Articles 356, 357 and 360 were omitted in their application to Jammu and Kashmir as per 1954 Order.

Thereafter comes Part XIX, MISCELLANEOUS (Articles 361-367). Exceptions was made in respect of Articles 362, 363, and 365 in the 1950 Order. Article 361 was applied with modification in that it would apply so far as it related to President and that article

364 would apply in so far as it related to the laws made by the parliament about major ports and aerodromes. Vide 1954 Order, however, situation had already been altered and after clause (4) of Article 361 clause (5) was added which read as under:

> "The provisions of this article shall apply in relation to the Sadar-i-Riyasat of Jammu and Kashmir as they apply in relation to a Rajpramukh, but without prejudice to the provisions of the Constitution of the State."

Articles 362 and 365 were omitted. In Article 366 clause (21) was omitted. This clause as it stood in the Indian Constitution in the year 1954 was finally deleted from the Constitution itself later in 1956.

A new clause was added to Article 367, i.e. clause (4) which read as under:

> "(4) For the purpose of this Constitution as it applies in relation to the State of Jammu and Kashmir:
>
> (a) Reference to this Constitution or to the provisions thereof shall be construed as references to the Constitution or the provisions thereof as applied in relation to the said State;
>
> (b) references to the Government of the said State shall be construed as including references to the Sadar-i-Rayasat acting on the advice of his Council of Ministers;
>
> (c) references to a High Court shall include references to a High Court of Jammu and Kashmir;
>
> (d) references the Legislature or the Legislative Assembly of the said State shall be construed as including references to the Constituent Assembly of the said State;
>
> (e) references to the permanent residents of the said State shall be construed as meaning persons who, before the commencement of the Constitution (Application to Jammu and Kashmir) Order, 1954, were recognised as State subjects under the law in force in the State or who are recognised by any law made by the Legislature of the State as permanent residents of the State; and
>
> (f) references to the Rajpramukh shall be construed as references to the persons for the time being recognised

> by the President as the Sadar-i-Riyasat of Jammu and Kashmir and as including references to any person for the time being recognised by the President as being competent to exercise the powers of the Sadar-i-Riyasat."

The provisions of Article 368 which is a sole Article of Part XX relate to power of Parliament to amend the Constitution and procedure therefor. In its application to the State of Jammu and Kashmir the following proviso was added:

> "Provided further that no such amendment shall have effect in relation to the State of Jammu and Kashmir unless applied by order of the President under clause (1) of Article 370."

From Part XXI, Articles 369, 371, 373, clauses 1, 2, 3 and 5 of Article 374. Article 376 and Article 392 were ordered to be omitted. This Part as earlier noted dealt with "Temporary, Transitional and Special Provisions" and this is the Part, which like other so-called transitory provisions, contains Article 370.

Article 370, part Article 372 and part Article 374 alone were applicable in the prescribed form to the State of Jammu and Kashmir. In Article 372, clauses (2) and (3) were to be deleted and references to laws in force in the territory of India would also include references to Hidayats, Ailans, Ishtihars, Circulars, Robkars, Irshad, Yadhasht, State Council Resolutions, Resolutions of the Constituent Assembly and other instruments having the force of law in the territory of the State of Jammu and Kashmir and reference to the commencement of the Constitution was construed to be reference to the commencement of the Application Order of 1954. In identical terms in Clause (4) of Article 374 the reference to the authority functioning as the Privy Council of a State was to be construed as a reference to the Advisory Board constituted under J&K Constitution Act Svt. 1996 and reference to the commencement of the Constitution here also was to be construed as reference to the commencement of the 1954 Order. From Part XXII, Articles 394 and 395 were omitted. The position regarding the application of Schedules appended to the Constitution that emerged as a result of the 1954 Order was as under:

(i) First Schedule	Applied
(ii) Second Schedule	Applied except paragraph 6

(iii)	Third schedule	Applied except Forms V, VI, VII and VIII
(iv)	Fourth Schedule Applied	
(v)&(vi)	Fifth and sixth Schedule	Not applied
(vii)	Seventh schedule	(a) Entries in the Union List as already noted above applied. (b) State list and the concurrent list stood omitted.
(viii)	Eighth Schedule	Applied
(ix)	Ninth Schedule	Applied

CHAPTER X

Erosion Continued Apace

The constitutional relationship between the State and the Union as it existed when the Constitution Application Order of 1950 was repealed and substituted by Constitution Application Order of 1954 has been detailed in the preceding chapter. There is no doubt that serious deviations were made and the position altered in some vital matters but for the time being we will only indicate what it is that had not been changed. In the legislative sphere of State-Union relationship, 1954 Order did not after the position insofar as non-application to the State of the Concurrent List and the State List of the Seventh Schedule was concerned. These two lists were completely excluded in their application in relation to the State of Jammu and Kashmir. This left Residuary Powers of legislation completely with the State Legislature and legislative power of the State was so extensive as to be capable of being available for all things not included in the Union List as applicable to the State of Jammu and Kashmir. Although the 1954 Order had increased the number of items to which the power of Parliament to legislate in respect of Jammu and Kashmir was extended but even so they were not as many as were subsequently added to it for effecting further erosion of autonomy by misuse of Article 370. The cumulative reading indicates that State's power to legislate on matters other than those ceded to the Union Parliament were quite wide and still left a great degree of autonomy with the State.

In Chapter II of Part XI dealing with administrative relations between the Union and the State. Article 256 was applied to the State in a modified form. This modification can be regarded as a normal and natural corollary of the State being a unit of the federation. This incidentally appears to be the spirit of clause 6 of the Instrument of Accession also.

Part VI did not apply with the result that State of Jammu and Kashmir was left free to frame its own Constitution for internal governance. This part also contained Chapter (V) which dealt with High Court in the States. The position in respect of the High Courts in the States also continued to be the same as it was at the time of passing of the 1950 Order. The continued non-application of this part of the Indian Constitution both in 1950 and 1954 Orders allowed the existing Constitution of Jammu and Kashmir State as amended upto 1950 to continue to remain a live document and also kept the prospect of State Constituent Assembly framing the Constitution of the State of Jammu and Kashmir alive and left the Constitution of the State as it was on 14th of May, 1954 undisturbed. It meant that the Head of the State and the Chief Executive continued to be Sadar-i-Riyasat and the Prime Minister respectively.

Provisions under Part XIV relating to services under the Union and the States were not applied to the State of Jammu and Kashmir either under 1950 or 1954 Order.

Likewise, provisions under Part XV regarding elections were restricted in their application to Jammu and Kashmir to the elections to parliament and offices of the President and Vice-President only. Also, provisions under Part XVI were restricted in their application to the J&K State to the Scheduled Castes only.

The next important Part that requires mention is Part XVIII. In this Part what was common between 1950 and 1954 Orders was non-application of Articles 356, 357 and 360. It, however, needs to be noted that the Order of 1954 did make Article 352 applicable in a modified form by addition of sub-clause (4) to Article 352 as mentioned earlier.

In the matter of financial relations many radical changes were made by the Constitution (Application to Jammu and Kashmir) Order, 1954. This inspite of the fact that no agreement could be reached in regard to the future financial relationship between the State and the Union under the Delhi Agreement of 1952.

Part XII (Articles 264-300) of the Indian Constitution was made applicable in essence as elaborated in the foregoing chapter.

The immenseness and the pace of erosion of State autonomy from 1953 onwards can be gauged from a perusal of the long list of Constitution Orders applying various provisions of the Indian Constitution to the State given below:

1. The Constitution (Application to J&K) Order, 1954 C.O. 48 Dated: 14.5.1954.
2. The Constitution (Application to J&K Amendment Order, 1956 C.O. 51 dated: 11.2.1956.
3. The Constitution (Application to J&K) Amendment Order, 1958 C.O. 55 dated: 16.1.1958.
4. The Constitution (Application to J&K) Second Amendment Order, 1958 C.O. 56 dated: 26.2.1958.
5. The Constitution (Application to J&K) Amendment Order 1959 C.O. 57 dated: 9.2.1959.
6. The Constitution (Application to J&K) Second Amendment Order, 1959 C.O. 59 dated: 23-04-1959.
7. The Constitution (Application to J&K) Amendment Order, 1960 C.O. 60 dated: 20-01-1960.
8. The Constitution (Application to J&K) Second Amendment Order, 1960 C.O. 61 dated: 22.6.1960.
9. The Constitution (Application to J&K) Amendment Order, 1961 C.O. 62 dated: 2.5.1961.
10. The Constitution (Application to J&K) Amendment Order, 1963 C.O. 66 dated: 28.9.1963.
11. The Constitution (Application to J&K) Amendment Order, 1964 C.O. 69 dated: 6.3.1964.
12. The Constitution (Application to J&K) Second Amendment Order, 1964 C.O. 70 dated: 2.10.1964.
13. The Constitution (Application to J&K) Third Amendment Order, 1964 C.O. 71 dated: 21.11.1964.
14. The Constitution (Application to J&K) Amendment Order, 1965 C.O. 72 dated: 17.5.1965.
15. The Constitution (Application to J&K) Second Amendment Order, 1965 C.O. 74 dated: 24.11.1965.
16. The Constitution (Application to J&K) Amendment Order, 1966 C.O. 75 dated: 29.6.1966.

17. The Constitution (Application to J&K) Amendment Order, 1967 C.O. 76 dated: 13.2.1967.
18. The Constitution (Application to J&K) Second Amendment Order, 1967 C.O. 77 dated: 5.5.1967.
19. The Constitution (Application to J&K) Third Amendment Order, 1967 C.O. 79 dated: 11.8.1967.
20. The Constitution (Application to J&K) Fourth Amendment Order, 1967 C.O. 80 dated: 26.12.1967.
21. The Constitution (Application to J&K) Amendment Order, 1968 C.O. 83 dated: 9.2.1968.
22. The Constitution (Application to J&K) Amendment Order, 1969 C.O. 85 dated: 17.2.1969.
23. The Constitution (Application to J&K) Second Amendment Order, 1969 C.O. 86 dated: 31.5.1969.
24. The Constitution (Application to J&K) Amendment Order, 1971 C.O. 89 dated: 24.8.1971
25. The Constitution (Application to J&K) Second Amendment Order, 1971 C.O. 90 dated: 8.11.1971
26. The Constitution (Application to J&K) Third Amendment Order, 1971 C.O. 91 dated: 29.11.1971
27. The Constitution (Application to J&K) Amendment Order, 1972 C.O. 92 dated: 24.2.1972.
28. The Constitution (Application to J&K) Second Amendment Order, 1972 C.O. 93 dated: 6.5.1972.
29. The Constitution (Application to J&K) Third Amendment Order, 1972 C.O. 94 dated: 2.8.1972.
30. The Constitution (Application to J&K) Fourth Amendment Order, 1972 C.O. 95 dated: 10.8.1972.
31. The Constitution (Application to J&K) Amendment Order, 1974 C.O. 97 dated: 1.5.1974.
32. The Constitution (Application to J&K) Second Amendment Order, 1974 C.O. 98 dated: 26.6.1974.
33. The Constitution (Application to J&K) Amendment Order, 1975 C.O. 100 dated: 29.6.1975.
34. The Constitution (Application to J&K) Second Amendment Order, 1975, C.O. 101 dated: 23.7.1975.
35. The Constitution (Application to J&K) Amendment Order, 1976 C.O. 103 dated: 2.3.1976.

36. The Constitution (Application to J&K.) Second Amendment Order, 1976 C.O. 104 dated: 25.5.1976.
37. The Constitution (Application to J&K) Third Amendment Order, 1976 C.O. 105 dated: 12.9.1976.
38. The Constitution (Application to J&K) Fourth Amendment Order, 1976 C.O. 106 dated: 31.12.1976.
39. The Constitution (Application to J&K) Amendment Order, 1977 C.O. 108 dated: 31.12.1977.
40. The Constitution (Application to J&K) Amendment Order, 1985 C.O. 122 dated: 4.6.1985.
41. The Constitution (Application to J&K) Second Amendment Order, 1985 C.O. 124 dated: 4.12.1985.
42. The Constitution (Application to J&K) Amendment Order, 1986 C.O. 129 dated: 30.7.1986.

Not all these Orders can be objected to. For instance, none can object to provision for direct elections to Parliament in 1966. Delimitation of Parliamentary constituencies, etc. It is the principle that matters. Constitutional limits are there to be respected, not violated. Amendments to the Constitution of India were extended as a matter of course to the State.

We have noticed above that in the eagerness to create an image of cementing closer relations, what followed 1954 is a series of Constitution (Application to J&K) Orders numbering 42 till now which were not conceived at any point of time either in 1950 or in 1952 or even later in May, 1954. Among the changes brought about the most important were in restricting the powers of legislature of the State, extension of powers of the Union Parliament, application to the State of financial provisions of the Constitution of India, provisions relating to emergency. All India Services, superintendence, direction and control of elections of the state legislature and several other matters.

The position having been so radically altered can be put in the following manner so as to indicate actual State-Union relationship which had emerged as a result of changes brought about.

(a) Almost all entries in the Union List are applicable to the State of Jammu and Kashmir with the result that Union Parliament's power to legislate extends to matters even beyond the three subjects on which the accession had originally been agreed upon. The list has gone far beyond 20 items of the list attached to the Instrument of Accession or even the Schedules to 1950 Order.

(b) Concurrent List of legislation in essence is applicable, even in regard to welfare legislation and essentially local matters.

(c) Most of the provisions about one of the wings of the State namely the Judiciary are now derivable or definable from the Country's Constitution rather than the Constitution of the State.

(d) Provision relating to All India Services is now applicable to the State.

(e) All the matters under Finance, Trade and Commerce are now applicable. Even the rudiments of financial autonomy have completely been swept away.

(f) Even the field of residuary legislation in the matter of law and order has been curtailed so far as the State is concerned and Entry 97 of the Union list too has been made applicable in curiously modified form to the detriment of the principle of political autonomy.

(g) All emergency powers including those in Article 356 and that too in their un-amended form and retrograde shape are applicable to the State and their misuse during the last eight to nine years has proved beyond doubt that apprehensions entertained in 1950's have come out to be true.

(h) Special provisions of Article 249 dealing with the Parliament's power of legislation in the State List have been extended to the State of Jammu and Kashmir quite surreptitiously in a brazen and clandestine manner by misinterpreting and misusing Article 370.

(i) Superintendence, direction and control of local elections now vests with the Central Election Commission.

Besides, some changes of far-reaching consequences including that of altering the mode of appointment of the Head of the State were effected in the Constitution of the State. The extent and the nature of autonomy which has been left with the

State as of now can be seen from the following table:

I.	Total No. of Articles	No. of Articles applied	Balance
	395	260	135*

*These relate to matters under Part VI of the Constitution of India which pertains to matters concerning the Executive, Legislature and High Courts of States of the Union and provisions whereof are identical to the provisions of the Constitution of Jammu and Kashmir.

II. Total No. of entries in the Union List	Entries applied	Balance
97	94	3*

*Entries 8.9 and 34 relating to CBI jurisdiction, preventive detention connected with Defence matters, and Courts of wards for the estates of Rulers of Indian States respectively.

III. Total No. of entries in the concurrent list	Entries applied	Balance
47	26	21*

*Entries 3, 5, 6, 7, 8, 9, 10, 14, 15, 17, 20, 21, 27, 28, 29, 31, 32, 37, 38, 41 and 44.

These entries relate mostly to matters of social legislation, charitable institutions, relief and rehabilitation of displaced persons, transfer of property etc.

IV.	Total No. of Schedules	No. of Schedules applied	Balance
	12	7	5*

*Schedule 5—Control of Scheduled Areas and S.T.

Schedule 6—Administration of Tribal Areas.

Schedule 10—Disqualification on grounds of defection except in so far it relates to members of Parliament.

Schedule 11—Powers of Panchayats (new provision of the Indian Constitution vide Seventy-third Amendment Act, 1992).

Schedule 12—Power and responsibilities of Municipalities (new provision of the Indian Constitution vide Seventy-fourth Amendment Act, 1992).

*Indicates provisions hithereto not applied to the State.

It is abundantly clear, therefore, that from 1953 onwards, especially in sixties, the process of erosion of the state autonomy was so rapid and on such a massive scale that entire Article 370 of the Constitution of India which was supposed to guarantee and preserve the special status of the State in the Indian Union was emptied of its substantive content with the result that the State's jurisdiction over the matters as envisaged by the Instrument of Accession of Oct. 1947 and the Delhi Agreement of 1952 was gradually diminished and systematically transferred to the Union.

Far from enjoying a special status, as Article 370 envisaged, the State was put in a status inferior to that of other States. One illustration suffices to demonstrate that Parliament had to amend the Constitution four times, by the 59th, 64th, 67th, 68th Constitution Amendments to extend President's rule imposed in Punjab on May 11, 1987. For the State of Jammu and Kashmir, the same result was accomplished by executive orders under Article 370.

The Union Home Minister. Mr. Gulzari Lal Nanda said on December 4, 1964 that Article 370 could well be used to serve as a "tunnel in the wall" in order to increase the Centre's powers. This was diametrically contrary to the clear intent underlying, and the objective of Article 370.

Another gross case illustrates the extent of misuse of Article 370. On July 30, 1986 the President made an Order under Article 370 extending to the State Article 249 of the Constitution in order to empower Parliament to legislate even on a matter in the State List on the strength of a Rajya Sabha resolution. "Concurrence" to this was given by the Centre's own appointee, Governor Jagmohan (*Indian Express*, August 17, 1986).

This is how C.O. 129 was made on July 30, 1986. It said that in Article 249, in clause (1) for the words "any matter enumerated in the State list specified in the resolution," the words "any matter specified in the resolution being a matter which is not enumerated in the Union List or in the concurrent list" shall be substituted. This was made "with the concurrence of the Government of the State of Jammu and Kashmir" when the State was under Governor's rule and no popular Government existed. This is a clear nullity.

Successive State governments had in the past accorded their "concurrence" for various reasons and under various political compulsions. No State would otherwise willingly accept curbs on its autonomy.

CHAPTER XI

Changes Effected in the Basic Structure of the State Constitution

This brings us to the perception which inspired both the State and the Union leadership in early fifties to envisage that the State of Jammu and Kashmir shall frame the Constitution of the State through a Constituent Assembly envisaged for it during the days of freedom struggle itself and recognised thereafter by a provision in the Constitution of India. This Constituent Assembly adopted a method of appointment of the Head of the State different from the one adopted by the Constituent Assembly of India in respect of the other States of the Union in as much as it provided for an elected Head (Sadar-i-Riyasat). Thus it brought to an end the era of hereditary rulership for all times to come and held out a promise for the future of a fully democratic Constitution for the State.

The Constitution finally adopted had the following features:

(a) An elected Head of the State.

(b) A chapter on Directive Principles ensuring equality, fraternity and social justice for all.

(A) An independent Judiciary.

(c) A Council of Ministers with a Prime Minister of the State at the Head.

(d) A Legislature consisting of two Houses with the Upper House based on absolute parity between the two regions of the State with very wide and effective powers.

(e) Another important feature of the Constitution adopted and enforced was and continues to be provided by Section 147. This section deals with power and procedure of amendment of the Constitution. This Section made some provisions of the Constitution of Jammu and Kashmir unalterable and among the unalterable provisions are the following:

(a) Section 147 itself.

(b) Section 3 defining the relationship of the State with the Union of India.

(c) Section 5 dealing with the extent of executive and legislative power of the State.

The State Constitution can be regarded as very rigid in this respect. This feature that it has provisions which are quite rigid and provisions which are flexible is not unique in the Constitution of the State alone. This is true of many Constitutions. Justice Anand has to say, in this regard, as follows:

> "The French Constitution declares that the Republican character of the Government cannot be changed and in the United States of America no federating State can secede and become independent."

In more than one ways, Sections 3, 4 and 5 in the Constitution of Jammu and Kashmir State can be regarded as the fundamental law on which in the words of His Lordship, Mr. Justice Adarsh Sen Anand, "the very structure of the Constitution has been erected".

Our purpose of making reference to these provisions of the Constitution of State of Jammu and Kashmir is to place on record how this fundamental law or the basic structure on which the Constitution is based has been subjected to changes. Even a casual study can indicate that despite the rigidity the requirement of the mandate of unalterable character of the provisions, politics has swayed someone to adopt measures which should not have been adopted at all.

The Amendment Acts of 1959 and 1965 were introduced respectively before and after the National Conference Party converted itself into a Pradesh Congress Committee, a branch in the State of Indian National Congress. The Constitution of Jammu and Kashmiri (Sixth Amendment) Act, 1960 introduced changes in Sections 2.27, 29, 30, 31, 32, 33, 51, 95, 100-A, 100-B and 126. As a result of the changes effected by this Amendment Act among various other provisions that suffered changes, was Section 147 also though declared by the Section itself as unalterable. Section 147 as it stood before the amendment was as follows:

> "An amendment of the Constitution may be initiated only by the introduction of a Bill for the purpose in the Legislative Assembly, and when the Bill is passed in the House by a majority of not less than two-thirds of the total membership of the House, it shall be presented to the Sadar-i-Riyasat for his assent and upon such assent being given to the Bill, the

Constitution shall stand amended in accordance with the terms of the Bill:

Provided that a Bill providing for the abolition of the Legislative Council may be introduced in the Legislative Assembly and passed by it by a majority of the total membership of the Assembly and by a majority of not less than two-thirds of the members of the Assembly present and voting.

Provided further that no Bill or Amendment seeking to make any change in—

(a) this section; or

(b) the provisions of Sections 3 and 5; or

(c) the provisions of the Constitution of India as applicable in relation to the State shall be introduced or moved in either House of the State Legislature."

Besides, an omnibus amendment in Section (2) by introduction of a sub-section (3) affected many other provisions. Sub-section (3) reads as under:

"Any reference in this Constitution to Sadar-i-Riyasat shall, unless the context otherwise requires, be construed as a reference to the Governor."

Section 147 vide Section (2) of the Sixth Amendment Act of the Constitution of Jammu and Kashmir State suffered change in that the word, 'Governor' was substituted for the word, 'Sadar-i-Riyasat' which could not have been made in view of the provision of the section. This amendment brings about fundamental changes in the core foundation of the Constitution of the State. This was done without considering the implication and so radically that the basic character of the Constitution was infringed upon just within eight years of its adoption and enforcement.

Incidentally, we may digress for a moment here and go to explanation part given at the end of sub-clause (b) of clause (1) of Article 370. This explanation originally was as under:

"For the purpose of this Article the Government of the State means the person for the time being recognised as Maharaja of Jammu and Kashmir acting on the advice of the Council of Ministers for the time being in office under Maharaja's proclamation dated 5th day of March, 1948."

The said explanation on the recommendation of the Constituent Assembly of the State of Jammu and Kashmir was changed by a Presidential Order vide C.O. 44 dated 17.11.1952 making Article 370 operative with a changed explanation with effect from 7th November, 1952. The substituted explanation reads as under:

"For the purpose of this Order, the Government of the State means the person for the time being recognised by the President on the recommendation of the Legislative Assembly of the State as Sadar-i-Riyasat of Jammu and Kashmir acting on the advice of the Council of Ministers of the State for the time being in office".

So, the part dealing with Maharaja's proclamation of 5th March, 1948 became Sadar-i-Riyasat recognised as such by President of India and acting on the advice of the Council of Ministers of the State for the time being in office with effect from 17th November, 1952. What then is Article 370 after the word 'Sadar-i-Riyasat' is substituted by the word Governor after the Sixth Amendment Act of the Constitution of the State of Jammu and Kashmir if the substitution is not part of the Indian Constitution? The word Sadar-i-Riyasat continues to exist in Article 370 for any kind of change in Article 370 cannot be brought about by making change in Jammu and Kashmir State Constitution and in the way it was brought about.

The power of the State Legislature can next be found to have been impinged upon insofar as its legal right to elect the Head of State subject to the recognition by the President of India got obliterated. This deprivation cannot but be recorded as a serious assault on the autonomous character of this unit of the federation. The recommendation to have an elected Head as the substitute for the hereditary ruler had been made by the Basic Principles Committee for the Constituent Assembly as early as 1952. This was mutually agreed upon by the State and the Union leaders. Consequently, the Sadar-i-Riyasat was duly elected in 1952 and thereafter every five years till the Constitution of State was amended in 1965. Why it was necessary in 1965 to deprive the

State of electing its Sadar-i-Riyasat and provide for a nominee of the Central Government as Governor need not be dwelt upon at length but, however, reference to 1984, 1986 and 1990 interludes in history must indicate that but for events happening at the behest of nominated Governors, ground situation in the State of Jammu and Kashmir would in all probability have been different. Why and to satisfy whom did the State leadership after in-coming of Congress into the State embark upon this mis-adventure shall always be regretted.

During 1948-65 the word Prime Minister of Jammu and Kashmir did not raise any storm in any cup of tea nor did it even remotely lead to any confusion with that of the Prime Minister of the Union. It was there in the State prior to 1947, had continued to be thereafter Maharaja's declaration of March 5th, 1948 and again after the adoption of interim Constitution in 1952, till the dismissal of the first elected Prime Minister in 1953 and again till March 1965. What has been achieved after writing it off alongwith the principle of election of the Head of the State as also the nomenclature of Sadar-i-Riyasat can now be seen from what has happened in very recent history of the State particularly to State's relationship with the Union.

This assault on State Autonomy must be and has to be undone. For this purpose appropriate amendments shall have to be made in the Constitution of Jammu and Kashmir and also consequential changes in the provisions of the Constitution of India as applicable to the State.

This requires to be done speedily to restore the faith of the people in the path chosen by them through their representatives in the course of deliberations in the Constituent Assembly of the State way back in 1951-53.

CHAPTER XII

Return of Sheikh Mohammad Abdullah to Power in 1975 and After

After the dismissal of Jenab Sheikh Mohammad Abdullah from the office of the Prime Minister of Jammu and Kashmir on August 8, 1953 in an unconstitutional and undemocratic manner he was kept under detention for over two decades. However, in February, 1975 due to the pursuation of Mrs. Indira Gandhi, he agreed to take over the state administration pending the next elections of the State Assembly with the support of the then Congress members of the State Legislature, although he insisted on the holding of Assembly elections before taking office. But, as it happened, in March, 1977, much before the due date of Assembly elections, the Congress party withdrew its support to him.

The Janata Party which was then in power at the Centre ordered fresh and fair elections in the State in the same year and the Jammu and Kashmir National Conference under the leadership of Sheikh Saheb won a thumping majority as a result of the fairest ever elections held in Jammu and Kashmir till then after 1953. However, unfortunately even the Historically held elections were not made best use of to deepen the roots of national mainstream politics by enlightened national leadership and by yielding to the people of Kashmir what they needed most, what they held to be their birth right, their right to be a special state of the Indian Union with unbridled powers of legislation in matters other than those ceded under Instrument of Accession or powers incidental or ancillary thereto.

After Sheikh Saheb's death in 1982, fresh elections to the J&K Legislative Assembly were held in June, 1983 and the National Conference under the leadership of Dr. Farooq Abdullah again won the elections with comfortable majority. But in 1984 the Government headed by him was dismissed unconstitutionally and undemocratically and another Government under the leadership of Shri Ghulam Mohammad Shah was installed by engineering defections in the National Conference with Congress Party support from outside.

This experiment also did not succeed. Congress Party withdrew support in March, 1986 and the G.M. Shah Government had to be dismissed. Governor's rule was imposed. In the Assembly elections held in 1987 National Conference under the leadership of Dr. Farooq Abdullah won the elections again. In January 1990 the Central Government brought back a Governor in the State who was unacceptable to the popularly elected State Government with the result that it resigned. Then followed a blood bath and massacre on large scale of innocent persons. Even the mourners of late Mir Waiz Moulvi Mohammad Farooq carrying his dead body were not spared. The situation deteriorated to such an extent that only after four months the Governor had to be replaced.

There were massive demonstrations by the people in Srinagar followed by eruption of militancy, which the Central Government thought fit to curb under its own auspices but failed to do so. The demand for Azadi (independence) was raised by a section of the angry youth in Kashmir. It was, however, late in the day that even the Union leadership realised that what is needed for this unit of the Union is autonomy and that "Sky should be the limit" in terms of the then Prime Minister of the Union Shri P.V. Narasimha Rao. The declaration did not, however, go beyond promises having been made so piously.

The United Front Government recognised the need and followed it up only by means of declaration in the Common Minimum Programme in 1996 by holding the prospect of "Greater Autonomy" as a live issue for bringing people of Kashmir back to the era of normalcy and Kashmir's political scenario back into the national mainstream. However, on the assurance of the central Government that it would consider favourably the demand for restoration of autonomy to the State and was prepared to enter into a dialogue with the elected representatives of the State, the National Conference went to the polls in September, 1996 on the autonomy platform with the following manifesto:

> "We pledge that if we are elected our Party will be bound to accomplish the following:
>
> Dignified undiluted and meaningful autonomy which has been inspiring our people will be restored and made unalterable. We will strive to bring it to the shape which was kept before us at the time of the Accession. We will also demand credible guarantees from the federal centre to keep constitutional relationship with the State in its pristine form so that the tragic events through which we have had to pass are not repeated in future."

The people of the State returned the Party to power with a two-thirds majority. It is in pursuance of this mandate of the electorate and assurance of the Central Government that the State Government appointed this Committee to examine the question of restoration of autonomy to the State of Jammu and Kashmir.

CHAPTER XIII

Recommendations

Change in the title of Part XXI and heading of Article 370

The word 'temporary' has been used in the title of part XXI and heading of Article 370 of the Constitution of India. In this context it would be relevant to mention as to how and why it came to be used therein. This was because of the provision contained in clause (3) of this Article which came into being at a time when the Constituent Assembly of the State had yet to be convened.

This Article could cease to be operative if the President of the Republic were to issue a notification to this effect on the basis of a recommendation of the State Constituent Assembly. It could also be made operative with modifications and exceptions by a similar process and from such date as may be specified by the President.

The Constituent Assembly ceased to exist after the Constitution for the State was adopted by it in November, 1956. It did not make any recommendation for the removal of this Article.

So it should have been indicated as early as 1956 that it would be a misnomer to call Article 370 'Temporary provision'. In fact, it had then become and had to continue as a special provision of the Indian Constitution applicable to the State of Jammu and Kashmir.

It would be appropriate to quote Jenab Sheikh Sahib's views expressed in this regard while addressing the State Constituent Assembly on 11th August, 1952:

> "Here I would like to point out that the fact that Article 370 has been mentioned as a temporary provision in the Constitution does not mean that it is capable of being abrogated, modified or replaced unilaterally. In actual effect, the temporary nature of this Article arises merely from the fact that the *power to finalise the Constitutional relationship between the State and the Union of India has been specifically vested in the Jammu and Kashmir Constituent Assembly. It follows that whatever modifications, amendments or exceptions that may become necessary either to Article 370 or any other Article in the Constitution of India in their application to the Jammu and Kashmir State are subject to decisions of this Sovereign Body."*

Accordingly, it is recommended as under:

(i) That the word 'temporary' be deleted from the title of Part XXI of the Constitution of India; and

(ii) That the word 'temporary' occurring in the heading of Article 370 be substituted by the word 'special'.

Legislative Relations (Part XI)

We have at length described that breath and soul of State-Union relationship initially was the Instrument of Accession and later this was replaced by provisions of the Indian Constitution as and when these became applicable. The Instrument of Accession was to be the basis. The Instrument conceded powers of legislation to the Federal Union in the matter of Defence. External Affairs and Communications and vide clause (3) this Instrument itself specified matters in the "schedule" thereto with respect to which the Dominion legislature could make laws for the State of Jammu and Kashmir. These scheduled matters were 20 in number and were grouped under sub-heads:

(a) Defence.

(b) External Affairs.

(c) Communications.

(d) Ancillary.

Dominion Legislature, therefore, could legislate with respect to the State of Jammu and Kashmir in respect of matters specified in the schedule to the Instrument of Accession.

Articles 1 and 370 became applicable to our State straightway and our State became part of the scheme of distribution of legislative powers enshrined in the Constitution of India. Seventh Schedule to the Constitution itemised the legislative field of operation in the following manner:

List I	Union list.
List II	State list.
List III	Concurrent list.

With the enforcement of Indian Constitution on 26.1.1950 and simultaneously application of Article 370 to the State of Jammu and Kashmir, Presidential Order of 1950 came to be issued on this very date. With its application relevant Union List items with omissions, exceptions and modifications became applicable from that very date. This was consistent with original terms of accession, conceding powers of legislation to Union Parliament in matters on which State sovereign had acceded to the Union.

The Union thereafter could legislate on items included in the Schedule to 1950 Order. The items which were excluded from the ambit of legislative power of Parliament in respect of the State of Jammu and Kashmir were as under:

> 7, 8, 23, 24, 32, 33, 34, 35, 36, 37, 38, 40, 42 to 71, 78 to 92 and 97.

The entries 22 and 76 were applied with modification. A casual examination of these would show that these were rightly not applied being beyond the border line of ceded items of Defence, External Affairs, Communications and Ancillary.

At this stage it would be pertinent to mention that Article 246 in its original form clearly laid down that in relation to the State of Jammu and Kashmir reference to clauses (2) and (3) in clause (1) of the Article and clauses (2) (3) and (4) of the Article shall not apply. This made ėxistence of State and Concurrent Lists only a matter of theoretical interest for our State. All that was yielded in Union List for federal legislation was thus known; rest of the powers were of the State and State alone. Such a decision was quite in keeping with the true spirit and context of federal polity. This is particularly so when application of Articles 248 and 249 were also excluded, the two having been completely omitted from the application to our State.

Their non-application ensured that residuary powers of legislation remained with the State unimpaired and Parliament could not legislate about any State matter even when there would have been a situation envisaged by Article 253.

It is note-worthy that all the entries made applicable particularly the substituted entry 97 read with modified Article 248 were not even remotely connected with Defence, External Affairs and Communications, nor can they in entirety or otherwise be regarded as ancillary to matters covered by these three subjects.

Changes from 1954 onwards, particularly in sixties were so

rapid that things started changing even beyond recognition. Encroachment on State jurisdiction was obvious, thereby reducing the State autonomy to a mockery.

Recommendations

In the legislative field, therefore, it is recommended as under:

(a) Matters in the Union list not connected with the three subjects of Defence, External Affairs and Communications and/or ancillary thereto but made applicable should be excluded from their application to the State.
(b) All modifications made in Article 246 in its application to the State subsequent to the 1950 Order should be rescinded.
(c) Articles 248, 249, 250 and 251 whether applied in original or substituted/modified form should be omitted in relation to the State.
(d) As in 1950 and 1954 List II (State) and List III (Concurrent) of the Seventh Schedule should not be applicable to the State.
(e) Article 254 be restored to the position it had in its application to our State in 1954.
(f) Articles 262 and 263 which were not applicable under 1950 Order but were subsequently extended to the State should cease to apply.

PART XV

Elections

(Articles 324 to 329)

Since elections to the State Legislature are held under laws made by the State Legislature, Article 324 should continue to apply in the manner and the way it was applicable in 1950/1954 Order. This is particularly so when the State Constitution had provisions relating thereto.

Recommendation

Therefore, change brought about in this Part after 1954 be reversed and consequential changes in other Articles in this Part be effected.

PART XVIII

Emergency Provisions

(Articles 352 to 360)

The following should be added to Clause 6 of Article 352.

Recommendation

(a) "provided that this request for concurrence of the Government of the State shall be subject to whatever decision the State Assembly may take within two months of declaration of emergency and failing any such decision, the proclamation of Emergency shall be deemed to have been revoked".

(b) Sub-clause (b) of clause (6) of this Article should be deleted.

(c) Articles 355, 356, 357, 358, 359 and 360 should be made non-applicable to the State of Jammu and Kashmir as was the position in 1954.

PART III

Fundamental Rights

(Articles 12 to 35)

Recommendation

This Part should be deleted. A separate chapter on Fundamental Rights needs to be included in the Jammu and Kashmir Constitution. Situation where Directive Principles do not apply and Fundamental Rights apply is not a happy one. Directive Principles in the State Constitution apply but in the absence of a provision these can hardly mean anything to Fundamental Rights which are enshrined in the Union Constitution. Fundamental Rights chapter in the State Constitution would add weight and worth to the organic law of the land and give the citizens satisfaction of even testing worth of Directive Principles for Legislation and for governance according to letter and spirit of law.

PART V

The Union

(Articles 52 to 151)

Very few Articles from this Part wer made applicable, in

1954 Order but the situation was changed with the passage of Constitution (Application to J&K) Order, 1960 and thereafter. Normally there can be no dispute now with the extended jurisdiction of the Supreme Court over matters in regard to our State, but it has got to be recorded that this aspect of State-Union relationship was not settled at the time of Delhi Agreement of 1952 and after the events of 1953 quick decisions were forced upon the flawed Constituent Assembly followed by a number of Constitution (Application to J&K) Orders. The position which ultimately has emerged is that the State of J&K has been accorded the same status as the rest of the States except for the above form of Articles 133 and 134 applied to the State. The judiciary of India has been unitary in character during the British rule and it remained so under the new Constitution of India adopted in 1950. Jammu and Kashmir too became part of it. notwithstanding the fact that strong views to have judicial autonomy were expressed during negotiations for Delhi Agreement, 1952. In any case divergent views were recorded.

The State had at that time a High Court whose judgements were subject to appeal/review before His Highness, advised in his judicial functions by a Board of Judicial Advisors consisting of eminent jurists/knowledgeable persons. That has not to be and reopening that chapter may not sound appropriate now except, of course, where adopting of provisions of the Union Judiciary for the State have in a way infringed upon the corresponding provisions of the State Constitution in regard to the State High Court.

Recommendation

(a) Article 72(1)(c), 72(3), 133, 134, 135, 136, 138, 145(1)(c) and 151(2) should be made non-applicable to the State as was the position in 1950 Order.
(b) Articles 149, 150 and 151 should apply to the State in the form in which they were in 1954.

PART VI

(Articles 152-237)

Article 124(4) of the Constitution of India mandates that a Supreme Court Judge shall not be removed from his office except by an Order of the President passed after an address by each

House of Parliament supported by a majority of the total membership of that House and by a majority of not less than two-thirds of the members of that House present and voting, has been presented to the President in the same session for such removal on the ground of proved misbehaviour or in capacity. Article 218 has in the course of time been applied to the J&K State. The position as it obtained prior to C.O. 60 was that under the State Constitution the removal of a judge of the High Court by the President for proved misbehaviour or incapacity could be on the basis of an address for removal supported by a majority of the total membership of each House of Legislature of the State and by the majority of not less than two-thirds of the members present and voting. But after the aforesaid application Order of 1960, the power to pass an address for such removal vests with the Parliament in accordance with Article 124 (4). Part VII of the State Constitutions deals with the State High Court. The Part starts with section 93 (Constitution of High Court) and ends with Section 108 (Officers and Servants of the High Court). Of these, we have Sec. 95 (Appointment and Tenure of Office of Judges) and Sec. 99 (Resignation and Removal of a Judge of the High Court). The aforementioned provision about removal till 1959 was sub-section (2) of section 99 of the State Constitution. The Constitution of Jammu and Kashmir (First Amendment) Act, 1959 vide its section 4 deleted this provision and the question of removal of a judge for proved misconduct or incapacity was left to be taken care of as in the rest of the country by resort to procedure in section 124 clause (4) thereof. This was so vide Constitution (Application to J&K) Order No. 60 of 1960.

All provisions about High Court having been retained in the State Constitution including one about administrative expenses, salaries, allowances and pensions continuing to remain a charge upon consolidated fund of the State, deletion of the above provision regarding removal by means of an address being the duty, right and obligation of State Legislature and not Parliament in terms of Section 124(4) is, to say the least, not justifiable. Article 218 conceded this right in respect of other High Courts to Parliament. It is because all other provisions like 93 to 108 of our State Constitution are in their case part of the Union Constitution itself. We would, therefore, recommend the following in this regard:

Recommendation

(i) Article 218 be omitted in its application to the State. That would enable the State Legislature to re-enact the provisions as they existed in sub-section (2) and (3) of Section 99 of the State Constitution before the enforcement of J&K Constitution (First Amendment) Act of 1959.

(ii) Articles 220, 222 and 226 should also be omitted in their application to J&K State.

PART XII

Finance, Property, Contracts and Suits

(Article 264 to 300 A)

We have seen that in 1952 during and after negotiations for Delhi Agreement that Article 266 (relating to the Consolidated Funds of India and public accounts of India and of the States), Articles 282 and 284 (relating to the Union or public account of India), Articles 298, 299 and 300 (relating only to the Union or Government of India) were applicable. Exception was made in respect of Articles 264 and 265, clause (2) of Article 267, Articles 268 to 281, Clause 2 of Article 283, Articles 286 to 291. Articles 293, 295, 296 and 297, C.O. 48 of 14th May 1954 made Articles 264, 265, 268, 272, 274-281, 285, 289, 293, 295 to 297 applicable to our State. Articles 269 and 286 were applied with amendments in 1958.

Law for imposition of tax burden is clearly laid down. The rule in federal polity generally is that if the Union levies a tax in respect of matters assigned to it, it retains the proceeds yielded by such imposition. Same is true of a unit in a federation. There are, however, a number of exceptions as under Articles 268 and 269 in the matter of distribution of income tax as also of whole or part of proceeds of excise duty. Our State also would collect excise and stamp duties as specified in entries 84 and 91 of list I and appropriate the net proceeds. Same is true as a result of application of Article 269 to our State in respect of levies collected thereunder. Even Article 270 applies to our State.

What has been incorporated in the Constitution of the State viz. Consolidated Fund and Contingency Fund of the State as also custody thereof, and Public Account of the State is covered by sections, 115, 116, 118 and 119 of the Constitution of our State. In fact the position that emerges from the application of various Constitution Orders is that the provisions of the Constitution of India identical to what has been incorporated in the State Constitution in sections 115, 116, 117, 118, 119, 120, 121, 122 and 123 do not apply and for the rest, by and large, provisions of Part XII of the Constitution of India apply to our State as to the rest of the States.

On the passage of Constitution (Application to J&K) Second Amendment Order 1958 (C.O. 56) jurisdiction of the Auditor General and Comptroller was extended. This brought entry 76 of list 1 into the picture in its application to the State.

Despite allocations available to the State at present, we are firmly of the opinion that in order that the State should be financially viable, it needs more financial resources and assistance. It may be recalled that during 1952 Delhi talks, the discussion on financial arrangement between the Union and the Sate remained inconclusive.

Recommendation

It is, therefore, recommended that the matter be discussed indepth between the State representatives and the Union Government.

PART XIV

Services under the Union and the States

(Articles 308-323)

Article 308 excluded application of this Part to our State. There is hardly any federation in the world where such provisions as those contained in Article 312 and legislative enactments thereunder are envisaged. These were not applicable to the State even in 1954 but have been made applicable thereafter.

Notwithstanding seemingly an attractive proposition one can say without any fear of contradiction that it has dwarfed local talent and made it difficult for local youth to aspire to compete for key civil posts on competitive basis. The weak-kneed attempt to organise Kashmir Civil Service is neither here nor there and increasing inflow of All India Services has meant pretty little in the field for which the services were apparently conceived. No imperial model of civil services in central cadre can be or could be a substitute for what the local youth could be expected to have, i.e. local patriotic feeling and passionate attachment for the service of those among whom they live. Ever since the application of these provisions of the Indian Constitution to our State the number of direct recruits from the State has been negligible. The problem has attained so unpleasant a shape, even in the national context, that demands of greater number of promotees from local services all over the country have assumed alarming proportions.

Recommendation

It is, therefore, recommended that in Article 312, the brackets and words "(including the State of Jammu and Kashmir)" inserted by the Constitution (Application to J&K) Order 1958 be omitted.

PART XVI

Special Provisions relating to certain classes

Articles 330 to 342

Article 339 regarding control of the Union over the administration of scheduled Areas and the Welfare of scheduled tribes was not applicable to the State till 1985. It was applied in a modified form to the State vide Constitution (Application to J&K) Order of 1985.

Likewise, Article 342 has been applied for the first time to the State in 1985.

Recommendation

(i) It is recommended that the powers in respect of aforesaid matters be restored to the State.

(ii) Articles 330, 331, 334, 335, 336 which were applied by 1950 Order should continue to be applicable Articles 338, 339, 340, 341 and 342 have been applied after 1950. Their application to the State should be omitted and corresponding provisions be made in the State Constitution.

PART XX

Amendment of the Constitution

(Article 368)

Needless to mention that unlike other states of the Union, the

State of Jammu and Kashmir has a Constitution of its own. Before the Constitution (Application to J&K) Second Amendment Order, 1975 (C.O. 101) the State Legislature had unfettered powers to amend it. But vide this Order Clause (4) was added to Article 368 of the Indian Constitution in its application to our State which reads as under:

> "(4) No law made by the Legislature of the State of Jammu and Kashmir seeking to make any change in or in the effect of any provision of the Constitution of Jammu and Kashmir relating to—
>
> (a) appointment, powers, functions, duties, emoluments, allowances, privileges or immunities of the Governor; or
>
> (b) superintendence, direction and control of elections by the Election Commission of India, eligibility for inclusion in the electoral rolls without discrimination, adult suffrage and composition of the Legislative Council, being matters specified in sections 138, 139 and 50 of the Constitution of Jammu and Kashmir shall have any effect unless such law has, after having been reserved for the consideration of the President, received his assent."

The addition of this clause in the Indian Constitution has restricted the power of the State Legislature to amend its own Constitution. This uncalled for clog on the constituent powers of State Legislature needs to be removed lock, stock, and barrel.

Recommendation

It is therefore recommended that:

(i) clause (4) of Article 368 added vide C.O. 101 be deleted;

(ii) clause (2) of Article 368 should apply with the proviso already introduced by 1954 Order and Clause (1) thereof which was not in existence in 1954 and was introduced in 1971 should remain omitted in its application to the State.

PART XXII

(Schedules First to Twelve)

The Indian Constitution has 12 schedules only some of which apply to our State with or without modifications relatable to some of the Articles of the Constitution of India. Each Schedule which is applicable to the State of Jammu and Kashmir being fathered by a specific Article in the Constitution of the country will naturally suffer modification, change/substitution depending upon what that Article contains in regard to its application to the State of Jammu and Kashmir.

SEVENTH SCHEDULE

Seventh Schedule derives its character and quality from what Article 246 of the Constitution reads like. Its corresponding quality in respect of Jammu and Kashmir State naturally will depend upon the form and the content that Article 246 of the Constitution of India will assume in its relation to the State of Jammu and Kashmir. In 1950, Article 246 of the Constitution of India had one character and quality/content in its application to the State of Jammu and Kashmir and that was reflected in the number of entries in the Union List in the Seventh Schedule in their application to the State of Jammu and Kashmir. Later on, this Article suffered changes and consequently various entries in the Union List and the Concurrent List also suffered radical changes.

Recommendation

It is recommended that:—

(a) entries in the Union List which were applied to the State by 1950 Application Order should continue and all other entries made applicable to the State by subsequent orders should be omitted;

(b) Concurrent List was not applicable under 1950 Order and it was also agreed in the Delhi Agreement that this should not apply to the State. Hence all subsequent orders applying various entries from this list should be rescinded.

In sum, it is recommended that consistent with the above, requisite changes as may become necessary consequent upon change in the Articles of the Constitution of India in their application to the State of Jammu and Kashmir as a result of this report be effected in the Schedules concerned.

Changes Required in the State Constitution

In view of what has been stated in chapter XI ante, this Committee recommends the repeal of:

(i) The Constitution of Jammu and Kashmir (First Amendment) Act, 1959 relating to superintendence, direction and control of elections to the State Legislature and provisions relating to the State High Court; and

(ii) The Constitution of Jammu and Kashmir (Sixth Amendment) Act, 1965 relating to the mode of appointment and nomenclature of the Head of the State and nomenclature of the head of the Executive.

CHAPTER XIV

Summary of Recommendations

1. Temporary, Transitional and Special Provisions (Part XXI)

(i) The word 'Temporary' be deleted from the title of part XXI of the constitution of India and the word 'temporary' occurring in the heading of Article 370 be substituted by the word 'special'.

2. Legislative Relations (Part XI)

(a) Matters in the Union List not connected with the three subjects of Defence, External Affairs and Communications and/ or Ancillary thereto but made applicable should be excluded from their application to the State.

(b) All modifications made in Article 246 in its application to the State subsequent to the 1950 order should be rescinded.

(c) Articles 248, 249, 250 and 251 whether applied in original or substituted/modified form should be omitted from their application to the State.

(d) As in 1950 and 1954, List II (State) and List III (Concurrent) of the Seventh Schedule should not be applicable to the State.

(e) Article 254 should be restored to the position it had in its application to the State in 1954.

(f) Articles 262 and 263 which were not applicable under 1950 Order but were subsequently extended to the State should cease to apply.

3. Elections (Part XV)

Changes brought about in this Part be reversed and consequential changes in other Articles in this Part be effected.

4. Emergency Provisions (Part XVIII)

(a) The following should be added to Cl. 6 of Articles 352 in its application to the State:

> "Provided that this request for concurrence of the Government of the State shall be subject to whatever decision the State Assembly may take within two months of declaration of emergency and failing any such decision, the proclamation of emergency shall be deemed to have been revoked."

(b) Sub-clause (b) of Cl. (6) of this Article should be deleted.

(c) Articles 355, 356, 357, 358, 359 and 360 should be made non-applicable to the State as was the position in 1954.

5. Fundamental Rights (Part III)

This part should be deleted. A separate chapter on Fundamental Rights be included in the State Constitution.

6. The Union (Part V)

(a) Articles 72(1)(c), 72(3), 133, 134, 135, 136, 138, 145(1)(c) and 151(2) should be made non-applicable to the State as was the position in 1950 Order.

(b) Articles 149, 150 and 151 should apply to the State in the form in which they were in 1954.

7. The States (Part VI)

(i) Article 218 be omitted in its application to the State and the position as it existed before the J&K Constitution (First Amendment Act) of 1959 restored.

(ii) Articles 220, 222 and 226 should also be omitted in their application to Jammu and Kashmir State.

8. Finance, Property, Contracts and Suits (Part XII)

The matter be discussed between the State representatives and the Union Government as agreed to during the talks in 1952 (Delhi Agreement)

9. Services under the Union and the States (Part XIV)

In Article 312 the brackets and words "including the State of Jammu and Kashmir" inserted by the Constitution (Application to J&K) Order 1958 be omitted.

10. Special Provisions relating to certain classes (Part XVI)

Application of Articles 338, 339, 340, 341 and 342 to the State should be omitted and corresponding provisions made in the State Constitution.

11. Amendment of the Constitution of India (Part XX)

(i) Clause (4) of Article 368 added vide C.O. 101 be deleted.

(ii) Clause (2) of the Article should apply with the proviso already introduced by 1954 order and clause (1) thereof which was not in existence in 1954 and was introduced in 1971 should remain omitted in its application to the State.

12. Schedules

In the Seventh Schedule entries in the Union List not applied to the State by the Constitution (Application to J&K) Order, 1950 should be omitted. Concurrent List which was not applicable to the State in 1950 but was applied by subsequent orders should cease to apply to the State.

13. Changes in the State Constitution

All amendments in the Constitution of Jammu and Kashmir made vide:

(i) Constitution of Jammu and Kashmir (First Amendment) Act, 1959 insofar as they relate to superintendence, direction and control of elections to the State Legislature and to the State High Court; and

(ii) Constitution of Jammu and Kashmir (Sixth Amendment) Act, 1965 relating to change of nomenclature of the Head of the State and State Executive, mode of appointment of the Head of the State and other consequential amendments

should be repealed and the original provisions of the Constitution of Jammu and Kashmir restored.

To sum up the provisions of the Constitution of India specified in the Second Schedule and the matters specified in the first Schedule to the Constitution (Application to J&K) Order, 1950 and the matters agreed to by the representatives of the State and the Union vide Delhi Agreement of 1952 should continue to apply to the State subject to the same exceptions and modifications as are specified in the said Order and the Delhi Agreement. All Orders issued thereafter under clause (1) of Article 370 of the Constitution of India by the President, applying various provisions and matters of the Constitution of India to the State whether in full or in modified form or making any change in the provisions or matters already applied by 1950 Order or agreed to under Delhi Agreement, should be rescinded and the provisions or matters so applied to the State should cease to apply.

Also the changes made in the State Constitution vide Constitution of Jammu and Kashmir (First Amendment) Act, 1959 and Constitution of Jammu and Kashmir (Sixth Amendment) Act, 1965 be repealed and the original provisions of the Constitution of Jammu and Kashmir as adopted by the State Constituent Assembly on November 17, 1956 be restored.

CHAPTER XV

Safeguards for Future

In the preceding chapters we have discussed in detail the extent of erosion caused to the State autonomy from time to time and also suggested remedial measures. That completes the job assigned to us by first item of the terms of reference. There are, however, two other items which require our consideration. The first is to ensure the "inviolability" of the final settlement, and the other is to keep in mind the need to maintain "harmonious" relations with the Centre.

A suggestion has been made that Article 258 should be invoked for entrusting to the State "functions in relation to any matter to which the executive power of the Union extends." This would put a seal on the record of the past. "Functions" so "entrusted" can always be recalled back. The issue is not one of executive "functions" but legislative "powers" apportioned between the Union and the State under two solemn compacts between them, the Instrument of Accession in 1947 and the Delhi Agreement of 1952 to which the President's Order of May 14, 1954 gave constitutional sanction besides, of course, Article 370 itself. To them must we return if popular sentiment is to be respected and resentments assuaged. It is first and foremost a moral issue. It also has important constitutional and political aspects. In the nature of things redress can only be through another compact between the Union and the State. Once the basic principles are agreed, there will be discussion on procedure. Forty years of unconstitutional practice have created a mess. The best course is for the President to repeal all Orders which are not in conformity with Constitution (Application to Jammu and Kashmir) Order, 1950 and the terms of the Delhi Agreement of 1952.

Ever since, Article 370 has acquired a dangerously ambiguous aspect. Designed to protect the State's autonomy, it has been used systematically to destroy it. A compact is necessary between the Union and the State which makes ample redress and finalizes their relationship by declaring a "Constitutional Understanding" that Article 370 of the Constitution of India can no longer be used to apply to the State of Jammu and Kashmir any other provisions of the Constitution of India beyond the ones extended under 1950 Order and the Delhi Agreement, 1952. This could be embodied in a new Article that specifies the agreement as part of the unamendable basic structure of the Indian Constitution.

Such constitutional understandings have been formulated in other democracies. The complexities of our situation render it the best, perhaps the only, course for removing the debris of an unhappy past and building, in its place, a relationship between the State of Jammu and Kashmir and the Union of India which reflects the most vital aspect of federalism -mutual trust and respect.

(Gh. Mohi-ud-Din Shah)
Chairman

(Abdul Ahad Vakil)
Member

(Abdul Rahim Rather)
Member

(Piyaray Lal Handoo)
Member

(Bodh Raj Bali)
Member

(Molvi I.H. Ansari)
Member

(Kushok Thiksay)
Member

(Mirza Ab. Rashid)
Member

(S. Teja Singh)
Member-Convenor

APPENDIX II—1

Names of Individuals and Organisations from whom Memorandums and Letters have been Received in Response to the State Autonomy Committee's Notification No. D 18/J-27/96 dated 14.12.1996

1. C.R. Khamitkar, consulting Engineer Journalist, Mysore sales D.B. Mahinderkar Building: Shroff Bassaweshwar Road, Bijapur-586101.
2. Rev. Dr. Kodumutti A.J. Nadar, MBBS, M. Divinity 7, Palaniappa Nagar, Salem-636007, India.
3. S. Sunil Kumar S/O P.S. Nair Indira Bhawan. Chambayil Road. Neyyattinkar. P.O. Pin No. 695-121, Trivandrum District, State Kerela.
4. A.A. Syed, Managing Director Sir Syed and Sons Engineering (P) Ltd., Room No. 67. 3rd Floor Development Cooperative Bank Building; Paltun Road, Crawford Market Bombay-400001.
5. President Social and Cultural Welfare Society, Portroad Shaynam, Leh 194101.
6. President of Educational and Cultural Organisation, Tukcha Leh-194101 (Ladakh) J&K State.
7. President of Ladakh Budhist Association.
8. G.M. Khan, R/O Aribal Shalimar, Srinagar.
9. Ladakh People's Forum.
10. President of Youth Wing L.B.A., Tashis Gatsal Chowlamsar, Leh Ladakh.
11. T.N. Saraf (IAS Retd) FAO Representative at the United Nations (Retd).
12. President of Ladakh, Budhist Association, Youth Wing, Leh Ladakh.
13. President of Lamdon Social Welfare Society, Leh-194101, Ladakh, J&K, India.
14. Ashwani Kumar, Convenor Panun Kashmir Movement (PKM).
15. President of Gonpathundal Tsogspa, Cultural and Welfare Society, Leh-Ladakh.

16. P.N. Tengloo, Organising Secretary All State Kashmiri Pandit Conference.
17. Pyari Lal Sharma of Baramulla, C/O Sanjay Sharma, 32-R. Rani Park, Jammu Tawi-180001.
18. Hari Om, Ph.D. Professor and Head of the Department of History and Centre for History and Culture.
19. Vinayak G. Madhavi, Usha V. Madhavi, Miss Sharmila V. Madhavi, Advocates High Court, Swami Nivas, Opp. Dena Bank, 315/3, Thakurdwar, Bombay-400002.
20. Jammu Mukti Morcha.
21. Tsering Samphel, President District Congress Committee (I), Leh, 194101. Ladakh, J&K.
22. Harbajan Singh S/O Kartar Singh, R/O Rafiabad, Tehsil Sopore, VIII, Sialkote, Distt. Baramulla.
23. Jammu and Kashmir Bhartiya Janta Party, PT, Prem Nath Dogra Bhawan, Kachi Chawani.
24. President Lothun Tsogspa, Phey Village Leh-Ladakh.
25. President of Nyamuthun Society Mane-Tselding, Leh-Ladakh.
26. Mr. Yog R. Sharma, 2329 B-l N, 11th St. Arlington VA 22201 USA.
27. President of Chang Thang Youth Welfare Association, Nyoma Block, Ladakh (J&K), India.
28. Dr. R.S. Kanwar, 245-L, Model Town, Jalandhar.
29. M.I. Ansari Compound, Agra Rd. Narpoli, Bhiwandi-421305, Distt. Thane, Mumbai.
30. Prof. M.L. Kapur, 342-Jiwan Shah Street, Shahidi Chowk, Jammu.
31. Bansi Lal Kaul, Chairman Committee to build response on Autonomy constituted by Kashmiri Pandit Global Smit, 232-C, Ram Vihar, Old Janipura, Jammu-180007.
32. Lawers of Jammu Mubark Mandi, Jammu.
33. Panun Kashmir C/o Raman and Pawan Steel Works, new Plots, Jammu-180005.
34. Syed Shahabuddin, IPS (Retd) Ex-MP, Advocate, Supreme Court of India
35. Shri Justice V.M. Tarkunde.
36. Swami Raj Sharma, IAS, (Retd) Advocate, J&K High Court, Jammu.

37. R.D. Kewal Ramani, Advocate, Supreme Court of India, 65 Lawyer's Chamber, Tilak Marg, New Delhi-110001.
38. Satish Sharma, S/10-6, Akhnoor.
39. Abdul Rehman, Tukro Secretary, Kashmir Council of Communist Party of India.
40. V. Veulcate Reddy, d2-76, K.R. Palem Seellureipate.
41. Contours of Autonomy of the State of Jammu and Kashmir by witness.

APPENDIX II—2

List of Members of Political Parties, Journalists, Jurists and other Eminent Persons with whom discussions were held in New Delhi in November, 1997

1. Shri Sharad Yadav, President Janta Dal Party, Janta Dal Party Office, 7-Jantar-Mantar Road, New Delhi.
2. Shri Harkrishan Singh Surjit, General Secretary, CPI(M).
3. Justice V.M. Tarkunde.
4. Congress M.P's.
   i. Shri G.R. Kar,
   ii. Shri P. Namgial
   iii. Shri Janak Raj Gupta, Ex-M.P.
5. CPI Secretaries
   i. Shri D. Raja
   ii. Shri Atulkumar Anjaan
   iii. Shri Shamim Faizi.
6. Shri A.G. Noorani.
7. Shri B.G. Verghese, Journalist.
8. Shri Shahab-ud-din, Ex-M.P.
9. Shri S.R. Kesri, President, Indian National Congress, 7-Purana Qila Road, New Delhi.
10. Shri Mulayam Singh Yadav, 2-Menon Road, New Delhi.
11. Justice V.R. Krishana Iyer, Former Judge, Supreme Court at Kerela House, New Delhi.

APPENDIX II—3-A

Maharaja of J&K's Letter Dated 26-10-1947 to Lord Mountbattan

My dear Lord Mountbatten,

I have to inform Your Excellency that a grave emergency has arisen in my State and request immediate assistance of your Government.

As your Excellency is aware the State of Jammu and Kashmir has not acceded to the Dominion of India or to Pakistan. Geographically my State is contiguous to both the Dominions. It has vital economic and cultural links with both of them. Besides my State has a common boundary with the Soviet Republic and China. In their external relations the Dominions of India and Pakistan cannot ignore this fact.

I wanted to take time to decide to which Dominion I would accede, or whether it is not in the best interests of both the Dominions and my State to sand independent, of course with friendly and cordial relations with both.

I accordingly approached the Dominions of India and Pakistan to enter into Standstill Agreement with my State. The Pakistan Government accepted this Agreement. The Dominion of India desired further discussions with representatives of my Government. I could not arrange this in view of the developments indicated below. In fact, the Pakistan Government are operating Post and Telegraph system inside the State.

Though we have got a Standstill Agreement with the Pakistan Government they have permitted steady and increasing strangulation of supplies like food, salt and petrol to my State.

Afridis, soldiers in plain clothes, and desperadoes with modern weapons have been allowed to infilter into the State at first in Poonch and then in Sialkot and finally in mass area adjoining Hazara District on the Ramkot side. The result has been that the limited number of troops at the disposal of the State had to bedispersed and thus had to face the enemy at several points simultaneously, that it has become difficult to stop the wanton destruction of life and property and lotting. The Mahora powerhouse which supplies the electric current to the whole of Srinagar has been burnt. The number of women who have been kidnapped and raped makes my heart bleed. The wild forces thus let loose on the State are marching on with the aim of capturing

Srinagar, the summer Capital of my Government, as first step to over running the whole State.

I hereby declare that I accede to the Dominion of India on the assurance that if an agreement is made between the Governor-General and the Ruler of this State whereby any function in relation to the administration in this State of any law of the Dominion Legislature shall be exercised by the Ruler of this State, then any such agreement shall be deemed to form part of this Instrument and shall be so construed and have effect accordingly.

The terms of this my Instrument of Accession shall not be varied by any amendment of the Act or the Indian Independence Act, 1947, unless such amendment is accepted by me by an Instrument supplementary to this Instrument.

Nothing in this Instrument shall empower the Dominion Legislature to make any law for this State authorising the compulsory acquisition of land for any purpose, but I hereby undertake that should the dominion for the purposes of a Dominion law which applies in this State deem it necessary to acquire any land, I will at their request acquire the land at their expense or if the land belongs to me transfer it to them on such terms as may be agreed, or, in default of agreement, determined by an arbitrator to be appointed by the Chief Justice of India.

Nothing in this Instrument shall be deemed to continue in anyway to acceptance of any future Constitution of India or to fetter my discretion to enter into arrangements with the Government of India under any such future constitution.

Nothing in this Instrument affects the continuance of my sovereignty in and over this State, or, save as provided by or under this Instrument, the exercise of any powers, authority and rights now enjoyed by me as Ruler of this State or the validity of any law at present in this State.

I hereby declare that I execute this Instrument on behalf of this State and that any reference in this Instrument to me or the Ruler of the State is to be construed as including a reference to my heirs and successors.

Given under my hand this 26th day of October, nineteen hundred and forty-seven.

HARI SINGH
Maharajadhiraj of
Jammu and Kashmir State

APPENDIX II—3B

Instrument of Accession of Jammu and Kashmir State

Whereas, the Indian Independence Act, 1947, provides that as from the fifteenth day of August, 1947, there shall be set-up an independent Dominion known as INDIA, and that the Government of India Act, 1935, shall with such omissions, additions, adaptations and modifications as the Governor-General may by order specify, be applicable to the Dominion of India;

And whereas the Government of India Act, 1935, as so adapted by the Governor-General provides that an Indian State may accede to the Dominion of India by an Instrument of Accession executed by the Ruler thereof;

Now, therefore, I Shriman Indar Mahandar Rajrajeshwar Maharajadhiraj Shri Had Singhji Jammu Kashmir Naresh Tatha Tibbet adi Deshadhipathi, Ruler of JAMMU AND KASHMIR State in the exercise of my sovereignty in and over my said State do hereby execute this my Instrument of Accession and—

1. I hereby declare that I accede to the Dominion of India with the intend that the Governor-General of India, the Dominion Legislature, the Federal Court and any other Dominion authority established for the purposes of the Dominion shall, by virtue of this my Instrument of Accession, but subject always to the terms thereof, and for the purposes of the Dominion, exercise in relation to the State of Jammu and Kashmir (hereinafter referred to as "this State") such functions as may be vested in them by or under the Government of India Act, 1935, as in force in the Dominion of India on the 15th day of August, 1947 (which Act as so in force is hereinafter referred to as "the Act").
2. I hereby assume the obligation of ensuring that due effect is given to the provisions of the Act within this State so far as they are applicable therein by virtue of this my Instrument of Accession.
3. I accept the matters specified in the Schedule hereto as

the matters with respect to which the Dominion Legislature may make laws for this State.

4. I hereby declare that I accede to the Dominion of India on the assurance that if an agreement is made between the Governor-General and the Ruler of this state whereby any functions in relation to the administration in this state of any law of the Dominion Legislature shall be exercised by the ruler of this State, then any such agreement shall be deemed to form part of this Instrument and shall be construed and have effect accordingly.
5. The terms of this my Instrument of Accession shall not be varied by any amendment of the Act or of the Indian independence Act, 1947, unless such amendment is accepted by an Instrument supplementary to this Instrument.
6. Nothing in this Instrument shall empower the Dominion Legislature to make any law for this State authorising the compulsory acquisition of land for any purpose, but I hereby undertake that should the Dominion for the purpose of a Dominion law which applied in this state deem it necessary to acquire any land, I will at their requisite acquire the land at their expense or if the land belongs to me transfer it to them on such terms as may be agreed, or in default of agreement, determined by an arbitrator to be appointed by the chief Justice of India.
7. Nothing in this Instrument shall be deemed to commit me in any way to acceptance of any future Constitution of India or to fetter my discretion to enter into arrangements with the Government of India under any such future constitution.
8. Nothing in this Instrument affects the continuance of my sovereignty in and over this State, or save as provided by or under this Instrument, the exercise or any powers, authority and rights now enjoyed by me as Ruler of this State or the validity of any law at present in force in this State.
9. I hereby declare that I execute this Instrument on behalf

of this State and that any reference in this Instrument to me or to the Ruler of the State is to be construed as including a reference to my heirs and successors.

Given under my hand this 26th day of October Nineteen Hundred and Forty-Seven.

(Sd.) HARI SINGH
Maharajadhiraj of Jammu and Kashmir State.

APPENDIX II—3C

Acceptance of Accession

Lord Mountbatten's Reply to Maharaja Sir Hari Singh, Dated 27th October 1947

My dear Maharajah Sahib,

Your Highness's letter, dated the 26th October, has been delivered to me by Mr. V.P. Menon. In the special circumstances mentioned by Your Highness, my Government have decided to accept the accession of Kashmir State to the Dominion of India. Consistent with their policy that, in the case of any State where the issue of accession has been the subject of dispute, the question of accession should be decided in accordance with the wishes of the people of the State, it is my Government's wish that, as soon as law and order have been restored in Kashmir and her soil cleared of the invader, the question of the State's accession should be settled by a reference to the people. Meanwhile, in response to your Highness's appeal for military aid, action has been taken today to send troops of the Indian Army to Kashmir to help your own forces to defend your territory and to protect the lives, property and honour of your people.

My Government and I note with satisfaction that your Highness has decided to invite Sheikh Abdullah to form an Interim Government to work with your Prime Minister.

Yours sincerely,
Sd/- Mountbatten of Burma

New Delhi
October 27, 1947.

APPENDIX II—4

[1]The Constitution (Application to Jammu and Kashmir) Order, 1950

C.O. 10

In exercise of the powers conferred by clause (1) of Article 370 of the Constitution of India, the President, in consultation with the Government of the State of Jammu and Kashmir, is pleased to make the following Order, namely:

1. (1) This Order may be called the Constitution (Application to Jammu and Kashmir) Order, 1950.

(2) It shall come into force at once.

2. For the purposes of sub-clause (b)(i) of clause (1) of article 370 of the Constitution, the matters specified in the First Schedule to this Order, being matters in the Union List, are hereby declared to correspond to matters specified in the Instrument of accession governing the accession of the State of Jammu and Kashmir to the Dominion of India as the matter with regard to which the Dominion Legislature may make laws for that State; and accordingly, the Power of Parliament to make laws for that State shall be limited to the matters specified in the said First Schedule.

3. In addition to the provisions of article 1 and article 370 of the Constitution, the only other provisions of the Constitution which shall apply in relation to the State of Jammu and Kashmir shall be those specified in the Second Schedule to this Order; and shall so apply subject to the exceptions and modifications specified in the said Schedule[2] and to the modification that all references in the said provisions to the Rajpramukh shall be construed as references to the Sadar-i-Riyasat of Jammu and Kashmir.

THE FIRST SCHEDULE
(See paragraph 2)

[Note—The number of each entry in this Schedule is the number of the corresponding entry in the Union List.]

1. Published with the Ministry of Law Notification No. C.O. 10, dated the 26th January, 1950, Gazette of India, Extraordinary, 1950, Part II, Section 3(i), page 673, superseded by CO. 48.
2. Added by C.O. 43 dated 15th November, 1952.

1. Defence of India and every part thereof including preparation for defence.
2. Naval, military and air forces; and other armed forces of the Union.
3. Delimitation of cantonment areas, local self-government in such areas the constitution and powers within such areas of cantonment authorities and the regulation of house accommodation (including the control of rents) in such areas.
4. Naval, military and air force works.
5. Arms, firearms, ammunition and explosives.
6. Atomic energy for the purpose of defence and mineral resources necessary for its production.
9. Preventive detention for reasons connected with Defence, Foreign Affairs or the security of India.
10. Foreign Affairs; all matters which bring the Union into relation with any foreign country.
11. Diplomatic, consular and trade representation.
12. United Nations Organisation.
13. Participation in international conferences, associations and other bodies and implementing of decisions made thereat.
14. Entering into treaties and agreements with foreign countries, and implementing of treaties, agreements and conventions with foreign countries.
15. War and peace.
16. Foreign jurisdiction.
17. Naturalisation and aliens.
18. Extradition.
19. Admission into, and emigration and expulsion from India; passports and visas.
20. Pilgrimages to places outside India.
21. Piracies and crimes committed on the high seas or in the air, offences against the law of nations committed on land or on the high seas or in the air.
22. Railways, but as respects any railway owned by the State of Jammu and Kashmir, and either operated by that State or operated on its behalf otherwise than in accordance with a contract with the State by the Government of India, limited to a regulation thereof in respect of safety, maximum and minimum rates and fares, station and service terminal charges, interchange of traffic and the responsibility of the

railway administrtion as carriers of goods and passengers, and as respects any railway which is wholly situate within the State and does not form a continuous line of communication with a railway owned by the Government of India, whether of the same guage or not, limited to the regulation thereof in respect of safety and the responsibility of the railway administration as carriers of goods and passengers.

25. Maritime shipping and navigation, including shipping and navigation on tidal waters; provision of education and training for the mercantile marine and regulation of such education and training provided by states and other agencies.
26. Light houses, including lightships, beacons and other provision for the safety of shipping and aircraft.
27. Ports declared by or under law made by Parliament or existing law to be major ports, including their delimitation, and the constitution and powers of ports authorities therein.
28. Port quarantine, including hospitals connected therewith; seamen's and marine hospitals.
29. Airways; aircraft and air navigation; provision of aerodromes; regulation and organisation of air traffic and of aerodromes; provision for aeronautical education and training and regulation of such education and training provided by States and other agencies.
30. Carriage of passengers and goods by railway, sea or air.
31. Posts and telegraphs, telephones, wireless, broadcasting and other like forms of communication.
41. Trade and commerce with foreign countries.
72. Elections to Parliament, and the offices of President and Vice-President; the Election Commission.
73. Salaries and allowances of members of Parliament, the Chairman and of the House of the People.
74. Powers, privileges and immunities of each House of Parliament and of the members and the committees of each House; enforcement of attendance of persons for giving evidence of producing documents before committees of Parliament or commissions appointed by Parliament.
75. Salaries and allowances of the Ministers for the Union; the salaries, allowances, and rights in respect of leave of absence

and other conditions of service of the Comptroller and Auditor-General.

76. Audit of the account of the Union.
77. Constitution and organisation of the Supreme Court, and the fees taken therein; persons entitled to practise before the Supreme Court.
80. Extension of the powers and jurisdiction of members of a police force belonging to any State to railway areas outside that State.
93. Offences against laws with respect to any of the matters aforesaid.
94. Inquiries and statistics for the purpose of any of the matters aforesaid.
95. Jurisdiction and powers of all courts, except the Supreme Court, with respect to any of the matters aforesaid, but, except with the consent of the State Government, not so as to confer any jurisdiction or powers upon any courts other than courts ordinarily exercising jurisdiction in, or in relation to, the State; admiralty jurisdiction.
96. Fees in respect of any of the matters aforesaid, but not including fees taken in any court.

THE SECOND SCHEDULE

(See paragraph 3)

Provisions of the Constitution applicable	*Exceptions*	*Modifications*
Part-V	Articles 72(1)(c), 72(3), 133, 134, 135, 136, 138, 145(1)(c) and 151 (2).	1) Articles 80 & 81 shall apply subject to the modification that the representatives of the State in the Council of States and the House of the People respectively, shall be chosen by the President in consultation with the Government of the State. [1](1A) Articles 54 & 55 shall apply subject to the modifications: (a) that the references therein to

1. Ins. by C.O. 39, dated 20th March, 1952.

		the elected members of both Houses oi Parliament and to each elected member of either House of Parliament shall be deemed to include, respectively, a reference to the representatives of the State in those Houses and to each such representative. (b) that the references to the elected members of the Legislative Assemblies of the States and to each such elected member shall be deemed to include, respectively, a reference to the members of the Constituent Assembly of the State and to each such member, and (c) that the population of the State shall be deemed to be forty-four Lakhs and ten thousands. (2) Articles 149 and 150 shall apply subject to the modification that the references therein to the State shall be construed as not including the State of Jammu and Kashmir.
Part XI	Articles 247 to 252, clauses (3) and (4) of article 257 and articles 260, 262 and 263.	(1) Clause (1) of article 246 shall apply subject to the provisions of paragraph (2) of this Order and clauses (2) and (3) of article 246 shall not apply in relation to the State. (2) Clause (1) of article 259 shall apply subject to the modification that after the words "until Parliament by law otherwise provides", the words "and the concurrence of the State to such law has been obtained" shall be deemed to be inserted.

Part XII	Articles 264 and 265, clause (2) of article 267, articles 268 to 281, clause (2) of article 283, articles 286 to 291, 293, 295, 296 and 297.	(1) Articles 266 shall apply only in so far as it relates to the Consolidated Fund of India and the public account of India. (2) Articles 282 and 284 shall apply only in so far as they relate to the Union or the public account of India. (3) Articles 298. 299 and 300 shall apply only in so far as they relate to the Union or the Government of India.
Part XV	Articles 325 to 329	Article 324 shall apply only in so far as it relates to elections to Parliament and to the offices of the President and Vice President.
Part XVI	Articles 332, 333 and 337 to 342	(1) Article 330 shall apply only in so far as it relates to seats reserved for Scheduled Castes. (2) Article 334 shall apply only in so far as it relates to the House of the People. (3) Article 335 shall apply only in so far as it relates to the Union.
Part XVII	Nil	The provisions of this Part shall Apply only in so far as they relate to the official language of the Union and to proceedings in the Supreme Court.
Part XIX	Articles 362, 363 and 365[1] and clause (21) of article 366].	(1) Article 361 shall apply only in so far as it relates to the President. (2) Article 364 shall apply only in so far as it relates to the Laws made by Parliament.
Part XX	Nil	Article 368 shall apply subject to the additional proviso: "Provided further that no such amendment shall have effect in relation to the State of Jammu and Kashmir unless applied by order of the President under clause (1) of article 370."

1. Inserted by C.O. 43 *infra*.

Part XXI	Articles 369, 371 and 373, clause (4) of article 374, articles [1]376, 378 and 386 and clause (2) of article 388.	(1) In clause (3) of article 379 after the words "Minister for any such State", the words "other than the State of Jammu and Kashmir" shall be deemed to be inserted. (2) Article 389 shall apply only in so far it relates to Bills pending in the Dominion Legislature. (3) Article 390 shall apply only in so far as it relates to the Consolidated Fund of India.
Part XXII	Nil	Nil
First Schedule	Nil	Nil
Second Schedule	Paragraph 6	Nil
Third Schedule	Forms V, VI, VII and VIII	Nil
Fourth Schedule	Nil	Nil
Eighth Schedule	Nil	Nil

1. Substituted *ibid*. for "376 and 378".

ANNEXURE II—5

Inaugural Speech made by Sher-I-Kashmir Sheikh Mohammad Abdullah in the Jammu and Kashmir Constituent Assembly on 5th November, 1951

"Mr. President:

Today is our day of destiny. A day which comes only once in the life of a nation. A day on which to remember the hosts of those gone before us, and of those yet to come, and we are humbled by the greatness of this day.

After centuries, we have reached the harbour of our freedom, a freedom, which, for the first time in history, will enable the people of Jammu and Kashmir, whose duly elected representatives are gathered here, to shape the future of their country after wise deliberation, and mould their future organs of Government. No person and no power stand between them and the fulfilment of this—their historic task. We are free, at last to shape our aspirations as people and to give substance to their ideals, which have brought us together here.

We meet here today, in this palace hall, once the symbol of unquestioned monarchial authority, as free citizens of the New Kashmir for which we have so long struggled.

I see about me in this hall, many companions—Hindus, Muslims, Buddhists, Harijans and Sikhs, who first trod with me that path which has brought us to this Constituent Assembly of 1951. We fought as one against tyranny and oppression. We survived privations and bitter struggles. The Jails of Hari Parbat, Bahu, Baderwah and those other jails, which only imprisoned our bodies but could not crush our spirit.

When we took back on these years, we see how our footsteps have taken us not among the privileges, but into the homes of the poor and downtrodden, we fought their battle against privilege and oppression and against these darker powers in the background which sought to set man against man on the ground of religion. Our movement grew and thrived side by side with the Indian National Congress and gave strength and inspiration to the people of the Indian States.

I may be forgiven if I feel proud that once again in the history of this State, our people have reached a peak of achievement through what I might call the classical Kashmiri genius for synthesis, born of toleration and mutual respect. Throughout the long tale of our history, the highest pinnacles of our achievement have been scaled when religious bigotry and intolerance ceased to cramp us and we have breathed the wider air of brotherhood and mutual understanding.

Our movement to freedom has been enacted against the background of this same old struggle. We stood for the brotherhood of men of all creeds and strengthened our union on the basic of common work and sacrifice. Against us were ranged the forces of religious bigotry centered in the Muslim League and its satellites, and the Hindu communalists from within and without the State. Ranged against us and often in alliance with communalism were the forces of the autocratic States, backed up on the one hand by British Imperialism, the paramount power, and on the other, by the rich Landowners and other beneficiaries of Court patronage.

We must remember that our struggle for power has now reached its successful climax in the convening of this Constituent Assembly. It is for you to translate the vision of New Kashmir into reality, and I would remind you of its opening words, which will inspire our labours:

> "We the people of Jammu, Kashmir, Ladakh and the Frontier regions, including Poonch and Chenani Illaqas—commonly known as Jammu and Kashmir State—in order to perfect our union in the fullest equality and self-determination, to raise ourselves and our children for ever from the abyss of oppression and poverty, degradation and superstition, from medieval darkness and ignorance, into the Sunlit Valleys of plenty, ruled by freedom, science and honest toil, in worthy participation of the historic resurgence of the peoples of the East, and the working masses of the world, and in determination to make this our country a dazzling gem of the snowy bosom of Asia, do propose and propound the following Constitution of our State."

This was passed at the 1944 Session of the National Conference in Srinager. Today, in 1951, embodying such aspirations, men and women from the four corners of the State in this Constituent Assembly has become the repository of its sovereign authority. This Assembly, invested with the authority of a constituent body, will be the fountain-head of basic laws, laying the foundation of a just social order and safeguarding the democratic rights of all the citizens of the State.

You are the sovereign authority in this State of Jammu and Kashmir; what you decide has the irrevocable force of law. The basic democratic principle of sovereignty of the nation, embodied ably in the American and French Constitution, is once again given shape in our midst. I shall quote the . . . famous words of Article 3 of the French Constitution of 1791:

> "The source of all sovereignty resides fundamentally in the nation... Sovereignty is one and indivisible, inalienable and imprescriptable. It belongs to the nation."

We should be clear about the responsibilities that this power invests us with. In front of us lie decision of the highest national importance, which we shall be called upon to take. Upon the correctness of our decisions depends not only the happiness of our land and people now, but the fate as well of generation to come.

What then are the main functions that this Assembly will be called upon to perform!

One great task before this Assembly will be to devise a constitution for the future governance of the country, Constitution-making is a difficult and detailed matter. I shall only refer to some of the broad aspects of the Constitution, which should be the product of the labours of this Assembly.

Another issue of vital importance to the nation involves the future of the Royal Dynasty. Your decision will have to be taken both with urgency and wisdom for on that decision rests the future form and character of the State.

The third major issue awaiting your deliberations arises out of the Land Reforms which the Government carried out with vigour and determination. Our "land to the tiller" policy brought light into the dark homes of the peasantry; but, side by side, it has given rise to the problem of the landowner's demand for compensation. The nation being the ultimate custodian of all wealth and resources, the representatives of the nation are truly the best jury for giving a just and final verdict on such claims. So in your hand lies the power of this decision

Finally, this Assembly will after full consideration of three alternatives that I shall state later, declare its reasoned conclusion regarding accession. This will help us to canalise our energies resolutely and with greater zeal in direction in which we have already started moving for the social and economic advancement of our country.

To take our first task, that of Constitution-making we shall naturally be guided by the highest principles of the democratic constitution of the world. We shall base our work on the principles of equality, liberty, and social justice, which are an integral feature of all progressive Constitution. The rule of law as understood in the democratic countries of the world should be the cornerstone of our political structure. Equality before the law and the independence of the Judiciary from the influence of the Executive or vital to use. The freedom of the individual in the matter of speech, movement and association should be guaranteed; freedom of the Press and of opinion would also be features of our Constitution. I need not refer in great detail to all those rights and obligations, already embodied in NEW KASHMIR, which are integral parts of democracy which has been defined as "an apparatus of social organization wherein people govern through their chosen representatives and are themselves guaranteed political and civil liberties."

You are no doubt aware of the scope of our present constitutionalities with India. We are proud to have our bonds with India, the goodwill of whose people and Government is available to us in unstinted and abundant measure. The Constitution of India has provided for a federal union and in the distribution of sovereign powers has treated us differently from other constitutional units. With the exception of the items grouped under Defence, Foreign Affairs and Communication in the Instrument of Accession, we have complete freedom to frame our constitution in the manner we like. In order to live and prosper as good partners in a common endeavour for the advancement of our peoples. I would advise that, while safeguarding our autonomy to the fullest extent so as to enable us to have the liberty to build our country according to the best traditions and genius of our people, we may also by suitable constitutional arrangements with the Union establish our right to seek and compel federal cooperation and assistance in this great task, as well as offer our fullest cooperation and assistance to the Union.

Whereas it would be easy for you to devise a document calculated to create a framework of law and order, as also a survey of the duties and rights of citizens, it will need more arduous labour to take concrete decision with regard to the manner in which we propose to bring about the rapid economic development of the State and more equitable distribution of our national income among the people to which we are pledged. Our National conference avows its faith in the principal that there is one thing common to meet of all castes and creeds, and that is their humanity. That being so, the one ailment which is ruthlessly sapping the vitality of human beings in Jammu and Kashmir is their appalling poverty, and if we merely safeguard their political freedom in solemn terms, it will not affect their lives materially unless it guarantees them economic and social justice.

NEW KASHMIR contains a statement of the objectives of our social policy. It given broadly a picture of the kind of life that we hope to make possible for the people of Jammu and Kashmir and manner in which the economic organization of the country will be geared to the purpose. These ideals you will have to integrate with the political structure which you will devise.

The future political set-up which you decide upon for Jammu and Kashmir must also take into consideration the existence of various sub-national groups in our State. Although culturally diverse, history has forged an uncommon unity between them; they all are pulsating with the same hopes and aspirations, sharing in each others joys and sorrows. While guaranteeing this basic unity of the State, our constitution must not permit the concentration of power and privilege in the hands of any particular group or territorial region. It must afford the fullest possibilities to each of these groups to grow and flourish in conformity with their cultural characteristics, without detriment to the integral unity of the state or the requirement of our social and economic policies.

Now let us take up an issue of basic importance which involves the fundamental character of the State itself. As an instrument of the will of a self-determining people who have now become sovereign in their own right, the Constituent Assembly will now re-examine and decide upon the future of the present ruling dynasty, in respect of its authority.

The present House of the Rulers of our state based its claim to authority on the treaty Rights granted to it by the British Government in 1846. To throw light on the nature of these rights it will be helpful to recall that the British power, in its drive for territorial expansion, achieved its objectives through a network of alliances with the Indian Princes, subsidiary and subordinate offensive and defensive. This mutually helpful arrangement enabled the British to consolidate their power and strengthened the grip of the princes, giving them military help in the event of rebellion by their exploited subjects. The Butler Committee Report on Treaty Rights in 1929, bears ample testimony to this save.

"The duty of the Paramount Power to protect the State against rebellion and insurrection is derived from the clause of treaties and snads from usage and from the promise of the King Emperor to maintain unimpaired the privileges, rights and dignities of the Princes. . . . The promise of the King Emperor to maintain unimpaired the privileges, rights and dignities of the Princes carries with it a duty to protect the Prince against attempt to eliminate him and substitute another form of Government."

In recognition of their services to the British Crown, the Indian Princess earned the rewards of a limited sovereignty over their States under the Protection and suzerainty of the Paramount power. It was in this way that their right, privileges and prerogatives were preserved.

Thus the pioneers of the British imperialism subjugated India, aided by the Indian Princes. This was hardly diplomacy it amounted to fraud and deceit: Mutual agreements arrived at for such ignoble purposes were invested with the sanctity of treaties. And it is from such "treaties that the Princes claimed their right to rule. Our own stage provides a classic example of this. One glance at a page of our history will lay bare the truth.

The State of Jammu and Kashmir came to be transferred to Maharaja Gulab Singh in 1846 after the Sikh Empire began to disintegrate. His failure to render competent assistance to the Sikh armies was duly noticed by the British as also his willingness to acknowledge their authority. This paved the way for the total occupation of Northern India by the British who were nor slow in recognizing Maharaja Gulab Singh's services to them in reward they sold him the territory of Jammu and Kashmir for 75 lakhs of rupees, and in the Treaty of Amritsar, the British Government made over the entire country independent possession of Maharaja Gulab Singh and the heirs mail of his body. In this way, the entire population of Jammu and Kashmir state came under his absolute authority. The peculiar indignity of the transaction naturally offended the national self-respect of our people who resisted the occupation of their country. But the direct intervention of the British troops helped the Maharaja to take possession of the territory.

This event in the history of the State had catastrophic consequences for the people. The old feudal order, which was bad enough, gave way to more exacting rule, in which the Maharaja assumed all proprietary rights over land. The entire state was plunged into a chaotic economic condition, aggravated by a heavy state of taxation, tributes and levies which were required to make up for the money given by the Maharaja to the British. This unrelieved despotism reduced the bulk of the people to the level of serials. There was general impoverishment in 1948, some 4000 artisans started on a trek to Lahore, with the object of permanently setting there. Even the British counseled the Maharaja to loosen his grip so as to avoid a total collapse of his administration. Perhaps the forefathers of the great poet philosopher son of Kashmir Iqbal, where also part of the same trail of migrants who left the State at this time. When his agony over the fate of the people of his homeland bruit out in immortal verse, his feelings are echoed in the heart of every Kashmiri:

> "O Wind, if you pass through Geneva, give this message to the comity of the people of the world. They sold the peasant, his field, his property and the roof over his head, in fact, they sold the entire nation and for what a paltry price."

Invested with this absolute authority acquired in 1846 the present ruling dynasty was in power for one hundred years. This sad and stern century of servitude has stultified the growth of our people, leaving them in the backwaters of civilization. While in British India, and even in some of the Indian States, many a measure of reform was introduced to alleviate the misery of the people, in this state the unenlightened absolutism of the Rulers drove them deeper and deeper into poverty and degradation. The conditions became increasingly intolerable they made determined efforts to wrest power from the hands of the Ruler.

By 1947, India had achieved independence and reached one of her historical watersheds. It was clear that with the withdrawal of the Paramount Power, the treaty rights of the Indian Princes would cease Sovereignty in that case should revert to the people: they wished, therefore, to be consulted about the arrangements to be made with regard to the transfer of power. But a strange situation arose. The Cabinet Mission, while admitting the claims of the Indian National Congress and the Muslim League in British India, completely refused a similar representation of the States people, who would not allow the right of the princes to speak on their behalf.

In our own state the National Conference had made it clear as early as February 10, 1946 that it was against any further continuance of the treaty rights of the princes which had been made in times and under circumstances which do not obtain now and which have been framed without seeking in consent of the state peoples. Under such circumstances no treaties or engagements which act as dividing wall between their progress and that of their brethren in British India, can be binding on the people.

It was in this connection that I invited the attention of the Cabinet Mission to the standing inquiry of the Treaty of Amritsar and sought its termination. I wrote to the Cabinet Delegation that:

> "As the mission is at the moment reviewing the relationship of the princes with the Paramount Power with reference to treaty rights, we wish to submit that for us in Kashmir re-examination of this relationship is a vital matter because a hundred years ago in 1846, the land and people of Kashmir were sold away by the British for 50 lakhs of British Indian Rupees. The people of Kashmir are determined to mould their destiny and we appeal to the Mission to recognise the justice and strength of our cause."

In the Memorandum submitted to the Cabinet Mission later by the National Conference the demand for independence from autocracy was reiterated. Today the National demand of the people of Kashmir is not merely the establishment of responsible

Government, but their right to absolute freedom from autocratic rule. This immensity of the wrong done to our people by the sale deed of 1646 can only be judged by looking into the actual living conditions of the people. It is the depth of our torment that has given strength to our protest.

The indifferent attitude of the Cabinet Mission to the claims of the States people convinced us that freedom would not be given to a hundred million people who were to be left to groan under the heel of autocratic rulers. Consequently the National Conference gave a call to the people to prepare themselves for fresh ordeals and new responsibilities in the final bid for the capture of power from the hands of autocracy. This call came on the eve of the transfer of power in India and was therefore in keeping with the spirit of the times.

The partition of India in 1947 brought many new problems and developments in its wake in Kashmir, the very foundations of the administration began to shake and the Government made frontal efforts to patch up the cracking structure its incompetence had become glaring with the tribal raids on the State in October, 1947, it was obvious that the Maharaja's authority had ceased to function and the real power lay in the hands of the peoples' organization, the National Conference even at this hour of grave national danger, the Ruler failed to see the wisdom of taking this organization into his confidence and he preferred escape to the dignity of a formal surrender. When the situation became critical, the unprecedented pressure of the people, forced him to call upon the representatives of the National Conference to deal with the emergency, when he himself had failed to handle the affairs of the State effectively.

The emergency Administration in the state marked in effect a revolutionary transfer of power from the Ruler to the people.

It was, however, the proclamation of March 5, 1948, which constituted the first step towards the completion of National emancipation. On this day, I, as leader of the largest party of the State, was entrusted with its Government being assisted by a cabinet with full powers to run the administration. The Maharaja's authority was limited to that of a constitutional ruler, making it imperative upon him to consult his Government on an issues relating to the governance of the State.

This was obviously an interim measure. The cabinet of the

peoples' representatives thus chosen functioned with the support and cooperation of the National Conference, but with the passage of time it became clear that the Maharaja could not reconcile himself to this democratic system of Government. He put positive impediments in the way of the Government. These threatened to block much needed reforms in various spheres of administration. It was, therefore, natural that following disagreement between him and the Government on matters of policy, that he should disconnect himself from the administration and leave the state. His young son Yuvaraj Karan Singh thereupon became the Regent and has functioned since as constitutional head of the state.

Today the Constituent Assembly having met, the time has come for the people's representatives to make fundamental decision about the future position of the present dynasty.

It is clear that this dynasty can no longer exercise authority, on the basis of an old discredited Treaty. During my trial for sedition in the "Quit Kashmir" movement I had clarified the attitude of my party when I said:

> "The future constitutional set-up in the State of Jammu and Kashmir cannot derive authority from the old source of relationship which was expiring and was bound to end soon. The set-up could only rest on the active will of the people of the State, conferring on the Head of the State the title and authority drawn from the true and abiding source of sovereignty, that is the people".

On this occasion, in 1946 I had also indicated the basis on which an individual could be entrusted by the people with the symbolic authority of a Constitutional head.

"The State and its Head represent the constitutional circumference and the centre of this sovereignty respectively, the Head of the State being the symbol of the authority with which the people may invest him for the realisation of their aspirations and the maintenance of their rights."

In consonance with these principles, and in supreme fulfilment of the peoples, aspirations, it follows that a constitutional Head of the state will have to be chosen to exercise the functions which this Assembly may choose to entrust to him.

So far as my party is concerned, we are convinced that the

institution of monarchy is incompatible with the spirit and needs of modern times which demand an egalitarian relationship between one citizen and an other. The supreme test of a democracy is the measure of equality of opportunity that it affords to its citizens to rise to the highest point of authority and position. In consequence, monarchies are fast disappearing from the world picture, as something in the nature of feudal anachronisms. In India, too, where before the partition, six hundred and odd princes exercised rights and privileges of rulership, the process of democratisation has been taken up and at present hardly ten of them exercise the limited authority of Constitutional Head of State.

After the attainment of complete power by the people, it would have been an appropriate gesture of goodwill to recognize Maharaja Hari Singh as the first constitutional head of the state. But I must say with regret that he has completely forfeited the confidence of every section of the people. His incapacity to adjust himself to changed conditions and his antiquated views on vital problems constitute positive disqualifications for him to hold the high office of a democratic Head of the State. Moreover, his past actions as a ruler have proved that he is not capable of conducting himself with dignity, responsibility and impartiality. The people still remember in with pain and regret this failure to stand by them in times of crisis, and his incapacity to afford protection to a section of his people in Jammu.

Saint Thomas Aquinas, as early as the thirteenth century described the consequences of a king refusing to realise his responsibilities in these wise words:

> "A king who is unfaithful to his duty forfeits the claim to obedience. It is not rebellion to depose him for he is himself a rebel whom the nation has a right to put down. But it is better to abridge his power that he may be unable to abuse it. All political authority is derived from the people, and all laws ought to be made by them or their own representation. There is no security for us so long as we depend upon the will of another man".

Because of his background, it would, therefore, be impossible to think of his being associated again with the administration of the State.

I am sure none of us is interested in a personal controversy with the Maharaja's family. In the conduct of public affairs, it is necessary that an impartial view of every individuals deeds should be taken. Our judgement should not be wrapped by ill will or personal rancour. During our association with Yuvaraj Karan Singh these last few years, I and my colleagues in the Government have been impressed by his intelligence, his broad outlook and his keen desire to serve the country. These qualities of the Yuvaraj singh prove him as a fit choice for the honour of being chosen the first Head of the State.

There is no doubt that Yuvaraj Karan Singh in his capacity as a citizen of the State, will prove a fitting symbol of the transition to a democratic system in which the ruler of yesterday becomes the first servant of the people, functioning under their authority and on their behalf.

The next issue before us is that of the compensation which we should or should not grant to those landowners who have been expropriated during the putting into operation of the land to the tiller legislation under which land was given, or given back to the man who actually cultivates it.

It is not possible for you to consider this question dispassionately unless you understand something of the history of land tenure in the state. For us the well-being of the peasants who from the vast majority of the population of this country is a top priority; we realize that on a sound organization of agriculture, and the elimination of debit and the evils of landlordism their ultimate welfare depends. We sincerely believe that our body politic cannot be healthy as long as their exists here an army of men doing little or no work and getting easy remuneration for it, and as long as we perpetuate the dangerous age old class division of our society that landlordism breeds. Our attempt has been to make our land-dwellers contented. We set about these fundamental reforms in the following way.

On Martyrs day, the 13th of July, 1950 the Government declared its policy of liquidating the big landed estates and transferring land to the tillers of the soil. On the 17th of October, 1950 was enacted the Big Landed Estates Abolition Act. By this Act, the right of ownership in respect of lands in excess of 22/34 acres of land excluding orchards, grass and fuel reserves was abolished and such land was decreed to be transferred to the actual tillers to the extent of their possession. In this way, the right of the cultivator to the ownership of land in his possession was recognized and enforced and no new class of intermediaries or rent receivers was allowed to come into being. The abolition of landlordism is thus an accomplished fact and, there is no going back on the decision already taken. The big landed Estates Abolition Act, however, provides for the Constituent Assembly to settle the question of compensation with respect to the land from which expropriation has taken place, that question is now before you for decision.

The system of individual ownership of land is of modern growth and originally, the land belonged in common to communities of kinsmen or to the State Before the British rule, the proprietors were by no means the real owners of the soil and of all method for the collection of revenue during that time, the most noteworthy was that of collecting it direct from the cultivators through the Headmen of the villages. There is very little evidence to show that in Mughal and Sikh times, there were many rent paying tenants. The Ain-I-Akbari not only contains no regulations about tenants, but also recognise no intermediary between the cultivator and the State. Nevertheless there were some types of intermediaries in the pre-British period and also in later times, and it is the existence......of these intermediaries, which led to the development of landlordism in the State. The revenue farmers were on class of such intermediaries and so were the different privileged classes of assignees, Jagirdars, muafidars and mukarraridars, all enjoying feudal concession, which were created during the Mughal and Sikh times and also during the Dogra Rule.

In the Jammu Province, ownership of land was granted by State Deeds during the Sikh Rule and the earlier period of the Dogra Rule. In the Kashmir Province, the ownership of land was held by the Ruler since 1846 when Maharaja Gulab Singh purchased Kashmir from the British. It was in 1933 as a result of the pressure of public opinion than proprietary right in land was conferred on the landholders in the Kashmir province including the Frontier Districts, but this concession to mass demand for transfer of proprietorship of land to the actual cultivators was reduced to a fiction inasmuch as large tracts of land, granted by earlier Rulers to influential persons. Rajas and Dewiness by state Deeds were construed and acted upon as grants of the right of proprietorship in land in this manner were created big proprietors who did not cultivate their land themselves, but had tenants who paid them rent in cash and kind. The small peasant proprietor who cultivated land with his own hands also existed, but there were cases where the cultivators who had originally acquired holders', right and were recorded as such were relegated to the position of tenants by the right of land holding being granted by the Ruler to some of his favourites who did not cultivate the land themselves and where pure and simple rent receivers.

While the land settlement in the State was rightly made with the peasant proprietors, the settlement with the peasant proprietors, the settlement with the intermediary proprietors was not made on their recognition as proprietors of the soil, but because of certain political and financial reasons. It was well understood, even by the successive settlement officers and Settlement Commissioner in the State that though the intermediary proprietors were to be declared the proprietors of the soil, their tenants really were no ordinary tenants, but were in most cases, the original and hereditary possessors of the soil. The First Regular Settlement conducted in the state had perhaps nothing to do with the determination of the historical and accurate theory of the intermediary proprietors' position, nor was its function to confer on the proprietors a position comparable to what they originally were. It appears that the task of the settlement authorities was only to legalize all the original acts of illegality and usurpation by which intermediary revenue framers or rent receivers had assumed great power and influence in the period or disorder, before a proper Revenue Administration came to the country.

At the first Regular Settlement the area of land not under cultivation was very large. In 1891 AD when the later Sir Walter Lawrence was in the State, every inducement was given to the cultivators to till the land and in this way large tracts of State land where brought under cultivation. But even such lands as had been reclaimed and brought under the plough by the cultivators where gifted away in proprietary right to influential person. There were grants of land known as Chaks made under orders No. 5 and 6, otherwise known as the Pratap Code. All these grants were subject to substantial concession in land revenue. There were grants in different kind, as for instance. State Official's Grants in perpetuity, Hindu, Grants and others. The vast majority of these concessionist landholders obtained their grants by virtue of the high positions they had acquired. The grants under the Pratap Code were entirely made to the clan and the kinsmen of the Royal House in whose favour were also released some State Forest Reserves and cultivable areas in some Game Reserves. With the demarcation of forests in the Suite, several areas where excluded from the forests and let out for cultivation and for purposes of agriculture. State lands were similarly permitted to be used as Grazing Ground. The reclaimed land out of the Wular Lake and in and around the Dal Lake, which was owned by the State, was also released for cultivation. And then under Raj Tilak Room No. 4 about 26 years ago. State waste lands were granted as Village Commons equivalent to the aggregate cultivated land of each village, with the same rights as the landholders enjoyed in respect of their existing holdings. Even after the First Regular Settlement, many estates were sold to speculators or given over to those who were prepared to meet the land revenue demand in cases where default was made by actual cultivators, and the right to own land was recognized as that of the revenue payer as against the actual cultivator who defaulted. The no cultivating land owners leased out their interests and the middlemen leased it out in turn, creating a long chain of rent receivers and rent payers, who intervened between the state and the actual cultivators.

It will thus be seen that a substantial portion of the landed property came to be owned from such land as was the property of the state before and in every case the acquisition of land was free from any encumbrance or payment of any consideration. It is in the light of this historical background, therefore that the Hon'ble Members of this House shall have to consider whether there is any justification for payment of any compensation to such land owners for lands from which they are expropriated under the Big landed Estates Abolition Act.

Finally, we come to the issue, which has made Kashmir an object of world interest, and has brought her before the forum of the United Nations. This simple issue has become so involved that people have begun to ask themselves, after three and a half years of tense expectancy. "Is there any solution?" Our answer is in the affirmative. Everything hinges round the genuineness of the will to find a solution. If we face the issue straight, the solution is simple.

The problem may be posed in this way. Firstly was Pakistan's action invading Kashmir in 1947 morally and legally correct, judged by any norm of international behaviour? Sir Owen Dixon's verdict on this issue is perfectly plain. In unambiguous terms he declared Pakistan an aggressor. Secondly, was the Maharaja is accession to India legally valid or not? The legality of the accession has not been seriously questioned by an irresponsible or independent person or authority.

These two answers are obviously correct. Then where is the justification of treating India and Pakistan at par in matters pertaining to Kashmir? In fact, the force of logic dictates the conclusion that the aggressor should withdraw his armed forces, and the United Nations should see that Pakistan gets out of the State.

In that event, India herself anxious to give the people of the state a chance to express their will freely would willingly cooperate with any sound plan of dimilitarization. They would withdraw their forces, only garrisoning enough posts to ensure against any repetition of that earlier treacherous attack from Pakistan.

These two steps would have gone a long way to bring about a new atmosphere in the State. The rehabilitation of displaced people, and the restoration of stable civic conditions would have allowed people to express their will and take the ultimate decision.

We as a Government are keen to let our people decide the future of our land in accordance with their own wishes. If these three preliminary processes were accomplished we should be happy to have the assistance of international observers to ensure fair play and the requisite conditions for a free choice by the people.

Instead invader and defender have been put on the same plan. Under various grabs, attempts have been made to side track the main issues. Sometimes, against all our ideals of life and way of living attempts to divide our territories have been made in the form of separation of our State religion-wise with ultimate plans of further disrupting its territorial integrity once an offer was made to police our country with Commonwealth forces, which threatens to bring in impartial control by the back door. Besides, the repugnance which our people have however, to the idea of inviting foreign troops on their soil, the very presence of Commonwealth troops could have reacted suspicion among our neighbours that we were allowing ourselves to be used as a base of possible future aggression against them. This could easily have made us in a second Korea.

We have watched all this patiently but we cannot be indifferent to the growing sufferings of our people we cannot any longer tolerate being banded about and left with an indefinite future. Not only has our patience been tried to its limits but our self-respect has been challenged by allegation that we are the stooges of India. And nobody in our own land that our influence rests on Indian bayonets that we are running a police state and various other taunts and fantastic allegations.

We, therefore, thought if best to call upon our own people to declare what future they seek. At last we, in October, 1950 decided to convoke a Constituent Assembly, which would pronounce upon the future affiliations of our state. We were, and are, convinced that whatever some groups or individuals in the world outside might have to say about this decision of ours, there are in every country many people who have faith in justice and straightforward dealing.

I have no doubt that our considered views will be understood and supported by freedom-losing, peace-loving and democratic minded people all over the world. I am sure too that Almighty God who guards all just causes will bestow. His blessings upon us and guide our footsteps towards correct and honest ends.

The problem, then of accession has to be considered against the background of history in particular, of the immediate past consequent on the British quitting India disappearance of the paramount power. The end of the war brought to ahead the question of Indian freedom. Let me recapitulate. The Cabinet Mission was sent to India to hammer out plans for the transfer of power. This mission had a series of consultations with parties and leaders of opinion in British India, but refused to agree to the people of the Indian States being represented by their popular leaders and instead backed up their old allies, the Indian princes and my colleagues had at that time raised our voice against this attitude in the following words of our Memorandum:

> "The fate of the Kashmiri nation is in the balance and in this hour of decision we demand our basic democratic right to send our selected representatives to the constitution-making bodies that will construct the framework of Free India. We emphatically repudiate the right of the Princely Order to represent the people of the Indian States of their right to nominate their personnel representatives as our spokesmen."

I have no doubt in my mind that if popular representatives from the Indian States had been included in the discussions they would have certainly helped in having many controversial issues resolved fairly and smoothly. But that was not to be. To our misfortune, and to the misfortune of millions of people in India and Pakistan, the Cabinet Mission as well as the Indian political parties seemed to have been swayed by various conflicting considerations, with the result that the Indian sub-continent which had acquired an organic unity through ages of social, cultural and economic intercourse, was suddenly vivisected into the two Dominions of India and Pakistan. I need not relate here the horrors that followed this unnatural operation. Millions of hearts in both countries still ache with wounds that will not heal.

The agony of this change over became all the more intense as a result of the position in which the Indian States were left under the Indian independence Act of the Brilish parliament the paramountcy of the British Crown, against which the princes had been leaning, lapsed, and it was made clear that it would not be transferred to either of the succeeding Dominions. There were three alternative courses open to them. They could accede to either of the two Dominions or remain independent. This gave the princes, themselves the option to decide the fate of their States.

Following the announcement of the 'Mountbaten plan' on June 3, some of the Indian States acceded to Pakistan and some to India by means of Instruments of Accession executed through their princes. There were also some who entered into stand still Agreements with either or both pending finalization of their decisions.

"The betrayal of the interests of the State people had been expected following the rejection of the Memorandum of the National Conference, and so we in Kashmir decided to place the issue before the people themselves.

This is how our well-known "Quit Kashmir" agitation began. The National Conference once again led the people through a great struggle, and once again the Ruler tried to curb it, this time with unprecedented severity. But when a whole people is on the move, it is not possible to repress them and they do not stop until they wrest freedom and justice for themselves from the unwilling hands of those above them.

The crucial date of Indian and Pakistani independence therefore, came when I and my colleagues were still behind prison bars. The whole sub-continent was in a state of high tension and disturbance. If at that time, the head of the State of Jammu and Kashmir had even the slightest sense of realism or a proper awareness of the danger lurking in the situation, he would have immediately taken the people into his confidence. By associating their representatives with administration, I am sure many of the complications that arose later could have been avoided.

Instead of that, the Maharaja's Government entered in Stand Still Agreement with Pakistan, and this was accepted without question by that Dominion. A similar arrangement was suggested to India, also but it is noteworthy that the Government of India insisted that it could not consider any agreement entered into by the Government of the State valid until it had the approval of the people's representatives.

While the leaders constantly refused to recognise vital issue of accession without first securing the approval of his people, the Muslim League and the Pakistan government supported the claims of the Rulers to speak for their States. The late Mr. Jinah took the position that after the lapse of Paramountcy, the Princes were completely independent and that they could themselves determine what relations they should have with the two Dominions. Throughout the struggles that the people of Kashmir waged against autocracy we should never forget that the Muslim League leadership had completely disassociated itself from them and that, during the upsurge of 1946 their local party organs had assisted the administration to suppress the movement.

At this crucial time, then, Pakistan was under strict cover of secrecy perfecting her own plans, and the Dawn, the Muslim League official organ in Karachi, was appealing to the Maharaja to accede to Pakistan on the grounds that he would have far greater freedom there than in India.

It was at this stage taking advantage of the isolation of the Kashmiris from the rest of the world, that Pakistan imposed an economic blockade upon us with a view to starving us into submission. Attempts were made even to excite communal hatred to disrupt our peaceful civic life. Even in the face of such provocation, the National Conference, I am proud to say, took an objective and democratic stand. Immediately on my release from imprisonment, I clarified the issue at a mass meeting in Srinagar. The first and fundamental issue before us was the establishment of a popular Government. Our objective might be summarised a "Freedom First." Then alone could we as a free people decide our future associations through accession. I also made it clear that the National Conference would consider this issue without prejudice to its political friends and opponets, and strictly in accordance with the best interests of the country as a whole. I said that in the state of tension and conflict that obtained both in India and Pakistan, it was difficult for the people here and now to predict what the final shape of both would be.

You will realize, therefore, that we could not be accused of being partial to one side or the other. During that period we openly discussed the matter with representatives of the Muslim League who had come to Srinagar for this purpose. We even sent one of our representatives to Lahore to acquaint the authorities in Pakistan, with our point of view. We were thus still struggling against autocracy and for freedom when the state was suddenly invaded from the state of Pakistan.

The overwhelming pressure of this invasion brought about a total collapse of the armed forces of the State as well as its administrative machinery, leaving the completely defenseless people at the mercy of invaders. It was not an ordinary type of invasion, inasmuch as no canons of warfare were observed. The bribement tribesmen who attacked the state in thousands, killed, burned, looted and destroyed whatever came their way and in this savagery no section of the people could escape. Even the nuns and nurses of a Catholic Mission were either killed, or brutally maltreated. As these raiders advanced towards Srinagar, the last vestige of authority, which lay in the person of the Maharaja, suddenly disappeared from the Capital. This created a strange vacuum, and would have certainly led the occupation of the whole state by Pakistani troops and tribesmen, if, at this supreme hour of crisis, the entire people of Kashmir had not risen like a solid barrier against the aggressor. They halted his onrush, but could not stop him entirely as the defenders, had not enough experience, training and equipment to fight back effectively. There is no doubt that some of them rose to great heights of heroism during these fateful days. Who can help being moved by the saga of crucified Sherwani. Abdul Aziz, Brigadier Rajendra Singh, Prempal Sardar Rangil Singh early Militia boys like Punshkar Nath Zadoo, Somnath Bira, Ismail among scores of other named and unnamed heroes of all communities. But we though rich in human material lacked war equipment and trained soldiers.

When the raiders were fast approaching Srinagar, we could think of only one way to save the State from total annihilation by asking for help from a friendly neighbour. The representative of the National Conference, therefore, flew to Delhi to seek help from the Government of India. But the absence of any constitutionalities between our State and India made it impossible for her to render us any effective assistance in meeting the aggressor. As I said earlier, India had refused to sign a standstill agreement with the State for the ground that she could not accept such an agreement until it had the approval of the people. But now, since the people's representatives themselves sought an alliance, the Government of India showed readiness to accept it. Legally the instrument of Accession had to be signed by the Ruler of the State. This the Maharaja did. While accepting that accession, the Government of India said that she wished that "as soon as law and order have been restored in Kashmir and her soil cleared of the invader, the question of the States accession should be settled by reference to the people."

Actuated by a sincere desire to avoid bloodshed and further conflict, the Government of India approached the Security Council in 1948 with a plant against Pakistan. The request was simple. The contention of India was that Pakistan was responsible for the invasion of Kashmir and was continuing to help the raiders who had been employed as mercenaries for this purpose. And it was further said that legally bound as India was to clear the Jammu and Kashmir State of raiders. She might be constrained to pursue the invaders to their bases in Pakistan, which might lead to a still bigger conflagration. India, therefore, wanted the Security Council to dispose of the case as quickly as possible in the interest of peace.

If this had been done, condition would have ifso facto came into being when the people of Jammu and Kashmir would have expressed their will with regard to the continuance of the accession to the Dominion they had joined. This was not to be.

This is the essential background, which we must fully take into account. Now I shall indicate some of the considerations which should be kept in view when you the Hon'ble Members of this august Assembly, shoulder the grave responsibility of giving your considered opinion on this issue of accession which effects not only the present generation of our people but generations yet to come.

The Cabinet Mission Plan has provided for three courses which may be followed by the Indian states when determining their future affiliations. A state can either accede to India or accede to Pakistan but, failing to do either, it still can claim the right to remain independent. These three alternatives are naturally open to our state, while the intention of the British Government was to secure the privileges of the Princes: the representatives of the people must have the primary consideration of promoting the greatest good of the common people. Whatever steps they take must contribute to the growth of a democratic social order wherein all invidious distinctions between group and creeds are absent. Judged by this supreme consideration, what are the advantages and disadvantages of our states accession to either India or Pakistan, or of having an independent status?

As a realist I am conscious that nothing is all black or all white, and there are many facts to each of the proposition before us. I shall first speak on the merits and demerits of the State's accession to India. In the final analysis, as I understand it, it is the kinship of ideals, which determines the strength of ties between two States. The Indian National Congress has consistently supported the cause of the State's Peoples' freedom. The autocratic rule of the Princes has been done away with the representative Governments have been entrusted with the administration. Steps towards democratization have been taken and these have raised the people's standard of living, brought about much needed social reconstruction, and, above all built up their very independence of spirit. Naturally, if we accede to India there is no danger of a revival of feudalism and autocracy. Moreover, during last four years, Government of India has never tried to interfere in our internal autonomy. This experience has strengthened our confidence in them as a democratic State.

The real character of a State is revealed in its Constitution. The Indian Constitution has set before the country the goal of secular democracy based upon justice freedom and equality for all without distinction. This is the bedrock of modern democracy. This should meet the argument that the Muslims of Kashmir cannot have security in India, where the large majority of the populations are Hindus. Any unnatural cleavage between religious groups is the legacy of Imperialism, find no Modern State can at ford to encourage artificial divisions if it is to achieve progress and prosperity. The Indian Constitution has amply and finally repudiated the concept of a religious State, which is a throwback to medievalism, by guaranteeing the equality of rights of all citizens irrespective of their religion, colour, caste and class.

The national movement in our State naturally gravitates towards these principles of secular democracy. The people here will ever accept a principle, which seeks to favour the interests of one religion or social group against another. This affinity in political principles, as well as in past association, and our common path of suffering in the cause freedom, must be weighed properly while deciding the future of the State.

We are also intimately concerned with the economic well-being of the people of this State. As I said before while referring to constitution-building, political ideals are often meaningless unless linked with economic plans. As a State, we are concerned mainly with agriculture and trade. As you know, and as I have detailed before, we have been able to put through our "land to the tiller" legislation and make of it a practical success. Land and all it means is an inestimable blessing to our peasants who have dragged along in servitude to the landlord and his allies for centuries without number. We have been able under present conditions to carry these reforms through; are we sure that in alliance with landlord ridden Pakistan, with so many feudal privileges intact, that these economic reforms of ours will be tolerated? We have already heard that news of our Land Reforms has travelled to the peasants of the enemy-occupied area of our State who vainly desire a like status, and like benefits. In the second place, our economic welfare is bound up with our arts and crafts. The traditional markets for these precious goods, for which we are justly known all over the world, have been centered in India. The volume of our trade, in spite of the dislocation of the last few years, shows this. Industry is also highly important to us. Potentially we are rich in minerals, and in the raw materials of industry; we need help to develop our resources in India, being more highly industrialized than Pakistan, can give us equipment, technical services and materials. She can help us too in marketing. Many goods also which it would not be partical for us to produce here for instance, sugar, cotton, cloth and otherwise essential commodities can be got by us in large quantities from India. It is around the efficient supply of such basic necessities that the standard of living of the man-in-the-street depends.

I shall refer now to the alleged disadvantages of accession to India.

To begin with, although the land frontiers of India and Kashmir are contiguous, an all-weather road-link as dependable as the one we have Pakistan does not exist. This must necessarily hamper trade and commerce to some extent, particularly during the snowy winter months. But we have studied this question, and with improvements in modern engineering, if the State wishes to remain with India the establishment of an all weather stable system of communication is both feasible and easy. Similarly, the use of the State rivers as a means of timber transport is impossible if we turn to India, except in Jammu where the river Chenab still carries logs to the plans. In reply to this argument, it may be pointed out that accession to India will open up possibilities of utilizing our forest wealth for industrial purposes and that, instead of timber, finished goods which will provide work for our carpenters and labourers, can be exported to India where there is a ready market for them. Indeed in the presence of our fleets of timber-carrying trucks, river transport is a crude system which inflicts a loss of some 20% to 35% in transit.

Still another factor has to be taken into consideration. Certain tendencies have been asserting themselves in India, which may in the future convert it into a religious State wherein the interests of Muslims will be jeopardized. This would happen if a communal organization had a dominant hand in the Government, and Congress ideals of the equality of all communities were made to give way to religious intolerance. This continued accession of Kashmir to India should, however, help in defeating this tendency.

From my experience of the last four years, it is my considered judgement that the presence of Kashmir in the Union of India has been the major factor in stabilizing relations between the Hindus and Muslims of India. Gandhiji was not wrong when he uttered words before his death which para-phrase; "I lift up mine eyes unto the hills, from whence cometh my help."

As I have said before, we must consider the question of accession with an open mind, and not let our personal prejudices stand in the way of balanced judgement. I will now invite you to evaluate the alternative of accession to Pakistan.

The most powerful argument, which can be advanced in her favour, is that Pakistan is a Muslim State, and a big majority of our people being Muslim the State must acceded to Pakistan. This claim of being a Muslim State is of course only a camouflage. It is a screen to dupe the common man, so that he may not see clearly that Pakistan is a feudal State in which a clique is trying by these methods to maintain itself in power. In addition to this, the appeal to religion constitutes a sentimental and a wrong approach to the question. Sentiment has its own place in life, but often it leads to irrational action. Some argue, as supposedly natural corollary to this that our acceding to Pakistan our annihilation or survival depends. Facts have disproved this. Right thinking men would point out that Pakistan is not an organic unity of all the Muslims in this sub-continent. It has on the contrary, caused the dispersion of the Indian Muslims for whose benefit it was claimed to have been created. There are two Pakistanis at least a thousand miles apart from each other. The total population of Western Pakistan which is contiguous to our state, is hardly 25 million, while the total number of Muslims resident in India is as many as 40 million. As one Muslim is as good as another, the Kashmiri Muslim if they are worried by such considerations should choose the forty millions living in India.

Looking at the matter too from a more modern political angle, religious affinities alone do not and should not normally determine the political alliances of State. We do not find a Christian bloc, a Buddhist bloc, or even a Muslim bloc, about which there is so much talk now-a-days in Pakistan. These day's economic interests and a community of political ideals more appropriately influence the policies of States.

We have another important factor to consider, if the State

decide to make this the predominant consideration. What will be the fate of the one million non-Muslims now in our State? As things stand at present, there is no place for them in Pakistan. Any solution which will result in the displacement or the total subjugation of such a large number of people will not be just or fair, and it is the responsibility of this House to ensure that the decision that it takes an accession does not militate against the interests of any religious group.

As regards the economic advantages, I have mentioned before the road and river links with Pakistan. In the last analysis, we must however remember that we are not concerned only with the movement of people but also with the movement of goods and the linking up of markets. In Pakistan there is a chronic dearth of markets for our products. Neither, for that matter, can she help us with our industrialization, being herself industrially backward.

On the debit side we have to take into account the reactionary character of her politics and State politics. In Pakistan, we should remember that the lot of the State subjects has not changed and they are still helpless and under the heel of their Rulers, who wield the same unbridled power under which we used to suffer here. This clearly runs counter to our own aspirations for freedom.

Another big obstacle to dispassionate evaluation of her policies is the lack of a constitution in Pakistan. As it stands at present, this state enjoys the unique position of being governed by a Constitution enacted by an outside Parliament which gives no idea whatsoever of the future shape of civic and social relations. It is reasonable to argue that Pakistan cannot have the confidence of a freedom loving and democratic people when it has failed to guarantee even fundamental rights of its citizens. The right of self-determination for nationalities is being consistently denied and those who fought against Imperialism for this just right are being suppressed with force. We should remember Badshah Khan and his comrades who laid down their all for freedom, also Khan Abdus Samad Khan and other fighters in Baluchistan. Our national movement in the State considers this right of self-determination inalienable, and no advantage however great, will persuade our people to forego it.

The third course open to us has still to be discussed. We have to consider the alternative of making ourselves an Eastern Switzerland, of keeping aloof from both States, but having friendly relations with them. This might seem attractive in that it would appear to pave the way out of the present deadlock. To us as a tourist country it could also have certain obvious advantages. But in considering independence we must not ignore practical consideration. Firstly, it is not easy to protect sovereignty and independence in a small country, which has not sufficient to strength, defend itself on our long and difficult frontiers bordering so many countries. Secondly, we must have the good will of all our neighbours. Can we find powerful guarantors among them to pull together always in assuring us freedom from aggression? I would like to remind you that from August 15 to October 22, 1947, our State was independent and the result was that our weakness was exploited by the neighbour with whom we had a valid standstill Agreement. The State was invalid. What is the guarantee that in future we may not be victims of a similar aggression?

I have now put the pros and cons of the three alternatives before you. It should not be difficult for men of discrimination and patriotism gathered in this Assembly to weigh all these in the scales of our national good and pronounce where the true well-being of the country lies in the future.

Mr. President, it will be fitting here if I on this solemn occasion remember the last words of one of our martyrs which still ring in my ears. In 1931, the State Police had fired on our demonstrators, and many lay wounded and dying in the grounds of the Jammu Mosque. One man, supported by his old mother and young wife, was nearing his last breath, and he comforted them in their misery, forgetting his own. Then he called for me. When I came to him he looked me straight in the eyes and said. "We have done our duty. Now it is for you and the nation to carry it through to a successful end." Perhaps the spirit of that hero is in this Hall today to see one fulfilment of his dreams of this land of Kashmir. Today is a day of fulfilment for all—a day when we finally and triumphantly assert our right to decide our own future, free from threats of force and outside dictation.

On this historic day, we remember the Prime Minister of India, our cherished friend and never failing comrade on this difficult journey and, besides, an illustrious son of Kashmir, the many friends in India and some even in Pakistan, who in the years before partition, helped us forward. We remember the Ahrars who went to jail in their thousands for us; Badshah Khan and our friends of the frontier, now in jails and fighting for their own freedom. Nor can we ever forget our kith and kin across the cease-fire line who are at present living under the heel of the enemy. There welfare is always dear to us and we shall continue to regard them as an integral part of ourselves.

For twenty years, Mr. President, we have journeyed to this day and our criterion in all we do must be the welfare of our people. This consideration alone must guide our decision.

Now again, I have put my deepest thoughts before you and may God, in His merey, lead us all forward on the right path.

ANNEXURE II—6

Constitutional Relationship between the Jammu and Kashmir State and the Indian Union

[1]*Speech made by Jenab Sheikh Mohammad Abdullah in Jammu and Kashmir Constituent Assembly on 11 August, 1952*

Sir, I crave permission to make a statement before the House in regard to constitutional relationship between the Jammu and Kashmir State and the Indian Union. As the Hon'ble Members are aware, during the last Session of the Constituent Assembly, the Basic Principles Committee had submitted a report making certain specific recommendations about the future Head of the State. The Drafting Committee will, no doubt, submit its report to the House during this Session.

Since the changes proposed by this Assembly involved corresponding adjustments in the Indian Constitution, the Government of India desired that it should have time to discuss with our representatives the proposals pending in this Assembly. Accordingly, a Delegation headed by Hon'ble M.A. Beg was sent by us to Delhi. The Government of India also availed of this opportunity to discuss with our representatives other matters pertaining to the constitutional relationship, it became necessary for me and some of my other colleagues in the Government to participate in the talks. I am now in a position to inform the House that certain broad principles have been laid down and certain decisions have been tentatively arrived at between the two Governments.

Before I apprise this House of the details of these tentative decision, I wish to review briefly the background of our relationship with India. For sometime past, there has been a good deal of discussions on this important question both here as well as outside. In the heat of public controversy, which this question aroused, the points at issue were sometime obscured.

May I mention here the developments which led to the establishment of our relationship with India in October, 1947?

1. Jammu & Kashmir Constituent Assembly (debates), Part I, Ist Vol. 1951-55, pp. 485-97.

After the Independence Act of 1947 was passed by the British Parliament, the Dominion Status was conferred on India and Pakistan; and the British Parliament having lapsed the Indian States became Independent. They were however, advised to join either of these two Dominions. It is a tragic commentary on these arrangements proposed by the British Government that the position of these Indian States, comprising one-fourth of the total population of the entire Indian sub-continent, was left absolutely vague and nebulous with the result that the future of the States people came to be subjected to the vagaries of their respective rules. Many of them acceded to either of the two Dominions after a good deal of procrastination while others hesitated and delayed the final decision to the detriment of the interests of the people living in these States.

The Jammu and Kashmir State was one of the States whose ruler had not taken a decision in regard to accession. While the State was in the condition of uncertainty and indecision and while the national movement was seeking transfer of complete power to the representatives of the people and the then State Government was indulging in repression in certain areas of the State particularly in Poonch, the State was suddenly invaded. Thousands of tribesmen from Pakistan as well as Pakistan nationals, launched a savage attack against the people of this State. The administration then in charge of its affairs proved singularly ineffective to cope with the grave emergency and consequently it collapsed all of a sudden. At that critical movement in the history of the State, the National Conference stepped into avert what looked like total annihilation at the hands of the raiders from Pakistan who were later proved to have been abetted by the Pakistan Government. The National Conference once mobilized all sections of the population in an effort to prevent conditions of chops and dislocation from spreading to the entire State. This factor was mainly responsible for the splendid moral displayed by the people of Kashmir who were inspired to heroic deeds in their resistance against the invaders.

It was, however, obvious that in face of the overwhelming number of the well armed raiders, unarmed people of Kashmir could not hold out for long. Consequently, it became urgently necessary for us to seek the assistance of the friendly neighbour which alone would enable us to throw back the invaders. In that critical moment, we could turn only to India where the Government and the people had demonstrated their sympathies for the ideals for which we were fighting the raiders.

But legal complications came in the way of India rendering the State any immediate help for its defence against aggression. The Government of India could send their army only if the State would acceded to that Dominion. In accordance with the Indian Independence Act of 1947, the Instrument of Accession had to be executed by the Ruler of the State in order to make it legally valid. Consequently, with the backing of the most popular organization in the country, the Maharaja signed the Deed of Accession on the 26th of October, 1947, and the State of Jammu and Kashmir became part of the Indian Dominion.

The basis of our relationship with India is the Instrument of Accession which enable our State to enter into a union with India. In accordance with the terms of the Instrument, certain powers were transferred to the Centre. The principle matters specified for this purpose in respect to which the Dominion Legislature could make laws for this State were:

(a) Defence,
(b) External Affairs, and
(c) Communications.

This arrangement involved a division of sovereignty which is the normal feature of a Federation. Beyond the powers transferred by it to the Dominion, the State enjoyed complete residuary Sovereignty.

These terms of the association of our State with the Dominion of India were maintained; and, subsequently, when the Constituent Assembly of India was charged with the task of framing a constitution, this overriding consideration was kept in view in determining the position of the State in the proposed Constitution earlier to this, it had been agreed between the two Governments that "in view of the special problems arising in respect of this State and the fact that the Government of India have assured its people that they would themselves finally determine their political future", a special position should be accorded to Jammu and Kashmir in the future Constitution so that a limited field of the Union Powers over the State is ensured. Four representatives were nominated from the Jammu and Kashmir State to the Constituent Assembly of India. These representatives participated in the deliberations of the Constituent Assembly of India at a time when the bulk of the Indian Constitution had already been adopted. It was at this stage that the constitutional position of the State was determined in the Constitution of India. The representatives of the Jammu and Kashmir State reiterated their views that our association with India should be based on the terms of the Instrument of Accession. It was also made clear that while the accession of the Jammu and Kashmir State with India was complete in fact and in law to the extent of the subjects enumerated in this instrument, the autonomy of the State with regard to all other subjects outside the ambit of the Instrument of Accession should be preserved.

Taking into account the special circumstances in which this State was placed, a special constitutional arrangement was evolved and provided in Article 370 of the Constitution which defines the position of Jammu and Kashmir as follows:

"Notwithstanding anything in this Constitution—

(a) the provisions of Article 238 shall not apply in relation to the State of Jammu and Kashmir;

(b) the power of parliament to make laws for the said States shall be limited to;

  (i) those matters in the Union list and the Concurrent list which, in consultation with the Government of the State, are declared by the President to correspond to matters specified in the instrument of Accession governing the accession of the State to the Dominion of India as the matters with respect to which the Dominion legislature may make laws for that State; and

  (ii) such other matters in the said lists as with the concurrence of the Government of the State, the President may by order specify.

Explanation: For the purposes of this Article; the Government of the State means the person for the time being recognized by the President as the Maharaja of

Jammu and Kashmir acting on the advice of the Council of Ministers for the time being in office under the Maharaja's proclamation dated: the fifth day of March, 1948;

(c) the provisions of Article 1 and of this article shall apply in relation to that State;

(d) such of the other provisions of this Constitution shall apply in relation to that State subject to such exceptions and modifications as the president may by order specify: Provided that no such order which relates to the matters specified in the Instrument of Accession of the State referred to in paragraph (1) of sub-clause (b) shall be issued except in consultation with the Government of the State:

Provided further that no such order which relates to matters other than those referred to in the last preceding proviso shall be issued except with the concurrence of the Government.

(2) If the concurrence of the Government of the State referred to in paragraph (ii) of sub-clause (b) of clause (1) or in the second proviso to sub-clause (d) of that clause be given before the Constituent Assembly for the purpose of framing the Constitution of the State is convened, it shall be placed before such Assembly for such decision as it may take thereon.

(3) Notwithstanding anything in the foregoing provisions of the Article, the President may by public Notification, declare that this Article shall cause to be operative or shall be operative only with such exceptions and modifications and from such date as he may specify:

Provided that the recommendation of the Constituent Assembly of the State referred to in clause (2) shall be necessary before the President issues such a Notification."

While the State of Jammu and Kashmir is included in the list of States in Part B of Schedule 1 of the Constitution, it is apparent from a perusal of this Article that the provisions of Article 238 relating to the Constitution of the States in Part B shall not apply to the State of Jammu and Kashmir. In view of the special position and character of the State and with a view to regulate the relationship of the State with the Union of India, Article 370 was devised.

The other important feature of this constitutional set-up is that the matters specified in the Instrument of Accession shall apply in relation to the Jammu and Kashmir State in consultation with the Government of Jammu and Kashmir State and all other matters which do not fall within the terms of the Instrument of Accession shall not apply in relation to our State except with the final concurrence of the Jammu and Kashmir Constituent Assembly.

Here I would like to point out that the fact that Article 370 has been mentioned as a temporary provision the Constitution does not mean that it is capable of being abrogated, modified or replaced unilaterally. In actual effect, the temporary nature of this Article arises merely from the fact that the power to finalize the Constitutional relationship between the State and the Union of India has been specifically vested in the Jammu and Kashmir Constituent Assembly. It follows that whatever modifications, amendments or exceptions that may become necessary either to Article 370 or any other Article in the Constitution of India in their application to the Jammu and Kashmir State are subject to decisions of this Sovereign Body.

Since a good deal of confuted thinking and uninformed criticism is indulged in by some interested people. I would like to point out here that the Constitution has confined the scope and jurisdiction of the Union Powers to the terms of Instrument of Accession with the proviso that they may be extended to such other matters also as the President may by order specify with the concurrence of the Jammu and Kashmir Constituent Assembly. The special problems facing the State were thus taken into account and under the Constitution the relationship approximated to that subsisting under the Instrument of Accession.

The Constitution of the Indian Union, therefore, clearly envisaged the convening of a Constituent Assembly for the Jammu and Kashmir State which would be finally competent to determine the ultimate position of the State in respect of the sphere of its accession which would be incorporated as in the shape of permanent provisions of the Constitution.

This briefly, is the position which the Constitution of India has accorded to our State. I would like to make it clear that any suggestions of altering arbitrarily this basis of our relationship with India would not only constitute a breach of the spirit and letter of the constitution, but it may invite serious consequences for a harmonious association of our State with India. The formula evolved with the agreement of the two Governments remains as valid today as it was when the Constitution was framed and reasons advanced to have this basis changed seem completely devoid of substance.

In arriving at this arrangement the main consideration before our Government was to secure a position for the State which would be consistent with the requirements of maximum autonomy for the local organs of State Power which are the ultimate source of authority in the State while discharging obligations as a unit of the Federation.

I would, therefore, plead that the validity of such constitutional arrangement should not be appraised academically but in the proper context of the extraordinary circumstances through which the State has been passing for the last five years or so. Since the State was invaded in 1947, the situation here has been bristling with such compelling urgencies as needed drastic administrative and economic changes. The revolutionary conditions prevailing in our State could be coped with only through extraordinary measures. The Government of the State was, therefore, called upon to take vital decisions which could not wait. Accordingly, it enacted laws which were calculated to transform the social and economic fabric of the common people. With the improvement in the internal situation of the country, the necessity for a legislature become obvious. Consequently, it was decided to convince a Constituent Assembly for the State elected on the basis of adult franchise. This Assembly accordingly came into being in October, 1951.

The Hon'ble members are aware that as the Leader of the National Conference Party, I indicated in my inaugural address the scope of the decisions which I felt the Constituent Assembly would have to take. I listed the four main issues as pertaining to the main functions to the Assembly, viz., the future of the Ruling Dynasty, payment of compensation for the land transferred to cultivators under the Big Landed Estates Act, Ratification of the State's accession to India as well as the framing of a Constitution for the State. While discussing these in my address to this House, I had given clear indications of my party views in regard to them. I had also an occasion to place my point of view on these issues before the representatives of the Government of India and I had the satisfaction that they approved of it.

When the Constituent Assembly commenced its labours, it had to tackle these issues in course of time. It took decisions in regard to payment of compensation to landlords and it came to the conclusion that no compensation was justified.

The Constituent Assembly has, at present, under its consideration the future of the Ruling Dynasty. In this connection the Basic Principles Committee recommended that the Institution of hereditary rulership in the State should be abolished and in future the office of the Head of the State should be elective. While accepting the recommendations of the Basic Principles Committee this Assembly charged the Drafting Committee to place before this House appropriate proposals for the implementation of these recommendations.

As I said in the beginning of my statement, such a fundamental decision involved corresponding adjustments in the Indian Constitution and in order to finalize the position in respect of this issue and other matters pertinent to it. I and my colleagues had discussions with the representatives of the Government of India as a result of which we arrived at some tentative agreements, the details of which I wish to place before the House.

The Government of India hold the view that the fact that the Jammu and Kashmir State was the constituent unit of the Union of India led inevitably to certain consequences in regard to some important matters, namely:

(a) Residuary powers;
(b) Citizenship;
(c) Fundamental Rights;
(d) Supreme Court of India;
(e) National Flag;
(f) The president of India;
(g) The Headship of the State;
(h) Financial Integration;
(i) Emergency Provisions; and
(j) Conduct of election to Houses of Parliament.

Permit me, Mr. President, now to deal with each one of these items and also the agreement arrived at between the Jammu and Kashmir Government and the Government of India in relation to them.

Residuary Powers

It was agreed that while under the present Indian Constitution, the Residuary Powers vested in the Centre in respect of all States other than Jammu and Kashmir, in the case of our State, they vested in the State itself. This position is compatible with Article 370 of the Indian Constitution and the Instrument of Accession on which this Article is based. We have always held that the ultimate source of sovereignty resides in the people. It is, therefore, from the people that all powers can flow. Under these circumstances, it is up to the people of Kashmir through this Assembly to transfer more powers for mutual advantage to the custody of the Union Centre.

Citizenship

It was agreed that in accordance with Article 5 of the Indian Constitution persons who have their domicile in the Jammu and Kashmir State shall be the citizens of India. It was further agreed that the State Legislature shall have power to define and regulate the rights and privileges of the permanent residents of the State, more especially in regard to acquisition of immovable property, appointments to services and like matters. Till then the existing State law would apply. It was also agreed that special provisions should be made in the laws governing citizenship to provide for the return of those permanent residents of Jammu and Kashmir State, who went to Pakistan in connection with the disturbances of 1947 or in fear of them as well as of those who have left for Pakistan earlier but could not return. If they returned, they should be entitled to the rights, and privileges and obligations of citizenship.

There are historic reasons which necessitate such constitutional safeguards as for centuries part, the people of the State have been victims of exploitation at the hands of their well-to-do neighbours. The Hon'ble Members are perhaps aware that in the late twenties, the people of Jammu and Kashmir agitated for the protection of their bonafide right against the superior competing interest of the non-residents of the State. It was in response to this popular demand that the Government of the day promulgated a Notification in 1927 by which a strict definition of the term "State Subject" was provided. I am glad to say that the Government of India appreciated the need for such a safeguard. No definition of the special rights and privileges of the residents of the State can afford to remain static. The need may arise at one stage or the other to liberalize such a definition. The importance of the fact that the State Legislature shall retain powers to be able to effect such modifications becomes obvious in this context.

There is yet another class of State Subjects whose interests had to be safeguarded. The Hon'ble Members of this House are aware that on account of the disturbances of 1947 and also as a consequence of the invasion of this country by Pakistan, large number of the residents of this State suffered dislocation. We have therefore, to visualize the possibility of their return to their homes and hearths as soon as normal conditions are restored. It has been suggested in certain quarters that this protection has been provided only for those residents of the State who are at present stranded in Pakistan. I would like to make it clear, as I have stated earlier, that this protection will operate only when the conditions are normal and such conditions naturally presume that the resettlement of the dislocated population, whether Muslims or Non-Muslims cannot be one sided or unilateral.

FUNDAMENTAL RIGHTS

It is obvious that while our Constitution is being framed, the Fundamental Rights and duties of a citizen have necessary got to be defined. It was agreed, however, that the Fundamental Rights, which are contained in the Constitution of India could not be conferred on the residents of Jammu and Kashmir State in their entirety taking into account the economic, social and political character of our movement as enunciated in the New Kashmir Plan. The need for providing suitable modification amendments and exceptions as the case may be in the Fundamental Rights Chapter of the Indian Constitution in order to harmonize those provisions with the pattern of our principles was admitted.

Particular care would have to be taken to preserve the basic character of the decisions taken by this House on the question of land compensation as well as the laws relating to the transfer of land to the tiller and other matters. The main point to be determined is whether the Chapter of our Fundamental Rights should form a part of the Kashmir Constitution on that or that of the Union Constitution.

Supreme Court

It was agreed that the Supreme Court should have original jurisdiction in respect of disputes mentioned in Article 131 of the Constitution of India. It was further agreed that the Supreme Court should have jurisdiction in regard to Fundamental Rights which are agreed to by the State.

On behalf of the Government of India, it was recommended that the Advisory Board in the State, designated "His Highness's Board of Judicial Advisors" should be abolished and the jurisdiction exercised by it should be vested in the Supreme Court of India. That is to say that the Supreme Court should be the final Court of Appeal in all civil and criminal matters as laid down in the Constitution of India.

We, however, felt that this would need a detailed examination and consequently it was agreed that we should have time to consider it further.

National Flag

We agreed that in view of the clarifications issued by me in my public statements while interpreting the resolution of this House according to which the old State flag was substituted by a new one. It was obvious that the new State flag was in no sense a rival of the National Flag. But for historical and other reasons connected with the freedom struggle in the State, the need for the continuance of this flag was recognized. The Union Flag to which we continue our allegiance as part of the Union will occupy the supremely distinctive place in the State.

President of India

It was agreed that the powers to grant reprieve commute

death sentences, etc. should also belong to the President of the Union.

Headship of the State

I am glad to inform this House that the Government of India have appreciated the principle proposed by the Basic Principles Committee as adopted by this Assembly in regard to the abolition of the hereditary rulership of the State. In order to accommodate this principle, the following arrangement was mutually agreed upon:

(i) The Head of the State shall be the person recognized by the President of the Union on the recommendation of the Legislature of the State;
(ii) He shall hold office during the pleasure of the President;
(iii) He may, by writing under his hand addressed to the President, resign his office; and
(iv) Subject to the foregoing provisions, the Head of the State shall hold office for a term of five years from the date he enters upon his office.

Financial Integration

In regard to this subject, we agreed that it would be necessary to evolve some sort of financial arrangement between the State and the Indian Union. But as this involved far reaching consequences, it was felt that a detailed and objective examination of this subject would be necessary.

Emergency Powers

On behalf of the Government of India, it was stated that the application of Article 352 of the Constitution was necessary as it related to vital matters affecting the security of the State. They did not press for the application of Article 356 or 360.

On behalf of the Kashmir Delegation, it was stated that the application of Article 352 to the State was not necessary. In the event of war on external aggression, item 1 in the Seventh Schedule relating to the defence of India applied and the Government of India would have full authority to take any steps in connection with defence, etc. In particular, we were averse to internal disturbance being referred to in this connection as even some petty internal disorder might be considered sufficient for the application of Article 352.

In reply it was pointed out that Article 352 could only be applied in a state of grave emergency and not because of some small disorder or disturbance.

In order to meet our view point, it was suggested on behalf of the Government of India that Article 352 might be accepted as it is with the addition at the end of the first paragraph (1) of the following words:

> "but in regard to internal disturbance at the request or with concurrence of the Government of the State".

We generally accepted this position, but wanted some time to consider the implications and consequences as laid down in Article 353, 358 and 359, which on the whole accepted. In regard to Article 354, we wanted to examine it further before expressing our opinion.

Conduct of Elections to Houses of Parliament

Article 324 of the Indian Constitution already applies to the State in so far as it relates to elections to Parliament and to the offices of the President and the Vice-President of India.

I have put before this House the broad indications of the agreement arrived at between us and the Government of India. As the Hon'ble Members will, no doubt, observe, the attitude of the Government of India has been most helpful. A satisfactory position has emerged and we are now able to assess the basic issues of our constitutional relationship with India in clearer terms. There has been a good deal of accommodation of our respective points of view. Both the representatives of Government of India and the Kashmir Delegation have been impelled by the desire to strengthen future the existing relationship to remove all security and vagueness. We are convinced, as ever before, that we have the full support both of the Government and the people of India in the fulfilment of our democratic ideals and the realization of our objectives.

This good will and amity, I am sure, will result in the consolidation of freedom and democracy in our country. I may however, emphasize, that the supreme guarantee of our relationship with India is the identity of the democratic and secular aspirations, which have guided the people of India as well as those of Jammu and Kashmir in their struggle for emancipation and before which all constitutional safeguards will take a secondary position.

It is of course, for the Constituent Assembly which is seized of these matters to determine the extent and scope of the State's accession to India. The Assembly may agree to continue this relationship on the present basis or extend its scope as it might like and consider feasible and proper. In the course of framing the Constitution for the State, the Hon'ble Members of this Assembly will have an opportunity of discussing these agreements and expressing their views thereon.

I thank you Sir, for affording me this opportunity to place before the Hon'ble Members of the House the result of our recent talks with the representatives of the Government of India.

APPENDIX II—7

[1]Statement of Pt. Jawahar Lal Nehru, Prime Minister of India in the House of People on July 24, 1952

". . . Now, the position since the Constitution was framed, is thus contained in Article 370 and in the President's Order following it. Article 370 was obviously of a transitional nature, and it allowed the President to make any additions to it, any variations to it, later on, the subject being that if any change or addition was required, we need not have to go through the cumbrous process of amending our Constitution, but the President was given authority to amend it in the sense of adding a subject, part of a subject, whatever it was to the other subjects in regard to Kashmir. But in Article 370, the old principle was repeated and emphasized that all these changes or any change required the approval of the Constituent Assembly of Jammu and Kashmir State. . . ."

". . . Now in regard to the talks we have had, the position, obviously the admitted position, is that the Jammu and Kashmir State is a constituent part or unit of the Indian Republic. It is a unit of India and is therefore a part of the territory of India. That is the basic position.

The question of citizenship arose obviously. Full citizenship applies there. But our friends from Kashmir were very apprehensive about one of two matters. For a long time past. In the Maharaja's time, there had been laws there preventing any outsider, that is, any person from outside Kashmir, from acquiring or holding land in Kashmir, if I may mention it in the old days the Maharaja was very much afraid of a large number of Englishmen coming and settling down there. Because the climate is delectable, and acquiring property. So, although most of their rights were taken away from the Maharaja under the British rule, the Maharaja stuck to this that nobody from outside should acquire land there. And that continues. And in the State Subjects notification by the Maharaja, they have defined four grades of subjects. Class number one, class two, class three and class four.

1. As per press release issued by Press Information of Bureau, Government of India dated July 24, 1952.

And unless you come in one of these classes, you just cannot acquire land there, or any immovable property. So the present Government of Kashmir is very anxious to preserve that right because, they are afraid, and I think rightly afraid, that Kashmir would be over run by people whose sole qualification might be the possession of too much money and nothing else, who might buy up and get the delectable places. Now they want to vary the old Maharaja's law to liberalize it, but nevertheless to have checks on the acquisition of lands by persons from outside. So far as we are concerned, I agree that under article 19, clause (5) of our Constitution we think it is clearly permissible both in regard to the existing law and any subsequent legislation. However, we agreed that this should be cleared up. The old State's subjects definition gave certain privileges regarding the acquisition of land, the services, and other minor things, I think, state scholarships and the rest. So, we agreed and noted down this.

The State Legislature shall have power to define and regulate the rights and privileges of the permanent residents of the State, more especially in regard to the acquisition of immovable property appointments to services and like matters. Till then the existing State law should apply.

Then there was another matter relating to citizenship because owing to these troubles in Kashmir since 1947 and little before and after there have been large number of people who have gone out of Kashmir but want to return. So there must be provision made for them to return. In fact in our own Constitution, some provision has been made and I might inform the House that this question was raised early this year or last year about the inclusion of a large number of migrants from East Bengal. We could not include them in our electoral rolls, because they came too late. We are including them now. Those that fulfil the conditions will all come in. So those who had gone away from Kashmir to Pakistan or elsewhere and who normally speaking might not be eligible for citizenship should be provided for, if they want to return so we said:

Special provision should be made in the laws governing citizenship for the return of those permanent residents of Jammu and Kashmir State, who went to Pakistan in connection with the disturbances of 1947 or earlier in fear of them, and could not return if they return they should be entitled to the rights and privileges and obligations of citizenship.

Then came the question of fundamental rights. Now there was general agreement that there should fundamental rights and these fundamental rights should apply to the State. But again there were great apprehensions in the minds of our friends from Kashmir. First of all, the question was how far these fundamental rights might not conic in the way of their land legislation now or any later development of it. Certainly we did not want them to come in the way of their land legislation. We like their land legislation. We thought it was very good, in fact it is quite impossible to upset a thing that has been done, but we said the matter should be cleared.

The second thing was this. Owing to all this business of invasion of Kashmir State, war, cease fire, all kinds of continuing tensions, difficulties due to infiltration, etc., constant attempts are made by infiltration, espionage cases are repeatedly heard. There is sabotage and the rest; but if you go to that State, you find normalcy there, that is to say, the state is functioning adequately normally, but behind that normalcy there is this tension, constant tension of an enemy trying to come in to create trouble, to disturb and all that. And the State Government has to be wary and watchful all the time and so we were told that it was possible that some part of the fundamental rights provisions might very well hamper the activities of the State Government from taking these precautions and these measures. We agreed that it was essential and in the interests of Kashmir situated as the State is now that the State Government should have that authority. So subject to this, further consideration can be given to it as to how this could be done, so that a fuller consideration of this and like matters was necessary so that the fundamental rights might be applied with such modifications and exceptions as might be considered necessary from this point of view, and agreed upon.

Then in regard to the Supreme Court it was agreed that the Supreme Court should have original jurisdiction in respect of disputes mentioned in Article 131 of the constitution of India. It was further agreed that the Supreme Court should have jurisdiction in regard to fundamental rights, which are applied to that State. On behalf of the Government of India we recommended that the advisory tribunal in the State which is designated as His Highness's Board of Judicial Advisors should be abolished and the jurisdiction exercised by it should be vested in the Supreme

Court of India that is to say that the Supreme Court should be the final Court of Appeal in all civil and criminal matters as laid down in the Constitution of India. The Kashmir Government delegation had no objection to this. They were prepared to agree but they said they would like to consider the matter in some detail further.

Now I come to the question which has been much discussed and referred to in the newspapers, the question of the Head of the State.

I might mention that apart from past history when this Constituent Assembly met in Kashmir the inaugural address to that Assembly stated quite clearly some of the policies that they were going to pursue, and among these policies was the election, by democratic process, of the head of the State. That has been the declared policy of the National Conference Organization in Kashmir for a long time. We had no objection with regard to the enunciation of that principle then. Now after careful consideration because we have always had to consider two matters: firstly, to give effect to the wishes of the people of the State, and secondly, to give effect to our own Constitution. We have come to an agreed formula. Of course, you will not attach too much importance to the language. A word here or there. For legal and constitutional purposes the words may be changed, but it describes the way we have been thinking and what we have agreed to. Now it was agreed (1) that the Head of the State shall be the person recognized by the President on the recommendation of the legislature of the State. How the Legislature of the state recommends is a matter for the Legislature. Whether it is by the process of election or not it is for them to decide; it may be by the process of a majority or two-thirds majority, it is entirely for them to decide. Anyhow they recommend and then it is for the President to recognize, (2) He that is Head of the State, shall hold office during the pleasure of the President, (3) He the Head of the State may by writing under his hand addressed to the President. Resign his office, and (4) Subject to the foregoing provisions of this article, the Head of the State shall hold office for a term of five years from the date he enters upon his office provided that he shall notwithstanding the expiration of his term, continue to hold office until his successor enters upon his office. That is so-far as the Head of the State is concerned.

Then there has been a good deal of misunderstanding in regard to the National Flag. This has been cleared up, I think, adequately by public statements made. Nevertheless, we thought that this should be further cleared up. Sheikh Abdullah, the Prime Minister of Jammu and Kashmir State had stated publicly that the question did not arise so far as they were concerned. Because the National Flag was the supreme flag and it had exactly the same status and position in the Jammu and Kashmir state as in any other part of India. The State flag was in no sense a rival to the National flag but for historical and sentimental reasons connected with their struggle for freedom in Kashmir, they wanted this state symbol to continue. This was agreed. It was added that this should be made clear in a formal manner, preferably by the Constituent Assembly of the State.

Thus in regard to the President of India, it was agreed that the powers to reprieve and commute death sentences, etc. should belong to the President of India.

There has been some talk about financial integration. It was decided that such financial arrangements between the State and the Government of India should be considered further and details worked out. The position as I said, is a dynamic changing one. Matters have to be gone into in some detail; so whatever the financial arrangements might be, we shall gradually work them out.

Then there is the question of emergency powers contained in our Constitution, more especially in our article 352 of the Constitution, it was agreed to; I will remind the House what article 352 is in case of invasion, external danger or internal disturbances, the President has power to declare a state of emergency and then various consequences flow from it. This parliament is then seized of the position. Now this was agreed to; but the friends from Kashmir were slightly apprehensive of what internal disturbances meant there. For the rest they have said, of course, if there is a grave emergency this should happen. So, with regard to adding some words to clear up, not to clear up that matter but rather to bring in the fact that in the case of internal disturbances any action taken should be with the concurrence of the Government of the State. It was agreed that article 352 of the Constitution should apply to the State with the addition at the end of the first paragraph of the following words:

"but in regard to internal disturbances, at the request or with the concurrence of the Government of the State."

That is the state of emergency will be declared with the concurrence of the Government of the State.

These are the principal things that have been discussed and I think that we have arrived at very satisfactory decisions, agreements which are in consonance with the wishes of the people of Kashmir and in consonance with our Constitution.

ANNEXURE II—8

Dr. Rajendra Prasad's note to Shri Jawahar Lal Nehru dated September 6, 1952

Rashtrapati Niwas
Simla
6th September 1952

My dear Prime Minister,

When you last saw me, I promised to send you a note on the legal and Constitutional aspect of the proposal to substitute a system of elected head for the Jammu and Kashmir State in place of the existing Rajpramukh. I now enclose a note for your consideration. In view of the complexity and importance of the issues involved, I have no doubt that the Attorney General and the Law Minister will be consulted.

I have received a memorial from the Maharaja, a copy of which, I understand, has also been received by you. Presumably, the Minister for States has also received a copy. I shall be glad in due course to have the comments of yourself and the Minister for States on this memorial.

I am leaving Simla on the morning of Sunday, the 7th September for places in the interior of Himachal Pradesh, but will be back by the evening of Tuesday, the 9th September.

I am sending copies of this letter with enclosure to the Ministers for Education, Defence and States.

Yours sincerely,

Rajendra Prasad

Shri Jawaharlal Nehru
Prime Minister

Enclosure:

The Prime Minister of Jammu and Kashmir has forwarded a copy of the resolution of the Constituent Assembly of the Jammu and Kashmir State relating to the substitution of a system of elected head of the state in place of Rajapramukh as at present with a request to the Government of India to take action to enable effect being given to the resolution. Along with the resolution two draft notifications to be issued by the President, one under clause (1) of that Article, have also been received. The former draft involves amendment of a provision of the Constitution of India and the latter contemplates a modification of two other provisions of the Constitution in its application to the State of Jammu and Kashmir. The proposal raises questions of considerable importance concerning the Constitutional scope of the proposed notifications and also about the competence of the President to have repeated recourse to the extraordinary powers conferred on him by the Article in question.

Before I take up this question it is very necessary to know whether any steps are being taken to amend the present Constitution of the State of Jammu and Kashmir. It appears from paragraph 6 of the resolution that there is already in existence the Jammu and Kashmir Constitution Act of 1996, which has been amended by Act No. XVII of 2008. Under this Constitution the Maharaja is presumably the head of the State, and it would obviously be necessary, as a first step, to amend that Constitution if it is decided to give immediate effect to the proposal now under consideration. Not having a copy of the Jammu and Kashmir Constitution Act, I am not in a position to say whether provision exists in that Constitution for its amendment, but inasmuch as it has been amended as recently as the Hindu Year 2008, I believe such provision does exist. I suggest that this question needs looking into.

The first draft notification enclosed with the letter of the Prime Minister of Jammu and Kashmir purports to be issued under clause (3) of Article 370. This clause is of a peculiar and exceptional nature in as much as it authorises amendments of Constitution by an executive act of the Government of India as distinguished from Parliament. The Constitution of India contemplates and lays down, apart from this article, two methods for its amendment. An amendment proper of the Constitution can be effected by the special procedure laid down in Article 368. There are certain other provisions in the Constitution in regard to which it is specially and specifically laid down that Parliament, by ordinary legislation can effect changes. In both these cases, it is the Parliament alone which can effect amendments. In the first case, even the power of Parliament to amend the Constitution is limited in as much as it can do so only if the special procedure in Article 368 is followed. In the second group of cases the Parliament is left free to pass legislation which may amount to amendment of the Constitution laid down. Nowhere else, as far as I can see is there any provision authorising the executive Government to make amendments in the Constitution, the temporary provisions contained in the Articles 391 and 392 having come to an end. There can be no doubt that Article 370, and particularly clause (3) thereof, is of an exceptional nature. While it safeguards in clause (2) the right of the Constituent Assembly of Jammu and Kashmir to revise or annul any action taken by the Government of that State in giving concurrence under clause 1(b)(ii) and the second proviso to clause l(d) of Article 370, it excludes altogether the Parliament of India from having any say regarding the Constitution of Jammu and Kashmir and places full power in the hands of the government including the power to amend the Constitution of India. It is therefore, necessary to examine the wording of this peculiar clause with some care for a correct appreciation of the comprehensive terms that:

> "Notwithstanding anything in the foregoing provisions of this article, the President may, by public notification, declare that this article shall cease to be operative or shall be operative only with such exceptions and modifications and from such date he may specify:
>
> "Provided that the recommendation of the Constituent Assembly of the State referred to in clause (2) shall be necessary before the President issues such a notification."

Clause (1) of this Article lays down that:

(a) the provisions of Article 238 shall not apply in relation to the State of Jammu and Kashmir;

(b) that the power of Parliament to make laws for the said State shall be limited to:

   (i) those matters in the Union list and the concurrent list which, in consultation with the Government of State, arc declared by the President to correspond to matters specified in the instrument of Accession governing the accession of the ate to the Dominion of India as the matter with respect to which the Dominion Legislature may make laws for that State; and

(ii) such other matters in the said Lists as with the concurrence of the Government of the State the President may by order specify.

Then follows explanation of the term "Government of the State" namely, the person for the time being recognized by the President as the Maharaja of Jammu and Kashmir acting on the advice under the Maharaja's proclamation dated the fifth day of March 1948.

The Article proceeds further to lay down in paragraph (c) and (d) of clause (1) that the provision(s) of Article 1 and of the Article shall apply in relation to that State; and that such of the other provisions of the Constitution shall apply in relation to that state subject to such exceptions and modifications as the President may by order specify: Provided that no such order which relates to the matter specified in the Instrument of Accession of the State referred to in paragraph (1) of sub-clause (b) shall be issued except in consultation with the Government of the State: and provided further that no such order which relates to matters other than those referred to in the last proceeding provision shall be issued with the concurrence of that Government.

The present proposal is to amend the Explanation in clause (1) by substituting for the words "as the Maharaja of Jammu and Kashmir acting the advice of the Council of Ministers for the time being in office under the Maharaja's Proclamation dated the fifth of March 1948." The word "as the Sadar-i-Riyasat of Jammu and Kashmir acting on the advice of the Council of Minister for the time being in office."

It is worthnothing that, while the proviso to clause (3) of Article 370 lays down that the recommendation of the Constituent Assembly of the State is a condition precedent to the issue of any notification by the President under the substantive provisions of the clause, it does not make it obligatory for the President to issue a notification to give effect to any recommendation that he may receive from the Constituent Assembly. Presumably it is deliberately so worded in order that the recommendation of the

Constituent Assembly could be examined on its merits before the President is advised to issue a notification under that clause. It is also worthnoting that the clause envisages two alternatives for the President, namely, either to declare that the whole of Article 370 shall cease to be operative or to declare that the whole of only with exceptions and modifications. In either case the President is further required to specify the date from which the notification is to take effect.

As I have already observed, the scope of this Article, if literally intercepted is exceedingly wide. Suppose the first alternative is adopted and whole of the Article is declared to be inoperative, what will be the result? One view would be that the Article being in the nature of an exception to the application of the Constitution of the State of Jammu and Kashmir, abrogation of the Article would result in the whole Constitution becoming applicable to the State of Jammu and Kashmir without any exception or modification. But the Article itself has been very peculiarly worded, for paragraph (c) of clause (I) of that Article expressly applies the provision of Article and of that Article to the State. In fact, it is because of this application of Article 1 to the State that the State is included within the territories of the Union. The abrogation of Article 370 abrogates along with the application of Article 1 to the State with the result that the State ceases to be part of the territory of India. I do not think that this could have been the intention of the framers of the Constitution for nowhere is the President empowered to exclude any portion of the territories of India from the Union. As a matter of fact, Article 2 contemplates the admission of fresh territories into the Union or the establishment of new States, but nowhere does the Constitution contemplate the exclusion of any territory from the territories of the Union.

Further, under the second alternative envisaged in clause (3), extensive power is conferred on the President to apply the Constitution to the State with such exceptions and modifications as may be specified in the notification and the question at once arises whether such an extensive power is exercisable from time to time or is exhausted by a single exercise thereof, judging by the language employed and by the very exceptional nature of the power conferred. I have little doubt myself that the intention is that the power is to be exercised only once, for then alone would it be possible to determine with precision which particular provisions should be excepted and which modified. The fact that President is also required to specify the date from which the notification is to take effect also tends to confirm this view. Although the phrase "exceptions modification" is used, there can be no doubt that what is involved is really an amendment by executive order of the Constitution in relation to the State of Jammu and Kashmir. Parliament could never have intended that such an extraordinary power of amending the Constitution by executive order was to be enjoyed without any limitation as to the number of times on which it could be exercised or as to the period within which it was exercisable or as to the scope and extent of the modifications and exceptions that could be made. It cannot be seriously maintained that for all time to come the application of our Constitution to Jammu and Kashmir would derive its authority from Article 370 to the complete exclusion of Parliament. The marginal note to Article 370 itself describes the nature of the Article as "Temporary Provision with respect to the State of Jammu and Kashmir". The conclusion, therefore, seems to me to be irresistible that clause (3) of Article 370 was not intended to be used from time to time. The correct view appears to be that recourse is to be had to this clause only when the Constituent Assembly of the State has been fully framed.

APPENDIX II—9

[1]The Constitution (Application to Jammu and Kashmir) Order, 1954
C.O. 48

In exercise of the powers conferred by clause (1) of article 370 of the Constitution, the President, with the concurrence of the Government of the State of Jammu and Kashmir, is pleased to make the following Order:

1. (1) This Order may be called the Constitution (Application to Jammu and Kashmir) Order, 1954.
   (2) It shall come into force on the fourteenth day of May 1954, and shall thereupon supersede the Constitution (Application to Jammu and Kashmir) Order, 1950.

2. The provisions of the Constitution which in addition to article 1 and article 370, shall apply in relation to the State of Jammu and Kashmir and the exceptions and modifications subject to which they shall so apply shall be as follows:

1. The preamble.
2. Part I: To article 3, there shall be added the following further proviso namely:

"Provided further that no Bill providing for increasing or diminishing the area of the State of Jammu and Kashmir or altering the name or boundary of that State shall be introduced in Parliament without the consent of the Legislature of that State."

3. Part II: (a) This part shall be deemed to have been applicable in relation to the State of Jammu and Kashmir as from the 26th day of January, 1950.

(b) To article 7, there shall be added the following further proviso namely:

1. Published in the Gazette of India, Extraordinary, Part II, Section 3, dated 14th May, 1954.

"Provided further that nothing in this article shall apply to a permanent resident of the State of Jammu and Kashmir who after having so migrated to the territory now included in the Pakistan, returns to the territory of that State under a permit for resettlement in that State or permanent return issued by or under the authority of any law made by the Legislature of that State, and every such person shall be deemed to be a citizen of India".

4. Part III: (a) In article 13, references to the commencement of the Constitution shall be construed as reference to the commencement of this Order.

(b) In clause (4) of article 15, the reference to Schedule Tribes shall be omitted.

(c) In clause (3) of article 16, the reference to the State shall be construed as not including a reference to the State of Jammu and Kashmir.

(d) In article 19, for a period of five years from the commencement of this order:

(i) in clauses (3) and (4), after the words "in the interest of" the words "the security of the State or" shall be inserted;

(ii) in clause (5) for the words "or for the protection of the interests of any Scheduled Tribes" the words "or in the interests of the security of the State" shall be substituted; and

(iii) the following new clause shall be added, namely:
'(7) The words "reasonable restrictions" occurring in clauses (2), (3), (4) and (5) shall be construed as meaning such restrictions as the appropriate Legislature deems reasonable'.

(e) In clauses (4) and (7) of article 22, for the word "Parliament", the words "the Legislature of the State" shall be substituted.

(f) In article 31, clauses (3), (4) and (6) shall be omitted; and for clause (5) there shall be substituted the following clause, namely:

"5 Nothing in clause (2) shall effect—

(a) the provisions of any existing law; or

(b) the provisions of any law which the State may hereafter make—

(i) for the purpose of imposing or levying any tax or penalty; or

(ii) for the promotion of public health or the prevention of danger to life or property; or

(iii) with respect to property declared by law to be evacuee property".

(g) In article 31-A, the proviso to clause (1), shall be omitted; and for sub-clause (a) of clause (2), the following sub-clause shall be substituted, namely:

'(a) "estate" shall mean land which is occupied or has been let for agricultural purposes or for purposes subservient to agriculture, or for pasture, and includes—

(i) sites of buildings and other structures on such land;

(ii) trees standing on such land;

(iii) forest land and wooded waste;

(iv) area covered by or fields floating over water;

(v) sites of jandars and gharats;

(vi) any jagir, inam, muafi or mukarrari or other similar grant; but does not include—

(i) the site of any building in any town, or town area or village abadi or any land appurtenant to any such building or site;

(ii) any land which is occupied as the site of a town or village; or

(iii) any land reserved for building purposes in a municipality or notified area or cantonment or town area or any area which a town planning scheme is sanctioned".

(h) In article 32, clause (3) shall be omitted; and after clause (2) the following new clause shall be inserted, namely:

"(2-A) Without prejudice to the powers conferred by clauses (1) and (2), the High Court shall have power throughout the territories in relation to which it exercises jurisdiction to issue to any person or authority, including in appropriate cases any Government within those territories, directions or orders or writs, including writs in the nature of *habeas corpus*, *mandamus*, prohibition, *quo warranto* and *certiorari*, or any of them, for the enforcement of any of the rights conferred by this Part."

(i) In article 35—

(i) references to the commencement of the Constitution shall be construed as reference to the commencement of this Order;

(ii) in clause (a) (i), the words, figures and brackets "clause (3) of article 16, clause (3) of article 32" shall be omitted; and

(iii) after clause (b), the following clause shall be added namely:

"(c) no law with respect to preventive detention made by the Legislature of the State of Jammu and Kashmir, whether before or after the commencement of the Constitution Application to Jammu and Kashmir) Order, 1954, shall be void on the ground that it is unconsistent with any of the provisions of this part, but any such law shall, to the extent of such unconsistency, cease to have effect on the expiration of five years from the commencement of the said Order, except as respects things done or omitted to be done before the expiration thereof.

(j) After article 35, the following new article shall be added namely:

'35-A. Saving of laws with respect to permanent residents and their right: Notwithstanding anything contained in this Constitution, no existing law in force in the State of Jammu and Kashmir, and no law hereafter enacted by the Legislature of the State,—

(a) defining the classes of persons who are, or shall be, permanent residents of the State of Jammu and Kashmir; or

(b) conferring on such permanent residents any special right and privileges or imposing upon other persons any restrictions as respects—

(i) employment under the State Government;
(ii) acquisition of immovable property in the State;
(iii) settlement in the State; or
(iv) right to scholarships and such other forms of aid as the State Government may provide,

shall be void on the ground that it is inconsistent with or takes away or abridges any rights conferred on the other citizens of India by any provision of this Part".

5. Part V: (a) In articles 54 and 55, references to the elected members of the House of the people and to each such member shall include references to the representatives of the State of Jammu and Kashmir in that House; and the population of the State shall be deemed to be forty-four lakhs and ten thousand.

(b) In the proviso to clause (1) of article 73, the words "or in any law made by Parliament" shall be omitted.

(c) Article 81 shall apply subject to the modification that the representatives of the State in the House of the people shall be appointed by the President on the recommendation of the Legislature of the State.

(d) In article 134, clause (2), after the words "Parliament may", the words "on the request of the Legislature of the State" shall be inserted.

(e) Articles 135, 136 and 139 shall be omitted.

(f) In articles 149 and 150, references to the States shall he construed as not including the State of Jammu and Kashmir.

(g) In article 151, clause (2) shall be omitted.

6. Part XI: (a) In article 246, the words, brackets and figures "Notwithstanding anything in clauses (2) and (3)" occurring in clause (1) and clauses (2), (3) and (4) shall be omitted.

(b) Articles 248 and 249 shall be omitted.

(c) In article 250, for the words "to any of the matters enumerated in the State List", the words "also to matters not enumerated in the Union List" shall be substituted.

(d) In article 251, for the words and figures, "articles 249 and 250", the word and figures "article 250" shall be substituted, and the words "under this Constitution" shall be omitted; and for the words "under either of the said articles", the words "under the said article" shall be substituted.

(e) To article 253, the following proviso shall be added, namely:

"Provided that after the commencement of the Constitution (Application to Jammu and Kashmir) Order, 1954, no decision affecting the disposition of the State of Jammu and Kashmir shall be made by the Government of India without the consent of the Government of that State".

(f) In article 254, the words, brackets and figure "or to any provision of an existing law with respect to one of the matters enumerated in the Concurrent List, then, subject to the provisions of clause (2)" and the words "or as the case may be, the existing law", occurring in clause (1), and the whole of clause (2) shall be omitted.

(g) Article 255 shall be omitted.

(h) Article 256 shall be renumbered as clause (1) of that article, and the following new clause shall be added thereto, namely:

"(2) The State of Jammu and Kashmir shall so exercise its executive power as to facilitate the discharge by the Union of its duties and responsibilities under the Constitution in relation to that State; and in particular, the said State shall, if so required by the Union, acquire or requisition property on behalf and at the expense of the Union, or if the property belongs to the State, transfer it to the Union on such terms as may be agreed, or in default of agreement, as may be determined by an arbitrator appointed by the Chief Justice of India."

(i) Article 259 shall be omitted.

(j) In clause (2) of Article 261, the words "made by Parliament" shall be omitted.

7. Part XII: (a) Clause (2) of article 267, article 273, clause 2 of article 283, articles 290 and 291 shall be omitted.

(b) In articles 266, 282, 284, 298, 299 and 300, references to the State or States shall be construed as not including references to the State of Jammu and Kashmir.

(c) In articles 277 and 295, references to the commencement of the Constitution shall be construed as references to the commencement of this Order.

8. Part XIII: (a) In clause (1) of article 303, the words "by virtue of any entry relating to trade and commerce in any of the Lists in Seventh Schedule" shall be omitted.

(b) In article 306, references to the commencement of the Constitution shall be construed as references to the commencement of this Order.

9. Part XIV: In article 308, after the words "First Schedule", the words "other than the State of Jammu and Kashmir" shall be added.

10. Part XV: (a) Article 324 shall apply only in so far as it relates to elections to Parliament and to the offices of President and Vice-President.

(b) Articles 235, 326, 327, 328 and 329 shall be omitted.

11. Part XVI: (a) In article 330, references to the "Scheduled Tribes" shall be omitted.

(b) Articles 331, 332, 333, 336, 337, 339 and 342 shall be omitted.

(c) In articles 334 and 335 references to the State or States shall be construed as not including references to the State of Jammu and Kashmir.

12. Part XVII: The provisions of this Part shall apply only in so far as they relates to—

(i) the official language of the Union;

(ii) the official language for communication between one State and another, or between a State and the Union; and

(iii) the language of the proceedings in the Supreme Court.

13. Part XVIII: (a) To article 352, the following new clause shall be added, namely:

"(4) No proclamation of Emergency made on grounds only of internal disturbance or imminent danger thereof shall have effect in relation to the State of Jammu and Kashmir (except as respects article 354) unless it is made at the request or with the concurrence of Government of that State."

(b) Articles 356, 357 and 360 shall be omitted.

14. Part XIX: (a) In article 361, after clause (4), the following shall be added, namely:

"(5) The provisions of this article shall apply in relation to the Sadar-i-Riyasat of Jammu and Kashmir as they apply in relation to a Rajpramukh, but without prejudice to the provisions of the Constitution of that State".

(b) Articles 362 and 365 shall be omitted.

(c) In article 366, clause (21) shall be omitted.

(d) To article 367, there shall be added, the following clause, namely:

(4) For the purposes of this Constitution as it applies in relation to the State of Jammu and Kashmir—

(a) references to this Constitution or to the provisions thereof shall be construed as references to the Constitution or the provisions thereof as applied in relation to the said State;

(b) references to the Government of the said State shall be construed as including references to the Sadar-i-Riyasat acting on the advice of his Council of Ministers;

(c) references to a High Court shall include references to the High Court of Jammu and Kashmir;

(d) references to the Legislature or the Legislative Assembly of the said State shall be construed as including references to the Constituent Assembly of the said State;

(c) references to the permanent residents of the said State shall be construed as meaning persons who, before the commencements of the Constitution (Application to Jammu and Kashmir) Order, 1954, were recognised as State subject under the law in force in the State or who are recognised by any law made by the Legislature of the State as permanent residents of the State; and

(f) references to the Rajpramukh shall be construed as references to the persons for the time being recognized by the President as the Sadar-i-Riyasat of Jammu and Kashmir and as including references to any person for the time being recognised by the President as being competent to exercise the powers of the Sadar-i-Riyasat".

15. Part XX: To article 368, the following proviso shall be added, namely:—

"Provided further that no such amendment shall have effect in relation to the State of Jammu and Kashmir unless applied by order of the President under clause (I) of Article 370".

16. Part XXI: (a) Articles 369, 371, 373, clauses (1), (2), (3) and (5) of article 374 and articles 376 to 392 shall be omitted.

(b) In article 372—

(i) clauses (2) and (3) shall be omitted;

(ii) references to the laws in force in the territory of India shall include references, to Hidayats, Ailans, Ishtihars, circulars, Robkars, Irshads, Yadashts, State, Council Resolutions, Resolutions of the Constitution Assembly, and other instruments having the force of law in the territory of the State of Jammu and Kashmir; and

(iii) references to the commencement of the Constitution shall be construed as references to the commencement of this Order.

(c) In clause (4) of article 374, the reference to the authority functioning as the Privy Council of a State shall be construed as a reference to the Advisory Board constituted under the Jammu and Kashmir Constitution Act, 1996, and references to the commencements of the Constitution shall be construed as references to the commencement of this Order.

17. Part XXII: Articles 394 and 395 shall be omitted.

18. First Schedule.

19. Second Schedule: Paragraph 6 shall be omitted.

20. Third Schedule: Forms V, VI, VII & VIII shall be omitted.

21. Fourth Schedule.

22. Seventh Schedule: (a) In the Union List—

(i) for entry 3, the entry "3. Administration of cantonments" shall be substituted;

(ii) entries 8, 9, 33 and 34, the words "trading corporations including" in entry 43, entries 44, 50, 52, 54, 55, 60, 67, 69, 78 and 79, the words "inter-State migration"' in entry 81, and entry 97 shall be omitted.

Appendix III

Gajendragadkar Commission Report

November 1968

CHAPTER I

Scope of the Inquiry

1.01. The Jammu and Kashmir Commission of Inquiry was appointed by the Government of Jammu and Kashmir, in consultation with the Union Government, by their Order No. 878-D of 1967, dated 6 November 1967. Its terms of reference were as follows:

"(i) To make an assessment of the development programmes apportioned to the various regions of the State and to recommend measures necessary to give assurance that the resources available to the State Government are being shared equitably and also to convey a feeling of equal participation in the integrated development of the State.

"(ii) To examine the recruitment policies of Government and to recommend measures for giving an equitable share in Government employment to the various regions and communities, having special regard to the claim of the Scheduled Castes and other economically, educationally and socially backward communities, classes and groups among the citizens of the State consistently with the maintenance of efficiency of administration.

"(iii) To examine the policies of the State Government

regarding admissions to institutions of higher education and the schemes of assistance by way of scholarships and loans, with a view to ensuring an equitable distribution of the available facilities to the various regions and communities, and having special regard to the claims of the Scheduled Castes and other economically, educationally and socially backward communities, classes and groups among the citizens of the State.

"(iv) To consider generally the causes that lead to irritations and tensions and to recommend remedial measures."

1.02. In considering the above matters, the Commission was required to take note of the provisions contained in Part III "Fundamental Rights", as well as other provisions of the Constitution of India as made applicable to the State of Jammu and Kashmir and of the Directive Principles of State Policy laid down in Part IV of the Constitution of Jammu and Kashmir and particularly of Section 23 thereof.

1.03. It took some time to secure the services of a senior and experienced officer to work as Secretary to the Commission. Mr. B.P. Bagchi, ICS, joined the Commission as its Secretary on 4 December 1967 and we held our first meeting in Delhi on the same day. We decided to call by public notice for memoranda from all parties, groups, associations, institutions, societies and individuals interested in the problems referred to the Commission, by 31 January 1968. We also decided that after the contents of the memoranda had been analysed, examined and collated, the Commission should visit Jammu and Srinagar for recording oral evidence. A Press-note to this effect was issued and paid advertisements published in most of the leading English dailies of the country and the local papers of the Jammu and Kashmir State.

1.04. In January 1968, the President of the Jammu and Kashmir Plebiscite Front wrote to the Chairman that his party "could not get necessary time to determine its attitude towards the Commission of Inquiry" or "to collect material required for submission to the Commission." He, therefore, requested that the last date for the submission, of memoranda be extended. Similar requests were received from the National Conference and from

Shri Kushak Bakula on behalf of the people of Ladakh and others. Many asked for an extension of time on grounds of the inclemency of the weather and the unusual severity of the winter in parts of the Jammu and Kashmir State which made them practically inaccessible. As these grounds were legitimate, the last date for the submission of memoranda was extended to 31 March 1968.

1.05. At three meetings held in Delhi on 15 December 1967, 5 and 6 January 1968 and 19 April 1968, we settled the various details pertaining to the functioning of the Commission's Secretariat and the programme and procedure of the Commission. The main decisions were:—

(i) That the Commission should first visit Srinagar for recording evidence and then go to Jammu. Later, the Commission should visit the Valley again for recording further evidence. The evidence of the parties belonging to the Valley and Ladakh should be recorded at Srinagar in June and that of the parties of Jammu in the second half of August. The Commission should also visit such other areas, including Ladakh... as it might consider necessary.

(ii) That the hearings by the Commission should be held in camera; but in order to expedite the collection of evidence the State Government should be requested to depute a senior officer to be present at the sittings so that he could immediately take steps to furnish such information as might be required.

(iii) That copies of memoranda received by the Commission should be supplied on payment of copying charges to those who had filed memoranda themselves and wished to give evidence before it.

1.06. We received in all 93 memoranda from different associations, groups and individuals. The list of those who submitted memoranda is given in Part A of Appendix 1. Certain parties first appeared before the Commission and subsequently submitted memoranda of supplementary memoranda or additional information, some of whom are listed in Part B of Appendix 1.

1.07. We also received a number of complaints or representations of a personal character. Some of these we referred to the State Government for such remedial action as they considered necessary and in response to certain others informed the persons concerned that the Commission was not going to deal with individual cases except those that might have relevance to its terms of reference.

1.08. Climatic conditions made it difficult for us to meet at Srinagar earlier than in June 1968. We held sittings daily at Srinagar from 6 June to 18 June 1968 (except on Sundays, 9 and 16 June) and heard the oral evidence of the associations, groups and individuals from Kashmir and Ladakh who had submitted memoranda and also of certain legislators and other individuals whom we had specially invited. A list of those who gave evidence at Srinagar is given in Appendix 2.

1.09. Sittings were held at Jammu daily from 22 August to 27 August 1968 for recording similar evidence. A list of those who appeared before us at Jammu is given in Appendix 3.

1.10. We assembled once again at Srinagar from 14 to 18 September 1968, mainly to hear, and hold discussions with, the Chief Minister and other Cabinet-Ministers of the State and senior officers of the State Government. A list of those who appeared before us during this session is given in Appendix 4.

1.11. Certain representatives from remote areas desired us to visit them to get a first-hand knowledge of the conditions there and their disabilities. It was not possible for the Commission as a whole to visit these areas. One of us, however, paid a visit to Ladakh in June 1968 and heard many officials and non-officials both at Leh and at Kargil. Two of us paid a brief visit to Poonch and Rajouri in August 1968 and to Doda, Kishtwar and Bhadarwah in September 1968 where they met certain local individuals and groups. Some memoranda and representations, dealing mainly with local problems, were also presented to them on these visits which have been considered by the Commission.

1.12. We finally met at Bombay from 25 to 29 November 1968 to complete our Report.

1.13. We received to utmost courtesy, co-operation and consideration from the Government of Jammu and Kashmir and we have pleasure in placing on record our appreciation and thanks to them. Our thanks are also due to the Union Government for their co-operation and assistance. Finally, we should like to thank to political parties, local organizations and associations and individuals who took the trouble to submit memoranda to us and to assist us by a frank discussion of the matters in issue. We are particularly grateful to those who, at considerable personal inconvenience, came from far-off places in the interior to place their views on the subjects before us.

CHAPTER II

Pleadings before the Commission

2.01. Of the 93 memoranda received by us, a little over one-third were from the Kashmir region, 51 from the Jammu region, four from Ladakh and six from outside the State. Only five (two from Jammu City, one each from Udhampur, Poonch and Srinagar) were from political parties while 12 were submitted by communal bodies. Of the rest, a little less than one-third were from associations, unions and communities, while the bulk of the remaining 47 were from individuals or groups of individuals. Forty memoranda were of a general nature and spoke only about the regions while 28 had a communal bias. In addition 12 were more or less unrelated to our terms of reference; 11 were from backward or depressed classes and the remaining two from Ex-Army personnel. Some parties who appeared before us subsequently presented memoranda or additional memoranda to supplement their oral evidence.

2.02. An analysis of the memoranda and the oral evidence recorded by the Commission shows that the grievances put forward by the memorialists and the witnesses can be broadly classified under four major Heads pertaining to (i) Development, (ii) Employment, (iii) Education, and (iv) Conditions giving rise to irritations and tensions. They can all be directly related to our terms of reference. Certain other grievances which fall in categories such as economic, fiscal, social and political, or those which pertain to a miscellaneous variety of subjects, such as tenancy laws, corruption in administration, breakdown of law and order, elections, discrimination in the issue of rations, etc. also have an inferential bearing on our terms of reference as causes tending to create irritations and tensions among the people.

2.03. *Development.—The* main complaint of several parties in regard to developmental matters was that planning was defective; that it showed a marked regional bias, as a result of which certain regions or areas, notably the Jammu region, Ladakh and the hilly, inaccessible areas of the State, had received altogether inadequate attention and their development had suffered in consequence. The alleged neglect of the tourist spots in the Jammu region was another grievance frequently voiced. It was represented that although the area of cultivable land in the Jammu region was larger than that in the Kashmir region, fewer irrigation schemes were taken up there for implementation and the expenditure incurred on them was disproportionately low. There were complaints that proper attention was not being paid towards the construction of roads and bridges in the backward areas of Jammu and Ladakh and that even drinking water facilities were not available in the Kandi areas of Jammu. The inadequacy of medical facilities, particularly the absence of mobile dispensaries, in the districts of Poonch and Kathua, was another grievance. The representatives from Ladakh pleaded that Ladakh was a delicate strategic area and needed special care and deft handling. Transport facilities, the prime need of this area, were woefully inadequate. They also stressed the need for providing enough electricity on a stable basis and for devising a suitable method whereby the funds allocated to Ladakh for developmental purposes were properly utilized and did not lapse. A suggestion was also made that the status of Ladakh in the State of Jammu and Kashmir should be formally recognized by including the word 'Ladakh' in the name of the State.

2.04. *Employment.*—Regarding employment in Government services, the complaints were of discrimination on communal and regional grounds in recruitment, favouritism and nepotism in promotions and lack of reservations for the Scheduled Castes and backward classes. Instances of unjust supersessions in the matter of promotions were cited. Many Jammu representatives felt aggrieved that the Jammu region was inadequately represented in the Secretariat and in various Government departments, and that frequently even peons, forest guards and Patwaries from Kashmir were posted in the Jammu region as though qualified persons to fill such posts could not be found locally: while, actually, it was alleged that Kashmiries with inferior qualifications were being preferred to better qualified persons of Jammu. Aspersion was also cast on the impartiality and fairness of the Public Service Commission. It was suggested that its members should be recruited from outside the State. Whereas region-wise representation in the services was advocated by the political parties, communal bodies wanted reservation to be made on a communal basis. Communities such as the Gujjars, Rajputs, Shias, Christians, etc. all desired special quotas and reservations of appointments for themselves on the ground of their backwardness.

2.05. *Education.*—The pleadings under the head 'Education' related to a lack of educational facilities in general; discrimination on the basis of regions and religions in the matter of admissions to higher educational and professional institutions; the lack of professional colleges in the Jammu region; discrimination in the grant of scholarships and selections for training abroad and an almost complete lack of encouragement to the backward classes to acquire higher education. Several parties from the Jammu region, particularly the Students' Congress, complained that all the technical colleges were located in Kashmir and pleaded for the establishment of such colleges in their own legion. A suggestion was also made by the Students' Congress for the establishment of a separate University in Jammu. The representatives from Ladakh pointed out that as the matriculation examination was held in Ladakh long after it was held in the rest of the State, their boys lost a whole term in the process of seeking admission to institutions of higher studies. They desired that something should be done to eliminate this loss of time.

2.06. *Causes of irritations and tensions.* Most of the representatives from Jammu and Ladakh complained that their legitimate regional aspirations were being ignored and that they had little share in the political power of the State. They stated that their regions were discriminated against in most matters, such as in the allocation of developmental funds, the provision of educational facilities, employment in Government services, etc.

2.07. No representative or individual who wrote to, or appeared before us questioned the constitutional or legal position of the State as an integral part of the Indian Union, or made out that this was a cause leading to the creation of tensions and irritation among the people. All of them on the contrary were at pains to emphasize that even the proposals or suggestions that they were making for greater decentralization of power to, or autonomy for, the various regions of the State; were subject to the overall consideration that they should in no way imperil or impair the unity and integrity of the State on the maintenance of which they laid great emphasis. Only one solitary organization, namely the Dogra Mandal, suggested the division of the State and the merger of the Jammu region with Himachal Pradesh.

2.08. Some parties pleaded for the abrogation of Article 370 of the Constitution which conferred a special status on the Jammu and Kashmir State, while certain others pressed for its continuance.

2.09. A number of parties were bitter that the general elections held in the past in the State had not been free and fair. We were also told that the elections to local bodies such as municipalities, town area committees, etc. had not been held for many years with the result that these bodies were no longer representative.

2.10. Representatives of the Zamindari and agriculturist interests were foud in their complaints about the iniquitous and anomalous features of the land and tenancy laws by which land had been expropriated without the payment of any compensation; a uniform ceiling for holdings had been fixed without reference to the quality and productivity of the land; and different rates had been prescribed for the sharing of the produce by land-holders owning more than 100 *Kanals* or less. Another cause of irritation pointed out by them was the great delay in the disposal of ejectment applications. They also complained that though the provisions of Section 45 of the Jammu and Kashmir Tenancy Act enabled the landlord to eject his tenant in possession on the ground that he required the land for personal cultivation, applications made by the landlords to enforce this right had been stayed, for the time being, till 31 December 1968 by a statutory notification. They urged that the notification should be rescinded.

2.11. Representatives of certain communities, such as Jats, Gujjars, Shias, Sikhs, Buddhists and Christians pleaded for adequate representation in the Cabinet, the legislature and the Public Service Commission.

2.12. A number of parties from the Jammu region were aggrieved that there was discrimination in the fixation of the quantum of rations and issue prices of foodgrains. Representatives from Ladakh complained of the lack of rationing facilities for the general population in their area, and of discrimination made between Ladakhi Government servants and others.

2.13. Several organizations of the Jammu region represented before us that all the State toll barriers were located in the Jammu region and that this had adversely affected its economy. Goods and traffic could, on the other hand, flow freely from any part of the Kashmir region to any other place within it.

2.14. Different views were expressed about the six-monthly move of the headquarters of the State Government between Srinagar and Jammu. Several representatives thought that the practice was inevitable even while conceding that it caused dislocation of work and waste of time.. A few representatives from Kashmir desired the discontinuance of this practice on the ground that it gave a feeling of isolation and neglect to Kashmir during the winter months when the Valley was snow-bound.

CHAPTER III

THE STATE OF JAMMU AND KASHMIR—A GENERAL BACKGROUND

3.01. In this Chapter we are giving some background information, gleaned from published and authentic sources, about the State of Jammu and Kashmir—the land and its people, their past history, the religions they follow, the languages they speak and the occupations they pursue. This may help to bring about a better understanding of the matters which fall within the scope of our inquiry.

3.02. State of Jammu and Kashmir occupies a position of great strategic importance in the north-west of India. It is separated from the rest of the country by mountains and uneven terrain. The State is composed of three distinct cultural units—Jammu, Ladakh and the Valley. It is the meeting place of the Hindu, Muslim and Buddhist cultures as living, co-existent forces. The Valley of Kashmir, apart from being justly famous for its natural scenery, has the distinction of possessing an ancient Sanskrit historical record. The ancient history of Jammu Province, however, is shrouded in mystery. There is no chronicle which throws light on the happenings thereof the period prior to the 18th century.

3.03. *Hindu Period.*—Till the 14th century, Kashmir was ruled by a series of Buddhist and Hindu dynasties whose annals are related in the celebrated versified Sanskrit chronicle known as 'Rajatarangini' by Kalhana. Its later chapters give a fairly reliable record of events from the 7th century to the middle of the 12th century. Kalhana's chronicles are continued by Pandit Jonaraja, who takes us to the beginning of the 15th century, and by Srivara and Prajyabhatta who bring the narration down to the Moghul conquest of Kashmir in 1586. The later history of the Valley can be found in the works of Birbal Kacheri and Diwan Kirpa Ram and certain British and European scholars noteworthy among them being Lawrence and Younghusband.

3.04. After the phase of local kings and rulers who extended their rule beyond the Valley into India and Central Asia, Asoka introduced Buddhism into Kashmir in the 3rd century B.C. This was later strengthened by Kanishka. In the early 6th century the control of the Valley passed to the Huns. The Valley regained freedom in 530 A.D., but soon after that came under the sway of the Ujjain Empire. Later, on the decline of the Vikramaditya dynasty, it once again had its own ruler, and there was a fusion of Hindu and Buddhist cultures. Lalitaditya (697-738 A.D.), who extended his hold up to Bengal in the east, Konkan in the south, Turkistan in the north-west and Tibet in the north-east, was the most famous of its Hindu rulers. While Lalitaditya was known for his building activity, King Avantivarman (855-83 A.D.), his successor, is remembered for the great progress in irrigation and drainage in the Valley made during his reign. By the beginning of the 14th century, "the Hindu kings had become incapable of their office" and Kashmir came to have Muslim rulers when Sinha Dev, the Hindu King, fled before a Tartar invasion.

3.05. *Muslim Period.*—Zainul Abedin (1417-69), Sikandar's second son, was not only the most famous of the Muslim rulers but the most illustrious ruler that Kashmir has known. Father and son were of entirely different temperaments; while the father was cruel and intolerant, the son was tolerant, wise and kind. When Zainul Abedin came to power, he completely reversed the policy of Sikandar. A man of secular outlook, he patronized all faiths and religions alike. He brought new life to the tortured Valley by putting an end to his father's rule of persecution and forcible conversions. He recalled those Hindus who had fled to distant places during Sikandar's regime and got the temples rebuilt and repaired. He banned cow-slaughter and removed the prohibition on the performance of Sati. In Zainul Abedin's time, handicrafts were introduced or stimulated, literature and the arts were pationized, canals and bridges were built and taxes were reduced. The reign of this enlightened ruler had an unhappy end for there was a struggle amongst his sons for succession to the throne. Eventually, his weak son, Haider Shah, fell a prey to the aggressive tribes from the north known as the Chaks. Sunni Muslims and Hindus alike were persecuted by the Chaks and they looked towards the Moghul Empire in India for a redress of their grievances. The Chak dynasty continued to rule till 1587 when Akbar invaded Kashmir and made it an apanage of the Moghul Empire; Kashmir then became the summer residence of Mughal Emperors for nearly 200 years. Akbar was followed by Jahangir, Shahjahan and Aurangzeb. Aurangzeb's successor was a weak ruler and in 1752, Kashmir passed from the feeble control of the Moghul emperor into the powerful grasp of Ahmed Shah Abdali of Afghanistan. For the next 67 years, it was held for the Pathans by a series of governors who were more or less independent of their kings and who behaved like tyrants.

3.06. *Sikh Rule.*—By the beginning of the 18th century, Sikh power had risen in the Punjab. The Kashmiris, harassed and exploited by the Pathan kings and unable to secure relief from their tyranny by their own efforts, sought outside assistance and looked forward to a Sikh invasion. In 1814, Ranjit Singh attempted an invasion by the Pir Panjal route, but was repulsed. A further personal appeal to him by Birbal Dai, a Brahmin who managed to escape from Srinagar to Lahore, resulted in another attack by the Sikhs. Misar Diwan Chand, one of Ranjit Singh's most competent generals, who was accompanied by Gulab Singh, was in command of the Sikh forces which in 1819 expelled the Afghans and brought Kashmir under the rule of the Sikhs.

3.07. *Dogra Rule.*—Till 1846, Kashmir remained under the Sikhs and was administered by their governors. The important governors during the Sikh regime were Moti Ram, Kirpa Ram, Sher Singh, Mian Singh, Ghulam Mohi-ud-Din and Imam-ud-Din, but all of them did not command the same respect in Kashmir. In fact the last two actually ruled after the death of Ranjit Singh but were too weak to assert themselves, and the decaying Sikh power, as one writer puts it, "exploded, disappearing in fierce but fading flames." Events leading to the transfer of Kashmir into the hands of the Dogras are closely related to the later history of the Sikhs, especially the prominent role played by Gulab Singh, who had earlier been a minister at Ranjit Singh's court. Gulab Singh belonged to a Rajput family. He was one of the three great-grand nephews of Ranjit Deva, a Dogra Chief of Rajput descent who ruled Jammu in the latter half of the 18th century.

3.08. As already stated, no record is available of the history of Jammu before the 18th century. It appears that during the 12th century when Mohammad Ghori had invaded India and overrun the Punjab, Rajputs, had taken refuge in the mountainous tracts of Jammu province and carved out separate estates and principalities such as Jammu, Kishtwar, Bhadarwah, Basohli, Reasi, etc. which they ruled as independent sovereigns. Very little information is available about the successive regimes which dominated the different regions of the province from time to time until Raja Ranjit Deva, son of Dhruv Deva, proclaimed himself as the ruler of the principality of Jammu in 1730 A.D.

3.09. On the death of Ranjit Deva in 1780, there ensued a struggle for succession. This gave the Sikhs an opportunity of turning Jammu and the neighbouring Hill tracts into a dependency. Gulab Singh, by then, had entered the service of Maharaja Ranjit Singh and had rendered such distinguished service that the Maharaja conferred the principality of Jammu on him with the hereditary title of Raja. During Ranjit Singh's lifetime, Gulab Singh remained loyal to the Lahore Court. However, on the death of Ranjit Singh and the consequent anarchy in the Sikh Court British penetration into north-western regions of India began. In subduing the Sikh power, they sought and secured the co-operation of Gulab Singh. In 1846, at the close of the first Sikh war, Gulab Singh appeared on the scene as a mediator between the British and the Lahore Durbar. On the condition of paying the war indemnity asked for by the British, Gulab Singh was made an independent ruler of Jammu and Kashmir. A separate treaty embodying this arrangement was concluded at Amritsar on 16 March 1846, under which Gulab Singh acknowledged the supremacy of the British-Government. This treaty thus marks the commencement of the history of the Jammu and Kashmir State as a political entity.

3.10. The treaty put Gulab Singh as Maharaja, in possession of all the hill country between the Indus and the Ravi, including Kashmir, Jammu, Ladakh and Gilgit, but excluding Lahaul, Kulu and certain other areas which, for strategical purposes, it was considered advisable to retain and for which a remission of Rs. 25 lakhs was made from the crore demanded, leaving Rs. 75 lakhs as the final amount to be paid by Gulab Singh. Gulab Singh had some difficulty in obtaining actual possession of the province of Kashmir. The last governor appointed by the Sikhs, Imamuddin, successfully resisted his efforts for a time, and it was only at the end of 1846 that Maharaja Gulab Singh with the aid of British troops was established in Kashmir.

3.11. No subsidiary force was imposed on Gulab Singh. Political relations between the Government of India and the State commenced in the year 1849 but these were conducted by the Punjab Government through the Maharaja's agent at Lahore and no representative of the Government of India was stationed in the State. It was not until the year 1852 that the first 'Officer on Special Duty' in the State was appointed. This officer resided in Kashmir only during the summer months. Maharaja Gulab Singh died in 1857 and was succeeded by his son Ranbir Singh. In 1885, after the death of Ranbir Singh and the accession to the *gaddi* of Maharaja Partap Singh, the designation of the 'Officer on Special Duty' was changed to 'Resident in Kashmir', who was permanently stationed at Srinagar. Partap Singh died in 1925 and was succeeded by his nephew, Hari Singh, the ruler who wielded authority till 1948.

3.12. *Independence.*—With the lapse of British Paramountcy on 15 August 1947, the Jammu and Kashmir State became free. It did not decide upon the issue of accession for more than two months after the British withdrawal from the sub-continent. The Maharaja, however, entered into a standstill agreement with Pakistan in order to ensure a free flow of trade and communications as before with the areas that constituted Pakistan. While negotiations for a standstill agreement with India were going on, Pakistan imposed an economic blockade to put pressure on the Maharaja into signing an Instrument of Accession in favour of Pakistan. This was supplemented by a massive armed tribal attack on the State. The people of Jammu and Kashmir, however, offered heroic resistance to the invaders. The invasion from Pakistan precipitated the issue of accession, and on 26 October 1947 the Government of India accepted the Instrument of Accession signed by the Maharaja with the popular backing of the people of the State led by Sheikh Mohammad Abdullah. Jammu and Kashmir thus became legally an integral part of India with overwhelming popular support.

3.13. *Location.—The* present State of Jammu and Kashmir presents a challenging subject for the study of economists, planners and social scientists of the country. Forming the northern most fringe of the country with a good part of the State separated from the rest of India by mountains and uneven terrain, it presents many special problems of its own, Lying between latitude 32.30 degree and 37.00 degree North and longitude 72.50 degree and 80.20 degree East, it forms the North-Western part of India. Its boundaries in the north are Soviet Turkistan and Chinese Sinkiang. In the west and the south-west, it is bounded by Afghanistan and Pakistan and in the east by Tibet while Himachal Pradesh and Punjab form the southern boundaries of the State.

3.14. *Physical features.—The* State falls into four natural regions described below:

(i) The Sub-montane and Semi-mountainous Tracts

This region consists of the plains bordering the Punjab and the broken mass of the foot-hills known locally as the 'Kandi' areas. The average height of this region is about 2,000 feet above sea-level. The river Chenab flows' through it. But on account of its being mostly stony and arid, cultivation here is scanty, scattered and wholly dependent on rain. The whole of Jammu district and a part of Kathua district fall in this tract.

(ii) The Outer Hills Region

The rest of Jammu province (i.e., the districts of Udhampur, Poonch, Doda and part of Kathua) falls in this region. It consists of low hills lying roughly to the south of the Pir Panjal range which separates the two provinces of Jammu and Kashmir. A large part of this area lies between 2,000 and 4,000 feet above sea-level. The river Chenab passes through this area also. Except in the fertile valleys formed by the river and its tributaries, cultivation is scarce and scattered and is done on small patches.

(iii) Jhelum Valley or Kashmir Valley Region

This region consists of the administrative districts of Anantnag, Srinagar and Baramulla. It is known as the Kashmir Valley. The river Jhelum with its numerous tributaries, pursuing a zigzag course, flows through the whole length of the Valley bisecting it almost into two-halves. The average height of the Valley is 5,500 feet above sea-level, while the mountains surrounding, it average 12,000 feet with a dip to about 9,000 feet, at Banihal pass. The region has a rich alluvial soil and paddy and fruit grow extensively there.

(iv) Indus Valley or Tibetan or Semi-Tibetan Tract

This area consists almost entirely of snow-capped mountains with plateaus, glaciers, rocky river valleys and wastes. The Indus is the main river of this region. There are a number of mountains over 20,000 feet in height. At present, it comprises Kargil and Leh divisions of the frontier district of Ladakh in Kashmir province. The whole of the area is dry and almost rainless. The cultivation of such crops as barley, maize and millets is, however, undertaken in this region with the help of irrigation from small canals known as 'Kuhls' which are fed by melting snow.

3.15. Administratively the State consists of three units, viz. Jammu, Kashmir and Ladakh—Doda, Udhampur, Jammu, Kathua and Poonch forming Jammu province and Anantnag, Srinagar and Baramulla the province of Kashmir, while Ladakh forms the frontier district of the State. The State comprises 6,726 villages and 43 towns of which Jammu and Srinagar are the most important industrial centres.

3.16. *Area and Population.*—According to the 1961 Census, the State has an area of about 139,000 square kilometres and a total population of 35.61 lakhs, giving a density of 26 per square kilometre, the lowest of all the States of the Indian Union, except for a few Union territories. The low density is explained by the fact that the frontier district of the State constitutes more than two-thirds of the area but has less than 2.5 per cent of the population. If the area and population of this district are excluded, the density would go up to 84 per square kilometre. In other words, the density of population for the residual area would be higher than that of Madhya Pradesh and Rajasthan. The fact, however, remains that the density of the State has been rising from decade to decade all along in the past.

3.17. The distribution of the area, population and density in the three administrative units is as under:—

Area, Population and Density—Based on 1961 Census

	Area		*No. of Towns*	*No. of Villages*	*Population*	*Density (Population)*	
	sq. miles	*sq. kms.*				*per sq. mile*	*per sq. km.*
1	*2*	*3*	*4*	*5*	*6*	*7*	*8*
Jammu	10073.1	26089.4	24	3485	1572887	156	60
Doda	4380.2	11344.7	6	661	268403	61	24
Udhampur	1731.6	4484.9	4	627	254061	147	57
Jammu	1248.6	3233.8	7	1050	516932	414	160
Kathua	1023.6	2651.2	4	585	207430	203	78
Poonch	1689.1	4374.8	3	562	326061	193	75
Kashmir	5838.0	15120.3	18	3003	1899438	325	126
Anantnag	2096.9	5430.9	6	1222	654368	312	120
Srinagar	1205.4	3121.2	3	714	640411	531	205
Baramulla	2536.0	6568.2	9	1067	604659	238	92
Ladakh	37753.8	97782.4	1	238	88651	2	0.9
Total	53664.9	138992.1	43	6726	3560976	66	26

Note: The figures exclude the area under unlawful occupation of Pakistan and China, where census could not be taken, and its population.

3.18. *Religions.*—The Jammu and Kashmir State presents a picture of a multi-racial society professing a variety of religions, speaking different languages and heir to a composite culture and customs. The State is inhabited by Hindus, Muslims, Sikhs, Christians, Buddhists and Jains. Muslims comprise about 68 per cent of the population, Hindus a little over 28 per cent, and Sikhs and Buddhists 1.8 arid 1.4 per cent respectively, while the total number of Christians is 2,848 and of Jains only 1,427. The percentage of population of Hindus and Muslims in Jammu province is 58:7 and 38.1 respectively. The districts of Udhampur, Jammu and Kathua have a concentration of Hindu population (78.9 per cent); Doda and Poonch have more of Muslims (72.9 per cent). Sikhs live mostly in Jammu and Poonch, and form 6.3 per cent of the population of Jammu and 2.5 per cent of that of Poonch. Kashmir has a majority of Muslims (94.4 per cent), the percentage in Anantnag, Srinagar and Baramulla being 95.4, 90.7 and 97.3 respectively. Hindus in the Valley constitute 4.7 per cent of the population. The maximum proportion of Hindus in the Valley (8.3 per cent) is found in Srinagar. Out of a total of 304 Christians, 230 live in Srinagar alone. About 54 per cent Buddhists and 45 per cent Muslims, besides about one per cent of Hindus and Sikhs, inhabit the territory of Ladakh. The district-wise distribution of population by religion is given in the table below:—

Percentage Distribution of Population by Religion—Based on 1961 Census

Region/ Religion	*Hindus*	*Muslims*	*Sikhs*	*Christians*	*Buddhists*	*Jains*	*Total*
1	2	3	4	5	6	7	8
Jammu	58.7	38.1	2.9	0.2	—	0.1	100.0
Doda	34.6	65:0	0.2	—	0.2	..	100.0
Udhampur	65.1	33.9	0.9	0.1	..	..	100.0
Jammu	83.0	10.0	6.3	04	—	0.3	100.0
Poonch	18.0	79.5	2.5	—	..	..	100.0
Kathua	85.7	13.0	1.2	0.1	..	—	100.0
Kashmir	4.7	94.4	0.9	—	—	—	100.0
Anantnag	3.7	95.4	.0.9	—	..	—	100.0
Srinagar	8.3	90.7	1.0	—	—	—	100.0
Baramulla	2.0	97.3	0.7	—	_	..	100.0
Ladakh	.0.7	45.4	0.1	—	53.8	..	100.0
Total	28.4	68.3	1.8	0.1	1.4	—	100.0

. . Nil.
—Negligible.

3.19. *Scheduled Castes.*—With the introduction of the Constitution of India, envisaging the establishment of a secular democracy, the 1961 Census for the first time dispensed with the details of the castes and sub-castes under the different religions, except for persons belonging to the Scheduled Castes. There are no Scheduled Tribes in the State and even the Scheduled Castes are found only in the five districts of Jammu province. The total population of the Scheduled Castes in the province is 2,84,131 (2,63,236 in rural areas and 20,895 in the urban areas). The district-wise proportion to population is given on next page.

Percentage of Scheduled Castes to Population

District	*Persons*	*Males*	*Females*
1	2	3	4
Doda	9.22	9.09	9.37
Udhampur	19.91	19.89	19.93
Jammu	29.31	29.53	29.06
Kathua	22.88	23.06	22.69
Poonch	3.01	2.94	3.10

The 1961 Census shows that the number of Scheduled Castes professing the Sikh religion is very small and that they mostly belong to the Basith, Chamar or Ramdasis and Megh or Kabirpanthi castes. All the others profess Hinduism. In fact, the population of Hindu Scheduled Castes is much larger than the entire population in the State of those professing Sikhism or Buddhism. It is six times that of the latter and more than four times the population of Sikhs. In the State as a whole, Hindu Scheduled Castes claim 28 per cent of the total Hindu population. The following table gives the percentage of Hindu Scheduled Castes to the total Hindu population and the total number of persons belonging to Sikh Scheduled Castes in Jammu province and its districts:—

	Percentage of Hindu Scheduled Castes Population to Total Hindu Population	*Total number of persons belonging to Sikh Scheduled Castes*
J & K State	28.0	168
Jammu Province	30.7	168
Doda District	26.7	10
Udhampur District	30.6	17
Jammu District	35.3	97
Kathua District	26.7	..
Poonch District	16.6	44

3.20. *Languages*—A number of languages are spoken in the State. The important languages spoken are Kashmiri in Kashmir; Dogri, Punjabi and Pahari-unspecified in Jammu and Ladakhi, Balti, Budhi and Tibetan in Ladakh. As the Valley is predominantly inhabited by Kashmiris, the mother tongue of over 90 per cent is Kashmiri, the other important languages spoken there are Punjabi (1.7 per cent) and Gojri (3.4 per cent). Although on the whole a little over 55 per cent speak Dogri in Jammu province, not less than 80 per cent in Jammu district, 77 per cent in Udhampur and 92 per cent in Kathua speak the same language.

In the whole of Jammu province, Punjabi is the mother tongue of only 5 per cent; 12 per cent speak Punjabi in Jammu district and 2.5 per cent in Poonch. There are only 11 per cent people in whole of Jammu province whose mother tongue is Kashmiri; in Doda, however, over 44 per cent of the people speak Kashmiri. Gojri is the mother tongue of 10 per cent of population in Udhampur and 9.3 per cent in Doda. Cher 26 per cent speak Gojri in Poonch, where the other important languages are Pahari-unspecified and Dogri which are spoken by 48.3 per cent and 13.2 per cent respectively. In Ladakh, over 56 per cent speak Ladakhi while the mother tongue of 37.1 percent is Balti and of 2.4 per cent Budhi; Tibetan is the mother tongue of only 2 per cent people in Ladakh. A few persons speak Kashmiri (0.7 per cent), Punjabi (0.2 per cent), and Dogri (0.2 per cent) as well. The region-wise proportion of languages spoken is given in the table below:—

Percentage Distribution of Population by Languages Spoken—Based on 1961 Census

Region/ Language	*Kashmiri*	*Punjabi*	*Dogri*	*Ladakhi*	*Budhi*	*Bakar-wali*	*Gojri*	*Others*	*Total*
1	*2*	*3*	*4*	*5*	*6*	*7*	*8*	*9*	*10*
Jammu	11.3	4.9	55.1	—	0.1	0.4	9.2	19.0	100.0
Doda	44.5	0.3	7.0	..	0.2	0.2	9.3	38.5*	100.0
Udhampur	8.8	1.4	77.6	..	..	1.0	10.0	1.2	100.0
Jammu	2.1	11.6	80 6	—	..	0.1	1.1	4.5	100.0
Kathua	1.8	1.9	92.3	..	..	0.3	1.6	2.1	100.0
Poonch	6.6	2.5	13.2	..	..	0.5	26.2	51.0†	100.0
Kashmir	90.4	1.7	0.1	—	—	..	3.4	4.4	100.0
Anantnag	93.3	1.1	0.1	—	—	..	4.2	1.3	100.0
Srinagar	95.1	1.6	0.1.	—	—	..	2.2	1.0	100.0
Baramulla	82.3	2.5	—	—	..	..	3.9	11.3	100.0
Ladakh	0.7	0.2	0.2	56.2	2.4	..	..	40.3‡	100.0
Total	53.3	3.1	24.4	1.4	0.1	0.2	5.9	11.6	100.0

. . Nil. —Negligible.

*Bhadrawahi 12.3 per cent; Pahari-unspecified 6.0 per cent. Siraji-Kashmiri 7.4 per cent; Kishtwari 4.3 per cent.

†Pahari-unspecified 48.3 per cent; Urdu 1.9 per cent.

‡Balti 37.1 per cent; Tibetan 2.1 per cent.

3.21. *Natural Resources.*—Of the natural resources of Kashmir Valley, forests need special mention. The forests of the State are renowned all over India for their grandeur; their lofty fir, deodar and pine trees; and varied flora and fauna. These forests are a very important source of revenue and yield large quantities of timber, firewood and minor forest products. They add grandeur to the landscape and are a means of protecting the land against erosion and ensuring the regular flow of water. It is estimated that out of the total forest area, about 28 per cent consists of coniferous forests and the rest of miscellaneous forests including high level pasturages. Of these the commercially exploitable forests comprise only 20 per cent; the rest are inaccessible at present. The other important natural resources of Jammu and Kashmir consist of minerals although only a small portion of the known deposits has as yet been surveyed in detail. It is now known, however, that the State has considerable deposits of gypsum and limestone and a geological survey reveals the existence of copper, lead and zinc also. In spite of the fact that the State occupies an important position because of its mineral resources in the whole of northwest India, its mineral industry has nevertheless remained undeveloped due to lack of suitable transport and power facilities.

3.22. *Literacy.* The basic problem of Kashmir for long has been its low income, poverty, disease, ignorance and unemployment. The State has all along been very backward, having the lowest incidence of literacy among all the States of India. According to the 1961 census, there are only 3.9 lakh literate persons in the State giving a literacy percentage of about 13 against the national average of 28 per cent. Urban areas, where greater facilities for education are available, however, claim a literacy percentage of 32.8 while in rural areas the literacy percentage is only 8.9. The largest number of literate persons is found in the cities of Jammu and Srinagar, the percentages being 45.0 and 24.8 respectively. The districts of Jammu and Srinagar have the highest percentage of literacy—22.3 for Jammu and 16.8 for Srinagar. The percentage of literacy in the various regions and districts of the State is indicated in the table on next page.

Percentage of Literacy*—Based on 1961 Census

Region	*Rural*			*Urban*			*Total*		
	M	*F*	*T*	*M*	*F*	*T*	*M*	*F*	*T*
Jammu	16.8	2.6	10.1	54.8	35.6	46.3	21.8	6.5	14.6
Doda	15.0	1.1	8.5	49.3	22.4	37.4	17.1	2.3	10.2
Udhampur	13.5	2.1	8.1	56.5	36.6	47.5	16.4	4.2	10.7
Jammu	21.4	4.5	13.4	56.2	39.2	48.7	30.7	12.8	22.3
Kathua	19.0	3.9	11.9	47.0	25.3	37.0	21.2	5.4	13.8
Poonch	13.7	1.2	7.8	55.2	29.7	43.6	15.9	2.6	9.6
Kashmir	13.5	1.2.	7.9.	36.4	14.9	26.5	18.3	4.1	11.8
Anantnag	14.6	1.3	8.5	30.3	7.2	20.0	15.7	1.7	9.3
Srinagar	11.4	1.1	6.7	38.4	17.0	28.5	23.7	8.5	16.8
Baramulla	13.7	1.1	7.9	30.8	9.6	21.2	15.3	1.9	9.2
Ladakh	16.2	0.9	8.7	42.0	7.6	24.9	17.3	1.2	9.4
Total	15.1	1.8	8.9	42.4	21.3	32.8	19.8	5.1	13.0

M: Males; F: Females; T: Total.
*Excludes population in age group 0-4.

3.23. *Economic*—Agriculture has been the main occupation of the State's population, the rural/urban ratio of population being 83:17; the proportion of workers to the total population is about 43 per cent according to the 1961 census. Over three-fourths of the workers are cultivators and agricultural labourers. About 6 per cent are engaged in household industries, 2 per cent each in manufacturing (other than household industry) and trade and commerce, while 9 per cent of the workers derive their livelihood from other services. The percentage distribution of workers in the different industries is given in the table on next page.

3.24. Agriculture is the mainstay of the State's economy, about 90 per cent of the population depending for their living on land. Rice is the staple food in the Kashmir Valley while in Jammu province people eat wheat, maize, barley and rice. A variety of fruit grow in the State: apples, pears, plums, cherry, etc. Walnuts, almonds and saffron are also among the other important products of the State. The produce of the various districts of the State, however, varies according to their altitude.

3.25. The cottage industries of the Jammu and Kashmir State like wood carving, wool weaving, shawl making, etc. are famous all over the world. Silk is found in abundance and silk goods are

Proportion of Workers in Different Industries—Based on 1961 Census

Region	*Total workers as per cent of population*	*As cultivator*	*As Agricultural labourer*	*Mining, quarrying etc.*	*Household industry*	*Manufacturing other than household industry*	*Construction*	*Trade and commerce*	*Transport, Storage and Communications*	*Other services*
Jammu	41.5	75.8	1.1	1.9	7.0	1.0	0.8	2.2	0.7	9 5
Doda	55.3	83.7	0.4	2.5	8.8	0.3	0.3	0.7	0.1	3 2
Udhampur	50.8	80.4	0.4	1.4	10.6	0.3	0.3	1.4	0.2	5.0
Jammu	32.3	58.1	2.6	1.3	3.0	3.0	1.9	5.1	2.1	22.9
Kathua	40.8	75.9	1.2	3.0	7.1	0.7	0.8	1.9	0.6	8.8
Poonch	38.0	85.4	0.7	1.8	6.3	0.4	0.2	0.9	0 2	4.1
Kashmir	42.7	74.9	1.3	1.5	5.6	3.3	0.4	2.3	1.1	9.6
Anantnag	43.9	81.8	1.5	1.4	6.8	4.2	0.4	1.7	0.5	4.7
Srinagar	37.9	56.2	1.0	1.5	6.4	8.3	0.6	4.3	2.6	19.1
Baramulla	46.7	84.1	1.4	1.6	3.8	1.0	0.2	1.3	03	6.3
Ladakh	66 1	85 .3	0.5	1.3	7.6	0.3	1.1	0.7	0.1	3.1
Total	42.8	75.7	1.2	1.7	6.3	2.2	0.6	2.2	0.8	9.3

a major export of Kashmir. The most important industry of the State is, however, Tourism. It is its main source of revenue. With beautiful tourist spots both in Jammu and Kashmir, the State attracts tourists from all over India and the world. The additional amenities provided by the Government in recent years for tourists have made for a substantial increase in their number.

3.26. The income of the State in 1965-66 (at 1955-56 prices) is estimated to be about Rs. 93 crores giving a per capita income of about Rs. 250. Agriculture, etc. constitute about 41.5 per cent of the State income while mining and manufacturing provide about 25.0 per cent. The contribution of commerce and transport is 9.1 per cent while other services absorb about 24.4 per cent of the State's income. Though the First and Second Five Year Plans witnessed a rise of 4 to 5 per cent per annum in the State's income, during the period, of the Third Five Year Plan the income, which was showing an annual growth of about 2.4 per cent till 1964-65, showed a decline of about 1/6 per cent in 1965-66 on account of a serious decline in agricultural production throughout the country caused by adverse weather conditions. With the better agricultural production expected in subsequent years, it is likely that the income growth may equal that prevailing in the First and the Second Five Year Plan periods. The State income at 1955-56 prices by industry of origin is shown in the table below:—

State Income at 1955-56 Prices by Industry of Origin

(In lakhs of rupees)

Industry	*1950-51*	*1955-56*	*1960-61*	*1965-66**	*1966-67†*
1. Agriculture, Animal Husbandry, Forestry, Fishing, etc.	2,605.5	3,374.1	4,084.3	3,876.0	4,464.2
2. Mining, Manufacturing and Small Enterprises	1,353.2	1,546.8	2,018.1	2,326.5	2,367.9
3. Commerce and Transport	635.4	689.2	764.8	853.6	865.3
4. Other services	960.2	1,187.3	1,736.5	2,272.6	2,409.0
5. Total	5,554.3	6,797.4	8,603.7	9,328.6	10,106.4
6. Per capita income (Rs.)	188.4	216.5	252.6	250.4	265.8

*Partially revised. †Preliminary.

Source: Directorate of Economics and Statistics, Jammu and Kashmir.

CHAPTER IV

Development Programmes

4.01. Our first term of reference requires us "to make an assessment of the development programmes apportioned to the various regions of the State and to recommend measures necessary to give assurance that the resources available to the State Government are being shared equitably and also to convey a feeling of equal participation in the integrated development of the State."

As is inevitable with any inquiry that involves making regional comparisons, each region tries to substantiate its claim that its interests have been neglected and that the other regions have prospered unduly over the years at its expense. We, therefore, took oral evidence and checked the statements made in evidence by reference to the statistical information obtained from the State Government and also other relevant material. The complaints of neglect were made mostly in the memoranda submitted by representatives from the Jammu Division and Ladakh though there were also some from the Kashmir Division. Besides, from the same region, allegations we're made that the urban areas had received more attention while the needs of the rural, hilly and inaccessible areas had been comparatively neglected.

4.02. *Resources of the Stole.* Before proceeding to discuss the apportionment of development programmes to the different regions, and the sharing of resources, by them, we propose to examine the budgetary resources, first of the State as a whole and then of the regions separately. The budgetary resources of a State are made up of the revenue receipts of the State and the grants-in-aid and loans given to it by the Centre in pursuance of the constitutional provisions as also for meeting its specific Plan needs. The resources of the State of Jammu and Kashmir are admittedly quite inadequate for its needs and the Union Government have had to supplement them to a considerable extent by giving grants-in-aid and loans. The following table, prepared for six consecutive years, gives an idea of how the revenue receipts of the State compare with the amount of Central assistance received by it in the form of grants and loans:

(In crores of rupees)

Year	Revenue Receipts of the State	Central		
		Grants	Loans	Total
1960-61	12.58	3.14	5.31	21 03
1961-61	12.59	9.48	6.64	28 71
1962-63	17.64	7.68	10 36	35.68
1963-64	18.36	8.19	9.07	35.62
1964-65	18.02	8.51	11.68	38.21
1965-66	19.76	11.91	12.83	44.50

Thus, Central assistance was nearly equal to the revenue receipts of the State in 1962-63 and 1963-64 and substantially exceeded the State's revenue in the years 1964-65 and 1965-66. The principal sources of revenue are: (a) forests, (b) road toll, (c) land revenue, (d) sales tax, and (e) excise.

4.03. *Allocation of resources to different regions.*—We shall now proceed to attempt an analysis of the regional breakdown of the State's revenue. This will give an idea of the revenue-earning capacity of each of the regions, viz., Jammu, Kashmir and Ladakh, and the contribution that each makes to the total revenue of the State. In arriving at the regional breakdown, certain assumptions have, however, to be made. This is be cause the figures relating to the State's revenue are not maintained region-wise. The apportionment of certain items of revenue to the regions is also not possible, for the point of collection of a tax may fall in one region while its incidence may fall in another. The receipts from road toll provide an illustration of this. The State of Jammu and Kashmir has a fairly extensive road system and road toll is an important source of revenue. Although the incidence of road toll is spread over the entire State, the collection points are all located in the Jammu region. It would thus be incorrect to show the entire receipts on this account as having been earned by the Jammu region merely because the toll barriers are all located there. There are a few other items of revenue also where the correct apportionment to the regions presents similar difficulties. There are still others where such apportionment is not possible at all. Nevertheless, after excluding such items as well as Central assistance and making suitable assumptions about the allocation of some of the other items of revenue to the regions, the State

Government have, at our request, made an analysis of the regional budgetary resources. This has been done for a few selected years, the years being 1960-61, 1963-64 and 1965-66. In overall, terms, the regional breakdown of resources for the years for which the analysis has been made; is as follows:

(In lakhs of rupees)

	1960-61	*1963-64*	*1965-66*
Jammu	389 21	462 51	453.98
Kashmir	322.94	490.38	46190
Ladakh	2.89	5.04	5.72
Total	715.04	957.93	921.60

The detailed breakdown for the three years in terms of individual items of revenue and the assumptions made in allocating them to the different regions are given in Appendix 5. The figures given above show that the resources of the Jammu region and the Kashmir region are about equal. No such large variation exists between them as would entitle one region to claim distinct superiority over the other in this respect. Ladakh is, however, in quite a different category. Its scanty resources require a great deal of additional support from the State and the Union Government.

4.04. *Apportionment of development programmes and expenditure.*—We now come to the development programmes of the State. Like the budgetary resources discussed in the preceding paragraph, the accurate apportionment of development programmes and developmental expenditure to the different regions is difficult. Many developmental schemes transcend regional boundaries and cannot be allocated to particular regions. Attempts have, however, been made by the State Government to allocate developmental expenditure to the different regions to the extent practicable and where it has not been possible to do so, they have shown such expenditure as common to two or more regions.

4.05. Development programmes in the State have been financed mainly out of its Plan budgets and only, to a limited extent out of its non-Plan budgets. We shall first consider the Plan budgets and then proceed to discuss the non-Plan budgets in so far as they relate to development.

4.06. The total Plan expenditure on development in the entire

State, during the three Plan periods, has been Rs. 10.681.25 lakhs. The expenditure on each Plan was as follows:—

(In lakhs of rupees)

First Five-Year Plan (1951-52 to 1955-56)	1,151.71
Second Five-Year Plan (1956-57 to 1960-61)	3,120.20
Third Five-Year Plan (1961-62 to 1965-66)	6,409.34
Total	10,681.25

As mentioned earlier, the resources of the State are quite inadequate for its needs and therefore the Union Government have had to make substantial assistance available to the State Government in the form of grants and loans for financing the State Plans. The quantum of assistance for the three Plans was as follows:—

(In lakhs of rupees)

	Total Plan expenditure	*Central assistance*	*Percentage of Central assistance to Plan expenditure*
First Plan	1,151.71	1,000.00	87
Second Plan	3,120.20	2,000.00	64
Third Plan	6,409.34	6,200.00	97
Total	10,681.25	9,200.00	86

Thus, the State Plans have largely been financed by the Union Government. A statement is given in Appendix 6 showing the quantum of Central assistance received by each State of the Union for each of the three Five-Year Plans, for purposes of comparison.

4.07. The apportionment of the Plan expenditure to the regions has been done by the State Government at our request. In respect of the First Plan however, it has not been possible to do so in the absence of sufficient details. It may be stated that the First Plan of the State did not represent any major developmental effort, the total expenditure during the five years being only Rs. 1,151.71 lakhs. The Second and the Third Plans were much larger and the per capita expenditure on development went up from Rs. 37.25 in the First Plan to Rs. 196.37 in the Third-Plan.

4.08. The expenditure under each Head of Development in the Second and Third Plans has been apportioned to the regions after taking into account the expenditure on the schemes included under that Head and the region that each such scheme is intended to serve. As stated in paragraph 4.04, in respect of certain schemes it has, however, not been possible to determine the particular region which derives benefit from them, and so such expenditure has been shown as common to the two regions of Jammu and Kashmir. Worked out thus, the allocation of expenditure on the Second and the Third Plan to the different regions would be as follows:

(In lakh of rupees)

	Total Plan expenditure	*Jammu region*	*Kashmir region*	*Common to Jammu and Kashmir regions*	*Ladakh region*
Second Plan	3,120.20	1.385,23	1,472.62	175.70	86.65
Third Plan	6,409.34	2,119.69	2,796.78	1,345.51	147.36
Total	9,529.54	3,504.92	4.269.40	1,521.21	234.01

This shows that Ladakh has received a much smaller share than either the Jammu or the Kashmir region and that as between the Jammu and Kashmir regions, the share of the latter in so far as Plan expenditure is concerned, has been about twenty-two per cent higher than that of the former. During the Second Five Year Plan period, the levels of expenditure in the Jammu and Kashmir regions were not markedly different and it was only in the Third Plan period that a substantially higher expenditure was incurred in the Kashmir region.

4.09. The details of Plan expenditure under each Head of Development for each region are given in Appendix VII. A scrutiny of the expenditure under these Heads of Development shows that the major regional disparities occur in a few of them as, for instance 'Agriculture', 'Irrigation', 'Power', 'Transport and Communication', 'Education' and 'Health and Family Planning'. The physical achievements in each of these will be discussed in later paragraphs.

4.10. Apart from the Plan expenditure, there is also a certain amount of non-Plan expenditure incurred on developmental schemes. The bulk of this expenditure has been incurred on the construction of roads. The allocation of non-Plan expenditure to the regions during the Second and the Third Plan periods is as follows:—

(In lakhs of rupees)

	Jammu region	*Kashmir region*	*Common to Jammu and Kashmir regions*	*Ladakh region*	*Total*
Second Plan	245.22	153.25	—	—	398.47
Third Plan	1,006.79	390.88	153.48	949.36	2,500 51
Total	1,252.01	544.13	153.48	949.36	2,898.98

The details of non-Plan expenditure under each Head of Development for each region are also given in Appendix VII.

4.11. If we take both Plan and non-Plan developmental expenditure into account, the overall position relating to expenditure on the different regions would be as follows:

(In lakhs of rupees)

	Jammu region	*Kashmir region*	*Common to Jammu and Kashmir regions*	*Ladakh region*	*Total*
A. Second Plan					
Plan Expenditure	1,385.23	1,472.62	175.70	86.65 3.	120.20
Non-Plan Expenditure	245.22	153.25			398.47
Total 'A' (Plan + Non-Plan Expenditure)	1,630.45	1,625,87	175.70	86.65 3	518.67
B. Third Plan					
Plan Expenditure	2,119.69	2796.78	1.345.51	147.36	6,409.34
Non-Plan Expenditure	1,006.79	390,88	153.48	949.36	2,500.51
Total 'B' (Plan + Non-Plan Expenditure) .	3,126.48	3.187.66	1,498.99	1,096.72	8.909.85
Grand Total: 'A' + 'B' (Plan+ Non-Plan Expenditure	4,756.93	4,813.53	1,674.69	1,183.37	12,428.52

Thus, on an overall assessment and leaving out of account the unallocable part of the expenditure, the development programmes during the Second and Third Plan periods, expressed in terms of expenditure, cannot be said to have been unequally shared between the Jammu and Kashmir regions. There does not, therefore, seem to be justification for the complaint of there having been deliberate discrimination exercised against either region. Ladakh's share has only been about one-fourth of that of the Jammu or Kashmir region; and besides, out of the total developmental expenditure of Rs. 1,183.37 lakhs there, one single item—construction of roads—accounts for as much as Rs. 934.44 lakhs.

4.12. Before drawing any conclusions, however, we should like to invite attention to the table that follows, giving certain statistical data relating to the State of Jammu and Kashmir and its three regions.

	Item	*Jammu region*	*Kashmir region*	*Ladakh region*	*Total J&K State*
1	*Geographical Area* (Sq Miles)	10,073.1	5,836.0	37,753.8	53,664.9
2	*Population* (Mid Plan) (*Figures in lakhs)*				
	First Plan (Projected)	12.78	17.32	0.82	30.92
	Second Plan (Projected)	14. 70	18.42	0.86	33.98
	Third Plan (Projected)	16.73	20.06	0.95	37.74
3	*Actual Development Expenditure* (excluding items common to Jammu and Kashmir regions)				
					(In Lakhs of rupees)
	First Plan period	Not available			1,151.71
	Second Plan period				
	Plan	1,3.85.23	1,47.62	86.65	2,944.50
	Non-Plan	245.22	153.2		398.4
	Total—Second Plan period (Plan+Non-Plan Expenditure)	1,630.45	1,625.87	86.65	3,342.97*

(In Lakhs of rupees)

	Item	Jammu region	Kashmir region	Ladakh region	Total J&K State
	Third Plan period:				
	Plan	2,119.69	2,796.78	147.36	5,063.83
	Non-Plan	1.006.79	190.88	949.36	2.347.03
	Total—Third Plan period (Plan+Non-Plan Expenditure)	3,126-48	3,187,66	1,096.72	7,410.86
4	*Per Capita Expenditure*		*(In rupees)*		
	First Plan				37.25
	Second Plan	110.91	88.27	100.75	98.38*
	Third Plan	186.87	158.91	1,154.44	196.37
5	*Expenditure per sq mile*		*(In rupees)*		
	First Plan				2,146
	Second Plan	16,186	27,850	229	6,229
	Third Plan	31,038	54,602	2,905	13,809

1. The figures exclude area under unlawful occupation of Pakistan and China and its population.
2. The figures marked with an asterisk do not take into account the developmental expenditure on items common to Jammu and Kashmir regions.

These figures show that the Jammu region's share of the total developmental expenditure has attained a certain parity with that of the Kashmir region. It does not, however, necessarily follow from this that in terms of actual performance also, the situation in the Jammu region is comparable to that in the Kashmir region. Similarly, the high per capita expenditure on Ladakh in the Third Plan period may not have much significance if the extremely low density of population of the area is kept in view.

4.13. The per capita developmental expenditure during the Third Plan period was Rs. 158.91 in the Kashmir region and Rs. 186.87 in the Jammu region while the developmental expenditure per square mile was Rs. 54,602 and Rs. 31,038 respectively. As an indication of development, the expenditure per unit of area is not a relevant factor in most sectors though it may have some relevance in those like Agriculture, Communication, etc. The lower figure per square mile for the Jammu region perhaps only indicates that the sparsely populated and under-developed area is larger in the Jammu region than in the Kashmir region. To obtain an integrated view of the progress made in different sectors of development, the foregoing data have to be related to other relevant information, such as the physical achievements made in each of the sectors of development. These are discussed below for the following sectors.

(a) Agricultural Programmes;
(b) Irrigation;
(c) Power;
(d) Industries;
(e) Transport and Communications;
(f) Education; and
(g) Health and Family Planning.

4.14. *Agricultural Programmes.*—The expenditure incurred during each of the Second and the Third Plan periods on Agricultural Programmes in the Jammu and Kashmir regions was as follows:

(In lakhs of rupees)

	Jammu region	*Kashmir region*	*Common to Jammu and Kashmir regions*	*Ladakh region*	*Total*
Second Plan period	66.49	88.10	12.11	2.77	16.9.47
Third Plan period	165.02	269.99	24.86	28.93	479.80
Total	231.51	349.09	36.97	31.70	649.27

Under Agricultural Programmes, the activities included are: Agriculture, Horticulture, Animal Husbandry, Sheep, Breeding and Wool Development, Dairying and Milk Supply, Fisheries and Forests and Soil Conservation. The figures shown above for the Second and Third Plans pertain to expenditure incurred on all these activities. These figures show that the expenditure during the period of the Second and Third Plans on Agricultural Programmes in the Kashmir region was approximately fifty per cent more than in the Jammu region. The activities included in Agricultural Programmes are discussed separately below:—

(i) Agriculture (including Horticulture).—The expenditure incurred on Agriculture in the Jammu and Kashmir regions during the Second and Third Plan periods was as follows:—

(In lakhs of rupees)

	Jammu region	*Kashmir region*	*Common to Jammu and Kashmir regions*	*Ladakh region*	*Total*
Second Plan period	15.00	30.97	7.48	—	53.45
Third Plan period	73.68	103.31	—	4.74	181.73
Total	88.68	134.28	7.48	4.74	235.I8

The area under cultivation in each of these regions in the years 1950-51 and 1964-65 was as follows:—

	Unit	*Year*	*Jammu region*	*Kashmir region*	*Ladakh region*	*Total*
1. Gross area under cultivation	000 acres	1950-51	780	780	40	1600
		1964-65	1211	863	42	2116
2. Net area under cultivation		1950-51	746	753	37	1536
		1964-65	797	819	42	1658

Thus, while the gross area under cultivation in the Jammu region increased considerably between 1950-51 and 1964-65 it increased only marginally in the Kashmir region. In Ladakh it remained almost static. Further, while the gross area under cultivation in the Jammu region is much larger than in the Kashmir region, the investment in Agriculture in the former has been substantially less than in the latter.

(ii) *Animal Husbandry (including Sheep Breeding and Wool Development, Dairying and Milk Supply).*—A considerable section of the population of the State is engaged on sheep breeding and cattle-rearing. The State Government made the investments, indicated below, on Animal Husbandry in each of the regions during the Second and the Third Plan periods:

(In lakhs of rupees)

	Jammu region	Kashmir region	Common to Jammu and Kashmir regions	Ladakh region	Total
Second Plan period	15.59	11.57	4.63	2.77	34.56
Third Plan period	33.16	68.98	4.95	16.21	123.30
Total	48.75	80.55	9.58	18.98	157.86

The progress achieved during the period of the three Plans is summarized in the following statement, which indicates the position immediately before the First Plan was launched and that at the end of the Third-Plan period:

Year	Indicator	Unit of measurement	Jammu region	Kashmir region	Ladakh region	Total
1950-51	1. Livestock population	Lakhs numbers	16.32	14.41	1.56	32.29
	2. Veterinary Hospitals and Dispensaries	Numbers	28	25	2	55
	3. Other Animal Husbandry Units	Numbers	3	2		5
1965-66	1. Livestock population	Lakhs numbers	23.50	14.86	2.43	40.79
	2. Veterinary Hospitals and Dispensaries	Numbers	65	71	4	142
	3. Other Animal Husbandry Units	Numbers	14	29	4	47

This table shows that though the livestock population in the Kashmir region is considerably smaller than in the Jammu region, the veterinary hospital facilities are better in the former and very much larger sums of money have been spent there than in the Jammu region or Ladakh.

(iii) *Forests and Soil Conservation.*—The activities of the State Government in this field of development can be judged from the following statistical tables:—

Expenditure

(In lakhs of rupees)

	Jammu region	*Kashmir region*	*Common to Jammu and Kashmir regions*	*Ladakh region*	*Total*
Second Plan period	34.39	40.54			74.93
Third Plan period	57.98	82.91	17.47	7.56	165.92
Total	92.37	123.45	17.47	7.56	240.85

Physical Achievements

	Unit of measurement	*Year*	*Jammu region*	*Kashmir region*	*Ladakh region*	*Total*
1. Sowing and planting of economic and industrial species	Acres	1956-57 to 1960-61	2,140	2,660	300	5,100
		1961-62 to 1965-66	1,039	4,654	N.A.	5,693
2. (a) Rehabilitation of degraded forest	Number of plants planted	1956-57 to 1960-61	35,000	65,000		100,000
(b) -do-	Acres	1961-62 to 1965-66	791	800		1,591
3. Soil Conservation on water-shed basis	Acres	1956-57 to 1960-61	40,862	13,381	660	54,903
		1961-62 to 1965-66	28,243	20,012	N.A.	48,255

N.A.: Not available.

Thus, in the field of forestry, the Kashmir region has received more attention than the Jammu region. In Jammu the emphasis has been on soil conservation. One wishes that more attention was paid to afforestation in Ladakh.

(iv) *Fisheries.*— The expenditure on Fisheries during the Second and the Third Plan periods in the different regions was as follows:—

(In lakh of rupees)

	Jammu region	*Kashmir region*	*Common to Jammu and Kashmir regions*	*Ladakh region*	*Total*
Second Plan period	1.51	5.02	—	—	6.53
Third Plan period	0.20	5.79	2.44	0.42	8.85
Total	1.71	10.81	2.44	0.42	15.38

Thus much higher investment was made in the Kashmir region than in either of the other two regions. In fact, in the Jammu region; there was a sharp decline in the investment during the Third Plan period. The higher expenditure in the Kashmir region is perhaps attributable to the fact that the scope for development of fisheries there was much greater than in the other regions.

4.15. *Irrigation.*—The amounts invested during the Second and the Third Five-Year Plan periods on irrigation and the results, as at the end of the Third Five-Year Plan period are as follows:

	Jammu region	*Kashmir region*	*Common to Jammu and Kashmir regions*	*Ladakh region*	*Total*
Expenditure during Second Plan period (In lakhs of rupees)	115.11	250.45	Nil	1.48	367.04
Expenditure during third Plan period (In lakhs of rupees)	169.05	527.16	120.98	4.07	821.26
Gross area under irrigation at the end of 1964-65 (In thousands of acres)	212	519		42	773

In irrigation, therefore, the Kashmir region is much better served than Jammu or Ladakh.

4.16. *Power:*—The expenditure incurred by the State Government on the development/purchase of power during the Second and the Third Five-Year Plan periods was as follows:

(In lakhs of rupees)

	Jammu region	*Kashmir region*	*Common to Jammu and Kashmir regions*	*Ladakh region*	*Total*
Second Plan period	152.68	219.06			371.74
Third Plan period	539.53	379 05	40.85		959.43
Total	692.21	598.11	40.85		1,331.17

The acutal achievement at the end of the Third Five-Year Plan period can be summarized thus:

	Unit of measure-ment	*Jammu region*	*Kashmir region*	*Ladakh region*	*Total*
Installed capacity	000 KW	3.50	24.00	Negligible	27.50
Electricity purchased	-do-	8.66	..	..	8.66
Towns and villages electrified	Actual number	177	349	Negligible	526

At the end of the Third Plan period, therefore, the availability of power in the Kashmir region was considerably more than in the Jammu region. In Ladakh it was almost negligible. The number of towns and villages electrified in the Kashmir region was almost double the number of those electrified in the Jammu region. The major Thermal/Hydel Projects under execution in the State are mentioned below:—

Jammu

(1) Chenani Hydro Electric Project with an ultimate capacity of 24 MW.

(2) Kalakote Thermal Power Project which is proposed to generate 22.5 MW.

Kashmir

(1) Lower Jehlum Hydro-Electric Project—Installed capacity 96 MW.

(2) Upper Sindh Hydel Project—intended to generate 34.5 MW

4.17. *Industries:*—There are certain natural disadvantages in setting up industries in this State. Cheap transport power and intrepreneurship are all lacking and the Government have had, therefore, to take the initiative in laying the foundation of its industrialization. Two companies were set-up in the public sector, viz., 'The Jammu and Kashmir Minerals Ltd.' and 'The Jammu and Kashmir Industries Ltd.' The following factories, arranged region-wise are functioning at present:

J&K Minerals Ltd.	*J&K Industries Ltd.*
Jammu	
1. Thermal Power Station, Kalakote	1. Sericulture
	2. Knitting Factory
2. Mining of Coal at Kalakote	3. Kashmir Willows
3. Padder Sapphire Mining Project	4. Rosin and Turpentine Factory
	5. Sole Leather Plant
	6. Arts Emporium
Kashmir	
1. Wuyan Cement Factory	1. Sericulture
2. Spun Pipe Factory	2. Woollen Mills
3. Prestressed Concrete Factory	3. Silk Weaving Factory
	4. Handloom Silk Weaving Factory
	5. Spinning Mill
	6. Joinery Mill
	7. Match Factory
	8. Pharmaceutical Works
	9. Leather Tanneries
	10. Bricks and Tiles Factory
	11. Arts Emporium

In addition, the following projects of the J&K Minerals Ltd. are under consideration:—

1. The Rayon Grade Pulp & Yarn Factory, Kashmir.
2. Cement Factories at Reasi and Basohli, Jammu.
3. A Paper Plant in Kashmir.

No factory has so far been located in Ladakh.

An idea of the performance of the six factories functioning under the J&K Minerals Ltd. can be had from Appendix 8 which is based on a note furnished by them.

There is not much industrial activity in the State and it is difficult to come to any definite, conclusions about it from the data furnished by the State Government in this region. The expenditure incurred on Industries during the Second Plan period has been split up by the State Government region-wise to some extent but the entire investment during the Third Plan period has been shown as being common to the two regions of Jammu and Kashmir. The expenditure during the two Plan periods was as follows:

(In lakhs of rupees)

	Jammu region	*Kashmir region*	*Common to Jammu and Kashmir regions*	*Ladakh region*	*Total*
Second Plan period	18.90	79.33	103.46		201.69
Third Plan period			864.07		864.07

The only conclusion that can be drawn from these figures is that Ladakh has not participated at all in the industrial development of the State.

The State Government have furnished some other information regarding the number of factories set-up in each region and the number of workers employed in them. The relevant data are reproduced below:—

	Jammu region		*Kashmir region*	
	1952	*1965*	*1952*	*1965*
Number of factories	19	78	27	113
Number of workers engaged	1,067	4,034	4,742	5,826

This shows that the Jammu region has received less attention than the Kashmir region in industrial development.

4.18. *Transport and Communications.—The* expenditure incurred on Transport and Communications in the Second and the Third Plan periods in the three regions of the State was as follows:

(In lakhs of rupees)

	Jammu region	*Kashmir region*	*Common to Jammu and Kashmir regions*	*Ladakh region*	*Total*
Second Plan period	693.77	449.11	6.52	63.74	1,213.14
Third Plan period	1,192.28	866.95	250.49	934.44	3,244.16
Total	1,886.05	1,316.06	257.01	998.18	4,457.30

Thus, considerable expenditure has been incurred by the State Government in this sector of development. Roads (including National Highways) and Bridges account for a substantial part of this expenditure. The important roads of the State are at present in the charge of three agencies, viz. the State Public Works Department, the Central Public Works Department and the Border Roads Development Board under the Ministry of Transport, Government of India. The financial outlays on the construction of roads and bridges in the Second and the Third Plan periods in the different regions of the State were as follows:

(In lakhs of rupees)

	Jammu region	*Kashmir region*	*Ladakh region*	*Total*
Second Plan period	487.12	245.48	63.74	796.34
Third Plan period	864.80	45.27	934.44	2,344.51
Total	1,351.92	790.75	998.18	3,140.85

The progress achieved in respect of roads under the State Public Works Department is shown on next page.

(In miles)

	Road milage at the beginning of the First Plan period			*Road milage at the end of the Third Plan period*		
	Jammu region	*Kashmir region*	*Ladakh region*	*Jammu region*	*Kashmir region*	*Ladakh region*
Motorable road milage (including jeepable roads)						
(i) Surlaccd	N.A.	416	—	715	1,201	Nil
(ii) Unsurfaced	N.A.	207	—	594	487	229
Total	432	623	—	1,309	1,168	229

N.A. : Not available.

These figures do not include the many miles of roads throughout the State which are in the charge of Central Government agencies.

In both the Jammu and Kashmir regions a number of places have been opened up and connected by new roads and the Suite and the Union Governments have applied themselves with vigour to this developmental activity. Much leeway has, however, still to be made up in the hilly and inaccessible areas of both the regions. In Ladakh, much road building activity has taken place recently but the Ladakhi people have not derived much benefit from them for lack of adequate civil transport facilities.

4.19. *Education.*—One significant feature of education in the Jammu and Kashmir State is that it is free from the kindergarten to the university stage. This has resulted in substantial growth in the education budget. The regional allocation of the State Government's expenditure on education during the last two Plan periods was as follows:—

(In lakhs of rupees)

	Jammu region	*Kashmir region*	*Common to Jammu and Kashmir regions*	*Ladakh region*	*Total*
Second Plan period	94.05	99.98	18.43	5.55	218.01
Third Plan period	234.99	325.61		12.33	572.93
Total	329.04	425.59	18.43	17.88	790.94

The progress made by the State Government in the matter of setting up of schools, colleges, professional institutions, etc. in the three regions during the period of the last three Plans may be judged from the following table showing the number of various types of educational institutions and the enrolment of students belonging to the different age groups in the years 1950-51 and 1965-66:—

Year 1950-51		*Jammu region*	*Kashmir region*	*Ladakh region*	*Total*
1.	Primary Schools	647	510	25	1,182
2.	Middle Schools	26	122	1	149
3.	High and Higher Secondary Schools	16	26	2	44
4.	Colleges (other than Medical, Engineering, Agricultural and Teachers' Training)	1	6		4
5.	Teachers' Training:				
	(a) T.T. Colleges	1	1	. .	2
	(b) T.T. Schools	N.A.	N.A.	N.A.	N.A.
6.	Enrolment				
	(a) 6-11- years age	20,000	35,000	1,000	56,000
	(b) 11-14 years age	3,000	18,000	100	21,100
	(c) 14-17 years age	4,000	3,000	20	4,020
Year 1965-66					
1.	Primary and Basic Schools	1,937	2,355	212	4,504
2.	Middle Schools	522	582	27	1,131
3.	High and Higher Secondary Schools	190	223	9	422
4.	Colleges (other than Medical, Engineering, Agricultural and Teachers' Training)	7	9		16
5.	Teachers' Training:				
	(a) T.T. Colleges	1	1		2
	(b) T.T. Schools	6	4	2	12
6.	Enrolment:				
	(a) 6-11 years age	1,42,000	1,44,000	5,000	2,91,000
	(b) 11-14 years age	38,000	48,000	1,000	87,000
	(c) 14-17 years age	16,000	25,000	300	41,300

N.A.: Not available.

It would also be worthwhile to compare the student-teacher ratios in high schools and colleges in the various regions:

	Jammu region	*Kashmir region*	*Ladakh region*	*Tolal*
High and Higher Secondary Schools:				
Year 1965-66:				
1. Number of High and Higher Secondary	190	223	9	422
2. Enrolment	63,867	65,606	935	1,30,408
3. Number of Teachers	2,734	3,363	77	6,174
4. Teachers per Institution	14.4	15.0	8.6	14.6
5. Students per Teacher	23	20	12	21
Colleges:				
Year 1965-66:				
1. Number of Colleges	7	9	..	16
2. Number of Teachers	245	367.	..	612
3. Enrolment	3.813	6840	..	10,653
4. Teachers per Institution	35	41	..	38
5. Students per Teacher	16	19	..	17

The data given above indicate the progress made in this vital field of development. They also show that in education, the Kashmir region has done better than the other regions. The student-teacher ratio for high, and higher secondary schools is smaller in the Kashmir region than in the Jammu region, though for colleges it is higher in the former. Enrolment in colleges is much higher in the Kashmir region—almost twice the enrolment in the Jammu region, though the former has only two more colleges. Professional institutions also are located mostly in the Kashmir region. The Agriculture College at Ranbirsinghpura in the Jammu Division has since been ordered to be closed.

4.20. *Health arid Family Planning.*—The steps taken by the State Government to improve the conditions of public health, which at the beginning of the First Five-Year Plan period were far from satisfactory, are summarized on next page.

(In lakhs of rupees)

	Jammu region	*Kashmir region*	*Common to Jammu and Kashmir regions*	*Ladakh region*	*Total*
Second Plan period	79.03	72.32	17.70	1.62	170.67
Third Plan period	140.13	208.43	8.41	6.51	363.48
Total	219.16	280.75	26.11	8.13	534.15

Physical Achievements:

Indicator	*Year*	*Jammu region*	*Kashmir region*	*Ladakh region*	*Total*
Number of Hospitals	1950-51	4	4	Nil	8
	1965-66	10	9	1	20
Number of Dispensaries		N.A.	N.A.	N.A.	11
		269	236	9	514
Number of Primary Health Centres		Nil	Nil	Nil	Nil
		23	30	Nil	53
Bed Strength		150	450	Nil.	600
		1,540	2,224	50	3,814
Number of Family Planning Centres		Nil	Nil	Nil	Nil
		8	10	1	19
Number of Doctors		86	98*	N.A.	184
		298	471	19	788

NA: Not available.
The figure marked with an asterisk includes the number of doctors in Ladakh region.

These tables show that at the end of the Third Plan period there was no great disparity between the Jammu and Kashmir regions in regard to the number of Hospitals, Dispensaries, Family Planning Centres and Primary Health Centres set-up. The number of Doctors was, however, almost 60 per cent more in the Kashmir region than in the Jammu region at the end of the Third Five-Year Plan period. It is also to be noted that even though the Kashmir region had only 9 hospital at the end of the Third Plan period as against 30 in the Jammu region, the bed-strength in the former was about 50 per cent more than in the latter. In Ladakh the facilities available appear to be extremely poor.

4.21. *Conclusions:* Thus, as we have said in paragraph 4.08, so far as developmental expenditure within the Plans is concerned, the expenditure incurred in the Kashmir-region has been about twenty-two per cent more than that incurred in the Jammu region. But it is only by taking into account the developmental, expenditure incurred outside the Plans also that some kind of arithmetical parity, between the two regions can be established. When we consider the items that constitute non-Plan developmental expenditure, we do not think that one should attach much importance to such parity. Appendix 7 shows that the non-Plan items are: Transport and Communications, National Highways and Colonies (Rehabilitation of Displaced Persons). In so far as: 'Transport and Communications' and 'National Highway' are concerned, it is difficult to say to what extent these may be deemed to serve purely regional needs and interests. It is doubtful whether the expenditure on the rehabilitation of displaced persons can be treated as developmental expenditure in the ordinary sense of the term. We have noticed that in most of the sectors of development discussed in paragraphs 4.14 to 4.20, judged by the physical achievements, the Kashmir region has done better than the other regions.

4.22. In absolute terms it is very difficult to define equitability as applied to the sharing of resources by different regions of a State and perhaps even more difficult to achieve it in practice. In judging this, several factors have to be taken into account such as population, area, specific needs, potential available, etc. Irrespective of the criteria that are adopted for the purpose, it is important that the people of each region should have a feeling of equal participation in the integrated development of the State. From the various memoranda and the oral evidence, we came to realize how strongly Jammu nurses a feeling of being discriminated against in developmental matters. It is not possible to ignore this feeling of dissatisfaction even allowing for the fact that much of it seems to be psychological. The position of Ladakh is somewhat similar. From the statistical and other data which we have examined in this Chapter; the conclusion seems fairly clear that the Kashmir region has on the whole received more attention than the other regions during the period of the three Plans. Even so, we do not think that on the basis of the material available to us, we would be justified in concluding that the State Government have deliberately discriminated against either Jammu or Ladakh.

4.23. In oral testimony as also in a number of memoranda, it was represented to us that within both the Jammu and Kashmir regions there are certain pockets which have remained much more backward than the rest of the region. These are the hilly and inaccessible parts of the State. It has not been possible to assess the extent of development, or the lack of it in these areas as district-wise details of development programmes and developmental expenditure are not maintained by the State Government. From the evidence produced before us, however, we feel that these areas deserve special attention and the Government should address themselves urgently to the task of developing them speedily.

4.24. The development in Ladakh during the period of the three plans has been inadequate. True, a number of roads have been constructed in the area but the public transport facilities still remain unsatisfactory. We feel that a vitally important border area like Ladakh should receive greater attention from both the State Government and the Union Government and that the Ladakhis should not be allowed to nurse a feeling that they are being left out in the State's march to prosperity.

4.25. *Recommendations.*—We have given thought to the question of how best to ensure that the resources available to the State Government are shared equitably by the regions so that they have a feeling of equal-participation in the integrated development of the State. It is not easy to lay down a rigid formula for the purpose nor do we think it is necessary to devise one. We should, however, like to visualize an arrangement whereby the regions can have the maximum opportunity to draw up their own developmental programmes and to implement them subject to the interests of the State as a whole.

4.26. We would suggest that there should be a statutory State Development Board and statutory Regional Development Boards for the three regions—Jammu, Kashmir and Ladakh. Each of the Regional Boards should be headed by the Chief Minister or the Planning Minister and should consist of legislators from the regions, economists, experts and concerned officials. . . The regions should be adequately represented on State Development Board which should be headed by the Chief Minister.

4.27. The functions of the Regional Development Boards should be:

(a) to draw up the regional Plans;

(b) to assign priority to schemes and projects included in the regional Plans; and

(c) to supervise the implementation of the regional Plans.

In discharging these functions it should be the special responsibility of the Regional Development Boards to look after the special needs of the backward areas in their respective regions.

4.28. The regional Plans prepared by the Regional Development Boards should be placed before the State Development Board which should carefully scrutinize them. The State Development Board should also prepare a residuary Plan of such schemes and projects as transcend regional boundaries or happen to be of an all-State, as opposed to regional, interest. With the regional Plans and the residuary Plan before it, the State Development Board should allocate Plan funds equitably (after taking into account the population, area and the specific, needs of each region) to the regional Plans and the residuary Plan of all-State interest.

4.29. We consider it very important that the general population should be kept correctly and adequately informed of the progress of development programmes and developmental expenditure. We would accordingly suggest that the State Development Board and each of the Regional Development Boards should prepare at the end of each year a report of their respective activities giving, details of the progress of the Plan programmes and Plan expenditure. At the end of each Plan, similar detailed reports should be prepared by the Boards indicating the physical and financial targets and the physical and financial achievements. All these reports should be laid before the Legislature as soon as may be after they are prepared.

CHAPTER V

RECRUITMENT **Pounds**

5.01. *Introduction.*—We shall now examine the recruitment policies of the State Government as required by our second term of reference. We have also to "recommend measures for giving an equitable share in the Government employment to the various regions and communities, having special regard to the claims of the Scheduled Castes and other economically, educationally and socially backward communities, classes and groups.

Several memorialists and representatives have complained that in the matter of recruitment to Government services there is discrimination on communal or religious grounds, or a lack of reservation for the Scheduled Castes and for those who claim to be economically educationally and socially backward. The question of giving an equitable representation in the services to the various communities of the State has a rather long history. In the late twenties and early thirties there were complaints that the Muslims, who formed the great majority of the population were not adequately represented in the State services and that this was also true of certain minority communities of the State.

5.02. *Glancy Commission.*—In November 1931, a Commission was appointed consisting of 4 non-official members, presided over by a European member, Mr. Bertrand J. Glancy of the Indian Civil Service (seconded to the then Indian Political Service), who was lent to the Jammu and Kashmir State by the Government of India, to enquire into and report on the various complaints, of religious or general nature already submitted to the State Government and also such complaints as might be directly laid before the Commission. It was from his name that the Commission derived its popular title of "the Glancy Commission."

5.03. *Recommendations.*—On the question of employment in the public services of the State, the Glancy Commission found that, generally the Muslims and certain minority communities were inadequately represented in the services. It made certain

1. Chapter IV of the Report of the Commission appointed under the Orders of His Highness the Maharaja Bahadur, dated the 13th November, 1931, to inquire into Grievances & Complaints, 2nd Edition, 1933 (hereafter referred to as the Report of the Glancy Commission).

recommendations with a view to achieving a more equitable method of recruitment to the services and affording to every community a fair chance of representation. Its principal recommendations on the subject are summarized below:

(i) While there need not be different standards for different communities, the standard should not be more exacting than efficiency demanded and those who possessed qualifications in excess of that standard should not be held to deserve appointment as a matter of right.

(ii) There was no need to change the age limit which was then thirty years.

(iii) Appointments and scholarships should be properly advertised and given as wide publicity as possible.

(iv) Due regard should be paid to the legitimate interests of every community in the matter of recruitment to Government services and the grant of scholarships for training provided that suitable candidates were forthcoming.

5.04. In regard to the claim that the Muslims, who constituted 78 per cent of the State's population, should be given a corresponding reservation in Government appointments, the Commission observed that it rested with the Muslims to work up the number of their representatives in State services by availing themselves of the opportunities to be pro-vided. It also observed that the hereditary occupation of a vast number of Muslims was agriculture and it was reasonable to suppose that the great majority of agriculturists would continue to prefer that occupation to any other. While no community should be allowed to acquire a stranglehold on State employment, the Commission wanted it to be recognized that certain communities were far in advance of others in [2]education.

5.05. It was claimed before the Glancy Commission that although no scholarships had been specifically reserved for Kashmiri Pandits, over 50 per cent of their numbers were literate (a far higher percentage than in any other community), that ministerial work had been their hereditary occupation and that they had no other means of subsistence readily available. The Commission recognized the force of this contention and

2. Page 24 of the Report of the Glancy Commission.

recommended that the need for other openings that could be legitimately provided for those who could not/be absorbed in State departments should receive the sympathetic attention of the Government. It should be carried out to the best of the Government's ability, for example, in the [3]field of industrial development, etc.

5.06. These recommendations of the Commission were accepted the then Ruler of the [4]State.

5.07. *Recruitment Rules Committee.*— The recommendations of the Glancy Commission did not bring about a final solution to the problem. A few years later a Committee was appointed to formulate proposals for recruitment to and training for, the services, the Recruitment Rules Committee was presided over by Mr. P.C. Mogha then Revenue Minister, and its members were the Chief Justice. Use Chief Secretary and the Accountant General of the State, besides Mr. M. Afzal Khan, Revenue Commissioner and later Home Minister of the State. The report of the Committee on the gazetted services was published in 1939 and that on the non-gazetted services in 1941.

5.08. *Main recommendations of the Committee.*—The Committee made detailed proposals regarding the classification of each service, gazetted and non-gazetted into classes and categories, the method of recruitment of each class and category and the qualifications required of the candidates. The main recommendations of the Committee which involved a departure from, or improvement on, the position under the Glancy Commission's Report are summarized below:—

(i) For direct recruitment the age limit should be reduced to 28 years, except for gazetted appointments in such departments as the Judicial, Education and Medical Departments where higher educational qualifications were required. In the Judicial and Education Departments, an age limit of 30 years was recommended and in the case of the Medical Department a still higher age limit of 32 years was [5]proposed.

3. Page 23 of the Report of the Glancy Commission.
4. Orders on the recommendations mentioned in the Report of the Glancy Commission.
5. Page 1 of the Interim Report of the Recruitment, Rules Committee re: Gazetted Services, 1939.

(ii) For gazetted services the normal method of recruitment should be by a competitive examination. Direct recruitment by nomination was provided for in most of the services but the Committee did not consider it desirable to fix a ratio between nomination and recruitment by competition as it thought that recruitment by nomination should be resorted to only exceptionally and should not be regarded as a normal method. The Committee recommended a proportion between direct appointments and promotions, including transfer, varying from 50 to 75 per cent according to the circumstances of each department. One consideration on recruitment was that it would give a better chance for regulating communal [6]represeniation.

(iii) For non-gazetted services the Committee recommended five methods of recruitment, namely, selection, nomination, competitive examination, promotion from a lower category or grade and transfer from another class. Recruitment partly by one method and partly by another was also recommended. The Report also indicated the proportion in which recruitment should be made direct, i.e., by selection, nomination or competitive examination, and by promotion or transfer. For technical departments such as the Medical and Public Works Departments, recruitment by competitive examination was not considered necessary and nomination or selection was considered [7]sufficient.

5.09. The Report of the Committee indicates that though no definite orders existed at the time on the subject of communal representation, 50 per cent representation for the Muslim community was supposed to be the [8]aim. This Committee also

6. Page 2 of the Interim Report of the Recruitment Rules Committee re: Gazetted Services, 1-939.
7. Pages 1-3 of the Report of the Committee appointed to formulate proposals for recruitment to Government services (Non-Gazetted Services), 1941.
8. Page 3 of the Interim Report of the Recruitment Rules Committee re: Gazetted Services, 1939.

suggested rules for the various competitive examinations recommended by it and detailed syllabuses for each of them.

5.10. *Position after introduction of popular rule.*—After the introduction of popular rule in the State in 1947, there was large expansion of the services as a result of accelerated developmental activities of the State Government. We have been advised by the State Government that between 1947 and 1953, recruitment was made in some Departments after observing the usual formalities but "there were cases where this 'was not done". In explanation, it has been stated that "recruitment could not probably be made strictly under the rules which were sanctioned as far back as in 1941". We have also been informed that immediately after 1947, some appointments in the higher ranks were also made from political cadres, though the number of such appointments was small.

5.11. *Jammu and Kashmir Public Services Reorganization Committee.*—To enable measures being taken towards the establishment of a State Public Service Commission as a statutory body, the State Government set-up.

The Committee does not seem to have submitted a report; the State Government have informed it that no copy of such a report is traceable.

5.12. *Jammu and Kashmir Public Service Recruitment Board:*—By an Order dated 31 December 1954 the Government appointed a Recruitment Board for recruitment to the superior services of the State. The powers and functions of this Board, designated as the Jammu and Kashmir Public service Recruitment Board, were laid down in a subsequent Order dated 2 May, 1955. It was required to advise the Government on the method, manner and principles governing direct recruitment to gazetted services and such non-gazetted superior services as might be specified by the Government from time to time, in accordance with the qualifications, standards, and other requirements laid down in the recruitment rules and other rules issued in that behalf. The activities of the Board were thus confined to cases of direct recruitment and promotion cases did not fall within its purview. We have been told by the State Government that while the Board made recommendations regarding direct recruitment to gazetted services from time to time, very few cases of non-gazetted establishment were referred to it. On the establishment of a Public

Service Commission in the State, the Recruitment Board was abolished on 2 September 1957.

5.13. *The Jammu and Kashmir Civil Services (Classification, Control and Appeal) Rules, 1956.* In June 1956, the State Government promulgated the Jammu and Kashmir Civil Services (Classification, Control and Appeal) Rules. These rules were originally framed in exercise of the powers conferred on the Government by the Jammu and Kashmir Civil Servants (Removal of Doubts and Declaration of Rights) Ordinance, 1956. When the Ordinance was replaced by a regular Act of the Legislature, the Jammu and Kashmir Civil Services (Classification, Control and Appeal) Rules were saved and they are still in force. Various representatives have complained that certain provisions of the Jammu and Kashmir Civil Services (Classification, Control and Appeal) Rules are being ignored or applied in such a way as to cause irritation and result in undue discrimination, the provisions which are alleged to be generally ignored are those relating to the prescription of qualifications for recruitment, seniority and promotions. Those which are alleged to be misused are the ones, relating to the reservation of posts for the backward classes and the provision that enables the Government to declare that the Jammu and Kashmir (Classification, Control and Appeal) Rules, 1956, shall not apply in whole or in part to a particular person or group of persons or to relax in individual cases and for reasons to be recorded in writing, any of those rules or any rules made thereunder if the Government is satisfied that a strict application of the rules would cause hardship to the individual concerned or confer undue benefit on him.

5.14. In order to judge whether the provisions of the rules of the Jammu and Kashmir Government have any unusual characteristics, they have been compared with the corresponding rules of the Union Government and of a few other States in the country. It has been found that so far as the procedure for consultation with the Public Service Commission is concerned the position in the Jammu and Kashmir State is on the whole similar to the position obtaining elsewhere. The differences, where they exist, are marginal. The only point which may be considered to make some difference is the exclusion of all appointments, promotions and transfers to non-gazetted services in Jammu and Kashmir from the purview of the Public Service Commission of the [9]State. But it is relevant to point out here that several categories of posts which would be included in the non-gazetted category in other States, are included in the gazetted category in Jammu and Kashmir.

5.15. In regard to the provisions of the Classification, Control and Appeal Rules also the position in Jammu and Kashmir does not appear to be materially different from the position at the Centre or in some other States.

5.16. The regulations relating to their Public Service Commission or the Jammu and Kashmir Civil Services (Classification, Control and Appeal) Rules do not, therefore, by themselves allow special scope for discrimination in the matter of recruitment, transfers, etc. of the State Government staff.

5.17. Coming to the complaints mentioned in paragraph 5.13, it may be mentioned that up-to-date recruitment rules do not exist for several services and posts. The absence of such rules has been the subject of criticism by the State Public Service Commission. They have complained that for a large majority of posts referred to them proper recruitment rules have not been framed and among those that exist, some are obsolete and require revision. They have also observed that for a large number of posts, qualifications have not been prescribed nor have the posts been [10]classified. This criticism has appeared in more than one Report of the Commission. The State Government are aware of this unsatisfactory position and steps are being taken to frame proper recruitment rules. According to available information, proper recruitment rules exist in the case of 4 State services only; for one service the rules require to be brought up to date; for 5 services the rules are still in the draft stage and for 10 other services no rules have been drafted so far. The progress of framing the recruitment rules needs to be speeded up.

5.18. *Results of competitive examinations.*—Here we should like to mention that some representatives demanded that the detailed subject-wise results of the competitive examinations held by the State Public Service Commission should be published for general information as was the practice before 1947. They thought that

9. Regulation 4 of the Jammu and Kashmir Public Service Commission (Limitation of Functions) Regulations, 1957.
10. Annual Reports of the Jammu and Kashmir Public Service Commission for the years 1963-64 and 1965-66.

such publication would remove any possible doubts with regard to the results and would also enable the public to judge whether or not the appointments had been made strictly on the basis of merit. In the course of his evidence before us, the Chairman of the State Public Service Commission stated that the Commission only published the aggregate marks of the candidates and that if it was the practice of the Union Public Service Commission to publish the detailed results, subject-wise, in respect of the examinations held by it, the State Public Service Commission would also consider doing so. He, however, added that a considerable time-lag in the publication of the detailed results would be unavoidable. In order to allay any misgivings in the mind of the public, we should like to recommend that the results, complete in all details, of all competitive examinations held by the State Public Service Commission, and any other Recruitment Board that may be set-up, should be published. These results should be sent to all the candidates who have taken the examination or, if this is not always feasible, they should at least be made available for scrutiny on request.

5.19. *Seniority Lists.*—The Annual Reports of the Public Service Commission also indicate that proper seniority lists are not always being [11]maintained. We have been told that the State Government are drawing up seniority lists, service by service. The State Government are having difficulty in doing so because of past neglect. It is needless to say that the drawing up of correct seniority lists and maintaining them up to date is a *sine qua non* for being able to deal with cases of promotion on a fair basis.

5.20. *Confidential rolls.*—Another defect pointed out in the Annual Reports of the Public Service Commission is that the confidential rolls of the members of the services are not always [12]submitted. When a question of supersession is involved this naturally makes it difficult for the Commission to judge whether the supersession is justified or not. Some of the memoranda presented to us have expressed the fear and suspicion that the remarks actually recorded in the character rolls were influenced

11. Annual Report of the Jammu and Kashmir Public Service Commission for the year 1964-65 and 1965-66.
12. Annual Report of the Jammu and Kashmir Public Service Commission for the year 1964-65.

by extraneous considerations. It is obviously necessary that the annual confidential rolls should be written up regularly and objectively and that provision should be made for review of the rolls by an authority superior to the reporting officer wherever such a provision does not already exist. We presume that adverse entries recorded in the confidential rolls of Government servants are communicated to them in accordance with the general practice in this matter. A procedure should be prescribed for dealing properly with representations of Government servants against such adverse entries.

5.21. *Viva Voce Tests.*—Complaints have been made to us that in the matter of recruitment to Government services, undue weightage is being given to *viva voce* tests, and that this leads to discrimination. No party, however, has been able to substantiate this charge. We obviously cannot recommend that *viva voce* tests should be dispensed with, nor do we consider that the weightage given by the State Government to such tests is disproportionately large.

5.22. *Communal Reservation.*—Our terms of reference require us to recommend measures for giving an equitable share in Government employment to the various regions and communities, having special regard to the claims of the Scheduled Castes and other economically, educationally and socially backward communities, classes and groups among the citizens of the State consistently with the maintenance of efficiency of administration. It has been enjoined on us that in considering this matter we should take note of the provisions contained in Part III—"Fundamental Rights" as well as other provisions of the Constitution of India as made applicable to the State of Jammu and Kashmir and of the Directive Principles of State Policy laid down in Part IV of the Constitution of Jammu and Kashmir and particularly of Section 23 thereof. As mentioned at the outset of this Chapter, the problem of affording equitable representation to the various communities of the State in the services is not a new one. Even the Glancy Commission and the Recruitment Rules Committee had occasion to deal with the matter many years ago.

5.23. The irritations and tensions mentioned in our fourth term of reference and which are likely to arise from various causes, including those that have given rise to our other three terms of reference, are not confined to the State of Jammu and Kashmir.

Irritations and tensions arising from similar causes exist in the minds of different communities and groups of citizens in other parts of India too; and it is the urgent and paramount duty of Indian democracy to remove the causes of such irritations and tensions. This problem has become more acute with the passage of time, the growth of population, the adoption-of the Welfare State ideology and the spread of mass education. Unless the socially and economically weaker sections of the Indian community, including the Scheduled Castes and the backward classes, as well as the members of linguistic and religious minorities residing in all parts of India, feel that the concept of equality of opportunity and justice—political, social and economic—has become a reality in their lives, these tensions and irritations are likely to continue. The goal set by the Constitution of India before Indian, democracy to afford equality before law to all citizens and to create a social and economic structure in which every citizen will be able to enjoy fully life, liberty, and happiness yet remains to be attained and it must be the earnest endeavour of Indian democracy to reach that goal as early as possible. We would like to emphasize, here that in the matter of irritations and tensions, whatever happens in the rest of India is bound to haw an immediate impact on the State of Jammu and Kashmir and *vice-versa*.. These general observations will apply to the further discussion of the problems which have been referred to us. How the causes for irritations and tensions existing in the minds of groups of citizens in the rest of India should be removed is a matter with which we are not concerned in the present inquiry.

5.24. We have obtained from the State Government statistical data regarding the communal and regional composition of the State Government staff as on 1 April 1967 as well as the communal and regional composition of the persons recruited to the State Government services, year by year, from 1961-62 to 1965-66. We have also had before us the statistical data furnished by the State Government to the High Court of Jammu and Kashmir in regard to the regional and communal composition of the gazetted and non-gazetted staff of the State Government as on 10 September 1963 in the case of Triloki Nath and another *Vs.* State of Jammu and Kashmir and others, a case to which we will make further reference in the subsequent paragraphs of this Chapter. Appendix IX is a summary of the data as compiled in the

Commission's Secretariat. It will be seen that region-wise, the position in the Kashmir Valley, taking both the rate of annual recruitment and the total strength of the staff, has improved while the corresponding position in Jammu has deteriorated. Though the Kashmir region's population is 53.3 per cent of the total population of the State, its share in the services as on 1 April 1967 was 60.9 per cent. The Jammu region's population is 44.2 per cent of the total population of the State but its share in the services on 1 April 1967 was only 36.1 per cent. The rate of recruitment of Ladakhis has shown a decline from 2.5 per cent in 1961-62 to 1.4 per cent in 1965-66. Their total share in the services as on 1 April 1967, however, was slightly in excess of the proportion of the population of Ladakh to the total population of the State. Community-wise the position of Muslims has shown an improvement though their total share in the services on 1 April 1967 was appreciably less than what it should be oh the basis of population. The position of Hindus has shown a decline though their share in the services as on 1 April 1967 was substantially higher than what was due to them according to their population. The annual intake of Buddhists has also shown a fall. The recruitment of Sikhs in the services has been fluctuating from year to year but their share on 1 April 1967 was considerably in excess of what was due to them on a population basis.

5.25. *Constitutional provision.*—Prior to the coming into force of the Constitution of India, reservations in the services, the legislatures, etc. in the country were made on the basis of religion. The recommendations of the Glancy Commission also seem to have followed the same pattern. Article 370 of the Constitution of India, which, came into force on 26 January 1950, makes a special provision with respect to the State of Jammu and Kashmir. The President issued an order under that Article on 14 May 1954 extending the application of the provisions of the Constitution of India to Jammu and Kashmir and indicating the exceptions and modifications subject to which they should [13]apply. This order made Article 15 of the Constitution, prohibiting discrimination on grounds of religion, race, caste, sex or place of birth, and Article 16, guaranteeing equality of opportunity in matters of public employment, applicable to the State of Jammu and Kashmir,

13. The Constitution (Application to Jammu and Kashmir) Order, 1954.

subject to the following modifications:—

(i) The reference to Scheduled Tribes in clause (4) of Article 15 is to be omitted; and

(ii) the reference to State in clause (3) of Article 16 is to be construed as not including a reference to the State of Jammu and Kashmir.

Article 29 dealing with protection of minorities became applicable without any modification. Section 10 of the Constitution of Jammu and Kashmir, which came into force on 17 November 1956, guarantees to the permanent residents of the State all the rights guaranteed to them under the Constitution of India, including the provisions, of Articles 15, 16 and 29. In Section 23, the Constitution of Jammu and Kashmir lays down a directive principle that the State shall guarantee to the socially and educationally backward sections of the people special care in the promotion of their educational, material and cultural interests and protection against social injustice.

5.26. *Position of Scheduled Castes and Scheduled Tribes.*—Apparently no tribe in Jammu and Kashmir is treated as a Scheduled Tribe. No special constitutional safeguards have been made for such tribes. For Scheduled Castes, the only Article—Article 335—in the Constitution of India dealing with the claims of the Scheduled Castes to services and posts has been rendered inapplicable to services and posts in connection with the affairs of the Jammu and Kashmir State by virtue of sub-para (11) of paragraph 2 of the Constitution (Application to Jammu and Kashmir) Order, 1954.

5.27. *Implementation of the Constitutional provisions by the State Government.*—The Government of Jammu and Kashmir do not appear to be following any clear-cut policy either in the classification of backward classes or in the matter of special benefits to be given to them. In February 1956 they issued a notification in which certain classes were recognized as 'backward classes'. The list has been amended from time to time. A copy of the list as it stands now is attached at Appendix 10. As far as we have been able to understand, this list, has been used only for the limited purpose of granting special scholarships to students belonging to the classes. In June 1956 the State Government issued the Jammu at Kashmir Civil Services (Classification, Control and

Appeal) Rules in which a clause was included to enable the State Government to make operations in Government services in favour of any backward class which, in the opinion of the Government, was not adequately represented in the services. It appears, however, that the term "backward classes" used for the purpose of recruitment did not have the same meaning as the one mentioned in the notification of February 1956, as amended from time to time. In fact the State Government do not appear to have issued any clear-cut orders, statutory or other, specifying which are the backward classes for the purpose of being accorded special facilities in the matter of recruitment to Government services. They have had some working rule which has been subject to modification from time to time to suit particular situations. The latest working rule, as it emerged from at affidavit filed by the State Government in a [14]writ petition submitted by two teachers to the Supreme Court, is apparently that 50 per cent of the posts are to be filled by Muslims from the entire State of Jammu and Kashmir and 40 per cent of them are to be filled by Jammu Hindus. The State Government sought to justify this working rule in the Supreme Court on the ground that Muslims as a community in the whole of the State of Jammu and Kashmir formed a "backward class" of citizens and they were not adequately represented in the services in the State; and that similarly; Hindus from the province of Jammu formed "a backward community" and were not adequately represented in the services of the State. Accordingly, reservation in the matter of appointments to posts and promotions in the services of the State was made in respect of both these classes.

5.28. *Supreme Court's Rulings.*—The Supreme Court examine the position at great length and observed as [15]follows:

> "Clause (4) of Art. 16 undoubtedly empowers the State to make reservation of appointments or posts in favour of any backward class of citizens so as to give the class an adequate representation in the services under the State. The provision

14. Writ Petition No. 107 of 1965 in the Supreme Court of India.
15. Judgement of the Supreme Court in Writ Petition No. 107 of 1965—Triloki Nath and another *Vs.* State of Jammu and Kashmir and others—delivered 23 April 1968.

making such reservation need not be by a statutory enactment; it may be made by an executive order or direction. But there is not even a formal executive order expressly dealing with reservation of posts and appointments in the Education Department. On behalf of the State it is claimed that as a matter of State Policy, in making appointments and promotions, reservations in fact have been made by the State as alleged by the petitioners with some variations. . . .

The expression backward class is not used as synonymous with 'backward caste' or 'backward community'. The members of an entire caste or community may in the social, economic and educational scale of values at a given time be backward and may on that account be treated as a backward class, but that is not because they are members of a caste or community, but because they form a class. In its ordinary connotation the expression 'class' means a homogeneous section of the people grouped together because of certain likenesses or common traits, who are identifiable by some common attributes such as the states, rank, occupation, residence in a locality, race, religion and the like. But for the purpose of Art. 16(4) in determining whether a section forms a class, a test solely based on caste, community, race, religion, sex, descent, place of birth or residence cannot be adopted, because it would directly offend the Constitution.

"In the voluminous evidence produced before the High Court a formal order making a provision for reservation of appointments or posts in favour of any backward class of citizens does not find a place. The only evidence to which our attention has been invited is the statement of Malik Ghulam Nabi, who deposed that the policy laid down by the Government in matters of the employment to the State services is that 50 per cent of the vacancies are reserved for the Muslims of Kashmir (for the entire State). Out of the remaining 50 per cent, 40 per cent are reserved for the Jammu Hindus and 10 per cent for the Kashmiri Hindus. There are a number of Government orders by which this policy has been laid down, but due to the short time at my disposal, I have been able to get only one copy of such order, which is signed by the Chief Secretary, whose handwriting I know and identify. In cross-examination Malik Ghulam Nabi stated that the order produced by him applied to all kinds of services under the State and it was being implemented even now and was still in force. The witness was unable to speak to the criteria on the basis of which the order was issued. . . It was recorded in paragraph-4 of the order that a Selection Board consisting of four Secretaries to the Government was set-up and they were asked to prepare a Select List on the basis of merit-*cum*-seniority, keeping in view the policy of adequate representation of such elements as are not adequately represented in the services and to pay due regard to provincial proportions. There is no reference in any of the clauses of the order to selection of officers on the basis that they belong to backward classes. The injunction to the Secretaries to select candidates keeping in view the policy of adequate representation of such elements as were not adequately represented in the services is not a provision making reservation of appointments or posts in favour of backward classes. Selections made, assuming that similar orders were passed enjoining the making of promotions to the gazetted, cadre in the Educational Service, could not be deemed to have been made on the basis of backwardness of the class to which they belonged.

"The State of Jammu and Kashmir had, it is admitted, from time to time framed lists of backward communities. . . But it is not claimed that in making promotions to the gazetted cadre in the Educational Service, the authorities acted in pursuance of the List. . . As already observed the normal rule contemplated by the constitutional provision is equality between aspirants to public employment, but in view of backwardness of certain classes it would be open to the State to make a provision for reservation of appointments or posts in their favour. When the State proceeds not to make reservations in favour of any backward class, but to distribute the total number of posts or appointments on the basis of community or place or residence, no reservation permitted by cl. (4) of Art. 16 can be said to be made. In effect the State policy which Malik Ghulam Nabi spoke to was a policy not of reservation of some appointments or posts: it was a scheme of distribution of all the posts community-wise. Distribution of appointments, posts or promotions made in implementation of that State policy is contrary to the constitutional guarantee under Art. 16(1) and (2) and is not saved by cl. (4).

"The promotions granted to respondents 3 to 83 are accordingly declared contrary to the provisions of Art. 16(1) and (4) of the Constitution and therefore void."

5.29. The Supreme Court had also occasion to examine the legality of reservation on a regional basis, in connection with a series of writ petitions filed against the policy of the Madras Government of allocating the seats in the Medical Colleges of the State to the various districts in the ratio of the population of each district to the total population of the State. It has [16]held that the allocation of seats on district-wise basis is *ultra vires* of Article 14 of the Constitution of India and has accordingly struck down the policy of the Madras Government. The principle enunciated by the Supreme Court in that case will, in our opinion, hold good in the case of recruitment to Government services and posts as well and any recommendation for fixing quotas for recruitment on a purely regional basis will be *ultra vires* of Article 16 of the Constitution of India as made applicable to the Jammu and Kashmir State.

5.30. The Muslims of the entire State together with the Hindus of Jammu province form 94.2 per cent of the total population of the State. When practically the entire population is treated as backward, there is bound to be considerable difference in the degree of backwardness between one class and another included in that population. The really backward classes which need protection have, therefore, to compete with those which are more advanced. This is bound to shut out the classes which are really backward from the services and we believe that this is what has happened in the State.

16. Judgement of the Supreme Court in Writ Petitions 194 of 1967 etc. and Civil Appeal No. 1456 of 1965—Minor P. Rajendran *Vs.* the State of Madras & others etc.—delivered on 17 January 1968.

5.31. While passing orders striking down the promotions of teachers in the Education Department, referred to in paragraphs 5.27 and 5.28, the Supreme Court has observed that its orders would not prevent the State Government from devising a scheme, consistent with the Constitutional guarantees, for the reservation of appointments, posts or promotions in favour of any backward class of citizens which in the opinion of the State is not adequately represented in the services under the State. In our opinion, the immediate requirement is to draw up afresh the list of backward classes in the State. The adoption of a single criterion or test of community, caste or region to which the persons concerned belong will be *ultra vires* of the Constitution. For identifying the backward classes in the State, therefore, a multiple test will have to be adopted; in other words, several criteria relating to economic, educational and social backwardness will have to be applied for determining which classes are really backward. Several witnesses who gave evidence before us were also of the same view.

5.32. Here, we should like to draw attention to the fact that clause (4) of Article 16 is in the nature of an exception, made in favour of the backward classes, to the basic principle enunciated in Article 14 and clauses (1) and (2) of Article 16, guaranteeing equality of opportunity to all citizens in matters relating to employment or appointment to any office under the State. In giving effect to the provisions of this clause, therefore, it is necessary to determine, for every State, which are the socially and educationally backward classes within its boundaries that deserve the protection of that clause. In India, some States are relatively advanced, socially and educationally, while certain others are comparatively backward. Even for a State that is relatively backward, socially and educationally, it is not permissible, in terms of Article 16(4), to treat the whole of the State as "backward" or a whole community as a community as "backward", without the application of the multiple test referred to in the previous paragraph. The attempt to identify the socially and educationally backward sections which deserve the protection of clause (4) of Article 16, involves making a comparison between different classes of citizens. Only such classes of citizens in the State can justifiably claim the protection of that clause as constitute socially and educationally the weakest section of the community. What we have stated here in relation to public employment applies equally to clause (4) of Article 15, which was introduced by way of a constitutional amendment in 1951; it provides for an exception to the basic principle contained in Article 14 and clauses (1) and (2) of Article 15, prohibiting, discrimination on grounds of religion, race, caste, sex or place of birth. This exception has been "made as a measure of protection to the backward classes and the Scheduled Castes and the Scheduled Tribes."

5.33. *Multiple criteria for determining backwardness.*—The problem of determining which are the backward classes is not simple. In its Report submitted to the Union Government in March 1955, the Backward Classes Commission has attempted to lay down certain criteria for general guidance in the matter. The tests recommended by the Commission, however, appeared to the Government to be too vague and wide to be of much practical value. It has been held by the Supreme Court in Balaji *Vs.* State of Mysore (A 1963 S.C. 649) that the appointment or recommendation of the Backward Classes Commission under Article 340 is not a condition precedent for the State to make special provisions for the backward classes under Article 15(4). In other words, the State is competent to classify classes of persons as "backward" by executive or legislative action so long as this has not already been determined after investigation by the Commission. This judgement of the Supreme Court indicates broadly, the factors that may be taken into account or the tests that may be applied in determining the social and educational backwardness of groups or classes of citizens. In considering social and educational backwardness, there is no escape from considering economic backwardness also. As the Backward Classes Commission has stated, "the economic backwardness had also to be kept in view in order to find out the ability of a community to take advantage of the available opportunities as also the recent trends in its advancement as a result of various measures initiated by State Governments during the last one or two decades." The Supreme Court has also, in the judgement referred to above, stated that "social backwardness is in the ultimate analysis the result of poverty to a very large extent. The classes of citizens who are deplorably poor automatically become socially backward." It follows, therefore, that the "means test" is one of the important tests for determining backwardness. The occupations of citizens may also contribute to make classes of citizens socially backward. To quote again, from the Supreme Court judgement: "There are some occupations which are treated as inferior, according to conventional beliefs and classes of citizens who follow these occupations are apt to become socially backward. The place of habitation also plays not a minor part in determining the backwardness of a community of persons". Thus, the occupation of citizens, and the place of their habitation are two other criteria for determining backwardness. As regards educational backwardness, a suitable criterion for determining it would be to consider the average of student population, per thousand in a particular class of citizens and to consider the class "backward" if this average is substantially below the State average. Moreover, in the case of certain classes, caste may also become a relevant factor in considering their backwardness although this cannot be made the sole or dominant test for the purpose.

5.34. To sum up, therefore, the following criteria should, in our opinion, be suitable for determining whether a certain class of citizens is socially and educationally backward:

(1) The economic backwardness of the class. [For this purpose, a suitable *ad hoc* figure of annual income may be adopted.]
(2) The occupation or occupations pursued by that class of citizens.
(3) Their place of habitation.
(4) The average of student population per thousand in that class. [This should be substantially below the State average.]
(5) Caste, in relation to Hindus.

5.35. *Revision of the list of backward classes.*—We recommended that the determination of classes which are backward on the basis of multiple criteria of the kind suggested in the previous paragraph be entrusted to high-powered Committee that would command general respect. On a Committee of this calibre there should at least be one or two persons who have expert knowledge and past experience of the subject. The reservation of posts and appointments in the services of the State Government should be made, available only to those classes that are included in the fresh list of backward classes drawn up on the basis of the Committee's recommendations. The percentage of posts and appointments so reserved should not exceed the proportion that the total population of the backward classes so listed form of the total population of the State, subject, however, to the condition that the total number of vacancies reserved for all classes of persons should not ordinarily exceed fifty percent. All direct recruitment to reserved vacancies, as well as to the general vacancies should be made strictly on the basis of merit from amongst the persons eligible for recruitment to the respective categories of vacancies.

5.36. *Reservation for Scheduled Castes.*—Representatives belonging to the Scheduled Castes have suggested to us that no vacancies in Government service are separately reserved for them and hence their representation in Government service is very low. As mentioned in paragraph 5.26, the provisions of Article 335 of the Constitution of India are not applicable to the Jammu and Kashmir State. Until recently no posts or vacancies in Government service seem to have been reserved for the Scheduled Castes as such. In July 1966, the State Government ordered that "all appointing authorities should know the district-wise population of Harijans in the State and while making appointments keep this in mind. If the post relates to a district or region the percentage of population in the district or region may be considered for fixing number of appointments to be reserved for Harijans. If it relates to the State as a whole, the percentage of population in the whole State may be considered." For admissions to technical and other institutions, the heads of the institutions and the selecting authorities have been similarly ordered to keep this ratio in view. A copy of the State Government's orders is at Appendix 11.

5.37. The above mentioned orders are not precise and they do not contain a clear directive. The position has, however, since been rectified to some extent by the issue of a notification by the State Government specifically providing for reservation for the Scheduled Castes in the services and posts in the State which shall, "as nearly as may be", be 5 per cent of the available vacancies, and for regulation of appointments to such services and posts accordingly. A copy of the notification is at Appendix 12.

5.38. We note that in order to provide for the reservation in services and posts for the Scheduled Castes, the State Government have had to include such Castes among the "backward classes of citizens of the State". Apparently, this was found necessary because the provisions of Article 335 of the Constitution of India relating to the claims of the Scheduled Castes to services and posts are not applicable to the Jammu and Kashmir State. We do not think that the conditions of the Scheduled Castes in the Jammu and Kashmir State are different from those of the Scheduled Castes in the other parts of the country. We, therefore, recommend that the provisions of Article 335 of the Constitution of India be made applicable to the Jammu and Kashmir State as well.

5.39. According to the 1961 census, the Scheduled Castes of the Jammu and Kashmir State formed 7.98 per cent of the total population of the State. Their share in the services of the Government is very much lower than is justified on the basis of their population. We consider that the reservation for the permanent resident Scheduled Castes in the services and posts under the State Government should be made in proportion to their population.

CHAPTER VI

EDUCATIONAL POLICIES

6.01. *Introduction.*—In this Chapter we propose to deal with the policies of the State Government regarding admissions to institutions of higher education and their schemes of assistance by way of scholarships and loans. The third of our terms of reference requires us to examine these policies "with a view to ensuring an equitable distribution of the available facilities to the various regions and communities, having special regard to the claims of the Scheduled Castes and other economically, educationally and socially backward communities, classes and groups among the citizens of the State."

Like the recruitment policies of the State Government discussed in the previous Chapter, these policies have also been the subject of much criticism. Complaints have been made to us of discrimination being exercised on the basis of regional and religious considerations in regard to admissions to higher educational and professional institutions and the grant of scholarships and selection for training abroad. There have also been complaints that no professional colleges are located in the

Jammu region and that the backward classes are not given any encouragement or facilities to pursue higher studies or receive professional training.

6.02. Complaints against the educational policies of the State are again not of recent origin. Of all the complaints made to the Glancy Commission (appointed in November 1931), one of the most widespread and insistent, according to it, was to the effect that certain communities, specially, the Muslim community, had not been given a fair chance in the matter of education. Some sixteen years prior to the appointment of the Glancy Commission, Mr. Sharp, Educational Commissioner with the Government of India, had visited Jammu arid Kashmir on the invitation of the State authorities and had advised them on the improvements required to be made in the Education Department of the State. While drawing attention to the suggestions of Mr. Sharp, the Glancy Commission recommended, *inter alia,* that care should be taken to see that the Muslims received all practicable encouragement in the matter of education; that the Principal of Shri Pratap Singh College, Srinagar, should be careful to see that Muslims were given a fair chance of admission to the science classes; that the special Mohammadan scholarships should be equated in value with merit scholarships; that in the matter of free studentships a due proportion should be allotted to all communities, care being taken to see that the rules prescribed were fairly carried out in practice, that the number of Muslim teachers and professors in High Schools and Colleges should be interviewed; that the post of Inspector for Mohammadan Education which had remained vacant should be revived and that the propagation of education among the depressed classes should receive due [1]attention.

6.03. In regard to Kashmiri Pandits, the Glancy Commission made the following observations:

> "It has been represented by the Kashmiri Pandits that special treatment should be afforded to them in the matter of technical training on the ground that as the proportion of clerical appointments falling to their community decreases they most have recourse to other outlets for employment. The Pandits like all other communities should be given a fair

1. Chapter III of the Report of the Glancy Commission.

chance in this matter and might receive special encouragement if they manifest an increased tends to take advantage of technical education for there are many reasons to suppose that they will not be in a position to compare successfully with other [2]students."

6.04. *Progress of education.*—The State of Jammu and Kashmir has been very backward in literacy and education. As late as 1941 the literacy percentage of the State was 6.9 only and the total number of women literates was less than 36,000. Since Independence and with the implementation of the Five Year Plans there has been great improvement. Education is now free throughout the State from the kindergarten to the university standard. The number of educational institutions and enrolment therein have registered marked progress, as the following table will [3]show:—

Sl. No.	*Heading*	*Position in 1950-51*	*Position in 1965-66*
1.	Number of Primary Schools	1,182	4,504
2.	Number of Middle Schools	149	1,131
3.	Number of High and Higher Secondary Schools	44	422
4.	Enrolment		
	(a) 6-11 years of age	56,000	2,91,000
	(b) 11-14 years of age	21,100	87,000
	(c) 14-17 years of age	4,020	41,300

6.05. Before Independence there were only 3 colleges in the State. The number of colleges has now risen to 17. The University of Jammu and Kashmir, which was established in 1948, started as a mere examining body. Now it is a full-fledged teaching University with several departments. It has two divisions, one at Jammu and the other at Srinagar. Both divisions provide for post-graduate studies in several subjects.

6.06. The percentage of literacy in the State rose to [4]13 (19.8 for males and 5.1 for females) by 1961. Even so, the percentage of literacy in Jammu and Kashmir is the lowest in the country.

2. Page 14 of the Report of the Glancy Commission.
3. Paragraph 4-19.
4. Page 133 of the Statistical Pocket Book of the Indian Union, 1966.

6.07. *Scholarships and Study Loans.*—Besides making education free from the kindergarten to the university stage, the State Government have also been granting scholarships and study loans on a liberal scale. The scholarships' are available to members of the Scheduled Castes and backward classes and to those of the remaining students who belong to the "lower income group" as defined by the Government of India. Educational loans are granted to students who are selected or nominated for various training and technical courses in and outside the State in terms of the Educational Loans Rules promulgated by the State Government in 1964. These loans are granted to hereditary State subjects "for courses of study, education or any other training approved by them". They carry no interest. The rate of loan admissible is normally Rs. 1,500 per annum for diploma courses, Rs. 2,500 per annum for technical/professional degree or post-graduate courses and Rs. 1,500 per annum for other courses. The initial grant of loan is also dependent upon the income of the parents or guardians of the students and the number of children dependent on them. Students whose parents or guardians have a monthly income exceeding Rs. 1,000 are not generally eligible for study loans. Loans are also granted to students who secure admissions privately in various courses of studies such as medicine, engineering and post-graduate courses in science subjects. The payment to the loanees is generally made for a period between 2 and 5 years, while the period for recovery of the loans extends up to 12 years. The following table shows the expenditure incurred by the State Government on this scheme during the last three years for which figures are available:

Year	*Amount*
1964-65	Rs. 29,95,536.10
1965-66	Rs. 34,74,790.32
1966-67	Rs. 38,02,363.80

6.08. So far as education at the school level or in the arts faculties at the university level is concerned, there is hardly any problem of finding places for intending scholars. Almost everyone who wants to join these courses is admitted. The position in professional and technical institutions is, however, different. The number of students seeking admission to such institutions is in excess of the number of places available in them and it has become necessary for the State to adopt a system of selection from among the eligible candidates.

4.09. *System of selection for admission.*—In 1963 and subsequent years, the practice followed by the State Government in respect of admissions, nominations to institutions for higher learning in and outside the State was as follows:

(i) For places reserved in institutions outside the State for degree and post-graduate degree courses in engineering, the Public Service Commission invited applications and submitted a merit list for final selection by the Chief Minister.

(ii) For places available for engineering courses in the Regional Engineering College, Srinagar, the Principal of the College invited applications and submitted a merit list for final selection by the Chief Minister.

(iii) For places available in the M.B.B.S., B.D.S., B.V.Sc., Ayurvedic and Unani courses and in the Polytechnics, whether within the State or outside, applications were invited by the Principals concerned and a Selection Committee selected the candidates. The list of candidates so selected was submitted to the Chief Minister for final approval.

(iv) For B.Sc. (Agri), the concerned Principals invited applications and submitted a merit list to the Agriculture Department for approval.

6.10. The procedure was modified in June 1966 and a Committee of two members was constituted for the selection of candidates for all the courses of training within and outside the State. It was open to the Committee to co-opt as adviser(s) any or all of the following:

(i) the Principal of the concerned institution;

(ii) the Secretary of the concerned Department of Government;

(iii) any person who might be considered suitable to act as an Adviser for the particular course of instruction.

The Committee scrutinised the applications of the candidates for each particular training course in accordance with the conditions governing admissions to the particular institution and thereafter interviewed the candidates to judge their physical fitness, personality, general knowledge and aptitude for the particular profession or it held a written test on general subjects "prescribed by a notification by the Committee." It was open to the Committee to hold the interview as well as the written test if it so desired. It then drew up the final list of the candidates to be selected for each course in order of merit of the candidates for each of the two regions, namely Jammu and Kashmir, having regard to the results of the interview and/or the written test and submitted the list to the Chief Minister for issuing orders in accordance with its recommendations. One hundred marks were assigned for the interview and the same number of marks for the written test.

6.11. The matter was reviewed again in July 1967 and instead of one Selection Committee for all the courses a separate Selection Committee was appointed for each of the technical courses such as Medicine, Ayurveda, Agriculture, Veterinary Science, Engineering, Polytechnic, Post-graduate education, etc. These Committees scrutinize the applications of the candidates in accordance with the conditions governing admissions to the particular institution and interview the candidates for judging their physical fitness, personality, general knowledge and aptitude for a particular profession. The Committees then draw up the final list of candidates to be selected for each of the two regions, namely, Jammu and Kashmir, in order of merit, having regard to the results of the interview and their academic merit as revealed by their performance in the basic qualifying examination, and submit the list to the Chief Minister for issuing orders in accordance with their recommendations. The interview carries 50 marks, allotted equally for physical fitness, personality, general knowledge and aptitude. One hundred marks are allotted for academic merit. The Regional Engineering College, Srinagar, being an autonomous body, was kept out of the purview of this procedure. Selection for admission to this institution is being made by an Admission Board set-up for the purpose by the Governing Body of the Regional Engineering College.

6.12. The revised procedure introduced in July 1967 for selection of candidates appears to us unexceptionable if the interview is conducted in a fair and objective manner. The selection of candidates on a regional basis, however, will offend the provisions of Article 14 of the Constitution of India, as indicated in paragraph 5.29. We shall have occasion to refer to this subject again later in this Chapter. If the procedure is correctly followed and the selection of candidates made strictly on merit, there is no justification for submitting such lists to the Chief Minister for approval.

6.13. *Reservation for backward classes and Scheduled Castes.*—We note that the State Government have made no formal provision for the reservation of places in educational and professional institutions either for backward classes or for the Scheduled Castes. This has also been pointed out by the High Court of Jammu and Kashmir State while delivering judgement in the case of Lalita Shuri Tikku *Vs.* State of Jammu and Kashmir and others (Writ Petition No. 66 of 1965 and allied Writ Petitions) relating to admissions to the Srinagar Medical College The relevant extract from the judgement is reproduced below:—

> "On the other hand, the Advocate General submitted that in the instant case, the selection was made on the basis of classification contemplated by Article 15(4) of the Constitution of India. He drew our attention to the affidavits of the Chief Secretary in various petitions which show that the selection was made, firstly, on the basis of candidates who were drawn from socially and educationally backward classes, secondly, of candidates who were residents of Jammu and thirdly, of candidates who were drawn from scheduled castes. It was, therefore, contended by the Advocate General that the affidavits of the Chief Secretary should be construed as a special provision falling within the permissible limits of Article 15 sub-clause 4 of the Constitution of India. We are, however, unable to agree with this argument.
>
> "Article 15(4) as already indicated, clearly contemplates that there must be a special provision for the classes mentioned in that Article, such a provision need not be made by a Legislative enactment and it can be made also by an executive order, but there must be some order or notification to show that the State having applied its mind to the various factors and the statistics of a particular class of citizens

> considers it to be a socially and educationally backward class for whose benefit provision has to be made. In the instant ease, no such provision at all appears to have been made by the State. For the first time, in answer to the petitions, the stand taken by the Chief Secretary, is that the selection has been made after taking into consideration the nature of the socially and educationally backward classes of citizens and of Scheduled Castes. Even in the affidavits, the Chief Secretary has hot disclosed the data statistics or the factors which go to make a particular class as a socially and educationally backward one. It has not even been indicated as to which is the class of citizens which has been declared to be socially and educationally backward. In these circumstances, therefore, we are constrained to hold that since no provision under Article 15(4) has been made, the selection has been made on a purely discriminatory basis."

6.14. In the course of our inquiry we came across instances where the selection of students for the technical and professional courses had been made in an arbitrary or discriminatory manner. There have been critical comments on such selections by the High Court of Jammu and Kashmir. In the case of Lalita Shuri Tikku *Vs.* State of Jammu and Kashmir and others, referred to in paragraph 6.13, the High Court made the following observations:

> "It is, therefore, manifest that a discrimination between members of the Scheduled Castes has also been made by the State and Kumari Bilori to have been subjected to hostile discrimination instead of her being considered on merits."

In another writ petition concerning admission to the Srinagar Medical College, filed before them in 1968 by Subash Mohan Jalali and others, the Court has observed as follows:

> "There appears to be discrimination in selecting the candidates even with respect to petitioner's belonging to same class namely residents of Jammu and those of Kashmir Province. . . . Thus it would appear that the selection has been made by the Committee either consciously or unconsciously in such a way as to discriminate (between) candidates even belonging to the same class of citizens."

6.15. We have scrutinized the statistical data pertaining to admissions of students to institutions of higher education furnished by the State Government. An abstract of these data is given in Appendix 13. We note that as between the Jammu region and the Kashmir region, the number of students belonging to Jammu selected for study in higher institutions was much smaller than the number of those belonging to Kashmir, but the share of Hindus has been much larger than that of Muslims in all the important courses of study.

6.16. It is unfortunate that the State Government do not maintain a separate record of admissions of students belonging to the backward classes. We are, therefore, unable to make any observation as to the extent to which the Directive Principles of State Policy laid down in Section 23 of the Constitution of Jammu and Kashmir have been followed by the State Government.

6.17. *Regional communal allocation of seats:*—The question whether any special provisions can be made in the matter of educational facilities on the basis of religion or region to which the persons concerned belong, has come up before the High Courts and the Supreme Court on a number of occasions and the Courts have given authoritative rulings. We should like to invite attention to the judgements in the following cases:

(i) M.R. Balaji *Vs.* State of Mysore in the Supreme Court;

(ii) R. Chitralekha *Vs.* State of Mysore in the Supreme Court;

(iii) Minor P. Rajendran *Vs.* State of Madras and other similar writ petitions in the Supreme Court; and

(iv) Lalita Shuri Tikku *Vs.* State of Jammu and Kashmir and other connected writ petitions in the High Court of Jammu and Kashmir.

6.18. It seems that special concessions, quotas or reservations for admission to educational and professional institutions can be made available only to the socially and educationally backward classes of citizens or to the Scheduled Castes and Scheduled Tribes: It is also clear that the classification of people as backward on the basis of their religion or region alone is repugnant to the provisions relating to fundamental rights in the Constitution of India as made applicable to Jammu and Kashmir. The remedy, therefore, is to draw up a list of backward classes on the basis of a multiple test as suggested by us in paragraphs 5.31 to 5.34, and provide for admission quotas or reservations for them in institutions of higher learning, which should not exceed the proportion that the population of the backward classes as a whole bears to the total population of the State. Similarly, reservations should also be made for the Scheduled Castes in proportion to their population. The total percentage of reservation for the backward classes and the Scheduled Castes should not, however, ordinarily exceed fifty. Subject to the reservation for the backward classes and the Scheduled Castes, the selection for admissions to educational institutions should be made strictly and solely on merit. Merit should also be the sole criterion for filling the seats reserved for the backward classes and the Scheduled Castes.

6.19. *Scholarships and study loans.*—We have not heard any serious complaints about the inadequacy of the scholarships or study loans granted by the State Government. On the other hand, complaints have been voiced by several parties that in the matter of distribution of the scholarships and study loans considerable discrimination is practised between the Jammu region and the Kashmir region and between one community and another. We have examined the statistical data made available to us by the State Government pertaining to the study loans given to students for study in institutions of higher education, during the three Five-Year Plan periods. An abstract of the data is given at Appendix 14. We note that region-wise, the students belonging to the Kashmir region have received a much larger amount, by way of study loans than the students belonging to the Jammu region. Community-wise, however, the Hindus have received a much larger share of study loans than the Muslims. The members of the Scheduled Casles have received no study loans whatsoever in the course of the entire period of the three Plans. Details of the study loans given to backward classes are not available as the figures for backward classes are included in those of their parent community.

6.20. As we have suggested for admissions, a certain proportion of the provision available for the grant of scholarships and study loans should be set apart for the backward classes and the Scheduled Castes. The provision should be separate for each of them and should not be less than the proportion that either of them bears to the total population of the State. The balance should be made available to the rest of the student population. In giving scholarships or loans, the means of the parent or guardian should be an important factor for determining the eligibility of the applicant and, other things being equal, merit should be the sole criterion for granting, them.

CHAPTER VII

Irritations and Tensions Remedies

7.01. *Introduction.*—We now come to the fourth and last of our terms of reference. This requires us "to consider generally the causes that lead 10 irritations and tensions and to recommend remedial measures." We shall begin by referring to certain recent facts of history which are responsible for some of the major irritations and tensions now existing among certain sections of the population.

7.02. We have mentioned in paragraphs 3.07 to 3.09 how Dogra rule came to be established in the Jammu and Kashmir State. Dogra rule was personal in character but several important developments in the State took place during this period. The Legislative Assembly, which was created in 1934, had thirty-five of its seventy-five members nominated by the Ruler and the electorate comprised only eight per cent of the population. In 1939, several constitutional reforms were carried out and the Constitution. Act came into force. It was, however, specifically provided in the Constitution that "nothing contained in this or any other act shall affect or be deemed to have affected the right and prerogative of His Highness to make laws, and issue proclamations, orders, and ordinances by virtue of his inherent authority". Besides, the legislature had no jurisdiction over a number of important matters which were included in the list of the Maharaja's reserved powers. In spite of the authoritarian nature of Dogra rule, certain sections of the population flourished and prospered during this period. The State Army was composed almost entirely of Dogra Rajputs for whom it provided the main source of employment. The educated and advanced Kashmiri Pandit community came gradually to monopolize the ministerial posts in the Government and occupy positions of influence in the civil administration after the State Government had yielded in 1925 to the pressure from the inhabitants of the State, and accepted the principle of recruiting only State subjects to Government posts,

These two communities were the main beneficiaries of Dogra rule along with a large number of Jagirdars, Chakdars and Shahukars (moneylenders).

7.03. With the introduction of democracy and popular rule in the State a complete break with the autocratic rule of the previous regime was inevitable. One of the first acts of the popular Government under Sheikh Mohammed Abdullah and one of its greatest achievements from the viewpoint of the peasants and the landless, who formed the overwhelming majority of the population, was to implement the programme of social and agrarian reforms as envisaged in the "New Kashmir" Plan. The new land reform laws which were introduced in the State meant not only the abolition of intermediary rights but also the redistribution of land and protection of the tenants. These land reforms dealt a heavy blow to the important and prosperous class of landholders, many of whom have not been able to reconcile themselves to this day to the altered situation. The expropriation of their land in excess of 182 *kanals* without payment of compensation was understandably a source of great distress and dissatisfaction to this class. Besides, in the haste with which the new land laws were enacted a number of serious anomalies crept into them and these have acted as additional irritants.

7.04. As we have already mentioned in paragraph 5.10, there was a large expansion of the services after the introduction of popular rule in the State in 1947. There were instances, as a result, where recruitment was made without observing the usual formalities; besides, some appointments in the higher ranks were also made from political cadres. We were told that the non-observance of the recruitment rules which started immediately after the introduction of popular rule adversely affected the people of the Jammu region in particular and was a source of irritation to that region. In evidence before us Bakshi Ghulam Mohammed unequivocally stated that merit could not be the only criterion in these matters, for merit were made the sole criterion there would be no place for Muslims, Jammu Dogras and other backward people in the State. He, therefore, introduced communal and regional representation for filling' Government posts and making admissions to educational institutions. When the Public Service Commission was established in 1957, it was also advised to keep these considerations in view and to suggest an equal number of candidates from the Jammu and Kashmir regions and also an equal number of candidates belonging to the Muslim and non-Muslim communities for filling vacancies in Government service. As a result of these new policies, the Kashmiri Pandit community lost its pre-eminent position in Government services. Since their main occupation was Government service, they could not easily adjust themselves to the changed situation and qualify themselves for the pursuit of other occupations for a living. Similarly, the Jammu Dogras who had traditionally sought, their career in the armed forces of the State lost this source of employment after Independence when the State Army, ceased to exist as a separate entity. They seem to have been caught unprepared by the change and did not equip themselves for other forms of employment.

7.05. The foregoing analysis shows how irritations and tensions have grown in certain communities and classes of the population because of their background and historical reasons. The Kashmiri Pandits seem to look back when they had almost a monopoly of the State services. Similarly, the Dogras of Jammu hark back to the days, when the ruler of the State belonged to their clan and they had a virtual, monopoly in the armed forces of the State. Neither of these communities, finds it easy to appreciate that with the establishment of democratic rule in the State the employment pattern in the public services was bound to change and that it was necessary to prepare oneself for other occupation. In Chapters V and VI, we have recommended reservation of posts in the services and admissions to institutions of higher education for the genuinely backward classes only, classified on the basis of certain multiple criteria. We venture to hope that when this is done and the rest of the employment and educational opportunities are made available on the basis of merit alone such grievances as these communities now have, will be largely removed.

7.06. We now proceed to deal with the causes of irritations and tensions which have been represented before us in the written memoranda and oral evidence. The alleged imbalance in development programmes and the policies-pursued by the State Government in the matter of recruitment to services and the provision of educational facilities are themselves some of the principal causes of irritation and tension. We have examined them in the three preceding chapters. In this Chapter we shall confine ourselves to the other matters. They are of varying degrees of importance. They range from such matters as the doubt and uncertainty which disturbs the minds of some people about the political future of their State or the bitterness which is engendered by real or imagined grievances of regional discrimination or the inequitable aspects of the land laws to the persistent complaints of general administrative inefficiency and corruption or such petty demands as the upgrading of a naib tehsil to a tehsil or the opening of a school here or a dispensary there. Some persons have also tried to ventilate their individual grievances in the garb of general complaints of irritation and tension. We propose to ignore petty and individual grievances and to deal in the paragraphs which follow only with those causes of irritation and tension which appear to us to be of consequence.

Political

7.07. *Ambivalence in regard to political policy.*—The people of the State, particularly those living in the Valley, feel that there is a certain degree of ambivalence about the political policy of the Union Government towards the State. Constant hostile propaganda from the other side of the sub-continent, the secessionist doctrines propagated by certain political leaders and parties of the State and the attempts of some political leaders of India to mediate in Jammu and Kashmir affairs, have created doubts in the mind of the people of the State about their political future. All the parties which appeared before us were however, unequivocal in their stand that the accession of the State to the Indian Union was final and irrevocable. Nevertheless, the effect of the propaganda carried on in the State by some elements which have not adjusted themselves to the realities of the situation cannot be ignored. Such propaganda is likely to create in the mind of the people in the Valley a general feeling of political uncertainty which is clearly a cause for creating tensions and irritations. The common man in the Valley as well as in Jammu and Ladakh is naturally vitally interested in his own betterment and in reaching a stage of economic development in which, he would be able to enjoy life, liberty and the pursuit of happiness more fully. This aim is undoubtedly hindered by the sense of uncertainty created by anti-Indian propaganda in the State. In judging the effect of this hostile propaganda in Jammu and Kashmir one has to bear in mind that

Pakistan has been ceaselessly challenging the validity of the State's accession to the Indian Union.

7.08. We noted with satisfaction that notwithstanding the delicate nature of the subject, the present State Government have allowed ample scope to freedom of expression to the citizens and have deliberately decided to deal with the challenge posed by these subversive treads in the State on a political plane. Our hope is that the public at large will extend their moral help to the State Government through the creation of sound public opinion to meet this challenge.

7.09. It would not be inappropriate to add here that the teachers in the University and the schools of Jammu and Kashmir, who form a cosmopolitan and progressive group and believe in the sense of values on which Indian democracy is founded and which form the basis also of the Constitution of Jammu and Kashmir, should play their legitimate role in guiding the impressionable minds of the younger generation in the State. If the intellectuals and educationists help the democratic forces in the State to tackle the situation created by subversive propaganda, the liberal policy adopted by the State Government is bound to be successful.

7.10. We gathered the impression that the University students in the Jammu and Kashmir State as in the rest of India and, indeed, in many parts of the world today, are unhappy and restive: Elements hostile to Indian democracy may well be tempted to exploit this frustration and restiveness. It should, we think, be possible for the teachers in the universities by means of close contact, and for the intellectuals in and outside the State through fruitful discussions, to assist in the process of inculcating in the minds of the students in Jammu and Kashmir an abiding faith in the basic values of life for which our Constitution stands, namely, justice—political, social and economic—secularism and the rule of law.

7.11. *Article* 370 *of the Constitution of India.*—Some parties feel that the special status conferred on the Jammu and Kashmir State by Article 370 of the Constitution of India is a major cause of irritation and tension. They desire that the provisions of that Article should be abrogated

They consider that this Article is being used to legalize unconstitutional acts by the State Government and that it encourages arbitrariness on their part. The validation of some of the State statutes, such as the Big Landed Estates Abolition Act, 1950, which provides for the expropriation of land without compensation, by the issue of a Presidential order under this Article of the Constitution is cited as an example. They also point out that its provisions are meant to be temporary and the Article is not meant to be a permanent feature of our Constitution.

On the other hand, another section considers that it is what it alleges to be the systematic erosion of the autonomy of the State guaranteed by this Article, that causes irritation and tension. It desires that the provisions of this Article should be strictly observed and that the Union Government should guarantee that, irrespective of which party is in power at the Centre, the special status conferred on the State by this Article should not be tampered with. The irredentism, chauvinism and revivalism preached by certain political and religious parties in other parts of the country have caused a genuine fear in the mind of this section about this.

7.12. Article 370, as its title itself indicates, is a temporary provision with respect to the State of Jammu and Kashmir. By means of this Article, the provisions in the Constitution of India relating to the Government of the States have been made inapplicable to the State of Jammu and Kashmir and a separate Constitution framed by the Constituent Assembly of the State has been enforced. The power of Parliament to make laws for the State of Jammu and Kashmir is limited to —

"(i) those matters in the Union List and in the Concurrent List which, in consultation with the Government of the State, are declared by the President to correspond to matters specified in the Instrument of Accession governing the accession of the State to the Dominion of India as the matters with respect to which the Dominion Legislature might make laws for that State; and

(ii) such other matters in the said Lists as, with the concurrence of the Government of the State, the President may by order specify."

It also provides for the application of such other provisions of the Constitution of India to the State of Jammu and Kashmir as the President may by order specify. The order may indicate the exceptions or modifications subject to which these provisions should be made applicable. Before issuing any such order, however, the President is required to consult the State Government in certain cases and obtain their concurrence in the other cases. For easy reference the full text of this Article is reproduced in Appendix 15.

7.13. It would be observed that the Jammu and Kashmir State has been granted by the Constitution of India a much larger measure of Autonomy within the Indian Union than the other States. There were reasons for according such-special treatment. According to the late N. Gopalaswami Ayyanger, who piloted the Article in the Constituent Assembly in 1949, "that particular State is not yet ripe for this kind of integration. It is the hope of everybody, here that in due course even Jammu and Kashmir will become ripe for the same sort of integration as has taken place in the case of other states". It was, however, inevitable that in course of time Article 370 should have been used to bring about uniformity of the State of Jammu and Kashmir with the rest of the country in matters of vital importance to the rights of individual citizens and the enforcement of the rule of law. But this has always been done in strict compliance with the letter and spirit of that Article.

7.14. Federal Financial Integration which had taken place in 1950 in the case of other Part B States was practically fully achieved in the Jammu and Kashmir State in 1954 as a result of the State Government agreeing to the application of a large number of items of the Constitution to that State. Consequently; Union Departments, like Customs, Central Excise, Posts and Telegraphs, Civil Aviation, All India Radio, etc. had their operation expended to the State just as to other States. The functions of the Comptroller and Auditor-General of India were extended to the State in 1958. In matters involving the interpretation of the Constitution, the Supreme Court has the same jurisdiction in respect of Jammu and Kashmir as in respect of the other States. The functions of the Election Commission of India now extend to Jammu and Kashmir not only for elections to Parliament and to the office of the President and of the Vice-President, but also for elections to the State Legislature. In December 1964, Articles 356 and 357 of the Constitution of India, containing provisions relating to the failure of the constitutional machinery in the States, were applied to Jammu and Kashmir. This brief and illustrative narration of the operation of Article 370 would show that the process adopted so far is consistent with the declared objectives of the Constitution of India and the Constitution of Jammu and Kashmir.

7.15. Article 370 has been introduced in the Constitution of India on account of the historical facts which led to the accession of the Jammu and Kashmir State to India. As we have already indicated, this Article guarantees to Jammu and Kashmir a very much larger measure of autonomy than is enjoyed by any other State. Arguments are often heard in India, and were repeated before us, both for repealing this Article and for retaining it. If the Article is repealed, it may raise nice questions of constitutional law as to the effect of such a step on the Constitution of Jammu and Kashmir. This may itself created, in the present circumstances, additional tensions in the mind of the majority community in the Valley. This is a consideration that has been emphasized before us by parties which want Article 370 to continue. On the other hand, those that want the Article to be removed from the Constitution have urged that it indirectly retards the process of the complete integration of the State of Jammu and Kashmir in the Indian Union which must be the ultimate objective. They stated that the time had come for abrogating his Article and placing the State of Jammu and Kashmir on the same footing as the other States in the Union. Those who advocated this view expressed their disapproval of the fact that citizens in India were not able to acquire property in Jammu and Kashmir unless they were permanent residents of the State as defined in Part III of the Constitution of Jammu and Kashmir while the persons belonging to the State were entitled to acquire property anywhere in the rest of India. It was also urged that no other State had an independent Constitution of its own and the existence of an independent Constitution for Jammu and Kashmir had an adverse, if indirect effect upon the process of complete integration of the State in the Indian Union.

7.16. We have given anxious consideration to this problem. We think that a present it would be inadvisable to recommend that Article 370 be abrogated. Keeping in view the progress which has already been made over the years in the integration of Jammu and Kashmir with the rest of India, we feel that it would be prudent to leave it to the Government and the people of the State of Jammu and Kashmir themselves to decide when this Article should be abrogated.

7.17. *Elections.*—Some representatives who appeared before us have cast doubts on the manner in which the elections have been conducted in the State in the past, particularly about the fairness of the last General Election. They have pointed out that at the last General Election, 141 nomination papers were rejected and 26 members were returned unopposed to the State Legislative Assembly and that the whole of Anantnag District failed to get an opportunity to go to the polls for electing its representatives to Parliament or to the State Legislature. These persons feel that all the elections held so far were systematically interfered with by the State authorities and that this has undermined the faith of the common man in democracy. The conduct of the elections, however, is now a matter which concerns the Election Commission and it is not for us to go into the question whether the last General Election was in fact interfered with. The proper forum to deal with it are the Election Tribunals and the Supreme Court. We were informed that a number of election petitions had been filed before the Election Tribunals in Jammu and Kashmir and some had already been disposed of. Some elections have been set aside by the Tribunals while certain others have been upheld by them. Though, as we have just observed, the forum to decide whether the elections were properly held or not is the Election Tribunals, we have mentioned this matter to indicate that a feeling does exist in the minds of some citizens that the elections were not free and fair. We should like to add that we have had an opportunity to examine 29 judgements delivered by the High Court of Jammu and Kashmir in Election Petitions filed before it. Out of these 29 petitions, 6 have been allowed while the rest have failed. It seems to us significant that in 12 out of these 29 cases, the nomination papers of non-Congress candidates were rejected on the ground that the said candidates had not subscribed and made the oath as required by law. In one case (Election Petitions Nos. 1 and 10 of 196: Ghulam Qadir Mir *V.* Ghulam Moh'd Rajpuri and others and Moh'd Shan Simnani *V.* Ghulam Moh'd Mir Rajpuri). Mr. Justice Anant Singh came to the conclusion that Mr. Kumar, the Returning Officer, and Mr. Safaya, the Assistant Returning Officer, appeared to have entered into a conspiracy to reject nomination papers of non-Congress candidates improperly with a view to facilitating the uncontested return of Mr. Rajpuri, who was a Congress candidate. According to the Judge, these two officers did not stop short of fabricating and tampering with the evidence. The Judge also felt that there was reasonable ground to suspect that Mr. Rajpuri, who was once a sitting Minister of Tourism under whom Mr. Safaya was working at Srinagar, had influenced the said two officers in that behalf. As a consequence of this finding, the Judge has directed that proceedings should be taken against the two officers under section 476 of the Criminal Procedure Code. The decisions of the High Court to which we have just referred are, of course, subject to appeal to the Supreme Court.

This is a cause of irritation and tension and a note of this feeling has to be taken. We should, therefore, like to add that as the Jammu and Kashmir State occupies a strategic area, it is necessary to nurture the faith of the common man in democracy and democratic institutions in the State. We hope that the State Government will do all they canto build up and sustain that faith.

7.18. We were told that the elections to local bodies such as Panchayats, town area committees, notified area committees and municipalities are long overdue and that these bodies are no longer, representative in character. Some parties have alleged that besides depriving the public of their fundamental right of franchise, this has resulted in the Government managing to have their own candidates elected to the Legislative Council from the local bodies constituencies. We think that it is necessary that the State Government should immediately take all steps to arrange for the holding of the elections to the local bodies as early as possible. We should also like to add that these elections should he held regularly in future.

7.19. *Civil liberties.*—We have heard complaints of the suppression of civil liberties in the State. For instance, it is alleged that the provisions of Section 144 of the Criminal Procedure Code are in force throughout the State that no public meeting can be held without prior permission of the Government authorities, and that the opposition Press has been muzzled. Discrimination is also alleged to be exercised in granting permission for holding public meetings. It is stated that while the ruling party gets the permission for the asking, the opposition parties find it difficult to secure it. We are not satisfied that these allegations are true.

We have been informed that the allegation that the provisions of Section 144 of the Criminal Procedure Code are in force throughout the State, is wrong. It is well known that the leaders of opposition parties are addressing public meetings in various parts of the State and are making statements to the Press. Some of them are very critical of the Government and some even question the finality of accession of the State to the Indian Union.

7.20. It seems appropriate at this stage to make a passing reference to the Kashmir Suite People's Convention held at Srinagar in October last. At this convention divergent opinions were freely and fully expressed. Some of the views which were ardently advocated appear to be plainly inconsistent with the correct constitutional position under the Constitution of India and the Constitution of Jammu and Kashmir. We feel that it is a tribute to the democratic way of life adopted by India, and by the State of Jammu and Kashmir as an integral part of the Union of India, that a Convention of this kind should have been called and such views openly, freely and fearlessly canvassed. We have already referred to the present State Government's decision—and we think the decision is correct and consistent with the democratic spirit of the Constitution—to allow full freedom of expression even to parties that do not see eye to eye with them or are opposed to their political ideology and commitments. Political trends, however, subversive they may appear to be, have necessarily to be countered on a political plane, and in a democratic country freedom of expression has to be granted to every citizen. This freedom does not mean the freedom to express views only in favour of the established order; it also means the freedom to express dissent so long as it is within the limits prescribed by the Constitution and the relevant provisions of the law. The fact that freedom of expression has been allowed to be exercised uninterruptedly in such a sensitive area as Jammu and Kashmir speaks volumes for the spirit and strength of Indian democracy.

7.21. *Autonomy of the State within the Union.—We* would now like to deal with the demand for a larger measure of autonomy for the State of Jammu and Kashmir within the Indian Union as such a demand was made before us. In dealing with it, several considerations have to be taken into account. The first consideration is that the demand for a larger measure of autonomy for the State of Jammu and Kashmir has not been made before us directly by any party from Jammu or Ladakh. Even amongst the parties belonging to the Valley that appeared before us only one or two raised the subject. We note, however, that some participants at the Convention, referred to in the preceding paragraph, made such a claim but it seems reasonable to conclude that the demand for a larger measure of autonomy for the State does not have the support of a substantial section of the population even of the Valley and has received little, if any, support from Jammu or Ladakh. While it may be conceded that this demand may give rise to certain tensions in the regions, it is one of those internal problems which arise between the Union Government and constituent States and in which no third party can have a *locus standi*. In fact, in any federal structure stresses and strains often occur between the federal Government and the constituent units and they have to be tackled in a democratic way by the parties concerned by evolving proper and healthy federal conventions.

7.22. The second consideration which is relevant in this connection is that the State of Jammu and Kashmir enjoys, as we have pointed out already, a much larger measure of autonomy than the other States in the Union of India. We have also indicated that this autonomy flows from Article 370 of the Constitution of India and have expressed the view that it should be for the Government and the people of the Jammu and Kashmir State to decide when this Article should be abrogated. In view of this constitutional position, we do not see any justification for considering the demand for an even larger measure of autonomy for the State in isolation without reference to the other States. The Centre-State relations which have emerged as a result of the fourth General Election held in 1967 has posed the question whether the Constitution of India should be amended to confer larger authority on the constituent States. Some of the State Governments have been pleading for a re-examination of the relevant provisions of the Constitution with a view to conferring greater authority on the States. It seems to us that if the Union Government decide to consider this question in the context of the newly evolving pattern of political life in this country, the case of the Jammu and Kashmir State should receive due consideration along with that of the other constituent States. Even in that event, as we have just indicated, the best way of dealing with such a problem in a democracy is to evolve appropriate conventions and traditions.

7.23. *Representation in Cabinet/Legislature.*—Several communities have complained to us that they are not adequately represented in the State Cabinet or the State Legislature or have no representation in them at all. The first comment that we should like to make on this demand is that with the exception of the Scheduled Castes and, in respect of nomination to the Legislative Council, of the backward classes, the suggestion that the communities as such are entitled in representation in the Cabinet or the Legislature is inconsistent with the provisions of the Constitution of India and the Constitution of Jammu and Kashmir. Besides, the number of communities in the State is large. Within the small size of the Cabinet or of the State Legislature it would be almost impossible to satisfy the demands of every community. It is for these communities to join the mainstream of politics of the State and avail themselves of the political advantages that this may offer.

Regional Aspirations

7.24. In the preceding chapters and the earlier paragraphs of this Chapter, we have dealt with several matters that agitate the minds of the people of the State. Even if all the matters were equitably settled, we feel that there would still be a measure of discontent unless the political aspirations of the different regions of the State were satisfied. In fact, we consider that the main cause of irritation and tension is the feeling of political neglect and discrimination real or imagined, from which certain regions of the State suffer.

7.25. Although the Jammu and Kashmir State has been a single political entity for over a hundred years, it cannot be denied that geographically, ethnically, culturally and historically, it is composed of three separate homogeneous regions, namely, Jammu, Kashmir and Ladakh. In fact, the Pir Panjal range forms a natural dividing line between the Jammu and Kashmir regions.

7.26. *Regional autonomy.*—We are glad to note that notwithstanding these differences and the regional political aspirations, no party or individual who has submitted a memorandum to us or appeared before us in person, with the solitary exception of the Dogra Mandal, has suggested a division of the State or the creation of a sub-State within the State. Even the idea of autonomy for the regions of the State is unacceptable to most of them. The Jammu Autonomy Forum is the sole protagonist from the Jammu region of regional autonomy for Jammu, Kashmir and Ladakh. The two individuals from Kashmir who supported autonomy for the regions also pleaded strongly for a greater measure of autonomy for the State as a whole within the Indian Union. The Dogra Mandal suggested that the Jammu region be merged with Himachal Pradesh.

7.27. We have given consideration to the proposal which was elaborately and ably presented before us by the delegation of the Jammu Autonomy Forum. It may theoretically be conceded that if the proposal represents the aspirations of a large majority of the population of the Jammu region—and we do not think that it does the satisfaction of their legitimate expectation in good time may lead to greater consolidation of the region with the rest of the State. On the other hand, it is quite likely that any recognition of the autonomy of a region of the State may whet its appetite for greater autonomy and accentuate separatist tendencies which may ultimately lead to the disintegration of the State itself. Besides, in dealing with the question of autonomy for the Jammu region, as in considering the question of autonomy for the State as a whole within the Indian Union, we cannot treat as irrelevant the impact that such a step is likely to have on the other regions constituting the State. This point is relevant and valid as all the parties which appeared before us, with one solitary exception, were agreed that nothing should be done that would impair or injure the unity and integrity of the State. On the basis of the evidence tendered before us, we have no doubt that the acceptence of the demand for autonomy made by the Jammu Autonomy Forum would make an adverse impact on the minds of the residents of the Kashmir region. Although there was general agreement among the parties which appeared before us for the establishment of Regional Development. Boards for developmental purposes, only two persons from the Kashmir region supported the demand for regional autonomy, and none from Ladakh supported it. As already stated, the Jammu Autonomy Forum was the only party from Jammu that advocated autonomy for the regions. After careful consideration of all the relevant factors, we have come to the conclusion that the demand made before us by the Jammu Autonomy Forum should not be accepted.

7.28. We have also given careful thought to the desirability of introducing a system of Regional Committees of the State Legislature of the type envisaged for certain States in Article 371 of the Constitution of India. Such Regional Committees existed for the Punjabi-speaking and the Hindi-speaking areas of the former Punjab State. The experiment did not work satisfactorily and the establishment of these Regional Committees did not prevent the eventual division of the former Punjab State into the new States of Punjab and Haryana. The reasons that we have already given for recommending the rejection of the demand made by the Jammu Autonomy Forum hold good also for rejecting the idea of introducing the system of Regional Committees of the State Legislature.

7.29. In paragraphs 4.25 to 4.29 we have suggested the establishment of a statutory State Development Board and statutory Regional Development Boards for the three regions—Jammu, Kashmir and Ladakh. This and certain other measures which we shall discuss in the subsequent paragraphs will, we hope, go a long way in satisfying the regional aspirations of the people of the State.

7.30. *Convention regarding composition of Cabinet.*—A convention should be established, that if the Chief Minister belongs to one region, there should be a Deputy Chief Minister belonging to the other region. By another convention, the number of Cabinet Ministers belonging to the two regions should be equal. There should also, in addition, be a full-fledged Cabinet Minister belonging to Ladakh.

7.31. *Decentralization of administration.*—The functions of each Head of Department should be divided on a regional basis in other words, each Department should have a Head and an Additional Head, one of them functioning in one region and the other in the other region. The Head of Department or Additional Head of Department, as the case may be will be responsible for all programmes in his region. The Additional Head of Department may correspond with the Secretariat direct on all matters concerning his region. He will, however, send copies of such correspondence to the Head of Department for record. Orders passes by the Government on the proposals of the Additional Head of Department will be sent to him direct with copies to the Head of Department. Matters of common interest and those requiring inter-regional coordination will be dealt with by Head of Department. It is understood that in certain departments, such as the Public Works Department there is a Chief Engineer for each region. What is suggested by us here is an extension of the principle to the other departments.

7.32. So far as the High Court of Jammu and Kashmir is concerned, when it functions at Srinagar, there should be at least one High Court Judge stationed at Jammu to dispose of matters that may arise in the Jammu region. Similarly, when the High Court functions at Jammu, there should be at least one High Court Judge stationed at Srinagar to deal with the cases arising in the Kashmir region.

7.33. *Regionalization of cadres.*—We are given to understand that all the service cadres of the State of whatever grade are State cadres and officials of every rank or class are liable to be transferred from any part of the State to any other part where there are posts of that rank or class in the service. For instance, we have been told that a peon or Patwari or forest guard may be transferred not only from one district to another but even from one region to another. It has been represented that when officers, particularly the low-paid ones, belonging to one region are posted to the other; they generally tend to count their days until they can get themselves transferred back to their own region and that, as a result, they fail to put their heart in their work in the other region. We feel that such transfers of low-paid staff are likely to cause hardship to them without any compensating administrative advantage. We would suggest that the posts in the various services should, where possible, be divided into three cadres; namely, a district-based cadre, a region-based cadre and a State-based cadre. Speaking in general terms, the inferior and non-gazetted (other than supervisory) posts should be district-based. In district-based cadres, transfers should be permissible only within the district. Supervisory non-gazetted posts, both clerical and non-clerical, and class III and class IV gazetted posts should generally form the regional cadre. In region-based cadres, transfers should be permissible only within the region. Members of State-based cadres alone should be liable to transfer anywhere within the State. Although we are recommending the division of the posts into three cadres—a district-based cadre, a region-based cadre and a State-based cadre—we should like to make it clear that the residents of the entire State will be eligible for appointment to the posts included in any of the cadres.

7.34. Members of district-based cadres on promotion to posts in the regional, cadre will become transferable anywhere within the region. Similarly, a person on promotion from a post in a regional cadre, to a post in the State cadre will become transferable to a place anywhere in the State.

7.35. The Kashmir Administrative Service, the Kashmir Civil Service (Judicial) and the Kashmir Police-Service are feeder services for the All India Services and the higher judiciary. Their incumbents should therefore, have wide experience of State administration. Members of these services and such other State services as the State Government may consider appropriate should in our opinion, be liable to work for a minimum specified period (say, five years) in one or two spells in each of the three regions, namely, Jammu, Kashmir and Ladakh.

7.36. *Regional and District Recruitment Boards.*—As a corollary to the proposal for the decentralization of cadres, a Regional Recruitment Board should be set-up for the Jammu region and another for the Kashmir region, and a District Recruitment Board for each district in the State, including Ladakh. The function of the Regional Recruitment Board should be to make recruitment to the regional cadres and that of the District Recruitment Boards to make recruitment to the district cadres. These Boards will concern themselves with filling only those posts which are outside the purview of the Public Service Commission. They could function on a part-time basis and be manned by suitable officers drawn from the regions or the districts, as the case may be.

Regional Discrimination

7.37. *Separate Universities for Jammu region and Kashmir region.*— We have heard complaints that the Jammu region has been discriminated against by being denied an equal number of University faculties and by not starting any technical and professional colleges there. We have compared the list of faculties existing on the Srinagar campus of the Jammu and Kashmir University with that of the faculties available on the Jammu campus. The former consists of one faculty more than the latter. We do not, therefore, agree that there has been any deliberate discrimination in the matter. There is, however, another matter which is stated to be agitating the mind of the student community in the Jammu region. We learn that the main university examinations in the Jammu region are held when the Kashmir region has its supplementary examinations and that its supplementary examinations are held when the Kashmir region has its main examinations. We would suggest that there should be a full-fledged university for each of Jammu and Kashmir regions. One of them should immediately start a faculty of law. Perhaps this could be done at Jammu first as there are no professional colleges there. We believe that it would soon become necessary to start law classes in the other university as well.

7.38. *Opening of technical and professional colleges.*— We note that technical and professional colleges, such as the Medical College, the Engineering College and the Agricultural College, are all located in the Kashmir region and the only professional college which were located in the Jammu region, namely, the Agricultural College at Ranbirsinghpura, has been closed down. This has caused some regional bitterness. As the existing professional colleges are all located in the Kashmir region; we consider that it would be appropriate to open a new Medical College at Jammu. The question of starting an Engineering College in the Jammu region may also be considered subsequently when the need for having a larger number of engineering graduates is felt.

7.39. *Matriculation examination.*— Another complaint of a regional nature that we have heard is that while the Matriculation Examination is held simultaneously in the Jammu region and the Valley, the dates on which the examination is held in Ladakh are different as a result of which the students of Ladakh lose a whole term when proceeding for higher studies. We would have recommended that the feasibility of holding the examination simultaneously in Jammu, Kashmir and Ladakh be examined by the State Government, had we not been informed by them that henceforth all the annual examinations of the Board of Secondary Education would be held, in the Jammu and Kashmir regions in March or April and in Ladakh district in April or May. We have also informed that with this change in dates, the Ladakhi students will not have to lose an academic session.

7.40. *Discrimination in rates of foodgrains.*—Several representatives from the Jammu and Ladakh regions have drawn our attention to the alleged discrimination in the sale of foodgrains at subsidized rates. The subsidized rates of foodgrains sold in

Srinagar City are lower than the corresponding rates in Jammu city. The State Government have explained to us that this is because' the prices of foodgrains, particularly rice, which is the staple food of the people of the Kashmir region have been traditionally low in the Valley; and that the procurement prices of paddy there are lower than elsewhere. We find it difficult to understand the explanation given by the State Government because the issue, prices of food-grains in the town and mofussils (other than Srinagar City) in the Valley are higher than the corresponding prices in the towns and mofussils of the Jammu region. We do not also understand the significance of the State Government's observation that the procurement prices of paddy in the Valley are lower. The procurement prices should, as far as possible, be linked with the cost of production; otherwise, there would be no incentive to the farmer to increase production. We recommend that the State Government should review their whole price policy, both for the procurement and for the issue of foodgrains, and introduce uniform issue prices for them throughout the two regions. We were told that the State Government were trying to fix a uniform price for coarse rice and also a higher uniform price for Basmati rice throughout the State.

7.41. *Quantum of rations.*—There is also some regional discrimination in the quantum of foodgrain rations that are issued. The quantum of monthly cereal ration in Srinagar City, is 11 kilograms of rice and 2 kilograms of Atta, making a total of 13 kilograms, while that in Jammu City is 3.45 kilograms of rice and 6.90 kilograms of Atta, making a total of 10.35 kilograms. The State Government explained this difference on the ground that rice is less nutritious (and made more so "by unscientific cooking") than wheat Atta and that on account of the colder climate of Srinagar the consumption of food is higher in Srinagar City than in Jammu City. So far as we are aware neither of such grounds would be tenable in any other part of the country for justifying a different scale of rations in rice-eating areas of in colder climates. We suggest that the quantum of rations at Srinagar and Jammu should be the same.

7.42. So far as the Ladakh district is concerned, it is not a statutorily rationed area. Rations are issued only to Government servants, both "locals" and "non-locals". The State Government have said that special rations are distributed in Ladakh on permits on the occasion of festivals or to needy persons. The scale of rations in the Ladakh district is stated to be uniform for both local and non-local Government servants, the scale being 14 kilograms per head per mensem. Out of the 14 kilograms, the "non-locals" get 9 kilograms of rice while no rice is issued to Government servants who belong to Ladakh. The State Government explained this distinction by saying that the local people take wheat Atta while "non-locals" generally consume only rice. We are not convinced by this explanation. We recommend that there should be no discrimination made between "non-locals" and "locals". If, however, non-locals want to take the whole or part of the rice ration in the form of wheat Atta they should be permitted to do so. If there is any similar discrimination made in the issue of relief rations to the indigent and needy, the State Government should examine the desirability of removing it.

7.43. The representatives of the State Government explained to us that as the staple food of the local population was grim barley (a cross between wheat and barley), there was no rationing in Ladakh for the general public and that a rationed supply of rice was likely to act as a disincentive to production. As, however, the district of Ladakh is deficit in foodgrains, some supplementary rationing should be introduced in the towns, of Ladakh, namely, Leh and Kargil, on a basis similar to that adopted for the towns of the Jammu and Kashmir regions, other than the cities of Srinagar and Jammu.

7.44. *Toll barriers.*—At present, all the State toll barriers are located in the Jammu region. There is not a single toll barrier in the entire Kashmir region. Representatives of Jammu complained that this was an instance of regional discrimination. The State Government have explained this by saying that the toll barriers have been so located as to make the collection of the tax convenient and evasion difficult. But as things stand the tell becomes payable in respect of goods and traffic moving within the Jammu region itself they have to cross any toll barrier while no toll is payable for movement anywhere within the Kashmir region. This is bound to place the economy of the Jammu region at a disadvantage. The State Government have informed us that they are considering the question of imposing a goods tax on goods moving within the Kashmir region and of those areas of the Jammu region that are not at present covered by toll barriers.

We recommend that the system of collection of tolls and the location of the toll barriers should be re-examined and rationalized so that neither region is placed at a disadvantage compared to the other.

Position of Ladakh

7.45. *Difficulties of Ladakh.* Ladakh District is in a somewhat unhappy position. It is one of the remotest districts of the country. It is cut off from the rest of the country for the major part of the year. Even when it is not so cut-off, access to it is difficult because of the inadequacy of means of transport. The number of civilian buses and trucks plying between Srinagar and Leh is indequate and the interior places in Ladakh are virtually unconnected. Government servants from other regions posted to the district try to get away from it as quickly as possible because of the rather forbidding terrain and climate. An adequate number of quilified Ladakhis for manning the services in the District is not yet available. We were told that few Ministers and senior officers of the State Government visit the District. In former days it used to have an appreciable trade and commerce with Tibet and the adjoining parts of China. This has now come to an end. There is not a single degree college in the whole of this far-flung district. By all accounts, therefore, the conditions in the Ladakh District are difficult, and its people have a feeling of isolation and neglect.

7.46. *Suggested remedies.*—We are conscious that both the State Government and the Union Government have done and are doing a great deal to improve these conditions. The people of Ladakh are appreciative of these efforts. But something special seems called for to remove the feeling of isolation and neglect from which Ladakh suffers. We recommend the following measures:—

(i) A degree College should be established immediately at Leh. Subsequently, a second college should be established at Kargil.

(ii) The transport facilities available to Ladakhi should be improved; in particular, the number of buses and trucks plying between Srinagar and Leh should be substantially increased and transport facilities made available to the interior places in Ladakh.

(iii) Suitable arrangements should be made for the stay at Kargil of persons travelling between Leh and Srinagar.

(iv) Stable and satisfactory arrangements for providing electricity to Leh and Kargil and other places of importance in Ladakh should be made.

(v) The single-line administration which was introduced in Ladakh some time ago should be revived in its entirety. The post of Development, Commissioner should be merged with that of the Deputy Commissioner and the incumbent of the post should function as the Head of all Departments in Ladakh, and the Ladakh Affairs Secretary should be the Secretary for all subjects so far as Ladakh is concerned. He should work under the Ladakhi Minister who could hold charge of the portfolio of Ladakh Affairs.

(vi) The headquarters of the Ladakh District (in area, one of the largest in India) lacks even the ordinary amenities and attributes of a district headquarters town. It is necessary that its status should be accorded due recognition by the construction of suitable buildings and roads, improving sanitary arrangements and such other measures. It would be appropriate if the old Raja's Palace were made into a museum for Ladakhi antiquities and arts and crafts.

7.47. It was represented to us that the procedure for sanctioning roads, irrigation and hydel schemes for Ladakh was extremely lengthy and dilatory and that such schemes had to pass through numerous stages before they could be implemented. We have had case studies made of a few such schemes and it does appear that they are undfit, delayed at certain stages both in the State Government and in the Central Government. It is doubtful, however, whether any of the stages can be eliminated altogether. Until recently, all such schemes of more than Rs. 3 lakhs had to be laid before the Council of Ministers for according administrative approval and this entailed delay. By a welcome amendment of the relevant Rules of Business administrative approval to schemes of over Rs. 20 lakhs can now be accorded with the Chief Minister's approval and to those of less with the approval of the Minister-in-charge. We were happy to observe that, in the cases which were studied by us, where more than one authority had to be consulted about any matter, action had generally been taken to consult them simultaneously and not successively. In the circumstances, as the working season in Ladakh is short and the need for speedy disposal great, we would recommend that all authorities concerned in the State and the Central Governments should be instructed to deal as expeditiously as possible with the schemes relating to Ladakh.

7.48. Incidentally, we may mention that some representatives of Ladakh painted out to us that in earlier times the State was referred to in certain documents as 'Jammu, Kashmir, Ladakh and Tibet-ha', 'Tibet-ha' being a Persian adaptation of Little Tibet. Subsequently, this usage seems to have fallen into disuse and reference to Ladakh and Tibet-ha was dropped. They, therefore, suggested that Ladakh should get its due place in the formal name of the State. We recommend that this plea should be taken into consideration by the State Government and some change made to meet the sentiments of the residents of Ladakh.

Land Reforms

7.49. *Wazir Committee recommendations.*—The subject which seems to be agitating the mind of people in the State most, irrespective of the region to which they may belong, concerns the abolition of big landed estates and the working of the provisions of the tenancy laws. Party after party which appeared before us had bitter things to say about them. There has been agitation in some form or other ever since the Big Landed Estates Abolition Act, 1950, and the amendments to the Tenancy Act came into force. In 1953, the State Government appointed a Committee to examine the working of land reforms and certain other matters under the chairmanship of Mr. Justice Janki Nath Wazir. In its report submitted the same year, the Committee pointed out several inconsistencies, anomalies and iniquities in the land reforms adopted by the State Government. We have been informed that no action was taken by the State Government on the recommendations of the Committee on matters relating to land reforms.

7.50. *Land Commission.*—The agitation seems to have continued. In 1963, the State Government appointed a Land Commission to go into the whole question of land reforms, including the conduct of settlement, the consolidation of holdings and the prevention of fragmentation and co-operative farming. We understand that the Land Commission has since submitted its report to the State Government.

7.51. *Removal of anomalies.*—We do not propose to go into the question of land reforms in detail. The expropriation of property without the payment of compensation and holding the landlord liable for mortgages on the land so expropriated are indeed unusual provisions. But they have been legally validated. Moreover, these provisions came into force eighteen years ago. Their operation can harldy be reversed now because that would lead to a fresh upheaval.

7.52. It should, however, be possible for the State Government, to remove some of the obvious anomalies. We suggest that the State Government should give due consideration to the recommendation of the Wazir Committee relating to land reforms and also to the recommendations of the subsequent Land Commission and take action to remove the anomalies, wherever possible. For instance, it is anomalous that if the extent of tenancy or tenancies under one landlord is not more than 100 *kanals* the rent payable by the tenant should be one-half, but as soon as the tenancy exceeds 100 *kanals*, the rent should be one-fourth in respect of the entire land including the first 100 *kanals*. This would mean that a landlord having more than 100 *kanals* under tenancy will in fact get less than what a landlord having 100 *kanals* will get. On the other hand, if a landlord owning singly more than 100 *kanals* dies and is succeeded by two or more heirs, the extent of the ownership of each heir and consequently the extent of the tenancy under each will be less than 100 *kanals*. In such cases, the heirs should be enabled to collect rent at the same rate at which any other landlord, owning less than 100 *kanals* can get under the law. But as the law stands, they can get a rent of only one-fourth. If, however, they are to get a rent of one-half, the tenant of tenants will be hard hit for no fault of theirs. We feel that the proper remedy is to fix a uniform rate of rent on a scientific basis.

7.53. *Applications for ejectment of tenancy.*—According to Section 44 of the Jammu and Kashmir Tenancy Act, 1923, a tenant can, subject to certain conditions, be ejected on any of the following grounds, namely:—

(i) that he has used the land comprised in the tenancy in a

manner which renders it unfit for the purpose for which it was let;

(ii) when rent is payable in kind, that he has without sufficient cause, failed to cultivate the land in the manner or to the extent customary in the locality in which the land is situate;

(iii) that a decree for arrears of rent in respect of the tenancy has been passed against him and remains unsatisfied without sufficient cause;

(iv) that being a tenant other than an occupancy tenant for a fixed term, he has sublet the land; and

(v) that the landlord requires the land for his personal cultivation.

We were told that though the applications for ejectment made in accordance with the above-mentioned provisions are meant to be disposed of in a summary manner by the revenue courts they drag on for long period's resulting in needless harassment to the landlords. We were also told that a very large number of such applications are awaiting disposal. Besides, action on about 5,000 applications made for ejectment of tenants on grounds of resumption for personal cultivation by the landlords has been stayed till 31 December 1968 by a statutory notification. We recommend that the notification staying the disposal of these applications should be rescinded, the Act under which, the notification has been issued be repealed and all pending applications for ejectment be disposed of as expeditiously as possible.

7.54. *Six-monthly move of the Secretariat.*—It has been pointed out to us that the practice of the six-monthly move of the headquarters of the State Government causes dislocation of work and is wasteful. We agree that this practice does cause dislocation and results in a waste of time. It would perhaps be logical to let the Secretariat of the State Government function at one place throughout the year allowing only a camp office to move to the other place for a limited period. If such a course were adopted, the permanent headquarters would probably be at Srinagar and the camp office would move to Jammu during the winter. Apart from other considerations, however, this arrangement would not be practicable for a long time to come for want of adequate heating arrangements which would be required in the office buildings and also at the residences of the officers and staff at Srinagar. Besides, in dealing with this question the impact of the proposed change on the minds of the residents of the Jammu region cannot be ignored. This arrangement has been in existence for very many years. For the reasons already indicated, therefore; we would not recommend its discontinuance.

7.55. *Rehabilitation of refugee's from non-liberated areas.*—The refugees who have migrated from the non-liberated areas of Jammu and Kashmir to the other part of the State have complained to us that they have not been properly rehabilitated though a period of twenty-one years has elapsed since they were uprooted. They contend that many of them were residents of Muzaffarabad and Uri which belong to Kashmir Province and that they should have been settled in the Kashmir region. They have stated that this was not done and that they were unjustifiably moved to the Jammu region. They have alleged that when lands were allotted to them, a sum of Rs. 2,500 per evacuee family was withheld from the rehabilitation grant, but they have not been given proprietary rights over their lands yet. They also desire that the registration of their claims for property left behind in the non-liberated areas of the State should be undertaken without further delay so that when there is an eventual political settlement their claims do not go by default for want of evidence. The problem requires to be handled with sympathy and understanding. We hope that the State Government will do all that they can to allay the apprehensions of these refugees.

7.56. *Clean and efficient administration.*—We have heard complaints of corruption, inefficiency and political interference in the State's administration. We are not directly concerned with these complaints. We have taken note of them only in so far as they tend to contribute to the irritations and tensions in the State. The allegations made before us were mostly of a general nature. We have no cause to think that the position in Jammu and Kashmir is worse than in many other parts of the country. The need for giving the people a clean and efficient administration cannot be over-emphasized, but as the Jammu and Kashmir State occupies a strategic area and there are already several other matters which are causing irritations and tensions in the State, the need for this in Jammu and Kashmir is even greater. We hope that the State Government will address themselves urgently to this important matter and that in this endeavour they will receive the unstinted support of the Services.

7.57. We have stressed the need forgiving the State of Jammu and Kashmir a clean and efficient administration which may inspire the faith of the common man in the impartiality and incorruptibility of its officers. It is obvious that in securing a clean and efficient administration for the State, its Services will have to play an important role. The members of the Services should be men of character and integrity who are able to act independently and fearlessly without running the risk of incurring the displeasure of their official superiors or political bosses. In order to give them a greater sense of security we should like to make certain specific recommendations.

7.58. We consider that fresh appointments to posts should as a rule be made only on the recommendation of the Public Service Commission or the Regional/District Recruitment Boards, the establishment of which we have recommended in paragraph 7.36. The tendency to make *ad hoc* appointments against newly created posts should be discouraged for such appointments cause dissatisfaction; besides, an *ad hoc* appointee gains an advantage over other candidates at the time of regular selection having worked against the post for some time and acquired the requisite experience. One method of eliminating such *ad hoc* appointments would be to ask the Public Service Commission and the proposed Regional District Recruitment Boards to maintain panels of eligible candidates for the common categories of posts. For the less common categories, the Commission or the Boards could make recommendations by issuing short-term advertisements and expediting the process of selection if an appointment to a post within the purview of the Public Service Commission has to be made in an emergency pending selection by the Commission, a temporary promotion from a panel prepared earlier by the concerned Departmental Promotion Committee may be made in preference to the *ad hoc* appointment of an outside candidate. In exceptional cases, however, when an *ad hoc* appointment of an outside candidate is unavoidable, the post should be filled as soon as possible by due selection in accordance with the relevant recruitment rules; no attempt should be made to get the *ad hoc* appointment "regularized" by the Public Service Commission in relaxation of the recruitment rules.

7.59. Regular meetings of the Departmental Promotion Committees, presided over by a Member of the Public Service Commission, should be held so that up-to-date panels of officers eligible for promotion to posts within the purview of the Commission are always available. *Ad hoc* promotions pending the approval of the Public Service Commission should be avoided. With a view to introducing greater objectivity in their deliberations and greater uniformity in the manner of their functioning, the Departmental Promotion Committees, whether presided over by a Member of the Public Service Commission or not, should invariably have a representative of the Services Department as a member.

7.60. The basic problem of the State as in several other parts of India has long been poverty, disease, ignorance and unemployment. In spite of the completion of three Five-Year Plans, the lot of the common man in the State does not seem to have substantially improved. Complaints were made before us that the large funds received from the Union Government over the years for the implementation of the State's developmental programmes had not been properly utilized and that the formulation and execution of many schemes and projects had been haphazard and defective. We feel that if developmental plans and programmes are formulated with due regard to the actual economic needs of the people and are implemented with vigour and efficiency, they would lead to their economic betterment and that would help the State Government to overcome the basic problem.

CHAPTER VIII

RECOMMENDATIONS

Development Programmes

1. There should be a statutory State Development Board and statutory Regional Development Boards for the three regions—Jammu, Kashmir and Ladakh. The Regional Boards should be headed by the Chief Minister or the Planning Minister and should consist of legislators from the regions, economists, experts and concerned officiate. The regions should be adequately represented on the State Development Board which should be headed by the Chief Minister.

The functions of the Regional Development Boards wiil be—

(a) to draw up the regional Plans;
(b) to assign priority to schemes and projects included in the regional Plans; and
(c) to supervise the implementation of the regional Plans.

In discharging these functions it should be the special responsibility of the Regional Development Boards to pay due regard to the special needs of the backward areas of their respective regions.

The State Development Board will scrutinize the regional Plans, prepare a residuary Plan of schemes and projects which transcend regional boundaries or happen to be of an all-State interest and allocate Plan funds equitably (after taking into account the population, area and the specific needs of each region) to the regional Plans and the residuary Plan of all-State interest. [Paragraphs 4.26 to 4.28]

2. The State Development Board and each of the Regional Development Boards will prepare at the end of each year a report of their respective activities giving details of the progress of the Plan programmes and Plan expenditure. At the end of each Plan, similar detailed reports should be prepared by the Boards indicating the physical and financial targets and the physical and financial achievements. All these reports should be laid before the Legislature as soon as may be after they are prepared. [Paragraph 4.29]

Recruitment Policies

3. Recruitment rules for all the State services for which they do not exist at present should be framed and promulgated as early as possible. Recruitment rules for other services also should be speedily framed. [Paragraph 5.17]

4. Complete, tabulated results of all competitive examinations held by the Public Service Commission and any other Recruitment Board that may be set-up, should be published. These results should be sent to all candidates who have taken the examination or, if this is not always feasible, the results should at least be made available for scrutiny on request. [Paragraph 5.18]

5. Seniority lists for ail services should be drawn up correctly and maintained up to date. [Paragraph 5.19]

6. The annual confidential reports on all Government servants should be written up regularly and objectively and maintained properly There should be provision for the review of the confidential rolls by an authority superior to the reporting officer. A proper procedure should be prescribed for dealing with representations of Government servants against adverse entries in their confidential rolls. [Paragraph 5.20]

7. The following-multiple criteria should be adopted for determining which classes should be treated as backward:

(1) The economic backwardness of the class.
(2) The occupation or occupations pursued by that class of citizens.
(3) Their place of habitation.
(4) The average of student population per thousand in that class.
(5) Caste, in relation to Hindus.

[Paragraphs 5.33 and 5.34]

8. The existing list of backward classes should be revised and a fresh list drawn up by a high-powered committee after applying the multiple criteria, mentioned above, relating to social, educational and economic backwardness. [Paragraph 5.35]

9. Article 335 of the Constitution of India should be made applicable to the Jammu and Kashmir State and reservation for the Scheduled Castes made in the services in proportion to their population. [Paragraphs 5.38 and 5.39]

10. Reservation in the services should also be made for the backward classes, as freshly determined, in proportion to their population, subject, however, to the condition that the total reservation for the backward classes and the Scheduled Castes should not ordinarily exceed fifty per cent.

The balance of the posts should be filled strictly and solely on the basis of merit. In filling the posts reserved for the backward classes and the Scheduled Castes, persons belonging to each of these categories should be selected on the basis of merit. [Paragraph 5.35]

Educational Policies

11. Reservation of places in educational and professional institutions should be made for the backward classes and the

Scheduled Castes in proportion to their respective population, subject to the condition that the total reservation does not ordinarily exceed fifty per cent. The balance of the places in such institutions should be filled strictly and solely on the basis of merit. In filling the places reserved for the backward classes and those reserved for the Scheduled Castes, merit should be the criterion for selecting the persons in each of these categories. [paragraph 6.18]

12. A certain proportion of the provision available for the grant of scholarships and study loans should be set apart for the backward classes and the Scheduled Castes. The provision should be separate for each of them and should not be less than the proportion that either of them bears to the population of the State. [Paragraph 6.20]

13. The balance of the provision for the grant of scholarships and study loans should be made available to the rest of the student population. In giving scholarships or loans, the means of the parent or guardian should be an important factor for determining the eligibility of the applicant and, other things being equal, merit should be the sole criterion for granting them. [Paragraph 6.20]

Irritations and Tensions

14. The Government and the people of the State of Jammu and Kashmir may themselves decide when Article 370 of the Constitution of India should be abrogated. [Paragraph 7.16]

15. The State Government should immediately take all steps to arrange for the holding of elections to the local bodies as early as possible. These election's should be held regularly in future. [Paragraph 7.18]

16. A convention should be established that if the Chief Minister belongs to one region, there should be a Deputy Chief Minister belonging to the other region. By another convention, the number of Cabinet Ministers belonging to the two regions should be equal. There should also be a full-fledged Cabinet Minister belonging to Ladakh. [Paragraph 7.30]

17. The functions of each Head of Department should be divided on a regional basis; in other words, each Department should have a Head and an Additional Head, one of them functioning in one region and the other in the other region. The Department will be under the overall control of the main. Head

who will also be responsible for the coordination of work between him and the Additional Head. [Paragraph 7.31]

18. When the High Court of Jammu and Kashmir functions at Srinagar, there should be at least one High Court Judge stationed at Jammu to dispose of the cases there. Similarly, when the High Court is functioning at Jammu, there should be at least one High Court Judge stationed at Srinagar to deal with the cases arising in Kashmir. [Paragraph 7.32]

19. Some of the cadres should be district-based, certain others region-based and the balance State-based. In district-based cadres transfers should be permissible only within the district and in region-based cadres transfers should be permissible only within the region. Members of State-based cadres alone should be transferable anywhere within the State. Generally speaking, the incumbents of inferior and non-gazetted (other than supervisory) posts should be district-based. Supervisory non-gazetted posts, both clerical and non-clerical, should belong to the regional cadres. Class III and Class IV gazetted posts should also generally be in the regional cadres. The residents of the entire State shall be eligible for appointment to the posts included in any of these cadres. [Paragraph 7.33]

20. The incumbent of a district-based post on promotion to a post in the regional cadre will become transferable anywhere within the region. Similarly, a person on promotion from a post in a regional cadre to a post in art all-State cadre will become liable to transfer to a place-anywhere in the State. [Paragraph 7.34]

21. Members of the Kashmir Administrative Service, the Kashmir Civil Service (Judicial) the Kashmir Police Service and such other State services as the State Government may consider necessary, shall be liable to serve for a minimum specified period say, 5 years in each of the three regions of Jammu, Kashmir and Ladakh. [Paragraph 7.35]

22. A Regional Recruitment Board should be set-up for each of the Jammu and Kashmir regions and a District Recruitment Board for each district in the State including Ladakh. The function of the Regional Recruitment Board will be to make recruitment to the regional cadres, and that of the District Recruitment Boards to make recruitment to the district cadres. These Boards will concern themselves with filling those posts which are outside the purview of the Public Service Commission. These Boards could

function part-time and be manned by suitable officers drawn from the regions or districts, as the case may be. [Paragraph 7.36]

23. There should be a separate full-fledged university in both the Jammu and Kashmir regions. One of them, preferably the one in Jammu, should immediately start a faculty of law. Subsequently, law classes will also have to be started in the other university. [Paragraph 7.37]

24. As all the professional colleges are located in Kashmir (the Agricultural College at Ranbirsinghpura also having been closed down recently) it will be proper to open a new-medical college at Jammu. The question of starting an engineering college in the Jammu region may also be considered when the need for turning out a larger number of engineering graduates is felt. [Paragraph 7.38]

25. The State Government should, review the entire policy of food-grain prices, both for procurement and for issue, and introduce uniform prices for foodgrains throughout the Jammu and Kashmir regions. [Paragraph 7.40]

26. The quantum of rations issued at Srinagar and Jammu should be the same. [Paragraph 7.41]

27. In the matter of rations issued to Government servants in the Ladakh District, no distinction should be made between "locals" and "non-locals"; if, however, non-locals want to take the whole or part of the rice ration in the form of wheat Atta, this should be permitted. [Paragraph 7.42]

28. Some supplementary rationing of foodgrains should be introduced at Leh and Kargil on a basis similar to that adopted for the towns of the Jammu and Kashmir regions other than the cities of Srinagar and Jammu. [Paragraph 7.43]

29. The system of collection of tolls and the location of the toll barriers in the State should be re-examined and rationalized so that neither the Jammu region nor the Kashmir region is placed at a disadvantage compared to the other. [Paragraph 7.44]

30. A degree college should be established immediately at Leh. Subsequently, a second college should be established at Kargil. [Paragraph 7.46]

31. The transport facilities available to Ladakh should be improved. In particular the number of buses and trucks plying between Srinagar and Leh should be substantially increased and transport facilities made available for access to the interior places, in Ladakh. [Paragraph 7.46]

32. Suitable arrangements should be made for the stay at Kargil of persons travelling between Leh and Srinagar. [Paragraph 7.46]

33. Stable and statisfactory arrangement's for providing electricity to Leh and Kargil and other places of importance in Ladakh should be made. [Paragraph 7.46]

34. The single-line administration which was introduced in Ladakh some time ago should be revived in its entirety. The post of Development Commissioner should be merged with that of the Deputy Commissioner and the incumbent of the post should function as the Head of all. Departments in Ladakh and the Ladakh Affairs Secretary should be the Secretary for all subjects so far as Ladakh is concerned. He should work under the Ladakhi Minister who could hold charge of the portfolio of Ladakh Affairs. [Paragraph 7.46]

35. The status of Leh should be accorded due recognition as the headquarters of a vast region by the construction of suitable buildings and roads, improving sanitary arrangements and other such measures. [Paragraph 7.46]

36. The sanctioning of roads, irrigation and hydel schemes for Ladakh entails much delay as they have to pass through several stages both in the State Government and in the Central Government. As the passage through these different stages is unavoidable, all the authorities concerned in the State and Central Government should be instructed to deal as expeditiously as possible with the schemes relating to Ladakh. [Paragraph 7.47]

37. The State Government should consider the request of the people of Ladakh for giving 'Ladakh' its due place in the formal name of the State. [Paragraph 7.48]

38. There are some obvious anomalies in the Big Landed Estates Abolition Act and the Tenancy Act. The Wazir Committee had in 1953 made certain recommendations for dealing with some of them. The Land Commission appointed in 1963 has recently submitted its report. The State Government should consider the recommendations of the Wazir Committee and the Land Commission and take action to remove the anomalies, wherever possible. [Paragraph 7.52]

39. The notification staying the disposal of applications made by the land-holders on grounds of resumption for personal cultivation should be rescinded, the Act under which the

notification has been issued should be repealed and all pending applications for ejectment should be disposed of as expeditiously as possible. [Paragraph 7.53]

40. The outstanding problems of refugees from non-liberated areas of the Jammu and Kashmir State should be examined sympathetically so that their apprehensions may be allayed. [Paragraph 7.55]

41. Fresh appointments to posts should, as a rule, be made only on the recommendation of the Public Service Commissionor the Regional/District Recruitment Boards and the tendency to make *ad hoc* appointments against newly created posts should be discouraged. [Paragraph 7.58]

42. Regular meetings of the Departmental Promotion Committees, presided over by a Member of the Public Service Commission, should be held so that panels of officers eligible for promotion to posts within the purview of the Commission are always available. *Ad hoc* promotions-pending the approval of the Public Service Commission should be avoided. The Departmental Promotion Committees should invariably have a representative of the Services Department as a member. [Paragraph 7.59]

Before we conclude we wish to express our sense of appreciation for the very valuable assistance given to us by Mr. B.P. Bagchi, the Secretary of the Commission, in organizing the work of the Commission and drafting the Report. We also wish to express our appreciation for the meritorious work done by the officers of the Commission, particularly Mr. R. Subrahmanian, who was of great help to the Secretary in the drafting of the Report. We also wish to thank the staff of the Commission for their help and co-operation.

P.B. GAJENDRAGADKAR
Chairman
SHANKAR PRASADA
Member
BADR-UD-DIN TYABJ
Member

(B.P. BAGCHI)
Secretary
Bombay
November 29, 1968.

APPENDICES

APPENDIX 1

PART A

NAMES OF BODIES ASSOCIATIONS/INDIVIDUALS WHO SUBMITTED WRITTEN MEMORANDA TO THE COMMISSION

1. Shri Abdul Aziz Shawl, Ex-MLA, P.O. Rajouri
2. Shri A. Bhatt, Rainawari, Srinagar
3. Shri Ali Mohd. Sheikh, Kakran, P.O. Kulgam, Kashmir
4. All J&K Backward Classes Union, Jammu
5. All J&K Bohra Sudhar Sabha, Srinagar
6. All J&K Christian Association, Jammu
7. All Jammu and.Kashmir National Conference, Srinagar
8. All J&K National Integration Front, Jammu
9. All Kashmir Hindu Action Committee
10. Anjuman Islamia, Jammu
11. Shri Badri Nath Parihar of Village Hadyal, Tehsil Kishtwar
12. Shri Bansi Lal Kohistani, Jammu
13. Beopar Mandal, Jammu
14. Bharatiya Depressed Classes League, Jammu
15. "Citizen of India", West Bengal
16. Congress Committee, Rajouri
17. Constructional Contractors Welfare Association, Srinagar
18. Shri D.C. Dubgotra, Palam Village, Delhi
19. District National Congress Committee, Udhampur
20. Dogra Mandal, Jammu
21. Dogra United Front, Jammu
22. Shri Durga Nath Raina, Chowgam, Tehsil Kulgam
23. Shri D. N. Raina, Chandigarh
24. Ex-Officers of the J & K Forces who retired before 1957, Jammu
25. Ex-Servicemen of J & K State, Jammu
26. Sofi Ghulam Ahmed Gash, Srinagar

27. Shri Ghulam Mohammad Wani, Nadihal-Bandipore, Member Kashmir Political Conference
28. Shri Ghulam Mohi-ud-Din, Srinagar
29. Shri Ghulam Rasool Matto, Srinagar
30. Government Officers belonging to Ladakh District
31. Gujar Samaj Sudhar Sabha, Poonch District
32. "Illegible (Kashmir)"
33. Choudhri Iqbal Azeem (Bakarwal), P.O. and Village Bhimri, Jammu
34. Jammu Autonomy Forum
35. Jammu Citizen's Council, Jammu
36. Janta Adhikar Raksha Samiti, Jammu
37. J & K Agriculturists' Association, Jammu
38. Jammu and Kashmir Ravidas Sabha, Jammu
39. J & K Shia United Front, Srinagar
40. Jammu and Kashmir State Gujjar Samaj Sudhar Sabha, Jammu
41. Jammu and Kashmir Students Congress (Shri K. Sharma)
42. Jammu and Kashmir Students Congress (Shri Preetam Singh)
43. Shri J.L.K. Jalali, Retired Assistant Governor, Srinagar
44. Shri J. R. Sethi of Jammu
45. Jat Sudhar Sabha, J & K State, Jammu
46. S/Shri Jivan Ram and Chabilal Kapoor of Village Chakcharat Ram, Baramulla
47. Kashmir Chamber of Commerce and Industry, Srinagar
48. Kashmir Fruit Association, Srinagar
49. "Kashmiri Hindus"
50. Kashmir Rajput Sabha, Mirhama, Kulgam (Kashmir)
51. (Two Memoranda)
52. Shri Khurshid Anwar Dogra, Jammu
53. Kisan Conference Doda, Jammu
54. Kshatriya Community of Jammu and Kashmir, Jammu
55. Ladakh Buddhist Association, Leh
56. Shri Mela Ram, Advocate, Jammu
57. S/Shri Mohan Lal and others, Clerks Dehat Sudhar Sabha, J&K Government
58. Shri Mohan Lal Motial, Jammu
59. Shri Mulk Raj Acharya, Jammu
60. Muslims Committee, Udhampur

61. Shri Nanak Chand Hieuntal, Border Security Force, Srinagar
62. Nehru Ekata Committee, Jammu
63. Shri Niranjan Nath Kaul, Batapura, Shopian (Kashmir)
64. "Observer"
65. Oilmen of Sopore town
66. Pleading Committee, Ladakh National Congress
67. Shri Poshkar Nath Dhar, Anantnag
68. Shri Prabhu Shoor, Poonch
69. Praja Socialist Party, Jammu and Kashmir State, Jammu
70. Shri Prathvi Nath, Srinagar
71. President, Nyaya-Bhavan, P.O. Banat, District Muzaffarnagar, U.P.
72. "Public" of Doda District
73. Raksha Samiti, Poonch
74. Shri Ram Chander Khajuria, Billawar, District Jammu
75. Refugees from Pakistan, District Kathua
76. Residents of Tehsil Biliawar
77. Rural Kashmiri Pandits, Kulgam
78. Secretary, Naya Bhawan, Jammu
79. Shri Shabbir Ahmed Salaria, Advocate, Jammu
80. Shri Shamim Ahmed Shamim, MLA, Srinagar
81. Shri Shiv Kumar Sharma, Sakhi Dafar, 7th Bridge, Srinagar
82. Singh Sabha, Jagir Sialkot, Village Balhama, Tehsil Sopore, District Baramulla
83. Siri Guru Singh Sabha Jammu, Akali Dal Jammu Province and Sikh Minority Board, Jammu and Kashmir, Jammu
84. Shri S. Norbo, MLC, Leh.
85. Shri Suraj Parkash Malgotra, Jammu
86. Shri Suresh Chander, Srinagar
87. Shri Tek Singh Dua, Jammu
88. "Traders of Gilgit etc."
89. "Uprooted Muslims of Tehsil Ramnagar, District Udhampur (Jammu)"
90. Walnut Dealers' Association, Srinagar
91. Without name and date
92. Shri Zafar Hussain, Jammu (Tawi)
93. Zamindara Association, Jammu

Part B

Parties/Associations/Individuals who Submitted Memoranda or Supplementary Memoranda Later

1. Shri Ali Mohd. Sheikh, P.O. Kulgam
2. All J&K Bhora Sudhar Sabha, Srinagar.
3. All Kashmir Hindu Action Committee
4. Anjuman Islamia, Jammu
5. Shri Bansi Lal Kohistani, Jammu
6. Beopar Mandal, Jammu
7. Dogra Mandal, Jammu
8. Dogra United Front, Jammu
9. Ex-J&K Militia Personnel
10. Ex-officers of the J&K Forces who retired before 1957
11. Ex-servicemen of J&K State, Jammu
12. Shri Ghulam Nabi Khyal, Srinagar
13. Shri Harbans Singh Azad, Chairman, Village and Khadi Industries Board, Srinagar
14. J&K Agriculturists' Association, Jammu
15. Jammu and Kashmir State Gujjar Samaj Sudhar Sabha, Jammu
16. Janta Adhikar Raksha Samiti, Jammu
17. Jat Sudhar Sabha, J&K State, Jammu
18. Kashmir Chamber of Commerce and Industry, Srinagar
19. Shri Mohan Lal Motial, Jammu
20. Major Piarsingh, MLC, P.O. Janglot (Kathua)
21. Oilmen of Sopore town
22. Pradesh Congress Refugee Advisory Committee, Jammu
23. President, Action Committee, Landless Jagirdars of Kashmir
24. Shri Guru Singh Sabha, Jammu, Akali Dal, Jammu Province, and Sikh Minority Board, Jammu and Kashmir, Jammu
25. Sharnarthi Action Committee, Jammu
26. Sharnarthi Pratinidhi Board, Jammu
27. Shri S. Norbo, MLC Leh
28. Mtr. Zainab Begum, Gagribal, Srinagar
29. Zamindara Association, Jammu

Appendix 2

Names or Parties/Associations/Individuals who gave Oral Evidence before the Commission at Srinagar

6 June 1968

1. Shri H.S. Azad, Chairman, Khadi and Village Industries Board, Srinagar
2. Shri Mohammad Muzaffar Khan, MLA, Tehsil Uri (Kashmir)
3. Shri Mohammad Younis, MLA, Tangdar (Kashmir)
4. The Jammu and Kashmir Shia United Front, Srinagar,
5. Shri Ali Mohammad Sheikh and other landowners of Kulgam (Kashmir)

7 June 1968

1. Syed Mir Qasim, President; Jammu and Kashmir Pradesh Congress
2. Shri R.K. Pandit, M.A., R/o Kakran, P.O. Kulgam (Kashmir) and others
3. The Kashmir Chamber of Commerce and Industry, Srinagar (Kashmir)

8 June 1968

1. Shri Mohammad Shafi, Deputy Minister for Animal Husbandry, Jammu and Kashmir
2. All Jammu and Kashmir National Conference, Srinagar
3. Shri Ghulam Rasool Matto, Srinagar
4. Singh Sabha, Village Balhama (Baramulla)

10 June 1968

1. Shri Ghulam Nabi 'Khayal', Editor 'Watan' and Secretary Swatantra Forum
2. Shri Jiwan Ram and Shri Chabilal Kapoor, Village Chakcharat Ram, Baramulla (Kashmir)

11 June 1968

All Jammu and Kashmir National Conference, Srinagar

12 June 1968

1. The Jammu and Kashmir State Gujjar Samaj Sudhar Sabha, Jammu
2. The Traders of Gilgit
3. Oilmen's Industrial Cooperative Society, Sopore
4. Shri Nanak Chand Hieuntal, Inspector, Border Security Force
5. (i) Shri Guru Singh Sabha, Jammu and Kashmir
   (ii) The Sikh Minority Board, and
   (iii) Sikh Riyasati Akali Dal, Jammu

13 June 1968

1. Shri G.R. Kar, Minister of State for Forests and Irrigation
2. Shri S.K. Kaul, MLA, Srinagar
3. Shri Motilal Misri, Secretary, Communist Party of India, Kashmir Branch, Srinagar
4. All Jammu and Kashmir Bhora Sudhar Sabha, Srinagar
5. Shri Soft Ghulam Ahmed Gash, Pleader, Bar Association, Srinagar
6. Shri Saifudin Soze, President, Backward Classes League, Baramulla
7. Kumari Veena Dhar

14 June 1968

All Kashmir Hindu Action Committee

15 June 1968

1. Mohtarma Zainab Begum, Srinagar
2. Agha Syed Ahmed, M.P., Srinagar
3. Professor D.N. Raina, Chandigarh
4. Shri Shamim Ahmed Shamim, MLA, Srinagar

17 June 1968

The Pleading Committee, Ladakh National Congress, Leh

18 June 1968

1. Shri Sonam Narboo, MLC, Leh
2. Kacho Mohammad Ali Khan, MLA, Kargil
3. Ladakh Buddhist Association, Leh

APPENDIX 3

Names of Parties/Associations/Individuals who gave Oral Evidence before the Commission at Jammu

22 August 1968

1. Shri Beli Ram, Deputy Speaker, Legislative Assembly
2. Shri Dharam Pal, MLA
3. Zamindara Association, Jammu
4. Shri Mohan Lal Motial, Jammu, and Others
5. Agriculturists' Association, Jammu
6. Janta Adhikar Raksha Samiti, Jammu

23 August 1958

1. Shri Parmanand, Deputy Minister, Transport
2. Shri Bhagat Chajoo Ram; MLA
3. Shri Guran Ditta Mal, MLA
4. Major Piarsingh, MLC
5. Shri Lachman Singh, MLC
6. Anjuman Islamia, Jammu
7. Jammu Citizens' Council, Jammu

24 August 1968

1. Shri Prem Nath Dogra, MLA
2. Shri Ram Nath Bhalgotra, MLA
3. Jammu and Kashmir Ex-Servicemens' Association, Jammu
4. Ex-Army Officers of Jammu and Kashmir State, Jammu
5. Jammu Autonomy Forum, Jammu
6. Raksha Samiti, Poonch
7. Shri Zaffar Hussain, Jammu
8. Ex-Jammu and Kashmir Militia personnel

25 August 1968

1. Shri Trilochan Dutta, MLA

2. Shri Bansi Lal Kohistani, MLA
3. Distt. National Congress Committee, Udhampur
4. Gujjar Samaj Sudhar Sabha, Jammu
5. Praja Socialist Party, Jammu and Kashmir State, Jammu
6. Shri Phulel Singh, Doda

26 August 1968

1. All J&K National Integration Front, Jammu
2. All J&K Backward Classes Union, Jammu
3. J&K Ravidas Sabha, Jammu
4. Shri Prabhu Shoor, Village Kangri, Distt. Rajouri
5. Jat Sudhar Sabha, Jammu and Kashmir State, Jammu
6. All J&K Kshatriya Sadar Sabha
7. Dogra Kashtriya Sadar Sabha, Jammu
8. Khukhran Bradri (Kashatriya Khukhran), Jammu
9. Beopar Mandal
10. Convener, Pradesh Congress Refugee Advisory Committee, Jammu

27 August 1968

1. Dogra United Front, Jammu
2. Dogra Mandal, Jammu
3. J & K Students Congress, Jammu
4. J & K Students Congress, Jammu
5. Residents of Tehsil Billawar/Basholi
6. All J&K Christian Association, Jammu

In addition to the persons mentioned above, Dr. Karan Singh, Union Minister for Tourism and Civil Aviation, met the Commission informally on 24 August 1968 at Jammu.

APPENDIX 4

List of Persons who Appeared before the Commission at Srinagar, in September, 1968

14 September 1968

1. Thakur Ranjit Singh, Minister of Works and Transport
2. Pir Gias-ud-Din, Minister of Industries and Power
3. Shri M.A. Khan, Minister of Health

15 September 1968

1. Chairman, Public Service Commission
2. Chief Secretary; Commissioner, Planning and Development Finance Secretary; Food Commissioner; Revenue Secretary; Additional Secretary, Education

16 September 1968

1. Shri G.L. Dogra, Minister of Revenue
2. Shri S.N. Fotedar, Chairman, Legislative Council

In addition to the persons mentioned above, the following persons met the Commission informally:

1. Shri Bhagwan Sahay, Governor of Jammu and Kashmir
2. Shri G.M. Sadiq, Chief Minister, Jammu and Kashmir
3. Shri Janki Nath Wazir, Retired Chief Justice of Jammu and Kashmir High Court

APPENDIX 5

Breakdown of Budgetary Resources

I. 1960-61

(In Lakhs of Rupees)

Sl. No.	*Head*	*Jammu*	*Kashmir*	*Ladakh*	*Total*
1.	Forests	190.72	171.13	0.16	362.01
2.	Excise	30.78	10.72	. .	41.50
3.	Entertainment Tax	2.81	2.16	. .	4.97
4.	Show Tax	. .	. .	. .	. .
5.	Road Toll Basic	24.6.6	16.43	. .	41.09
6	Road Toll Addl.	27.29	32.41	1.71	61.41
7.	Sales Tax (Gen)	*5.60*	4.83	. .	10.43
8	Sales Tax (Motor Spirit)	9.27	4.92	. .	14.19
9.	Passenger Tax	. .	. .	. .	. .
10.	Property Tax	. .	. .	. .	. .
11.	Stamps	5.38	7.82	0.05	13.25
12.	Electricity	6.56	6.56	. .	. .
13.	Irrigation	4.44	1.00	. .	5.44
14.	Rents and Misc. P.W.D. Receipts	2.35	12.03	. .	14.38
15.	Land Revenue	24.65	42.10	0.97	67.72
16.	Fees under Motor Vehicles Act	0.52	1.77	. .	2.29
17.	Taxes under Motor Vehicles Taxation Act	4.05	3.10	. .	7.15
18.	Transport	46.73	15.58	. .	62.31
19.	Water Rates	3.40	3.50	. .	6.90
	Total	389.21	322.94	2.89	715.04

(Contd.)

APPENDIX 5 (*Contd.*)

II. 1963-64

(In Lakhs of Rupees)

Sl. No.	*Head*	*Jammu*	*Kashmir*	*Ladakh*	*Total*
1.	Forests	167.10	203.50	N.A.	370.60
2.	Excise	48.65	15.55	..	64.20
3.	Entertainment Tax	4.06	3.03	..	7 06
4.	Show Tax	0.37	0.23	..	0.60
5:	Road Toll Basic	36.84	24.56	..	61.40
6	Road Toll Addl.	59.22	70.34	3.70	133.26
7.	Sales Tax (Gen)	27.89	15.03	..	42.92
8.	Sales Tax (Motor Spirit)	15.84	12.94	..	28.78
9.	Passenger Tax	4.76		..	12.53
10.	Property Tax	0.56	23	..	0.79
11.	Stamps	8.46	11.47	0.14	20.07
12.	Electricity	(–)3.40	36.24	..	32.84
13.	Irrigation	3.12	2.23	..	5.35
14.	Rents and Misc. P.W.D. Receipts	4.27	13.55	..	17.82
15.	Land Revenue	25.51	33.06	1.20	59.77
16.	Fees under Motor Vehicles Act	2.23	7.90	..	10.13
17.	Taxes under Motor Vehicles Taxation Act	6.91	5.93	..	12.84
18.	Transport	48.54	25.10	..	73.64
19.	Public Health	1.58	1.75	..	3.33
	Total	462.51	490.38	5.04	957.93

(*Contd.*)

APPENDIX 5 (*Contd.*)

III. 1965-66

(In Lakhs of Rupees)

Sl. No.	*Head*	*Jammu*	*Kashmir*	*Ladakh*	*Total*
1.	Forests	137.19	177.40	N.A.	314.59
2.	Excise	72.63	17.96	..	90.59
3.	Entertainment Tax	4.22	3.26	..	7.48
4.	Show Tax	0.38	0.22	..	0.60
5.	Road Toll Basic	51.37	34.25	..	85.62
6.	Road Toll Addl.	71.30	8.4.64	4.46	160.40
7.	Sales Tax (Gen)	35.44	16.10	..	51.54
8.	Sales Tax (Motor Spirit)	13.36	13.50	..	26.86
9.	Passenger Tax	4.72	6.35	..	11.07
10.	Property Tax	1.07	0.92	..	1.99
11.	Stamps	7.63	13.20	0.11	20.94
12.	Electricity	3.30	32.03	..	35.33
13.	Irrigation	3.47	2.00	..	5.47
14	Rents and Misc. P.W.D. Receipts	6.25	10.70	..	16.95
15.	Land Revenue	18.29	24.27	1.08	43.64
16.	Fees under Motor Vehicles Act	6.23	9.13	..	15.36
17.	Taxes Under Motor Vehicles Taxation Act	9.17	7.59	..	16.76
18.	Transport	5.83	6.19	0.07	12.09
19.	Public Health	2.13	2.19	..	4.32
	Total	453.98	461^90	5.72	921.60

(*Contd.*)

Appendix 5 (*Contd.*)

IV. Allocation of Resources: Assumptions

(a) The allocation of total resources to different regions has by and large, been made on the basis of the point of collection, though there is no bar to remitting the revenue of one region in the Treasury of another region.

(b) For 'road toll' which is a significant item of revenue of the State, the points of collection are all located in Jammu, though the incidence of the toll is spread all over the State. The location of the toll points is done after taking into account the convenience of collection and ensuring that all possible points of leakage are plugged. The allocation of road-toll has been done by the State Government on the following basis:

(1) *Basic Toll:* 60 percent for Jammu and 40 percent for Kashmir.

(2) *Additional Toll* has been allocated to three regions in proportion to the population of each region.

(c) In respect of receipts under the 'Electricity Department', which is a commercial department, the figures have been worked out by deducting from the gross receipts collected in each region, the working expenses incurred in that region.

(d) With regard to receipts under the Transport Department, (which is also a commercial department) the net receipts for the entire State have been worked out by deducting from the gross receipts the working expenses of the year. The net receipts so arrived at have been allocated to the different regions in the proportion of gross receipts 'collected from each region.' While doing so, the receipts accruing from Pathankot have been added to those of Jammu region even though these receipts are on account of services rendered to the Army for carriage of goods from Pathankot to places in the Kashmir Division or Ladakh District. The same procedure has been followed in the case of foodgrains transported from Pathankot to Srinagar.

APPENDIX 6

Plan Outlay and Central Assistance—State-wise

(In crores of Rupees)

State		First Plan			Second Plan			Third Plan (Provisional)		
		Plan outlay	*Central Assistance*	*Col. (3) as % of Col. (2)*	*Plan. outlay*	*Central Assistance*	*Col. (6) as % of Col. (5)*	*Plan outlay*	*Central Assistance*	*Col. (9) as % of Col. (8)*
1	2	3	4	5	6	7	8	9	10	11
1.	Andhra Pradesh	107	61	57.0	181	96	53.0	349	220	63.0
2.	Assam	28	22	78 6	63	31	49.2	132	100	75.8
3.	Bihar	102	55	53.9	177	84	47.5	332	216	65.4
4	Gujarat	99	32	32.3	147	50	34.0	240	112	46.7
5.	Jammu & Kashmir	11.52	10	86.8.	31.20	20	64.1	64.09	62	967
6.	Kerala	44	24	54.5	79	38	48.1	182	122	67.0
7.	Madhya Pradesh	94	61	64.9	145	96	66.2	287	219	76.3
8.	Madras	85	42	49.4	187	95	50.8	342	187	54.7
9.	Maharashtra	125	48	.38.4	214	74	34.6	435	167	38.4
10.	Mysore	94	47	50.0	139	67	48.2	264	156	59.1
11.	Nagaland	..	..	..	..	..	..	11	11	100.0
12.	Orissa	85	77	90.6	89	66	74.2	224	137	61.2
13.	Punjab	163	141	86.5	151	88	58.3	252	134	53.2
14.	Rajasthan	66	60	90.9	109	59	59. 0	213	161	75.6
15.	Uttar Pradesh	166	87	52.4	223	121	53.1	557	356	63.9
16.	West Bengal	154	113	73.4	156	73	46.8	305	155.	.50.8

Note: The figures of Plan outlay shown for Jammu and Kashmir have been furnished by the State Government. The figures for the other States are those furnished by the Union Ministry of Finance.

APPENDIX 7

Development Programme (Plan): Second Five Year Plan

Sl. No.	Head of Development	Total Plan Outlay	Jammu Region	Kashmir Region	Common to Jammu and Kashmir Region	Ladakh Region	Total
1	2	3	4	5	6	7	8
1.	Agricultural Programme	267.74	66.49	88.10	12.11	..	166.70
2.	Co-operation and C.D.	228.78	170.00	173.81	2.99	..	346.80
3.	Irrigation	495.45	115.11	250.45	..	..	365.56
4.	Power	329.24	152.68	219.06	..	..	371.74
5.	Village and Small Scale-Industries }	341.24	18.90	79.33	103.46	..	201.69
6.	Industry and Mining }						
7.	Transport and Communications	665.00	502.31	295.86	6.52	..	804.69
8.	Education	281.68	94.05	99.98	18.43	..	212.46
9.	Health	285.00	79.03	72.32	17.70	..	169.05
10.	Water Supply (Rural)	81.07	59.47	21.63	..	..	81.10
11.	Urban Water Supply		19.62	15.12	..	..	34.74
12.	Housing	95.00	43.46	58.60	..	..	102.06
13.	Labour and Labour Welfare	9.97	4.66	4.94	..	..	9.60
14.	Welfare of Scheduled Castes and other Backward Classes	38.95	33.32	4.85	..	..	38.17
15.	Social Welfare	21.47	1.79	1.74	..	..	3.53
16.	Development of backward area	94.73	..	23.67	..	86.65	110.32
17.	Local Bodies	132.05	24.34	63.16	..	..	87.50
18.	Plan Publicity	15.20	..	..	11.43	..	11.43
19.	Statistical Schemes	9.50	..	..	3.06	..	3.06
	Total	3392.07	1385.23	1472.62	175.70	86.65	3120.20

(*Contd.*)

APPENDIX 7 *(Contd.)*

Development Expenditure Outside Plan: Second Five-Year Plan (1956-61)

(In lakhs of Rupees)

Sl. No.	Head of Development	Jammu Region	Kashmir Region	Common to Jammu and Kashmir Region	Ladakh Region	Total
1	2	3	4	5	6	7
1.	Transport and Communications	120.46	88.52	..	..	208.98
2.	National Highways	71.00	64.73	..	..	135.73
3.	Colonies (Rehabilitation of Displaced Persons)	53.76	—	..	..	53.76
	Total	245.22	153.25	..	..	398.47

(Contd.)

APPENDIX 7 *(Contd.)*

Development Programme (Plan): Third Five Year Plan

(In lakhs of Rupees)

Sl. No.	Head of Development	Total Plan Outlay	Jammu Region	Kashmir Region	Common to Jammu and Kashmir Region	Ladakh Region	Total
1	2	3	4	5	6	7	8
1.	Agriculture Programmes excluding minor irrigation	675.40	165.02	260.99	24 .86	..	450.87
2.	Co-operation and C.D.	513.51	156.18	142.76	168.83	..	467.77
3.	Irrigation (including minor irrigation)	1625.00	169.05	527.16	120.98	..	817.19

1	2	3	4	5	6	7	8
4.	Power	997.00	539.53	379.05	40.85	..	959.43
5.	Village and Small Scale Industries						
6.	Industry and Mining	906.00	..	..	864.07	..	864.07
7.	Transport and Communications	9.31.59	412.05	494.51	97.00	..	1003.57
8.	Education (including Cultural activities)	498.02	234.99	325.61	..	..	560.60
9.	Health and Family Planning	351.00	140.13	208.43	8..41	..	156.97
10.	Water Supply						
	(a) Rural	227.44	117.26	122.98	..	..	240.24
	(b) Urban	..	61.32	84.98	..	..	146.30
11.	Housing	200.00	54.32	126.84	..	..	181.16
12.	Labour and Labour Welfare	30.00	15.29	11.78	..	..	27.07
13.	Welfare of	24.00	30:68	12.46	..	..	..
	Scheduled Castes and other Backward Classes	24.00	30.68	12.46	..	..	43.14
14.	Social Welfare	13.69	4.03	2.30	..	..	6.33
15.	Public Co-operation	4.45	0.29	..	..	..	0.29
16.	Area Development	402.00		50.35 (Sonawari)		147.36	197.71
17.	Local Bodies	75.00	17.74	45.23		..	62.97
18.	Plan Publicity	13.00			8.48	..	8.48
19.	Government Presses	5.00	1.81	1.35		..	3.16
20.	Statistical Schemes	7.90	..	..	1.47	..	1.47
21.	Metric Systems of weights	..	..	..	10.55	..	10.55
	Total	7500.00	2119.69	2796.78	1345.51	147.36	6409.34

(*Contd.*)

APPENDIX 7 *(Contd.)*

Development Expenditure Outside Plan: Third Five-Year Plan (1961-66)

(In lakhs of Rupees)

Sl. No.	*Head of Development*	*Jammu Region*	*Kashmir Region*	*Common to Jammu and Kashmir Region*	*Ladakh Region*	*Total*
1	2	3	4	5	6	7
1.	Transport and Communications	618.61	285.95	153.48	934.44	1992.03
2.	National Highways	162.07	86.49	..	..	248.56
3.	Local Bodies	16.64	18.44	..	..	29.08
4.	Ladakh Development	..	..	..	14.92	44.92
5.	Colonies (Rehabilitation of displaced Persons)	215.92	..	..	..	215.92
	Total	1006.79	390.88	153.48	949.36	2500.51

APPENDIX 8

A Note on J & K Minerals Ltd.

J & K Minerals Ltd. was established in February, 1960 for exploration of mineral resources in the State of J & K and for the development of mineral-based industries including generation of thermal power, etc.

The projects which are being managed by the Corporation at present and the targets and achievements of each are given below:—

(i) Wuyan Cement Factory

Investment:		Rs. 136.64 lakhs
Installed capacity:		18,000 tonnes per year
Production:		
1963-64	=	14,554.42 tonnes
1964-65	=	9,756.95 tonnes
1966-67	=	8,845.90 (clinker)
	=	8,030.98 (Cement)
1967-68	=	7,660.24 (clinker)
	=	5,826.01 (Cement)
Target production for 1968-69		12,000 tonnes of cement.

The factory was set-up in February, 1963 with an initial production capacity of 60 tonnes per day. The plant installed in the factory is the only plant of its type and size in Asia. The factory meets the bulk of the requirements of cement in the Kashmir Valley and the sale price has been so fixed that it is slightly lower than the price of cement obtained from the plains. Because of frequent shut-downs of electricity and low voltage, the production of the factory has remained low. The Corporation has recently purchased its own 860 KVA generating set to reduce: the effect of the power shut-downs and low voltage. It is proposed to expand the production capacity of the factory to 120 tonnes per day as the demand for cement in the valley is said to be on the increase. During 1968-69, the target production of cement in the factory is expected to be 12,000 tonnes.

(ii) Spun Pipe Factory

Investment:		Rs. 6,61,277
Installed capacity: 6′	=	100% efficiency— 9600 Nos.—57,600 rft.
8′	=	100% efficiency — 8640 Nos.—69,120 rft.
Production: 1964-65	=	41,344 rft.
1965-66	=	51,648 rft.
1966-67	=	66,832 rft.
1967-68	=	74,152 rft.
Target for 1968-69	=	75,000 rft.

The factory went into commercial production on 1-4-1964 and its performance is stated to be satisfactory. Since the demand for spun pipes in the valley is said to be steadily on the increase, the production capacity of the factory is proposed to be expanded so as to obtain a capacity, of 2.5 to 3 lacs rft. of pipes per annum. During financial year 1968-69, the target production of 75,000 rft. of pipes has been fixed for the factory.

(iii) Prestressed Concrete Factory

Investment	=	Rs. 12,93,266
Installed capacity	=	Capacity as per project report 30′/350 lb — 3,700 Nos. Poles 32′/380 lb — 3,300 " " 36′/400 lb— 2,000 " "
Actual Capacity	=	22′/250 lb — 1,725 " " 27′/400 lb — 1,494 " " 30′/350 lb — 1,264 " " 32′/500 lb — 632 " " 34′/400 lb — 575 " "

Production

	22'/250	*27'/400*	*32'/500*	*30'/350*	*30'/500*	*34'/400*	*Total*
1962-63	60	52	66	..	..		178
1963-64	960	182	66	66	..	198	1.472
1964-65	..	52	..	814	100	..	966
1965-66	720	416	..	44	80	..	1,260
1966-67	720	104	22	572	60	..	1,478
1967-68	175	252	..	..	20	..	453
Target for—1968-69 — 2.000 poles							

The factory with a capacity for manufacturing 9,000 P.C.C. poles, per-year went into production on 1-4-1963. The factory, which was mainly designed for the manufacture of P.C.C. poles for the State Electrical-Department has been facing considerable difficulties from us very inception, due to lack of orders from that Department. The State Government has been apprised of the problem from time to time. Plans are stated, to be under preparation for utilisation of the idle capacity of the factory by diverting some of its sheds for manufacture of some other P.C.C. products.

(iv) Thermal Power Stations — Kalakot

Investment = Rs. 365.76 lakhs fending March, 1966)

Capacity = 22.5 M.W.

The power house is under construction at Kalakot and the first 7.5 M.W. has been commissioned on trial basis recently.

(v) Padder Saphire Mining Project

Production =	1963-64	50,000 grams
	1964-65	2,00,000 grams
	1965-66	2,24,839 grams
	1966-67	1,84,950 grams
	1967-68	1,88,672 grams

The extraction of saphire made at present is mainly from the debris. It is expected that operations connected with the extraction of saphire corundums from Padder area will be taken-up on a larger scale during the year 1968-69.

(vi) Mining of Coal at Kalakot

Bergoa Mining Project:

Investment: Rs. 61.59 lakhs (ending March, 1966)

Production:	1962-63	=	17,458 tonnes
	196.3-64	=	19,717 tonnes
	1964-65	=	8,558 tonnes inclusive of Metka and Jangalgali
	1965-66	=	743.5 tonnes

The coal extracted from Bergoa mines is being, reserved. For Thermal Power Station, Kalakot. It is stated that other connected mines, i.e., Melka and Chakkar coalfields are under study at present, and some exploratory mining is being done

(vii) New Projects

The Corporation has also been entrusted with setting up of new units, subject to economic and technical feasibility, like Rayon Grade Pulp and Yarn Plant in Kashmir Valley, and cement plants at Reasi and Basholi in Jammu Province. It is stated that detailed investigations regarding these projects have already been taken up in hand and a firm of consultants namely, M/s. C.M.D.C. are busy at present in preparing the project reports of these projects. The report for the Reasi Cement-Plant has already been received from the Consultants and is under detailed scrutiny at present. The project reports for other schemes are expected to be submitted by the Consultant during the year 1968-69. Besides, the Government has also entrusted the work of preparation of a project report for a paper plant of a capacity of 10 tonnes per day to M/s. National Industrial Development Corporation.

APPENDIX 9

Recruitment of Government Employees during 1961-62 to 1965-66 and Position as on 10-9-1963 and 1-4-1967

I. Regional Composition

(Based on material supplied by the State Government upto 22-11-68)

	Jammu				*Kashmir*				*Ladakh*				*Outside the State*				*Total*			
	G	*NG*	*CIV*	*T*	*G*	*NG*	*CIV*	*T*	*G*	*NG*	*CIV*	*T*	*G*	*NG*	*CIV*	*T*	*G*	*NG*	*CIV*	*T*
1961-62	116	1943	519	2578	234	3164	661	4049	3	105	63	173	12	30	..	32	355	1212	1235	..
Percentage	32.7	37.1	41.7	37.7	63.1	60.5	53.1	59.3	0.8	2.0	5.2	2.5	3.4	0.4		0.5	100.0	100.0	100.0	100.0
1962-63	140	1356	368	2554	232	2768	645	3670	..	103	47	150	12	60	42	64	390	..	72.2	..
Percentage	30.6	38.7	45.9	39.7	66.1	58.1	50.3	57.0	..	2.2	3.7	2.3	3.3	4.0	0.1	1.0	100.0	100.0	100.0	100.0
1963-64	133	1601	517	2114	280	3175	669	4124	..	56	46	102	8	41	24	..	828	138	1234	..
Percentage	31.6	32.4	41.9	34.1	66.5	65.7	54.3	63.7	..	1.1	3.7	1.5	1.9	6.8	0.1	6.7	100.0	100.0	100.0	100.1
1964-65	255	2771	711	3639	315	3981	369	4874	1	92	400	198	2	12	1	45	475	..	..	..
Percentage	33.3	42.2	42.3	41.7	66.3	56.4	51.7	55.8	0.2	1.5	5.9	2.3	0.4	0.2	0.1	0.2	100.0	100.0	100.0	100.0
1965-66	249	3456	900	4635	432	7912	956	9305	3	126	72	511	..	2	..	2	684	1154	..	..
Percentage	25.4	39.2	46.7	32.8	63.2	68.7	49.6	65.8	0.4	1.1	3.7	1.4	..	..	..	..	100.0	100.0	100.0	100.0
10-9-1963	762	15612	4353	21727	1424	25749	6108	33281	NA	NA	NA	NA	177	7	21	235	2363	4238	1342	..
Percentage	32.2	39.2	41.5	39.3	60.3	60.7	58.3	69.2	NA	NA	NA	NA	7.5	0.1	0.2	0.5	100.0	100.0	100.0	100.0
1-4-1967	1074	23673	5250	29927	2038	40512	7986	50526	27	1750	543	7290	58	54	36	145	3112	65836	12285	..
Percentage	32.2	35.9	38.1	36.1	65.1	61.4	57.9	69.9	0.9	2.7	3.7	2.8	1.8	..	0.3	0.2	100.0	100.0	100.0	100.0
				1572387				1899438				88651								
Percentage				44.2				53.3				2.5								100.0

G: Guaranted; NG: Non-Guaranteed; CIV: Class IV; T: Total; NA: Not applicable.

APPENDIX 9 (*Contd.*)

II. Communal Composition

(Based on material supplied by the State Government upto 22-11-68)

	Muslims			*Hindus*				*Sikhs*				*S. Castes*							
												Hindus				*Sikhs*			
	NG	*CIV*	*T*	*G*	*NG*	*CIV*	*T*	*G*	*NG*	*CIV*	*T*	*G*	*NG*	*CIV*	*T*	*G*	*NG*	*CIV*	*T*
1961-62	2559	716	3411	202	2145	377	2724	16	302	48	366	..	155	63	218	..	4	..	4
Percentage	48.9	57:5	49.9	56.9	41.0	30 3	39 9	4.5	5.8	3.9	5.3	..	3.0	5.0	3.2	..	0.1	..	0.1
1962-63	2264	753	3156	202	2070	392	2664	18	259	69	346	..	124	37	161	..	18	..	18
Percentage	47.2	58.7	49.0	56.3	43.1	30.6	41.4	5.0	.5.4	5.4	5.4	..	2.6	2.9	2.5	..	0.4	..	0.3
1963-64	2667	717	3557	232	2004	379	2615	16	335	49	400	..	89	43	132	..	5	..	5
Percentage	51.9	58.1	52.4	55.1	39.0	30.7	38.5	3.8	6.6	4.6	5.9	..	1.7	3.8	1.9	..	0.1	..	0.1
1964-65	3379	96.3	4530	263	2758	514	3535	23	251	59	333	..	120	68	188	..	8	1	9
Percentage	51.4	57.3	51.9	55.4	42.0	30.6	40.5	4.8	3.8	3.5	3.8	..	1.8	4.0	2.2	..	0.1	0.1	0 1
1965-66	7197	1068	8498	405	3615	567	4587	33	446	45	524	6	181	120	307	..	12	..	12
Percentage	62.4	55.4	60.1	59.2	31.3	29.5	32.4	4.8	3.9	2.3	3.7	0.9	1.6	6.2	2.2	..	0.1	..	0.1
10-9-1963	19115	5955	25963	1175	19878	3682	24735	106	2454	387	2947	NA	NA	NA	NA	NA	NA	NA	NA
Percentage	45.1	56.8	47.0	49.7	46.9	35.1	44.8	4.5	5.8	3.7	5.3								
1-4-1967	34300	7810	43441	1565	26305	4412	32282	180	3255	451	3886	12	1142	694	1848	..	77	6	83
Percentage	52.0	56.7	52.4	50.2	39.9	32.0	38.9	5.8	4.9	3.3	4.7	0.4	1.7	5.0	2.2	..	0.1	..	0.1
			243267				729,230				62,901				283963				168
Percentage			68.3				20.4				3.8				8.0				—

G: Guaranted; NG: Non-Guaranteed; CIV: Class IV; T: Total; NA: Not applicable.

APPENDIX 9 (*Contd.*)

II. Communal Composition

(Based on material supplied by the State Government up 22-11-68)

	Buddhists				*Others*				*Total*			
		NG	*CIV*	*T*	*G*	*NG*	*CIV*	*T*	*G*	*NG*	*CIV*	*T*
1961-62	..	41	26	67	1	26	15	42	355	5232	1245	68.32
Percentage	..	0.7	2.1	1.0	0.3	0.5	1.2	0.6	100.0	100.0	100.0	100.0
1962-63	..	39	15	54	..	23	16	39	359	47.7	128.2	6438
Percentage	..	0.8	1.2	0.8	..	0.5	1.2	0.6	100.0	100.0	100.0	100.0
1963-64	..	25	27	52	..	11	18	29	431	51.36	1233	6790
Percentage	..	0.5	2.2	0.8	..	0.2	1.5	0.4	100.0	100.0	100.0	100.0
1964-65	1	36	40	77	..	18	36	54	475	6520	1681	8726
Percentage	0.2	0.6	2.4	0.9	..	0.3	2.1	0.6	100.0	100 0	100.0	100.0
1965-66	3	56	27	86	4	24	101	129	684	11551	1928	14143
Percentage	0.4	0.5	1.4	0.6	0.6	0.2	5.2	0.9	100.0	100 0	100.0	100.0
10-9-1963	NA	NA	NA	NA	189	951	458	1598	2363	42398	10482	55243
Percentage					8.0	2.2	4.4	2.9.	100.0	100.0	100.0	100.0
1-4-1967	10	591	198	799	19	316	214	549	3117	65986	13785	82885
Percentage	0.3	0.9	1.4	1.0	9.6	0.5	1.6	0.7	100.0	100.0	100.0	100.0
				48.360				4287				3560976
Percentage				1.4				.0.1				100.0

G: Guaranted; NG: Non-Guaranteed; CIV: Class IV; T: Total; NA: Not applicable.

Appendix 10

List of Backward Classes other than Scheduled Castes Recognized in the State of Jammu and Kashmir

Acharji; Arikasha (Sawer); Alqa (Patigur); Aknoon (Maktab teacher)

Bhjojki; Bafand (Weaver); Baba Fquir; Beggar; Bede* and Bon (Drum and flute player); Bhands; Bazigar; Banjara; Biloch; Bawria; Bakarwals; Bharmunje; Bohrees (Kashmir Hindus)

*Champas (Nomadic people of Chushul)

Dubduba; Dhobi; Dosali; Derazi (Village Darzi)

Kul Faqir (Gypsies)

*Guraj (blacksmith); Gujjars; Gharate (Kashmir Pohol); Gorkahn (Grave digger); Geseoni; Gaddis; Gosains

Hajam

Jhiwar; Jullaha; Jogi

Kamboh; Kumar; Kanwai (village Nanwai) Kaligar (village Kaligar) Kawaj

Lohar; Lubhana

Madari; Mirasi; Mochi; Manjie (including Gad Hanjis); Malyar; Markban

Nalband; Nadar (Kashmir Doom)

Pakhtoons; Pathira (Khist saz); Pandit Goar

Qasab

Reshi (Maliyar); Rangreez; Razire

*Ladakh District.

Sansi; Sikligar; Shaksar; Sheer Gujar; Sangtrash (stone-cutter); Shaw Faqir; Shippies; Sochies

Teli; Tarkhans; Thanthur

Watal (Sweepers, Shupri Watal); Waza (village Waza)

Zalooger (Durkigar); Zargar (village Zargar)

List of Scheduled Castes

1. Barwals
2. Basith
3. Batwal
4. Chamar or Ramdasia
5. Chura
6. Phyar
7. Doom or Mahasha
8. Gardi
9. Jolaha
10. Megh or Kabirpanthi
11. Ratal
12. Saryara
13. Watal

APPENDIX 11

Government of Jammu and Kashmir General Department

Circular

Rule 19 of Civil Services (Classification, Control and Appeal Rules provide for securing of adequate representation of various communities in the State in services. In pursuance of this Rule, Government have been contemplating to determine certain reservation of posts for Scheduled Castes. It has now been decided that with a view to achieve this purpose:—

1. all appointing authorities should know the district-wise population of Harijans in the State and while making appointments keep this in mind. If the post relates to a district or region the percentage of population in the district or region may be considered for fixing number of appointments to be reserved for Harijans. If it relates to the State as a whole the percentage of population in the whole State may be considered;
2. for this purpose the population figures as given in the Census Report 1961 are brought to the notice of appointing authorities.

State/Division/District	*Total Population (in lakh)*	*Scheduled Castes*
Jammu and Kashmir	35.67	2.84
lammu Division	15.72	2.84
Udhampur, District	2.54	0.51
Doda District	2.68	0.25
Jammu District	5.17	1.52
Kathua District	2.07	0 47
Poonch Rajouri District	3.26	0.09

Similarly in the case of allotment of seats for technical or other institutions, heads of the institutions and the selecting authorities should keep the above ratio in view.

The undersigned is directed that the above policy should be strictly followed while making appointments.

(Sd). E.N. Mangat Rai,
Chief Secretary to Government.

APPENDIX 11 *(Contd.)*

No. GD(ADM) 4/65-SW(i) Dated: -7-1966

Copy for information and necessary action forwarded to the:

1. All Secretaries to Govt.
2. Secretary to Governor.
3. Secretary to Chief Minister.
4. Secretary Public Service Commission.
5. All Head of Departments.
6. All Provincial Heads.
7. Superintendent Govt. Press for publication in the three consecutive issues of the Govt. Gazette.

APPENDIX 12

Government of Jammu and Kashmir Civil Secretariat—General Department

NOTIFICATION

No. 1034-D of 1968 Dated 20-7-1968

Whereas on the basis of the facts, figures and data given in the Census Report and those available from other sources including public records, the Government is of the opinion that the permanent residents of Ladakh District and the permanent resident Scheduled Castes are backward classes of citizens of the State and are not adequately represented in the services under the State:

Now, therefore, the Government hereby directs that reservations shall be made in the services and posts under the State in favour of these classes which shall, as nearly as may be, bear such proportion to the available vacancies as is specified below against each such class and appointment to such services and posts shall be regulated accordingly:

(a)	Permanent residents Scheduled Caste	5%
(b)	Permanent residents of Ladakh Distt.	2%

Provided that if a sufficient number of candidates belonging to any class specified above is not available for filling up the available vacancies reserved for such classes, the remaining vacancies shall lapse and shall be filled up on merit from amongst other candidates.

This order shall apply to all cases in which recruitment action has not been completed.

Explanation:—For purposes of this order "available vacancies", means the vacancies in the service or in respect of posts under the State which are to be filled.

By Order of the Government of Jammu and Kashmir.

(Sd.) (Isher Dass Gupta)
Deputy Secretary to Government,
General Department.

APPENDIX 12 *(Contd)*

No. GD (Adm.) 382/68-SW dated 20-7-1968.

Copy for information and necessary action forwarded to the:

1. All Secretaries to Government.
2. All Heads of Departments.
3. Divisional Commissioner, Kashmir/Jammu.
4. Secretary, Public Service Commission.
5. Secretary to Governor, Jammu and Kashmir State.
6. Secretary, Legislative Assembly.
7. Secretary, Legislative Council.
8. Manager, Government Press, Srinagar for publication in the Government Gazette.

Index